COLLINS-SPURRELL
WELSH
DICTIONARY

COLLINS-SPURRELL
WELSH
DICTIONARY

Re-edited by
HENRY LEWIS

COLLINS
LONDON AND GLASGOW

GENERAL EDITOR: J. B. FOREMAN
FIRST PUBLISHED 1960

Reprint 10 9 8 7 6 5 4 3 2 1

ISBN 0 00 433402 7
© *William Collins Sons & Co. Ltd. 1960*
PRINTED IN GREAT BRITAIN
COLLINS CLEAR-TYPE PRESS

CONTENTS

	page
A FOREWORD *by D. Lloyd George*	6
PREFACE *by Henry Lewis*	7
THE WELSH LANGUAGE	8
NOTES ON PRONUNCIATION	10
LIST OF ABBREVIATIONS	12
WELSH-ENGLISH DICTIONARY	13
PERSONAL NAMES	168
PLACE NAMES	169
ENGLISH-WELSH DICTIONARY	171

(Reprinted from *Spurrell's Welsh Dictionary*)

FOREWORD

The making of a good Dictionary is a contribution of the highest order to the welfare of a language. It clarifies and stabilises the pronunciation, orthography and meaning of its words; garners and stores the varied wealth of its vocabulary. To the farmer, his barn; to the manufacturer, his warehouse; to all who use and love their native tongue, a dictionary.

I deeply appreciate the great service which the firm of W. Spurrell & Son have rendered over a long period to the Welsh language by producing successive editions of their Welsh Dictionary. I myself have found their last edition invaluable, and I am delighted that it has been once more revised and brought up to date, and that the words with which the Welsh language, like every other language, has been enriched during recent years can now be included. I congratulate both Editor and Publisher upon their effort, and I trust this new Dictionary will prove a treasured aid to all who study our beautiful and historic tongue.

D. Lloyd George

PREFACE

In planning this book the original intention was to prepare a revised edition of the *Schools' Dictionary* edited by Bodvan Anwyl and first published in 1919. Later, as it became apparent that a new edition of *Spurrell's English-Welsh and Welsh-English Dictionary*, published in 1937, could not be issued for some time, it was decided that a general purpose edition, midway between the two, should be produced. It now appears as the *Collins-Spurrell Welsh Dictionary*.

There is no need to enlarge upon the debt which was owed to the late Bodvan Anwyl for his valuable work in connection with Spurrell's Dictionaries. In particular the Welsh-English Dictionary, of which eight editions appeared between 1914 and 1937, was of great assistance to students of Welsh of all grades. In this re-edition his plan has been followed, as it had adequately proved its soundness. The aim has been to provide the general reader with as much assistance as possible, within concise limits, in reading current literature, while also supplying material of use to those engaged in wider study of the language. Many words are included in the Welsh-English section which are no longer in use, but which are likely to occur in the earlier literature which such readers desire to peruse.

The increasing interest in the use of Welsh in schools, and by scholars in more advanced studies, has led to the necessity for extending what is called the "technical terms" in several subjects. It should be remembered that very many of the new words are offered as suggestions, and no doubt a large number will eventually come into common use, while others will not be so readily adopted. The proof of the pudding is the eating of it, and we must wait to see what the final reaction of the writers of Welsh in these various branches of study will be before we can confidently give dictionary space to these terms.

As in former editions, parts of words only are given, in bold type, when they suffice. The plural is in italics. It should be noted that a noun ending in **-iwr** or **-wr** in the singular ends in *-wyr* in the plural. Thus **derbyniwr,** (*-wyr*), **-nnydd,** (*-ynyddion*) is to be read **derbyniwr** (*derbynwyr*), **derbynnydd** (*derbynyddion*). Also a singular noun in **-ydd** may form its plural by substituting *-wyr* for **-ydd.** Thus **emynydd,** (*-ion, -wyr*) should read **emynydd** (*emynyddion, emynwyr*). The plurals of **mynach** are *mynaich* and *mynachod*; of **Undodwr,** *Undodwyr* and *Undodiaid*. **Deheubarth -dir** stands for **Deheubarth, Deheudir; mynyddig, -og** for **myny-, ddig, mynyddog.** The space saved by this method of indicating plurals has been used to provide a larger vocabulary than would otherwise have been possible.

Henry Lewis

THE WELSH LANGUAGE

Most of the languages of Europe, and some of the languages of Asia, can be traced back to a common ancestor to which the name Indo-European is commonly given. From this ancestor were derived a dozen or so branches, one of which is called Celtic. This branch probably had its beginning in the upper Danube valley, and from there spread in many directions over Europe, and even to Galatia in Asia Minor. As the Celtic-speaking people became scattered, changes naturally occurred in the language, resulting in the growth of dialects. Of these the best known on the continent is that which was spoken in Gaul, to which the name Gaulish is given. Gaulish became extinct in the early Christian period, and was displaced by Latin.

In the meantime people speaking different forms of Celtic had crossed over from the Continent to the British Isles. One group established itself in Ireland. This is known as the Goidelic or Gaelic group, and from it descended the Irish language, which spread from Ireland to the Isle of Man, developing later to Manx, and also to Scotland, eventually becoming Scottish Gaelic. The other group prevailed in Britain and the language is called British or Brythonic or Brittonic. Prior to the Roman Conquest this language was spoken throughout what later became England, Wales and southern Scotland. It was from this descendant of the original Common Celtic language that ultimately sprang the Welsh, Cornish and Breton languages.

The language of the Goidelic group is referred to also as Q Celtic, and that of the British group as P Celtic. The reason for this is that the Indo-European consonant written 'qu' has given 'c' in the former and 'p' in the latter. An example is found in the forms corresponding to the English interrogative pronoun 'who', which in Irish is 'cia' or 'cé', in Welsh 'pwy', and in Latin 'quis'. It may be mentioned that Gaulish shows the same development as the British languages. Thus whereas the word for 'head, end' is in Irish 'ceann' (earlier 'cenn'), it is in Welsh 'pen', while the corresponding form is found in Gaulish 'penne' in a compound name.

One of the oldest poems in Welsh literature is a eulogy to Cynan Garwyn, son of Brochwel Ysgithrog. Cynan's son Selyf is known to have been killed as he led the Welsh in the battle of Chester about the year 615. The eulogy is attributed to Taliesin, whom persistent tradition acclaims as author of eulogies and elegies to princes in southern Scotland and northern England who struggled against the Saxon invader in the late sixth century. Another name that has been handed down from these early times is Aneirin, whose long poem *Y Gododdin* refers to a great tragic exploit at Catraeth, somewhere in the neighbourhood of Catterick. These early traditions have tenaciously persisted throughout the long story of Welsh poetic literature.

Recorded Welsh prose goes back to the early ninth century. The earliest remains are scanty, but it can hardly be contested that prose writing must have long preceded what little has had the good fortune to escape oblivion. It is free from the crudeness that would be expected from initial efforts, and the way in which difficult and somewhat abstruse material is expressed with clarity, economy and directness goes a long way to prove that the writers were inheritors rather than initiators. The splendour and exactness of medieval Welsh prose, quite apart from its literary content, is striking evidence of the mastery of the writers of the prose medium. These qualities appear not least in the unlikely realm of legal writing.

During its long history the Welsh language has naturally undergone changes, but far from the extent to which English, for example, has changed since the days of Chaucer. He was a contemporary of Dafydd ap Gwilym, but whereas Chaucer has to be practically translated into Modern English, Dafydd is using to all intents the same language as any present-day poet expressing himself in the same type of poem. Similarly, if most of the earlier prose literature were printed in accordance with modern orthographical usage, the reader would not experience excessive difficulty in comprehending it. There have been changes in syntax, and still more in vocabulary. Idiomatic expressions have become obsolete from age to age, and new ones have grown. But substantially the literary language has been strikingly uniform.

The vocabulary has naturally been greatly affected from time to time by contact with peoples speaking a different language. Like many other languages Welsh has rarely been afraid of borrowing words from foreign languages. In the period of Roman occupation, and later under the influence of the Church, hundreds of Latin words were borrowed and submitted to the same treatment as native words. The same is to a less extent true of the period of contact with Anglo-Saxons. Then came the influence of the Normans, followed ultimately by the great pressure of English. All these accretions have been from non-Celtic sources, but the Welsh vocabulary is not without borrowings taken from time to time from Irish.

The written, and especially the printed, literary language always tends to be more static and conservative than the spoken. This results in the retention in the literary language of forms which have long since vanished completely from everyday colloquial speech, thus giving the printed literary language a somewhat artificial appearance. But the spoken language also differs from area to area. Indeed a brook seems a sufficient barrier to create divergence in expression between the inhabitants on either side. It is well known that speakers of dialect in one locality can hardly understand compatriots speaking another dialect of the same language. To secure, therefore, that all speakers, of whatever dialects, should have access to all that is of value in enlightened minds, the standard literary language must retain a high level of permanence, but should also avoid pedantic rigidity and scholastic snobbery.

NOTES ON THE PRONUNCIATION OF WELSH

Vowels

They are sounded, long or short, as the vowels in the English words given.

A   p*a*lm, p*a*t.
E   g*a*te (without diphthongisation), g*e*t.
I   f*ee*t, f*i*t.
O   m*o*re, n*o*t.
U   (1) North Wales: like French *u* or German *ü* without rounding lips.
     (2) South Wales: as I.
W   c*oo*l, f*u*ll.
Y   (1) In monosyllables generally, and in final syllables, as U (the 'clear' sound).
     (2) In all but final syllables, and in **y, yr** (the), **fy** (my), **dy** (thy), **yn, yng, ym** (in), the adverbial **yn,** the preverbal and relative particle **y, yr** (**y'm, y'th** etc), **syr** (sir), **nyrs** (nurse), as English f*u*n, (the 'obscure' sound).

Diphthongs

(1) Falling diphthongs, in which the second sound is consonantal: the two vowels have the sound noted above: **ae, oe, ai, oi**, the diphthong **ei** as English b*y*, **aw, ew, iw, ow, uw, ŵy, yw.**

(2) Rising diphthongs, in which the first sound is consonantal: **ia, ie, io, iw, iy,** ('obscure' y); **wa, we, wi, wo, wy,** ('clear' y), **wy,** ('obscure' y).

Consonants

Only such as differ from English need be noted.

CH   (following C in the alphabet), as Scottish lo*ch.*
DD   (following D in the alphabet), as *th* in English *th*is, brea*the.*
F   as English *v.*
FF   as English *f.*
G   always as in English *g*o.
NG   (following G in the alphabet), as in English si*ng.* In some words (e.g. **dangos**), however, it is sounded *ng-g*, as in English lo*ng*er. Alphabetically this follows after N.
LL   produced by placing the tongue to pronounce *l*, then emitting breath without voice.
PH   (following P in the alphabet), as English *f.*
TH   always as th in English *th*in.

10

Accent

Welsh words are generally accented on the last syllable but one. There are certain exceptions:

(1) The reduplicated personal pronouns **myfi, tydi, efe, efô, hyhi, nyni, chwychwi, hwynt-hwy**, accented on the final syllable.

(2) Verbs in **-(h)au, -(h)oi, -eu**, accented on the final syllable.

(3) A few dissyllabic words beginning with **y** + consonant, accented on the final syllable.

(4) Certain polysyllabic words with a diphthong resulting in contraction in the final syllable, such as **Cymraeg**.

(5) Some late borrowings accented as in the language of origin, generally English.

Initial Mutations

Certain initial consonants are mutated under certain conditions, as shown in the following table. Only the radical form is given in the dictionary.

Sounds	EXAMPLES			
	Radical	*Soft*	*Nasal*	*Spirant*
p	*p*ren	*b*ren	*mh*ren	*ph*ren
t	*t*ad	*d*ad	*nh*ad	*th*ad
c	*c*am	*g*am	*ngh*am	*ch*am
b	*b*aich	*f*aich	*m*aich	
d	*d*yn	*dd*yn	*n*yn	
g	*g*ŵr	-ŵr	*ng*ŵr	
ll	*ll*ais	*l*ais		
rh	*rh*es	*r*es		
m	*m*am	*f*am		

11

ABBREVIATIONS: BYRFODDAU

a.	adjective	: ansoddair
adv.	adverb	: adferf
c.	conjunction	: cysylltiad
c.n.	collective noun	: enw torfol
f.	feminine	: benywaidd
i.	interjection	: ebychiad
imper.	imperative	: gorchmynnol
m.	masculine	: gwrywaidd
n.d.	noun dual	: enw deuol
pl.	plural	: lluosog
pn.	pronoun	: rhagenw
pr.	preposition	: arddodiad
px.	prefix	: rhagddodiad
rel.	relative	: perthynol
s.	singular	: unigol
v.	verb	: berf
v.i.	intransitive verb	: berf gyflawn
v.t.	transitive verb	: berf anghyflawn

GEIRIADUR CYMRAEG A SAESNEG

a, interrogative particle: preverbal particle: *rel. pn.* who, that, which

a, ac, *c.* and

â, ag, *c.* as

â, ag, *pr.* with

a, *i.* ah, oh,

ab, ap, *n.m.* son (before name, in place of surname, like 'Mac' and 'Fitz')

âb, (*abau, -iaid*), *n.m.f.* ape

abad, (*-au*), *n.m.* abbot

abadaeth, (*-au*), *n.f.* abbacy, abbot-ship

abades, (*-au*), *n.f.* abbess

aball, *n.f.* destruction; postilence; failure

abar, *n.m.* corpse

abatir, (*-oedd*), *n.m.* abbey-land

abaty, (*abatai*), *n.m.* abbey

aber, (*-oedd, ebyr*), *n.m.* confluence; mouth of river, estuary; brook, stream

aberfa, (*-oedd*), *n.f.* mouth of river, estuary

abergofiant, *n.m.* forgetfulness

aberth, (*-au, ebyrth*), *n.m.* sacrifice

aberthged, *n.f.* oblation; offering of fruits

aberthol, *a.* sacrificial

aberthu, *v.* sacrifice

aberthwr, (*-wyr*), *n.m.* sacrificer

aberu, *v.* flow into, disembogue

abid, *n.m.f.* apparel; dress of religious order

abl, *a.* able; well-off

abladol, *a.* ablative

abledd, *n.m.* ability; plenty

abo, abwy, *n.m.* prey; carcase

abred, *n.m.* release; state of evil

abrwysg, *a.* clumsy, drunken

abrwysgl, *a.* huge; dreadful

absen, *n.m.* absence; slander

absennol, *a.* absent

absennu, *v.* backbite, slander

absennwr, (*absenwyr*), *n.m.* back-biter

absenoldeb, *n.m.* absence

absenoli, *v.* absent

abwyd, -yn, (*-od*), *n.m.,* worm; fishing-bait

ac, a, *c.* and

acen, (*-ion*) *n.f.* accent

aceniad, *n.m.* accentuation

acennod, *n.f.* accent-mark

acennu, *v.* accent, stress

acenyddiaeth, *n.f.* accentuation

acer, (*-i*), *n.f.* acre

acses, *n.m.f.* access (of fever); ague

act, (*-au*) *n.f.* act

actio, *v.* act

acw, *adv.* there, yonder

ach, *i.* ugh

ach, (*-au, -oedd*), *n.f.* degree of kin-ship; (*pl.*) pedigree, ancestry

achenog, (*-ion*), *n.m.* beggar

aches, *n.m.* tide, flood; eloquence

achlân, *adv.* wholly, entirely

achles, (*-oedd*), *n.f.* succour, protec-tion; manure

achlesol, *a.* succouring

achlesu, *v.* succour, cherish; man-ure

achlod, *n.m.* shame, disgrace

achlust, *n.m.* rumour: *a.* attentive

achlysur, (*-on*) *n.m.* occasion

achlysuro, *v.* occasion

achlysurol, *a.* occasional

achor, *n.m.* fear; tumult

achos, (*-ion*), *n.m.* cause, case

achos, *c.* because, for

achosi, *v.* cause

achre, *n.m.* shivering

achub, *v.* seize, snatch; save, rescue. **—a. y blaen,** forestall. **a. y cyfle,** seize the opportunity

achubiaeth, *n.f.* salvation

achubol, *a.* saving

achubwr, (*-wyr*), **-ydd,** (*-ion*), *n.m.* saviour, rescuer

achudd, *n.m.* seclusion, retreat

achul, *a.* thin, emaciated

achwre, ach(f)re, *n.* under-thatch, protection; covering, garment

achwyn, *v.* complain: (*-ion*), *n.m.* complaint, plaint

achwyngar, *a.* querulous

achwyniad, (*-au*), *n.m.* complaint, accusation

achwynwr, (*-wyr*), *n.m.* complainer; complainant, plaintiff

achwynyddes, (*-au*), *n.f.* complainant

achydd, (*-ion*), *n.m.* genealogist

achyddiaeth, *n.f.* genealogy

achyddol, *a.* genealogical

adail, *n.f.* building, edifice, structure

adain, aden, (*adenydd*), *n.f.* wing; fin; spoke

adamant, *n.m.* adamant, diamond

adamantaidd, *a.* adamantine

adameg, *n.f.* speech; riddle; tale

adar, *n.pl.* (**aderyn,** *n.m.*), birds, fowls. —**a. drudwy, a. yr eira,** starlings. **a y to,** sparrows

adara, *v.* catch birds, fowl

adardy, (*-dai*) *n.m.* aviary

adargi, (*-gwn*), *n.m.* retriever, setter, spaniel

adargraffiad, (*-au*), *n.m.* reprint

adargraffu, *v.* reprint

adarwr, (*-wyr*), *n.m.* fowler

adarwriaeth, *n.f.* fowling

adarydd, (*-ion*), *n.m.* ornithologist

adaryddiaeth, *n.f.* ornithology

adblaned, (*-au*), *n.f.* satellite

ad-dalu, *v.* repay, requite

ad-drefnu, *v.* rearrange

adeg, (*-au*), *n.f.* time, occasion, opportunity

adeilad, (*-au*), *n.m.f.* building, edifice

adeiladaeth, *n.f.* building; edification

adeiladol, *a.* edifying

adeiladu, *v.* build, edify

adeiladwr, (*-wyr*), **-ydd,** (*-ion*), *n.m.* builder

adeiniog, *a.* winged

aden, (*-ydd, edyn*), *n.f.* wing (**adain**)

adenedigaeth, *n.f.* regeneration

adeni, *v.* regenerate

adennill, *v.* regain, recover

aderyn, (*adar*), *n.m.* bird

adfach, (*-au*), *n.m.* barb; liver-fluke

adfail, (*-feilion*), *n.m.* ruin

adfant, *n.m.* emptiness: *a.* vain; sad

adfeddiannu, *v.* repossess

adfeiliad, *n.m.* decay, ruin

adfeiliedig, *a.* decayed, in ruins

adfeilio, *v.* decay, moulder

adfer, -u, -yd, *v.* restore

adferf, (*-au*), *n.f.* adverb

adferfol, *a.* adverbial

adferiad, *n.m.* restoration

adferol, *a.* restorative

adferwr, (*-wyr*), *n.m.* restorer

adflas, *n.m.* after-taste, bad taste

adfyd, *n.m.* adversity

adfydus, *a.* adverse, miserable

adfynach, *n.m.* renegade monk

adfyw, *a.* half alive, half dead

adfywhau, *v.* revive, reanimate

adfywiad, (*-au*), *n.m.* revival

adfywio, *v.* revive, resuscitate

adfywiol, *a.* refreshing

adg-. See **atg-**

adiad, *n.m.* drake

adio, *n.m.* addition: *v.* add

adladd, adlodd, *n.m.* aftermath

adlais, (*-leisiau*), *n.m.* echo

adlam, (*-au*), *n.m.* home; rebound

adlaw, (*-iaid*), *n.m.* inferior person or thing

adleisio, *v.* resound

adlewyrch, -iad, (*-au*), *n.m.* reflection

adlewyrchu, *v.* reflect

adlo, *n.* account, reason

adlog, (*-au*), *n.m.* compound interest

adloniadol, *a.* of or for entertainment

adloniant, *n.m.* recreation, entertainment

adlonni, *v.* entertain, refresh

adnabod, *v.* know, recognize

adnabyddiaeth, *n.f.* knowledge, acquaintance

adnabyddus, *a.* known, familiar

adnabyddwr, *n.m.* knower

adnau, (*adneuon*), *n.m.* deposit, pledge

adneuo, *v.* deposit

adneuol, *a.* depositing

adnewyddiad, (*-au*), *n.m.* renewal, renovation

adnewyddu, *v.* renew, renovate

adnewyddwr, (*-wyr*), *n.m.* renewer, renovator

adnod, (*-au*), *n.f.* verse

adnoddau, *n.pl.* resources

adolygiad, (*-au*), *n.m.* review

adolygu, *v.* review

adolygydd, (*-ion*), *n.m.* reviewer

adran, (*-nau*), *n.f.* division, section

adref, *adv.* homewards, home

adrodd, *v.* relate, repeat, recite

adroddgan, (*-au*), *n.f.* recitative

adroddiad, (*-au*), *n.m.* report; recitation

adroddwr, (*-wyr*), *n.m.* narrator, reciter

adrywedd, *n.m.* track, scent

ads-. See **ats-**

adundeb, *n.m.* reunion

aduno, *v.* reunite

adwaith, (*-weithiau*), *n.m.* reaction

adwedd, *n.m.* death; resting-place; flight; return

adwr, *n.m.* coward, churl

adwythig, *a.* cruel; evil, bareful; sore, sick; harmful

adwy, (*-au, -on*), *n.f.* gap, breach; pass

adwyth, (*-au*), *n.m.* evil, misfortune, illness

adyn, (*-od*), *n.m.* wretch

adyrgop, -yn, *n.m.* spider

adysgrif, (*-au*), *n.f.* copy, transcript

adysgrifio, *v.* copy, transcribe

addail, *n.pl.* foliage; grass; salad

addas, *a.* suitable, proper

addasrwydd, *n.m.* suitableness, fitness

addasu, *v.* suit, adapt, fit

addaw, addo, *v.* promise

addawol, *a.* promising

addawydd, (*-ion*), *n.m.* promiser

addef, *v.* acknowledge, own, admit

addef, *n.m.* home, dwelling

addefedig, *a.* admitted, confessed

addefiad, *n.m.* admission, confession

addewid, (*-ion*), *n.f.* promise

addfain, *a.* slender, shapely

addfed. See **aeddfed**

addfwyn, *a.* gentle, meek, mild

addfwynder, *n.m.* gentleness, meekness

addien, *a.* fair, beautiful

addod, *n.m.* ŵy a., nest-egg

addoed, *n.m.* death, hurt

addoedi, *v.* delay, postpone, prorogue

addoediad, *n.m.* prorogation

addoer, *a.* sad, cruel; chilling

addoldy, (*-dai*), *n.m.* place of worship

addolgar, *a.* devout, reverent

addolgarwch, *n.m.* devoutness, reverence

addoli, *v.* worship, adore

addoliad, *n.m.* worship

adduned, (*-au*), *n.f.* vow

addunedu, *v.* vow

addurn, (*-au, -iadau*), *n.m.* ornament

addurniad, *n.m.* ornamentation

addurno, *v.* adorn, ornament

addurnol, *a.* ornamental, decorative

addurnwr, (*-wyr*), *n.m.* decorator

addysg, *n.f.* education, instruction

addysgiadol, *a.* instructive

addysgiaeth, *n.f.* instruction, training

addysgiaethwr, (*-wyr*), *n.m.* educationist

addysgol, *a.* educational

addysgu, *v.* educate, instruct

addysgwr, (*-wyr*), **-ydd,** (*-ion*), *n.m.* educator, instructor, tutor

aeddfed, *a.* ripe, mature

aeddfedrwydd, *n.m.* ripeness, maturity

aeddfedu, *v.* ripen

ael, (*-iau*), *n.f.* brow

aelaw, *n.m.* wealth: *a.* frequent, rich, generous

aele, *a.* sad, wretched

aelgerth, -geth. See **elgeth**

aelod, (*-au*), *n.m.* member, limb

aelodaeth, *n.f.* membership

aelodi, *v.* become a member; enrol

aelwyd, (*-ydd*), *n.f.* hearth, fireside

aer, (*-ion*), *n.m.* heir

aer, *n.m.* air

aeres, (*-au*), *n.f.* heiress

aerfa, *n.f.* slaughter, battle

aeron, *n.pl.* fruit, fruits, berries

aerwy, (*-au, -on*), *n.m.* collar, torque; neck-chain

aes, *n.f.* shield

aeth, *n.m.* pain, grief, fear, shock

aethnen, *n.f.* aspen, poplar

aethus, *a.* poignant, grievous, severe

afal, (*-au*), *n.m.* apple

afaleua, *v.* gather apples

afallen, (*-nau*), *n.f.* apple-tree

afan, *n.pl.* (*-en, n.f.*), raspberries

afanc, (*-od*), *n.m.* beaver

afar, *n.m.* sorrow, grief

afiach, *a.* unwell, unhealthy, morbid

afiachus, *a.* sickly; unwholesome

afiaith, *n.m.* zest, mirth, glee

afiechyd, (*-on*), *n.m.* disease, malady

afieithus, *a.* mirthful, gleeful

aflafar, *a.* harsh, unmelodious

aflan, *a.* unclean, polluted, foul

aflawen, *a.* fierce; sad, cheerless, dismal; 'awful'

aflednais, *a.* immodest, indelicate

afledneisrwydd, *n.m.* immodesty, indelicacy

aflendid, *n.m.* uncleanness; pollution

aflêr, *a.* untidy, slovenly

aflerwch, *n.m.* untidiness, slovenliness

afles, *n.m.* disadvantage, hurt

aflesol, *a.* disadvantageous, unprofitable

afliwiog, *a.* pale, colourless

aflonydd, *a.* unquiet, restless

aflonyddu, *v.* disquiet, disturb, molest

aflonyddwch, *n.m.* disturbance, unrest

aflonyddwr, (*-wyr*), *n.m.* disturber

afloyw, *a.* turbid; opaque

afluniaidd, *a.* mis-shapen, deformed

aflunio, *v.* disfigure, deform

aflwydd, *n.m.* misfortune, calamity

aflwyddiannus, *a.* unsuccessful

aflwyddiant, *n.m.* failure

aflwyddo, *v.* fail   [archy

aflywodraeth, *n.f.* misrule, anaflywodraethus, *a.* ungovernable

afon, (*-ydd*), *n.f.* river

afonfarch, (*-feirch*), *n.m.* hippopotamus

afonig, *n.f.* rivulet, streamlet, brook

afradlon, *a.* wasteful, prodigal

afradlonedd, *n.m.* prodigality

afradloni, afradu, *v.* waste, lavish, squander

afraid, *a.* unnecessary, needless:

afreidiau, *n.m.* superfluity

afrasol, *a.* graceless, impious

afreidiol, *a.* needless, superfluous

afreol, *n.f.* misrule, disorder

afreolaidd, *a.* irregular; disorderly

afreoleidd-dra, *n.m.* irregularity

afreolus, *a.* unruly, disorderly

afresymol, *a.* unreasonable

afresymoldeb, *n.m.* unreasonableness

afrifed, *a.* innumerable

afrllad, -en, (*-au, -ennau,*) *n.f.* wafer

afrosgo, *a.* clumsy, unwieldy

afrwydd, *a.* difficult, stiff, awkward

afrwyddo, *v.* obstruct, hinder

afrywiog, *a.* perverse, cross-grained, improper

afrywiogrwydd, *n.m.* churlishness, roughness,

afu, liver: *n.m.f.* —*a.* (**g**)**las,** gizzard

afwyn, (*-au*), *n.f.* rein

affeithiad, *n.m.* affection (in grammar)

afflau, *n.m.* grip, hug, embrace

affliw, *n.m.* shred, particle

ag, *c.* as: *pr.* with. See **â**

agen, (*-nau*), *n.f.* cleft, chink, fissure

agendor, *n.m.f.* gulf, abyss

agennu, *v.* split, crack

ager, agerdd, *n.m.* steam, vapour

agerfad, (*-au*), *n.m.* steamboat

agerlong, (*-au*), *n.f.* steamship, steamer

ageru, *v.* steam, evaporate

agerw, *a.* bitter, fierce

agor, -yd, *v.* open, expand

agored, *a.* open; liable

agorfa, (*-oedd*), *n.f.* opening, orifice

agoriad, (*-au*), *n.m.* opening; key

agoriadol, *a.* opening, inaugural

agorwr, (*-wyr*), **-ydd,** (*-ion*), *n.m.* opener

agos, *a.* near, nigh

agosaol, *a.* approaching

agosatrwydd, *n.m.* intimacy

agosáu, *v.* draw near, approach

agosrwydd, *n.m.* nearness, proximity

agwedd, (*-au*), *n.f.* form; aspect; attitude

agweddi, *n.m.* dowry, marriage gift

agwrdd, *a.* strong, mighty

angall, *a.* unwise, foolish

angau, *n.m.f.* death

angel, (*angylion, engyl*), *n.m.* angel

angen, (*anghenion*), *n.m.* need, want

angenoctid, *n.m.* indigence, want

angenrheidiol, *a.* necessary, needful

angenrheidrwydd, *n.m.* necessity

angerdd, *n.m.* heat; passion; force

angerddol, *a.* ardent, intense, passionate

angerddoldeb, *n.m.* vehemence, intensity

angeu. See **angau**

angeuol. See **angheuol**

anghaffael, *n.m.* mishap; defect, flaw

anghallineb, *n.m.* unwisdom, imprudence

angharedig, *a.* unkind

angharedigrwydd, *n.m.* unkindness

anghariadoldeb, *n.m.* uncharitableness

anghefnogi, *v.* discourage

anghelfydd, *a.* unskilful, clumsy

anghenfil, (*angenfilod*), *n.m.* monster

anghenraid, (*angenrheidiau*), *n.m.* necessity

anghenus, *a.* needy, necessitous, indigent

angheuol, *a.* deadly, mortal, fatal

anghlod, *n.m.* dispraise, dishonour

anghoelio, *v.* disbelieve

anghofio, *v.* forget

anghofrwydd, *n.m.* forgetfulness

anghofus, *a.* forgetful, oblivious

anghred, *n.f.* unbelief, infidelity

anghredadun, (*anghredinwyr*), *n.m.* unbeliever

anghrediniaeth, *n.f.* unbelief, infidelity

anghrediniol, *a.* unbelieving

anghredu, *v.* disbelieve

anghrefyddol, *a.* irreligious

anghrist, (*-iau*), *n.m.* antichrist

anghryno, *a.* incompact, prolix

anghwrtais, *a.* discourteous

anghydfod, *n.m.* disagreement, discord

Anghydffurfiaeth, *n.f.* Nonconformity

Anghydffurfiwr, (*-wyr*), *n.m.* Nonconformist

anghydnaws, *a.* uncongenial

anghydsynio, *v.* dissent, disagree

anghydweddol, *a.* incompatible

anghyfaddas, *a.* unsuitable, unfit

anghyfaddasu, *v.* unfit, disqualify

anghyfamodol, *a.* uncovenanted

anghyfanhedd-dra, *n.m.* desolation

anghyfanheddle, (*-aneddleoed*), *n.m.* desolate place

anghyfanheddol, *a.* desolating; desert

anghyfannedd, *a.* uninhabited, desert

anghyfansoddiadol, *a.* unconstitutional

anghyfartal, *a.* unequal, uneven

anghyfartaledd, *n.m.* disparity

anghyfarwydd, *a.* unfamiliar, unskilled**

anghyfeillgar, *a.* unfriendly

anghyfiaith, *a.* foreign, alien

anghyfiawn, *a.* unjust, unrighteous

anghyfiawnder, *n.m.* injustice

anghyflawn, *a.* incomplete

anghyfleus, *a.* inconvenient

anghyfleustra, (*-terau*), *n.m.* inconvenience

anghyflogaeth, *n.m.* unemployment

anghyfnewidiol, *a.* immutable

anghyfraith, *n.f.* transgression, crime

anghyfranogol, *a.* incommunicable

anghyfreithlon, *a.* unlawful, illegal, illegitimate

anghyfrifol *a.* irresponsible

anghyffredin *a.* uncommon, rare

anghyffyrddus, *a.* uncomfortable

anghymedrol, *a.* immoderate

anghymen, *a.* rash, coarse, untidy

anghymeradwy, *a.* unacceptable

anghymeradwyo, *v.* disapprove

anghymesur, *a.* inordinate

anghymharol, *a.* incomparable

anghymharus, *a.* ill-matched

anghymhendod, *n.m.* foolishness, indelicacy, untidiness

anghymhwyso, *v.* unfit, disqualify

anghymhwyster, *n.m.* incapacity, disqualification

anghymodlawn, -lon, *a.* implacable

anghymwys, *a.* unfit, unsuitable

anghynefin, *a.* unfamiliar

anghynefindra, *n.m.* unfamiliarity

anghynnes, *a.* odious, loathsome

anghysbell, *a.* out-of-the-way; remote

anghyson, *a.* inconsistent

anghysondeb, -der, (*-au*), *n.m.* inconsistency

anghysur, (*-on*), *n.m.* discomfort

anghysuro, *v.* discomfort

anghysurus, *a.* uncomfortable

anghytbwys, *a.* unbalanced, lopsided

anghytgord, (*-iau*), *n.m.* discord, dissension

anghytrig, *a.* non-resident, corresponding

anghytûn, *a.* not agreeing, discordant

anghytundeb, *n.m.* disagreement

anghytuno, *v.* disagree

anghywair, *a.* ill-equipped; discordant: *n.m.* disrepair

anghyweithas, *a.* froward, uncivil

anghywir, *a.* incorrect, inaccurate, false

anghywirdeb, (*-au*), *n.m.* inaccuracy, falseness

anghywrain, *a.* unskilful; slovenly

angladd, (*-au*), *n.m.f.* burial, funeral

angof, *n.m.* forgetfulness, oblivion

angor, (*-au, -ion*), *n.m.* anchor

angorfa, (*-oedd, -feydd*), *n.f.* anchorage

angori, *v.* anchor

angylaidd, *a.* angelic

angyles, (*-au*), *n.f.* female angel

ai, *adv.* is it? what? —**ai e?** is it so?

ai, *c.* or; either; if

aidd, *n.m.* zeal, ardour, zest

aig, *eigiau,* *n.f.* host, shoal

aig, *n.f.* (late corrupt form) sea, ocean

ail, *a.* second: *adv.* a second time, again

ailadrodd, *v.* repeat

ailadroddiad, (*-au*), *n.m.* repetition

ailenedigaeth, *n.f.* rebirth

aileni, *v.* bear again, regenerate

Ailfedyddiwr, (*-wyr*), *n.m.* Anabaptist

ail-law, *a.* second-hand

aillt, *n.m.* vassal, villain, slave

ais, *n.pl.* (**eisen,** *n.f.*), laths; ribs

alaeth, *n.m.* wailing, lamentation, grief

alaethu, *v.* lament

alaethus, *a.* mournful, lamentable

alaf, (*-oedd, elyf*), *n.m.* herd of cattle; wealth

alarch, (*-od, elyrch*), *n.m.* swan

alaru, *v.* surfeit; loathe

alaw, (*-on*), *n.f.* lily; air, melody, tune

Albanwr, (*-wyr*), *n.m.* Scot
alcam, *n.m.* tin
alch, (*-au, eilch*), *n.f.* grate, grill
algebra, *n.m.* algebra
Almaeneg, *n.f.* German
Almaenwr, (*-wyr*), *n.m.* German
almon, *n.m.* almond
aloi, (*aloeon*), *n.m.* alloy
allan, *adv.* out
allanol, *a.* outward, external
allforio, *v.* export
allfro, *n.* foreigner; foreign land
allgarwch, *n.m.* altruism
allor, (*-au*), *n.f.* altar
allt, (*elltydd*), *n.f.* hill; cliff; wood
alltud, (*-ion*), *n.m.* alien; exile
alltudiaeth, *n.f.* banishment, exile
alltudio, *v.* banish, exile
allwedd, (*-au, -i*), *n.f.* key, cleff (music)
am, *pr.* round, about; for; at; on: *c.* for, because; so long as
am. See **ym** [ture
amaeth, *n.m.* husbandman; agricul-
amaethdy, (*-dai*), *n.m.* farm-house
amaethu, *v.* farm, till
amaethwr, (*-wyr*), *n.m.* farmer
amaethwraig, *n.f.* farm-wife
amaethyddiaeth, *n.f.* agriculture
amaethyddol, *a.* agricultural
amarch, *n.m.* disrespect, dishonour
amau, *v.* doubt, suspect; (*-heuon*), *n.m.* doubt
ambell, *a.* occasional.—**a. waith,** sometimes
amcan, (*-ion*), *n.m.* purpose, aim; guess
amcangyfrif, *v.* estimate: (*-on*), *n.m.* estimate
amcanu, *v.* purpose; aim; guess
amdlawd, *a.* very poor, impoverished
amdo, (*-oeau*), *n.m.* shroud, winding-sheet
amdoi, *v.* shroud, enshroud
amdorch, (*-dyrch*), *n.f.* chaplet, wreath
amddifad, *a.* destitute, orphan
amddifadrwydd, *n.m.* destitution, privation

amddifadu, *v.* bereave, deprive
amddifaty, (*-tai*), *n.m.* orphanage
amddifedi, *n.m.* destitution, privation
amddiffyn, *v.* defend, protect, shield: (*-ion*), *n.m.* defence
amddiffynfa, (*-feydd*), *n.f.* fortress
amddiffyniad, *n.m.* protection, defence
amddiffynnwr, (*-ynwyr*), **-ynydd,** (*-ynyddion*), *n.m.* defender, protector
amddyfrwys, *a.* mighty, rugged; marshy
ameu. See **amau**
amgáu, *v.* enclose, shut in
amgen, *a. & adv.* other, else, otherwise; different.—**nid a.,** that is to say, namely
amgenach, *a. & adv.* otherwise; better
amgueddfa, (*-feydd*), *n.f.* museum
amgyffred, *v.* comprehend, comprise: (*-ion*), *n.m.* comprehension
amgyffrediad, *n.m.* comprehension
amgylch, (*-oedd*), *n.m.* circuit; environs, surroundings.—**o (oddi) amgylch,** round about, about
amgylchedd, *n.m.* circumference
amgylchfyd, *n.m.* environment
amgylchiad, (*-au*), *n.m.* circumstance; occasion
amgylchiadol, *a.* circumstantial
amgylchu, *v.* surround
amgylchynol, *a.* surrounding
amgylchynu, *v.* surround
amharch. See **amarch**
amharchu, *v.* dishonour, disrespect
amharchus, *a.* disrespectful, disreputable
amhariad, *n.m.* impairment, damage
amharod, *a.* unprepared, unready
amharodrwydd, *n.* unreadiness
amharu, *v.* impair, harm, injure, damage
amhechadurusrwydd, *n.m.* sinlessness
amhendant, *a.* indefinite, vague
amhenderfynol, *a.* irresolute

amhenodol, a. indefinite
amherchi, v. dishonour, insult
amherffaith, a. imperfect
amherffeithrwydd, n.m. imperfection
amhersonol, a. impersonal
amherth(y)nasol, a. irrelevant
amheuaeth, n.f. doubt, scepticism
amheugar, a. suspicious; sceptical
amheuol, a. doubting, doubtful
amheus, a. doubting, doubtful, dubious
amheuthun, a. dainty, savoury: (-ion), n.m. dainty, delicacy, treat
amheuwr, (-wyr), n.m. doubter, sceptic
amhiniog, (-au, -ion), n.m. doorpost, threshold; architrave; borderer
amhlantadwy, a. childless, barren
amhleidiol, amhleitgar, a. impartial
amhoblog, a. sparsely populated
amhoblogaidd, a. unpopular
amhosibl, a. impossible
amhriodol, a. improper
amhrisiadwy, a. priceless
amhrofiadol, a. inexperienced
amhrydlon, a. unpunctual
amhûr, a. impure, foul
amhwrpasol, a. irrelevant
amhwyllo, v. lose one's senses, go mad
aml, a. frequent, abundant: adv. often
amlder, amldra, n.m. abundance
amldduwiad,(-iaid), n.m. polytheist
amldduwiaeth, n.f. polytheism
amleiriog, a. wordy, verbose, prolix
amlen, (-ni), n.f. envelope, wrapper
amlhad, n.m. increasing, increase
amlhau, v. increase, multiply
amlinelliad, (-au), n.m. outline
amlochrog, a. many-sided
amlosgfa, n.f. crematorium
amlosgi, v. cremate
amlwg, a. plain, clear, manifest, evident, prominent
amlwreigiaeth, n.f. polygamy

amlwreigiwr, (-wyr), n.m. polygamist
amlygiad, (-au), n.m. manifestation
amlygrwydd, n.m. prominence
amlygu, v. manifest, reveal, evince
amlymu, v. trim, clear
amnaid, (-neidiau), n.f. beck, nod
amneidio, v. beckon, nod
amod, (-au), n.m.f. condition
amodi, v. covenant, stipulate
amodol, a. conditional
amrant, (-au, -rannau), n.m. eyelid
amrantiad, n.m. wink, twinkling, second
amreiniol, a. unprivileged
amrwd, a. uncooked, raw, crude
amryddawn, a. versatile
amryfal, a. sundry, manifold
amryfus, a. erroneous, inadvertent
amryfusedd, (-au), n.m. error, oversight
amrygyr, a. busy, restless
amryliw, a. variegated
amryw, a. several, sundry, various
amrywiad, (-au), n.m. variant
amrywiaeth, n.f. variety, diversity
amrywio, v. vary, differ
amrywiol, a. sundry
amrywion, n.pl. varieties
amser, (-oedd, -au), n.m.f. time
amseriad, (-au), n.m. timing, dating, date
amserlen, (-ni), n.f. time-table
amserol, a. timely; temporal
amseru, v. time, date
amserydd, (-ion), n.m. chronologist
amseryddiaeth, n.f. chronology
amseryddol, a. chronological
amwisg, (-oedd), n.f. covering, shroud
amwisgo, v. enwrap, shroud
amwyn, v. contend, seize, defend, support
amwys, a. ambiguous
amwysedd, n.m. ambiguity
amyn, c. & pr. unless, except, but
amynedd, n.m. patience
amyneddgar, a. patient
an-, px. un-, in-, de-, dis-

anach, (-au), n.m.f. impediment, disadvantage

anachaidd, a. unlawful, incompatible

anad, a. **Yn a.,** above all, more than

anadferadwy, a. irreparable

anadl, (-au, -on), n.f.m. breath

anadliad, n.m. breath, breathing

anadlu, v. breathe

anadnabyddus, a. unknown

anaddas, a. unfit, unsuitable

anaddasu, v. unfit, disqualify

anaeddfed, anaddfed, a. unripe

anaeddfedrwydd, n.m. unripeness

anaele, a. awful, direful; incurable

anaf, (-au), n.m. blemish, defect; wound

anafu, v. blemish, maim

anafus, a. maimed, disabled

anair, (-eiriau), n.m. ill report, slander

anallu, n.m. inability

analluog, a. unable

analluogi, v. disenable; disable

anaml, a. infrequent, rare: adv. rarely, seldom [uous

anamlwg, a. obscure, inconspic-

anamserol, a. untimely, mistimed

anap, (-hapon), n.m.f. mischance, mishap

anarchiaeth, n.m. anarchy

anarferol, a. unusual, extraordinary

anarfog, a. unarmed

anawdd, a. hard, difficult (also **anhawdd**)

anchwiliadwy, a. unsearchable

ancr, n.m.f. anchorite, anchoress

ancwyn, (-ion), n.m. dinner, supper; delicacy

andras, n.m. curse; devil, deuce

andwyo, v. spoil, ruin, undo

andwyol, a. harmful, ruinous

anedifeiriol, a. impenitent

aneddfa. See **anheddfa**

aneffeithiol, a. ineffectual

aneglur, a. indistinct; illegible

aneirif, a. innumerable

anelu, v. bend, aim

anenwog, a. unrenowned, ignoble, mean

anerchiad, (-au), n.m. salutation, address

anesboniadwy, a. inexplicable

anesgusodol, a. inexcusable

anesmwyth, a. uneasy, restless

anesmwythder, -dra, n.m. uneasiness, unrest

anesmwytho, v. be or make uneasy

anesmwythyd, n.m. uneasiness, disquiet

anewyllysgar, a. unwilling

anfad, a. wicked, nefarious

anfadrwydd, n.m. wickedness, villainy

anfadwaith, n.m. villainy

anfadwr, (-wyr), n.m. villain, scoundrel

anfaddeugar, a. unforgiving

anfaddeuol, a. unpardonable

anfanol, -wl, a. rough, uncouth

anfantais, (-teision), n.f. disadvantage

anfanteisiol, a. disadvantageous

anfarwol, a. undying, immortal

anfarwoldeb, n.m. immortality

anfedrus, a. unskilful

anfedrusrwydd, n.m. unskilfulness

anfeddyginiaethol, a. incurable

anfeidrol, a. infinite

anfeidroldeb, n.m. infinity

anferth, a. huge, monstrous

anferthedd, n.m. hugeness, monstrosity

anfodlon, a. unwilling

anfodloni, v. discontent, dissatisfy

anfodlonrwydd, n.m. discontent

anfodd, n.m. unwillingness, displeasure

anfoddio, v. displease, disoblige

anfoddlon, &c. See **anfodlon**

anfoddog, a. discontented, dissatisfied

anfoddogrwydd, n.m. discontentment

anfoesgar, a. unmannerly, rude

anfoesgarwch, n.m. rudeness, incivility

anfoesol, a. immoral

anfoesoldeb, n.m. immorality

anfon, *v.* send, transmit, dispatch

anfoneddigaidd, *a.* ungentlemanly

anfonheddig, *a.* ignoble, discourteous

anfoniad, *n.m.* sending, transmission

anfri, *n.m.* disrespect, dishonour

anfucheddol, *a.* immoral

anfuddiol, *a.* unprofitable

anfwriadol, *a.* unintentional

anfwyn, *a.* unkind, ungentle, uncivil

anfynud, *a.* rough, unrefined

anfynych, *a.* infrequent, seldom, rare

anffaeledig, *a.* infallible

anffaeledigrwydd, *n.m.* infallibility

anffafriol, *a.* unfavourable

anffawd, (*-ffodion*), *n.f.* misfortune

anffodus, anffortunus, *a.* unfortunate

anffrwythlon, *a.* unfruitful, barren

anffurfio, *v.* disfigure, deform

anffurfiol, *a.* deformed; informal

anffyddiaeth, *n.f.* infidelity, atheism

anffyddiwr, (*-wyr*), *n.m.* infidel, atheist

anffyddlon, *a.* unfaithful

anguriol, angiriol, *a.* fearful, painful, dire

anhaeddiannol, *a.* unmerited

anhaeddiant, *n.m.* demerit, unworthiness

anhapus, *a.* unhappy, unlucky

anhardd, *a.* unhandsome, unseemly

anharddwch, *n.m.* uncomeliness

anhawdd, *a.* hard, difficult

anhawddgar, *a.* unamiable, unlovely

anhawster, (*anawsterau*), *n.m.* difficulty

anheddfa, (*aneddfaoedd*), *n.f.*, **-le,** (*aneddleoedd*), *n.m.f.* dwellingplace

anhepgor, (*-ion*), *n.m.* essential

anhepgorol, *a.* indispensable

anhoffter, *n.m.* hatred, dislike

anhraethadwy, *a.* unutterable

anhraethol, *a.* unspeakable, ineffable

anhrefn, *n.m.* disorder, confusion

anhrefnu, *v.* disorder, disarrange

anhrefnus, *a.* disorderly, untidy

anhreiddiol, *a.* impervious, impenetrable

anhreuliedig, *a.* undigested; unspent

anhrugarog, *a.* unmerciful, merciless

anhuddo, *v.* cover

anhunedd, *n.m.* wakefulness, disquiet

anhwyldeb, *n.m.* disorder, complaint

anhwylus *a.* unwell; inconvenient

anhwylustod, *n.m.* inconvenience

anhyblyg, *a.* inflexible, stiff, rigid

anhydawdd, *a.* insoluble

anhyder, *n.m.* distrust, diffidence

anhyderus, *a.* diffident

anhydrin, *a.* unmanageable

anhydyn, *a.* intractable, obstinate

anhyddysg, *a.* unversed, ignorant

anhyfryd, *a.* unpleasant

anhyfrydwch, *n.m.* unpleasantness

anhygar, *a.* unpleasant, unamiable

anhygoel, *a.* incredible

anhygyreh, *a.* inaccessible

anhylaw, *a.* unhandy, unwieldy

anhynod, *a.* indistinctive; uncertain

anhysbys, *a.* unknown; unversed

anhywaith, *a.* intractable, refractory

anial, *a.* desert, wild: *n.m.* wilderness

anialwch, *n.m.* wilderness

anian, (*-au*), *n.f.* nature, instinct, genius

anianawd, *n.m.* temperament, disposition

anianol, *a.* natural

anianyddol, *a.* physical

anifail, (*-feiliaid*), *n.m.* animal, beast

anifeilaidd, *a.* beastly, brutish

anifeileiddio, *v.* animalize, brutalize

anifeilig, *a.* animal, of animals

anlwc, *n.m.* bad luck, misfortune

anlwcus, *a.* unlucky

anllad, *a.* wanton, lascivious, lewd

anlladrwydd, *n.m.* wantonness, lewdness

anlladu, *v.* wanton

anllygradwy, *a.* incorruptible

anllygredig, *a.* incorrupt, incorruptible

anllygredigaeth, *n.f.* incorruption

anllythrennog, *a.* illiterate

anllywodraeth, *n.f.* misrule, anarchy

annaearol, *a.* unearthly, weird

annatodol, *a.* indissoluble

annaturiol, *a.* unnatural

annealladwy, *a.* unintelligible

anneallus, *a.* unintelligent

annedwydd, *a.* unhappy, miserable

annedwyddwch, *n.m.* unhappiness

annedd, *(anheddau), n.f.* dwelling

anneddfol, *a.* lawless

annefnyddiol, *a.* useless; immaterial

annelwig, *a.* shapeless, unformed; vague

anner, *(aneirod, -i, -au), n.f.* heifer

annerbyniol, *a.* unacceptable

annerch, *v.* salute, greet, address; *(anerchion), n.m.* salutation, greeting

annewisol, *a.* ineligible, undesirable

annhebyg, *a.* unlike, dissimilar

annhebygol, *a.* unlikely, improbable

annhebygolrwydd, *n.m.* improbability

annhebygrwydd, *n.m.* unlikeness

annheg, *a.* unfair

annhegwch, *n.m.* unfairness

annheilwng, *a.* unworthy

annheilyngdod, *n.m.* unworthiness

annherfynol, *a.* endless; infinitive

annhirion, *a.* ungentle, cruel

annhosturiol, *a.* pitiless, ruthless

annhuedd, *n.f.* disinclination

annhueddol, *a.* disinclined, indisposed

anniben, *a.* slow; untidy, slovenly

annibendod, *n.m.* slowness; untidiness

annibyniaeth, *n.f.* independence

annibynnol, *a.* independent

Annibynnwr, *(-ynwyr), n.m.* Independent

annichellgar, *a.* guileless, simple

annichon, -adwy, *a.* impossible

anniddan, *a.* comfortless, miserable

anniddig, *a.* peevish, irritable, fretful

anniddigrwydd, *n.m.* peevishness

anniddos, *a.* leaky, comfortless

annifeiriol, *a.* innumerable

anniflanedig, *a.* unfading, imperishable

annifyr, *a.* miserable

annifyrrwch, *n.m.* misery

anniffoddadwy, *a.* unquenchable

annigonedd, *n.m.* insufficiency

annigonol, *a.* insufficient, inadequate

annigonolrwydd, *n.m.* inadequacy

annileadwy, *a.* indelible, ineffaceable

annilys, *a.* unauthentic, spurious

annillyn, *a.* inelegant

annioddefol, *a.* unbearable, intolerable

anniogel, *a.* unsafe, insecure

anniolchgar, *a.* unthankful, ungrateful

anniolchgarwch, *n.m.* ingratitude

annirnadwy, *a.* incomprehensible

annisgrifiadwy, *a.* indescribable

annisgwyliadwy, *a.* unexpected

anniwair, *a.* unchaste, incontinent, lewd

anniwall, *a.* insatiable

anniweirdeb, *n.m.* unchastity, incontinence

anniwylliedig, *a.* uncultured

annoeth, *a.* unwise, imprudent

annoethineb, *n.m.* unwisdom, folly

annog, *v.* incite, urge; exhort

annormal, *a.* abnormal

annos, *v.* incite, set (a dog) on

annosbarthus, *a.* unruly, disorderly

annuw, -iad, (-iaid), n.m. atheist

annuwiaeth, n.f. atheism

annuwiol, a. ungodly, godless

annuwioldeb, n.m. ungodliness

annwn, n.m. the underworld, abyss, hell

annwyd, (anwydau, -on), n.m. cold

annwyl, a. dear, beloved

annyledus, a. undue, wrongful

annymunol, a. unpleasant, disagreeable

annynol, a. inhuman, cruel

annysgedig, a. unlearned

anobaith, n.m. despair

anobeithio, v. despair

anobeithiol, a. hopeless

anocheladwy, a. unavoidable, inevitable

anodd, a. hard, difficult

anoddefgar, a. impatient, intolerant

anoddun, n.m. abyss

anogaeth, (-au), n.f. admonition, exhortation

anolrheinadwy, a. unsearchable

anolygus, a. unsightly

anonest, a. dishonest

anonestrwydd, n.m. dishonesty

anorchfygol, a. irresistible

anorfod, a. insuperable, unavoidable

anorffen, a. endless, unending

anorffennol, a. uncompleted; imperfect

anorthrech, a. invincible

anrasol, a. graceless

anrhaith, (-rheithiau), n.f. prey, spoil, booty

anrheg, (-ion), n.f. present, gift

anrhegu, v. present, give

anrheithio, v. prey, spoil, plunder

anrheithiwr, (-wyr), n.m. spoiler

anrhydedd, (-au), n.m. honour

anrhydeddu, v. honour

anrhydeddus, a. honourable

anrhydeddwr, (-wyr), n.m. honourer

ansad, a. unsteady, unstable

ansadrwydd, n.m. instability

ansafadwy, a. unstable; fickle

ansathredig, a. untrodden, unfrequented

ansawdd, (-soddau), n.m.f. quality, state

ansefydlog, a. unsettled: unstable; fickle

ansefydlogi, v. unsettle

ansicr, a. uncertain, doubtful

ansicrwydd, n.m. uncertainty, doubt

ansoddair, (-eiriau), n.m. adjective

ansoddi, v. qualify

ansyber, a. untidy, slovenly

anterliwt, (-iau), n.m.f. interlude

anterth, n.m. meridian, zenith, prime

antur, (-iau), n.m. attempt, venture; adventure. —**ar a.,** at random

anturiaeth, (-au), n.f. adventure, enterprise

anturiaethus, a. adventurous, enterprising [turer

anturiaethwr, (-wyr), n. adventurio,

anturio, v. venture, adventure

anturus, a. adventurous

anthem, (-au), n.f. anthem

anudon, (-au), n.m. false oath, perjury

anudoniaeth, n.f. perjury

anudonwr, (-wyr), n.m. perjurer

anufudd, a. disobedient

anufudd-dod, n.m. disobedience

anufuddhau, v. disobey

anundeb, n.m. disunion

anunion, a. crooked; unjust

anuniondeb, n.m. injustice, iniquity

anurddo, v. spoil, mar, disfigure

anwadal, v. unstable, fickle, changeable

anwadalu, v. waver, vacillate

anwadalwch, n.m. fickleness

anwar, a. wild, barbarous, savage

anwaraidd, a. uncivilized, barbarous

anwarddyn, (-wariaid), n.m. barbarian, savage

anwareidd-dra, n.m. barbarity

anwastad, a. uneven, unstable, fickle

anwe, (-oedd), n.f. woof

an-wedd, a. enormous

anwedd, n.m. vapour, steam

anweddaidd, a. unseemly, indecent

anweddus, a. improper, indecent

anweledig, a. unseen, invisible

anwes, n.m. indulgence; caress

anwesog, a. pampered, affectionate

anwesu, v. fondle, caress, pamper, indulge

anwir, a. untrue, lying, false; wicked

anwiredd, (-au), n.m. untruth; iniquity

anwireddu, v. falsify

anwireddus, a. untruthful, false, lying

anwr, (-wyr), n.m. wretch, coward

anwybod, n.m. ignorance, discourtesy

anwybodaeth, n.f. ignorance

anwybodus, a. ignorant

anwybyddu, v. ignore

anwydog, a. cold, chilly; having a cold

anwydwst, n.f. influenza

anwyldeb, n.m. belovedness, dearness

anwyliaid, n.pl. beloved ones, favourites

anwylo, v. cherish, fondle, caress

anwylyd, (-liaid), n.m. beloved

anwylyn, n.m. favourite

anwythiad, n.m. induction

anwythol, a. inductive

anymarferol, a. impractical, impracticable

anymddiried, v. & n.m. mistrust, distrust

anymwybodol, a. unconscious

anymwybyddiaeth, n.f. unconsciousness

anynad, a. peevish, petulant; brawling

anysbryd, (-oedd), n.m. evil spirit

anysgrifenedig, a. unwritten

anysgrythurol, a. unscriptural

anystwyth, a. stiff, rigid

anystwytho, v. stiffen

anystyriaeth, n.f. heedlessness, rashness

anystyriol, a. heedless, reckless, rash

anystywallt, -ell, a. unmanageable

apêl, (apelion), n.m.f., **apeliad,** (-au), n.m. appeal

apelio, v. appeal

apostol, (-ion), n.m. apostle

apostolaidd, -ig, a. apostolic

apostoliaeth, n.f. apostleship

apwyntio, v. appoint

âr, n. ploughed land, tilth; ground

ar, pr. on, upon, over

arab, a. facetious, merry, pleasant

arabedd, n.m. facetiousness, wit

arabus, a. witty

aradr, (erydr), n.m. plough

araf, a. slow, soft, gentle, still

arafu, v. slow; quiet; moderate

arafwch, n.m. slowness; moderation

arail, v. guard, care for, foster: a. attending

araith, (areithiau), n.f. speech

arall, (eraill), a. & pn. another, other; else

aralleg, (-au), n.f.m. allegory

aralleiriad, (-au), n.m. paraphrase

aralleirio, v. paraphrase

araul, a. sunny, sunlit; serene

arawd, n.f. speech, oration

arbed, v. spare, save

arbedol, a. sparing, saving

arbenigrwydd, n.m. speciality, prominence

arbennig, a. special

arch, (eirchion), n.f. request, petition; bidding

arch, (eirch), n.f. ark, coffin; trunk, waist

archadeiladydd, n.m. architect

archaeoleg, n.f. archaeology

archangel, (-ylion), n.m. archangel

archdeyrnaeth, (-au), n.f. monarchy, despotism

archddiacon, (-iaid), n.m. archdeacon

archeb, (*-ion*), *n.f.* order
archebu, *v.* order
archen, *n.f.*, **-ad,** *n.m.* shoe; clothing
archesgob, (*-ion*), *n.m.* archbishop
archesgobaeth, (*-au*), *n.f.* archbishopric
archiad, *n.m.* bidding
archoffeiriad, (*-iaid*), *n.m.* high priest
archoll, (*-ion*), *n.f.* wound
archolli, *v.* wound
archwaeth, *n.m.* taste, appetite
archwaethu, *v.* taste, savour
archwilio, *v.* examine, audit; explore
archwiliwr, (*-wyr*), *n.m.* auditor; explorer
ardal, (*-oedd*), *n.f.* region, district
ardalydd, (*-ion*), *n.m.* marquis
ardreth, (*-i,*) *n.f.* rent
ardrethol, *a.* rented, hired
ardrethu, *v.* rent
ardwy, *n.m.* protection; ruler
ardystiad, (*-au*), *n.m.* pledge, attestation
ardystio, *v.* pledge, attest
arddangos, *v.* show, exhibit, indicate
arddangosfa, (*-feydd*), *n.f.* show
arddel, *v.* avow, own
arddeliad, *n.m.* unction
ardderchog, *a.* excellent, noble, splendid
ardderchowgrwydd, *n.m.* excellency
arddodi, *v.* prefix; impose
arddodiad, (*-iaid*), *n.m.* preposition
arddodiad, (*-au*), *n.m.* imposition
arddu, *v.* plough (properly **aredig**)
arddull, (*-iau*), *n.f.* style
ardduniant, *n.m.* sublimity
arddunol, *a.* sublime
arddwr, (*-wyr*), *n.m.* ploughman
arddwrn, (*-ddyrnau*), *n.m.* wrist
aredig, *v.* plough
areitheg, *n.f.* rhetoric
areithfa, *n.f.* pulpit, platform
areithio, *v.* speak, make a speech
areithiwr, (*-wyr*), *n.m.* speaker, orator

areithyddiaeth, *n.f.* oratory; elocution
aren, (*-nau*), kidney; (*pl.*) reins
arf, (*-au*), *n.m.f.* weapon, (*pl.*) arms; tool
arfaeth, (*-au*), *n.f.* purpose; decree
arfaethu, *v.* purpose
arfdy, (*-dai*), *n.m.* armoury
arfeddyd, *n.m.* purpose, intention
arfer, *v.* use, accustom: (*-ion*), *n.f.m.* use, custom, habit
arferiad, *n.m.f.* use, custom, habit
arferol, *a.* usual, customary
arfod, *n.f.* stroke of a weapon, fight; armour
arfod, *n.m.* guard; opportunity, occasion
arfog, *a.* armed
arfogaeth, *n.f.* armour
arfogi, *v.* arm
arfoll, (*-au*), *n.m.* pledge, oath; welcome reception
arfordir, (*-oedd*), *n.m.* coast
arffed, (*-au*), *n.f.* lap
arffedog, (*-au*), *n.f.* apron
argae, (*-au*), *n.m.* dam, embankment; enclosed place
argeisio, *v.* seek
argel, *n.m.f.* concealment, refuge: *a.* hidden, occult
arglwydd, (*-i*), *n.m.* lord
arglwyddaidd, *a.* lordly
arglwyddes, (*-au*), *n.f.* lady
arglwyddiaeth, (*-au*), *n.f.* lordship, dominion
arglwyddiaethu, *v.* have dominion
argoed, (*-ydd*), *n.m.* enclosure of trees
argoel, (*-ion*), *n.f.* sign, token, omen
argoeli, *v.* betoken, portend, augur
argoelus, *a.* ominous
argraff, (*-ion*, *-au*), *n.f.* print, impression
argraffiad, (*-au*), *n.m.* impression; edition
argraffty, (*-tai*), *n.m.* printing-house
argraffu, *v.* print, impress
argraffwasg, *n.f.* printing-press

argraffwr, (*-wyr*), **-ydd,** (*-ion*), *n.m.* printer

argyfwng, (*-yngau, -yngoedd*), *n.m.* crisis

argyhoeddi, *v.* reprove; convince, convict

argyhoeddiad, (*-au*), *n.m.* conviction

argyhoeddiadol, *a.* convincing

argyllaeth, *n.m.* grief, mourning

argymell, *v.* urge, recommend

argyswr(w), *n.m.* fear

argywedd, *n.m.* harm, hurt

arholi, *v.* examine

arholiad, (*-au*), *n.m.* examination

arholwr, (*-wyr*), *n.m.* examiner

arhosfa, *n.f.* abode; stay

arhosiad, *n.m.* staying, stay

arhosol, *a.* abiding, permanent

arial, *n.m.f.* vigour, mettle

arian, *n.m.* silver: *c.n.* money, cash. **—a. breiniol,** currency. **—a. treigl,** current money

ariandy, (*-dai*), *n.m.* bank

ariangar, *a.* fond of money, avaricious

ariangarwch, *n.m.* love of money, avarice

ariannaid, *a.* silver, silvern

ariannaidd, *a.* silvery

ariannog, *a.* moneyed, wealthy, rich

ariannol, *a.* financial, monetary

ariannu, *v.* silver

ariannydd, (*arianyddion*), *n.m.* banker

arlais, (*-leisiau*), *n.f.* temple

arloesi, *v.* clear, prepare the way

arloesydd, (*-wyr*), *n.m.* pioneer

arlun, (*-iau*), *n.m.* portrait, painting, drawing

arluniaeth, *n.f.* portraiture, painting

arlunio, *v.* draw, paint, portray

arlunydd, (*-wyr*), *n.m.* artist

arlwy, (*-au, -on*), *n.m.f.* provision, feast

arlwyo, *v.* prepare, provide; cook

arlywydd, (*-ion*), *n.m.* president

arlywyddiaeth, *n.f.* presidency

arlliw, (*-iau*), *n.m.* varnish, tint

arlliwio, *v.* colour, tint, paint

arllwys, *v.* pour out, empty

arllwysfa, *n.f.* outfall, outlet, vent

armel, *n.m.* second milk

armes, *n.f.* prophecy, calamity

arnodd, (*-au*), *n.m.f.* plough-beam

arobryn, *a.* worthy, prize-winning

arofun, *v.* intend, purpose

arogl, (*-au*), **aroglau,** (*-euau*), *n.m.* scent, smell

arogl-darth, *n.m.* incense

arogldarthu, *v.* burn incense

arogli, arogleuo, *v.* scent; smell

arogliad, *n.m.* smelling, sense of smell

arolwg, *n.m.* survey

arolygiaeth, *n.f.* superintendency

arolygu, *v.* superintend

arolygwr, (*-wyr*), **-ydd,** (*-ion*), *n.m.* superintendent, inspector

aros, *v.* wait, await, stay, stop, tarry, abide, remain

arswyd, *n.m.* dread, terror, horror

arswydo, *v.* dread; shudder

arswydus, *a.* fearful, terrible, dreadful

arsyllfa, (*-feydd*), *n.f.* observatory

artaith, (*-teithiau*), *n.f.* torture, torment, pang

arteithglwyd, *n.f.* rack

arteithio, *v.* torture, rack

arteithiol, *a.* racking, excruciating

arth, (*eirth*), *n.m.f.* bear

arthes, (*-au*), *n.f.* she-bear

arthio, -u, *v.* bark, growl

aruchel, *a.* lofty, sublime

arucheledd, *n.m.* loftiness, sublimity

aruthr, *a.* marvellous, strange

aruthredd, *n.m.* amazement, horror

aruthrol, *a.* huge, prodigious

arwaesaf, *n.m.* warrant, guarantor, protector

arwain, *v.* conduct, lead, guide, carry

arwedd, (*-au, -ion*), *n.f.* bearing, aspect

arweddu, *v.* bear

arweddwr, (*-wyr*), *n.m.* bearer

arweiniad, *n.m.* guidance; introduction

arweiniol, *a.* leading, introductory

arweinydd, (*-ion*), *n.m.* guide, leader; conductor

arweinyddiaeth, *n.f.* leadership

arwerthiant, (*-iannau*), *n.m.* auction

arwerthu, *v.* sell by auction

arwerthwr, (*-wyr*), *n.m.* auctioneer

arwest, *n.f.* string; minstrelsy

arwisgiad, *n.m.* investiture

arwisgo, *v.* enrobe, array, invest

arwr, (*-wyr*), *n.m.* hero

arwraidd, *a.* heroic, epic

arwres, (*-au*), *n.f.* heroine

arwrgerdd, (*-i*), *n.f.* epic poem

arwriaeth, *n.f.* heroism

arwrol, *a.* heroic, gallant

arwyar, *a.* bloodstained

arwybod, *n.m.* awareness

arwydd, (*-ion*), *n.m.f.* sign, signal: ensign

arwyddair, (*-eiriau*), *n.m.* motto

arwyddlun, (*-iau*), *n.m.* emblem, symbol   [bolic

arwyddluniol, *a.* emblematic, sym-

arwyddnod, (*-au*), *n.m.* mark, token

arwyddo, *v.* sign; signify

arwyddocâd, *n.m.* signification

arwyddocaol, *a.* significant

arwyddocáu, *v.* signify, denote

arwyl, (*-ion*), *n.f.* funeral rites

arwylo, *v.* mourn over the dead

arwynebedd, *n.m.* surface, superficies

arwynebol, *a.* superficial

arwyrain, *n.m.f.* praise, panegyric: *v.* rise, extol

arwystlo, *v.* pledge, mortgage

arynaig, *n.m.* fear, dread

arysgrif, (*-au*), **-en,** (*-nau*), *n.f.* inscription, epigraph

asb, (*-iaid*), *n.f.* asp

asbri, *n.m.* animation, vivacity, spirits

asbrïol, *a.* animated, vivacious, spirited

asen, (*-nau, ais*), *n.f.* rib

asen, (*-nod*), *n.f.* she-ass

aseth, *n.f.* stake, spar, lath

asgell, (*esgyll*), *n.f.* wing, fin. —**a. fraith,** chaffinch

asgellog, *a.* winged

asglod, asglodion, *n.pl.* (**asglodyn,** *n.m.*), chips

asgre, *n.f.* bosom, heart

asgwrn, (*esgyrn*), *n.m.* bone

asiedydd, (*-ion*), *n.m.* joiner

asio, *v.* join, weld; solder; cement

astalch, (*estylch*), *n.f.* shield

astell, (*estyll, ystyllod*), *n.f.* plank, shelf. **a. ddu,** black-board

astrus, *a.* abstruse, difficult

astud, *a.* attentive

astudiaeth, (*-au*), *n.f.* study

astudio, *v.* study

astudrwydd, *n.m.* attentiveness

aswy, *a.* left

aswyno, *v.* beseech; charm, conjure

asyn, (*-nod*), *n.m.* he-ass

asynnaidd, *a.* asinine

at, *pr.* to, towards; for; at; by

atafaeliad, *n.m.* confiscation, distraint

atafaelu, *v.* distrain, confiscate

atal, *v.* stop, hinder, withhold: (*-ion*), *n.m.* hindrance, impediment. —**a. dweud,** stammering

atalfa, (*-feydd*), *n.f.* check; stoppage

ataliad, (*-au*), *n.m.* stoppage

ataliol, *a.* preventive

atalnod, (*-au*), *n.f.* stop, point

atalnodi, *v.* point, punctuate

atblygol, *a.* reflexive

atbor, (*-ion*), *n.m.* leavings, scraps

ateb, *v.* answer, reply: (*-ion*), *n.m.* answer

atebol, *a.* answerable, responsible

ateg, (*-ion*), *n.f.* prop, stay, support

ategol, *a.* confirming; auxiliary

atgas, *a.* odious, hateful

atgasrwydd, *n.m.* odiousness, hatefulness

atgenhedliad, *n.m.* regeneration

atgenhedlu, *v.* regenerate

atgno, (*-oeau, -oeon*), *n.m.* remorse

atgof, (*-ion*), *n.m.* remembrance, reminiscence

atgofio, *v.* recollect, remember, remind

atgoffa, *v.* recall, remind

atgyfnerthion, *n.pl.* reinforcements

atgyfnerthu, *v.* reinforce

atgyfodi, *v.* rise or raise again

atgyfodiad, *n.m.* resurrection

atgynhyrchu, *v.* reproduce

atgyweiriad, (*-au*), *n.m.* repair

atgyweirio, *v.* repair, mend

atgyweiriwr, (*-wyr*), *n.m.* repairer, mender

atodi, *v.* add, append, affix

atodiad, (*-au*), *n.m.* addition, appendix

atodlen, (*-ni*), *n.f.* supplement; schedule

atolwg, atolygu, *v.* pray, beseech

atom, (*-au*), *n.m.f.* atom

atreg, *n.m.* remorse, delay, support

atsain, (*-seiniau*), *n.f.* echo; *v.* echo

atseinio, *v.* resound, echo

atwf, (*atyfion*), *n.m.* second growth

atyniad, (*-au*), *n.m.* attraction

atyniadol, *a.* attractive

atynnu, *v.* attract

athrawaidd, *a.* apt to teach

athrawes, (*-au*), *n.f.* teacher, governess

athrawiaeth, (*-au*), *n.f.* doctrine

athrawiaethol, *a.* doctrinal

athrawiaethu, *v.* teach

athrawus, *a.* apt to teach

athrist, *a.* very sad, pensive, sorrowful

athro, (*athrawon*), *n.m.* teacher, master

athrod, (*-ion*), *n.m.* slander, libel

athrodwr, (*-wyr*), *n.m.* slanderer, libeller

athrofa, (*-feydd*), *n.f.* college, academy

athrofaol, *a.* academic

athroniaeth, *n.f.* philosophy

athronydd, (*-ion, -wyr*), *n.m.* philosopher

athronyddol, *a.* philosophical

athronyddu, *v.* philosophize

athrylith, (*-oedd*), *n.f.* genius

athrylithgar, *a.* of genius, talented

athrywyn, *n.m.* mediation, intervention: *v.* mediate, arbitrate

aur, *n.m.* gold

awch, *n.m.* edge; ardour, zest; relish, appetite

awchlym, *a.* sharp, keen, acute

awchlymu, *v.* sharpen, whet

awchus, *a.* sharp, keen; eager; greedy

awdl, (*-au, odlau*), *n.f.* ode

awdur, (*-on, -iaid*), *n.m.* author

awduraidd, *a.* classic

awdurdod, (*-au*), *n.m.f.* authority

awdurdodi, *v.* authorize

awdurdodol, *a.* authoritative

awdures, (*-au*), *n.f.* authoress

awduriaeth, *n.f.* authorship

awdwr, (*-wyr*), *n.m.* author

awel, (*-on*), *n.f.* breeze, wind

awelog, *a.* breezy, windy

awen, (*-au*), *n.f.* muse

awen, (*-au*), *n.f.* rein

awenydd, (*-ion*), *n.m.* poet

awenyddes, (*-au*), *n.f.* poetess

awenyddiaeth, *n.f.* poetry, poesy

awenyddol, *a.* poetical

awenyddu, *v.* poetize

awgrym, (*-au, -iadau*), *n.m.* hint, suggestion

awgrymiadol, *a.* suggestive

awgrymu, *v.* hint, suggest

awr, (*oriau*), *n.f.* hour

awrlais, (*-leisiau*), *n.m.* clock

Awst, *n.m.* August

awydd, (*-au*), *n.m.* desire, eagerness

awyddfryd, *n.m.* vehement desire, zeal

awyddu, *v.* desire

awyddus, *a.* desirous, eager, zealous

awyr, *n.f.* air, sky

awyrdrom, (*-au*), *n.f.* aerodrome

awyren, (*-nau, -ni*) *n.f.* balloon, aeroplane

awyrendy, (*-dai*) *n.m.* hangar

awyrgylch, (*-au, -oedd*), *n.m.f.* atmosphere

awyriad, *n.m.* ventilation

awyrlong, (*-au*), *n.f.* airship

awyro, -u, *v.* air, ventilate

B

baban, (-*od*), *a.* baby
babanidd, *a.* babyish
babandod, *n.m.* babyhood, infancy
bacas, (*bacs*(*i*)*au*), *n.f.* footless stocking; hair on horse's fetlocks
baco, *n.m.* tobacco
bacwn, *n.m.* bacon
bach, (-*au*), *n.m.* hook. —**bachau petryal,** square brackets
bach, *a.* little, small
bachell, (-*au*, -*ion*), *n.f.* nook, corner; snare
bachgen, (*bechgyn*), *n.m.* boy
bachgendod, *n.m.* boyhood
bachgennaidd, *a.* boyish
bachgennes, (-*au*), *n.f.* young girl
bachgennyn, (*bechgynnos*), *n.m.* little boy
bachigyn, (*bachigion*), *n.m.* little bit, diminutive
bachog, *a.* hooked
bachu, *v.* hook, grapple
bad, (-*au*), *n.m.* boat
badwr, (-*wyr*), *n.m.* boatman
badd, (-*au*), **baddon,** (-*au*), *n.m.* bath
bae, (-*au*), *n.m.* bay
baedd, (-*od*), *n.m.* boar
baeddu, *v.* beat, buffet; soil
baetio, *v.* bait, maltreat
bagad, (-*au*), *n.m.* cluster; troop, multitude
bagl, (-*au*), *n.f.* crook; crutch; leg
baglor, (-*ion*), *n.f.* bachelor
bagloriaeth, *n.f.* bachelorship
baglu, *v.* entangle, ensnare, trip
bagwy, (-*au*, -*on*), *n.m.* cluster, bunch; point
bai, (*beiau*), *n.m.* fault, vice; defect; blame
baich, (*beichiau*), *n.m.* burden, load
bais, *n.* bottom, ford; walking
bala, *n.m.* efflux of river from lake
balc, (-*iau*), *n.m.* balk
balcio, *v.* balk
balch, *a.* proud; glad
balchder, *n.m.* pride

balchdra, *n.m.* joy, gladness
balchïo, *v.* pride
baldordd, *n.m.* babble, balderdash
baldorddi, *v.* babble
baled, (-*i*), *n.f.* ballad
baledwr, (-*wyr*), *n.m.* ballad-monger
balm, *n.m.* balm
balmaidd, *a.* balmy
balleg, *n.f.* hamper, net, purse
ballegrwyd, (-*au*), *n.f.* drag-net
ban, (-*nau*), *n.m.f.* peak; horn; corner; stanza
banadl, *n.pl.* (**-badlen,** *n.f.*), broom
banc, (-*iau*), *n.m.* bank
banc, (*bencydd*), *n.m.* bank, mound, hill
bancaw, (-*iau*), *n.m.* band, tuft
baner, (-*au*, -*i*), *n.f.* banner, flag
banerog, *a.* with banners, bannered
banerwr, (-*wyr*), *n.m.* standard-bearer; ensign
banffagl, (-*au*), *n.f.* bonfire, blaze
bangaw, *a.* eloquent, melodious, skilful
bangor, (-*au*, *bengyr*), *n.f.m.* upper row of rods in wattle fence; monastery
baniar, (-*ieri*) *n.m.f.* shout; banner
banllaw, (-*lloriau*), *n.m.* platform
banllef, (-*au*), *n.f.* loud shout
bannod, (*banodau*), *n.f.* article
bannog, *a.* elevated, conspicuous; horned
banon, *n.f.* queen
bar, (-*rau*), *n.m.* bar
bâr, *n.m.* fury, greed
bara, *n.m.* bread
baran, *n.m.* fury, rage
barbaraidd, *a.* barbarous
barbareidd-dra, *n.m.* barbarity
barbareiddio, *v.* barbarize
barbariad, (-*iaid*), *n.m.* barbarian
barbariaeth, *n.m.* barbarism
barbwr, (-*wyr*), *n.m.* barber
barcer, (-*iaid*), *n.m.* tanner
barclod, (-*iau*), *n.m.* apron
barcud, (-*iaid*), **barcutan,** (-*od*), *n.m.* kite
bardd, (*beirdd*), *n.m.* bard, poet

barddas, *n.m.f.* bardism
barddol, *a.* bardic
barddoni, *v.* compose poetry, poetize
barddoniaeth, *n.f.* poetry, verse
barddonol, *a.* poetic, poetical
barf, (*-au*), *n.f.* beard, whiskers
barfog, *a.* bearded
barfwr, (*-wyr*), *n.m.* barber
bargeinio, bargenna, *v.* bargain
bargen, (*-einion*), *n.f.* bargain
bargod, (*-ion*), *n.m.* eaves
bargyfreithiwr, (*-wyr*), *n.m.* barrister
bariaeth, *n.f.m.* evil, grief, wrath
baril, (*-au*), *n.f.* barrel
barilaid, (*-eidiau*), *n.f.* barrelful
bario, *v.* bar, bolt
barlad, *n.m.* drake
barlys, *n.m.* barley
barn, (*-au*), *n.f.* judgment; opinion: sentence
barnais, *n.f.* varnish
barnedigaeth, (*-au*), *n.f.* judgment
barneisio, *v.* varnish
barnol, *a.* judicial, condemnatory, annoying
barnu, *v.* judge
barnwr, (*-wyr*), *n.m.* judge
baromedr, *n.m.* barometer
barrug, *n.m.* hoar-frost
barugo, *v.* cast hoar-frost
barugog, *a.* white with hoar-frost
barus, *a.* voracious, greedy
barwn, (*-iaid*), *n.m.* baron
barwnes, (*-au*), *n.f.* baroness
barwniaeth, (*-au*), *n.f.* barony
barwnig, (*-iaid*), *n.m.* baronet
bas, *a.* shallow: (*bais, beis*), *n.pl.* shallows
bas, *a. & n.m.* bass
basged, (*-i, -au*), *n.f.* basket
basgedaid, (*-eidiau*), *n.f.* basketful
basgedwr, (*-wyr*), *n.m.* basket-maker
basgerfiad, (*-au*), *n.m.* bas-relief
basle, (*-oedd*), *n.m.* shoal
bastard, (*-iaid*), *n.m.* bastard
bastardiaeth, *n.f.* bastardy
batri, *n.m.* battery

bath, (*-au*), *n.m.* kind, sort; stamp; coin
bathdy, (*-dai*), *n.m.* mint
bathodyn, (*-odau*), *n.m.* medal
bathol, *a.* coin, coined
bathu, *v.* coin
baw, *n.m.* dirt, mire, dung, filth
bawaidd, *a.* dirty, vile; sordid, mean
bawd, (*bodiau*), *n.f.* thumb; toe
bechan, *a.*, f. of **bychan**
bechgynnos, *n.pl.* little boys, youngsters
bedw, *n.pl.* (*-en, n.f.*) birch
bedydd, *n.m.* baptism
bedyddfa, (*-fâu, -feydd*), *n.f.* baptistry
bedyddfaen, (*-feini*), *n.m.* font
bedyddio, *v.* baptize
bedyddiol, *a.* baptismal; baptized
Bedyddiwr, (*-wyr*), *n.m.* Baptist
bedd, (*-au*), *n.m.* grave, tomb, sepulchre
beddargraff, (*-iadau*), *n.m.* epitaph
beddfaen, (*-feini*), *n.m.* tombstone
beddgell, (*-oedd*), *n.f.* vault, catacomb
beddrod, (*-au*), *n.m.* tomb, sepulchre
Beibl, (*-au*), *n.m.* Bible
Beiblaidd, *a.* Bible, biblical
beichio, *v.* burden; low; sob
beichiog, *a.* pregnant
beichiogi, *v.* conceive
beichus, *a.* burdensome, oppressive
beiddgar, *a.* daring, audacious
beiddgarwch, *n.m.* daring, audacity
beiddio, *v.* dare, presume
beili, (*beiliaid*), *n.m.* bailiff
beio, *v.* blame, censure
beirniad, (*-iaid*), *n.m.* adjudicator; critic
beirniadaeth, (*-au*), *n.f.* adjudication; criticism
beirniadol, *a.* critical
beirniadu, *v.* adjudicate; criticize
beisgawn, (*-au*), *n.f.* stack, heap of corn sheaves
beiston, *n.f.* sea-shore, beach: surf

beius, *a.* faulty; blameworthy

bellach, *adv.* now, at length

ben, (*-ni*), *n.f.* wain, waggon, cart

bendigaid, bendigedig, *a.* blessed

bendigedigrwydd, *n.m.* blessedness

bendith, (*-ion*), *n.f.* blessing, benediction

bendithio, *v.* bless

bendithiol, *a.* conferring blessings

benthyca, -io, *v.* borrow; lend

benthyciwr, (*-wyr*), *n.m.* borrower, lender

benthyg, *n.m.* loan

benyw, *a.* female: (*-od*), *n.f.* female, woman

benywaidd, *a.* feminine; effeminate

benywol, *a.* feminine, female

ber, *a.,* f. of **byr**

bêr, (*berau, -i*), *n.m.* spear; roasting-spit

bera, *n.f.m.* rick; pyramid

berdys, *n.pl.* (**-yn,** *n.m.,* **-en,** *n.f.*) shrimps

berf, (*-au*), *n.f.* verb. —**b. anghyflawn,** transitive verb. —**b. gyflawn,** intransitive verb

berfa, (*-fâu, -feydd*), *n.f.* barrow

berth, *a.* beautiful, valuable

berthog, *a.* wealthy, fair

berw, *n.m. & a.* boiling, seething, ebullition

berwedig, *a.* boiling

berwedydd, (*-ion*), *n.m.* boiler

berwedd-dy, (*-dai*), *n.m.* brewery

berweddu, *v.* brew

berwi, *v.* boil, seethe, effervesce

berwr, *c.n.* cress

bery, (*-on*), *n.m.* bird of prey, kite

betgwn, *n.m.f.* bedgown

betws, *n.m.* oratory, chapel; birch grove

beudy, (*-dai*), *n.m.* cow-house, shippon

beunoeth, beunos, *adv.* nightly, every night

beunydd, *adv.* daily, every day, always

beunyddiol, *a.* daily, quotidian

bidog, (*-au*), *n.f.* dagger; bayonet

bil, (*-iau*), *n.m.* bill

bilidowcar, *n.m.* cormorant

bilwg, (*-ygau*), *n.m.* billhook

bîr, *n.m.* beer

biswail, *n.m.* dung

blaen, *a.* fore, foremost, first; front: (*-au, -ion*), *n.m.* point, end, top, tip; front, van, priority, precedence; edge [taste

blaenbrawf, (*-brofion*), *n.m.* fore-

blaendal, *n.m.* prepayment

blaendarddu, *v.* sprout

blaenddodi, *v.* prefix

blaenddodiad, (*-iaid*), *n.m.* prefix

blaenffrwyth, *n.m.* first-fruits

blaengar, *a.* prominent, progressive

blaengroen, (*-grwyn*), *n.m.* foreskin

blaenllaw, *a.* forward, prominent

blaenllym, *a.* sharp, keen

blaenllymu, *a.* sharpen, whet

blaenor, (*-iaid*), *n.m.* leader; elder

blaenori, *v.* lead, precede

blaenoriaeth, *n.f.* preference; precedence

blaenorol, *a.* previous, antecedent

blaenu, *v.* point; outrun; precede

blaenwr, (*-wyr*), *n.m.* leader; forward

blagur, *c.n.* sprouts, buds, shoots

blaguro, *v.* sprout, bud; flourish

blaguryn, *n.m.* sprout, bud, shoot

blaidd, (*bleiddiaid, bleiddiau*), *n.m.* wolf

blas, *n.m.* taste, savour, relish

blasio, -u, *v.* taste

blasus, *a.* tasty, savoury, delicious

blawd, (*blodion, -iau*), *n.m.* flour, meal

blêr, *a.* untidy, slovenly

blerwm, *n.m.* blabberer; blab-blab

blew, *n.pl.* (**-yn,** *n.m.*), hairs; hair; fur

blewog, *a.* hairy, shaggy

bliant, *n.m.* lawn, fine linen

blif, (*-iau*), *n.m.* catapult

blingo, *v.* skin, flay

blin, *a.* tired, weary: peevish, irritable

blinder, (*-au*), *n.m.* weariness; trouble

blinderog, -derus, *a.* wearisome

blinfyd, *n.m.* tribulation

blino, *v.* tire, weary; trouble, vex

blith, (*-ion*), *n.m.* milk: *a.* milch

blithdraphlith, *adv.* helter-skelter

blodeugerdd, (*-i*), *n.f.* anthology

blodeuglwm, *n.m.* bunch, nose-gay

blodeuo, *v.* flower, bloom, flourish

blodeuog, *a.* flowery; flourishing

blodeuyn, blodyn, (*blodau*), *n.m.* flower

blodiog, *a.* floury, mealy

bloddest, *n.f.* rejoicing, acclamation

bloedd, (*-iau, -iadau*), *n.f.* shout

bloeddio, -ian, *v.* shout

bloeddiwr, (*-wyr*), *n.m.* shouter

bloesg, *a.* lisping, faltering, indistinct

bloesgi, *v.* lisp, falter, speak indistinctly

bloneg, *n.m.* **-en,** *n.f.* lard, grease

blwch, (*blychau*), *n.m.* box

blwng, *a.* sullen, cheerless

blwydd, (*-au, -i*), *n.f. and a.* year of age; year-old

blwydd-dal, *n.m.* annuity, pension

blwyddiad, (*-iaid*), *n.m.* yearling, annual

blwyddiadur, (*-on*), *n.m.* year-book, annual

blwyddyn, (*blynyddoedd*), *n.f.* year

blychaid, (*-eidiau*), *n.m.* boxful

blynedd, *n.pl.f.* years (after numerals)

blynyddol, *a.* annual, yearly

blys, (*-iau*), craving, lust

blysig, *a.* greedy, lustful

blysigrwydd, *n.* greediness

blysio, *v.* crave, lust

bocs, (*-ys*), *n.m.* box

bocsach, *n.m.* vaunt, boast, brag

boch, (*-au*), *n.f.* cheek

bochgoch, *a.* rosy-cheeked

bod, *v.* be, exist: (*-au*), *n.m.* being, existence

boda, *n.m.f.* buzzard

bodio, *v.* thumb, finger

bodlon, *a.* content, willing

bodloni, *v.* satisfy, content; be content

bodlonrwydd, *n.m.* contentment

bodolaeth, *n.f.* existence

bodoli, *v.* exist

bodd, *n.m.* pleasure, will, consent

boddfa, *n.f.* flood

boddhad, *n.m.* pleasure, satisfaction

boddhaol, *a.* pleasing, satisfactory

boddhau, *v.* please, satisfy

boddhaus, *a.* pleased

boddi, *v.* drown; flood

boddio, *v.* please, satisfy

boddlon, &c. See **bodlon**

bogail, (*-eiliau*), *n.m.f.* navel; boss, hub

boglwm, (*-lymau*), **-lyn,** (*-lynnau*), *n.m.* boss, knob, stud

bol, bola, (*boliau*), *n.m.* belly

bolaid, (*-eidiau*), *n.m.* bellyful

bolera, *v.* gorge, guzzle; sponge

bolerwr, (*-wyr*), *n.m.* sponge, parasite

bolgi, (*-gwn*), *n.m.* gourmand, glutton

bolgno, *n.m.,* **-fa,** *n.f.* gripes, colic

bolheulo, *v.* bask in the sun

bolio, *v.* belly, gorge

boliog, *a.* big-bellied, corpulent

boloch, *n.* pain, anxiety; destruction

bolrwth, *a.* gluttonous, greedy

bolrwym, *a.* costive, constipated

bollt, (*-au, -ydd, byllt*), *n.f.* bolt

bolwst, *n.f.m.* gripes, colic

bol(y)sothach, *n.m.* hotchpotch; jargon

bôn, (*bonau, bonion*), *n.m.* bottom; stump

boncath, (*-od*), *n.m.* buzzard

bonclust, (*-iau*), *n.m.* box on the ear

boncyff, (*-ion*), *n.m.* stump, trunk, stock

bondigrybwyll, *adv.* forsooth

bondo, *n.m.* eaves

bonedd, *n.m.* gentility, nobility

boneddigaidd, *a.* noble; gentlemanly

boneddigeiddrwydd, *n.m.* gentlemanliness

boneddiges, (-au), n.f. lady

bonesig, n.f. lady; Miss

bonet, (-i), n.f. bonnet

bongam, a. bandy-legged

bonheddig, a. noble, gentle, gentlemanly; (boneddigion), n.m.pl. gentlemen

bonheddwr, (-wyr), n.m. gentleman

bonllef, (-au), n.f. shout

bonllwm, a. bare-bottomed, breechless

bonyn, (bonion), n.m. stump

bord, (-ydd, -au), n.f. table, board

bore, (-au), n.m. morning: a. early

boreddydd, n.m. day-break, morning

borefwyd, n.m. breakfast

boreol, n. morning

bors, n.f. hernia

bos, n.f. palm of the hand

bost, (-iau), n.m. boast, brag

bostio, v. boast, brag

botas, -en, (-asau), n.f. boot

botwm, (-ymau), n.m. button

botymog, a. buttoned

botymu, v. button

both, (-au), n.f. nave of wheel; boss

brac, a. free, frank, talkative

bracso, v. wade, paddle

bracty, (-tai), n.m. malt-house, brewery

brad, (-au), n.m. treason; plot

bradfwriadu, v. plot, conspire

bradlofrudd, (-ion), n.m. assassin

bradlofruddiaeth, (-au), n.f. assassination

bradlofruddio, v. assassinate

bradwr, (-wyr), n.m. traitor

bradwriaeth, (-au), n.f. treason, treachery

bradwrus, a. traitorous, treacherous

bradychu, v. betray

braen, a. rotten, corrupt

braenar, (-au), n.m. fallow

braenaru, v. fallow

braenu, v. rot, putrify

braf, a. fine

brag, n.m. malt

bragad, n.f. army, battle; offspring

bragaldian, v. jabber, gabble, prate

bragod, (-au, -ydd), n.m. bragget

bragu, v. malt, brew

bragwair, n.m. moorland hay, coarse grass

bragwr, (-wyr), n.m. maltster, brewer

braich, (breichiau), n.f. arm; branch

braidd, adv. rather, somewhat

braint, (breintiau), n.f. privilege

braisg, a. gross, thick, large; pregnant

braith, a., f. of **brith**

brân, (brain), n.f. crow, rook, raven

bras, (breision), a. fat; coarse; rich; luxuriant

brasáu, v. grow fat or gross

brasbwytho, v. baste, tack

brasgamu, v. stride

braslun, (-iau), n.m. sketch, outline

braslunio, v. sketch, outline

brasnaddu, v. rough-hew

baaster, n.m. fat

brasterog, a. fat, greasy

brat, (-iau), n.m. rag, clout; pinafore

bratiaith, n.f. debased language

bratiog, a. ragged, tattered

brath, (-au), n.m. stab, wound; sting; bite

brathog, a. that bites; biting

brathu, v. stab, wound; sting; bite

brau, a. brittle, frail, fragile; kindly; prompt

braw, (-iau), n.m. terror, dread, fright

brawd, (brodyr), n.m. brother; friar

brawd, (brodiau), n.f. judgment

brawdgarwch, n.m. brotherly love

brawdle, (-oedd), n.f.m. judgment-seat

brawdlys, (-oedd), n.f.m. assize-court

brawdmaeth, n.m. foster-brother

brawdol, a. brotherly, fraternal

brawdoliaeth, (-au), n.f. brotherhood, fraternity

brawddeg, (-au), n.f. sentence

brawddegu, v. construct sentences

brawl, *n.m.* boast, brag; gabble, tattle

brawychu, *v.* frighten, terrify

brawychus, *a.* frightful, terrible

bre, (-*on*, -*oedd*), *n.f.* hill, highland

brebwl, (-*yliaid*), *n.m.* blockhead; prattler

breci, *n.m.* wort; spree

brecwast, (-*au*), *n.m.f.* breakfast

brecwasta, *v.* breakfast

bredych, (-*au*, -*ion*), *n.m.* betrayal; fear; rascal

brech, *n.f.* eruption, pox

brech, *a.* f. of **brych**

brechdan, (-*au*), *n.f.* slice of bread and butter

bref, (-*iadau*), *n.f.* lowing; bleat; bray

breferad, (-*au*), *n.m.* bellowing

brefiad, (-*au*), *n.m.* lowing; bleating

brefu, *v.* low; bleat; bray

breg, *n.m.* guile, blemish, breach: *a.* fragile, faulty

bregliach, *v.* jabber

bregus, *a.* frail, brittle, rickety

breichled, (-*au*), *n.f.* bracelet

breichrwy(f), (-*au*), *n.m.f.* bracelet

breinio, *v.* privilege, enfranchise

breiniol, *a.* privileged, free

breinlen, (-*ni*), *n.f.* charter

breintal, *n.m.* bonus; royalty

breintiedig. *a.* patented, patent

breintio, *v.* privilege, favour

brenhinaidd, *a.* kingly, regal

brenhindod, *n.m.* royalty

brenhindref, (-*i*), *n.f.* royal city

brenhindy, (-*dai*), *n.m.* royal palace

brenhines, (*breninesau*), *n.f.* queen

brenhinfainc, *n.f.* throne

brenhiniaeth, (*breniniaethau*), *n.f.* kingdom

brenhinol, *a.* royal, regal

brenin, (-*hinoedd*), *n.m.* king

brest, (-*iau*), *n.f.* breast, chest

bresych, *n.pl.* (-*en*, *n.f.*), cabbages

brethyn, (-*nau*), *n.m.* cloth

brethynnwr, (-*ynwyr*), *n.m.* clothier

breuan, (-*au*), *n.f.* quern; print of butter

breuder, *n.m.* brittleness, frailty

breuddwyd, (-*ion*), *n.m.f.* dream. **b. gwrach,** wishful thinking

breuddwydio, *v.* dream

breuddwydiol, *a.* dreaming, dreamy

breuddwydiwr, (-*wyr*), *n.m.* dreamer

brëyr, (*brehyrion*, -*iaid*), *n.m.* nobleman, chief, baron

bri, *n.m.* honour, renown, distinction

briallu, *n.pl.* (**briallen,** *n.f.*), primroses

bribys, *n.pl.* fragments, scraps

brifo, *v.* hurt

brig, (-*au*), *n.m.* top; (*pl.*) twigs

briger, (-*au*), *n.m.* hair of head; top

brigo, *v.* top; branch

brigog, *a.* branching; flourishing

brigwyn, *a.* white-topped, white-crested

brigyn, (*brigau*), *n.m.* twig

brith, *a.* mottled, speckled: *f.* **braith**

britho, *v.* mottle, speckle; dazzle

Brithwr, (-*wyr*), *n.m.* Pict

brithyll, (-*od*, -*iaid*), *n.m.* trout

briw, *a.* broken, bruised, sore: (-*iau*), *n.m.* wound, sore

briwlio, *v.* broil

briwo, *v.* wound, hurt

briwsion, *n.pl.* (-*yn*, *n.m.*), crumbs

briwsioni, *v.* crumble

briwsyn, (*briwsion*), *n.m.* crumb, morsel

bro, (-*ydd*), *n.f.* land; region; vale

broch, *n.m.* badger

broch, *n.m.* froth, anger, tumult

brochi, *v.* chafe, fume; bluster

brochus, *a.* fuming; blustering

brodio, *v.* embroider; darn

brodor, (-*ion*), *n.m.* native

brodorol, *a.* native

broga, (-*od*), *n.m.* frog

brol, *n.f.* boast, brag

brolio, *v.* boast, brag, vaunt

broliwr, (-*wyr*), *n.m.* boaster, braggart

bron, (-*nau*, -*nydd*), *n.f.* breast

bron, *adv.* almost, nearly. —**o'r bron,** completely, in succession

bronfraith, (*-freithod*), *n.f.* thrush

brongoch, (*-iaid*), *n.f.m.* robin redbreast

bronwen, *n.f.* weasel

bru, *n.m.* womb

brud, (*-iau*), *n.m.* chronicle; divination

brudio, *v.* prognosticate, divine

brudiwr, (*-wyr*), *n.m.* wizard, soothsayer

brwd, *a.* hot, fervent: *n.m.* boil, heat

brwdfrydedd, *n.m.* ardour, enthusiasm

brwdfrydig, *a.* ardent, enthusiastic

brwmstan, *n.m.* brimstone, sulphur

brwmstanaidd, *a.* brimstony, sulphury

brwnt, *a.* foul, nasty, dirty; harsh: *f.* **bront**

brwyd, (*-au*), *n.m.* embroidering frame; skewer

brwyd, *a.* variegated; bloodstained; shattered

brwydo, *v.* embroider

brwydr, (*-au*), *n.f.* battle, combat

brwydro, *v.* battle, combat

brwydrwr, (*-wyr*), *n.m.* fighter, combatant

brwydwaith, *n.m.* embroidery

brwylio, *v.* broil

brwyn, *n.m.* grief, sadness

brwynen, (*brwyn*), *n.f.* rush

brwynog, *a.* rushy

brwysg, *a.* drunk; vigorous

brycan, brecan, (*-au*), *n.f.m.* blanket, rug

brych, *a.* mottled, brindled, freckled: *f.* **brech**: *n.m.* the after-birth of a cow

brychau, *n.pl.* (**-euyn,** *n.m.*), spots, freckles

brycheulyd, *a.* spotted, brindled

brychni, *n.m.* spots, freckles

brychu, *v.* spot, freckle

bryd, *n.m.* mind, heart, will

brydio, *v.* burn, inflame, boil, throb

brygawthan, *v.* jabber, prate, rant

bryn, (*-iau*), *n.m.* hill

bryncyn, (*-nau*), *n.m.* hillock

bryniog, *a.* hilly

brynti, bryntni, *n.m.* filthiness, filth

brys, *n.m.* haste, hurry

brysio, *v.* hasten, hurry

brysiog, *a.* hurried, hasty

bryslythyr, (*-au*), *n.m.* dispatch

brysneges, (*-au*), *n.f.* telegram

brytheirio, *v.* belch

Brython, (*-iaid*), *n.m.* Briton, Welshman

Brythoneg, *n.f.* British language, Welsh

brythwch, *n.m.* storm, tumult; groan

bryweddu, *v.* brew

brywes, *n.m.* brewis

bual, (*buail*), *n.m.* buffalo

buan, *a.* fast, quick, swift, fleet; soon

buander, -dra, *n.m.* swiftness, speed

buandroed, *a.* swift-footed

buarth, (*-au*), *n.m.* yard

buchdraeth, (*-au*), *n.f.* biography, memoir

buchedd, (*-au*), *n.f.* life, conduct

bucheddol, *a.* right-living, virtuous

bucheddu, *v.* live, flourish

buches, (*-au*), *n.f.* herd of cows

buchfrechu, *v.* vaccinate

budr, *a.* dirty, filthy, foul, vile

budreddi, *n.m.* filthiness, filth

budro, *v.* dirty, soil, foul

budd, (*-ion*), *n.m.* benefit, profit, gain

buddai, (*-eiau*), *n.f.* churn

buddel, (*-wydd*), *n.m.f.* cow-house post

buddiant, (*-iannau*), *n.m.* interest

buddio, *v.* profit, avail

buddiol, *a.* profitable, beneficial, useful

buddioldeb, *n.m.* profitableness

buddsodd, (*-ion*), **-iad,** (*-au*), *n.m.* investment

buddsoddi, *v.* invest

buddugol, *a.* winning, victorious

buddugoliaeth, (*-au*), *n.f.* victory

buddugoliaethus, *a.* victorious, triumphant

buddugwr, (-*wyr*), *n.m.* winner, victor

bufrechiad, *n.m.* vaccination

bugail, (-*eiliaid*), *n.m.* shepherd; pastor

bugeiles, (-*au*), *n.f.* shepherdess

bugeiliaeth, (-*au*), *n.f.* pastorate

bugeilio, -a, *v.* watch, shepherd

bugeiliol, *a.* pastoral

bugunad, *n.m.* bellowing, roar

bun, *n.f.* maid, maiden

burgyn, (-*nod*, -*iaid*), *n.m.* carcass, carrion

burman, burum, *n.m.* barm, yeast

busnes, (-*ion*), *n.m.f.* business

busnesa, *v.* interfere, meddle

busnesgar, busneslyd, *a.* meddlesome

bustach, (-*tych*), *n.m.* bullock, steer

bustachu, *v.* buffet about, bungle

bustl, *n.m.* gall, bile

bustlaidd *a.* like gall; bitter as gall

buwch, (*buchod*), *n.f.* cow

bwa, (*bwâu*), *n.m.* bow; arch

bwaog, *a.* arched, vaulted

bwbach, (-*od*), *n.m.* bugbear, bogey, scarecrow

bwced, (-*i*), *n.m.f.* bucket

bwci, (-*ïod*), *n.m.* bugbear, bogey, ghost

bwcl, (*byclau*), *n.m.* buckle

bwcled, (-*au*), *n.f.* buckler

bwch, (*bychod*), *n.m.* buck. —**b. gafr,** he-goat

bwgan, (-*od*), *n.m.* bogey, ghost, scarecrow

bwgwl, (*bygylau*), *n.m.* threat, menace

bwgwth. See **bygwth, bygythio**

bwhwman, *v.* beat about; vacillate

bŵl, (*bylau*), *n.m.* globe, ball, knob

bwlch, (*bylchau*), *n.m.* gap; pass; notch

bwled, (-*i*), *n.f.* bullet

bwn, (*bynnoedd, byniaid*) *n.m.* bittern

bwndel, (-*i*), *n.m.* bundle

bwngler, (-*iaid*), *n.m.* bungler

bwnglera, *v.* bungle

bwngleraidd, *a.* bungling, clumsy

bwnglerwaith, *n.m.* bungle, botch

bwnglerwch, *n.m.* clumsiness

bwr, (*byr*), *a.* fat, big, strong

bwrdais, (-*deisiaid*), *n.m.* burgess

bwrdeistref, (-*i*), *n.f.* borough

bwrdd, (*byrddau*), *n.m.* table; board

bwriad, (-*au*), *n.m.* purpose, intention

bwriadol, *a.* intentional

bwriadu, *v.* purpose, intend

bwrlwm, (*byrlymau*), *n.m.* bubble: gurgling

bwrn, (*byrnau*), *n.m.* burden, incubus

bwrw, *v.* cast, shed; strike; imagine, suppose; spend: *n.m.* cast, throw; woof

bwtler, (-*iaid*), *n.m.* butler

bwtri, *n.m.* buttery, pantry, dairy

bwth, (*bythod*), *n.m.* hut, booth, cot

bwthyn, (*bythynnod*), *n.m.* cottage, cabin, hut

bwyall, -ell, (-*eill, -yll*), *n.f.* axe

bwyd, (-*ydd*), *n.m.* food

bwyda, bwydo, *v.* feed

bwyd-offrwm, (-*ymau*), *n.m.* meat-offering

bwydwr, (-*wyr*), *n.m.* feeder

bwygilydd, *adv.* (from one) to the other

bwylltid, (-*au*), *n.m.* swivel

bwyllwr(w), (-*yriau*), *n.m.* provisions for journey

bwysel, (-*au, -i*), *n.m.* bushel

bwystfil, (-*od*), *n.m.* (wild) beast

bwystfilaidd, *a.* beastly, brutish

bwystfiles, (-*au*), *n.f.* beast

bwyta, *v.* eat; corrode

bwytadwy, *a.* eatable, edible

bwytawr, (-*wyr*), *n.m.* eater

bwyteig, *a.* greedy, voracious

bychan, *a.* little, small: *f.* **bechan**

bychander, -dra, *n.m.* littleness, smallness

bychanu, *v.* belittle, minimize

bychanus, *a.* derogatory

byd, (-*oedd*), *n.m.* world; state; life

bydaf, (-*au*), *n.m.f.* beehive

bydio, *v.* live, fare

bydol, *a.* worldly, secular

bydolddyn, (-*ion*), *n.m.* worldling

bydolrwydd, *n.m.* worldliness

bydwraig, (*-wragedd*), *n.f.* midwife

bydysawd, *n.m.* universe

byddag, (*-au*), *n.f.* running knot, noose

byddar, *a.* deaf: (*-iaid, byddair*), *n.m.* deaf person

byddardod, *n.m.* deafness

byddarol, *a.* deafening

byddaru, *v.* deafen, stun

byddin, (*-oedd*), *n.f.* army, host

byddino, *v.* set army in array, embattle

byddinog, *a.* with armies

bygwth, *v.* threaten, menace: (*-ython, -ythiau*), *n.m.* threat, menace

bygylu, *v.* threaten, intimidate

bygythio. *v.* threaten, menace

bygythiol, *a.* threatening, menacing

bylchog, *a.* gapped, gappy; notched

bylchu, *v.* make a gap, breach; notch

bynnag, *pn.* -ever, -soever

byr, *a.* short, brief: *f.* **ber**

byrbryd, (*-iau*), *n.m.* luncheon

byrbwyll, *a.* impulsive, rash

byrbwylltra, *n.m.* impulsiveness

byrder, -dra, *n.m.* shortness, brevity

byrdwn, *n.m.* burden, refrain, chorus

byrddaid, (*-eidiau*), *n.m.* tableful

byrddio, *v.* board

byrddiwr, (*-wyr*), *n.m.* boarder

byrfyfyr, *a.* impromptu

byrhau, *v.* shorten, abridge

byrhoedlog, *a.* short-lived

byrlymu, *v.* bubble, gurgle

byrllysg, (*-au*), *n.m.f.* mace

bys, (*-edd*), *n.m.* finger; toe; hand of dial

bysaid, (*-eidiau*), *n.m.* pinch

bysio, *v.* finger

bysled(r), (*-au*), *n.m.* finger-stall

byth, *adv.* ever, for ever: *n.m.* eternity

bytheiad, (*-aid*), *n.m.* hound

bytheirio, *v.* belch

bythfywiol, *a.* everliving

bythgofiadwy, *a.* ever-memorable

bythol, *a.* everlasting, eternal, perpetual

bytholi, *v.* perpetuate

bytholwyrdd, (*-ion*), *a. & n.m.* evergreen

bythynnwr, (*-ynwyr*), *n.m.* cottager

byw, *v.* live; *a.* alive, living, quick: *n.m.* life

bywgraffiad, (*-au*), *n.m.* biography

bywgraffiadol, *a.* biographical

bywgraffydd, (*-ion*), *n.m.* biographer

bywgraffyddol, *a.* biographical

bywhau, bywiocáu, *v.* animate, vivify, quicken

byw(i)ad, *n.m.* soft part of bread

bywiog, *a.* lively, animated, vivacious

bywiogi, *v.* enliven, animate

bywiol, *a.* living, animate

bywoliaeth, (*-iolaethau*), *n.f.* living

bywyd, (*-au*), *n.m.* life

bywydeg, *n.f.* biology

bywydfad, (*-au*), *n.m.* lifeboat

bywydol, *a.* of life, vital

bywyn, (*-nau*), *n.m.* pith, core

C

caban, (*-au*), *n.m.* cabin

cabidwl, *n.m.* consistory, chapter

cabl, (*-au*), *n.* blasphemy, reviling

cabledd, (*-au*), *n.m.* blasphemy

cableddus, *a.* blasphemous

cablu, *v.* blaspheme, revile

cablwr, (*-wyr*) **-ydd,** (*-ion*), *n.m.* blasphemer

caboli, *v.* polish

cacamwci, *n.m.* burdock

cacen, (*-nau, -ni*), *n.f.* cake

cacwn, *n.pl.* (**cacynen,** *n.f.*), wasps; wild bees

cad, (*-au, -oedd*), *n.f.* battle; army, host

cadach, (*-au*), *n.m.* cloth, kerchief, clout

cadair, (*-eiriau*), *n.f.* chair, seat; cradle; udder

cadarn, (*cedyrn*), *a.* strong, mighty; firm

cadarnhaol, *a.* affirmative

cadarnhau, *v.* strengthen, confirm

cadben. See **capten**

cadeirfardd, (*-feirdd*), *n.m.* chaired bard

cadeirio *v.* chair

cadeiriog, *a.* chaired

cadeiriol, *a.* chair, cathedral

cadeirydd, (*-ion, -wyr*), *n.m.* chairman

cadernid, *n.m.* might; stability

cadfarch, (*-feirch*), *n.m.* war-horse

cadfridog, (*-ion*), *n.m.* general

cadfwyall, (*-eill, -yll*), *n.f.* battle-axe

cadlas, (*-lesydd*), *n.f.* close, enclosure

cadlong, (*-au*), *n.f.* warship, battle-ship

cadlys, (*-oedd*), *n.f.* camp, enclosure

cadno, (*cedny, cadnoid, cadnawon*), *n.m.* fox

cadnöes, cadnawes, (*-au*), *n.f.* vixen

cadoediad, (*-au*), *n.m.* armistice, truce

cadofydd, (*-ion*), *n.m.* tactician, strategist

cadofyddiaeth, *n.f.* tactics, strategy

cadofyddol, *a.* tactical, strategic

cadr, *a.* handsome, powerful

cadw, *v.* keep, preserve, save; hold

cadwedig, *a.* saved

cadwedigaeth, *n.f.* salvation

cadw-mi-gei, *n.m.* money-box

cadwraeth, *n.f.* keeping; observance

cadwyn, (*-au, -i*), *n.f.* chain

cadwyno, *v.* chain

cadwynog, *a.* chained, in chains

caddug, *n.m.* darkness; mist, fog

caddugo, *v.* darken, obscure

cae, (*-au*), *n.m.* field; fence, hedge

caead, (*-au*), *n.m.* cover, lid: *a.* shut, closed

caeadle, (*-oedd*), *n.m.* enclosure

caeëdig, *a.* closed, fenced

cael, *v.* have; get; find

caen, (*-au*), *n.f.* surface; peel; coating

caenen, (*-nau*), *n.f.* layer, film, flake

caentach, (*-au*), *n.f.* wrangle, grumbling: *v.* wrangle, grumble

caer, (*-au, ceyrydd*), *n.f.* wall; castle; city

caerfa, (*-feydd*), *n.f.* fortress, fort

caeriwrch, *n.m.* roebuck

caerog, *a.* walled, fortified; brocaded

caeth, *a.* bond; confined, close: (*-ion*), *n.m.* bondman, slave

caethder, *n.m.* strictness; restraint

caethes, (*-au*), *n.f.* bondmaid, slave

caethfab, (*-feibion*), *n.m.* bondman, slave

caethfasnach, *n.f.* slave-trade

caethferch, (*-ed*), *n.f.* bondmaid, slave

caethforwyn, (*-forynion*), *n.f.* bondmaid, slave

caethglud, *n.f.* captivity

caethgludiad, (*-au*), *n.m.* captivity

caethgludo, *v.* lead captive

caethiwed, *n.m.* slavery, bondage, captivity

caethiwo, *v.* bind, confine, enslave

caethiwus, *a.* confining; confined, tied

caethlong, (*-au*), *n.f.* slave-ship, slaver

caethwas, (*-weision*), *n.m.* bondman, slave

caethwasanaeth, -wasiaeth, *n.m.* slavery

cafell, (*-au*), *n.f.* cell; sanctuary, oracle

cafn, (*-au*), *n.m.* trough, gutter

cafnio, -u, *v.* hollow out, scoop, gouge

cafod. See **cawod**

caffael, *v.* get, obtain

caffaeliad, (*-au*), *n.m.* acquisition; prey, spoil

caffio, *v.* snatch, grapple

cafflo, *v.* cheat; entangle

cagl, *n.m.* clotted dirt

caglu, *v.* befoul, bedraggle

cangell, (*-hellau*), *n.f.* chancel

cangelloriaeth, *n.f.* chancellorship

cangen, (*-hennau, cangau*), *n.f.* branch, bough

canghellor, (*cangellorion*), *n.m.* chancellor

canghennog *a.* branching

canghennu, *v.* branch, ramify

caib, (*ceibiau*), *n.f.* pickaxe, mattock

cail, (*ceiliau*), *n.f.* sheepfold, flock of sheep

caill, (*ceilliau*), *n.f.* testicle

cain, *a.* fair, fine, elegant

cainc, (*cangau, ceinciau*), *n.f.* branch; strand; strain

cais, (*ceisiadau*), *n.m.* application; attempt; try

calan, (*-nau*), *n.m.* first day of month. —Y c., New-year's day

calch, *n.m.* lime

calchen, *n.f.* limestone; lump of lime

calchfaen, (*-feini*), *n.m.* limestone

calchiad, *n.m.* plaster

calcho, calchu, *v.* lime

caled, *a.* hard; severe; harsh; dry

caledi, *n.m.* hardness; hardship

caledu, *v.* harden, dry

caledwch, *n.m.* hardness

calen, (*-nau, -ni*), *n.f.* whetstone; bar

calendr, *n.m.* calendar

calennig, *n.m.f.* new-year's gift

calon, (*-nau*), *n.f.* heart

calondid, *n.m.* encouragement

calon-dyner, *a.* tender-hearted

calon-galed, *a.* hard-hearted

calon-galedwch, *n.m.* hard-heartedness

calonnog, *a.* hearty; high-spirited

calonogi, *v.* hearten, encourage

call, *a.* wise, sensible, rational

callestr, *n.f.* flint

callineb, *n.m.* wisdom, sense

cam, (*-au*), *n.m.* step

cam, *a.* crooked, wry; wrong: (*-au*), *n.m.* injury, wrong

cam-, *px.* wrong, mis-

camarfer, *v.* misuse, abuse: (*-ion*), *n.m.f.* misuse, malpractice

camargraff, *n.f.m.* wrong impression

camarwain, *v.* mislead

camarweiniol, *a.* misleading

cambren, (*-ni*), *n.m.* swingletree

camchwarae, *n.m.* foul play

camder, -dra, *n.m.* crookedness

cam-drefn, *n.f.* disorder

camdreuliad, *n.m.* indigestion

camdreulio, *v.* mis-spend

cam-drin, *v.* ill-treat, abuse

camdriniaeth, (*-au*), *n.f.* ill-treatment

camdystiolaeth, (*-au*), *n.f.* false witness

camdystiolaethu, *v.* bear false witness

camddeall, *v.* misunderstand

camddealltwriaeth, *n.m.* misunderstanding

camddefnydd, *n.m.* misuse

camddefnyddio, *v.* misuse

camedd, *n.m.* bend, curvature

cameg, (*-au, cemyg*), *n.f.* felloe

camel, (*-od*), *n.m.* camel

camenw, (*-au*), *n.m.* misnomer

camenwi, *v.* misname

camfa, (*-feydd*), *n.f.* stile

camfarnu, *v.* misjudge

camgred, (*-au*), *n.f.* misbelief, heresy

camgredu, *v.* misbelieve

camgwl, *n.m.* penalty, fine; blame

camgyfrif, *v.* miscalculate

camgyhuddiad, (*-au*), *n.m.* false accusation

camgyhuddo, *v.* accuse falsely

camgymeriad, (*au*), *n.m.* mistake

camgymryd, *v.* mistake, err

camlas, (*-au, -lesydd*), *n.f.m.* canal

camliwio, *v.* misrepresent

camlwrw, *n.m.* forfeit; evil, disorder

camog, (*-au*), *n.f.* felloe

camp, (*-au*), *n.f.* feat, exploit; game; prize

campfa, (*-feydd*), *n.f.* gymnasium

campio, *v.* gambol, frolic, frisk

campus, *a.* excellent, splendid, grand

campwr, (*-wyr*), *n.m.* champion

camre, *n.m.* walk, footstep(s)

camsyniad, (*-au*), *n.m.* mistake

camsynied, *v.* mistake

camsyniol, *a.* mistaken

camu, *v.* bow, bend, stoop

camu, *v.* step, stride

camwedd, (*-au*), *n.m.* iniquity, transgression

camweddu, *v.* transgress

camwri, *n.m.* injury, wrong

camymddwyn, *v.* misbehave

camymddygiad, (*-au*), *n.m.* misconduct

camystyr, (*-on*), *n.f.* wrong sense

cân, (*canau, caniadau, caneuon*), *n.f.* song

can, *a.* white: *n.m.* flour

cancr, *n.m.* canker; cancer

cancro, *v.* canker, corrode

candryll, *a.* shattered, wrecked

canfed, *a.* hundredth

canfod, *v.* see, perceive, behold

canfyddadwy, *a.* perceptible

canfyddiad, *n.m.* perception

canhwyllbren, (*canwyllbrenni, -au*), *n.m.f.* candlestick

canhwyllwr, (*canhwyllwyr*), *n.m.* chandler

caniad, *n.m.* singing; ringing; crowing

caniad, (*-au*), *n.f.* song, poem

caniadaeth, *n.f.* singing, psalmody

caniatâd, *n.m.* leave, permission, consent

caniataol, *a.* permissive; granted

caniatáu, *v.* permit, allow

caniedydd, (*-ion*), *n.m.* singer, songster

canig, (*-ion*), *n.f.* song, glee

canlyn, *v.* follow, pursue

canlyniad, (*-au*), *n.m.* consequence, result

canlynol, *a.* following, consequent

canlynwr, (*-wyr*), *n.m.* follower

canllaith, *a.* tender, kind, calm

canllaw, (*-iau*), *n.f.m.* hand-rail, parapet

canmlwyddiant, *n.m.* centenary

canmol, *v.* praise, commend

canmoladwy, *a.* praiseworthy

canmoliaeth, (*-au*), *n.f.* praise, commendation

canmoliaethus, *a.* eulogistic, complimentary

cannaid, *a.* white, bright, luminous

cannu, *v.* whiten, bleach

cannwr, (*canwyr*), *n.m.* bleacher

cannwyll, (*canhwyllau*), *n.f.* candle

canol, *a.*: (*-au*), *n.m.* middle, centre, midst

canolbarth, (*-au*), *n.m.* middle part, midland

canolbwynt, (*-iau*), *n.m.* centre

canolbwyntio, *v.* centre

canoldir, (*-oedd*), *n.m.* inland region

canolddydd, *n.m.* mid-day, noon

canolfan, (*-nau*), *n.m.f.* centre

canoli, *v.* centre

canolig, *a.* middling

canolog, *a.* central

canolradd, (*-ol*), *a.* intermediate

canolwr, (*-wyr*), *n.m.* mediator; centre (in football)

canon, (*-au*), *n.f.m.* (*-iaid*), *n.m.* canon

canonaidd, *a.* canonical

canoneiddio, *v.* canonize

canoniaeth, (*-au*), *n.f.* canonry

canonwr, (*-wyr*), *n.m.* canon, canonist

canrif, (*-oedd*), *n.f.* century

cansen, (*-ni*), *n.f.* cane

cant, (*-au*), *n.m.* circle, ring, rim; tyre

cant, (*cannoedd*), *n.m.* hundred

cantawd, *n.f.* cantata

cantel, (*-au*), *n.m.* rim, brim

cantor, (*-ion*), *n.m.* singer

cantores, (*-au*), *n.f.* songstress, singer

cantref, (*-i, -ydd*), *n.m.* hundred

cantwr, (*-orion*), *n.m.* singer, songster

cantwraig, *n.f.* songstress, singer

canu, *v.* sing, chant; play; crow; ring

canwr, (*-wyr*), *n.m.* singer
canwriad, (*-iaid*), *n.m.* centurion
canwyr, (*-au, -ion*), *n.m.* plane
canys, *c.* because, for
cap, (*-iau*), *n.m.* cap
capan, (*-au*), *n.m.* cap; lintel
capel, (*-i, -ydd, -au*), *n.m.* chapel
capelwr, (*-wyr*), *n.m.* chapel-goer
caplan, (*-iaid*), *n.m.* chaplain
caplaniaeth (*-au*), *n.f.* chaplaincy
capteiniaeth, *n.f.* captaincy
capten, (*-einiaid*), *n.m.* captain
car, (*ceir*), *n.m.* car
câr, (*ceraint*), *n.m.* friend; relation
carbwl, *a.* clumsy, awkward
carco, *v.* take care   [ful
carcus, *a.* solicitous, anxious, care-
carchar, (*-au*), *n.m.* prison; restraint
carchardy, (*-dai*), *n.m.* prison-
house
carchariad, *n.m.* imprisonment
carcharor, (*-ion*), *n.m.* prisoner
carcharores, (*-au*), *n.f.* prisoner
carcharu, *v.* imprison
cardod, (*-au*), *n.f.* charity, alms,
dole
cardota, *v.* beg
cardotyn, (*-wyr*), *n.m.* beggar
cardydwyn, -odwyn, *n.m.,* **-wen,**
n.f. weakest of brood or litter
cardd, *n.m.* shame, disgrace
caredig, *a.* kind
caredigrwydd, *n.m.* kindness
caredd, (*-au*), *n.f.* sin, crime
caregan, (*-gos*), *n.f.* stone, pebble
caregog, *a.* stony
caregu, *v.* stone; petrify
carennydd, *n.m.* friendship; kin-
ship
cares, (*-au*), *n.f.* female friend;
kinswoman
carfaglog, *a.* clumsy
carfan, (*-au*), *n.f.* beam
cariad, (*-au*), *n.m.* love
cariad, (*-au, -on*), *n.c.* lover, sweetheart
cariadfab, *n.m.* lover, sweetheart
cariadferch, *n.f.* sweetheart, mistress

cariadlawn, *a.* full of love, loving
cariadus, *a.* loving, beloved, dear
cariadwledd, (*-oedd*), *n.f.* love-
feast
cario, *v.* carry, bear
carlam, (*-au*), *n.m.* prance, gallop
carlamu, *v.* prance, gallop
carlwm, (*-lymod*), *n.m.* ermine,
stoat
carn, (*-au*), *n.m.* hoof; hilt, haft,
handle
carn, (*-au*), **carnedd,** (*-au*), *n.f.*
cairn
carnog, -ol, *a.* hoofed
carol, (*-au*), *n.m.f.* carol
caroli, *v.* carol
carp, (*-iau*), *n.m.* clout, rag
carped, (*-au, -i*), *n.m.* carpet
carpiog, *a.* ragged, tattered
carrai, (*careiau*), *n.f.* lace, thong
carreg, (*cerrig*), *n.f.* stone
carrog, *n.f.* stream
cartref, (*-i, -ydd*), *n.m.* home, abode
cartrefle, (*-oedd*), *n.m.* abode
cartreflu, *n.m.* militia
cartrefol, *a.* homely, domestic,
home; family
cartrefu, *v.* make one's home,
settle
carth, (*-ion*), *n.m.* tow, oakum; off-
scouring
carthen, (*-ni, -nau*), *n.f.* winnowing-sheet
carthffos, (*-ydd*), *n.f.* sewer
carthu, *v.* cleanse, purge, scavenge
carthwr, (*-wyr*), *n.m.* cleanser,
scavenger
caru, *v.* love; like; court
caruaidd, *a.* loving, kind
carw, (*ceirw*), *n.m.* stag, deer
carwden, (*-ni*), *n.f.* back-chain;
tall awkward fellow
carwr, (*-wyr*), *n.m.* lover, wooer
carwriaeth, (*-au*), *n.f.* courtship
cas, *a.* hateful, odious; nasty, disagreeable: *n.m.* hatred, aversion
cas, (*caseion*), *n.m.* hater, foe,
enemy
casáu, *v.* hate, detest, abhor
casáwr, (*-wyr*), *n.m.* hater

casbeth, (*-au*), *n.m.* aversion, nuisance

caseg, (*cesig*), *n.f.* mare

casgen, (*-ni, casgiau*), *n.f.* cask

casgl, *n.f.m.* collection

casgliad, (*-au*), *n.m.* collection; gathering

casglu, *v.* collect, gather; infer

casglwr, (*-wyr*), **-ydd**, (*-ion*), *n.m.* collector

casineb, *n.m.* hatred

cast, (*-iau*), *n.m.* vice, knack

castan, (*-au*), *n.f.* chestnut

castanwydd, *n.pl.* (**-en**, *n.f.*), chestnut-trees

castell, (*cestyll*), *n.m.* castle

castellog, *a.* castled, castellated

castellu, *v.* castle, encamp

castio, *v.* trick, cheat; cast, calculate

castiog, *a.* full of tricks, tricky

casul, (*-(i)au*), *n.m.f.* chasuble, cassock

caswir, *n.m.* unpalatable truth

cat, (*-iau*), *n.m.* bit, piece, fragment; pipe

catel, *c.n.* chattels; cattle

catgor, (*-(i)au*), *n.m.* ember day(s)

catrawd, (*-rodau*), *n.f.* regiment

cath, (*-od, -au*), *n.f.* cat

cathl, (*-au*), *n.f.* melody, hymn, lay

cathlu, *v.* sing, hymn

cathod, *n.f.* cathode

catholig, *a.* catholic

catholigrwydd, *n.m.* catholicity

cau, *a.* hollow, concave

cau, *v.* shut, close, enclose

caul, (*ceulion*), *n.m.* maw; rennet; curd

caw, (*-(i)au*), *n.m.* band, swaddling-clothes

cawci, (*-Iod*), *n.m.f.* jackdaw

cawdel, *n.m.* hotchpotch, mess

cawdd, (*coddion*), *n.m.* wrath, offence, affliction

cawell, (*cewyll*), *n.m.* hamper, basket, cradle [ful

cawellaid, (*-eidiau*), *n.m.* hamper-

cawellwr, (*-wyr*), *n.m.* basket-maker

cawg, (*-iau*), *n.m.* basin, bowl, pitcher

cawl, *n.m.* broth, soup; hotchpotch

cawn, *n.pl.* (**-en**, *n.f.*) reeds

cawod, (*-ydd*), *n.f.* shower

cawodi, *v.* shower

cawodog, *a.* showery

cawr, (*cewri*), *n.m.* giant

cawraidd, *a.* gigantic

cawres, (*-au*), *n.f.* giantess

cawrfil, (*-od*), *n.m.* elephant

caws, *n.m.* cheese; curd

cawsai, cawsi, *n.f.m.* causeway

cawsaidd, *a.* cheesy, caseous

cawsellt, (*-ydd, -i, -au*), *n.m.* cheese-vat

cawsio, *v.* curd, curdle

cawsiog, *a.* curdled

cebystr, (*-au*), *n.m.* tether, halter

cecren, (*-nod*), *n.f.* shrew, scold

cecru, *v.* wrangle, bicker

cecrus, *a.* cantankerous, quarrelsome

cecryn, (*-nod*), *n.m.* wrangler, brawler

ced, (*-oedd, -au, -ion*), *n.f.* bounty, boon

ceden, (*-od, -au*), *n.f.* nap

cedrwydd, *n.pl.* (**-en**, *n.f.*) cedars

cefn, (*-au*), *n.m.* back; garden bed; support

cefndedyn, *n.m.* mesentery; diaphragm, pancreas

cefnder, (*-dyr*), *n.m.* first cousin

cefnen, (*-nau*), *n.f.* night-line

cefnfor, (*-oedd*), *n.m.* main sea, ocean

cefngrwm, *a.* hump-backed

cefnllwm, *a.* bare-backed

cefnog, *a.* well-off, well-to-do

cefnogaeth, *n.f.* encouragement, support

cefnogi, *v.* encourage, support

cefnogol, *a.* encouraging

cefnu, *v.* back, turn the back, forsake

ceffyl, (*-au*), *n.m.* horse

ceg, (*-au*), *n.f.* mouth

cega, *v.* mouth, prate

cegaid, (*-eidiau*), *n.f.* mouthful

cegen, (-nau), n.f. gullet, windpipe

cegid, n.pl. (-en, n.f.) hemlock

cegid, -en, (-au), n.f. green woodpecker, jay

cegin, (-au), n.f. kitchen

ceginwrych, n.m. hair standing on end, agitation

cegrwth, a. gaping

cegyr, n.pl. hemlock

cengl, (-au), n.f. band; girth; hank

cenglu, v. hank; girth; wind

cei, (-au), n.m. quay

ceibio, v. pick with pickaxe

ceibiwr, (-wyr) n.m. picker, digger, navvy [iour

ceidwad, (-aid), n.m. keeper, saviour

ceidwadaeth, n.f. conservatism; conservancy

ceidwadol, a. conservative

Ceidwadwr, (-wyr), n.m. Conservative

ceiliagwydd, (-au), n.m. gander

ceiliog, (-od), n.m. cock. —c. rhedyn grasshopper

ceinach, (-od), n.f. hare

ceincio, v. branch out, ramify

ceinciog, a. branched, branching

ceinder, n.m. elegance, beauty

ceiniad, (-iaid), n.m. singer

ceinioca, v. gather pence; beg

ceiniog, (-au), n.f. penny

ceiniogwerth, (-au, -i), n.f. pennyworth

ceinion, n.pl. beauties, gems

ceinmyg, a. honourable, praiseworthy

ceintach, v. grumble, croak

ceintachlyd a. querulous

ceintachwr, (-wyr), n.m. grumbler, croaker

ceirch, n.m. & c.n. oats, oat

ceirchen, n.f., -yn, n.m. grain of oats

ceirios, n.pl. (-en, n.f.), cherries

ceisbwl, (-byliaid), n.m. catchpole, bailiff

ceisiedydd, (-ion), n.m. seeker; applicant

ceisio, v. seek; ask; try, attempt, endeavour; fetch, get

ceisiwr, (-wyr), n.m. seeker

cêl, a. hidden, concealed; n.m. concealment

celain, (celanedd, celaneddau), n.f. dead body

celanedd, c.n.f. carnage, slaughter

celc, n.m.f. concealment; hoard

celf, (-au), n.f. art, craft

celfi, n.pl. (-cyn, n.m.), tools, gear; furniture

celfydd, a. skilled, skilful

celfyddgar, a. ingenious; artistic

celfyddwr, (-wyr), n.m. artificer, artist

celfyddyd, (-au), n.f. art, craft; skill

celfyddydol, a. artificial

celffaint, (-einiau), n.m. decayed stump, dilapidated thing

celi, Celi, n.m. heaven, God

celu, v. hide, conceal

celwrn, (-yrnau), n.m. tub, bucket, pail

celwydd, (-au), n.m. lie, falsehood, untruth

celwyddog, a. lying, mendacious; false

celwyddwr, (-wyr), n.m. liar

celyn, n.pl. (-nen, n.f.), holly

cell, (-oedd, -au), n.f. cell, chamber

celli, (celliau, -ïoedd), n.f. grove

cellwair, v. jest, trifle: n.m. fun

cellweiriwr, (-wyr), n.m. jester, trifler

cellweirus, a. playful, jocular

cemeg, n.m. chemistry

cen, c.n. skin, peel, scales, scurf, film, lichen

cenadwri, n.f. message

cenau, (cenawon), n.m. cub, whelp; rascal

cenedl, (-hedloedd), n.f. nation; gender

cenedlaethol, a. national

cenedlaetholdeb, n.m. nationalism

cenedlaetholi, v. nationalize

cenedlaetholwr, (-wyr), n.m. nationalist

cenedl-ddyn, (-ion), n.m. gentile

cenfaint, (-feiniau), n.f. herd

cenfigen, (*-nau*), *n.f.* envy, jealousy

cenfigennu, *v.* envy

cenfigennus, -enllyd, *a.* envious, jealous

cenhadaeth, (*cenadaethau*), *n.f.* mission

cenhadol, *a.* missionary

cenhadu, *v.* permit

cenhadwr, (*-hadon*), *n.m.* missionary

cenhaty, (*-tai*), *n.m.* mission-house

cenhedlaeth, (*cenedlaethau*), *n.f.* generation

cenhedlig, *a.* gentile, pagan

cenhedlu, *v.* beget, generate

cenllif, *n.m.* flood, torrent, deluge

cenllysg, *c.n.m.* hailstones, hail

cennad, (*-hadau, -hadon*), *n.f.* leave; messenger

cennin, *n.pl.* (**-hinen,** *n.f.*), leeks

cennog, *a.* scaly, scurfy

cennu, *v.* scale, scurf

cêr, *n.f.* gear, tools, trappings

cerbyd, (*-au*), *n.m.* chariot, coach, car

cerbydres, (*-i*), *n.f.* railway train

cerbydwr, (*-wyr*), *n.m.* coachman

cerdyn, (*cardiau*), *n.m.* card

cerdd, (*-i*), *n.f.* song, poem; music, poetry

cerdded, *v.* walk; go; travel

cerddediad, *n.m.* walking, going; pace

cerddgar, *a.* harmonious, musical

cerddin, cerdin, *n.pl.* (**-en,** *n.f.*) rowan

cerddor, (*-ion*), *n.m.* singer, musician

cerddorfa, (*-feydd*), *n.f.* orchestra

cerddoriaeth, *n.f.* music

cerddorol, *a.* musical

cerddwr, (*-wyr*), *n.m.* walker

cerfddelw, (*-au*), *n.f.* graven image, statue

cerfio, *v.* carve

cerflun, (*-iau*), *n.m.* statue; engraving

cerfluniaeth, *n.f.* sculpture

cerflunydd, (*-lunwyr*), *n.m.* sculptor

cerfwaith, *n.m.* carving, sculpture

cern, (*-au*), *n.f.* cheek, jaw

cernod, (*-iau*), *n.f.* buffet

cernodio, *v.* buffet

cerpyn, (*carpiau*), *n.m.* clout, rag

cerrynt, *n.m.f.* course, road; current

cert, (*-i*), *n.f.* cart

certiwr, (*-wyr*), *n.m.* carter

certwain, (*-weiniau*), **certwyn,** (*-i*), *n.f.* cart, wain

certh, *a.* right; awful

cerub, ceriwb, (*-iaid*), *n.m.* cherub

cerwyn, (*-i*), *n.f.* tub; vat; winepress

cerydd, (*-on*), *n.m.* correction, chastisement; rebuke, reproof, censure

ceryddol, *a.* chastising, chastening

ceryddu, *v.* correct, chastise; rebuke

ceryddwr, (*-wyr*), *n.m.* chastiser; rebuker

cesail, (*-eiliau*), *n.f.* arm-pit; bosom

cesair, *n.pl. & c.n.* hailstones, hail

cest, (*-au*), *n.f.* belly, paunch

cestog, *a.* corpulent

cetyn, (*catiau*), *n.m.* piece, bit; pipe

cethern, *c.n.f.* fiends, furies

cethin, *a.* dark, fierce, ugly

cethr, (*-au, -i*), **-en,** (*-nau*), *n.f.* nail, spear

cethrenu, cathrenu, *v.* drive, goad

ceubren, (*-nau*), *n.m.* hollow tree

ceubwll, (*-byllau*), *n.m.* pit

ceudod, *n.m.* cavity; abdomen; thought, heart

ceufad, (*-au*), *n.m.* canoe

ceuffordd, (*-ffyrdd*), *n.f.* tunnel

ceuffos, (*-ydd*), *n.f.* drain, ditch

ceulan, (*-nau, -lennydd*), *n.f.* bank, brink

ceulo, *v.* curdle, coagulate

ceunant, (*-nentydd*), *n.m.* ravine, gorge

cewyn, (*-nau, -non, cawiau*), *n.m.* swaddling clothes

ci, (*cŵn*), *n.m.* dog, hound

ciaidd, *a.* dog-like, houndish; brutal

cib, (*-au*), *n.m.* pod, husk

cibddall, *a.* purblind

cibo, *v.* frown, scowl

cibog, *a.* scowling

cibws, cibwst, *n.f.* kibes, chilblains

cibyn, (*-nau*), *n.m.* shell; husk; half a bushel

cic, (*-iau*), *n.m.f.* kick

cicio, *v.* kick

cidwm, (*-ymiaid, -ymod*), *n.m.* wolf; rascal

cieidd-dra, *n.m.* houndishness, brutality

cig, (*-oedd*), *n.m.* flesh, meat

cigfran, (*-frain*), *n.f.* raven

cignoeth, *a.* touching to the quick, caustic

cigog, *a.* fleshy

cigwain (*-weiniau*), *n.f.* flesh-hook

cigydd, (*-ion*), *n.m.* butcher

cigyddiaeth, *n.f.* butchery

cigyddio, *v.* butcher, slaughter

cigyddlyd, *a.* brutal, murderous

cil, (*-iau, -ion*), *n.m.* back; retreat; corner

cilagor, *v.* open partly

cilagored, *a.* ajar

cilbost, (*cilbyst*) *n.m.* gate-post

cilchwyrn, *n.pl.* (*-en, n.f.*), (*-au, -od*), *n.m.* glands

cildrem, (*-iau*), *n.f.* leer

cildremio, *v.* leer

cildwrn, cil-dwrn, *n.m.* tip, bribe

cildyn, *a.* obstinate, stubborn

cildynnu, *v.* be obstinate

cildynnus, *a.* obstinate, stubborn

cildynrwydd, *n.m.* obstinacy

cilddant, (*-ddannedd*), *n.m.* molar

cilfach, (*-au*), *n.f.* nook; creek, bay

cilgnoi, *v.* chew the cud, ruminate

cilgwthio, *v.* push, shove, jostle

cilio, *v.* retreat, recede, swerve

cilwen, (*-au*), *n.f.* half smile

cilwenu, *v.* simper, smile, leer

cilwg, (*-ygon*), *n.m.* frown, scowl

cilydd, (*-ion*), *n.m.* fellow, companion

cilyddol, *a.* reciprocal

cimwch, (*-ychiaid*), *n.m.* lobster

cingroen, *n.f.* stink-horn

ciniawa, *v.* dine

cinio, (*ciniawau*), *n.m.* dinner

cip, (*-ion*), *n.m.* pluck, snatch;

cipdrem, (*-iau*), *n.f.m.* glance, glimpse

cipedrych, *v.* glance, glimpse

cipio, *v.* snatch

cipiwr, (*-wyr*), *n.m.* snatcher

cipolwg, *n.m.f.* glance, glimpse

ciprys, *v. & n.m.* scramble

ciried, *n.f.m.* generosity, bounty

cis, (*-iau*), *n.m.f.* buffet; slap, touch

cist, (*-iau*), *n.f.* chest, coffer, box; bin

ciwb, *n.m.* cube

ciwdod, *n.f.* tribe, clan, nation

ciwed, *c.n.f.* rabble, mob, crew

ciwt, *a.* cute, clever, ingenious

claddedigaeth, (*-au*), *n.f.m.* burial

claddfa, (*-feydd*), *n.f.* burial-ground, cemetery

claddu, *v.* bury

claear, *a.* lukewarm, tepid; mild; cool

claearineb, *n.m.* lukewarmness

claearu, *v.* make mild or tepid; soothe

claer, *a.* clear, bright, shining

claerder, *n.m.* clearness, brightness

claf, (*cleifion*), *a.* sick, ill: *n.m.* sick person, patient

clafdy, (*-dai*), *n.m.* hospital, infirmary

clafr, *n.m.* itch, mange

clafychu, *v.* sicken, fall ill

clai, (*cleiau*), *n.m.* clay

clais, (*cleisiau*), *n.m.* stripe; bruise

clamp, (*-iau*), *n.m.* mass, lump; monster

clandro, *v.* calculate, reckon

clap, (*-iau*), *n.m.* lump

clapgi, (*-gwn*), *n.m.* telltale

clapio, *v.* lump; strike; gossip

clapiog, *a.* lumpy

clas, *n.m.* monastic community, cloister, college

clasur, (*-on*), *n.m.* classic

clasurol, *a.* classical

clau, *a.* quick, swift, soon; true; audible

clawdd, (*cloddiau*), *n.m.* hedge; dyke, embankment

clawr, (*cloriau*), *n.m.* face, surface; cover, lid; board

clebar, cleber, *n.f.m.* idle talk, gossip, tattle

clebran, *v.* chatter, gossip, tattle

clebryn, *n.m.,* **clebren,** *n.f.* tattler

clec, (*-iau, -s*), *n.f.* click; clack; crack; gossip

cleci, (*-cwn*), *n.m.* telltale

clecian, *v.* click; clack; crack, snap

cledr, (*-au*), *n.f.* pole; rail; palm (of hand)

cledren, (*-nau, -ni*), *n.f.* pale, pole, rail

cledrffordd, (*-ffyrdd*), *n.f.* railway

cleddyf, cleddau, cledd, (*cleddyf-au*), *n.m.* sword; brace

cleddyfwr, (*-wyr*), *n.m.* swordsman

clefyd, (*-au*), *n.m.* disease; fever

clegar, *v.* clack, cluck, cackle

clegyr, clegr, *n.m.* rock; cairn, stony place

cleiog, *a.* clayey

cleiriach, *n.m.* decrepit one

cleisio, *v.* bruise

cleisiog, *a.* bruised

clem, (*-iau*), *n.f.* slice, sole-piece; notion: *pl.* grimaces

clemio, *v.* patch sole of boot

clep, (*-iau*), *n.f.* clack, clap; gossip

clepgi, (*-gwn*), *n.m.* babbler; telltale

clepian, *v.* clap; slam; blab

clêr, *c.n.f.* itinerant minstrels; bards

clêr, *n.pl.* (**cleren,** *n.f.*), flies

clera, *v.* stroll as minstrels

clerc, (*-od*), *n.m.* clerk

clercio, *v.* serve as clerk

clerigol, *a.* clerical

clerigwr, (*-wyr*), *n.m.* clergyman

clerwr, (*-wyr*), *n.m.* itinerant minstrel

clerwriaeth, *n.f.* minstrelsy

clewt, (*-iau*), *n.m.* clout

clewtian, *v.* clout

clicied, (*-au*), *n.f.* clicket; trigger

cliciedu, *v.* latch, fasten

clindarddach, *v.* crackle: *n.m.* crackling

clir, *a.* clear

clirio, *v.* clear

clo, (*cloeau, cloeon*), *n.m.* lock, conclusion

cloadur, *n.m.* closure

clobyn, *n.m.,* **cloben,** *n.f.* monster

cloc, (*-iau*), *n.m.* clock

clocian, *v.* cluck

clocsiau, *n.pl.* (**clocsen,** *n.f.*) clog

cloch, (*clych, clychau*), *n.f.* bell

cloch, *n.f.* clock (of time of day only)

clochaidd, *a.* sonorous, noisy

clochdar, *v.* cluck, cackle

clochdy, (*-dai*), *n.m.* belfry, steeple

clochydd, (*-ion*), *n.m.* bell-man; sexton

clod, (*-ydd*), *n.m.f.* praise, fame, renown

clodfori, *v.* praise, extol

clodwiw, *a.* commendable, praiseworthy

cloddfa, (*-feydd*), *n.f.* quarry, mine

cloddio, *v.* dig, delve; quarry, mine

cloddiwr, (*-wyr*), *n.m.* digger, navvy

cloëdig, *a.* locked, closed

cloer, (*-(i)au*), *n.m.f.* locker; niche, embrasure

cloff, *a.* lame

cloffi, *v.* lame, halt; *n.m.* lameness

cloffni, *n.m.* lameness

cloffrwym, (*-au*), *n.m.* fetter, hobble. —**c. y cythraul, c. y mwci,** great bindweed

clog, (*-au*), *n.m.f.* cloak

clog, (*-au*), *n.f.* rock, precipice

clogwyn, (*-i*), *n.m.* cliff, crag, precipice

clogwynog, *a.* craggy, precipitous

clogyrnaidd, *a.* rough, rugged, clumsy

cloi, *v.* lock

clonc, *n.f.* clank; gossip: *a.* addled

clopa, (*-âu*), *n.f.m.* noddle; knob; club

cloren, (*-nau*), *n.f.* rump, tail

clorian, (*-nau*), *n.m.f.* pair of scales

cloriannu, *v.* weigh, balance
cloron, *n.pl.* **(-en,** *n.f.***),** potatoes
clos, (*-ydd*), *n.m.* yard
clos, (*closau*), *n.m.* pair of breeches
clòs, *a.* close
closio, *v.* close, near
clud, *n.m.f.* luggage, baggage
cludadwy, *a.* portable
cludair, (*-eiriau*), *n.f.* heap, load, wood-pile
cludiad, *n.m.* carriage
cludo, *v.* carry, convey
cludwr, (*-wyr*), **-ydd,** (*-ion*), *n.m.* porter
clùl, (*-iau*), *n.m.* knell
clun, (*-iau*), *n.f.* hip, haunch, thigh, leg   [wood
clun, *n.m.* meadow, moor; brush-
cluro, *v.* rub, smear
clust, (*-iau*), *n.f.m.* ear; handle
clustfeinio, *v.* prick up the ears; eavesdrop
clustgyffes, *n.f.* auricular confession
clustlws, (*-lysau*), *n.m.* ear-ring
clustog, (*-au*), *n.f.m.* cushion, pillow
clwb, (*clybiau*), *n.m.* club
clwc, *a.* addled
clwcian, *v.* cluck
clwm, (*clymau*), *n.m.* knot, tie
clwff, (*clyffiau*), *n.m.* lump, chunk
clwpa, (*-od*), *n.m.* knob, boss; club; dolt
clws, *a.* pretty, nice: *f.* **clos**
clwstwr, (*clystyrau*), *n.m.* cluster
clwt, (*clytiau*), *n.m.* patch, clout, rag
clwyd, (*-au,* *-i,* *-ydd*), *n.f.* hurdle; gate; roost
clwydo, *v.* roost
clwyf, (*-au*), *n.m.* wound; disease
clwyfo *v.* wound
clwyfus, *a.* wounded; sore; sick
clybodeg, *n.f.* accoustics
clyd, *a.* warm, sheltered, snug, cosy
clydwch, clydwr, *n.m.* warmth, shelter
clyfar, *a.* clever; pleasant, agreeable
clymblaid, (*-bleidiau*), *n.f.* clique, cabal

clymog, *a.* knotty, entangled
clymu, *v.* knot, tie
clytio, *v.* patch, piece
clytiog, *a.* patched; ragged
clytwaith, *n.m.* patchwork
clyw, *n.m.* sense of hearing
clywadwy, *a.* audible
clywed, *v.* hear; feel: taste; smell
clywedigaeth, *n.f.* hearing
clywedydd, (*-ion*), *n.m.* hearer, auditor
cnaf, (*-on,* *-iaid*), *n.m.* knave, rascal
cnafaidd, *a.* knavish, rascally
cnaif, (*cneifion*), *n.m.* shearing, fleece
cnap, (*-iau*), *n.m.* lump, knob, boss
cnapan, (*-au*), *n.m.* ball, bowl
cnapiog, *a.* lumpy
cnau, *n.pl.* **(cneuen,** *n.f.***),** nuts
cnawd, *n.m.* flesh
canwdol, *a.* carnal, fleshly, fleshy
cneifio, *v.* shear, fleece
cneifiwr, (*-wyr*), *n.m.* shearer
cneua, *v.* nut
cneuen, (*cnau*), *n.f.* nut
cnewyll, *n.pl.* **(-yn,** *n.m.***),** kernels
cnith, (*-iau,* *-ion*), *n.m.* slight touch, blow; pluck
cno, *n.m.* bite, chewing, gnawing
cnoc, (*-iau*), *n.m.f.* knock
cnocio, *v.* knock
cnofa, (*-feydd*), *n.f.* gnawing, pang
cnoi, *v.* gnaw, chew, bite; ache
cnot, (*-iau*), *n.m.* knot, bunch
cnu, (*-au*), **cnuf,** (*-iau*), *n.m.* fleece
cnud, (*-oedd*), *n.f.* pack (of wolves, etc.)
cnùl, (*-iau*), *n.m.* knell
cnwd, (*cnydau*), *n.m.* crop; covering
cnydfawr, *a.* fruitful, productive
cnydio, *v.* crop, yield increase
cnydiog, *a.* fruitful, productive
cob, (*cobau*), *n.f.* coat, cloak
còb, (*-iau*), *n.m.* cop, embankment
coban, (*-au*), *n.f.* **c. nos,** night-shirt   [imp
coblyn, (*-nod*), *n.m.* sprite, goblin,
cocos, *n.pl.* cogs. **—olwyn g.,** cog-wheel
cocos, cocs, *n.pl.* **(cocsen,** *n.f.***),** cockles

coch, *a. & n.m.* red
coch-gam, *n.f.* robin
cochi, *v.* redden, blush
cochi, cochder, *n.m.* redness
cochl, (*-au*), *n.m.f.* mantle, cloak
cod, (*-au*), *n.f.* bag, pouch
codaid, (*-eidiau*), *n.f.* bagful
codi, *v.* rise, raise, lift, erect
codiad, (*-au*), *n.m.* rise, rising
codog, *a.* baggy: (*-ion*) *n.m.f.* rich man; miser
codwm, (*codymau*), *n.m.* fall, tumble
codwr, (*-wyr*), *n.m.* riser; raiser, lifter. **-c.canu,** precentor
codded, *n.m.* anger; grief
coddi, *v.* anger, offend
coed, (*-ydd*), *c.n.m.* wood, timber, trees
coeden, (*coed*), *n.f.* tree
coedio, *v.* timber
coediog, *a.* wooded, wood
coedwig, (*-oedd*), *n.f.* wood, forest
coedwigwr, (*-wyr*), *n.m.* woodman, forester
coedd, *a.* public
coeg, *a.* empty, vain; one-eyed, blind
coegddyn, (*-ion*), *n.m.* fop, coxcomb, fool
coegedd, *n.m.* emptiness, silliness
coegen, (*-nod*), *n.f.* minx, coquette
coegennaidd *a.* coquettish
coegfalch *a.* vain, foppish
coegi, *v.* jeer at, mock
coeglyd, *a.* vain, sarcastic
coegni, *n.m.* vanity: spite; sarcasm
coegwr, (*-wyr*), *n.m.* fool
coegwych, *a.* gaudy, garish, tawdry
coegyn, (*-nod*), *n.m.* coxcomb
coel, (*-ion*), *n.f.* belief, trust, credit
coelbren, (*-nau, -ni*), *n.m.* lot
coelcerth, (*-i*), *n.f.* bonfire, blaze
coelfain, *n.m.* reward; good news
coelgrefydd, (*-au*), *n.f.* superstition
coelgrefyddol, *a.* superstitious
coelio, *v.* believe, credit, trust
coes, (*-au*), *n.f.* leg, shank: *n.m.f.* handle; stem, stalk
coetgae, *n.m.* hedge; enclosure

coetref, *n.f.* woodland homestead
coeth, *a.* fine, refined; elegant
coethder, *n.m.* refinement, elegance
coethi, *v.* refine; chastise; babble
coethwr, (*-wyr*), *n.m.* refiner
cof, (*-ion*), *n.m.* memory; remembrance
cofadail, (*-eiladau*), *n.f.* monument
cofeb, (*-ion*), *n.f.* memorandum, memorial
cofgolofn, (*-au*), *n.f.* monument
cofiadur, (*-on, -iaid*), *n.m.* recorder
cofiadwy, *a.* memorable
cofiannydd, (*-anyddion*), *n.m.* biographer
cofiant, (*-iannau*), *n.m.* memoir, biography
cofiedydd, (*-ion*), *n.m.* remembrancer
cofio, *v.* remember, recollect
cofl, (*-au*), *n.f.* embrace; bosom
coflaid, (*-eidiau*), *n.f.* armful; bundle
coflech, (*-au*), *n.f.* memorial tablet
cofleidio, *v.* embrace, hug
coflyfr, (*-au*), *n.m.* record, chronicle
cofnod, (*-ion*), *n.m.* memorandum, minute
cofnodi, *v.* record, register
cofrestr, (*-au*), *n.f.* register, roll
cofrestrfa, *n.f.* registry
cofrestru, *v.* register
cofrestrydd, (*-ion*), *n.m.* registrar
cofus, *a.* mindful
coffa, *v.* remember: *n.m.* remembrance
coffâd, *n.m.* remembrance
coffadwriaeth, *n.f.* remembrance, memory
coffadwriaethol, *a.* memorial
coffáu, *v.* remember; remind; commemorate
coffi, *n.m.* coffee   [chest
coffr, (*-au*), *n.m.* coffer, trunk,
cog, (*-au*), *n.f.* cuckoo
cog, (*-au*), *n.m.* cook
coginiaeth, *n.f.* cookery
coginio, *v.* cook
cogio, *v.* cog; sham, feign, pretend
cogor, *v.* chatter, caw, croak: *n.m.* chattering

cogwrn, (-_yrnau_, _cegyrn_), _n.m._ knob, cone; cock (of corn); shell

cogydd, (-_ion_), _n.m._ **cogyddes,** (-_au_), _n.f._ cook

cogyddiaeth, _n.f._ cookery

congl, (-_au_), _n.f._ corner

côl, _n.f._ bosom, embrace

col, (-_ion_), _n.m._ awn, beard

coledd, -u, _v._ cherish, foster

coleddwr, (-_wyr_), _n.m._ cherisher, fosterer

coleg, (-_au_), _n.m._ college

colegol, _a._ collegiate

colegwr, (-_wyr_), _n.m._ collegian

coler, (-_i_), _n.f.m._ collar

colfen, (-_nau_, -_ni_), _n.f._ bough, branch; tree

colofn, (-_au_), _n.f._ column, pillar

colomen, (-_nod_), _n.f._ dove, pigeon

colomendy, (-_dai_), _n.m._ dove-cot

colomennaidd, _a._ dove-like

coluddion, _n.pl._ (-**yn,** _n.m._), bowels

coluro, _v._ colour, paint; conceal

colwyn, (-_od_), _n.m._ puppy

colyn, (-_nau_), _n.m._ pivot; sting

colynnog, _a._ stinging

colynnu, _v._ sting

coll, (-_iadau_), _n.m._ loss; failing, defect

colladwy, _a._ perishable

colled, (-_ion_), _n.m.f._ loss

colledigaeth, _n.f._ perdition

colledu, _v._ occasion loss

colledus, _a._ fraught with loss

colledwr, (-_wyr_), _n.m._ loser

collen, (_cyll_), _n.f._ hazel

collfarn, (-_au_), _n.f._ doom, condemnation

collfarnu, _v._ condemn

colli, _v._ lose; be lost, perish; spill, shed

collnod, (-_au_), _n.m._ apostrophe

collwr, (-_wyr_), _n.m._ loser

comed, (-_au_), _n.f._ comet

comedi, (-_ïau_), _n.f.m._ comedy

comfforddus, _a._ comfortable

comiwnyddiaeth, _n.f._ communism

compod, (-_au_), _n.m._ compass

conach, _v._ grumble

concro, _v._ conquer

concwerwr, (-_wyr_), _n.m._ conqueror [victory

concwest, (-_au_), _n.f._ conquest,

condemniad, _n.m._ condemnation

condemnio, _v._ condemn

conffirmasiwn, _n.m._ confirmation

conffirmio, _v._ confirm

cono, _n.m._ rascal; wag; old fogey

consuriaeth, _n.f._ conjuring

consurio, _v._ conjure

consuriwr, (-_wyr_), _n.m._ conjurer

cop, copyn, (-_nod_, -_nau_), _n.m._ spider

copa, (-_âu_), _n.f._ top, crest; head

copi, (-_ïau_), _n.m._ copy; copy-book

copïo, _v._ copy, transcribe

copïwr, (-_wyr_), _n.m._ copyist, transcriber

copr, _n.m._ copper

côr, (_corau_), _n.m._ choir; stall, pew

cor, (-_rod_), _n.m._ dwarf; spider

corawl, _a._ choral

corbwll, (-_byllau_), _n.m._ whirlpool; puddle

corcyn, (_cyrc_), _n.m._ cork

cord, (-_iau_), _n.m._ cord; chord

cordeddu, _v._ twist, twine

cordwal, _n.m._ cordwain, Cordovan leather

corddi, _v._ churn; turn: agitate

corddiad, (-_au_), _n.m._ churning

corddwr, (-_wyr_), _n.m._ churner

cored, (-_au_), _n.f._ weir, dam

corfan, (-_nau_), _n.m._ metrical foot

corfaniaeth, _n.f._ scansion

corff, (_cyrff_), _n.m._ body

corfflu, (-_oedd_), _n.m._ corps

corffol, _a._ corpulent

corffolaeth, _n.f._ bodily form; stature

corfforaeth, (-_au_), _n.f._ corporation

corffori, _v._ embody, incorporate

corfforol, _a._ bodily, corporeal, corporal

corgan, côr -gân, (-_au_), _n.f._ chant

corganu, _v._ chant

corgi, (-_gwn_), _n.m._ cur

corgimwch, (-_ychiaid_), _n.m._ prawn

corhwyad, (-_aid_), _n.f._ teal; moorhen

corlan, (-nau), n.f. fold
corlannu, v. fold
corn, (cyrn), n.m. horn; pipe; tube; roll; corn
cornant, (-nentydd), n.m. brook, rill
cornboer, n.m. phlegm
cornchwiglen, (-chwiglod), n.f. lapwing
cornel, (-i, -au), n.f.m. corner
cornelu, v. corner
cornicyll, (-od), n.m. lapwing, plover, peewit
cornio, v. horn, butt
corniog, a. horned
cornwyd, (-ydd), n.m. boil, abscess, sore
corodyn, n.m. trifle, toy; baggage
coron, (-au), n.f. crown
coroni, v. crown: n.m. coronation
coroniad, n.m. coronation
coronog, a. crowned
corpws, n.m. body (facetious)
corrach, (corachod), n.m. dwarf, pygmy
corryn, (corynnod), n.m. spider
cors, (-ydd), n.f. bog, swamp
corsen, (-nau, cyrs), n.f. reed; stem, stalk; cane
cortyn, (-nau), n.m. cord, rope
corun, (-au), n.m. crown of the head; tonsure
corwg(l), (-yg(l)au), n.m. coracle
corwynt, (-oedd), n.m. whirlwind
cosb, (-au), n.f. punishment, penalty
cosbadwy, a. punishable
cosbedigaeth, n.f. punishment
cosbi, v. punish
cosbol, a. punitive, penal
cosbwr, (-wyr), n.m. punisher
cosfa, (-feydd), n.f. itch, itching; thrashing
cosi, v. scratch, itch: n.m. itching
cost, (-au), n.f. cost, expense
costio, v. cost
costog, (-ion), n.m. mastiff; cur: a. surly
costrel, (-au, -i), n.f. bottle
costrelaid, (-eidiau), n.f. bottleful
costrelu, v. bottle
costus, a. costly, expensive

cosyn, (-nau, -nod), n.m. a cheese
côt, cot, (cotiau), n.f. coat
cotwm, n.m. cotton
cowlas, (-au), n.m.f. bay of building; hay-mow
cowyll, (-au, -ion), n.m. maidenhood-fee; clothing
cowyn, (-nau), n.m. plague, pestilence
crac, (-iau), n.m. crack
cracio, v. crack
craciog, a. cracked
crach, n.pl. (-en, n.f.), scabs: a. scabby; petty: **-ach,** n.pl. snobs
crachboer, n.m. phlegm
crachfardd, (-feirdd), n.m. poetaster
crachfeddyg, (-on), n.m. quackdoctor
crachfonheddwr, (-wyr), n.m. snob
craf, c.n. garlic
crafangio, -u, v. claw, grab
crafanc, (-angau), n.f. claw; talon; clutch
crafiad, (-au), n.m. scratch
crafog, a. cutting, sarcastic
crafu, v. scrape; scratch: n.m. itch
crafwr, (-wyr), n.m. scraper
craff, a. close; keen; sagacious: n.m. hold, grip
craffter, n.m. keenness, sagacity
craffu, v. look closely, observe intently
craffus, a. keen, sagacious
cragen, (cregyn), n.f. shell
crai, a. new, fresh, raw
craidd, (creiddiau), n.m. middle, centre
craig, (creigiau), n.f. rock
crair, (creiriau), n.m. relic
craith, (creithiau), n.f. scar
cramen, (-nau), n.f. crust, scab
cranc, (-od), n.m. crab
crand, a. grand
crandrwydd, n.m. grandeur, finery
crap, (-iau), n.m. hold; smattering
crapio, v. grapple; pick up
cras, (creision), a. parched, dry; harsh

crasiad, *n.m.* baking
craslyd, *a.* harsh, grating
craster, *n.m.* dryness; harshness
crasu, *v.* parch, scorch; bake
crau, *(creuau),* *n.m.* hole, eye, socket
crau, *n.m.f.* blood, gore
crau, *(creuau),* *n.m.* sty; stockade
crawcian, crawcio, *v.* croak, caw
crawen, *(-nau),* *n.f.* crust
crawn, *n.m.* matter, pus
crawni, *v.* gather, suppurate
crawnllyd, *a.* purulent
cread, *n.m.* creation
creadigaeth, *(-au),* *n.f.* creation
creadigol, *a.* creative
creadur, *(-iaid),* *n.m.* creature; animal
creadures, *(-au),* *n.f.* female creature
creawdwr, *(-wyr),* *n.m.* creator
crebach, *a.* shrunk, withered
crebachlyd, *a.* crabbed, wrinkled
crebachu, *v.* shrink, shrivel, wrinkle, pucker
crebwyll, *(-ion),* *n.m.* invention, fancy
crecian, *v.* cluck; crackle
crechwen, *n.f.* loud laughter, guffaw
crechwenu, *v.* laugh loud, guffaw
cred, *(-au),* *n.f.* belief; trust; pledge; troth
credadun, *(credinwyr),* *n.m.* believer
credadwy, *a.* credible
crediniaeth, *n.f.* belief
crediniol, *a.* believing
credo, *(-au),* *n.m.f.* creed, belief
credu, *v.* believe
credwr, *(-wyr),* *n.m.* believer
cref, *a.,* f. of **cryf**
crefu, *v.* crave, beg, implore
crefydd, *(-au),* *n.f.* religion
crefydda, *v.* profess or practise religion
crefyddol, *a.* religious, pious
crefyddolder, *n.m.* religiousness, piety
crefyddwr, *(-wyr),* *n.m.* religioner, religionist

crefft, *(-au),* *n.f.* handicraft, trade
crefftwr, *(-wyr),* *n.m.* craftsman
cregyn, *n.pl.* (**cragen,** *n.f.*), shells
creider, *n.m.* freshness
creifion, *n.pl.* scrapings
creigiog, *a.* rocky
creigiwr, *(-wyr),* *n.m.* quarryman
creigle, *(-oedd),* *n.m.* rocky place
creinio, *v.* wallow, lie or fall down; cringe
creirfa, *(-oedd),* *n.f.* reliquary; museum
crempog, *(-au),* *n.f.* pancake
crensio, *v.* grind (the teeth)
crepach, *a.* numb: *n.f.* numbness
crest, *n.m.* crust, scurf
creu, *v.* create
creulon, *a.* cruel
creulondeb, *(-derau),* *n.m.* cruelty
crëwr, *(crewyr),* *n.m.* creator
crëyr, *(crehyrod),* *n.m.* heron
cri, *(-au),* *n.m.* cry, clamour
cri, *a.* new, fresh, raw; unleavened
criafol, -en, *n.f.* mountain ash
crib, *(-au),* *n.f.m.* comb, crest; ridge
cribddeilio, *v.* grab, extort
cribddeiliwr, *(-wyr),* *n.m.* extortioner
cribin, *(-iau),* *n.f.m.* rake; skinflint
cribinio, *v.* rake
cribo, *v.* comb; card
crimog, *(-au),* **crimp,** *n.f.* (-(i)au), *n.m.* shin
crin, *a.* withered, sear, dry
crino, *v.* wither, dry up
crintach, -lyd, *a.* niggardly, stingy
crintachrwydd, *n.m.* niggardliness
crintachu, *v.* scrimp, skimp, stint
crio, *v.* cry, weep
cripio, *v.* scratch; climb, creep
crisbin, *a.* crisp, parched; withered
cris-groes, *n.f.* criss-cross
crisial, *(-au),* *n.m.* & *a.* crystal
Cristion *(-ogion),* *n.m.* Christian
Cristionogaeth, *n.f.* Christianity
Cristionogol, *a.* Christian
criw, *(-iau),* *n.m.* crew
crïwr, *(-wyr),* *n.m.* crier
crocbont, *(-ydd),* *n.f.* suspension bridge

crocbren, (-ni), n.m.f. gallows, gibbet

crocbris, (-iau), n.m. exorbitant price

croch, a. loud, vehement

crochan, (-au), n.m. pot, cauldron

crochanaid, (-eidiau), n.m. potful

crochenydd, (-ion), n.m. potter

croen, (crwyn), n.m. skin, hide; peel, rind

croeni, -io, v. form skin, skin over

croes, (-au), n.f. cross: n.m. transept

croes, (-ion), a. cross, contrary

croesan, (-(i)aid, -od), n.m. jester; buffoon

croesanair, (-eiriau), n.m. obscenity, insult, mockery

croesaw. See **croeso**

croesawgar, a. hospitable

croesawiad, n.m. welcome, reception

croesawu, v. welcome

croesawus, a. hospitable

croesbren, (-nau), n.m.f. cross

croesffordd, (-ffyrdd), n.f. cross-road

croesgad, (-au), n.f. crusade

croesgadwr, (-wyr), n.m. crusader

croeshoeliad, n.m. crucifixion

croeshoelio, v. crucify

croesholi, v. cross-examine

croesholiad, (-au), n.m. cross-examination

croesi, v. cross

croeso, croesaw, n.m. welcome

croesymgroes, a. criss-cross; vice-versa

croew. See **croyw**

crofen, (-nau, -ni), n.f. rind, crust

crog, (-au), n.f. cross, rood: a. hanging

crogi, v. hang, suspend

croglath, (-au), n.f. springe, snare

Croglith, n.m.f. **Dydd Gwener y G.,** Good Friday

croglofft, (-ydd, -au), n.f. garret; rood-loft

crogwr, (-wyr), n.m. hangman

cronglwyd, (-ydd), n.f. **tan fy ngh.,** under my roof

crombil, (-iau), n.f. crop; gizzard; bowels

cromen, (-ni, -nau), n.f. dome

cromfach, (-au), n.f, bracket, parenthesis

cromlech, (-au), n.f. cromlech

cron, a., f. of **crwn**

cronfa, (-feydd), n.f. reservoir; fund

cronicl, (-au), n.m. chronicle

croniclo, v. chronicle

cronnell, (cronellau), n.f. sphere, globe

cronni, v. collect, hoard; dam

cropian, v. creep, crawl, grope

crosiet, (-au, -i), n.m. crotchet

croth, (-au), n.f. womb; calf (of leg)

croyw, a. clear, plain, distinct; fresh

croywder, n.m. clearness; freshness

croywi, v. clear; freshen

crud, (-au), n.m. cradle

crug, (-iau), n.m. hillock; tumulus; heap; multitude; abscess, blister

cruglwyth, (-i), n.m. heap, pile

cruglwytho, v. heap, pile up; overload

crugo, v. fester, vex, plague

crwban, (-od), n.m. tortoise, turtle

crwbi, (-iod), n.m. hump

crwc, (cryciau), n.m. pail

crwca, a. crooked, bowed, bent

crwm, a. convex, curved, bowed: f. **crom**

crwn, a. round; complete: f. **cron**

crwner, (-iaid), n.m. crowner, coroner

crwst, (crystiau), n.m. crust

crwth, (crythau), n.m. crowd, fiddle; purring; hump

crwybr, n.m. honeycomb; mist; hoarfrost

crwydr, n.m. wandering. **—ar g.,** astray

crwydro, v. wander, stray, roam

crwydrol, crwydrus, a. wandering

crwydrwr, (-wyr), n.m. wanderer, rover

crwydryn, (-riaid), n.m. vagrant, tramp

crwynwr, (*-wyr*), *n.m.* skinner, currier

crwys, *n.f.,n.pl.* cross, crucifix. **-dan ei g.**, laid out for burial

crybwyll, *v.* mention: (*-ion*), *n.m.* mention

crybwylliad, *n.m.* mention, notice

crych, *a.* rippling; curly; quavering

crychlais, (*-leisiau*), *n.m.* trill, tremolo

crychlyd, *a.* wrinkled, puckered

crychnaid, (*-neidiau*), *n.f.* leap, gambol

crychneidio, *v.* skip, frisk

crychni, *n.m.* curliness; wrinkle

crychu, *v.* wrinkle, pucker; ruffle, ripple

cryd, (*-iau*), *n.m.* shivering; fever; ague

cryd. See **crud**

crydd, (*-ion*), *n.m.* cobbler, shoe-maker

crydda, *v.* cobble

cryddiaeth, *n.f.* shoemaking

cryddu, *v.* shrink, pine

cryf, *a.* strong: *f.* **cref**

cryfder, -dwr, *n.m.* strength

cryfhaol, *a.* strengthening

cryfhau, *v.* strengthen; grow strong

cryg, *a.* hoarse: *f.* **creg**

cryglyd, *a.* hoarse, raucous

crygni, *n.m.* hoarseness

crygu, *v.* hoarsen

cryman, (*-au*), *n.m.* reaping-hook, sickle

crymanwr, (*-wyr*), *n.m.* reaper

crymu, *v.* bow, bend, stoop

cryn, *a.* considerable, much

crŷn, *n.m. & a.* shivering

crynder, *n.m.* roundness

cryndod, *n.m.* trembling, shivering

crynedig, *a.* trembling, tremulous

crynfa, (*-feydd*), *n.f.* tremble, tremor

crynhoad, (*-noadau*), *n.m.* collection, digest

crynhoi, *v.* gather together, collect

cryno, *a.* compact; neat, tidy

crynodeb, (*-au*), *n.m.* summary

crynswth, *n.m.* mass, bulk, whole

crynu, *v.* shiver, tremble, quake

Crynwr, (*-wyr*), *n.m.* Quaker

crys, (*-au*), *n.m.* shirt

crysbais, (*-beisiau*), *n.f.* jacket, jerkin

crystyn, (*crystiau*), *n.m.* crust

crythor, (*-ion*), *n.m.* fiddler, violin-ist

cryw, (*-iau*), *n.m.* creel; weir

cu, *a.* dear, fond, kind

cuall, *a.* quick, rash, foolish: *n.m.* blockhead, fool

cuan, (*-od*), *n.f.* owl

cuchio, *v.* scowl, frown

cuchiog, *a.* scowling, frowning

cudyll, (*-od*), *n.m.* hawk

cudyn, (*-nau*), *n.m.* lock (of hair), tuft

cudd, *a.* hidden, concealed

cuddfa, (*-feydd*), *n.f.* hiding-place; hoard

cuddiad, *n.m.* hiding

cuddiedig, *a.* hidden, concealed

cuddio, *v.* hide, conceal   [tive

cuddswyddog, (*-ion*), *n.m.* detec-

cuedd, *n.m.* Papal indulgence

cuert, *n.m.* shelter

cufydd, (*-au*), *n.m.* cubit

cul, (*-ion*), *a.* narrow, lean

culfor, (*-oedd*), *n.m.* strait

culhau, *v.* narrow; grow lean

culni, *n.m.* narrowness

cun, -iad, (*-iaid*), *n.m.* lord

cun, *a.* dear, beloved; lovely

cunnog, (*cunogau*), *n.f.* pail

cur, *n.m.* throb, ache, pain; care, trouble

curad, (*-iaid*), *n.m.* curate

curadiaeth, (*-au*), *n.f.* curacy

curfa, (*-feydd*), *n.f.* beating, flogging

curiad, (*-au*), *n.m.* beat, throb, pulse

curio, *v.* pine, waste

curlaw, *n.m.* pelting rain

curn, (*-au*), **curnen**, (*-nau*), *n.f.* mound, core, rick

curnennu, *v.* heap, stack

curo, *v.* beat, strike, knock; throb; clap

curwr, (*-wyr*), *n.m.* beater
curyll, (*-od*), *n.m.* hawk
cusan, (*-au*), *n.f.m.* kiss
cusanu, *v.* kiss
cut, (*iau*), *n.m.* hovel, shed, sty
cuwch, (*cuchiau*), *n.m.* scowl, frown
cwafrio, *v.* quaver, trill
cwar, (*rau*), *n.m.* quarry
cward, (*-i*), *n.m.* pane
cwbl, *a. & n.m.* all, whole, total
cwblhad, *n.m.* fulfilment
cwblhau, *v.* fulfil, complete, finish
cwcw, *n.f.* cuckoo
cwcwallt, (*-iaid*), *n.m.* cuckold
cwcwalltu, *v.* cuckold
cwcwll, (*cycyllau*), *n.m.* hood, cowl
cwch, (*cychod*), *n.m.* boat; hive
cwd, (*cydau*), *n.m.* pouch, bag
cweryl, (*-on*), *n.m.* quarrel
cweryla, *v.* quarrel
cwerylgar, *a.* quarrelsome
cwestiwn, (*-iynau*), *n.m.* question
cwffio, *v.* fight, box
cwgn, (*cygnau*), *n.m.* knot; knuckle; joint
cwhwfan. See **cyhwfan**
cwfert, *n.m.* cover, shelter
cŵl, (*cyliau*), *n.m.* offence, wrong
cwla, *a.* poorly, feeble
cwlbren, (*-ni*), *n.m.* bludgeon
cwlff, -yn, (*cylffiau*), *n.m.* chunk
cwlwm. See **clwm**
cwlltwr, (*cylltyrau*), *n.m.* coulter
cwm, (*cymau, cymoedd*), *n.m.* valley
cwman, *n.m.* rump; stoop
cwmni, (*-iau, -ïoedd*) *n.m.* company
cwmnïaeth, *n.f.* companionship
cwmpas, (*-oedd*), *n.m.* round.—**o.g.**, about
cwmpasog, *a.* round about, circuitous
cwmpasu, *v.* round, wind, surround
cwmpawd, (*-odau*), *n.m.* compass
cwmpeini, cwmpni, *n.m.* company
cwmwd, (*cymydau*), *n.m.* commot
cwmwl, (*cymylau*), *n.m.* cloud
cŵn. See **ci**
cwndid, (*-au*), *n.m.* song, carol

cwndid, (*-au*), *n.m.* conduit; channel
cwndid, *n.m.* escort, safe-conduct
cwningen, (*-ingod*), *n.f.* rabbit
cwnsel, (*-au, -oedd, -i*), *n.m.* council; counsel, advice, secret
cwnsler, (*-iaid*), *n.m.* counsellor
cwnstabl, (*-iaid*), *n.m.* constable
cwpan, (*-au*), *n.m.f.* cup
cwpanaid, (*-eidiau*), *n.m.f.* cupful, cup
cwpl, (*cyplau*), *n.m.* couple; tie-beam
cwplâd, cwpláu. See **cwblhad, cwblhau**
cwpled, (*-i, -au*), *n.m.* couplet
cwplws, (*cyplysau*), *n.m.* coupling; brace [board
cwpwrdd, (*cypyrddau*), *n.m.* cup-
cwr, (*cyrrau*), *n.m.* edge, border, skirt
cwrcwd, *n.m.* stooping; squatting
cwrdd, (*cyrddau*), *n.m.* meeting
cwrdd, cwrddyd, *v.* meet, touch
cwrel, *n.m.* coral
cwrlid, (*-au*), *n.m.* coverlid
cwrnad, (*-au*), *n.m.f.* hubbub: *v.* bawl, nag
cwrrach, (*cwrachau, -od*), *n.m.* tattered volume
cwrs, (*cyrsiau*), *n.m.* course; fit
cwrt, (*cyrtiau*), *n.m.* court
cwrtais, *a.* courteous
cwrteisi, cwrteisrwydd, *n.m.* courtesy
cwrw, (*cyrfau*), *n.m.* ale, beer
cwrwg(l). See **corwg(l)**
cwsg, *n.m.* sleep
cwsmer, (*-iaid*), *n.m.* customer
cwsmeriaeth, *n.f.* custom
cwt, (*cytiau*), *n.f.m.* tail, skirt, queue
cwt, (*cytiau*), *n.m.* hut, sty
cwta, *a.* short, curt
cwter, (*-i, -ydd*), *n.f.* gutter, channel
cwtogi, *v.* shorten, curtail
cwtws, (*cytysau*), *n.m.* lot, portion
cwtws, *n.f.* tail
cwthr, (*cythrau*), *n.m.* anus, rectum
cwthwm, (*cythymau*), *n.m.* puff of wind, storm

cwymp, (-au), n.m. fall, tumble
cwympo. v. fall; fell
cwyn, (-ion), n.m.f. complaint, plaint
cwynfan, v. complain, lament
cwynfanllyd, a. querulous
cwynfanus, a. plaintive, mournful
cwyno, v. complain, lament
cwynos, (-au), n.m.f. supper, meal
cwyr, n.m. wax
cwyro, v. wax
cwys, (-au, -i), n.f. furrow-slice, furrow
cybôl, n.m. nonsense, rubbish
cybolfa, n.f. hotchpotch, medley
cyboli, v. muddle; talk nonsense; mess; bother
cybydd, (-ion), n.m. miser, niggard
cybydda, v. stint, hoard
cybydd-dod, -dra, n.m. miserliness
cybyddlyd, a. miserly
cycyllog, a. hooded, cowled
cychaid, (-eidiau), n.m. boatful; hiveful
cychwîor, a. & n.m. like, equal; mate
cychwr, (-wyr), n.m. boatman
cychwyn, v. rise, stir, start
cychwynfa, n.f. start, starting-point
cychwyniad, (-au), n.m. start, beginning
cyd, a. joint, united, common; fellow: px. together
cydaid, (-eidiau), n.m. bagful
cydbwysedd, n.m. balance
cyd-destun, (-au), n.m. content
cydfod, n.m. agreement, concord
cydfyned, v. go with, concur, agree
cydffurfio, v. conform
cydgordio, v. agree, harmonize
cydio, v. join; bite; take hold
cydnabod, v. acknowledge: n.m. acquaintance
cydnabyddiaeth, n.f. acquaintance; recognition
cydnabyddus, a. acquainted; familiar
cydnaws, a. congenial
cydnerth, a. well set

cydol, n.f.m. & a. whole
cydradd, a. equal
cydraddoldeb, n.m. equality
cydrych(i)ol, a. present
cyd-rhwng, pr. between
cydsyniad, n.m. consent
cydsynio, v. consent
cydwastad, a. level (with), even
cydweddog, a. conjugal
cydweddu, v. accord, agree
cydweithrediad, n.m. co-operation
cydweithredu, v. co-operate
cydweled, v. agree
cydwladol, a. international
cyd-wladwr, (-wyr), n.m. compatriot
cydwybod, (-au), n.f. conscience
cydwybodol a. conscientious
cydymaith, (cymdeithion), n.m. companion
cydymdeimlad, n.m. sympathy
cydymdeimlo, v. sympathize
cydymffurfiad, n.m. conformity
cydymffurfio, v. conform
cydymgais, n.m. competition, rivalry
cydymgeisydd, (-wyr), n.m. rival
cyfadran, (-nau), n.f. faculty (in college); period (in music)
cyfaddas, a. fit, suitable, convenient
cyfaddasiad, (-au), n.m. adaptation
cyfaddaster, n.m. fitness, suitability
cyfaddasu, v. fit, adapt
cyfaddawd, (-odau), n.m. compromise
cyfaddef, v. confess, own, admit
cyfaddefiad, (-au), n.m. confession, admission
cyfaenad, n.m. & a. harmonious song
cyfagos, a. near, adjacent, neighbouring
cyfaill, (-eillion), n.m. friend
cyfair, (-eiriau), n.m. acre
cyfair, -er, n.m. direction. **—ar g.,** for; opposite
cyfalaf, n.m. capital
cyfalle(dd) n.m.f. union, spouse

cyfallwy, *a.* adequate, perfect, sharp

cyfamod, (*-au*), *n.m.* covenant

cyfamodi, *v.* covenant

cyfamodol, *a.* federal: covenanted

cyfamodwr, (*-wyr*), *n.m.* covenanter

cyfamser, *n.m.* meantime

cyfamserol, *a.* timely; synchronous

cyfan, *a. & n.m.* whole

cyfandir, (*-oedd*), *n.m.* continent

cyfanfor, (*-oedd*), *n.m.* main sea, ocean

cyfanfyd, *n.m.* whole world, universe

cyfangorff, *n.m.* whole, bulk, mass

cyfan gwbl, *a.* **yn g.,** altogether, quite

cyfanheddol, *a.* habitable, inhabited

cyfanheddu, *v.* dwell, inhabit

cyfannedd, *a.* inhabited: (*-anheddau*), *n.f.* inhabited place, habitation

cyfannu, *v.* make whole, complete

cyfanrwydd, *n.m.* wholeness, entirety

cyfansawdd, *a.* composite, compound

cyfansoddi, *v.* compose, constitute

cyfansoddiad, (*-au*), *n.m.* composition; constitution

cyfansoddiadol, *a.* constitutional

cyfansoddwr, (*-wyr*), *n.m.* composer

cyfanswm, (*-symiau*), *n.m.* total

cyfarch, *v.* greet, salute, address

cyfarchiad, (*-au*), *n.m.* greeting, salutation

cyfarchwel, -chwyl, *n.m.* shelter, care, oversight

cyfarchwylio, *v.* observe, survey

cyfaredd, (*-ion*), *n.f.* charm, spell

cyfareddol, *a.* enchanting

cyfareddu, *v.* charm, enchant

cyfarfod, *v.* meet: (*-ydd*), *n.m.* meeting

cyfarfyddiad, (*-au*), *n.m.* meeting

cyfarpar, *n.m.* provision, equipment; diet. —**c. rhyfel,** munitions of war

cyfartal, *a.* equal, even

cyfartaledd, *n.m.* proportion, average

cyfartalu, *v.* proportion, equalize

cyfarth, *v.* bark

cyfarws, -wys, (*-au*), *n.m.* gift, reward

cyfarwydd, *a.* skilled; familiar

cyfarwyddo, *v.* direct; become familiar

cyfarwyddwr, (*-wyr*), *n.m.* director

cyfarwyddyd, (*-iadau*), *n.m.* direction, instruction

cyfatal, *a.* unsettled, hindering

cyfateb, *v.* correspond, agree, tally

cyfatebiaeth, (*-au*), *n.f.* correspondence, analogy

cyfatebol, *a.* corresponding, proportionate

cyfathrach, (*-au*), *n.f.* affinity; intercourse

cyfathrachu, *v.* have intercourse

cyfathrachwr, (*-wyr*), *n.m.* kinsman

cyfddydd, *n.m.* day-break, dawn

cyfeb, cyfebr, *a.* pregnant (of mare, ewe)

cyfeddach, (*-au*), *n.f.* carousal

cyfeddachwr, (*-wyr*), *n.m.* carouser

cyfeiliant, *n.m.* musical accompaniment

cyfeilio, *v.* accompany

cyfeiliorn, *n.m.* error.—**ar g.,** astray

cyfeiliornad, (*-au*), *n.m.* error, heresy

cyfeiliorni, *v.* err, stray

cyfeiliornus, *a.* erroneous, mistaken

cyfeilydd, (*-ion*), *n.m.* accompanist

cyfeillach, (*-au*), *n.f.* fellowship; fellowship-meeting

cyfeillachu, *v.* associate

cyfeilles, (*-au*), *n.f.* female friend

cyfeillgar, *a.* friendly

cyfeillgarwch, *n.m.* friendship

cyfeiriad, (*-au*), *n.m.* direction; reference

cyfeirio, *v.* point; direct; refer

cyfelin, (*-au*), *n.f.* cubit, eighteen inches

cyfenw, (*-au*), *n.m.* surname; namesake

cyfenwi, *v.* surname

cyfer, *n.m.* **ar g.,** for; opposite

cyferbyn, *a.* opposite

cyferbyniad, (*-au*), *n.m.* contrast

cyferbyniol, *a.* opposing, opposite

cyferbynnu, *v.* contrast, compare

cyfergyr, *n.f.* contest, battle

cyfernod, *n.m.* coefficient

cyfiaith, *a.* of the same language

cyfiawn, *a.* just, righteous

cyfiawnder, (*-au*), *n.m.* justice, righteousness

cyfiawnhad, *n.m.* justification

cyfiawnhau, *v.* justify

cyfieithiad, (*-au*), *n.m.* translation, version

cyfieithu, *v.* translate, interpret

cyfieithydd, (*-wyr*), *n.m.* translator, interpreter

cyfisol, *a.* of the present month, instant

cyflafan, (*-au*), *n.f.* outrage; massacre

cyflafareddiad, *n.m.* arbitration

cyflafareddu, *v.* arbitrate

cyflafareddwr, (*-wyr*), *n.m.* arbitrator

cyflaith, *n.m.* toffee

cyflawn, *a.* full, complete

cyflawnder, *n.m.* fullness; abundance

cyflawni, *v.* fulfil, perform, commit

cyflawniad, (*-au*), *n.m.* fulfilment, performance

cyfle, (*-oedd*) *n.m.* place; chance, opportunity

cyfled, *a.* as broad as

cyflegr, (*-au*), *n.m.* gun, cannon, battery

cyflenwad, (*-au*), *n.m.* supply

cyflenwi, *v.* supply

cyfleu, *v.* place, set; convey

cyfleus, *a.* convenient

cyfleustra, (*-terau*), *n.m.* opportunity, convenience

cyflin, *a.* parallel

cyflo, *a.* in calf

cyflog, (*-au*), *n.m.f.* hire, wage; wages

cyflogi, *v.* hire; engage in service

cyflogwr, (*-wyr*), *n.m.* hirer, employer

cyflwr, (*-lyrau*), *n.m.* condition, case

cyflwyniad, *n.m.* presentation, dedication

cyflwyno, *v.* present; dedicate

cyflychwr, -wyr, *n.m.* evening, twilight, dusk

cyflym, *a.* quick, fast, swift

cyflymder, -dra, *n.m.* swiftness, speed

cyflymu, *v.* speed, accelerate

cyflyru, *v.* condition

cyfnerthu, *v.* confirm; aid, help

cyfnesaf, (*-iaid, -eifiaid*), *n.m.f.* next of kin, kinsman: *a.* next, nearest

cyfnewid, *v.* change, exchange

cyfnewidfa, (*-oedd, -feydd*), *n.f.* exchange

cyfnewidiad, (*-au*), *n.m.* change, alteration

cyfnewidiol, *a.* changeable

cyfnewidiwr, (*-wyr*), *n.m.* changer, trader

cyfnither, (*-oedd*), *n.f.* female cousin

cyfnod, (*-au*), *n.m.* period

cyfnodol, *a.* periodic(al): **-yn,** (*-ion*), *n.m.* periodical publication

cyfnos, *n.m.* evening twilight, dusk

cyfochredd, *n.m.* parallelism

cyfochrog, *a.* parallel

cyfodi, *v.* rise, arise; raise

cyfodiad, *n.m.* rise, rising

cyfoed, *a.* coeval, contemporary: (*-ion*), *n.m.* contemporaries

cyfoesi, *v.* be contemporary

cyfoeswr, (*-wyr*), *n.m.* contemporary

cyfoeth, *n.m.* power; riches, wealth

cyfoethog, *a.* powerful; rich, wealthy

cyfoethogi, *v.* make or grow rich

cyfog, *n.m.* sickness

yfogi, v. vomit

yfor, n.m. flood, abundance; rim, brim, edge: a. entire, brim-full

yforiog, a. brim-full, overflowing

yfosodiad, n.m. opposition

yfradd, (-au), n.f. rate. —**c. log,** rate of interest: a. of equal rank

yfraid, (-reidiau), n.m. necessity

yfraith, (-reithiau), n.f. law

yfran, (-nau), n.f. part, portion, share

yfranc, (-rangau), n.f.m. meeting; combat; incident; story, tale

yfranddaliwr, (-wyr), n.m. shareholder

yfraniad, (-au), n.m. contribution

yfrannog, a. participating, partaking

yfrannol, a. contributing

yfrannu, v. contribute; impart

yfrannwr, (-anwyr), n.m. contributor

yfranogi, v. participate, partake

yfranogol, a. communicable

yfranogwr, (-wyr), n.m. partaker

yfreithio, v. go to law, litigate

yfreithiol, a. legal

yfreithiwr, (-wyr), n.m. lawyer

yfreithlon, a. lawful, legitimate

yfreithlondeb, n.m. lawfulness

yfreithloni, v. legalize; justify

yfres, (-i), n.f. series

yfresymiad, (-au), n.m. syllogism

yfrgolli, v. lose utterly, damn

yfrif, v. count, reckon; account; impute: (-on), n.m. account, reckoning

yfrifiad, (-au), n.m. counting; census

yfrifol a. of repute; responsible

yfrifoldeb, (-au), n.m. responsibility

yfrifydd, (-ion), n.m. reckoner, accountant

yfrin, a. secret, subtle

yfrinach, (-au), n.f. secret

yfrinachol, a. secret, private, confidential

yfrinfa, n.f. lodge of friendly society

cyfrin-gyngor, (-nghorau), n.m. privy council

cyfriniaeth, n.f. mystery; mysticism

cyfriniol, a. mysterious, mystic

cyfriniwr, (-wyr), n.m. mystic

cyfrodedd, a. twisted, twined

cyfrodeddu, v. twist, twine

cyfrol, (-au), n.f. volume

cyfrwng, (-ryngau), n.m. medium, means

cyfrwy, (-au), n.m. saddle

cyfrwyo, v. saddle

cyfrwys, a. cunning

cyfrwystra, n.m. cunning

cyfrwywr, (-wyr), n.m. saddler

cyfryngdod, n.m. mediation, intercession; mediatorship

cyfryngiad, n.m. mediation; intervention

cyfryngol, a. mediatorial

cyfryngu, v. mediate; intervene

cyfryngwr, (-wyr), n.m. mediator

cyfryngwriaeth, n.f. mediatorship

cyfrysedd, (-au), n.m.f. conflict, strife, battle

cyfryw, a. like, such

cyfundeb, (-au), n.m. union; connexion

cyfundebol, a. connexional

cyfundrefn, (-au), n.f. system

cyfundrefnol, a. systematic

cyfundrefnu, v. systematize

cyfuniad, (-au), n.m. combination

cyfuno, v. unite, combine

cyfunol, a. united

cyfuwch, a. as high

cyfwerth, a. equivalent

cyfwng, (-yngau), n.m. space; interval

cyfwrdd, v. meet

cyfyng, a. narrow, confined

cyfyngder, (-au), n.m. trouble, distress

cyfyngdra, n.m. narrowness; distress

cyfyng-gyngor, n.m. perplexity

cyfyngu, v. narrow, confine, limit

cyfyl, n.m. neighbourhood. —**ar ei g.** near him

cyfymliw, *v.* reproach, expostulate

cyfyrder, (*-dyr*), *n.m.* second cousin

cyfys, *n.m.* temple (of the forehead)

cyfystlys, *a.* side by side

cyfystyr, *a.* synonymous

cyfystyron, *n.pl.* synonyms

cyff, (*-ion*), *n.m.* stock

cyffaith, (*-ffeithiau*), *n.m.* confection

cyffelyb, *a.* like, similar

cyffelybiaeth, (*-au*), *n.f.* likeness, similitude

cyffelybiaethol, *a.* figurative

cyffelybrwydd, *n.m.* likeness, similarity

cyffelybu, *v.* liken, compare

cyffer. See **cyffur**

cyffes, (*-ion*), *n.f.* confession

cyffesgell, (*-oedd*), *n.f.* confessional

cyffesu, *v.* confess

cyffeswr, (*-wyr*), **-ydd,** (*-ion*), *n.m.* confessor

cyffin, (*-iau, -ydd*), *n.f.m.* border, confine

cyffio, *v.* stiffen; fetter

cyffion, *n.pl.* stocks

cyffoden, (*-nod*), *n.f.* concubine, mistress

cyffordd, (*-ffyrdd*), *n.f.* (railway) junction

cyffredin, *a.* common; general

cyffredinol, *a.* general, universal

cyffredinoli, *v.* universalize

cyffredinolrwydd, *n.m.* universality

cyffredinwch, *n.m.* commonness

cyffro, (*-adau*), *n.m.* motion, stir; excitement

cyffroi, *v.* move, excite; provoke

cyffrous, *a.* exciting; excited

cyffryd, *n.m.* trembling, shaking

cyffur, (*-iau*), *n.m.f.* ingredient, drug

cyffuriwr, (*-wyr*), *n.m.* apothecary, druggist

cyffwrdd, *v.* meet, touch

cyffylog, (*-od*), *n.m.* woodcock

cyffyrddiad, (*-au*), *n.m.* touch, contact

cyffyrddus, *a.* comfortable

cygnog, *a.* knotted, gnarled

cyngaf, cyngaw, *n.m.* burdock; burs

cyngan, *a.* suitable, harmonious

cynganeddol, *a.* in *cynghanedd*

cynganeddu, *v.* form *cynghanedd*; harmonize

cyngaws, (*cynghawsau, -ion*), *n.m.* lawsuit, action

cyngerdd, (*-ngherddau*), *n.m.f.* concert

cynghanedd, (*cynganeddion*), *n.f.* music, harmony: Welsh metrical alliteration

cynghorfynt, *n.m.* jealousy, envy, malice

cynghori, *v.* counsel, advise; exhort

cynghorwr, (*-wyr*), *n.m.* councillor, counsellor; exhorter

cynghrair, (*-eiriau*), *n.m.f.* alliance, league

cynghreiriad, (*-iaid*), *n.m.* confederate, ally

cynghreirio, *v.* league, confederate

cynghreiriwr, (*-wyr*), *n.m.* confederate, ally

cyngor, (*-nghorion*), *n.m.* counsel, advice: (*-nghorau*), *n.m.* council

cyngres, (*-au, -i*), *n.f.* congress

cyngwystl, ¡(*-(i)on*), *n.m.f.* wager, pledge

cyhoedd, *a. & n.m.* public

cyhoeddi, *v.* publish, announce

cyhoeddiad, (*-au*), *n.m.* publication; announcement; (preaching) engagement

cyhoeddus, *a.* public

cyhoeddusrwydd, *n.m.* publicity

cyhoeddwr, (*-wyr*), *n.m.* publisher

cyhuddiad, (*-au*), *n.m.* accusation, charge

cyhuddo, *v.* accuse, charge

cyhuddwr, (*-wyr*), *n.m.* accuser

cyhwfan, *v.* wave, heave

cyhyd, *a.* as long, so long

cyhydedd, *n.m.* equator

cyhyr, (*-au*), *n.m.* flesh, muscle

cyhyrog, *a.* muscular

cyhyryn, *n.m.* piece of flesh; muscle

cylch, (*-au, -oedd*), *n.m.* round, circle, sphere, hoop

cylchdaith, (*-deithiau*), *n.f.* circuit

cylchdro, (*-eon, -adau*), *n.m* orbit

cylchdroi, *v.* rotate, revolve

cylched, (*-au*), *n.m.* coverlet, blanket

cylchedd, (*-au*), *n.m.f.* compass, circle, circuit

cylchgrawn, (*-gronau*), *n.m.* magazine

cylchlythyr, (*-au*), *n.m.* circular

cylchredeg, *v.* circulate

cylchrediad, *n.m.* circulation

cylchres, (*-i*), *n.f.* round, rota

cylchwyl, (*-iau*), *n.f.* anniversary, festival

cylchynol, *a.* surrounding

cylchynu, *v.* surround, encompass

cylion, *n.pl.* (*-yn,* *n.m.* *-en,* *n.f.*), flies, gnats

cylymu, *v.* knot, tie

cyll, *n.pl.* (**collen,** *n.f.*), hazel-trees

cylla, (*-on*), *n.m.* stomach

cyllell, (*-yll*), *n.f.* knife

cyllid, (*-au*), *n.m.* revenue, income

cyllideb, (*-au*), *n.f.* budget

cyllidwr, (*-wyr*), **cyllidydd,** (*-ion*), *n.m.* taxgatherer, revenue or excise officer, financier

cymaint, *a.* as big, as much, as many; so big, etc.

cymal, (*-au*), *n.m.* joint

cymalwst, *n.f.* rheumatism

cyman, *n.f.* assembly, host: *a.* complete, entire

cymanfa, (*-oedd*), *n.f.* assembly; festival

cymanwlad, *n.f.* commonwealth

cymar, (*-heiriaid*), *n.m.* fellow

cymathiad, *n.m.* assimilation

cymathu, *v.* assimilate

cymdeithas, (*-au*), *n.f.* society, association

cymdeithasfa, (*-oedd*), *n.f.* association

cymdeithasgar, *a.* sociable

cymdeithasol, *a.* social

cymdeithasu, *v.* associate

cymdeithion, *n.pl.* (**cydymaith,** *n.m.*), companion

cymedrol, *a.* moderate, temperate

cymedroldeb, *n.m.* moderation, temperance

cymedroli, *v.* moderate

cymedrolwr, (*-wyr*), *n.m.* moderator; moderate drinker

cymell, *v.* urge, press, persuade, induce

cymen, *a.* wise, skilful, neat, becoming

cymer, (*-au*), *n.m.* confluence

cymeradwy, *a.* acceptable, approved

cymeradwyaeth, *n.f.* approval; applause

cymeradwyo, *v.* approve; recommend

cymeradwyol, *a.* commendatory

cymeriad, (*-au*), *n.m.* character, reputation

cymeryd. See **cymryd**

cymesur, *a.* proper, proportionate

cymesuredd, *n.m.* proportion

cymesurol, *a.* commensurate, proportionate

cymhares, (*cymaresau*), *n.f.* one of a pair

cymhariaeth, (*cymariaethau*), *n.f.* comparison

cymharol *a.* comparative

cymharu, *v.* pair; compare

cymhelliad, (*-hellion*), *n.m.* motive, inducement

cymhendod, *n.m.* knowledge; proficiency; tidiness; eloquence; affectation

cymhennu, *v.* put in order, trim; scold, reprove

cymhercyn, *a.* limping, infirm

cymhorthdal, (*cymorthdaloedd*), *n.m.* subsidy, grant.

cymhleth, *a.* complicated; complex

cymhwysiad, *n.m.* application

cymhwyso, *v.* apply

cymhwyster, (*cymwysterau*), *n.m.* fitness, suitability; (*pl.*) qualifications

cymod, *n.m.* reconciliation

cymodi, *v.* reconcile; be reconciled

cymodol, *a.* reconciliatory, propitiatory

cymodwr, (*-wyr*), *n.m.* reconciler

cymon, *a.* orderly, tidy; seemly

cymorth, *v.* assist, aid, help: *n.m.* assistance, aid, help

Cymraeg, *n.f.m. & a.* Welsh

Cymraes, *n.f.* Welshwoman

cymrawd, (*-odyr*), *n.m.* comrade, fellow

Cymreig, *a.* Welsh

Cymreigaidd, *a.* Welshy

Cymreiges, (*-au*), *n.f.* Welshwoman

Cymreigio, *v.* translate into Welsh

Cymreigydd, (*-ion*), *n.m.* Welsh scholar

Cymro, (*Cymry*), *n.m.* Welshman

Cymroaidd, *a.* Welsh, Welshy

cymrodedd, *n.m.* arbitration; compromise

cymrodor, (*-ion*), *n.m.* consociate, fellow

cymrodoriaeth, *n.f.* fellowship

Cymru, *n.f.* Wales

cymrwd, *n.m.* mortar, plaster

Cymry. See **Cymro**

cymryd, *v.* take, accept. **—c. ar,** pretend

cymun, -deb, *n.m.* communion, fellowship

cymuned, *n.f.* community

cymuno, *v.* commune

cymunwr, (*-wyr*), *n.m.* communicant

cymŵedd, *v.* jest, mock

cymwy, (*-au*), *n.m.* affliction

cymwynas, (*-au*), *n.f.* kindness, favour

cymwynasgar, *a.* obliging, kind

cymwynasgarwch, *n.m.* obligingness, kindness

cymwynaswr, (*-wyr*), *n.m.* benefactor

cymwys, *a.* fit, proper, suitable; exact

cymwysiadol, *a.* applicable

cymydog, (*cymdogion*), *n.m.* neighbour

cym(y)dogaeth, (*-au*), *n.f.* neighbourhood

cym(y)dogaethol, *a.* neighbouring

cym(y)doges, (*-au*), *n.f.* neighbour

cym(y)dogol, *a.* neighbourly

cymylog, *a.* cloudy, clouded

cymylu, *v.* cloud, dim, obscure

cymyndod, *n.m.* committal

cymynrodd, (*-ion*), *n.f.* legacy, bequest

cymynroddi, *v.* bequeath

cymynu, *v.* hew, fell

cymynwr, (*-wyr*), *n.m.* hewer, feller

cymynnu, *v.* commend; command

cymyrredd, *n.m.* dignity; pride, arrogance

cymysg, *a.* mixed

cymysgedd, *n.m.f.* mixture

cymysgfa, *n.f.* mixture, medley, hotchpotch

cymysgliw, *a.* motley

cymysglyd, *a.* muddled, confused

cymysgryw, *a.* mongrel; heterogeneous

cymysgu, *v.* mix, blend; confuse

cymysgwr, (*-wyr*), *n.m.* mixer, blender

cyn, *px.* before, previous: *px.* first, previous, former, pre-, ex-

cyn, *adv.* **-cyn wynned â,** as white as

cŷn, (*cynion*), *n.m.* wedge, chisel

cynadledda, *v.* meet in conference

cynamserol, *a.* premature, untimely

cynaniad, *n.m.* pronunciation

cynanu, *v.* pronounce

cynbrawf, (*-brofion*), *n.m.* foretaste

cyndad, (*-au*), *n.m.* forefather, ancestor

cyndyn, *a.* stubborn, obstinate

cyndynnu, *v.* be obstinate

cyndynrwydd, *n.m.* stubbornness, obstinacy

cynddaredd, *n.f.* madness: rabies

cynddeiriog, *a.* mad, rabid

cynddeiriogi, *v.* madden, enrage

cynddeiriogrwydd, *n.m.* rage, fury

cynddrwg, *a.* as bad

cynddydd, *n.m.* day-break, dawn

cynefin, *a.* acquainted, accustomed, familiar: *n.m.* haunt, habitat

cynefindra, *n.m.* use, familiarity

cynefino, v. get used, become accustomed

cynefinol, a. usual, accustomed

cynefod, (-au), n.f. custom, usage

cynfas, (-au), n.f.m. (bed) sheet; canvas

cynfyd, n.m. primitive world, antiquity

cynfyl, n.m. strife, contention

cynffon, (-nau), n.f. tail

cynffonna, v. fawn, toady, cringe

cynffonnwr, (-onwyr), n.m. toady, sycophant

cynhadledd, (cynadleddau), n.f. conference

cynhaeaf, (cynaeafau), n.m. harvest

cyn(h)aeafa, v. dry in the sun

cyn(h)aeafu, v. harvest

cyn(h)aeafwr, (-wyr), n.m. harvester [port

cynhaliaeth, n.f. maintenance, support

cynhaliol, a. sustaining

cynhaliwr, (-wyr), n.m. supporter, sustainer

cynhebrwng, (-yngau), n.m. funeral

cynhenid, a. innate

cynhennu, v. contend, quarrel

cynhennus, a. contentious, quarrelsome

cynhennwr, (-henwyr), n.m. wrangler

cynhesol, a. agreeable, amiable

cynhesrwydd, n.m. warmth

cynhesu, v. warm, get warm

cynhorthwy, (cynorthwyon), n.m. help, aid

cynhwynol, a. natural, congenital, innate

cynhwysfawr, a. comprehensive

cynhwysiad, n.m. contents

cynhyrchiol, a. productive

cynhyrchu, v. produce

cynhyrfiad, (cynyrfiadau), n.m. stirring, agitation

cynhyrfiol, a. stirring, thrilling

cynhyrfu, v. stir, agitate

cynhyrfus, a. agitated; exciting

cynhyrfwr, (-wyr), n.m. agitator, disturber [fortune

cynhysgaeth, n.f. dower, portion,

cyni, n.m. anguish, distress, adversity

cynifer, a. & n.m. as many, so many

cynigiad, (-au), n.m. proposal, motion

cynigiwr, (-wyr), **-ydd,** (-ion), n.m. proposer, mover

cynildeb, n.m. frugality, economy

cynilion, n.pl. savings

cynilo, v. save, economise

cynio, v. chisel, gouge

cynired, v. go to and fro, resort

cyniwair, v. go to and fro, frequent

cyniweirfa, (-feydd), n.f. resort, haunt

cyniweirydd, n.m. wayfarer

cynllun, (-iau), n.m. pattern; plan

cynllunio, v. plan, design

cynllunydd, (-ion, -wyr), n.m. designer

cynllwyn, v. plot, conspire: (-ion), n.m. plot

cynllwynwr, (-wyr), n.m. conspirator

cynnal v. hold, uphold, support, sustain

cynnar, a. early

cynnau, v. kindle, light

cynneddf, (cyneddfau), n.f. quality, faculty

cynnen, (cynhennau), n.f. contention, strife

cynnes, a. warm

cynnig, v. offer; attempt; propose, move; bid; apply: (cynigion), n.m. offer; attempt; motion

cynnil, a. economical; delicate

cynnor, (cynhorau), n.f. door-post

cynnud, n.m. firewood, fuel

cynnull, v. collect, gather, assemble

cynnwrf, n.m. stir, commotion, agitation

cynnwys, v. contain, include, comprise, comprehend: n.m. content(s)

cynnydd, n.m. increase, growth, progress

cynnyrch, (cynhyrchion), n.m. produce, product; (pl.) productions cynorthwyo, v. help, assist

cynorthwyol, a. auxiliary; assistant

cynorthwywr, (-wyr), n.m. helper, assistant

cynrhon, n.pl. (-yn, n.m.), maggots

cynrhoni, v. breed maggots

cynrhonllyd, a. maggoty

cynrychiolaeth, n.f. representation

cynrychioli, v. represent

cynrychiolwr, (-wyr), -ydd, (-ion), n.m. representative, delegate

cynt, a. earlier, sooner, quicker: adv. See gynt

cyntaf, a. & adv. first

cyntedd, (-au), n.m. court; porch

cyntefig, a. prime, primitive

cyntun, n.m. nap

cynulleidfa, (-oedd), n.f. congregation

cynulleidfaol, a. congregational

cynulliad, (-au), n.m. gathering

cynuta, v. gather fuel

cynyddol, a. increasing, growing

cynyddu, v. increase

cynysgaeddu, v. endow, endue

cyplu, cyplysu, v. couple

cyraeddadwy, a. attainable

cyraeddiadau, n.pl. attainments

cyrains, cyrans, n.pl. currants

cyrbibion, n.pl. atoms, smithereens

cyrcydu, v. squat, cower

cyrch, (-au), n.m. attack

cyrchfa, (-feydd), n.f. resort

cyrchu, v. go, resort, repair

cyrhaeddgar, a. telling, incisive

cyrhaeddiad, (cyraeddiadau), n.m. reach, attainment

cyrhaeddyd, v. reach

cyrliog, a. curly

cyrraedd, v. reach, attain; arrive

cysawd, (-odau), n.m. system; constellation

cysefin, a. original, primordial

cysegr, (-au,-oedd), n.m. sanctuary

cysegredig, a. consecrated, sacred

cysegredigrwydd, n.m. sacredness

cysegriad, (-au), n.m. consecration

cysegr-ladrad, n.m. sacrilege

cysegr-lân, a. holy

cysegru, v. consecrate, dedicate, devote

cysetlyd, a. fastidious

cysgadrwydd, n.m. sleepiness, drowsiness

cysgadur, (-iaid), n.m. sleeper

cysglyd, a. sleepy

cysgod, (-au, -ion), n.m. shade, shadow; shelter; type

cysgodi, v. shadow, shade; shelter

cysgodol, a. shady, sheltered

cysgogi, v. shake, move

cysgu, v. sleep

cysgwr, (-wyr), n.m. sleeper

cysidro, v. consider

cysodi, v. set type, compose

cysodydd, (-ion, -wyr), n.m. compositor

cyson, a. consistent, constant

cysondeb, n.m. consistency; regularity

cysoni, v. harmonize; reconcile

cysonwr, (-wyr), -ydd, (-ion), n.m. harmonist

cystadleuaeth (-au), n.f. competition

cystadleuol, a. competitive

cystadleuwr, -ydd, (-wyr), n.m. competitor

cystadlu, v. compete; compare

cystal, a. as good, so good: adv. as well, so well

cystrawen, (-nau), n.f. construction, syntax

cystudd, (-iau), n.m. affliction; illness

cystuddiedig, a. afflicted, contrite

cystuddio, v. afflict, trouble

cystuddiol, a. afflicted

cystuddiwr, (-wyr), n.m. afflicter, oppressor

cystwyo, v. chastise, castigate, trounce

cysur, (-on), n.m. comfort, consolation

cysuro, v. comfort, console

cysurus, a. comfortable

cysurwr, (-wyr), n.m. comforter

cyswllt, (-ylltiadau), n.m. joint, junction

cysylltair, (-eiriau), cysylltiad, (-iaid), n.m. conjunction

cysylltiad, (-au), n.m. joining, connexion

cysylltiol, a. connecting; connected

cysylltu, v. join, connect

cytbwys, a. of equal weight

cytgan, (-au), n.m.f. chorus

cytgord, n.m. concord

cytio, v. pen, sty

cytir, (-oedd), n.m. common

cytras, a. allied, related; cognate

cytsain, (-seiniaid), n.f. consonant

cytûn, a. agreed, of one accord, unanimous

cytundeb, (-au), n.m. agreement, consent

cytuno, v. agree, consent

cythlwng, n.m. fasting, fast, hunger

cythraul, (-euliaid), n.m. devil, demon

cythreules, (-au), n.f. she-devil, fury

cythreulig, a. devilish, fiendish

cythrudd, n.m. annoyance, irritation

cythruddo, v. annoy, provoke, irritate

cythrwfl, n.m. uproar, tumult

cythryblu, v. trouble, agitate

cythryblus, a. troubled, agitated

cyw, (-ion), n.m. young bird, chick, chicken

cywain, v. convey, carry; garner

cywair, (-eiriau), n.m. order; key; tune

cywarch, n.m. hemp

cyweirio, v. set in order; prepare, dress

cyweirnod, (-au), n.m. key-note

cyweithas, n.m. company, society: a. sociable, kind, gentle

cywely, n.c. bedfellow

cywen, (-nod), n.f. pullet, young hen

cywilydd, n.m. shame; shyness

cywilyddgar, a. bashful, shy

cywilyddio, v. shame; be ashamed

cywilyddus, a. shameful, disgraceful

cywir, a. correct, accurate, true, faithful

cywirdeb, n.m. correctness; integrity

cywiriad, (-au), n.m. correction

cywiro, v. correct; make good, perform

cywirwr, (-wyr), n.m. corrector

cywrain, a. skilful; curious

cywreinbeth, (-au, -einion), n.m. curiosity

cywreinfa, (-feydd), n.f. museum

cywreinrwydd, n.m. skill; curiosity

cywydd, (-au), n.m. alliterative Welsh poem so called

CH

chwa, (-on), n.f. puff, gust, breeze

chwaer, (chwiorydd), n.f. sister

chwaeth, (-au), n.f. taste

chwaethach, adv. much less

chwaethu, v. taste

chwaethus, a. tasteful; decent

chwaith, adv. nor either, neither

chwalfa, (-feydd), n.f. upset, rout

chwalu, v. scatter, spread

chwalwr, (-wyr), n.m. scatterer

chwaneg, a. & n.m. more

chwanegu, v. add, augment, increase

chwannen, (chwain), n.f. flea

chwannog, a. desirous; addicted

chwant, (-au), n.m. desire, craving, lust

chwanta, v. desire, lust, covet

chwantus, a. lustful

chwarae, chware, v. play; (-on), n.m. play

chwaraedy, (-dai), n.m. playhouse, theatre

chwaraefwrdd, (-fyrddau), n.m. stage

chwaraegar, a. playful, sportive

chwaraegerdd, (-i), n.f. drama

chwaraewr, (-wyr), n.m. player

chwaraeydd, (-ion), n.m. actor

chwarddiad, n.m. laugh

chwarel, (-au, -i, -ydd), n.f. quarry

chwarel, (*-au*), *n.f.* pane of glass

chwarelwr, (*-wyr*), *n.m.* quarryman

chwareus, *a.* playful

chwarren, (*-arennau*), *n.f.* gland; kernel

chwart, (*-iau*), *n.m.* quart

chwarter, (*-i, -au*), *n.m.* quarter

chwarterol, *a.* quarterly

chwarteru, *v.* quarter

chwe, *a.* six (before a noun)

chwech, *a.* six: (*-au*), *n.m.* six; sixpence

chwecheiniog, (*-au*), *n.m.* sixpence

chwedl, (*-au*), *n.f.* story, tale

chwedleua, *v.* talk, gossip

chwedleugar, *a.* talkative

chwedloniaeth, *n.f.* mythology

chwedlonol, *a.* mythical, mythological

chwedlonydd, (*-wyr*), *n.m.* mythologist

chwedyn, *adv.* **-na chynt na ch.,** neither before nor after

Chwefror, Chwefrol, *n.m.* February

chweg, *a.* sweet, pleasant

chwegr, *n.f.* mother-in-law

chwegrwn, *n.m.* father-in-law

chwennych, chwenychu, *v.* covet, desire

chwephlyg, *a.* sixfold

chwerthin, *v.* laugh: *n.m.* laughter

chwerthiniad, (*-au*), *n.m.* laugh

chwerthinial, *v.* laugh, titter, giggle, snigger

chwerthinllyd, *a.* laughable, ridiculous

chwerw, *a.* bitter

chwerwder, *n.m.* bitterness

chwerwi, *v.* grow bitter, embitter

chweugain, *a.* six score: *n.m.* ten shillings

chwi, *pn.* you

chwiban, *v. & n.m.* whistle

chwibaniad, *n.m.* whistling, whistle

chwibanogl, (*-au*), *n.f.* whistle, flute

chwibanu, *v.* whistle

chwidr, *a.* wild, foolish, rash

chwifio, *v.* wave, flourish, brandish

chwiffiad, *n.m.* whiff, jiffy

chwil, (*-od*), *n.m.f.* beetle, chafer

chwil, *a.* whirling, reeling

chwilboeth, *a.* scorching, piping hot

chwildroi, *v.* whirl, spin

chwilen, (*chwilod*), *n.f.* beetle

chwilenna, *v.* rummage; pry; pilfer   [scrutiny

chwilfa, (*-feydd*), *n.f.* search,

chwilfriw, *a.* smashed to atoms

chwilfriwio, *v.* smash, shatter

chwilfrydedd, *n.m.* curiosity

chwilfrydig, *a.* curious, inquisitive

chwilgar, *a.* curious, inquisitive

chwilgarwch, *n.m.* inquisitiveness

chwilgi, (*-gwn*), *n.m.* prying dog, busybody

chwilio, *v.* search; examine

chwiliwr, (*-wyr*), *n.m.* searcher

chwil-lys, *n.m.* inquisition

chwilota, *v.* rummage, pry

chwim, *a.* nimble, quick, agile

chwimder, -dra, *n.m.* nimbleness

chwimio, *v.* move, stir

chwimwth, *a.* nimble, brisk

chwinciad, *n.m.* twinkling, trice

chwiorydd. See **chwaer**

chwip, (*-iau*), *n.f.* whip; whipping

chwipio, *v.* whip

chwipyn, *adv.* instantly

chwirligwgan, *n.f.* whirligig

chwisgi, *n.m.* whisky

chwistrell, (*-au, -i*), *n.f.* squirt, syringe

chwistrellu, *v.* squirt, syringe, inject

chwit-chwat, *a.* fickle, inconstant

chwith, *a.* left; wrong; sad; strange

chwithau, *pn.c.* you (on your part), you also

chwithdod, -dra, *n.m.* strangeness

chwithig, *a.* strange, wrong, awkward

chwithigrwydd, *n.m.* awkwardness

chwitho, *v.* feel dismayed or offended

chwithrwd, *v.* rustle, hiss

chwiw, (*-iau*), *n.f.* fit, attack, malady

chwiwbigo, *v.* pilfer

chwiwgi, (*-gwn*), *n.m.* sneak; thief; rogue

chwiwladrata, *v.* pilfer

chwiwleidr, (*-ladron*), *n.m.* pilferer

chwychwi, *pn.* you yourselves

chwŷd, chwydiad, *n.m.* vomit

chwydu, *v.* vomit, spue

chwydd, chwyddi, *n.m.* swelling

chwyddo, *v.* swell, increase, magnify

chwyddwydr, (*-au*), *n.m.* microscope

chwŷl, *n.m.f.* turn, rotation

chwyldro, (*-ion*), *n.m.* rotation; orbit

chwyldroad, (*-au*), *n.m.* revolution

chwyldroadol, *a.* revolutionary

chwyldroi, *v.* whirl, revolve, rotate

chwyn, *n.pl. & c.n.* weeds

chwynnog, *a.* weedy

chwynnu, *v.* weed

chwynnwr, (*-ynwyr*), *n.m.* weeder

chwyrlïo, *v.* whirl, spin, speed

chwyrn, *a.* rapid, swift

chwyrndra, *n.m.* rapidity, swiftness

chwyrnellu, *v.* whirl, whiz

chwyrnu, *v.* hum; snore; snarl

chwyrnwr, (*-wyr*), *n.m.* snorer; snarler

chwys, *n.m.* sweat, perspiration

chwysigen, (*-igod*), *n.f.* blister, vesicle

chwysigennu, *v.* blister

chwyslyd, *a.* sweaty

chwystyllau, *n.pl.* pores

chwysu, *v.* sweat, perspire; exude

chwyswr, (*-wyr*), *n.m.* sweater

chwyth, chwythad, *n.m.* breath

chwythbib, (*-au*), *n.f.* blowpipe

chwythu, *v.* blow, blast; breathe; hiss

chwythwr, (*-wyr*), *n.m.* blower

D

da, *a.* good, well: (*-oedd*), *n.m.* good; goods; stock, cattle.

da-da, *n.m.* sweets

dacw, *adv.* there is, are; behold there

dad- dat-, *px.* un-, dis- re-, back

dadannudd, *n.m.* disclosure, uncovering

dadansoddi, *v.* analyse

dadansoddiad, (*-au*), *n.m.* analysis

dadansoddwr, (*-wyr*), *n.m.* analyst

dadebru, *v.* resuscitate, revive

dadeni, *v.* regenerate, reanimate: *n.m.* rebirth, renascence, renaissance

dadfachu, *v.* unhook

dadfathiad, *n.m.* dissimulation

dadfeilio, *v.* fall to ruin, decay

dadflino, *v.* rest (after exertion)

dadl, (*-euon*), *n.f.* debate; doubt; plea

dadlaith, *v.* thaw; dissolve

dadlau, *v.* argue, debate: plead

dadleniad, (*-au*), disclosure, exposure

dadlennu, *v.* disclose, expose

dadleuol, *a.* controversial, polemical

dadleuwr, (*-wyr*), **-ydd,** (*-ion*), *n.m.* debater, controversialist; advocate

dadluddedu, *v.* rest (after exertion)

dadlwytho, *v.* unload, unburden

dadmer, *v.* thaw; dissolve

dadolwch, *n.m.* propitiation: *v.* worship, seek forgiveness

dadorchuddio, *v.* unveil, uncover

dadsefydliad, *n.m.* disestablishment

dadsefydlu, *v.* disestablish

dadwaddoli, *v.* disendow

dadwaddoliad, *n.m.* disendowment

dadwneuthur, *v.* undo, unmake

dadwrdd, *n.m.* noise, uproar, hubbub

dadymchwel, -yd, *v.* overturn, overthrow [soil

daear, (*-oedd*), *n.f.* earth, ground,

daeardy, (*-dai*), *n.m.* dungeon

daeareg, *n.f.* geology

daearegol, *a.* geological

daearegwr, (*-wyr*), **-ydd,** (*-ion*), *n.m.* geologist

daeargi, (*-gwn*), *n.m.* terrier

daeargryn, (*-fâu*), *n.m.f.* earthquake

daearol, *a.* terrestrial, earthly, earthy

daearu, *v.* earth; inter

daearyddiaeth, *n.f.* geography

daearyddol, *a.* geographical

daearyddwr, (*-wyr*), *n.m.* geographer

daer, *n.f.* earth

dafad, (*defaid*), *n.f.* sheep; wart

dafaden, (*-ennau*), *n.f.* wart

dafn, (*-au*), *n.m.* drop

dagrau, *n.pl.* (**deigryn,** *n.m.*), tears

dangos. See **dan-**

dail, *n.pl.* (**dalen, deilen,** *n.f.*), leaves

daint, (*dannedd*), *n.m.* tooth

daioni, *n.m.* goodness, good

daionus, *a.* good; beneficial; beneficent

dal, -a, *v.* hold; catch; arrest; last

dalen, (*-nau, dail*), *n.f.* leaf

dalfa, (*-feydd*), *n.f.* hold; arrest, custody

daliad, (*-au*), *n.m.* holding; tenet; spell

dall, (*deillion*), *a.* blind

dallbleidiaeth, *n.f.* bigotry

dallbleidiol, *a.* bigoted

dallbleidiwr, (*-wyr*), *n.m.* bigot

dallgeibio, *v.* blunder

dallineb, *n.m.* blindness

dallu, *v.* blind; dazzle

damcaniaeth, (*-au*), *n.f.* theory

damcaniaethol, *a.* theoretical

damcanu, *v.* theorize, speculate

dameg, (*-hegion*), *n.f.* parable

damhegol, *a.* parabolic(al), allegorical

damnedigaeth, *n.f.* damnation, condemnation

damnio. *v.* damn

damniol, *a.* damning, damnatory

damsang, *v.* tread, trample

damwain, (*-weiniau*), *n.f.* accident, chance, fate

damweinio, *v.* befall, happen

damweiniol. *a.* accidental, casual

dan. See **tan**

danadl, *n.pl.* (**danhadlen,** *n.f.*), nettles

danas, *c.n.* deer. —**bwch d.,** buck

danfon, *v.* send, convey; escort

dangos, *v.* show

dangoseg, (*-ion*), *n.f.* index

dannod, *v.* reproach, upbraid, taunt, twit

dannoedd, *n.f.* toothache

dansoddol, *a.* abstract

dant, (*dannedd*), *n.m.* tooth

danteithfwyd, (*-teithion*), *n.m.* dainty

danteithiol, *a.* dainty, delicious

darbod, *v.* prepare, provide: (*-ion*), *n.m.* provision

darbodaeth, *n.f.* providence, thrift

darbodus, *a.* provident, thrifty

darbwyllo, *v.* persuade, convince

darfelydd, *n.m.* imagination

darfod, *v.* finish, end; perish; happen

darfodedig, *a.* perishable, transient

darfodedigaeth, *n.m.* consumption

darganfod, *v.* discover

darganfyddiad, (*-au*), *n.m.* discovery

darganfyddwr, (*-wyr*), *n.m.* discoverer

darlith, (*-iau, -oedd*), *n.f.* lecture

darlithio, *v.* lecture

darlithiwr, (*-wyr*), **-ydd,** (*-ion*), *n.m.* lecturer

darlun, (*-iau*), *n.m.* picture

darluniad, (*-au*), *n.m.* portrayal, description [trated

darluniadol, *a.* pictorial, illus-

darlunio, *v.* portray, depict, describe

darllaw, *v.* brew

darllawdy, (*-dai*), *n.m.* brewery

darllawydd, (*-ion, -wyr*), *n.m.* brewer

darllen *v.* read

darllenadwy, *a.* readable, legible

darllenfa, (*-feydd*), *n.f.* reading room; reading-desk; lectern

darllengar, *a.* fond of reading, studious

darlleniad, (*-au*), *n.m.* reading

darllenwr, (*-wyr*), **-ydd,** (*-ion*), *n.m.* reader

darn, (*-au*), *n.m.* piece, fragment, part

darnguddio, *v.* conceal or withhold a part

darnio, *v.* cut up, hack

darnodi, *v.* distinguish, denote, define

darnodiad, (*-au*), *n.m.* definition

darogan, *v.* predict, foretell, forebode: (*-au*), *n.f.* prediction, foreboding　　　　　　　　　　[ject

darostwng, *v.* lower; subdue; sub-

darostyngiad, *n.m.* humiliation; subjection

darpar, (*-ion*, *-iadau*), *n.m.* preparation, provision: *a.* intended, elect

darpariaeth, (*-au*), *n.f.* preparation, provision

darparu, *v.* prepare, provide

darparwr, (*-wyr*), *n.m.* provider

darwden, *n.f.* ringworm

das, (*-au*, *deisi*), *n.f.* rick, stack

dat-, *px.* See **dad-**

datblygiad, (*-au*), *n.m.* development, evolution

datblygu, *v.* develop, evolve

datgan, *v.* declare; recount: render

datganiad, (*-au*), *n.m.* declaration; rendering

datganu, *v.* declare; sing, render

datgeiniad, (*-iaid*), *n.m.* singer

datgloi *v.* unlock

datgorffori *v.* dissolve (parliament)

datgorfforiad, *n.m.* dissolution

datguddiad, (*-au*), *n.m.* revelation, disclosure

datguddio, *v.* reveal, disclose

datguddiwr, -ydd, (*-wyr*), *n.m.* revealer

datgyffesiad, *n.m.* recantation

datgyffesu, *v.* recant

datgysylltiad, *n.m.* disestablishment

datgysylltu, *v.* disconnect: disestablish

datgysylltwr, (*-wyr*), *n.m.* disestablisher

datod, *v.* undo, untie, dissolve

datrys, *v.* solve

datseinio, *v.* resound, reverberate

dathliad, (*-au*), *n.m.* celebration

dathlu, *v.* celebrate

dau, *a. & n.m.* two: *f.* **dwy**

dau-, deu-, *px.*, two, bi-

daw, (*dofion*), *n.m.* son-in-law

dawn, (*doniau*), *n.m.f.* gift, talent

dawns, (*-iau*), *n.f.* dance

dawnsio, *v.* dance

dawnsiwr, (*-wyr*), *n.m.* dancer

dawnus, *a.* gifted, talented

de. See **deau**

deall, *v.* understand: *n.m.* understanding, intellect, intelligence

dealladwy, *a.* intelligible

deallgar, *a.* intelligent

deallol, *a.* intellectual

dealltwriaeth, (*-au*), *n.f.* understanding, intelligence

deallus, *a.* understanding, intelligent

deau, *a. & n.m.* right; south

decplyg, *a.* tenfold

dectant, *n.m.* ten-stringed instrument

dechrau, *v.* begin: *n.m.* beginning

dechreuad, (*-au*), *n.m.* beginning

dechreunos, *n.f.* nightfall, dusk

dechreuol, *a.* initial

dechreuwr, (*-wyr*), *n.m.* beginner

dedfryd, (*-au*), *n.f.* verdict; sentence

dedfrydu, *v.* sentence

dedwydd, *a.* happy, blessed

dedwyddwch, -yd, *n.m.* happiness, bliss

deddf, (*-au*), *n.f.* law, statute, act

deddfol, *a.* legal, lawful

deddfoldeb, *n.m.* legality

deddfu, *v.* legislate, enact

deddfwr, (*-wyr*), *n.m.* legislator

deddfwriaeth, *n.f.* legislation, legislature

defion, *n.pl.* rights; rites, customs

defni, *v.* drip, trickle

defnydd, (*-iau*), *n.m.* material, stuff; use

defnyddio, *v.* use, utilize, employ

defnyddiol, *a.* useful

defnyddioldeb, *n.m.* usefulness, utility

defnyn, (*-nau*), *n.m.* drop

defnynnu, *v.* drop, drip, dribble, distil

defod, (*-au*), *n.f.* custom; rite, ceremony

defodaeth, *n.f.* ritualism

defodol, *a.* ritualistic

defodwr, (*-wyr*), *n.m.* ritualist

defosiwn, (*-ynau*), *n.m.* devotion

defosiynol, *a.* devotional, devout

deffiniad, -io. See **diff-**

deffro, deffroi, *v.* rouse; wake

deffroad, (*-au*), *n.m.* awakening

deg, *a.* ten: (*-au*), *n.m.* ten

degwm, (*-ymau*), *n.m.* tenth, tithe

degymu, *v.* tithe

deng, *a.* ten (before certain words)

dengyn, *a.* strong, mighty, stubborn

dehau, deheu. See **deau**

deheubarth, -dir, *n.m.* southern region, south

deheuig, *a.* dexterous, skilful

deheulaw, *n.f.* right hand

deheuol, *a.* southern

deheurwydd, *n.m.* dexterity, skill

deheuwr, (*-wyr*), *n.m.* southerner, southman

deheuwynt, *n.m.* south wind

dehongli, *v.* interpret

dehongliad, (*-au*), *n.m.* interpretation

dehonglwr, (*-wyr*), **-ydd,** (*-ion*), *n.m.* interpreter

deifio, *v.* singe, scorch; blast

deifiol, *a.* scorching, scathing

deigryn, (*dagrau*), *n.m.* tear

deildy, (*-dai*), *n.m.* bower, arbour

deilen, (*-dail*), *n.f.* leaf

deiliad, (*-on, deiliaid*), *n.m.* tenant; subject

deilio, *v.* leaf

deiliog, *a.* leafy

deillio, *v.* proceed, emanate, issue

deincod, *n.m.* teeth on edge

deincryd, *n.m.* chattering or gnashing of teeth

deintydd, (*-ion*), *n.m.* dentist

deintyddiaeth, *n.f.* dentistry

deirton, *n.f.* (tertian) ague

deiryd, *v.* pertains, belongs

deiseb, (*-au*), *n.f.* petition

deisebu, *v.* petition

deisebwr, -ydd, (*-wyr*), *n.m.* petitioner

deisyf, deisyfu, *v.* desire, wish; beseech, entreat

deisyfiad, (*-au*), *n.m.* request, petition

del, *a.* pretty, neat

delfryd, (*-au*), *n.m.* ideal

delfrydol *a.* ideal

delff, *n.m.* churl, oaf, dolt, rascal

delio, *v.* deal

delw, (*-au*), *n.f.* image; form, mode, manner

delweddu, *v.* portray

dellt, *n.pl.* (**-en,** *n.f.*), laths, lattice, splinters

dengar, *a.* attractive

dengarwch, *n.m.* attractiveness

deniadau, *n.pl.* attractions, allurements

deniadol, *a.* attractive

denu, *v.* attract, allure, entice

deon, (*-iaid*), *n.m.* dean

deondy, (*-dai*), *n.m.* deanery

deoniaeth, (*-au*), *n.f.* deanery

deor, *v.* brood, hatch, incubate

dera, *n.f.* fiend; the staggers

derbyn, *v.* receive; accept; admit

derbyniad, (*-au*), *n.m.* receipt; reception

derbyniol, *a.* acceptable

derbyniwr, (*-wyr*), **nnydd,** (*-ynyddion*), *n.m.* receiver, acceptor

derbynneb, (*-ynebau, -ynebion*), *n.f.* receipt, voucher

dernyn (*-nau*), *n.m.* piece, scrap

derwen, (*derw, deri*), *n.f.* oak-tree, oak

derwydd, (*-on*), *n.m.* druid

derwyddiaeth, *n.f.* druidism

derwyddol, *a.* druidic(al)

desg, (*-iau*), *n.f.* desk

destlus, *a.* neat

destlusrwydd, *n.m.* neatness

dethol, *v.* select, pick, choose: *a.* select

detholiad, (*-au*, *detholion*), *n.m.* selection

deu-. See **dau-**

deuawd, (*-au*), *n.m.f.* duet

deublyg, *a.* double, twofold

deuddeg, *a. & n.m.* twelve

deugain, *a. & n.m.* forty

deunaw, *a. & n.m.* eighteen

deune, *a.* twice the colour or brightness of

deunydd, (*-iau*), *n.m.* stuff, material

deuol, *a.* dual

deuparth, *n.d.* two-thirds

deurudd, *n.d.* the cheeks

deutu, *n.d.* **-o dd.,** about

dewin, (*-iaid*), *n.m.* diviner, magician, wizard

dewines, (*-au*), *n.f.* witch, sorceress

dewiniaeth, *n.f.* divination, witchcraft

dewinio, *v.* divine

dewis, *v.* choose, select: *n.m.* choice

dewisiad, *n.m.* choice, option

dewisol, *a.* choice, desirable

dewr, *a.* brave: (*-ion*), *n.m.* brave man, hero

dewrder, *n.m.* bravery, valour

di-, *neg. px.* without, not, un-, non-, -less

diacon, (*-iaid*), *n.m.* deacon

diacones, (*-au*), *n.f.* deaconess

diaconiaeth, *n.f.* diaconate

diadell, (*-au*, *-oedd*), *n.f.* flock

diadlam, *a.* not to be recrossed

diaddurn, *a.* unadorned, plain, rude

diaelodi, *v.* dismember; expel a member

diafol, (*diefyl*, *dieifl*), *n.m.* devil

dianghenraid, *a.* unnecessary, needless

di-ail, *a.* unequalled, unrivalled

dial, *v.* avenge, revenge: *n.m.* vengeance, revenge

dialedd, (*-au*), *n.m.* vengeance, nemesis

dialgar, *a.* revengeful, vindictive

dialgarwch, *n.m.* vindictiveness

dialwr, (*-wyr*), **-ydd,** (*-ion*), *n.m.* avenger

diamau, *a.* doubtless

diamheuol, *a.* undoubted, indisputable

diamodol, *a.* unconditional, unqualified

diamwys, *a.* unambiguous

diamynedd, *a.* impatient

dianc, *v.* escape

dianwadal, *a.* unwavering, immutable

dianwadalwch, *n.m.* immutability

diannod, *a.* without delay, forthwith   [undress

diarchenu, *v.* take off one's shoes,

diarddel, *v.* expel, excommunicate

diarddeliad, *n.m.* expulsion, excommunication

diarfogi, *v.* disarm

diarfogiad, *n.m.* disarmament

diarffordd, *a.* out of the way, inaccessible

diargyhoedd, *a.* blameless

diarhebol, *a.* proverbial

diasbad, *n.f.* cry, scream

diasbedain, *v.* resound, ring

diatreg, *a.* immediate

diau, *a.* true, certain; doubtless

diawl, (*-iaid*), *n.m.* devil

di-baid *a.* unceasing, ceaseless

diball, *a.* unfailing, infallible, sure

diben, (*-ion*), *n.m.* end, purpose, aim

dibennu, *v.* end, conclude, finish

diberfeddu, *v.* disembowel, eviscerate

dibetrus, *a.* unhesitating

dibl, (*-au*), *n.m.* border, edge

dibrin, *a.* abundant, plentiful

dibriod, *a.* unmarried, single

dibris, *a.* reckless, contemptuous

dibrisio, *v.* depreciate, despise

dibristod, *n.m.* depreciation, contempt

dibwys, *a.* trivial, unimportant

dibyn, (*-nau*), *n.m.* steep, precipice

dibyniad, *n.m.* dependence

dibynnol, *a.* depending; subjunctive

dibynnu, *v.* depend, rely

dibynnydd, (*dibynyddion*), *n.m.* dependant

dicllon, *a.* wrathful, angry

dicllonrwydd, *n.m.* wrath, indignation

dicra, *a.* squeamish, fastidious, slow

dicter, *n.m.* anger, wrath, displeasure

dichell, (*-ion*), *n.f.* wile, craft, guile

dichellddrwg, *a.* cunning and malicious

dichellgar, *a.* wily, crafty, cunning

dichlyn, *v.* choose, pick: *a.* careful, circumspect, exact

dichlynaidd, *a.* well-behaved, circumspect

dichon, *v.* be able; it may be

dichonadwy, *a.* possible, practicable

didaro, *a.* unaffected, unconcerned, cool

diden, (*-nau*), *n.f.* nipple, teat

didoli, *v.* separate, segregate

didoliad, *n.m.* separation, segregation

didolnod, (*-au*), *n.m.f.* diæresis

di-dor, *a.* unbroken, uninterrupted

didoreth, *a.* shiftless, silly, fickle

didoriad, *a.* unbroken, untamed, rough

diduedd, *a.* impartial, unbiassed

didwyll, *a.* guileless, sincere

didwylledd, *n.m.* guilelessness, sincerity

didwyllo, *v.* undeceive, disillusion

di-ddadl, *a.* unquestionable, indisputable

diddan, *a.* amusing, diverting, pleasant

diddanion, *n.pl.* pleasantries, jokes

diddanu, *v.* amuse, divert; comfort

diddanwch, *n.m.* comfort, consolation

diddanwr, (*-wyr*), **-ydd,** (*-ion*), *n.m.* comforter

diddig, *a.* contented, pleased

diddigrwydd, *n.m.* contentment, placidity

diddim, *a. & n.m.* void

diddordeb, *n.m.* interest

diddori, *v.* interest

diddorol, *a.* interesting

diddos, *a.* watertight, sheltered; snug

diddosi, *v.* shelter

diddosrwydd, *n.m.* shelter, safety

diddwythiad, *n.m.* deduction

diddyfnu, *v.* wean

diddymdra, *n.m.* nothingness, void

diddymiad, -iant, *n.m.* annihilation

diddymu, *v.* annihilate, abolish

dieflig, *a.* devilish, diabolical, fiendish

diegwyddor, *a.* unprincipled

dieisiau, *a.* unnecessary, needless

dieithr, *a.* strange, alien, foreign: (*-iaid*), *n.m.* stranger

dieithrio, *v.* estrange, alienate

dieithrwch, *n.m.* strangeness

dienaid, *a.* soulless, senseless

dienyddiad, (*-au*), *n.m.* execution

dienyddio, *v.* put to death, execute

dienyddiwr, (*-wyr*), *n.m.* executioner

dieuog, *a.* guiltless, innocent

dieuogrwydd, *n.m.* innocence

difa, *v.* consume, destroy, devour

difai, *a.* blameless, faultless

difalch, *a.* humble

difancoll, *n.f.* total loss, perdition

difannu, *v.* disappear, vanish

difant, *n.m.* perdition, loss

difaol, *a.* consuming, devouring

difater, *a.* indifferent, unconcerned

difaterwch, *n.m.* indifference, apathy

difeddiannu, *v.* dispossess, deprive

difeio, *v.* exculpate

difeius, *a.* blameless, faultless

difenwi, *v.* revile, abuse, belittle

diferiog, *a.* wily, crafty

diferol, *a.* dripping, dropping

diferu, *v.* drip, drop, dribble, distil

diferyn, (*-nau, diferion*), *n.m.* drop

di-feth, *a.* infallible

difetha, *v.* destroy, spoil, waste

difethdod, *n.m.* destruction, waste

difethgar, *a.* wasteful

Difiau, *n.m.* Thursday

diflanedig, *a.* evanescent, fleeting

diflannu, v. vanish, disappear

diflanrwydd, n.m. evanescence

diflas, a. insipid, dull, wearisome

diflastod, n.m. disgust

diflasu, v. disgust; weary, surfeit

diflin, -o, a. untiring, indefatigable

difodi, v. annihilate, exterminate

difodiad, -iant, n.m. annihilation

di-foes, a. rude, unmannerly

difraw, a. indifferent, apathetic

difrawder, n.m. indifference, apathy

difreiniad, n.m. disfranchisement

difreinio v. disfranchise, deprive

difriaeth, n.f. abuse, calumny

difrif, n.m. seriousness, earnestness

difrifddwys, a. solemn

difrifol, a. serious, earnest, solemn, grave

difrifoldeb. See **difrifwch**

difrifoli, v. sober, solemnize

difrifwch, n.m. seriousness, earnestness, solemnity

difrïo, v. scold, abuse, malign

difrod, n.m. waste, havoc, damage

difrodi, v. waste, spoil, ravage

difrodwr, (-wyr), n.m. spoiler, devastator

difrycheulyd, a. spotless, immaculate

di-fudd, a. unprofitable, useless, futile

difuddio, v. deprive, bereave

di-fwlch, a. without a break, continuous

difwyno, v. mar, soil, sully, defile

difyfyr, a. impromptu

difyr, a. pleasant, diverting, amusing

difyrion, n.pl. diversions, amusements

difyrru, v. divert, amuse, beguile

difyrrus, a. diverting, amusing

difyrrwch, n.m. diversion, amusement, fun

difyrrwr, (-yrwyr), n.m. entertainer

diffaith, a. waste, desert; base, mean: (-ffeithydd), n.m. wilderness, desert

diffeithio, v. lay waste

diffeithwch, n.m. desert, wilderness

diffiniad, (-au), n.m. definition

diffinio, v. define

diffodd, -i, v. quench, extinguish

diffoddiad, n.m. quenching, extinction

diffoddwr, (-wyr), **-ydd,** (-ion), n.m. quencher

diffrwyth, a. barren; numb, paralysed

diffrwythdra, n.m. barrenness; numbness

diffrwytho, v. make barren; paralyse

diffuant, a. unfeigned, sincere, genuine

diffuantrwydd, n.m. genuineness

diffwys, a. wild, waste; high, steep; huge, awful

diffyg, (-ion), n.m. defect, want, lack; eclipse

diffygio, v. fail; faint, weary

diffygiol, a. defective; faint, weary

diffyndollaeth, n.f. protectionism

diffyndollwr, (-wyr), n.m. protectionist

diffynnydd, (-ynyddion), n.m. defendant

diffynyddes, (-au), n.f. defendant

dig, a. angry, wrathful: n.m. anger, wrath

digalon, a. disheartened, depressed, dejected, sad   [tion

digalondid, n.m. depression, dejec-

digalonni, v. dishearten, discourage

digamsyniol, a. unmistakable

digasedd, n.m. hatred, enmity

digasog, a. hating, hateful, hated

digio, v. anger, offend: take offence

di-glem, a. inept

digllon. See **dicllon**

digofaint, n.m. anger, wrath, indignation

digofus, a. angry, indignant

digolledu, v. indemnify, compensate

digon, n.m., a. & adv. enough: done (of cooking)

digonedd, n.m. abundance, plenty

digoni, v. suffice; satisfy: cook

digonol, a. satisfying; sufficient, adequate; satisfied

digonolrwydd, n.m. sufficiency, abundance

digrif, -ol, a. mirthful, funny

digrifwch, n.m. mirth, fun

digwydd, v. befall, happen, occur

digwyddiad, (-au), n.m. happening, occurrence, event

digyrrith, a. unstinted, liberal

digywilydd, a. impudent

digywilydd-dra, n.m. impudence

dihafal, a. unequalled, peerless

dihafarch, a. brave, powerful

dihangfa, (diangfâu), n.f. escape

dihangol, a. escaped, safe

dihalog, a. undefiled, pure

dihareb, (diarhebion), n.f. proverb

dihatru, v. strip, undress

diheintio, v. disinfect

dihenydd, n.m. end, death, execution. —**Yr hen Dd.,** the Ancient of Days

diheuro, v. excuse, apologize

dihewyd, n.m. desire; devotion

dihidlo, v. drop, distil; shed

dihiryn, (-hirod) n.m. rascal, scoundrel

dihoeni, v. languish, pine

dihuno, v. wake, rouse

dihysbydd, a. inexhaustible

dihysbyddu, v. empty, exhaust

dil, (-iau), n.m. **-dil mêl,** honeycomb

dilead, n.m. abolition, deletion

dilechdid, n.m. dialectic

diledryw, a. pure, genuine

dileu, v. blot out, delete; abolish

dilewyrch, a. dismal; unprosperous

dilin, a. refined

dilorni, v. abuse, revile

di-lun, a. slovenly

diluw. See **dilyw**

dilychwin, a. unsullied, spotless

dilyn, v. follow, pursue; imitate

dilyniad, n.m. following; imitation

dilynol, a. following; consequent

dilynwr, (-wyr), n.m. follower; imitator

dilys, a. sure, certain; genuine

dilysrwydd, n.m. genuiness

dilysu, v. certify, warrant, guarantee

di-lyth, a. unflagging, unfailing

dilyw, n.m. flood, deluge

dillad, (-au), n.m. clothes, clothing

dilladu, v. clothe

dilledydd, n.m. clothier

dilledyn, n.m. garment

dillyn, a. refined, elegant, chaste

dillynder, n.m. refinement, elegance

dillynion, n.pl. beauties, gems

dim, a. any; (with negative understood) no: n.m. anything; none, nothing

dimai, (-eiau), n.f. halfpenny

dimeiwerth, (-au), n.f. halfpennyworth

di-nam, a. faultless

dinas, (-oedd), n.f. city

dinasyddiaeth, n.f. citizenship

dincod. See **deincod**

dinesig, a. civil, civic

dinesydd, (dinasyddion), n.m. citizen

dinistr, n.m. destruction

dinistrio, v. destroy

dinistriol, a. destroying, destructive

dinistrydd, (-ion), n.m. destroyer

diniwed, a. harmless, innocent

diniweidrwydd, n.m. innocence

dinod, a. insignificant, obscure

dinodedd, n.m. insignificance, obscurity

dinoethi, v. bare, denude, expose

diod, (-ydd), n.f. drink, beverage

diodi, v. give drink

dioddef, v. suffer, bear; wait: (-iadau), n.m. suffering

dioddefaint, n.m. suffering, passion

dioddefgar, -efus, a. patient

dioddefgarwch, n.m. patience

dioddefwr, -ydd, (-wyr), n.m. sufferer, patient

di-oed, a. without delay, immediate

diofal, a. careless

diofalwch, n.m. carelessness

diofryd, n.m. vow; ban, taboo

diofrydu, *v.* vow, devote; ban, taboo

diog, *a.* slothful, indolent, lazy

diogel, *a.* safe, secure; sure, certain

diogelu, *v.* make safe, secure

diogelwch, *n.m.* safety, security

diogi, *v.* be lazy, idle: *n.m.* laziness

dioglyd, *a.* lazy, sluggish, indolent

diogyn, *n.m.* lazy one, idler, sluggard

diolch, *v.* thank, give thanks: (*-iadau*), *n.m.* thanks, thanksgiving

diolchgar, *a.* thankful, grateful

diolchgarwch, *n.m.* thankfulness, gratitude

diolwg, *a.* ugly

diorseddu, *v.* dethrone, depose

diosg, *v.* undress, put off, strip, divest

diota, *v.* tipple   [house

dioty, (*-tai*), *n.m.* ale-house, public-

diotwr, (*-wyr*), *n.m.* drinker, tippler

dipton, (*-au*), *n.f.* dipthong

dir, *a.* certain, necessary

diraddio, *v.* degrade

diraddiol, *a.* degrading

dirboen, (*-au*), *n.f.* extreme pain, torture

dirdynnol, *a.* excruciating

dirdynnu, *v.* rack, torture

direidi, *n.m.* mischievousness, mischief

direidus, *a.* mischievous

direol, *a.* unruly, disorderly

dirfawr, *a.* vast, huge, immense, enormous

dirgel, *a.* secret: (*-ion*), *n.m.* secret

dirgeledig, *a.* hidden, secret; mystical

dirgelu, *v.* secrete, conceal, hide

dirgelwch, *n.m.* secrecy, mystery, secret

dirgryniad, (*-au*), *n.m.* tremor, vibration

dirgrynu, *v.* tremble, vibrate

diriaethol, *a.* concrete

dirmyg, *n.m.* contempt, scorn

dirmygu, *v.* despise, scorn

dirmygus, *a.* contemptuous; contemptible

dirnad, *v.* discern, comprehend

dirnadaeth, *n.f.* discernment, comprehension

dirprwy, (*-on*), *n.* deputy; delegate

dirprwyaeth, (*-au*), *n.f.* commission; deputation

dirprwyol, *a.* vicarious

dirprwywr, (*-wyr*), *n.m.* commissioner

dirwasgiad, (*-au*), *n.m.* depression

dirwest, *n.m.f.* abstinence, temperance

dirwestol, *a.* temperate

dirwestwr, (*-wyr*), *n.m.* abstainer

dirwy, (*-on*), *n.f.* fine

dirwyn, *v.* wind, twist, twine

dirwynwr, (*-wyr*), *n.m.* winder

dirwyo, *v.* fine

di-rym, *a.* powerless, void

dirymu, *v.* nullify, annul, cancel

dirywiad, *n.m.* degeneration, deterioration

dirywio, *v.* degenerate, deteriorate

dis, (*-iau*), *n.m.* die, dice

di-sail, *a.* groundless, baseless

disbaddu, *v.* castrate, geld, spay

disbaddwr, (*-wyr*), *n.m.* castrator

disbaidd, *a.* castrated

disberod, *n.m.* -ar dd., wandering, astray

disglair, *a.* bright, brilliant

disgleirio, *v.* shine, glitter, sparkle

disgleirdeb, **-der**, *n.m.* brightness, brilliance

disgleirio, *v.* shine, glitter

disgloff, *a.* free from lameness

disgrifiad, (*-au*), *n.m.* description

disgrifiadol, *a.* descriptive

disgrifio, *v.* describe

disgwyl, *v.* look, expect, wait

disgwylfa, (*-feydd*), *n.f.* watchtower

disgwylgar, *a.* watchful, expectant

disgwyliad, (*-au*), *n.m.* expectation

disgybl, (*-ion*), *n.m.* disciple, pupil

disgyblaeth, *n.f.* discipline

disgyblu, *v.* discipline

disgyn, *v.* descend; fall, drop; let down   [declivity

disgynfa, (*-feydd*), *n.f.* descent,

disgyniad, (-au), n.m. descent
disgynnydd, (-ynyddion), n.m. descendant
disgyr, n.f. shout, cry
disgyrchiant, n.m. gravitation
—**craidd d.,** centre of gravity
disgyrchu, v. gravitate
di-sigl, a. unshaken, steadfast, firm
disodli, v. trip up, supplant
dist, (-iau), n.m. joist, beam
distadl, a. insignificant, low, base, mean
distadledd, n.m. insignificance, obscurity
distain, (-einiaid), n.m. steward
distaw, a. silent, quiet
distawrwydd, n.m. silence, quiet
distewi, n. silence; calm, quiet
distryw, n.m. destruction
distrywgar, a. destructive, wasteful
distrywio, v. destroy
distrywiwr, (-wyr), n.m. destroyer
distyll, n.m. ebb; **-iad,** distillation
distyllio, v. distil
di-sut, a. unwell; small
diswta, a. sudden, abrupt
diswyddiad, (-au), n.m. dismissal
diswyddo, v. dismiss from office, discharge
disychedu, v. quench thirst
di-syfl, a. immovable, impregnable
disyfyd, a. sudden, instantaneous
disyml, a. simple, artless, ingenuous
disymwth, a. sudden, instantaneous
disynnwyr, a. senseless
diwair, a. chaste
diwall, a. satisfied, full, perfect
diwallu, v. satisfy, supply
diwarafun, a. unforbidden, ungrudging
diwedd, n.m. end, conclusion
diweddar, a. late, modern
diweddaru, v. modernise
diweddarwch, n.m. lateness
diweddeb, n.f. cadence
diweddglo, n.m. conclusion
diweddu, v. end, finish, conclude

diweirdeb, n.m. chastity
diwethaf, a. last
diwinydd, (-ion), n.m. divine, theologian
diwinyddiaeth, n.f. divinity, theology
diwinyddol, a. theological
diwreiddio, v. uproot, eradicate
diwrnod, (-iau), n.m. day
diwryg, a. feeble, anaemic
diwyd, a. diligent, industrious
diwydiannol, a. industrial
diwydiant, (-iannau), n.m. industry
diwydrwydd, n.m. diligence, industry
diwyg, n.m. form, dress, garb
diwygiad, (-au), n.m. reform, reformation; revival
diwygiadol, a. reformatory; revivalistic
diwygiedig, a. reformed; revised
diwygio, v. amend, reform, revise
diwygiwr, (-wyr), n.m. reformer; revivalist
diwylliadol, a. cultural
diwylliant, n.m. culture
diwylliedig, a. cultured
diwyllio, v. cultivate
diwyno, v. mar, spoil, sully, soil
diymadferth, a. helpless
diymhongar, a. unassuming
diymwad, a. undeniable, indisputable
diysgog, a. steadfast, firm, stable
diysgogrwydd, n.m. steadfastness, stability
diystyr, a. contemptuous; contemptible
diystyrllyd, a. contemptuous, disdainful
diystyru, v. disregard, despise
diystyrwch, n.m. contempt, disdain, scorn
do, adv. yes (to questions in preterite tense)
doctor, (-iaid), n.m. doctor
doctora, v. doctor
doctoraidd, a. doctoral, doctorial
dod. See **dyfod**
dodi, v. put, place; give

dodrefn, *n.pl.* (**-yn,** *n.m.*), furniture
dodrefnu, *v.* furnish
dodrefnwr, (*-wyr*), *n.m.* furnisher
dodwy, *v.* lay eggs
doe, *adv.* yesterday
doeth, (*-ion*), *a.* wise
doethineb, *n.m.f.* wisdom
doethlyd, *a.* sophisticated
dof, *a.* tame, domesticated; garden
dofednod, *n.pl.* fowls, poultry
dofi, *v.* tame, domesticate; assuage
dofn, *a.*, *f.* of **dwfn**
Dofydd, *n.m.* God
dogfen, (*-ni, -nau*), *n.f.* document
dogn, (*-au*), *n.m.* share, portion; dose
dogni, *v.* ration
dôl, (*dolydd, dolau*), *n.f.* meadow
dolef, (*-au*), *n.f.* cry
dolefain, *v.* cry out
dolefus, *a.* wailing, plaintive
dolen, (*-nau*), *n.f.* loop, link, ring, bow
dolennog, *a.* ringed, looped; winding
dolennu, *v.* loop; wind, meander
doler, (*-i*), *n.f.* dollar
dolur, (*-iau*), *n.m.* sore; ailment; grief
dolurio, *v.* hurt, wound; grieve
dolurus, *a.* sore
donio, *v.* endow, gift
doniol, *a.* gifted; witty, humorous
dôr, (*dorau*), *n.f.* door
dosbarth, (*-au, -iadau*), *n.m.* reason; class; district
dosbarthiad, *n.m.* distribution
dosbarthu, *v.* class, classify; distribute
dosbarthwr, (*-wyr*), *n.m.* distributor
dosran, (*-nau*), *n.f.* division, section
dosrannu, *v.* separate, analyse
dot, (*-iau*), *n.m.f.* dot
dot, *n.f.* giddiness, vertigo
dotio, *v.* dote
dracht, (*-iau*), *n.m.* draught (of liquor)
drachtio, *v.* drink deep
draen, (*drain*), *n.f.* prickle, thorn

draenen, (*drain*), *n.f.* thorn
draenog, (*-od*), *n.m.* hedgehog
dragio, *v.* drag, tear, mangle
draig, (*dreigiau*), *n.f.* dragon
drain. See **draen, draenen**
draw, *adv.* yonder, away
dreng, *a.* morose, surly, sullen, harsh
drewi, *v.* & *n.m.* stink
drewllyd, *a.* stinking
dringad, *v.* & *n.m.* climb
dringfa, (*-feydd*), *n.f.* climb, ascent
dringhedydd, (*dringedyddion*), *n.m.* climber
dringo, *v.* climb
dringwr, (*-wyr*), *n.m.* climber
dros. See **tros**
drud, *a.* dear, precious, costly; reckless
drudaniaeth, *n.m.f.* dearth, scarcity
drudfawr, *a.* costly, expensive
drudwen, *n.f.*, **drudwy,** *n.m.* starling
drwg, *a.* evil, bad, naughty, wicked: (*drygau*), *n.m.* evil, harm, hurt
drwgdybiaeth, (*-au*), *n.f.* suspicion
drwgdybio, *v.* suspect
drwgdybus, *a.* suspicious
drwgweithredwr, (*-wyr*), *n.m.* evildoer
drws, (*drysau*), *n.m.* door
drwy. See **trwy**
drycin, (*-oedd*), *n.f.* foul weather
drycinog, *a.* stormy
drych, (*-au*), *n.m.* spectacle; mirror; object, pattern
drychfeddwl, (*-yliau*), *n.m.* idea
drychiolaeth, (*-au*), *n.f.* apparition, phantom
drygair, *n.m.* ill report; scandal
drygfyd, *n.m.* adversity
drygioni, *n.m.* badness, wickedness
drygionus, *a.* bad, wicked
drygu, *v.* hurt, harm, injure
dryll, (*-iau*), *n.m.* piece; part; *n.m.f.* gun, rifle
drylliad, (*-au*), *n.m.* breaking; wreck
dryllio, *v.* break in pieces, shatter

drylliog, *a.* broken, contrite

drysi, *n.pl.* (**-ïen,** *n.f.*), thorns, briers

dryslyd, *a.* perplexing; confused

drysor, (**-ion**), *n.m.* door-keeper, porter

drysu, *v.* tangle; perplex; be confused

dryswch, *n.m.* tangle; perplexity; confusion

drythyll, *a.* well-fed; high-spirited; lascivious

dryw, (**-od**), *n.m.f.* wren

du, *a. & n.m.* black

duc, dug, (**-iaid**), *n.m.* duke

dueg, *n.f.* spleen, melancholy

dulio, *v.* beat, bang, thump, hammer

dull, (**-iau**), *n.m.* form, manner, mode

duo, *v.* black, blacken

dur, *n.m.* steel

duw, (**-iau**), *n.m.* god. —**Duw,** God

düwch, *n.m.* blackness

duwdod, *n.m.* godhead, divinity, deity

duwies, (**-au**), *n.f.* goddess

duwiol, (**-ion**), *a. & n.m.* godly, pious

duwioldeb, *n.m.* godliness, piety

duwiolfrydedd, *n.m.* godliness, piety

duwiolfrydig, *a.* god-fearing, pious

dwbio, *v.* daub, plaster

dwbl, *a.* double

dweud, dweyd. See **dywedyd**

dwfn, *a.* deep, profound: *f.* **dofn**

dwfr, dŵr, (**dyfroedd**), *n.m.* water

dwl, *a.* dull, stupid, foolish

dwndwr, *n.m.* din, babble, hubbub

dwned, *n.m.* grammar

dŵr. See **dwfr**

dwrdio, *v.* scold

dwrn, (**dyrnau**), *n.m.* fist; knob, handle, hilt

dwsin, (**-inau**), *n.m.* dozen

dwthwn, *n.m.* day

dwy. See **dau**

dwyfol *a.* divine

dwyfoldeb, *n.m.* divinity, deity

dwyfoli, *v.* deify

dwyfron, (**-nau**), *n.f.* breast, chest

dwyfronneg, *n.f.* breastplate

dwyieithog, *a.* bilingual, duoglot

dwylaw, -lo, *n.d. & pl.* two hands, hands

dwyn, *v.* bear; bring; steal

dwyrain, *n.m. & a.* east

dwyreiniol, *a.* easterly, eastern, oriental [oriental

dwyreiniwr, (**-wyr**), *n.m.* eastern,

dwys, *a.* dense, grave, deep, intense

dwysáu, *v.* deepen, intensify

dwyster, *n.m.* gravity, solemnity

dwywaith, *adv.* twice

dy, *pn.* thy, thine

dyblu, *v.* double; repeat

dyblyg, *a.* twofold, double

dyblygu, *v.* double, fold

dybryd, *a.* sore, dire; flagrant

dychan, (**-au**), *n.f.* lampoon, satire

dychangerdd, (**-i**), *n.f.* satirical poem, satire

dychanu, *v.* lampoon, satirize, revile

dychanwr, (**-wyr**), *n.m.* satirist

dychlamu, *v.* throb, palpitate, flutter

dychmygol, *a.* imaginary

dychmygu, *v.* imagine

dychryn, (**-iadau**), *n.m.* fright, terror: *v.* frighten

dychrynllyd, *a.* frightful, terrible

dychrynu, *v.* frighten, be frightened

dychweledigion, *n.pl.* converts

dychweliad, (**-au**), *n.m.* return; conversion

dychwelyd, *v.* return

dychymyg, (**dychmygion**), *n.m.* imagination, fancy; riddle, device

dydd, (**-iau**), *n.m.* day

dyddfu, *v.* flag, pine, faint

dyddgwaith, *n.m.* a (certain) day

dyddhau, *v.* become day, dawn

dyddiad, (**-au**), *n.m.* date

dyddiadur, (**-on**), *n.m.* diary, journal

dyddio, *v.* become day, dawn; date

dyddiol, *a.* daily

dyddiwr, (**-wyr**), *n.m.* daysman, arbitrator

dyddlyfr, (-*au*), *n.m.* diary, journal

dyfais, (-*feisiau*), *n.f.* device, invention

dyfal, *a.* diligent

dyfalbara, *v.* persevere: *n.m.* perseverance

dyfalbarhad, *n.m.* perseverance

dyfalbarhau, *v.* persevere

dyfaliad, (-*au*), *n.m.* guess, conjecture

dyfalu, *v.* guess, conjecture

dyfalwch, *n.m.* diligence, assiduity

dyfarniad, (-*au*), *n.m.* decision, verdict

dyfarnu, *v.* adjudge

dyfeisio, *v.* devise, invent, imagine; guess

dyfn, *a.* deep

dyfnder, (-*au*, -*oedd*), *n.m.* deep, depth

dyfndra, *n.m.* deepness, depth

dyfnhau, *v.* deepen

dyfod, dod, *v.* come, become

dyfodfa, *n.f.* access, entrance

dyfodiad, *n.m.* coming, arrival, advent

dyfodiad, (-*iaid*), *n.m.* comer, stranger   [future

dyfodol, *a.* coming, future: *n.m.*

dyfradwy, *a.* watered; watering

dyfrffos, (-*ydd*), *n.m.* canal, watercourse

dyfrgi, (-*gwn*), *n.m.* otter

dyfrgist, (-*iau*), *n.f.* cistern, tank

dyfrglwyf, *n.m.* dropsy

dyfrhau, dyfrio, *v.* water

dyfrllyd, *a.* watery

dyfyniad, (-*au*), *n.m.* citation, quotation

dyfynnod, (-*ynodau*), *n.m.* quotation mark

dyfynnu, *v.* cite, quote; summon

dyffryn, (-*noedd*), *n.m.* valley

dygiad, *n.m.* bearing, upbringing

dygiedydd, (-*ion*), *n.m.* bearer

dygn, *a.* hard, severe, grievous, dire

dygwyl, *n.m.* holiday, feast day

dygyfor, *v. & n.m.* surge, muster

dygymod, *v.* agree (with), put up (with)

dyhead, (-*au*), *n.m.* aspiration

dyheu, *v.* pant; long, yearn, aspire

dyhiryn. See **dihiryn**

dyhuddiant, *n.m.* propitiation, consolation

dyhuddo, *v.* propitiate, console

dyladwy, *a.* due

dylanwad, (-*au*), *n.m.* influence

dylanwadol, *a.* influential

dylanwadu, *v.* influence

dyled, (-*ion*), *n.f.* debt, obligation

dyledog, *a.* in debt, indebted

dyledus, *a.* due

dyledwr, (-*wyr*), *n.m.* debtor

dyletswydd, (-*au*), *n.f.* duty, obligation

dylif, *n.m.* flood, deluge: *n.f.* warp

dylifo, *v.* flow, stream, pour

dyludo, *v.* flock, throng

dylyfu gên, *v.* yawn, gape

dylluan. See **tylluan**

dyma, *adv.* here is, here are; this is, these are

dymchweliad, *n.m.* overthrow

dymchwelyd, *v.* overthrow, upset, subvert

dymuniad, (-*au*), *n.m.* wish, desire

dymuno, *v.* wish, desire

dymunol, *a.* desirable, agreeable, pleasant

dyn, (-*ion*), *n.m.* man, person

dyna, *adv.* there is, there are; that is, those are

dynad, *n.pl.* nettles

dyndod, *n.m.* manhood, humanity

dynes, *n.f.* woman

dynesiad, *n.m.* approach

dynesu, *v.* draw near, approach

dyngarol, *a.* philanthropic

dyngarwch, *n.m.* philanthropy

dyngarwr, (-*wyr*), *n.m.* philanthropist

dyniawed, (-*iewaid*), *n.m.* yearling, stirk

dynin, *n.m.* carcass, corpse

dyn-laddiad, *n.m.* manslaughter

dynodi, *v.* denote, signify

dynofyddiaeth, *n.f.* anthropology

dynol, *a.* human; man-like; manly

dynoliaeth, *n.f.* humanity

dynolryw, *c.n.* mankind

dynwared, *v.* imitate, mimic

dynwarediad, *(-au)*, *n.m.* imitation, mimicry

dynwaredol, *a.* imitative

dynwaredwr, *(-wyr)*, *n.m.* imitator, mimic

dyrchafael, *v.* rise, ascend: *n.m.* ascension

dyrchafiad, *n.m.* elevation, promotion

dyrchafol, *a.* elevating

dyrchafu, *v.* raise, elevate; rise, ascend

dyri, *(-ïau)*, **dyrif,** *(-au)*, *n.f.* ballad, lyric

dyrnaid, *(-eidiau)*, *n.m.* handful

dyrnfedd, *(-i)*, *n.f.* hand-breadth, span

dyrnfol, *(-au, -fyl)*, *n.f.* gauntlet; mitten

dyrnod, *(-iau)*, *n.m.f.* blow, stroke

dyrnu, *v.* thump; thresh

dyrnwr, *(-wyr)*, *n.m.* thresher

dyrys, *a.* tangled; difficult; perplexing

dyrysbwnc, *(-bynciau)*, *n.m.* problem

dyryslyd, dyrysu, dyryswch. See **dryslyd, drysu, dryswch**

dysg, *n.m.f.* learning

dysgawdwr, *(-wyr)*, *n.m.* teacher

dysgedig, *(-ion)*, *a.* learned

dysgeidiaeth, *n.f.* teaching, doctrine

dysgl, *(-au)*, *n.f.* dish

dysglaid, *(-eidiau)*, *n.f.* dishful, dish

dysglöen, *n.f.* splinter

dysgu, *v.* learn, teach

dysgwr, *(-wyr)*, *n.m.* learner, teacher

dywal, *a.* fierce, brave, cruel

dywalgi, *(-gwn)*, *n.m.* tiger

dywediad, *(-au)*, *n.m.* saying

dywedwst, *a.* taciturn: *n.m.* taciturnity

dywedyd, *v.* say, speak, tell

dyweddi, *(-ïau)*, *n.f.* betrothal: *n.c.* betrothed

dyweddïad, *n.m.* betrothal

dyweddïo, *v.* betroth

dywenydd, *n.m.* pleasure, happiness

E

eang, *a.* wide, broad, immense

eangder, eangu. See **ehangder, ehangu**

eb, ebe, ebr, *v.* said, quoth

ebargofi, *v.* forget

ebargofiant, *n.m.* oblivion

ebargofus, *a.* oblivious

ebill, *(-ion)*, *n.m.* auger, borer; peg

ebillio, *v.* bore

ebol, *(-ion)*, *n.m.* colt, foal

eboles, *(-au)*, *n.f.* foal, filly

ebran, *(-nau)*, *n.m.* provender, fodder

Ebrill, *n.m.* April

ebrwydd, *a.* quick, swift, soon

ebryfygu, *v.* forget

ebwch, *(-ychau)*, *n.m.* gasp

ebychiad, *(-au)*, *n.m.* interjection, ejaculation

ebychu, *v.* gasp, interject, ejaculate

economeg, *n.f.* economics

echdoe, *adv.* day before yesterday

echel, *(-au)*, *n.f.* axle, axletree; axis

echen, *n.f.* source, family, tribe

echnos, *adv.* night before last

echrydus, *a.* fearful, frightful, shocking

echryslon, *a.* direful, horrible, shocking

echryslonrwydd, *n.m.* frightfulness

echwyn, *(-ion)*, *n.m.* loan

echwynna, *v.* borrow, lend

echwynnwr, *(-wynwyr)*, *n.m.* lender, creditor

edau, *(edafedd)*, *n.f.* thread; *(pl.)* yarn, wool

edfryd, *v.* restore

edifar, *a.* penitent, sorry

edifarhau, -faru, *v.* repent, be sorry

edifarus, -feiriol, *a.* repentant, penitent   [tence

edifeirwch, *n.m.* repentance, peni-

edliw, v. upbraid, reproach, taunt
edliwgar, a. taunting, reproachful
edlych, (-od), n.m. weakling, starveling
edmygedd, n.m. admiration
edmygu, v. admire   [mirer
edmygwr, -ydd, (-wyr), n.m. admedn, (-od), n.c. fowl, bird
edrych, v. look, examine
edrychiad, n.m. look
edrychwr, (-wyr), n.m. beholder, spectator
edwi, edwino, v. fade, wither, decay
eddi, n.pl. thrums; fringe
ef, efe, pn. he, him; it
efallai, adv. perhaps, peradventure
efengyl, (-au), n.f. gospel
efengylaidd, a. evangelical
efengyles, (-au), n.f. female evangelist
efengylu, v. evangelize
efengylwr, -ydd, (-wyr), n.m. evangelist
efelychiad, (-au), n.m. imitation
efelychu, v. imitate
efelychwr, (-wyr), n.m. imitator
efô, pn. he, him; it
efo, pr. with
efrau, n.pl. tares
efrydiaeth, (-au), n.f. study
efrydu, v. study
efrydydd, (-ion, -wyr), n.m. student
efrydd, (-ion), a. maimed, crippled
efydd, n.m. bronze, copper, brass
effaith, (-eithiau), n.f. effect
effeithio, v. effect, affect
effeithiol, a. effectual, effective, efficient
effeithioli, v. render effectual
effeithiolrwydd, n.m. efficacy
effro, a. awake, vigilant
egin, n.pl. (-yn, n.m.), germs, sprouts
egino, v. germinate, shoot, sprout
eglur, a. clear, plain, evident
eglurdeb, -der, n.m. clearness
eglureb, (-au), n.f. illustration
eglurhad, n.m. explanation, demonstration

eglurhaol, a. explanatory
egluro, v. make clear, explain
eglwys, (-i, -ydd), n.f. church
eglwysig, a. church, ecclesiastical
eglwyswr, (-wyr), n.m. churchman
eglwyswraig, (-wragedd), n.f. churchwoman
egni, (-ïon), n.m. effort, might, energy
egnïol, a. energetic   [cheeky
egr, a. sharp; sour; severe; savage;
egroes, n.pl. (-en, n.f.), hips
egru, v. grow stale or acid
egwan, a. weak, feeble
egwyd, (-ydd), n.f. fetlock; fetter
egwyddor, (-ion, -au), n.f. rudiment; principle; alphabet
egwyddori, v. instruct, ground, initiate
egwyddorol, a. high-principled
egwyddorwas, (-weision), n.m. apprentice
egwyl, n.f. lull, respite; opportunity
enghraifft, (-eifftiau), n.f. example, instance
englyn, (-ion), n.m. Welsh alliterative stanza
englynwr, (-wyr), n.m. composer of *englynion*
engyl. See **angel**
ehangder, (eangderau), n.m. breadth, immensity
ehangu, v. enlarge, extend
ehedeg, v. fly; run to seed
ehedfa, (-feydd), n.f. flight
ehedfan, v. hover, fly
ehediad, (-au), n.m. flight
ehediad, (-iaid), n.m. fowl, bird
ehedydd, (-ion), n.m. lark
ehofndra, n.m. fearlessness, boldness
ehud, a. rash, simple, foolish
ehudrwydd, n.m. rashness, folly
ei, pn. his, hers; its
eich, pn. your
eidion, (-nau), n.m. ox
eiddew, c.n. ivy
eiddgar, a. zealous, ardent
eiddgarwch, n.m. zeal, ardour
eiddigedd, n.m. jealousy; zeal

eiddigeddu, v. be jealous, envy; have zeal

eiddigeddus, a. jealous, envious

eiddigus, a. jealous; zealous

eiddil a. slender, feeble

eiddilo, v. enfeeble

eiddilwch, n.m. slenderness, feebleness

eiddiorwg, c.n. ivy

eiddo, n.m. property, possessions: pn. his, &c.

eidduno, v. desire, wish, pray

Eifftaidd, a. Egyptian

Eifftiwr, (-wyr), **Eifftiad,** (-iaid), n.m. Egypt

eigion, n.m. depth, ocean

eingion, (-au), n.f. anvil

eil-, px. second (**ail**)

eilchwyl, adv. again

eiliad, (-au), n.m.f. second, moment

eilio, v. weave, plait; sing; second

eiliw, n.m. hue, glimmer; appearance, image

eiliwr, (-wyr), n.m. seconder

eilun, (-od), n.m. image, idol

eilunaddolgar, a. idolatrous

eilunaddoli, v. worship idols

eilunaddoliad, n.m. **-iaeth,** n.f. idolatry

eilunaddolwr, (-wyr), n.m. idolator

eilwaith, adv. again

eillio, v. shave

eilliwr, (-wyr), n.m. shaver, barber

ein, p.a. our

einioes, n.f. life, lifetime

einion, (-au), n.f. anvil

eira, eiry, n.m. snow

eirchion. See **arch**

eirian, a. bright, beautiful

eirias, a. burning, glowing, fiery

eirin, n.pl. (-en, n.f.), plums

eiriol, v. plead, pray, intercede

eiriolaeth, n.f. intercession

eiriolwr, (-wyr), n.m. intercessor, mediator

eirlaw, n.m. sleet

eisen, (ais), n.f. rib; lath

eisglwyf, n.m. pleurisy

eisiau, n.m. want, need, lack

eisin, c.n. bran, husk

eisoes, adv. already

eistedd, v. sit, seat

eisteddfa, (-oedd, -fâu), n.f. seat

eisteddfod, (-au), n.f. session; eisteddfod

eisteddiad, (-au), n.m. sitting, session

eisteddle, (-oedd), n.m. seat, sitting, pew

eithaf, (-ion), a. & n.m. extreme; superlative

eithafoedd, n.pl. extremes, extremities

eithafol, a. extreme

eithafwr, (-wyr), n.m. extremist

eithin, n.pl. (-en, n.f.), furze, gorse

eithinog, a. furzy

eithr, pr. except; besides: c. but

eithriad, (-au), n.m. exception

eithrio, v. except, exclude

eleni, adv. this year

elfen, (-nau), n.f. element

elfeniad, (-au), n.m. analysis

elfennol, a. elementary

elfennu, v. analyse

elgeth, n.f. chin

eli, (elïau), n.m. ointment, salve

eliffant, (-od, -iaid), n.m. elephant

eliffantaidd, a. elephantine

elin, (-au, -oedd), n.f. elbow; angle, bend

elino, v. elbow

elinog, a. angular

elïo, v. anoint

elor, (-au), n.f. bier

elusen, (-nau), n.f. alms

elusendy, (-dai), n.m. almshouse

elusengar, a. charitable, benevolent

elusengarwch, n.m. charity, benevolence

elusennol, a. eleemosynary

elusennwr, (-enwyr), n.m. almoner

elw, n.m. possession, gain, profit

elwa, v. gain, profit

elwlen, (-wlod), n.f. kidney

Ellmynaidd, a. German

Ellmynwr, (-wyr), n.m. German

ellyll, (-on), n.m. fiend

ellyllaidd, a. fiendish

ellylles, (*-au*), *n.f.* fury

ellyn, (*-au, -od*), *n.m.* razor

emyn, (*-au*), *n.m.* hymn

emynydd, (*-ion, -wyr*), *n.m.* hymnist

emynyddiaeth, *n.f.* hymnody, hymnology

enaid, (*eneidiau*), *n.m.* life, soul

enbyd, -us, *a.* dangerous, perilous

enbydrwydd, *n.m.* peril, danger, jeopardy

encil, (*-ion*), *n.m.* retreat, flight

enciliad, (*-au*), *n.m.* retreat; desertion

encilio, *v.* retreat; desert

enciliwr, (*-wyr*), *n.m.* retreater; deserter

encyd, *n.m.* space; while

eneideg, *n.f.* psychology

eneiniad, (*-au*), *n.m.* anointing, unction

eneinio, *v.* anoint

eneiniog, *a. & n.m.* anointed

enfawr, *a.* enormous, huge, immense

enfys, (*-au*), *n.f.* rainbow

engiriol, *a.* nefarious, cruel, terrible

enhuddo. See **anhuddo**

enillfawr, *a.* lucrative, remunerative

enillgar, *a.* gainful; winsome

enillwr, -ydd, (*-wyr*), *n.m.* gainer, winner

enllib, (*-ion, -iau*), *n.m.* slander, libel

enllibaidd, *a.* slanderous, libellous

enllibio, *v.* slander, libel

enllibiwr, (*-wyr*), *n.m.* slanderer, libeller

enllibus, *a.* slanderous, libellous

enllyn, *n.m.* relish eaten with bread

ennaint, (*eneiniau*), *n.m.* ointment

ennill, *v.* gain, win, earn: (*enillion*), *n.m.* gain, profit; (*pl.*) earnings

ennyd, *n.m.f.* while, moment

ennyn, *v.* kindle, burn, inflame; excite

ensyniad, (*-au*), *n.m.* insinuation

ensynio, *v.* insinuate

entrych, (*-oedd*), *n.m.* firmament, height, zenith

enw, (*-au*), *n.m.* name; noun

enwad, (*-au*), *n.m.* denomination, sect

enwadaeth, *n.f.* sectarianism

enwadol, *a.* sectarian; nominative

enwadwr, (*-wyr*), *n.m.* sectarian, sectary

enwaediad, *n.m.* cirumcision

enwaedu, *v.* circumcise

enwebu, *v.* nominate

enwedig, *a.* **Yn e.,** particularly, especially

enwi, *v.* name

enwog, (*-ion*), *a.* famous, renowned, noted

enwogi, *v.* make famous

enwogrwydd, *n.m.* fame, renown

enwyn, *n.m.* **-llaeth e.,** buttermilk

eynfa, *n.f.* inflammation; itching

eyniad, (*-au*), *n.m.* inflammation

eynnol, *a.* inflammatory; inflamed

eofn, *a.* fearless, bold

eog, (*-iaid*), *n.m.* salmon

eos, (*-au*), *n.f.* nightingale

eosaidd, *a.* like a nightingale

epa, (*-od*), *n.m.* ape, monkey

epil, *n.m.* offspring, brood

epilgar, *a.* prolific, teeming

epilio, *v.* bring forth, teem, breed

epistol, (*-au*), *n.m.* epistle

eples, *n.m.* leaven, ferment

eplesiad, *n.m.* fermentation

eplesu, *v.* leaven, ferment

er, *pr.* for, in order to; since: *c.* though

eraill. See **arall**

erbyn, *v.* receive, meet: *pr.* against, by

erch, *a.* speckled; frightful

erchi, *v.* ask, pray, command, demand

erchwyn, (*-ion*), *n.m.* side, bed-side

erchyll, *a.* hideous, horrible

erchyllter, (*-au*), *n.m.* atrocity

erchylltod, -tra, *n.m.* hideousness, horror

eres, *a.* wonderful, strange

erestyn, *n.m.* minstrel, buffoon

erfin, *n.pl.* (**-en,** *n.f.*), turnips

erfyn, *v.* beg, pray, implore, expect

erfyniad, (-*au*), *n.m.* prayer, petition

ergyd, (-*ion*), *n.m.f.* blow, stroke; shot; cast

ergydio, *v.* strike; throw, cast

ergydiwr, (-*wyr*), *n.m.* striker

erioed, *adv.* ever

erledigaeth, (-*au*), *n.f.* persecution

erlid, *v.* persecute: (-*iau*), *n.m.* persecution

erlidiwr, (-*wyr*), *n.m.* persecutor

erlyn, *v.* pursue, prosecute

erlyniad, *n.m.* prosecution

erlynydd, (-*ion*), *n.m.* prosecutor

ermyg, (-*ion*), *n.m.* instrument, organ

ern, ernes, (-*au*), *n.f.* earnest, pledge

ers, *pr.* since (**er ys**)

erthwch, *n.m.* grunt, pant

erthygl, (-*au*), *n.f.* article

erthyl, (-*od*), *n.m.* abortion

erthylu, *v.* abort, miscarry

erw, (-*au*), *n.f.* acre

erwydd, *n.pl.* stave (in music)

eryr, (-*od*), *n.m.* eagle; shingles

eryraidd, *a.* eagle-like, aquiline

esboniad, (-*au*), *n.m.* explanation; commentary

esboniadaeth, *n.f.* exposition, exegesis

esboniadol, *a.* expository, explanatory

esbonio, *v.* explain, expound

esboniwr, (-*wyr*), *n.m.* expositor, commentator

esgair, (-*eiriau*), *n.f.* shank, leg; ridge

esgeulus, *a.* neglectful, negligent

esgeuluso, *v.* neglect

esgeulustod, -tra, *n.m.* negligence

esgeuluswr, (-*wyr*), *n.m.* neglecter

esgid, (-*iau*), *n.f.* boot, shoe

esgob, (-*ion*), *n.m.* bishop

esgobaeth, (-*au*), *n.f.* bishopric, see, diocese

esgobol, *a.* episcopal; episcopalian

esgobyddiaeth, *n.f.* episcopalianism

esgobyddol, *a.* episcopalian

esgor, *v.* bring forth, bear

esgud, *a.* quick, swift, active

esgus, (-*ion*), *n.m.* excuse, pretext

esgusawd, (-*odion*), *n.m.* excuse, apology

esgusodi, *v.* excuse

esgusodol, *a.* excusable, excused

esgyn, *v.* ascend, rise

esgynbren, (-*nau*), *n.m.* perch

esgynfa, (-*feydd*), *n.f.* ascent, rise

esgynfaen, *n.m.* horse-block

esgyniad, *n.m.* ascension

esgynlawr, (-*loriau*), *n.m.* platform, stage

esgynnol, *a.* ascending

esgyrn. See **asgwrn**

esgyrnygu, *v.* gnash or grind the teeth

esiampl, (-*au*), *n.f.* example

esillydd, *n.m.* offspring, descendant

esmwyth, *a.* soft, smooth; easy

esmwythâd, *n.m.* ease, relief

esmwythder, -dra, *n.m.* ease

esmwytho, -áu, *v.* ease, soothe, soften

esmwythyd, *n.m.* ease, luxury

estron, (-*iaid*), *n.m.* foreigner, alien

estronaidd, *a.* strange, foreign, alien

estrones, (-*au*), *n.f.* alien woman

estronol, *a.* strange, foreign, alien

estrys, (-*iaid*), *n.m.f.* ostrich

estyll, *n.pl.* (**-en,** *n.f.*), planks, boards

estyn, *v.* extend, reach; stretch, prolong

estyniad, *n.m.* extension, prolongation

estheteg, *n.m.f.* aesthetics

etifedd, (-*ion*), *n.m.* heir, inheritor

etifeddeg, *n.m.f.* heredity

etifeddes, (-*au*), *n.f.* heiress

etifeddiaeth, (-*au*), *n.f.* inheritance

etifeddol, *a.* hereditary

etifeddu, *v.* inherit

eto, *c.* yet, still: *adv.* again; yet, still

ethnig, *n.m.* heathen

ethnydd, (-*ion*), *n.m.* ethnologist

ethnyddiaeth, *n.f.* ethnology

ethnyddol, *a.* ethnological

ethol, *v.* elect
etholadwy, *a.* eligible
etholaeth, (*-au*), *n.f.* constituency
etholedig, (*-ion*), *a.* elect
etholedigaeth, *n.f.* election (theol.)
etholfraint, (*-freintiau*), *n.f.* franchise
etholiad, (*-au*), *n.m.* election
etholiadol, *a.* electoral, elective
etholydd, (*-ion*), **-wr,** (*-wyr*), *n.m.* elector
eu, *pn.* their
eunuch, (*-iaid*), *n.m.* eunuch
euog, *a.* guilty
euogrwydd, *n.m.* guiltiness, guilt
euraid, -aidd, *a.* golden, (of) gold
eurgrawn, *n.m.* treasury
euro, *v.* apply or bestow gold; gild
eurof, (*-aint*), *n.m.* goldsmith
eurych, (*-od*), *n.m.* goldsmith; tinker
ewig, (*-od*), *n.f.* hind
ewin, (*-edd*), *n.m.f.* nail, talon, claw; hoof
ewino, *v.* claw
ewinog, *a.* having nails or claws
ewinrhew, *n.f.* frost-bite
ewyllys, (*-iau*), *n.f.* will
ewyllysgar, *a.* willing, obliging
ewyllysgarwch, *n.m.* willingness
ewyllysio, *v.* will, wish
ewyllysiwr, (*-wyr*), *n.m.* wisher
ewyn, *n.m.* foam, froth, surf
ewynnog, *a.* foaming, foamy, frothy
ewynnu, *v.* foam, froth
ewythr, (*-edd*), *n.m.* uncle

F

fagddu, *n.f.* **-y f.,** gross darkness
fe, *pn.* he, him: also used formally before verbs
feallai, *adv.* perhaps, peradventure
fel, *adv.,* *c. & pr.* so, as, that, thus, like; how
felly, *adv.* so, thus
festri, (*-ïoedd*), *n.f.* vestry
ficer, (*-iaid*), *n.m.* vicar
ficerdy, (*-dai*), *n.m.* vicarage

ficeriaeth, (*-au*), *n.f.* vicariate, vicarage
finegr, *n.m.* vinegar
folum (*-au*), *n.m.* volume
fory, *adv.* to-morrow (**yfory**)
fry, *adv.* above, aloft
fwltur, (*-iaid*), *n.m.* vulture
fy, *pn.* my
fyny, *adv.* up, upwards

FF

ffa, *n.pl.* (**ffäen, ffeuen,** *n.f.*), beans
ffacbys, *n.pl.* fitches, vetches
ffactri, (*-ïoedd*), *n.f.* factory, mill
ffaeledig, *a.* fallible
ffaeledigrwydd, *n.m.* fallibility
ffaeledd, (*-au*), *n.m.* failing, defect, fault
ffaelu, *v.* fail
ffaeth, *a.* luxuriant
ffafr, (*-au*), *n.f.* favour
ffafraeth, *n.f.* favouritism
ffafrio, *v.* favour
ffafriol, *a.* favourable
ffagl, (*-au*), *n.f.* blaze, flame; torch
ffaglog, *a.* blazing, flaming
ffaglu, *v.* blaze, flame
ffair, (*ffeiriau*), *n.f.* fair, exchange
ffaith, (*ffeithiau*), *n.f.* fact
ffald, (*-au*), *n.f.* fold; pound
ffals, (*ffeilsion*), *a.* false, deceitful
ffalsedd, *n.m.* falsehood, deceit
ffalsio, *v.* fawn, cringe
ffalsiwr, (*-wyr*), *n.m.* flatterer, toady
ffalster, *n.m.* deceitfulness, cunning
ffansi, *n.f.* fancy
ffansïo, *v.* fancy
ffansïol, *a.* fanciful, pleasing to the fancy
ffarm, (*ffermydd*), *n.f.* farm
ffarmio, *v.* farm
ffarmwr, (*ffermwyr*), *n.m.* farmer
ffarmwraig, (*-wragedd*), *n.f.* farm-woman
ffarwel, *n.f.* farewell
ffarwelio, *v.* bid farewell
ffasiwn, (*-iynau*), *n.m.* fashion

ffasiynol, *a.* fashionable

ffatri, (-ïoedd), *n.f.* factory, mill

ffau, (*ffeuau*), *n.f.* den

ffawd, (*ffodion*), *n.f.* fortune, fate

ffawydd, *n.pl.* (**-en,** *n.f.*), beech trees

ffedog. See **arffedog**

ffei, *i.* fie

ffeil, *n.f.* file

ffein, ffeind, *a.* fine

ffeirio, *v.* barter, exchange

ffel, *a.* sharp, sly, cunning

ffelwm, *n.m.* whitlow

ffenestr, (-i), *n.f.* window

ffêr, (*fferau*), *n.f.* ankle

fferins, *n.pl.* sweets

fferllyd, *a.* chilly

ffermdy, (-dai), *n.m.* farm-house

fferru, *v.* congeal, freeze; perish with cold

fferyllfa, (-feydd), *n.f.* dispensary

fferylliaeth, *n.f.* pharmacy

fferyllydd, (-wyr), *n.m.* chemist, pharmacist

ffest, *a.* fast

ffest, *n.f.* feast

ffetan, (-au), *n.f.* sack, bag

ffiaidd, *a.* loathsome, abominable

ffidil, (*ffidlau*), *n.f.* fiddle

ffidler, (-iaid) *n.m.* fiddler

ffidlo, *v.* fiddle

ffieiddbeth, (-au), *n.m.* abomination

ffieidd-dra, *n.m.* abomination

ffieiddio, *v.* loathe, abominate, abhor

ffieiddrwydd, *n.m.* abhorrence, disgust

ffigur, (-au), *n.f.* figure, type

ffigurol, *a.* figurative

ffigys, *n.pl.* (**-en,** *n.f.*), figs

ffigysbren, (-nau), *n.m.* fig-tree

ffilm, (-iau), *n.f.* film

ffiloreg, *n.f.* rigmarole, nonsense

ffin, (-iau), *n.f.* boundary, limit

ffinio, *v.* border (upon), abut

ffiol, (-au), *n.f.* vial; cup

ffiseg, *n.m.* physics

ffisig, *n.m.* physic, medicine

ffisigwr, (-wyr), *n.m.* physician

ffisigwriaeth, *n.m.* physic, medicine

fflach, (-iau), *n.f.*, **fflachiad,** (-au), *n.m.* flash

fflachio, *v.* flash

fflangell, (-au), *n.f.* scourge

fflangellu, *v.* scourge, whip, flog

fflaim, *n.f.* lance, fleam

fflam, (-au), *n.f.* flame

fflamio, *v.* flame, blaze

fflamllyd, *a.* flaming, blazing

fflat, *a.* flat: (-iau), *n.m.* flat-iron; (-au, -iau), *n.f.* a flat

fflatio, *v.* flat, flatten

fflaw, fflewyn, *n.m.* splinter, mote

fflodiad, -iart, *n.f.* floodgate

fflwch, *a.* full, bountiful

fflyd, (*oedd*), *n.f.* fleet

ffo, *n.m.* flight [refugee

ffoadur, (-iaid), *n.m.* fugitive,

ffodus, *a.* fortunate, lucky

ffoedigaeth, *n.f.* flight

ffoi, *v.* flee

ffôl, *a.* foolish, silly

ffoledd, *n.m.* foolishness, folly, fatuity

ffolen, (-nau), *n.f.* buttock

ffoli, *v.* infatuate, dote; fool

ffolineb, *n.m.* foolishness, folly

ffolog, (-od), *n.f.* silly woman

ffon, (*ffyn*), *n.f.* stick, staff

ffonnod, (*ffonodiau*), *n.f.* stroke, blow, stripe

ffonodio, *v.* cudgel, beat

fforc, (*ffyrc*), *n.f.* (table) fork

fforch, (-au, *ffyrch*), *n.f.* fork

fforchi, *v.* fork

fforchog, *a.* forked, cleft, cloven

fforchogi, *v.* fork; divide (hoof)

ffordd, (*ffyrdd*), *n.f.* way, road; distance

fforddio, *v.* afford

fforddol, (-ion), *n.m.* wayfarer, passer-by

fforest, (-ydd, -au), *n.f.* forest

fforffedu, *v.* forfeit

fforio, *v.* explore, spy, scout

fforiwr, (-wyr), *n.m.* explorer

ffortiwn, (-iynau), **-un,** (-au), *n.f.* fortune

ffortunus, *a.* fortunate

ffos, (*-ydd*), *n.f.* ditch, trench

ffosi, *v.* ditch, trench

ffrae, (*-au*), *n.f.* quarrel

ffraegar, *a.* quarrelsome

ffraeo, *v.* quarrel

ffraeth, *a.* fluent; witty, facetious

ffraetheb, (*-ion*), *n.f.* joke, witticism

ffraethineb, *n.m.* wit, facetiousness

Ffrangeg, *n.f.* French

ffrâm, (*fframiau*), *n.f.* frame

fframio, *v.* frame

fframwaith, *n.m.* framework

Ffrancwr, (*-wyr*, *Ffrancod*), *n.m.* Frenchman

ffrawddunio, *v.* crave, wheedle

Ffrengig, *a.* French. —**Llygod Ff.,** rats

ffres, *a.* fresh

ffresni, *n.m.* freshness

ffreutur, *n.f.* refectory

ffrewyll, (*-au*), *n.f.* whip, scourge

ffrewyllio, -u, *v.* whip, scourge

ffridd, (*-oedd*), *n.f.* mountain pasture, sheep-walk

ffrind, (*-iau*), *n.m.* friend

ffrïo, (*-iau*), *v.* fry; hiss

ffroch, ffrochwyllt, *a.* furious

ffroen, (*-au*), *n.f.* nostril; muzzle (of gun)

ffroeni, *v.* snort, snuff, sniff

ffroenuchel, *a.* haughty, disdainful

ffrog, (*-iau*), *n.f.* frock

ffrois, *n.pl.* (*-en,* *n.f.*), pancake

ffrom, *a.* angry, irascible, testy, touchy

ffromi, *v.* fume, chafe, rage

ffromllyd, *a.* testy, irascible

ffrost, *n.m.* boast, vaunt

ffrostio, *v.* boast, brag, vaunt

ffrostiwr, (*-wyr*), *n.m.* boaster, braggart

ffrwd, (*ffrydiau*), *n.f.* stream, torrent

ffrwgwd, (*ffrygydau*), *n.m.* squabble

ffrwst, *n.m.* hurry, haste, bustle

ffrwydriad, (*-au*), *n.m.* explosion

ffrwydro, *v.* explode

ffrwydrol *a.* explosive

ffrwyn, (*-au*), *n.f.* bridle

ffrwynglymu, *v.* tether

ffrwyno, *v.* bridle, curb

ffrwyth, (*-au*, *-ydd*), *n.m.* fruit; vigour, use

ffrwythlon, *a.* fruitful, fertile

ffrwythlondeb, *n.m.* fruitfulness, fertility

ffrwythloni, *v.* become fruitful; fertilize

ffrwytho, *v.* bear fruit

ffrydio, *v.* stream, gush

ffrydlif, *n.m.f.* stream, flood, torrent

ffrystio, *v.* hurry, hasten

ffuantu, *v.* feign, pretend, sham

ffuantus, *a.* insincere, disingenuous

ffuantwr, (*-wyr*), *n.m.* dissembler

ffug, *a.* fictitious, false, sham: (*-ion*), *n.m.* fiction, sham

ffugchwedl, (*-au*), *n.f.* novel

ffugenw, (*-au*), *n.m.* pseudonym

ffugio, *v.* feign; forge

ffugiwr, (*-wyr*), *n.m.* impostor; forger

ffumer, (*-au*), *n.m.* chimney, funnel

ffun, *n.f.* breath

ffunen, (*-ni*), *n.f.* lace, fillet; kerchief

ffunud, *n.m.* form, manner. (After *un* only

ffured, (*-au*), *n.f.* ferret

ffureta, *v.* ferret

ffurf, (*-iau*), *n.f.* form, shape

ffurfafen, *n.f.* firmament, sky

ffurfiad, (*-au*), *n.m.* formation

ffurfio, *v.* form

ffurfiol *a.* formal

ffurfioldeb, *n.m.* formality, formalism

ffurfiolwr, (*-wyr*), *n.m.* formalist

ffurflen, (*-ni*), *n.f.* form (to fill)

ffurflywodraeth, *n.f.* constitution, polity

ffurfwasanaeth, (*-au*), *n.m.* liturgy

ffust, (*-iau*), *n.f.* flail

ffustio, -o, *v.* beat

ffustion, *n.m.* fustian

ffwdan, *n.f.* fuss, bustle, flurry

ffwdanu, *v.* fuss, bustle

ffwdanus, *v.* fussy, fidgety, flurried

ffŵl, (*ffyliaid*), *n.m.* fool

ffwlbart, (*-iaid*), *n.m.* polecat

ffwlbri, *n.m.* fudge, nonsense, tom-foolery

ffwlcyn, *n.m.* fool, ninny, nincom-poop

ffwndro, *v.* founder, become confused

ffwndrus, *a.* confused, bewildered

ffwndwr, *n.m.* confusion, hurly-burly

ffwr, *n.m.* fur

ffwrdd, *n.m.* way, **I ff.,** away

ffwrn, (*ffyrnau*), *n.f.* furnace, oven

ffwrnais, (*-eisiau*), *n.f.* furnace

ffwrwm, (*ffyrymau*), *n.f.* form, bench

ffydd, *n.f.* faith

ffyddiog, *a.* strong in faith, trustful

ffyddlon, *a.* faithful

ffyddlondeb, *n.m.* faithfulness, fidelity

ffyddloniaid, *n.pl.* faithful ones

ffynadwy, -edig, *a.* prosperous

ffynhonnell, (*ffynonellau*), *n.f.* fount, source

ffyniant, *n.m.* prosperity

ffynidwydd, *n.pl.* (**-en,** *n.f.*), fir-trees, pine-trees

ffynnon, (*ffynhonnau*), *n.f.* fountain, well, spring

ffynnu, *v.* prosper, thrive

ffyrf, *a.* thick, stout: *f.* **fferf**

ffyrfder, *n.m.* thickness, stoutness

ffyrling, (*-au, -od*), *n.f.* farthing

ffyrnig, *a.* fierce, savage, ferocious

ffyrnigo, *v.* grow fierce; enrage

ffyrnigrwydd, *n.m.* fierceness, ferocity

G

gadael, gadu, *v.* leave, forsake; let, allow

gaeaf, (*-au, -oedd*), *n.m.* winter

gaeafaidd, -ol, *a.* wintry

gaeafu, *v.* winter, hibernate

gafael, -yd, *v.* hold, grasp: (*-ion*), *n.f.* hold, grasp

gafaelgar, *a.* gripping, tenacious

gafl, (*-au, geifl*), *n.f.* fork; stride

gafr, (*geifr*), *n.f.* goat

gafrewig, (*-od*), *n.f.* gazelle, antelope

gagendor. See **agendor**

gaing, (*geingau*), *n.f.* chisel. —**g. gau,** gouge

gair, (*geiriau*), *n.m.* word

galanas, (*-au*), *n.f.* murder, mass-acre

galanastra, *n.m.* slaughter

galar, *n.m.* mourning, grief, sorrow

galarnad, (*-au*), *n.f.* lamentation

galarnadu, *v.* bewail, lament

galaru, *v.* mourn, grieve, lament

galarus, *a.* mournful, lamentable, sad

galarwr, (*-wyr*), *n.m.* mourner

galw, *v.* call: *n.m.* call, demand

galwad, (*-au*), *n.m.f.* call, calling, demand

galwedigaeth, (*-au*), *n.f.* calling

galwyn, (*-i*), *n.m.* gallon

gallt, (*gelltydd*), *n.f.* hill; cliff; wood

gallu, *v.* be able: (*-oedd*), *n.m.* power, ability

galluog, *a.* able, powerful, mighty

galluogi, *v.* enable, empower

gan, *pr.* with, by; of, from

gar, (*-rau*), *n.f.m.* thigh, ham

garan, (*-od*), *n.f.* heron, crane, stork

Garawys, *n.m.* Lent

gardas, -ys, (*-ysau*), *n.m.f.* garter

gardd, (*gerddi*), *n.f.* garden; garth, yard

garddio, -u, *v.* garden: *n.m.* gardening

garddwr, (*-wyr*), *n.m.* gardener

garddwriaeth, *n.f.* horticulture

gargam, *a.* knock-kneed

garlant, (*-au*), *n.m.* garland

garlleg, *n.pl.* (**-en,** *n.f.*), garlic

gartref, *adv.* at home (mut. of **cartref**)

garth, *n.m.* hill; enclosure

garw, (*geirwon*), *a.* coarse, rough, harsh

garwedd, *n.m.* roughness

garwhau, *v.* roughen; ruffle

gast, (*geist*), *n.f.* bitch

gau, *a.* false

gefail, (*-eiliau*), *n.f.* smithy

gefel, (*-eiliau*), *n.f.* tongs, pincers

gefell, (*-eilliaid*), *n.c.* twin

gefyn, (*-nau*), *n.m.* fetter, shackle

gefynnu, *v.* fetter, shackle

geingio, *v.* chisel, gouge

geilwad, (*-waid*), *n.m.* caller

geirddadl, *n.f.* cavil, quibble

geirfa, (*-oedd*), *n.f.* vocabulary, glossary

geiriad, *n.m.* wording, phraseology

geiriadur, (*-on*), *n.m.* dictionary, lexicon

geiriadurol, *a.* lexicographical

gairiadurwr, (*-wyr*), *n.m.* lexicographer

geirio, *v.* word, phrase

geirlyfr, (*-au*), *n.m.* word-book, dictionary

geirwir, *a.* truthful, truth-speaking

geirwiredd, *n.m.* truthfulness

gelau, gelen, (*gelod*), *n.f.* leech

gelyn, (*-ion*), *n.m.* foe, enemy

gelyniaeth, *n.f.* enmity, hostility

gelyniaethus, *a.* hostile, inimical

gelynol, *a.* hostile, adverse

gellyg, *n.pl.* (**-en,** *n.f.*), pears

gem, (*-au*), *n.f.* gem, jewel

gêm, *n.f.* game

gemog, *a.* gemmed, jewelled

gemydd, (*-ion*), *n.m.* jeweller

gên, *n.f.* jaw, chin

genau, (*-euau*), *n.m.* mouth, orifice

genau-goeg, (*-ion*), *n.f.* lizard, newt

genedigaeth, (*-au*), *n.f.* birth

genedigol, *a.* native

geneth, (*-od*), *n.f.* girl

genethaidd, *a.* girlish

genethig, *n.f.* little girl, maiden

geni, *v.* be born

genni, *v.* be contained

genwair, (*-eiriau*), *n.f.* fishing-rod

genweirio, *v.* angle, fish

genweiriwr, (*-wyr*), *n.m.* angler

gêr, *c.n.* gear, tackle; rubbish

ger, *pr.* by, near

gerain, *v.* whine, whimper

gerbron, *pr.* before (place)

gerfydd, *pr.* by

geri, *n.m.* bile, gall. —**g. marwol,** cholera morbus

gerllaw, *pr.* near: *adv.* at hand

gerwin, *a.* rough, severe, harsh

gerwindeb, -der, *n.m.* roughness, severity

gerwino, *v.* roughen

geudeb, -edd, *n.m.* falsity

gewyn, (*-nau, gïau*), *n.m.* sinew, tendon

gewynnog, *a.* sinewy

gïach, (*-od*), *n.m.* woodcock

gieuol, *a.* of the nerves, neural

gieuwst, *n.f.* neuralgia

gildio, *v.* yield; gild

gilydd, *n.m.* **-ei g.,** each other.-**gyda'i g.,** together

gimbill, *n.f.* gimlet

glafoerio, *v.* drivel, slobber

glafoerion, *n.pl.* drivel, slobber

glaif, gleifiau, *n.m.* lance, sword, glaive

glain, (*gleiniau*), *n.m.* gem, jewel; bead

glân, *a.* clean; holy; fair, beautiful

glan, (*-nau, glennydd*), *n.f.* bank, shore

glanhad, *n.m.* cleansing, purification

glanhaol, *a.* cleansing, purging

glanhau, *v.* cleanse, purify

glaniad, *n.m.* landing, disembarkation

glanio, *v.* land, disembark

glanwaith, *a.* cleanly

glanweithdra, *n.m.* cleanliness

glas, (*gleision*), *a.* blue, green grey: *n.m.* blue

glasgoch, *a. & n.m.* purple

glaslanc, (*-iau*), *n.m.* youth, stripling

glasog, (*-au*), *n.f.* crop, gizzard

glastwr, *n.m.* milk and water

glastwraidd, *a.* milk-and-water

glasu, *v.* become blue, green, or grey; turn pale

glaswellt, *c.n.* green grass

glaswelltyn, *n.m.* blade of grass; tigridia

glaw, (*-ogydd*), *n.m.* rain

glawio, *v.* rain

glawlen, (-ni), n.f. umbrella

glawog, a. rainy

gleisiad, (-iaid), n.m. salmon

gleision, n.pl. whey

glendid, n.m. cleanness; fairness; beauty

glesni, n.m. blueness, verdure

glew, (-ion), a. brave, daring; astute

glewdra, n.m. courage, resource

glin, (-iau), n.m. knee

glo, n.m. coal   [ling

gloddest, (-au), n.m. carousal, revel-

gloddesta, v. carouse, revel

gloddestwr, (-wyr), n.m. reveller

gloes, (-au, -ion), n.f. pang; qualm

glofa, (-feydd), n.f. colliery

glowr, (-wyr), n.m. collier

glowty, (-tai), n.m. cow-house, shippon

glöyn, n.m. coal. —**g. byw**, butterfly

gloyw, (-on), a. bright, clear; shiny, glossy

gloywder, n.m. brightness, clearness

gloywi, v. brighten, polish

glud, (-ion), n.m. glue; bird-lime

gludio, v. glue, cement

gludiog, a. sticky

glwth, (glythau), n.m. couch

glwth, (glythion), a. gluttonous: n.m. glutton

glwys, a. fair; holy

glyn, (-noedd), n.m. glen, valley

glynu, v. stick, adhere, cleave

glythineb, glythni, n.m. gluttony

glythinebu, glythu, v. glut, gormandize

glyw, n.m. governor, lord

gnawd, a. customary, usual

gne, n.m. colour, hue

gnif, n.m. toil, effort

go, adv. rather, somewhat

goachul, a. lean; puny; sickly, poorly

gobaith, (-eithion), n.m. hope

gobeithio, v. hope

gobeithiol, a. hopeful

gobeithlu, (-oedd), n.m. Band of Hope

gobennydd, (-enyddiau), n.m. bolster, pillow

goblygu, v. fold, wrap

gochel. See **gochelyd**

gocheladwy, a. avoidable

gochelgar, a. wary, cautious

gocheliad, n.m. avoidance. —**ar ei o.**, on his guard

gochelyd, v. avoid, shun

godard, (godardau), n.f. cup, mug

godidog, a. excellent, splendid

godidowgrwydd, n.m. excellence

godineb, n.m. adultery

godinebu, v. commit adultery

godinebus, a. adulterous

godinebwr, (-wyr), n.m. adulterer

godre, (-on), n.m. skirt, border, edge

godriad, (-au), n.m. milking

godro, v. milk

godrudd, a. wild, furious

goddaith, (-eithiau), n.f. fire, bonfire

goddau, n.m. purpose, intention

goddef, v. bear, suffer, allow, permit

goddefgar, a. forbearing, tolerant

goddefgarwch, n.m. forbearance, tolerance

goddefiad, (-au), n.m. license; toleration

goddefol, a. tolerable; passive

goddiweddyd, goddiwes, v. over-take   [mar]

goddrych, n.m. subject (in gram-

goddrychol, a. subjective

gof, (-aint), n.m. smith

gofal, (-on), n.m. care, charge

gofalu, v. care, mind, take care

gofalus, a. careful

gofaniaeth, n.f. smith's craft

gofeg, n.f. mind; speech, utterance

gofer, (-oedd, -ydd), n.m. overflow of well; rill

gofid, (-iau), n.m. grief, sorrow, trouble

gofidio, v. afflict, grieve, vex

gofidus, a. grievous, sad

gofod, n.m. space

gofwy, (-on), n.m. visitation

gofwyo, v. visit

gofyn, v. ask, demand, require: (-ion), n.m. demand, requirement

gofyniad, (*-au*), *n.m.* question, query

gofynnod, (*-ynodau*), *n.m.* note of interrogation

gofynnol, *a.* necessary, requisite

gogan, *n.f.* defamation, satire

goganu, *v.* defame, satirize, lampoon

goganwr, (*-wyr*), *n.m.* satirist

goglais, *v. & n.m.* tickle

gogledd, *n.m. & a.* north

gogleddol, *a.* northern

gogleddwr, (*-wyr*), *n.m.* northman

gogleisio, *v.* tickle

goglyd, *n.m.* dependence, trust

gogoneddiad, *n.m.* glorification

gogoneddu, *v.* glorify

gogoneddus, *a.* glorious

gogoniant, *n.m.* glory

gogor, (*-ion*), *n.f.* fodder, provender

gogr, (*-au*), *n.m.* sieve, riddle

gogrwn, gogryn, *v.* sift, riddle, bolt

gogwydd, *n.m.* slant, inclination, bent

gogwyddiad, (*-au*), *n.m.* inclination

gogwyddo, *v.* incline, slope, lean

gogyfer, *a.* opposite; for, by

gogyfuwch, *a.* equal, even

gogyhyd, *a.* of equal length

gogymaint, *a.* equal in size

gohebiaeth, (*-au*), *n.f.* correspondence

gohebol, *a.* corresponding

gohebu, *v.* correspond

gohebydd, (*-wyr*), *n.m.* correspondent, reporter

gohiriad, (*-au*), *n.m.* postponement

gohirio, *v.* delay, postpone, defer

golaith, *v.* avoid, evade

golau, *a., n.m. & v.* light

golau-leuad, *n.m.* moonlight

golch, (*-ion*), *n.m.* wash, lye

golchdy, (*-dai*), *n.m.* wash-house, laundry

golchfa, *n.f.* wash; lathering

golchi, *v.* wash; lather

golchiad, (*-au*), *n.m.* washing; plating, coating

golchion, *n.pl.* slops; suds

golchwr, (*-wyr*), **-ydd,** (*-ion*), *n.m.* washer

golchwraig, (*-wragedd*), *n.f.* washerwoman

golchyddes, (*-au*), *n.f.* laundress

goledd(f), *n.m.* slant, slope

goleuad, (*-au*), *n.m.* light, luminary

goleudy, (*-dai*), *n.m.* lighthouse

goleuni, *n.m.* light [ate

goleuo, *v.* light, enlighten, illumin-

golo, *v.* conceal, bury

golosg, *n.m.* coke

golud, (*-oedd*), *n.m.* wealth, riches

goludog, *a.* wealthy, rich

golwg, (*-ygon*), *n.f.m.* sight, look; (*pl.*) eyes

golwyth, (*-ion*), *n.m.* chop, slice, cut

golygfa, (*-feydd*), *n.f.* scene, view; (*pl.*) scenery

golygiad, (*-au*), *n.m.* view

golygu, *v.* view; mean; edit

golygus, *a.* sightly, comely, handsome

golygwedd, (*-au*), *n.f.* feature, aspect

golygydd, (*-ion, -wyr*), *n.m.* editor

golygyddiaeth, *n.f.* editorship

golygyddol, *a.* editorial

gollwng, *v.* drop, loose, let go; discharge; dismiss; leak

gollyngdod, *n.m.* release; absolution

gomedd, *v.* refuse

gomeddiad, *n.m.* refusal; omission

gonest. See **onest**

gonestrwydd, *n.m.* honesty

gôr, *n.m.* pus

gor-, *px.* over-, super-

gorau, (*-euon*), *a.* best. **—o'r g.** very well

gorawen, *n.f.* joy, ecstasy

gorblu, *n.pl.* immature feathers

gorbwyso, *v.* outweigh, overweigh

gorcharfan, (*-au*), *n.f.* jaw, gum

gorchest, (*-ion*), *n.f.* feat, exploit

gorchestol, *a.* excellent, masterly

gorchfygu *v.* overcome, conquer

gorchfygwr, (*-wyr*), *n.m.* victor; conqueror

gorchudd, (*-ion*), *n.m.* cover, covering, veil

gorchuddio, *v.* cover

gorchwyl, (*-ion*), *n.m.* employ, task

gorchymyn, *v.* command: (*gorchmynion*), *n.m.* command, commandment

gordoi, *v.* overspread, cover

gordd, (*gyrdd*), *n.f.* hammer, mallet

gordderch, (*-adon*), *n.f.* concubine

gorddin, *n.m.* oppression, violence, attack

gorddwy, *n.m.* oppression

gorddyfnder, (*-au*), *n.m.* deep

goresgyn, *v.* overrun, invade; conquer

goresgyniad, *n.m.* invasion; conquest

goresgynnydd, *n.m.* invader; conqueror

goreu. See **gorau**

goreuro, *v.* gild

gorflwch, (*-flychau*), *n.m.* goblet, cup

gorfod, *v.* be obliged: *n.m.* obligation, necessity [pulsion

gorfodaeth, *n.f.* obligation, com-

gorfodi, *v.* oblige, compel

gorfodol, *a.* obligatory, compulsory

gorfoledd, *n.m.* joy, rejoicing, triumph

gorfoleddu, *v.* rejoice, triumph

gorfoleddus, *a.* jubilant, triumphant

gorfynt, *n.m.* envy, jealousy, pride: *a.* proud, jealous, ambitious

gorffen, *v.* finish, complete, conclude

gorffeniad, *n.m.* finishing, finish

Gorffennaf, *n.m.* July

gorffennol, *a. & n.m.* past

gorffwyll, *a.* mad, frenzied

gorffwyllo, *v.* rave

gorffwyllog, *a.* mad, insane

gorffwylltra, *n.m.* madness, insanity

gorffwys, *v. & n.m.* rest, repose

gorffwysfa, (*-oedd*), *n.f.* resting-place, rest

gorffwysiad, (*-au*), *n.m.* rest, pause

gorffwyso, **gorffwystra.** See **gorffwys**

gorhendaid, *n.m.* great-great-grandfather

gorhennain, *n.f.* great-great-grandmother

gori, *v.* hatch

gorifyny, *n.m.* ascent, hill, steep climb

goris, *pr.* below, beneath, under

goriwaered, *n.m.* descent, declivity

gorlawn, *a.* superabundant

gorlenwi, *v.* overfill

gorliwio, *v.* colour too highly, exaggerate

gorllewin, *n.m.* west

gorllewinol, *a.* westerly, western

gorllewinwr, (*-wyr*), *n.m.* western

gorllwyn, *v.* wait for, watch

gormail, *n.m.* oppression, tyranny

gormes, *n.m.* oppression, tyranny

gormesol, *a.* oppressive, tyrannical

gormesu, *v.* oppress, tyrannize

gormeswr, (*-wyr*), **-ydd,** (*-ion*) *n.m.* oppressor, tyrant

gormod, (*-ion*), *n.m.* too much, excess

gormodedd, *n.m.* excess, superfluity

gormodiaith, *n.f.* hyperbole, exaggeration

gormodol, *a.* excessive

gormwyth, *n.m.* catarrh

gornest. See **ornest**

goroesi, *v.* outlive, survive

goroesiad, (*-au*), *n.m.* survival

goroeswr, (*-wyr*), *n.m.* survivor

goror, (*-au*), *n.m.* confine, border, coast

gorsaf, (*-oedd*), *n.f.* station

gorsedd, (*-au*), *n.f.* **gorseddfa,** (*-oedd, n.f.,* **gorseddfainc,** (*-feinciau*), *n.f.* throne

gorseddu, *v.* throne, enthrone, install

gorsin, gorsing, (*-au*), *n.f.* doorpost

gorthrech, *n.m.* oppression; coercion

gorthrechu, v. oppress; coerce

gorthrwm, n.m. oppression

gorthrymder, n.m. oppression, tribulation

gorthrymedig, a. oppressed

gorthrymu, v. oppress

gorthrymus, a. oppressive

gorthrymwr, -ydd, (-wyr), n.m. oppressor

goruchaf, a. most high, highest

goruchafiaeth, n.f. supremacy; triumph

goruchel, a. high, supreme, exalted

goruchelder, n.m. summit, height

goruchwyliaeth, (-au), n.f. oversight; dispensation; operation; process

goruchwylio, v. oversee, supervise

goruchwyliwr, (-wyr), n.m. overseer, steward

gorun, n.m. noise; battle

goruwch, pr. above, over

goruwchnaturiol, a. supernatural

goruwchreoli, v. overrule

gorwedd, v. lie

gorweddfa, (-oedd), **-fan,** (-nau), n.f. bed, couch

gorweddian, v. lounge, loll

gorweddiog, a. bedridden

gorwel, (-ion), n.m. horizon

gorwych, a. gorgeous

gorwydd, (-ŵy-), n.m. horse

gorwydd, (-wŷ-), n.m. border of trees, wooded slope

gorwyr, (-ion), n.m. great-grandson

gorwyres, (-au), n.f. great-grand-daughter   [cession

gorymdaith, (-deithiau), n.f. procession

gorymdeithio, v. procession

gorynys, (-oedd), n.f. peninsula

gosber, (-au), n.m. vespers

gosgedd, (-au), n.m. form, figure

gosgeiddig, a. comely, graceful

gosgordd, (-ion), n.f. retinue, train, escort

gosgorddlu, (-oedd), n.m. body-guard

gosgymon, n. fuel

goslef, (-au), n.f. tone, intonation (**oslef**)

gosod, v. put, set; let; appoint: a. false, artificial

gosodiad, (-au), n.m. proposition, thesis

gosteg, (-ion), n.f. silence; (pl.) banns

gostegu, v. silence, still, quell

gostwng, v. lower, reduce; bow; put down, humble

gostyngedig, a. humble

gostyngeiddrwydd, n.m. humility

gostyngiad, n.m. reduction; humiliation

gotoyw, n.m. spur

gradell, (gredyll), n.f. griddle

gradd, (-au), n.m.f. grade, degree, stage

graddedigion, n.pl. graduates

graddfa, (-feydd), n.f. scale

graddio, v. graduate

graddol, a. gradual

graddoli, v. grade, graduate

graean, c.n. (**greyenyn,** n.m.), gravel

graeanu, v. granulate

graeanwst, n.f. gravel (complaint)

graen, n.m. grief; fear; a. sad, grievous, ugly

graen, n.m. grain, gloss, lustre

graenus, a. of good grain, glossy, sleek

gramadeg, (-au), n.m. grammar

gramadegol, a. grammatical

gramadegu, v. grammaticize, parse

gramadegwr, -ydd, (-wyr), n.m. grammarian

gran, (-nau), n.m. cheek

gras, (-au, -usau), n.m. grace

graslawn, -lon, a. full of grace, gracious

graslonrwydd, n.m. graciousness, grace

grasol, grasusol, a. gracious

grât, (gratiau), n.m. grate

grawn, n.pl. (**gronyn,** n.m.), grain; grapes; roe

grawnwin, n.pl. grapes

Grawys, n.m. Lent

gre, (-oedd), n.f. stud, flock

greddf, (-au), n.f. instinct, intuition

greddfol, *a.* instinctive, intuitive, rooted

greddfu, *v.* become ingrained

greidio, *v.* scorch

gresyn, *n.m.* pity

gresyni, *n.m.* misery, wretchedness

gresynu, *v.* commiserate, pity

gresynus, *a.* miserable, wretched

gridyll, (*-au*), *n.m.f.* griddle

griddfan, *v.* groan, moan: (*-nau*), *n.m.* groan

grillian, -io, *v.* squeak, creak; chirp; crunch

gris, (*-iau*), *n.m.* step, stair

grisial, *n.m.* crystal

grisialaidd, *a.* crystal, crystalline

gro, *c.n.* (**gröyn,** *n.m.*), gravel, pebbles

Groeg, *n.f.* Greek; Greece: *a.* Greek

Groegaidd, *a.* Grecian, Greek

Groeges, (*-au*), *n.f.* Greek woman

Groegwr, (*-wyr, -iaid*), *n.m.* Greek, Grecian

gronell, *n.f.* roe

gronyn, (*-nau*), *n.m.* grain, particle; while

grot, (*-iau*), *n.m.* groat, fourpence

grual, *n.m.* gruel

grud, *n.m.* grit

grudd, (*-iau*), *n.f.* cheek

gruddfan. See **griddfan**

grug, *n.m.* heather

grugiar, (*-ieir*), *n.f.* moor-hen, grouse

grugog, *a.* heathery

grwgnach, *v.* grumble, murmur

grwgnachlyd, *a.* given to grumbling

grwgnachwr, (*-wyr*), *n.m.* grumbler

grwn, (*grynnau*), *n.m.* ridge

grŵn, grwndi, *n.m.* purr

grwnan, *v.* croon, purr

grwndwal, (*-au*), *n.m.* foundation

gryd, *n.m.* shout, tumult; battle

grydian, *v.* murmur; grunt

grym, (*-oedd*), *n.m.* force, power, might

grymial, *v.* mutter, murmur, grumble

grymus, *a.* strong, powerful, mighty

grymuso, *v.* strengthen

grymuster, -tra, *n.m.* power, might

grynio, *v.* ridge

gwacáu, *v.* empty

gwacsaw, *a.* trivial, frivolous, giddy

gwacsawrwydd, *n.m.* levity, vanity

gwacter, *n.m.* emptiness, vacuity

gwachul. See **goachul**

gwad, *n.m.* denial, disavowal

gwadn, (*-au*), *n.m.* sole

gwadnu, *v.* sole; foot it

gwadu, *v.* deny, disown; renounce, forsake

gwadwr, (*-wyr*), *n.m.* denier

gwadd, (*-od*), *n.f.* mole

gwadd. See **gwahodd**

gwaddod, (*-ion*), *n.m.* sediment, lees, dregs

gwaddodi, *v.* deposit sediment

gwaddol, (*-ion, -iadau*), *n.m.* endowment; dowry

gwaddoli, *v.* endow, dower

gwae, (*-au*), *n.m.f.* woe

gwaed, *n.m.* blood, gore

gwaedlif, *n.m.* hæmorrhage, dysentery

gwaedlyd, *a.* bloody, sanguinary

gwaedoliaeth, *n.f.* blood, consanguinity

gwaedu, *v.* bleed

gwaedd, (*-au*), *n.f.* cry, shout

gwaeddi. See **gweiddi**

gwaeg, (*gwaëgau*), *n.f.* buckle, clasp

gwael, *a.* poor, vile; poorly, ill

gwaelder, -dra, *n.m.* poorness, vileness

gwaeledd, *n.m.* illness; meanness

gwaelod, (*-ion*), *n.m.* bottom; (*pl.*) sediment

gwaelodi, *v.* settle, deposit sediment

gwaelu, *v.* sicken

gwaell, (*gwëyll, gweill*), *n.f.* rod: knitting-needle   [down

gwaered, *n.m.* descent. **—I w.,** [worse

gwaeth, *a.* worse   [worse

gwaethwaeth, *adv.* worse and

gwaethygu, *v.* worsen

gwaew. See **gwayw**

gwag, *(gweigion),* *a.* empty, vacant, vain

gwagedd, *n.m.* emptiness, vanity

gwagelog, *a.* wary, circumspect

gwagen, *(-i),* *n.f.* waggon

gwagenwr, *(-wyr),* *n.m.* waggoner

gwagfa, *(-feydd),* *n.f.* vacuum

gwagle, *(-oedd),* *n.m.* space, void

gwagu, *v.* empty

gwahân, *n.m.* **-ar w.,** apart, separately

gwahangleifion, *n.pl.* lepers

gwahanglwyf, *n.m.* leprosy

gwahanglwyfus, *a.* leprous: *n.m.* leper

gwahaniaeth, *(-au),* *n.m.* difference

gwahaniaethol, *a.* distinguishing

gwahaniaethu, *v.* differ; distinguish

gwahanlen, *(-ni),* *n.f.* veil of temple

gwahanol, *a.* different

gwahanu, *v.* divide, part, separate

gwahardd, *v.* forbid, prohibit

gwaharddiad, *(-au),* *n.m.* prohibition, veto

gwahodd, *v.* invite

gwahoddedigion, *n.pl.* guests

gwahoddiad, *(-au),* *n.m.* invitation

gwahoddwr, *(-wyr),* *n.m.* inviter, host

gwain, *(gweiniau),* *n.f.* sheath, scabbard

gwair, *(gweiriau),* *n.m.* hay

gwaith, *(gweithiau),* *n.m.* work

gwaith, *(gweithiau),* *n.f.* time

gwâl, *(gwalau),* *n.f.* couch, bed; lair

gwal, *(-iau, gwelydd),* *n.f.* wall

gwala, *n.f.* enough, plenty

gwalch, *(gweilch),* *n.m.* hawk; rogue, rascal

gwaled, *(-au),* *n.f.* wallet

gwalio, *v.* wall, fence

gwall, *(-au),* *n.m.* defect, want; mistake, error

gwallgof, *a.* mad, insane

gwallgofdy, *(-dai),* *n.m.* madhouse, lunatic asylum

gwallgofddyn, *(-gofiaid),* *n.m.* madman

gwallgofi, *v.* go mad, rave

gwallgofrwydd, *n.m.* madness, insanity

gwallt, *(-iau),* *n.m. & c.n.* hair of the head

gwalltog, *a.* hairy

gwallus *a.* faulty, incorrect, inaccurate

gwamal, *a.* fickle, frivolous

gwamalio, -u, *v.* waver; behave frivolously   [levity

gwamalrwydd, *n.m.* frivolity,

gwan, *(gweiniaid, gweinion),* *a.* weak, feeble

gwanaf, *(-au),* *n.f.* layer; row, swath

gwanc, *n.m.* greed, voracity

gwancio, *v.* gorge, glut

gwancus, *a.* greedy, voracious

gwaneg, *(-au, gwenyg),* *n.f.* wave, billow

gwangalon, *a.* faint-hearted

gwangalonni, *v.* lose heart

gwanhau, *v.* weaken, enfeeble

gwanllyd, gwannaidd, *a.* weakly, delicate

gwant, *n.m.* caesura

gwantan, *a.* unsteady, fickle; feeble, poor

gwanu, *v.* pierce, stab

gwanwyn, *n.m.* spring

gwanychu, *v.* weaken, enfeeble

gwâr, *a.* tame, gentle

gwar, *(-rau),* *n.m.f.* (nape of) neck; back

gwaradwydd, *(-iadau),* *n.m.* shame, reproach

gwaradwyddo, *v.* shame, reproach

gwaradwyddus, *a.* shameful, disgraceful

gwarafun, *v.* forbid, refuse, grudge

gwaraidd, *a.* gentle, civilized

gwarant, *(-au),* *n.f.* warrant

gwarantu, *v.* warrant, guarantee

gwarchae, *v.* besiege: *n.m.* siege

gwarcheidiol, *a.* guardian, tutelary

gwarcheidwad, *(-waid),* *n.m.* guardian

gwarchod, v. watch, ward, mind
gwarchodaeth, n.f. ward, custody
gwarchodlu, (-oedd), n.m. garrison, guards
gward, (-iau), n.m.f. ward
gwarden, (-deiniaid), n.m. warden
gwarder, n.m. mercy, tenderness, kindness
gwared, v. rid, deliver, redeem
gwaredigaeth, (-au), n.f. deliverance
gwaredigion, n.pl. redeemed, ransomed
gwaredu, v. save, deliver, redeem, rid
gwaredwr, (-wyr), -ydd, (-ion), n.m. saviour
gwaredd, n.m. mildness, gentleness
gwareiddiad, n.m. civilization
gwareiddiedig, a. civilized
gwareiddio, v. civilize
gwargaled, a. stiffnecked, stubborn
gwargaledwch, n.m. stubbornness
gwargam, a. stooping
gwargamu, v. stoop
gwarged, n.m. remains
gwargrwm, a. round-shouldered
gwargrymu, v. stoop
gwario, v. spend
gwarogaeth. See gwrogaeth
gwarth, n.m. shame, disgrace, reproach
gwarthaf, n.m. top, summit. —ar w., on top of, upon
gwarthafl, (-au), n.f. stirrup
gwartheg, n.pl. cows, cattle
gwarthnod, (-au), n.m. stigma
gwarthnodi, v. stigmatize
gwarthol, (-ion, -aflau), n.f. stirrup
gwarthrudd, n.m. shame, disgrace
gwarthruddo, v. shame, disgrace
gwarthus, a. shameful, disgraceful
gwas, (gweision), n.m. lad: servant
gwasaidd, a. servile, slavish
gwasanaeth, (-au), n.m. service
gwasanaethferch, (-ed), n.f. handmaid
gwasanaethgar, a. serviceable; obliging
gwasanaethu, v. serve, minister

gwasanaethwr, (-wyr), n.m. manservant, servant
gwasanaethwraig, (-wragedd), n.f. maidservant
gwasanaethydd, (-ion), n.m. servant
gwasanaethyddes, (-au), n.f. handmaid
gwaseidd-dra, n.m. servility
gwasg, (-au, -oedd, gweisg), n.f. press: n.m. waist; bodice
gwasgar, n.m. dispersion. —ar w., scattered, dispersed
gwasgaredig, (-ion), a. scattered
gwasgarog, a. scattered; divided
gwasgaru, v. scatter, disperse; spread
gwasgarwr, (-wyr), n.m. scatterer; spreader
gwasgfa, (-feydd, -feuon), n.f. squeeze; fit
gwasgod, (-au), n.f. waistcoat
gwasgod, n.m. shade, shelter
gwasgu, v. press, squeeze, crush, wring
gwasod, a. in heat (of a cow)
gwastad, a. level, flat; even; constant, continual
gwastadedd, (-au), n.m. plain
gwastadol, a. continual, perpetual
gwastadrwydd, n.m. evenness
gwastatáu, v. make even, level; settle
gwastatir, (-oedd), n.m. level ground, plain
gwastraff, n.m. waste, extravagance
gwastraffu, v. waste, squander
gwastraffus, a. wasteful, extravagant
gwastraffwr, (-wyr), n.m. waster, spendthrift
gwastrawd, (-odion), n.m. groom, ostler
gwastrodaeth, -odi, v. groom; discipline
gwatwar, v. mock; mimic: n.m. mockery
gwatwareg, n.f. sarcasm, satire, irony

gwatwariaith, *n.f.* irony

gwatwarus, *a.* mocking, scoffing

gwatwarwr, (*-wyr*), *n.m.* mocker, scoffer

gwau, *v.* weave, knit

gwaudd, *n.f.* daughter-in-law

gwaun, (*gweunydd*), *n.f.* moor, meadow

gwawch, (*-iau*), *n.f.* **-io**, *v.* scream, yell

gwawd, *n.m.* scoff, scorn, ridicule

gwawdiaeth, *n.f.* ridicule

gwawdio, *v.* mock, scoff, jeer, ridicule

gwawdiwr, (*-wyr*), *n.m.* mocker, scoffer

gwawdlyd, *a.* mocking, jeering, sneering

gwawl, *n.m.* light

gwawl-lun, (*-iau*), *n.m.* photograph

gwawn, *n.m.* gossamer

gwawr, *n.f.* dawn, day-break; hue, nuance

gwawrio, *v.* dawn

gwayw, (*gwewyr*), *n.m.* pang, pain, stitch

gwaywffon, (*-ffyn*), *n.f.* spear

gwden, (*-ni, gwdyn*), *n.f.* withe

gwddf, (*gyddfau*), *n.m.* neck, throat

gwdihŵ, *n.m.* owl

gwe, (*-oedd*), *n.f.* web; texture

gwead, *n.m.* weaving, knitting; texture

gwedi, *pr.* after: *adv.* after, afterwards

gwedd, (*-au*), *n.f.* aspect, form; appearance

gwedd, (*-oedd*), *n.f.* yoke; team

gweddaidd, *a.* seemly, decent

gweddeidd-dra, *n.m.* seemliness, decency

gwedder, (*gweddrod*), *n.m.* wether, **Cig g.**, mutton

gweddgar, *a.* plump, sleek

gweddi, (*-Iau*), *n.m.* prayer

gweddigar, *a.* prayerful

gweddill, (*-ion*), *n.m.* remnant, remainder, rest; (*pl.*) remains

gweddillio, *v.* leave spare, leave a remnant

gweddïo, *v.* pray

gweddïwr, (*-ïwyr*), *n.m.* pray-er

gweddol, *a.* fair, fairly

gweddu, *v.* suit, become, befit

gweddus, *a.* seemly, decent, proper

gweddustra, *n.m.* decency, propriety

gweddw, *a.* single; widow, widowed. **—gŵr g.**, widower: (*-on*), *n.f.* widow

gweddwdod, *n.m.* widowhood

gweddwi, *v.* widow

gwefl, (*-au*), *n.f.* lip (usu. of animal)

gwefr, *n.m.* amber; electricity; thrill

gwefreiddio, *v.* electrify, thrill

gwefreiddiol, *a.* thrilling

gwefus, (*-au*), *n.f.* (human) lip

gwefusol, *a.* of the lip, labial

gwegi, *n.m.* vanity, levity

gwegian, *v.* sway, totter

gwegil, *n.m.f.* nape of neck; back

gwehelyth, *n.m.f.* lineage, pedigree

gwehilion, *n.pl.* refuse, trash, riff-raff

gwehydd, (*-ion*), *n.m.* weaver

gwehynnu, *v.* draw, pour, empty

gweiddi, *v.* cry, shout

gweilgi, *n.f.* sea, torrent

gweili, *a.* empty, idle

gweini, *v.* serve, minister; be in service

gweinidog, (*-ion*), *n.m.* minister, servant

gweinidogaeth, (*-au*), *n.f.* ministry, service

gweinidogaethol, *a.* ministerial

gweinidogaethu, *v.* minister

gweinidoges, (*-au*), *n.f.* minister's wife

gweinio, *v.* sheathe

gweinyddes, (*-au*), *n.f.* attendant, nurse [stration

gweinyddiaeth, (*-au*), *n.f.* admini-

gweinyddol, *a.* administrative

gweinyddu, *v.* administer, officiate

gweirglodd, (*-iau*), *n.f.* meadow

gweitied, -io, *v.* wait

gweithdy, (*-dai*), *n.m.* workhouse; workshop

gweithfa, (-oedd, -feydd), n.f. works

gweithfaol, a. industrial

gweithgar, a. hard-working, industrious

gweithgaredd, (-au), -garwch, n.m. activity

gweithio, v. work; ferment; purge

gweithiwr, (-wyr), n.m. workman, worker

gweithred, (-oedd), n.f. act, deed, work

gweithrediad, (-au), n.m. action, operation

gweithredol, a. active, actual, virtual

gweithredu, v. act, work, operate

gweithredwr, (-wyr), n.m. doer

gweithredydd, (-ion), n.m. doer, factor, agent

gweladwy, a. perceptible, visible

gweled, gweld, v. see, perceive

gwelediad, n.m. sight, appearance

gweledig, a. seen, visible

gweledigaeth, (-au), n.f. vision

gweledydd, (-ion), n.m. seer

gweli, (-ïau), n.m. wound, sore

gwelw, a. pale

gwelwi, v. pale

gwely, (-au, gwelâu), n.m. bed

gwell, a. better, superior

gwella, v. better, mend, improve

gwellau, (-eifiau), n.m. shears

gwellen, (gweill), n.f. knitting-needle

gwellhad, n.m. bettering, improvement

gwellhau, v. better, improve

gwelliant, (-iannau), n.m. amendment, improvement

gwellt, c.n. grass; sward; straw

gwelltglas, n.m. grass, greensward

gwelltog, a. grassy, green

gwelltyn, n.m. blade of grass; a straw

gwellwell, adv. better and better

gwên, (gwenau), n.f. smile

gwen, a., f. of gwyn

gwenci, (-ïod), n.f. stoat, weasel

gwendid, (-au), n.m. weakness, frailty

Gwener, n.f. Venus. —Dydd G., Friday

gwenerol, a. venereal

gwenfflam, a. blazing, ablaze

gweniaith, n.f. flattery

gwenieithio, v. flatter

gwenieithiwr, (-wyr), n.m. flatterer

gwenieithus, a. flattering

gwenith, n.pl. (-en, n.f.), wheat

gwenithfaen, n.m. granite

gwennol, (gwenoliaid), n.f. swallow, martin; shuttle

gwenu, v. smile

gwenwisg, (-oedd), n.f. surplice

gwenwyn, n.m. poison, venom; jealousy

gwenwynig, -wynol, a. poisonous, venomous

gwenwynllyd, a. peevish; jealous

gwenwyno, v. poison; fret; be jealous

gwenyn, n.pl. (-en, n.f.), bees

gwep, n.f. visage, grimace

gwêr, n.m. tallow, suet, or the like

gŵer, n.m. shade

gwerchyr, n.m. cover, lid, valve

gwerdd, a., f. of gwyrdd

gwerin, c.n.f. men, people; democracy; crew

gweriniaeth, (-au), n.f. democracy; republic

gwerinlywodraeth, (-au), n.f. republic

gwerinol, a. plebeian, vulgar

gwerinos, c.n.f. the rabble, the mob

gwerinwr, (-wyr), n.m. democrat

gwern, (-i, -ydd), n.f. swamp, meadow; alder-grove

gwern, n.pl. (-en, n.f.), alder-trees

gwerog, a. tallowy, suety

gwers, (-i), n.f. verse; lesson

gwersyll, (-oedd), n.m. camp, encampment

gwersyllu, v. encamp

gwerth, n.m. worth, value; sale

gwerthfawr, a. valuable, precious

gwerthfawredd, n.m. preciousness

gwerthfawrogi, v. appreciate

gwerthfawrogiad, n. appreciation

gwerthu, v. sell

gwerthwr, (-*wyr*), *n.m.* seller

gwerthyd, (-*au*), *n.f.* spindle, axle

gweryd, (-*au*), *n.m.* earth, soil; sward

gweryriad, *n.m.* neighing

gweryru, *v.* neigh

gwestai, (-*eion*), *n.m.* guest

gwesty, (-*au, -tai*), *n.m.* inn, hotel

gweu, *v.* weave, knit

gwewyr. See **gwayw**

gwg, *n.m.* frown, scowl; wrath

gwgu, *v.* frown, scowl, lower

gwialen, (*gwiail*), *n.f.* rod, switch

gwialennod, (-*enodiau*), *n.f.* stroke, stripe

gwialenodio, *v.* beat with a rod

gwib, *n.f.* wandering, jaunt: *a.* wandering

gwibdaith, (-*deithiau*), *n.f.* excursion

gwiber, (-*od*), *n.f.* viper

gwibio, *v.* flash, flit, rove, gad, wander

gwibiog, *a.* flitting, wandering

gwiblong, (-*au*), *n.f.* cruiser

gwich, *n.f.* squeak; creak; wheeze, wheezing

gwichiad, (-*iaid*), *n.m.* periwinkle

gwichian, *v.* squeak, squeal; creak; wheeze

gwichlyd, *a.* creaking; wheezy

gwiddon, (-*od*), *n.f.* witch

gwiddon, *n.pl.* mites

gwif, (-*iau*), *n.m.* lever, crowbar

gwig, (-*oedd*), *n.f.* wood

gwingo, *v.* wriggle, fidget; writhe; kick, struggle

gwin, (-*oedd*), *n.m.* wine

gwinau, *a.* bay, brown, auburn

gwinc, (-*od*), *n.f.* chaffinch

gwinegr, *n.m.* vinegar

gwinllan, (-*noedd, -nau*), *n.f.* vineyard

gwinllannwr, -nydd, *n.m.* vinedresser

gwinwryf, (-*oedd*) *n.m.* wine-press

gwinwydd, *n.pl.* (-*en, n.f.*), vines

gwir, *a.* true: *n.m.* truth

gwireb, (-*au, -ion*), *n.f.* truism, axiom

gwireddu, *v.* verify, substantiate

gwirfodd, *n.m.* goodwill; own accord

gwirfoddol, *a.* voluntary, spontaneous

gwirfoddolwr, (-*wyr*), *n.m.* volunteer

gwirio, *v.* verify

gwirion, (-*iaid*), *a.* innocent; silly

gwiriondeb, *n.m.* innocence; silliness

gwirionedd, (-*au*), *n.m.* truth, verity, reality   [ine

gwirioneddol, *a.* true, real, genu-

gwirioni, *v.* infatuate, dote

gwirionyn, *n.m.* simpleton

gwirod, (-*ydd*), *n.m.* liquor, spirits

gwisg, (-*oedd*), *n.f.* dress, garment, robe

gwisgi, *a.* brisk, lively, nimble; ripe

gwisgo, *v.* dress; wear

gwisgwr, (-*wyr*), *n.m.* wearer

gwiw, *a.* fit, meet; worthy

gwiwer, (-*od*), *n.f.* squirrel

gwlad, (*gwledydd*), *n.f.* country, land

gwladaidd, *a.* countrified

gwladeiddio, *v.* blush

gwladfa, (-*oedd*), *n.f.* colony, settlement

gwladgar. See **gwlatgar**

gwladgarol, *a.* patriotic

gwladgarwch, *n.m.* patriotism

gwladgarwr, (-*wyr*), *n.m.* patriot

gwladol, *a.* of a country, civil, state

gwladoli, *v.* nationalize

gwladweiniaeth, *n.f.* statesmanship

gwladweinydd, (-*ion, -wyr*), *n.m.* statesman

gwladwr, (-*wyr*), *n.m.* countryman, peasant

gwladwriaeth, (-*au*), *n.f.* state

gwladwriaethol, *a.* state, political

gwladychfa, (-*oedd*), *n.f.* settlement, colony

gwladychu, *v.* inhabit, settle, colonize

gwladychwr, (-*wyr*), *n.m.* settler, colonist

gwlân, (*gwlanoedd*), *n.m.* wool
gwlana, *v.* gather wool
gwlanen, (*-ni*), *n.f.* flannel
gwlanog, *a.* woolly
gwlatgar, *a.* patriotic
gwlaw. See **glaw**
gwledig, *a.* countrified, country, rural
gwledig, *n.m.* lord, prince, ruler
gwledd, (*-oedd*), *n.f.* feast, banquet
gwledda, *v.* feast
gwleddwr, (*-wyr*) *n.m.* feaster
gwleidiadaeth, *n.f.* politics
gwleidiadol, *a.* political
gwleidydd, (*-ion*), *n.m.* politician, statesman
gwleidyddiaeth, *n.f.* politics
gwleidyddol, *a.* political
gwleidyddwr, (*-wyr*), *n.m.* politician
gwlith, (*-oedd*), *n.m.* dew
gwlitho, *v.* dew, bedew
gwlithog, *a.* dewy
gwlithyn, *n.m.* dewdrop
gwlyb, (*-ion*), *a.* & *n.m.* wet, fluid, liquid
gwlybaniaeth, *n.m.* wet, moisture
gwlybwr, *n.m.* wet, moisture, liquid, fluid
gwlybyrog, *a.* wet, damp, rainy
gwlych, *n.m.* wet. —**rhoi yng ng.,** steep
gwlychu, *v.* wet, moisten; get wet; dip
gwlydd, *n.pl.* & *c.n.* (**-yn,** *n.m.*), haulm
gwn, (*gynnau*), *n.m.* gun
gŵn, (*gynau*), *n.m.* gown
gwndwn. See **gwyndwn**
gwneud, gwneuthur, *v.* do, make
gwneuthuriad, *n.m.* make, making
gwneuthurwr, (*-wyr*), *n.m.* maker, doer
gwnïad, *n.m.* sewing, stitching, seam
gwniadur, (*-iau*), *n.m.f.* thimble
gwniadwraig, *n.f.* stitcher, seamstress
gwniadyddes, (*-au*), *n.f.* seamstress

gwnïo, *v.* sew, stitch
gwniyddes, (*-au*), *n.f.* seamstress
gwobr, (*-au*), *n.f.m.*, **gwobrwy,** (*-au, -on*), *n.m.* reward, prize
gwobrwyo, *v.* reward
gwobrwywr, (*-wyr*), *n.m.* rewarder
gŵr, (*gwŷr*), *n.m.* man; husband
gwra, *v.* seek or marry a husband
gwrach, (*-ïod*), *n.f.* hag, witch. **Breuddwyd g.,** wishful thinking
gwrachïaidd, *a.* old-womanish
gwraidd, (*gwreiddiau*), *c.n.* roots
gwraig, (*gwragedd*), *n.f.* woman; wife
gwrandaw, -do, *v.* hearken, listen
gwrandawiad, *n.m.* listening, hearing
gwrandawr, (*-wyr*), *n.m.* listener, hearer
gwrcath, (*-od*), *n.m.* tom-cat
gwregys, (*-au*), *n.m.* girdle, belt, zone; truss
gwregysu, *v.* girdle, gird
gwrêng, *n.m.* & *c.n.* (one of the) common people
gwreica, *v.* seek or marry a wife
gwreichion, *n.pl.* (**-en,** *n.f.*), sparks
gwreichioni, *v.* emit sparks, sparkle
gwreiddio, *v.* root
gwreiddiol, *a.* radical, rooted; original
gwreddioldeb, *n.m.* originality
gwreiddyn, (*gwreiddiau, gwraidd*), *n.m.* root
gwreigaidd, *a.* womanish, womanly
gwres, *n.m.* heat, warmth
gwresfesurydd, (*-ion*), *n.m.* thermometer
gwresog, *a.* warm, hot; fervent
gwresogi, *v.* warm, heat
gwrhyd, (*-oedd*), **gwryd,** *n.m.* fathom
gwrhydri, *n.m.* exploit, valour
gwrid, *n.m.* blush, flush
gwrido, *v.* blush, flush
gwridog, gwritgoch, *a.* rosy-cheeked, ruddy
gwrm, *a.* dun, dark blue, brown
gwrogaeth, *n.f.* homage

gwrogi, v. do homage

gwrol, a. brave, courageous

gwroldeb, n.m. bravery, courage

gwroli, v. hearten

gwron, (-iaid), n.m. hero

gwroniaeth, n.f. heroism

gwrtaith, (-teithiau), n.m. manure; culture   [ture

gwrteithiad, n.m. cultivation, cul-

gwrteithio, v. manure; cultivate, culture

gwrth-, px. counter-, contra-, anti-

gwrthban, (-au), n.m. blanket

gwrthblaid, n.f. (party in) opposition

gwrthbrofi, v. disprove, refute

gwrthbwynt, n.m. counterpoint

gwrthdaro, v. clash, collide

gwrthdrawiad, (-au), n.m. collision

gwrthdystiad, (-au), n.m. protest

gwrthdystio, v. protest

gwrthddadl (-euon), n.f. objection

gwrthddadlau, v. object, controvert

gwrthddywediad, (-au), n.m. contradiction

gwrthddywedyd, v. contradict

gwrthgiliad, (-au), n.m. backsliding

gwrthgilio, v. backslide, secede

gwrthgiliwr, (-wyr), n.m. backslider, seceder

gwrthglawdd, (-gloddiau), n.m. rampart

gwrthgyferbyniad, (-au), n.m. contrast, antithesis

gwrthgyferbynnu, v. contrast

gwrthladd, v. resist, repel

gwrthnaws, n.m. antipathy: a. repugnant

gwrthnysig, a. obstinate, stubborn

gwrthnysigrwydd, n.m. obstinacy

gwrthod, v. refuse, reject

gwrthodedig, a. rejected, reprobate

gwrthodiad, n.m. refusal, rejection

gwrthodwr, (-wyr), n.m. refuser, rejecter

gwrthol, n.m. & adv. back. —**ôl a g.,** to and fro

gwrthrych, (-au), n.m. object; subject (of biography)

gwrthrychol, a. objective

gwrthryfel, (-oedd), n.m. rebellion, mutiny

gwrthryfela, v. rebel

gwrthryfelgar, a. rebellious, mutinous

gwrthryfelwr, (-wyr), n.m. rebel, mutineer

gwrthsafiad, n.m. resistance

gwrthsefyll, v. withstand, resist

gwrthun, a. repugnant, odious, absurd

gwrthuni, n.m. odiousness, absurdity

gwrthuno, v. mar, deform, disfigure

gwrthweithio, v. counteract

gwrthwyneb, n.m. opposite, contrary

gwrthwynebiad, (-au), n.m. objection

gwrthwynebol, a. opposed

gwrthwynebu, v. resist, oppose

gwrthwynebus, a. repugnant

gwrthwynebwr, -ydd, (-wyr), n.m. opponent, adversary

gwrych, (-oedd), n.m. hedge

gwrych, n.pl. & c.n. (-**yn,** n.m.), bristles

gwryd. See **gwrhyd**

gwryd, n.m. valour

gwryf, (-oedd), n.m. press

gwrym, (-iau), n.m. seam; wale

gwrysg, n.pl. (-**en,** n.f.), stalks, haulm

gwryw, a. male: (-od), n.m. male

gwrywaidd, -ol, a. masculine

gwrywgydiwr, (-wyr), n.m. sodomite

gwth, n.m. push, thrust, shove; gust

gwthio, v. push, thrust, shove, obtrude

gwthiwr, (-wyr), n.m. pusher

gwyar, n.m. gore, blood

gwybed, n.pl. (-**yn,** n.m.), flies

gwybod, v. know: (-au), n.m. knowledge. —**gwybodau,** studies

gwybodaeth, (-au), n.f. knowledge
gwybodeg, n.m. epistemology
gwybodus, a. knowing
gwybyddus, a. known
gwybyddwr, (-wyr), n.m. knower
gwych, a. fine, splendid, brilliant
gwychder, n.m. splendour, pomp
gwŷd, (gwydiau), n.m. vice
gwydn, a. tough
gwydnwch, n.m. toughness
gwydr, (-au), n.m. glass
gwydraid, (-eidiau), n.m. glassful, glass
gwydro, v. glaze
gwydrwr, (-wyr), n.m. glazier
gwydryn, (gwydrau), n.m. drinking-glass
gŵydd, n.m. presence
gŵydd, (gwyddau), n.m. goose
gŵydd, a. wild
gwŷdd, (gwehyddion, gwyddion), n.m. loom; plough
gwŷdd, n.pl. (**gwydden,** n.f.), trees
gwyddbwyll, n.f. chess
Gwyddel, (-od, Gwyddyl), n.m. Irishman
Gwyddeleg, n.f. Irish
Gwyddeles, (-au), n.f. Irishwoman
Gwyddelig, a. Irish
gwyddfa, n.f. tumulus, grave
gwyddfid, n.m. honeysuckle
gwyddfod, n.m. presence
gwyddoniadur, (-on), n.m. encyclopædia
gwyddoniaeth, n.f. science
gwyddonol a. scientific
gwyddonydd, (-wyr), n.m. scientist
gwyddor, (-ion), n.f. rudiment; science.—**yr w.,** the alphabet
gwyddori, v. instruct, ground
gwyfyn, (-od), n.m. moth
gwŷg, c.n. vetch
gwygl, a. sultry
gŵyl, a. bashful, modest
gŵyl, (-iau), n.f. holiday, feast, festival
gwylaidd, a. bashful, modest
gwylan, (-od), n.f. sea-gull
gwylder, n.m. bashfulness, modesty

gwyldy, (-dai), n.m. watch-house
gwyleidd-dra, n.m. bashfulness, modesty
gwylfa, (-fâu, -feydd), n.f. watch
gwyliadwriaeth, n.m. watchfulness, caution: (-au), n.f. watch; guard
gwyliadwrus, a. watchful, cautious
gwyliedydd, (-ion), n.m. watchman, sentinel
gwylio, v. watch, mind, beware
gwyliwr, (-wyr), n.m. watchman, sentinel
gwylmabsant, (-au), n.f. wake
gwylnos, (-au), n.f. watch-night, wake, vigil
gwyll, n.m. darkness, gloom
gwylliad, (-iaid), n.m. robber, bandit
gwyllt, a. wild, savage, mad; rapid: (-oedd), n.m. wild
gwylltineb, n.m. wildness; rage, fury   [passion
gwylltio, -u, v. frighten; fly into a
gwymon, n.m. seaweed
gwymp, a. fine, fair
gwyn, a. white; blessed: f. **gwen**
gwŷn, (gwyniau), n.m.f. ache, smart; lust
gwynder, -dra, n.m. whiteness
gwyndwn, n.m. unploughed land
gwyneb. See **wyneb**
gwynegon, n.m. rheumatism
gwynegu, v. throb, ache
gwynfa, n.f. paradise
gwynfyd, (-au), n.m. blessedness, bliss; (pl.) beatitudes
gwynfydedig, a. blessed, happy, beatific
gwyngalchog a. whitewashed
gwyngalchu, v. whitewash
gwyniad, (-iaid), n.m. whiting
gwynias, a. white-hot
gwynio, v. throb, ache
gwynnu, v. whiten, bleach
gwynnwy, n.m. white of egg
gwynt, (-oedd), n.m. wind; breath; smell
gwyntell, (-i), n.f. round basket without handle

gwyntio, v. smell
gwyntog, a. windy
gwyntyll, (-au), n.f. fan
gwyntylliad, n.m. ventilation
gwynytyllio, -u, v. ventilate, winnow
gŵyr, a. crooked, oblique, sloping
gwŷr. See **gŵr**
gwyrdraws, a. perverse
gwyrdro, (-ion), n.m. perversion
gwyrdroi, v. pervert, distort
gwyrdd, (-ion), a. & n.m. green
gwyrddlas, a. green, verdant
gwyrddlesni, n.m. verdure
gwyrddni, n.m. greenness, verdure
gwyrgam, a. crooked   [ness
gwyrni, n.m. crookedness, perverse-
gwyro, v. swerve; slope; stoop,
bend
gwyrth, (-iau), n.f. miracle
gwyrthiol, a. miraculous
gwyry, gwyryf, (gwyryfon), n.f.
virgin
gwyryfdod, n.m. virginity
gwyryfol, a. virgin
gwŷs, (gwysion), n.f. summons
gwysio, v. summon
gwystl, (-on), n.m. pledge; hostage
gwystlo, v. pledge, pawn
gwystno, v. dry, wither, flag
gwŷth, n.m. anger, wrath
gwythen, (-nau), n.f. vein
gwythi, n.pl. (-ïen, n.f. (-iennau)
veins.—**cwlwm g.,** cramp
gwythlon, a. angry, wrathful
gwythwch, n.m. wild pig
gwyw, a. withered, faded, sear
gwywo, v. wither, fade
gyda, -g, pr. with
gyddfol, a. guttural
gyferbyn, pr. over against, opposite
gylfin, (-od), n.m. bill, beak
gylfinir, n.m. curlew
gynfad, (-au), n.m. gunboat
gynnau, adv. a little while ago, just
now
gynt, adv. formerly, of yore
gyr, (-roedd), n.m. drove
gyrfa, (-oedd, -feydd), n.f. race;
course; career

gyriedydd, (-ion), n.m. driver
gyrru, v. drive; send; work, forge
gyrrwr, (gyrwyr), n.m. driver;
sender
gyrwynt, (-oedd), n.m. hurricane,
tornado
gysb, n.m. staggers

H

ha, i. ha
hac, (-iau), n.f. cut, notch, hack
hacio, v. hack
had, (-au), n.m. & c.n. (**hedyn,**
n.m.), seed
hadu, v. seed
hadyd, c.n. seed-corn
haeach, adv. almost; hardly
haearn, (heyrn), n.m. iron. —**h.
bwrw,** cast iron. —**h. gyr,**
wrought iron
haearnaidd, a. like iron
haeddiannol   a.   meritorious;
merited   [desert
haeddiant, (-iannau), n.m. merit,
haeddu, v. deserve, merit
hael, a. generous, liberal
haelfrydedd, n.m. liberality
haelfrydig, a. generous, free
haelioni, n.m. generosity
haelionus, a. generous, liberal
haen, (-au), n.f. layer, stratum;
seam
haenen, (-nau), n.f. layer, film
haenu, v. stratify
haeriad, (-au), n.m. assertion
haerllug, a. importunate; impudent
haerllugrwydd, n.m. importunity;
impudence
haeru, v. affirm, assert
haf, (-au), n.m. summer
hafaidd, a. summer-like, summery
hafal, a. like, equal
hafan, n.f. haven
hafn, (-au), n.f. hollow, gorge,
ravine
hafod, (-ydd), n.f. summer dwelling,
farm

hafog, *n.m.* havoc

hafoty, (*-tai*), *n.m.* summer residence

hagen, *c.* but, moreover, however

hagr, *a.* ugly

hagru, *v.* mar, disfigure

hagrwch, *n.m.* ugliness

haid, (*heidiau*), *n.f.* swarm, drove, horde

haidd, (*heiddiau*), *n.m. & c.n.* barley

haig, (*heigiau*), *n.f.* shoal

haint, (*heintiau*), *n.m.f.* pestilence, faint

halen, *n.m.* salt, brine

halog, -edig, *a.* defiled, polluted

halogi, *v.* defile, profane, pollute

halogrwydd, *n.m.* defilement, pollution

halogwr, (*-wyr*), *n.m.* defiler, profaner

halwyn, (*-au*), *n.m.* salt(s)

hallt, *a.* salt, salty; severe

halltedd, -rwydd, *n.m.* saltness, saltiness

halltu, *v.* salt

halltwr, (*-wyr*), *n.m.* salter

hambwrdd, (*-byrddau*), *n.m.* tray

hamdden, *n.f.* leisure, respite

hamddenol, *a.* leisurely, deliberate

hanerob, (*-au*), *n.f.* flitch of bacon

haneru, *v.* halve

hanes, (*-ion*), *n.m.* history, story, account

hanesgerdd, (*-i*), *n.f.* epic poem

hanesiaeth, *n.f.* history

hanesydd, (*-wyr*), *n.m.* historian

hanesyddiaeth, *n.f.* history

hanesyddol, *a.* historical

hanesyn (*-nau*), *n.m.* anecdote

hanfod, *v.* descend, issue: *n.m.* essence

hanfodol, *a.* essential

haniad, *n.m.* derivation, descent

haniaeth, *n.f.* abstraction

haniaethol, *a.* abstract

hanner, (*hanerau*), *n.m., a. & adv.* half [descended

hanu, *v.* proceed, be derived, be

hapus, *a.* happy

hapusrwydd, *n.m.* happiness

hardd, *a.* beautiful, handsome

harddu, *v.* beautify, embellish, adorn

harddwch, *n.m.* beauty

harnais, (*-eisiau*), *n.m.* harness

harneisio, *v.* harness

hatling, (*-au, -od*), *n.f.* mite, half a farthing

hau, *v.* sow, disseminate

haul, (*heuliau*), *n.m.* sun

hawdd, *a.* easy

hawddamor, *n.m. & i.* good luck, welcome

hawddfyd, *n.m.* ease, prosperity

hawddgar, *a.* amiable; comely

hawddgarwch, *n.m.* amiability

hawl, (*-iau, holion*), *n.f.* claim; right. **-h. ac ateb,** question and answer

hawlio, *v.* claim, demand

hawlydd, (*-ion*), *n.m.* claimant, plaintiff

haws, *a.* easier

heb, *pr.* without

heblaw, *pr.* beside(s)

hebog, (*-au*), *n.m.* hawk, falcon

Hebraeg, *n.f. & a.* Hebrew

Hebreaidd, Hebreig, *a.* Hebrew, Hebraic

Hebrees, (*-au*), *n.f.* Hebrew woman

Hebreigydd, (*-ion*), *n.m.* Hebraist

Hebrëwr, (*-wyr*), *n.m.* a Hebrew

hebrwng, *v.* conduct, convey, escort

hebryngydd, (*-ion*), *n.m.* conductor

hedeg, *v.* fly; run to seed

hedegog, *a.* flying; high-flown

hedfa, (*-feydd*), *n.f.* flight

hedfan, *v.* fly, hover

hedydd, (*-ion*), *n.m.* lark

hedyn, (*hadau*), *n.m.* seed, germ

hedd, *n.m.* peace, tranquillity

heddgeidwad, (*-waid*), *n.m.* policeman

heddiw, *adv.* to-day

heddlu, *n.m.* police force

heddwas, (*-weision*), *n.m.* policeman

heddwch, *n.m.* peace, quiet, tranquillity

heddychlon, *a.* peaceful, peaceable

heddychol, *a.* peaceable, pacific

heddychu, *v.* pacify, appease

heddychwr, (*-wyr*), *n.m.* pacifier, peace-maker

hedd-ynad, (*-on*), *n.m.* justice of the peace

heddyw. See **heddiw**

hefelydd, *a.* similar

hefyd, *adv.* also, besides

heffer, (*heffrod*), *n.f.* heifer

hegl, (*-au*), *n.f.* leg, shank

heglog, *a.* leggy, long-legged

heglu, *v.* foot it, 'hook it'

heibio, *adv.* past

heidio, *v.* swarm, throng, flock

heidden, *n.f.* grain of barley, barleycorn

heigio, *v.* shoal, team

heini, *a.* active, lively, nimble, brisk

heintio, *v.* infect

heintus, *a.* infectious, contagious

heislan, (*-od*), *n.f.* hackle, hatchel

heislanu, *v.* hackle flax

hel, *v.* gather, collect; drive, chase

hela, *v.* hunt. —**cŵn h.,** hounds

helaeth, *a.* ample, abundant, extensive

helaethrwydd, *n.m.* abundance

helaethu, *v.* enlarge, extend, amplify

helaethwych, *a.* sumptuous

helbul, (*-on*), *n.m.* trouble

helbulus, *a.* troubled, troublous

helcyd, *v.* hunt: *n.m.* worry, trouble

helfa, (*-fâu, -feydd*), *n.f.* hunt, catch

helfarch, (*-feirch*), *n.m.* hunter

helgi, (*-gwn*), *n.m.* hound

heli, *n.m.* salt water, brine

heliwr, (*-wyr*), *n.m.* hunter, huntsman

helm, (*-au*), *n.f.* helm, helmet, stack

help, *n.m.* help, aid, assistance

helpio, -u, *v.* help, aid, assist

helwriaeth, *n.f.* game, hunting; chase

helyg, *n.pl.* (*-en, n.f.*), willows

helynt, (*-ion*), *n.f.* trouble, fuss, bother

helltni, *n.m.* saltiness, saltness

hem, *n.m.* rivet

hem, (*-iau*), *n.f.* hem, border

hen, *a.* old, aged, ancient, of old

henadur, (*-iaid*), *n.m.* alderman

Henaduriad, (*-iaid*), *n.m.* Presbyterian

henaduriaeth, (*-au*), *n.f.* presbytery

Henaduriaeth, *n.f.* Presbyterianism

Henadurol, *a.* Presbyterian

henafgwr, henafol. See **hy-**

henaint, *n.m.* old age

hendaid, (*-deidiau*), *n.m.* great-grandfather

hender, *n.m.* oldness

hendref, (*-i, -ydd*), *n.f.* winter dwelling

heneiddio, *v.* grow old, age

henfam, *n.f.* grandmother

hennain, (*heneiniau*), *n.f.* great-grandmother

heno, *adv.* to-night

henuriad, (*-iaid*), *n.m.* elder, presbyter

henuriaeth, *n.f.* presbytery

heol, (*-ydd*), *n.f.* road

hepgor, *v.* spare, dispense with: (*-ion*), *n.m.* what may be dispensed with

hepian, *v.* slumber, doze

her, (*-iau*), *n.f.* challenge

herc, (*-iau*), *n.f.* hop; limp

hercian, *v.* hop, hobble, limp

heresi, (*-ïau*), *n.f.* heresy

heretic, (*-iaid*), *n.m.* heretic

hereticaidd, *a.* heretical

herfeiddio, *v.* dare, brave, defy

herfeiddiol *a.* daring, defiant

hergwd, *n.m.* push, thrust, shove, lunge

herio, *v.* challenge, dare, brave, defy

herlodes, (*-i*), *n.f.* damsel, girl

herw, *n.m.* raid; outlawry

herwa, *v.* scout, prowl, raid

herwhela, *v.* poach, (game)

herwr, (*-wyr*), *n.m.* scout, raider; outlaw

herwydd. See **oherwydd**

hesb, *a.*, f. of **hysb**

hesben, (*-nau*), *n.f.* hasp

hesbin, (*-od*), *n.f.* yearling ewe

hesbwrn, (*-yrniaid*), *n.m.* young ram

hesg, *n.pl.* (**-en,** *n.f.*), sedge, rushes

het, (*-iau*), *n.f.* hat

heulo, *v.* shine (as the sun); sun

heulog, *a.* sunny

heulwen, *n.f.* sunshine

heuwr, (*-wyr*), *n.m.* sower

hi, *pn.* she, her; it

hidio, *v.* heed

hidl, *a.* **-wylo yn h.,** weep abundantly

hidl, (*-au*), *n.f.* strainer, sieve

hidlo, *v.* distil, run; strain, filter

hil, *n.f.* race, lineage, posterity

hilio, *v.* bring forth, teem, breed

hiliogaeth, *n.f.* offspring, issue, posterity

hin, *n.f.* weather

hinfynegydd, (*-ion*), *n.m.* barometer

hiniog, (*-au*), *n.f.* door-frame, threshold

hinon, *n.f.* fair weather

hinsawdd, (*-soddau*), *n.f.* climate

hinsoddol, *a.* climatic

hir, *a. & px.* long

hiraeth, *n.m.* longing, nostalgia, grief; homesickness

hiraethu, *v.* long, yearn, sorrow

hiraethus, *a.* longing; homesick

hirbell, *a.* **-o h.,** from afar

hirben, *a.* long-headed, shrewd

hirhoedledd, *n.m.* longevity

hirhoedlog, *a.* long-lived

hir-ymarhous, *a.* longsuffering

hirymaros, *n.m.* longsuffering

hithau, *pn.c.* she (on her part), she also

hobaid, (*-eidiau*), *n.f.* peck

hoced, (*-ion*), *n.f.* deceit, fraud

hocedu, *v.* cheat, deceive, defraud

hocedwr, (*-wyr*), *n.m.* cheat, fraud

hocys, *n.pl.* mallows

hodi, *v.* shoot, ear

hoe, *n.f.* spell, rest

hoeden, (*-nau*) *n.f.* hoyden

hoedl, (*-au*), *n.f.* lifetime, life

hoel, -en, (*-ion*), *n.f.* nail

hoelio, *v.* nail

hoeliwr, (*-wyr*), *n.m.* nailer

hoen, *n.f.* joy, gladness; vigour

hoenus, *a.* joyous, blithesome, gay

hoenusrwydd, *n.m.* liveliness, sprightliness

hoenyn, (*-nau*), *n.m.* snare

hoew. See **hoyw**

hofran, *v.* hover

hoff, *a.* dear, fond; favourite

hoffi, *v.* like, love

hoffter, *n.m.* fondness; delight

hoffus, *a.* lovable, amiable, affectionate

hogen, (*-nod*), *n.f.* girl; **-naidd,** *a.* girlish

hogfaen, (*-feini*), *n.m.* whetstone, hone

hogi, *v.* sharpen, whet

hogyn, (*hogiau*), *n.m.* boy, lad

hongian, *v.* hang, dangle

holgar, *a.* inquisitive, curious

holi, *v.* ask, question, inquire, examine

holiad, (*-au*), *n.m.* interrogation, question

holwr, (*-wyr*), *n.m.* interrogator; catechist

holwyddoreg, (*-au*), *n.f.* catechism

holwyddori, *v.* catechize

holl, *a.* all, whole

hollalluog, *a.* almighty, omnipotent

hollalluowgrwydd, *n.m.* omnipotence

hollbresennol, *a.* omnipresent

hollbresenoldeb, *n.m.* omnipresence

hollddoeth, *a.* all-wise

hollfyd, *n.m.* universe

hollgyfoethog, *a.* almighty

holliach, *a.* whole, sound

hollol, *a.* quite

hollt, (*-au*), *n.f.* split, slit, cleft

hollti, *v.* split, cleave, slit

holltwr, (*-wyr*), *n.m.* splitter

hollwybodaeth, *n.f.* omniscience

hollwybodol, *a.* omniscient

homili, (*-ïau*), *n.f.* homily

hon, *pn.*, f. of **hwn**

honcian, *v.* waggle; jolt; limp

honedig, *a.* alleged

honiad, (*-au*), *n.m.* claim, assertion, allegation

honni, *v.* assert, allege, profess, pretend

honno, *pn.*, f. of **hwnnw**

hopran, (*-au*), *n.f.* mill-hopper; mouth

hosan, (*-au*), *n.f.* stocking

hoyw, *a.* alert, sprightly, lively, gay

hoywdeb, -der, *n.m.* sprightliness

hoywi, *v.* brighten, smarten

hual, (*-au*), *n.m.* fetter, shackle

hualog, *a.* fettered. shackled

hualu, *v.* fetter, shackle

huan, *n.f.* the sun

huawdl, *a.* eloquent

hud, *n.m.* magic, illusion, charm, enchantment

hudlath, (*-au*), *n.f.* magic wand

hudo, *v.* charm, allure, beguile

hudol, *a.* enchanting: (*-ion*) *n.m.* enchanter

hudoles, (*-au*), *n.f.* enchantress, sorceress

hudoliaeth, (*-au*), *n.f.* enchantment, allurement

hudolus, *a.* enchanting, alluring

hudwr, (*-wyr*), *n.m.* enticer, allurer

huddygl, *n.m.* soot

hufen, *n.m.* cream

hugan, (*-au*), *n.f.* cloak, covering; rug

hulio, *v.* cover, spread

hun, (*-au*), *n.f.* sleep, slumber

hun, *p.n.* self.—**ei dŷ ei h.**, his own house

hunan, (*-ain*), *pn.* self: *px.* self-

hunan-dyb, *n.m.* self-conceit

hunangar, *a.* self-loving, selfish

hunaniaeth, *n.f.* identity

hunanladdiad, *n.m.* self-murder, suicide

hunanleiddiad, (*-iaid*), *n.m.* suicide

hunanol, *a.* selfish, conceited

hunanoldeb, *n.m.* selfishness; conceit

hunanymwadiad, *n.m.* self-denial

hunanymwadu, *v.* deny oneself

hunell, (*-au*), *n.f.* wink (of sleep)

hunllef, *n.f.* nightmare

huno, *v.* sleep

huodledd, *n.m.* eloquence

hur, (*-iau*), *n.m.* hire, wage

hurio, *v.* hire

huriwr, (*-wyr*), *n.m.* hirer; hireling

hurt, *a.* hurt, stunned, stupid

hurtio, *v.* stun, stupefy

hurtrwydd, *n.m.* stupidity

hurtyn, (*-nod*), *n.m.* stupid, blockhead

huw, *n.m.* lullaby

hwb, (*hybiau*), *n.m.* push; effort; lift

hwde, (*hwdiwch*), *v. imper.* take, accept

hwn, *a. & pn.* this (one): f. **hon**

hwnnw, *a. & pn.* that one (absent): f. **honno**

hwnt, *adv.* beyond, away, aside.— **tu h.**, beyond

hwp, *n.m.* push; **-io, -o**, *v.* push

hwrdd, (*hyrddod*), *n.m.* ram

hwrdd, (*hyrddiau*), *n.m.* impulse, stroke

hwre, *v.* **hwde**

hwsmon, (*-myn*) *n.m.* farm-bailiff

hwtio, *v.* hoot, hiss

hwy, *pn.* they, them

hwyad, -en, (*hwyaid*), *n.f.* duck.

hwyhau, *v.* lengthen, elongate

hwyl, (*-iau*) *n.f.* sail; humour; religious fervour

hwylbren, (*-nau, -ni*), *n.m.* mast

hwylio, *v.* prepare, order; sail

hwyliog, *a.* fervent, eloquent

hwylus, *a.* easy, convenient, comfortable

hwyluso, *v.* facilitate

hwylustod, *n.m.* ease, facility, convenience

hwynt, *pn.* them, they

hwynt-hwy, *pn.* they, they themselves

hwyr, *a.* late: *n.m.* evening

hwyrach, *adv.* perhaps

hwyrdrwm, *a.* sluggish, drowsy, dull

hwyrfrydig, *a.* slow, tardy, reluctant

hwyrfrydigrwydd, *n.m.* tardiness, reluctance

hwyrhau, *v.* get late

hwyrol, *a.* evening

hwythau, *pn.c.* they (on their part), they also

hy, *a.* bold

hyawdl, -edd. See **hu-**

hybarch, *a.* venerable

hyblyg, *a.* flexible, pliant, pliable

hybu, *v.* improve in health

hyblygrwydd, *n.m.* flexibility, pliancy

hyd, (*-au, -oedd*), *n.m.* length: *pr.* to, till, as far as

hyder, *n.m.* confidence, trust

hyderu, *v.* confide, rely, trust

hyderus, *a.* confident

hydr, *a.* strong, powerful, bold

hydred, (*-ion*), *n.m.* longitude

hydredol, *a.* longitudinal

hydref, (*-au*), *n.m.* autumn. **—H.,** October

hydrefol, *a.* autumnal

hydrin, *a.* tractable, docile

hydwyll, *a.* gullible

hydwylledd, *n.m.* gullibility

hydwyth, *a.* elastic

hydwythedd, *n.m.* elasticity

hydyn, *a.* tractable, docile

hydd, (*-od*), *n.m.* stag

hyddysg, *a.* well versed, learned

hyf. See **hy**

hyfder, -dra, *n.m.* boldness

hyfedr, *a.* expert, skilful, clever

hyfhau, *v.* wax bold

hyfryd, *a.* pleasant, delightful, agreeable

hyfrydu, *v.* delight

hyfrydwch, *n.m.* delight, pleasure

hyfwyn, *a.* kindly, genial

hyfforddi, *v.* direct, instruct, train

hyfforddiadol, *a.* training

hyfforddiant, *n.m.* instruction, training

hyfforddus, *a.* trained

hyfforddwr, (*-wyr*), *n.m.* guide, instructor

hygar, *a.* amiable

hygarwch, *n.m.* amiability

hyglod, *a.* celebrated, renowned, famous

hyglyw, *a.* audible

hygoel, *a.* credible; credulous

hygoeledd, *n.m.* credibility; credulity

hygoelus, *a.* credulous, gullible

hygyrch, *a.* accessible

hyhi, *pn.f.* emphat. of **hi**

hylaw, *a.* handy, convenient; dexterous

hylif, (*-au*), *n.m.* & *a.* fluid, liquid

hylithr, *a.* fluent

hylosg, *a.* combustible, inflammable

hylwydd, *a.* prosperous

hyll, *a.* ugly, hideous

hylltra, *n.m.* ugliness

hyllu, *v.* mar, disfigure

hymn, (*-au*), *n.f.* hymn

hyn, *a.* & *pn.* this; these: that

hynafgwr, (*-gwyr*), *n.m.* old man, elder

hynafiad, (*-iaid*), *n.m.* ancestor

hynafiaeth, (*-au*), *n.f.* antiquity

hynafiaethol, *a.* antiquarian, archæological

hynafiaethwr, -ydd, (*wyr*), *n.m.* antiquary

hynafol, *a.* ancient

hynaws, *a.* kind, genial

hynawsedd, *n.m.* kindness, geniality   [ity

hynny, *a.* & *pn.* that; those

hynod, *a.* noted, notable, remarkable

hynodi, *v.* distinguish, characterize

hynodion, *n.pl.* peculiarities

hynodrwydd, *n.m.* peculiarity

hynt, (*-iau, -oedd*), *n.f.* way, course

hyrddio, -u, *v.* hurl, impel

hyrddwynt, (*-oedd*), *n.m.* hurricane

hyrwydd, *a.* expeditious, convenient

hyrwyddo, *v.* facilitate, promote

hyrwyddwr, (*-wyr*), *n.m.* sponsor, promoter

hysain, *a.* euphonious, sonorous

hysb, *a.* dry, barren: *f.* **hesb**

hysbio, v. dry
hysbyddu, v. exhaust, drain
hysbys, a. known, manifest, evident
hysbyseb, (-*ion*), n.f. advertisement
hysbysebu, v. advertise
hysbysebwr, (-*wyr*), n.m. advertiser
hysbysiad, (-*au*), n.m. announcement, advertisement
hysbysrwydd, n.m. information
hysbysu, v. inform, announce
hysbyswr, (-*wyr*), n.m. informant, informer
hysian, -io, v. hiss; set on, incite
hyswïaeth, n.f. housewifery
hytrach, a. rather
hywaith, a. industrious, dexterous
hywedd, a. trained, tractable

I

i, pr. to, into
i, pn.sup. I, me
iâ, n.m. ice
iach, a. healthy, well
iachâd, n.m. healing
iacháu, v. heal; save
iachawdwr, (-*wyr*), n.m. saviour
iachawdwriaeth, n.f. salvation
iachawr, (-*wyr*), n.m. healer
iachus, -ol, a. healthy, healthful, wholesome
iachusrwydd, n.m. healthfulness
iad, (-*au*), n.f. pate
iangwr, (-*wyr*), n.m. youth, knave
iaith, (*ieithoedd*), n.f. language.—**yr i. fain,** English
iâr, (*ieir*), n.f. hen
iard, (*ierdydd*), n.f. yard
iarll, (*ieirll*), n.m. earl
iarllaeth, (-*au*), n.f. earldom
iarlles, (-*au*), n.f. countess
ias, (-*au*), n.f. boiling; shiver; thrill
Iau, n.m. Jupiter. —**Dydd I.,** Thursday
iau, (*ieuau*), n.m. liver
iau, (*ieuau, ieuoedd*), n.f. yoke
iawn, a. right: n.m. right: atonement: adv. very

iawndal, n.m. compensation
iawnder, (-*au*), n.m. right, equity
iawnol, a. atoning, expiatory
Iddew, (-*on*), n.m. Jew
Iddewaeth, n.f. Judaism
Iddewaidd, a. Jewish
Iddewes, (-*au*), n.f. Jewess
Iddewig, a. Jewish
iddwf, n.m.—**tân i.,** erysipelas
ie, adv. yes, yea
iechyd, n.m. health; salvation
iechydfa, (-*feydd*), n.f. sanatorium
iechydiaeth, n.f. hygiene, sanitation
iechydol, a. hygienic, sanitary
iechydwriaeth, n.f. salvation, healing
ieitheg, n.f. philology
ieithegydd, (-*ion*, -*wyr*), n.m. philologist
ieithwedd, (-*au*, -*ion*), n.f. idiom, style
ieithydd, (-*ion*), n.m. linguist
ieithyddiaeth, n.f. linguistics, philology
ieithyddol, a. linguistic, philological
iet, (-*au*, -*iau*), n.f. gate
ieuanc, (-*ainc*), a. young; unmarried
ieuenctid, n.m. youth
ieuo, v. yoke
ifanc, (-*ainc*), a. young
ifori, n.m. ivory
ig, (-*ion*), n.m. hiccup
igam-ogam, a. zigzag
igian, v. hiccup
ing, (-*oedd*), n.m. distress, agony, anguish
ingol, a. agonizing, agonized
ill, pn. they.—**i. dau,** they both
impio, v. sprout, shoot; bud, graft
impyn, n.m. scion, shoot, graft
inc, n.m. ink
incil, n.m. tape
incwm, n.m. income
iod, n.m. iota, jot
Iôn, n.m. the Lord
Ionawr, n.m. January
Iôr, n.m. the Lord

iorwg, *n.m.* ivy
ir, *a.* fresh, green, raw
irai, *n.m.* ox-goad
iraid, (*ireidiau*), *n.m.* grease
iraidd, *a.* fresh, succulent, luxuriant
irder, *n.m.* freshness, greenness
ireidd-dra, *n.m.* freshness, vigour
ireiddio, *v.* freshen
irllawn, *a.* irate, wrathful
iro, *v.* grease, smear, rub, anoint
irwr, (*-wyr*), *n.m.* greaser
is, *a.* inferior, lower: *pr.* below, under: *px.* under-, sub-, vice-
isel, *a.* low; base; humble; depressed
iselder, (*-au*), *n.m.* lowness, depth; depression
iselfryd, *a.* humble-minded
iselfrydedd, *n.m.* humility, condescension
iselhau, -u, *v.* lower, abase, degrade
is-gadeirydd, *n.m.* vice-chairman
is-ganghellor, *n.m.* vice-chancellor
is-gapten, (*-iaid, -einiaid*), *n.m.* lieutenant
isiarll, (*-ieirll*), *n.m.* viscount
isiarllaeth, (*-au*), *n.f.* viscounty
islaw, *pr.* below, beneath
isod, *adv.* below, beneath
isop, *n.m.* hyssop
isradd, (*-au*), *n.m.* inferior
israddol, *a.* inferior
israddoldeb, *n.m.* inferiority
iswasanaethgar, *a.* subservient
isymwybyddiaeth, *n.f.* subconsciousness
ithfaen, *n.m.* granite
iwrch, (*iyrchod*), *n.m.* roebuck

J

jac-y-do, *n.m.* jackdaw
jam, *n.m.* jam: **-io,** *v.* preserve
jar, (*-iau*), *n.f.* jar
ji-binc, (*-od*), *n.f.* chaffinch
job, (*-sys*), *n.f.* job
joben, *n.f.* **jobyn,** *n.m.* job
jôc, *n.f.* joke
jocan, *v.* joke

joch, (*-iau*), *n.m.* gulp
jwg, (*jygiau*), *n.f.* jug

L

lafant, *n.m.* lavender
lamp, (*-au*), *n.f.* lamp
lapio, *v.* lap, wrap
larwm, *n.m.* alarm
lawnt, (*-iau*), *n.f.* lawn
lefain, *n.m.* leaven
lefeinio, *v.* leaven
lefel, *n.f.* level
lefeinllyd, *a.* leavened
letys, *n.pl.* (**-en,** *n.f.*) lettuce
lifrai, *n.m.f.* livery
lili, *n.f.* lily
lindys, *n.m.* caterpillar
locust, (*-iaid*), *n.m.* locust
lodes. See **herlodes**
loetran, *v.* loiter
lol, *n.f.* nonsense
lolian, *v.* talk nonsense
lôn, (*lonydd*), *n.f.* lane
lori, (*-ïau*), *n.f.* lorry
lot, (*-iau*), *n.f.* lot
lwans, lwfans, *n.m.* allowance
lwc, *n.f.* luck
lwcus, *a.* lucky
lwfer, (*-au*), *n.m.* louver, chimney
lwmp, (*lympiau*), *n.m.* lump

LL

llabed, (*-au*), *n.f.* lappet, lapel, flap
llabwst, (*-ystiau*), *n.m.* lubber, lout
llabyddio, *v.* stone
llac, *a.* slack, loose, lax
llacio, *v.* slacken, loosen, relax
llacrwydd, *n.m.* slackness, laxity
llach, (*-iau*), *n.f.* lash, slash
llachar, *a.* bright, brilliant, flashing
llachio, *v.* lash, slash
Lladin, *n.f.* Latin
lladmerydd, (*·ion*), *n.m.* interpreter
lladrad, (*-au*), *n.m.* theft, robbery
lladradaidd, *a.* stealthy, furtive
lladrata, *v.* thieve, steal

lladron. See **lleidr**
lladrones, (-au), n.f. female thief
lladronllyd, a. thievish, pilfering
lladd, v. cut; kill, slay, slaughter
lladd-dy, (-dai), n.m. slaughter-house
lladdedig, (-ion), a. killed, slain
lladdedigaeth, (-au), n.f., **lladdfa,** (-fâu, -feydd), n.f. slaughter
lladdwr, (-wyr), n.m. killer, slayer
llaes, a. long, loose. —**Y treiglad ll.,** spirant mutation
llaesod(r), n.f. litter
llaesu, v. slacken, loosen, relax, droop, flag
llaeth, n.m. milk
llaetha, v. yield milk
llaethdy, (-dai), n.m. milk-house, dairy
llaethog, a. rich in milk; milky
llafar, n.m. utterance, speech: a. vocal; loud
llafariad, (-iaid), n.f. vowel
llafn, (-au), n.m. blade
llafnes, (-au, -i), n.f. big girl, etc.
llafrwyn, n.pl. (-en, n.f.) bulrushes
llafur, (-iau), n.m. labour; corn
llafurfawr, a. elaborate
llafurio, v. labour, toil; till
llafurus, a. laborious, toilsome, painstaking
llafurwr, (-wyr), n.m. labourer, husbandman
llai, a. smaller
llaid, n.m. mud, mire
llain, (lleiniau), n.f. patch, piece, narrow strip
llais, (lleisiau), n.m. voice, vote
llaith, a. damp, moist
llaith, n.m. death
llall, (lleill), pn. other, another
llam, (-au), n.m. stride, leap, jump, bound
llamhidydd, (llamidyddion), n.m. porpoise
llamsachus, a. prancing, frisky
llamu, v. stride, leap, bound
llan, (-nau), n.f. church; village
llanastr, n.m. lumber, confusion, mess

llanc, (-iau), n.m. young man, youth, lad
llances, (-au, -i), n.f. young woman, lass
llancesig, n.f. maiden, lassie
llannerch, (llennyrch), **llanerchau** (-i, -ydd), n.f. spot, patch, glade
llanw, n.m. flow (of tide): v. flow, fill
llariaidd, a. mild, meek, gentle
llarieidd-dra, n.m. meekness, gentleness
llarieiddio, v. soothe, mollify
llarp, (-iau), n.m. shred, clout
llarpio, v. rend, tear, mangle, maul
llarpiog, a. tattered, ragged
llaswyr, (-au), n.m. psalter
llatai, (-eion), n.c. love-messenger
llath, (-au), n.f. yard, wand
llathen, (-ni), n.f. yard
llathr, a. bright, glossy, smooth
llathraidd, a. smooth; of fine growth
llathru, v. polish
llau, n.pl. (**lleuen,** n.f.), lice
llaw, (dwylaw, dwylo), n.f. hand
llawcio, v. gulp, gorge, gobble
llawchwith, a. left-handed
llawdr, (llodrau), n.m. breeches, trousers
llawdde, a. dexterous
llawddryll, (-iau), n.m. pistol, revolver
llawen, a. merry, joyful, glad, cheerful
llawenhau, v. rejoice, gladden
llawenychu, v. rejoice
llawenydd, n.m. joy, gladness, mirth
llawer, (-oedd), n.m., a. & adv. many, much
llawes, (llewys), n.f. sleeve
llawfaeth, a. reared by hand
llawfeddyg, (-on), n.m. surgeon
llawfeddygaeth, n.f. surgery
llawfeddygol, a. surgical
llaw-fer, n.f. shorthand
llawforwyn, (-forynion), n.f. hand-maid
llawfrydedd, n.m. sadness

llawffon, (*-ffyn*), *n.f.* walking-stick

llawn, *a.* full: *adv.* quite

llawnder, -dra, *n.m.* fullness, abundance

llawnodi, -iad. See **llof-**

llawr, (*lloriau*), *n.m.* floor, ground, earth

llawryf, (*-oedd*), *n.m.* laurel, bay

llawryfog, -ol, *a.* laureate

llawysgrif, (*-au*), *n.f.* manuscript

llawysgrifen, *n.f.* handwriting

lle, (*-oedd, llefydd*), *n.m.* place

lleban, (*-od*), *n.m.* clown, lubber

llecyn, (*-nau*), *n.m.* place, spot

llech, (*-au, -i*), *n.f.* slab, flag, slate

llechgi, (*-gwn*), *n.m.* sneak

llechres, (*-i*), *n.f.* table, catalogue, list

llechu, *v.* hide, shelter; lurk, skulk

llechwedd, (*-au, -i*), *n.f.* slope, hillside

llechwraidd, *a.* stealthy, underhand, insidious

lled, (*-au*), *n.m.* breadth, width

lled, *adv.* partly, rather

lledaenu, *v.* spread, disseminate, circulate

lleden, (*lledod*), *n.f.* flat-fish

lledfegin, (*-od*), *n.m.* domesticated animal, petted youth

llediaith, *n.f.m.* foreign accent

llednais, *a.* modest, delicate; meek

lledneisrwydd, *n.m.* modesty, delicacy

lled-orwedd, *v.* recline, lounge, loll

lledr, (*-au*), *n.m.* leather

lledred, (*-ion*), *n.m.* latitude

lledrith, *n.m.* magic, illusion, phantasm

lledrithio, *v.* appear, haunt

lledrithiol, *a.* illusory, illusive

lledrwr, (*-wyr*), *n.m.* leathermerchant   [spread

lledu, *v.* widen, broaden, expand,

lleddf, *a.* slanting; flat, minor; plaintive

lleddfu, *v.* flatten; soften, soothe, allay

llef, (*-au*), *n.f.* voice, cry

llefain, *v.* cry

llefaru, *v.* speak, utter

llefarwr, (*-wyr*), **-ydd,** (*-ion*), *n.m.* speaker

lleferydd, *n.m.f.* utterance, voice, speech

llefn, *a.,* f. of **llyfn**

llefrith, *n.m.* sweet milk, new milk

llegach, *a.* weak, feeble, infirm, decrepit

lleng, (*-oedd*), *n.f.* legion

lleiaf, *a.* least, smallest

lleiafrif, (*-au*), *n.m.* minority

lleian, (*-od*), *n.f.* nun

lleiandy, (*-dai*), *n.m.* nunnery, convent

lleibio, *v.* lap, lick

lleidiog, *a.* miry

lleidr, (*lladron*), *n.m.* thief, robber

lleiddiad, (*-iaid*), *n.m.* slayer

lleihad, *n.m.* diminution, decrease

lleihau, *v.* lessen, diminish, decrease

lleill. See **llall**

lleisio, *v.* sound, utter; bawl

lleisiol, *a.* vocal

lleisiwr, (*-wyr*), *n.m.* vocalist

lleithder, -dra, *n.m.* damp, moisture

lleithig, *n.f.* couch; footstool

lleitho, *v.* damp, moisten

llem, *a.,* f. of **llym**

llemain, *v.* hop, skip, leap, dance

llên, *n.f.* literature, lore, learning

llen, (*-ni*), *n.f.* sheet; veil, curtain

llencyn, *n.m.* stripling, lad

llengar, *a.* literary, learned

llengig, *n.f.* diaphragm, midriff

llenor, (*-ion*), *n.m.* literary man

llenwi, *v.* fill; flow in

llenydda, *v.* practise literature

llenyddiaeth, (*-au*), *n.f.* literature

llenyddol, *a.* literary

lleol, *a.* local

lleoli, *v.* locate; localize

lleoliad, *n.m.* location; localization

llercian, *v.* lurk, loiter

lles, *n.m.* benefit, profit, good, advantage.—**y wladwriaeth les,** the welfare state

llesâd, *n.m.* advantage, profit, benefit

llesáu, *v.* benefit, advantage

llesg, *a.* feeble, faint; languid, sluggish

llesgáu, *v.* weaken, languish, faint

llesgedd, *n.m.* weakness, languor, debility

llesiant, *n.m.* benefit, advantage

llesmair, (*-meiriau*), *n.m.* faint, swoon

llesmeirio, *v.* faint, swoon

llesol, *a.* advantageous, profitable, beneficial

llestair, llesteirio, *v.* hinder, impede, baulk

llesteiriant, *n.m.* frustration

llestr, (*-i*), *n.m.* vessel

lletchwith, *a.* awkward, clumsy

lletbai, *a.* askew, awry; oblique

lletem, (*-au*), *n.f.* wedge, stud, rivet

lletraws, *n.m.* diagonal

llety, (*-au*), *n.m.* lodging(s)

lletya, *v.* lodge

lletygar, *a.* hospitable

lletygarwch, *n.m.* hospitality

lletywr, (*-wyr*), *n.m.* lodger; host

lletywraig, (*-wragedd*), *n.f.* landlady [ing

llethol, *a.* oppressive, overpower-

llethr, (*-au*), *n.f.* slope, declivity

llethrog, *a.* sloping, steep, declining

llethu, *v.* overlie; smother; oppress, overpower, overwhelm

lleuad, (*-au*), *n.f.* moon

lleuog, *a.* lousy

llew, (*-od*), *n.m.* lion.—**dant y ll.,** dandelion

llewa, *v.* eat, devour

llewaidd, *a.* lionlike, leonine

llewes, (*-au*), *n.f.* lioness

llewpart, (*-pardiaid*), *n.m.* leopard

llewych, *n.m.* light, brightness

llewyg, (*-on*), *n.m.* faint, swoon

llewygu, *v.* faint, swoon

llewyrch, *n.m.* brightness, radiance, gleam

llewyrchu, *v.* shine

llewyrchus, *a.* flourishing, prosperous

lleyg, (*-ion*), *a.* lay

lleygwr, (*-wyr*), *n.m.* layman

lliain, (*-einiau*), *n.m.* linen; cloth; towel

lliaws, *n.m.* host, multitude

llibin, *a.* limp, feeble; awkward, clumsy

llid, *n.m.* wrath; irritation, inflammation

llidiart, (*-ardau*), *n.m.* gate

llidio, *v.* be angry, chafe, inflame

llidiog, *a.* angry, wrathful; inflamed [nation

llidiowgrwydd, *n.m.* wrath, indig-

llidus, *a.* inflamed

llieiniwr, (*-wyr*), *n.m.* linen-draper

llif, (*-iau*), *n.f.* saw

llif, (*-ogydd*), *n.m.* stream, flood, current

llifddor, (*-au*), *n.f.* floodgate

llifddwfr, (*-ddyfroedd*), *n.m.* flood, torrent

llifeiriant, (*-iaint*), *n.m.* flood

llifeirio, *v.* flow, stream

llifeiriol, *a.* streaming, overflowing

llifio, *v.* saw

llifiwr, (*-wyr*), *n.m.* sawyer

llifo, *v.* flow, stream

llifo, *v.* grind (tool)

llifo, *v.* dye

llifwr, (*-wyr*), *n.m.* dyer

llin, *n.m.* flax.—**had ll.,** linseed

llinach, (*-au*), *n.f.* lineage, pedigree

llindagu, *v.* strangle, throttle, choke

llinell, (*-au*), *n.f.* line

llinglwm, *n.m.*—**cwlwm ll.,** tight knot

lliniaru, *v.* ease, soothe, allay

llinorog, *a.* eruptive; purulent, suppurating

llinos, (*-od*), *n.f.* linnet

llinyn, (*-nau*), *n.m.* line, string, twine

llinynnu, *v.* string

lliosog. See **lluosog**

llipa, *a.* limp, flabby

llipryn, (*-nod*), *n.m.* hobbledehoy

lliprynnaidd, *a.* limp, flabby

llith, *n.m.* mash

llith, (*-iau, -oedd*), *n.f.* lesson, lecture

llithio, v. entice, allure, seduce; feed
llithriad, (-au), n.m. slip, glide
llithrig, a. slippery, glib, fluent
llithrigrwydd, n.m. slipperiness, glibness
llithro, v. slip, glide, slide
lliw, (-iau), n.m. colour, hue, dye
lliwio, v. colour, dye
lliwiog, a. coloured
llo, (lloi, lloeau), n.m. calf
lloches, (-au), n.f. refuge, shelter, den
llochesu, v. harbour, shelter
llochi, v. stroke, caress, fondle
llodig, a. in heat (of a sow)
llodrau, n.pl. trousers, breeches
lloer, (-au), n.f. moon
lloerig, a. & n.m. lunatic
llofnod, -iad, (-au), n.m. signature
llofnodi, v. sign
llofrudd, (-ion), n.m. murderer
llofruddiaeth, (-au), n.f. murder
llofruddio, v. murder
llofruddiog, a. guilty of murder
lloffa, v. glean
lloffion, n.pl. gleanings
llofft, (-ydd), n.f. loft, bedroom, gallery
lloffwr, (-wyr), n.m. gleaner
lloffyn, n.m. bundle of gleanings
llog, (-au), n.m. interest: **-i**, v. hire
llogell, (-au), n.f. pocket
llogwr, (-wyr), n.m. hirer
llong, (-au), n.f. ship
llongddrylliad, (-au), n.m. shipwreck
llongwr, (-wyr), n.m. sailor
llongwriaeth, n.f. seamanship
llom, a. f. of **llwm**
llon, a. glad, merry
llonaid, llond, n.m. full
llonder, n.m. gladness, joy
llongyfarch, v. congratulate
llongyfarchiad, (-au, -archion), n.m. congratulation
lloniant, n.m. joy, cheer
llonni, v. cheer, gladden
llonydd, a. quiet, still: n.m. quiet, calm
llonyddu, v. quiet, still, calm

llonyddwch, n.m. quietness, quiet
llorio, v. floor
llorp, (-iau), n.f. cart-shaft
llosg, n.m. & a. burning
llosgach, n.m. incest
llosgfa, (-fâu, -feydd), n.f. burning
llosgfynydd, (-oedd), n.m. volcano
llosgi, v. burn, scorch; smart
llosgwrn, (-yrnau), n.m. tail
llosgyrnog, a. tailed
llostlydan, (-od), n.m. beaver
llu, (-oedd), n.m. host
lluched, n.pl. (-en, n.f.), lightning
lluchio, v. throw, fling, pelt
lluchiwr, (-wyr), n.m. thrower
lludlyd, a. ashy
lludu, lludw, n.m. ashes, ash
lludded, n.m. weariness, fatigue
lluddedig, a. wearied, tired, fatigued
lluddedu, v. tire, weary
lluddias, -io, v. hinder; forbid
lluest, (-au), n.m. tent, booth
lluestfa, (-feydd) n.f. encampment
lluestu, v. encamp
lluesty, (-tai), n.m. tent, booth
llugoer, a. lukewarm
lluman, (-au), n.m. banner, standard, ensign
llumon, n.m. chimney, stack
llun, (-iau), n.m. form, image, picture
Llun, Dydd Llun, n.m. Monday
lluniaeth, n.m. food, nourishment
lluniaethu, v. order, ordain, decree
lluniaidd, a. shapely
llunio, v. form, shape, fashion
lluniwr, (-wyr), n.m. former, maker
lluosi, v. multiply
lluosiad, n.m. multiplication
lluosill, -afog, a. polysyllabic
lluosog, a. numerous; plural
lluosogi, v. multiply
lluosogiad, n.m. multiplication
lluosydd, n.m. multiplier
llurgunio, v. mangle, mutilate
llurguniwr, (-wyr), n.m. mangler, mutilator
llurig, (-au), n.f. coat of mail, cuirass

llurigog, *a.* mail-clad
llus, *n.pl.* (**-en**, *n.f.*), bilberries
llusern, (*-au*), *n.f.* lantern, lamp
llusg, (*-ion*), *n.m.* draught; drag
llusgfad, (*-au*), *n.m.* tugboat
llusgo, *v.* drag; trail; crawl; drawl
llusgwr, (*-wyr*), *n.m.* dragger, slow-coach
llutrod, *n.m.* mire, ashes, debris
lluwch, *n.m.* dust; spray; snow-drift
lluydd, *n.m.* host, army
llw, (*-on*), *n.m.* oath
llwch, *n.m.* dust, powder
llwdn, (*llydnod*), *n.m.* young of animals
llwfr, *a.* timid, cowardly
llwfrdra, *n.m.* cowardice
llwfrddyn, **-gi**, *n.m.* coward
llwfrhau, *v.* faint
llwglyd, *a.* hungry, famished
llwgr, *n.m.* corruption: *a.* corrupt
llwgrwobrwy, (*-on*), *n.m.* bribe
llwgrwobrwyo, *v.* bribe
llwgu, *v.* starve, famish
llwm, *a.* bare; destitute; poor: *f.* **llom**
llwnc, *n.m.* gulp, swallow; gullet
llwncdestun, *n.m.* toast (health)
llwr, llwrw, *n.m.* track.—**ll. ei ben**, headlong.—**ll. ei gefn**, backwards
llwy, (*-au*), *n.f.* spoon, ladle
llwyaid, (*-eidiau*), *n.f.* spoonful
llwybr, (*-au*), *n.m.* path, track
llwybreiddio, *v.* direct, forward
llwybro, *v.* walk
llwyd, *a.* brown; grey; pale; hoary
llwydaidd, *a.* greyish, palish
llwydi, **llwydni**, *n.m.* greyness; mould, mildew
llwydnos, *n.f.* dusk, twilight
llwydo, *v.* turn grey; become mouldy
llwydrew, *n.m.* hoar-frost
llwydrewi, *v.* cast hoar-frost
llwydd, **-iant**, *n.m.* success, prosperity
llwyddiannus, *a.* successful, prosperous
llwyddo, *v.* succeed, prosper

llwyfan, (*-nau*), *n.m.f.* platform, stage
llwyfen, (*llwyf*), *n.f.* elm
llwyn, (*-i*), *n.m.* grove; bush
llwyn, (*-au*), *n.f.* loin
llwynog, (*-od*), *n.m.* fox
llwynoges, (*-au*), *n.f.* vixen
llwynwst, *n.f.* lumbago
llwyo, *v.* use a spoon; ladle
llwyr, *a.* entire, complete, total: *adv.* entirely, altogether: *px.* total
llwyredd, *n.m.* entireness, completeness
llwyrymatal, **-ymwrthod**, *v.* abstain totally
llwyth, (*-au*), *n.m.* tribe, clan
llwyth, (*-i*), *n.m.* load, burden
llwytho, *v.* load, burden
llwythog, *a.* laden, burdened
llychlyd, *a.* dusty
llychwino, *v.* spot, tarnish, soil, sully
llychyn, *n.m.* particle of dust, mote
llydan, *a.* broad, wide
llydnu, *v.* bring forth, foal
llyfn, *a.* smooth, sleek: *f.* **llefn**
llyfnder, **-dra**, *n.m.* smoothness, sleekness
llyfndew, *a.* plump, sleek
llyfnhau, *v.* smooth, level
llyfnu, *v.* smooth, level; harrow
llyfr, (*-au*), *n.m.* book
llyfrbryf, (*-ed*), *n.m.* bookworm
llyfrdy, (*-dai*), *n.m.* library
llyfrfa, (*-oedd*), *n.f.* library; book-room
llyfrgell, (*-oedd*), *n.f.* library
llyfrgellydd, (*-ion*), *n.m.* librarian
llyfrwerthwr, (*-wyr*), *n.m.* book-seller
llyfryddiaeth, *n.f.* bibliography
llyfryn, (*-nau*), *n.m.* booklet, pamphlet
llyfu, *v.* lick
llyffant, (*-od, llyffaint*), *n.m.* frog, toad
llyffethair, (*-eiriau*), *n.f.* fetter, shackle
llyffetheirio, *v.* fetter, shackle
llyg, (*-od*), *n.m.f.* shrew(-mouse)

llygad, (*llygaid*), *n.m.* eye
llygad-dynnu, *v.* bewitch
llygadog, *a.* eyed, sharp-eyed
llygadrwth, *a.* wide-eyed, staring
llygadrythu, *v.* stare
llygadu, *v.* eye
llygatraff, *a.* keen-eyed, sharp-sighted
llygedyn, *n.m.* ray of light
llygeidiog, *a.* eyed
llygoden, (*llygod*), *n.f.* mouse.—**ll. fawr, ll. ffrengig,** rat
llygota, *v.* catch mice
llygotwr, (*-wyr*), *n.m.* mouser, ratter: *f.* **llygotwraig**
llygradwy, *a.* corruptible
llygredig, *a.* corrupt, depraved, degraded
llygredigaeth, (*-au*), *n.f.* corruption
llygredd, *n.m.* corruptness, depravity
llygriad, (*-au*), *n.m.* corruption, adulteration
llygru, *v.* corrupt, adulterate
llygrwr, (*-wyr*), *n.m.* corrupter, adulterator
llynges, (*-au*), *n.f.* fleet, navy
llyngeswr, (*-wyr*), *n.m.* navy-man
llyngesydd, (*-ion*), *n.m.* admiral
llyngyr, *n.pl.* (**-en,** *n.f.*), (intestinal) worms
llym, *a.* sharp, keen, severe: *f.* **llem**
llymaid, (*-eidiau*), *n.m.* sip, drink
llymarch, (*llymeirch*), *n.m.* oyster
llymder, *n.m.* sharpness, keenness, severity
llymder, -dra, *n.m.* bareness, poverty
llymeitian, -io, *v.* sip, tipple
llymeitiwr, (*-wyr*), *n.m.* tippler, sot
llymhau, *v.* make bare (from **llwm**)
llymhau, *v.* sharpen (from **llym**)
llymriaid, *n.pl.* (**-ïen,** *n.f.*), sand-eels
llymrieita, *v.* catch sand-eels
llymrig, *a.* crude, raw, slipshod
llymru, *n.m.* flummery
llymu, *v.* sharpen, whet

llyn, (*-noedd*), *n.m.* lake, pond, pool; drink
llynciad, (*-au*), *n.m.* draught, gulp
llynclyn, (*-noedd*), *n.m.* vortex, gulf
llyncu, *v.* swallow, gulp, absorb
llyncwr, (*-wyr*), *n.m.* swallower, guzzler
llynedd, *n.f.* last year
llyo, *v.* lick
llys, (*-oedd*), *n.m.* court, hall, palace
llysaidd, *a.* courtly, polite
llysblant, *n.pl.* step-children
llyschwaer, *n.f.* step-sister
llysenw, (*-au*), *n.m.* nickname
llysenwi, *v.* nickname
llysfab, *n.m.* step-son
llysfam, *n.f.* step-mother
llysferch, *n.f.* step-daughter
llysfrawd, *n.m.* step-brother
llysgenhadaeth, *n.f.* embassy, legation
llysgenhadol, *a.* ambassadorial
llysgenhadwr, llysgennad, (*-genhadon*), *n.m.* ambassador
llysiau, *n.pl.* (**-ieuyn,** *n.m.*), herbs, vegetables
llysieueg, *n.f.* botany
llysieuol, *a.* herbal, vegetable
llysieuydd, (*-ion, -wyr*), *n.m.* botanist
llysnafedd, *n.m.* snivel, slime
llystad, *n.m.* step-father
llysu, *v.* reject
llysywen, (*llysywod*), *n.f.* eel
llysywenna, *v.* catch eels
llythrennol, *a.* literal
llythyr, (*-au*), *n.m.* letter, epistle
llythyrdoll, (*-au*), *n.f.* postage
llythyrdy, (*-dai*), *n.m.* post-office
llythyren, (*llythrennau*), *n.f.* letter, type
llythyrnod, (*-au*), *n.m.* postage-stamp
llythyrwr, (*-wyr*), *n.m.* letter-writer
llyw, (*-iau*), *n.m.* ruler; rudder, helm
llywaeth, *a.* hand-fed, tame, pet
llywiawdwr, (*-wyr*), *n.m.* ruler, governor

llywio, *v.* rule, govern, direct, steer
llywionen, *n.f.* canvas sheet
llywiwr, (*-wyr*), *n.m.* steersman, helmsman [ment
llywodraeth, (*-au*), *n.f.* govern-
llywodraethol, *a.* governing, dominant
llywodraethu, *v.* govern, rule
llywodraethwr, (*-wyr*), *n.m.* governor, ruler
llywydd, (*-ion*), *n.m.* president
llywyddiaeth, (*-au*), *n.f.* presidency
llywyddol, *a.* presidential
llywyddu, *v.* preside

M

mab, (*meibion*), *n.m.* boy, son; man, male
mabaidd, *a.* filial
maban, (*-od*), *n.m.* babe, baby
mabandod, *n.m.* childhood, infancy
mabinogi, *n.m.* tale, story
mabmaeth, (*-au*, *-od*), *n.m.* foster-son
maboed, *n.m.* childhood, infancy, youth
mabolaeth, *n.f.* sonship; boyhood, youth
mabolaidd, *a.* youthful, boyish
mabolgamp, (*-au*), *n.f.* game, sport, feat
mabsant, *n.m.* patron saint
mabwysiad, *n.m.* adoption
mabwysiadol, *a.* adoptive; adopted
mabwysiadu, *v.* adopt
macrell, (*mecryll*), *n.f.m.* mackerel
macwy, (*-aid*), *n.m.* youth, page
mach, (*meichiau*), *n.m.* surety, bail
machlud, -o, *v.* set, go down —**machlud haul,** sunset
machludiad, *n.m.* setting, going down
machnïydd, *n.m.* mediator
mad, *a.* good, goodly
madalch, madarch, *n.m.* toadstool

madrondod, *n.m.* giddiness, stupe-faction
madroni, *v.* make or become giddy
madru, *v.* putrefy, fester, rot
madruddyn, *n.m.* cartilage.—**m. y cefn,** spinal cord
maddau, *v.* pardon, forgive, remit
maddeuant, *n.m.* pardon, forgive-ness
maddeugar, *a.* of a forgiving disposition
maddeuol, *a.* pardoning, forgiving
maddeuwr, (*-wyr*), *n.m.* pardoner
mae, *v.* is, are; there is, there are
maeden, *n.f.* slut, jade
maeddu. See **baeddu**
mael, (*-ion*), *n.f.* gain, profit; traffic
maelfa, (*-oedd*), *n.f.* shop
maen, (*meini*), *n.m.* stone
maenol, maenor, (*-au*), *n.f.* manor
maentumio, *v.* maintain
maer, (*-od, meiri*), *n.m.* mayor
maeres, (*-au*), *n.f.* mayoress
maerol, *a.* mayoral
maeryddiaeth, *n.f.* mayoralty
maes, (*meysydd*), *n.m.* field.—**Im.,** out
maeslywydd, (*-ion*), *n.m.* field-marshal
maestir, (*-oedd*), *n.m.* open country, plain
maestref, (*-i, -ydd*), *n.f.* suburb
maeth, *n.m.* nourishment, nutri-ment
maethgen, (*-nau*), *n.f.* beating
maethlon, *a.* nourishing, nutri-tious
maethu, *v.* nourish, nurture
maethydd, (*-ion*), *n.m.* nourisher
mafon, *n.pl.* (**-en,** *n.f.*), raspberries
magl, (*-au*), *n.f.* snare; mesh
maglu, *v.* snare, mesh, trip
magnel, (*-au*), *n.f.* gun, cannon
magnelwr, (*-wyr*), *n.m.* gunner
magu, *v.* breed, rear, nurse; gain, acquire [ture
magwraeth, *n.f.* nourishment, nur-
magwyr, (*-ydd*), *n.f.* wall
maharen, (*meheryn*), *n.m.* ram; wether

Mai, *n.m.* May

mai, *c.* that it is

maidd, *n.m.* whey

mail, (*meiliau*), *n.f.* bowl, basin

main, (*meinion*), *a.* fine, slender, thin.—**m. y cefn,** small of the back

mainc, (*meinciau*), *n.f.* bench, form, seat

maint, *n.m.* size, quantity, number

maintioli, *n.m.* size, stature

maip, *n.pl.* (**meipen,** *n.f.*), turnips

maith, (*meithion*), *a.* long, tedious

malais, *n.m.* malice

maldod, *n.m.* dalliance, affectation

maldodi, *v.* pet, pamper, indulge

maleisus, *a.* malicious

malio, *v.* care, mind, heed

malu, *v.* grind, mince, chop, smash

malurio, *v.* pound; crumble, moulder

malurion, *n.pl.* fragments, debris

malwod, *n.pl.* (**-en, malwen,** *n.f.*), snails

malwr, (*-wyr*), *n.m.* grinder

mall, *n.f.* blight.—**y f.,** Belial, perdition

malltod, *n.m.* rot, blight, blast

mallu, *v.* rot, blast

mam, (*-au*), *n.f.* mother.—**mam-gu** grandmother

mamaeth, (*-od*), *n.f.* nurse

mamog, (*-iaid*), *n.f.* dam, sheep with young

man, (*-nau*), *n.m.f.* place, spot; blemish

mân, *a.* small, fine, petty

maneg, (*menig*), *n.f.* glove, gauntlet

mangre, *n.f.* place, spot [tiæ

manion, *n.pl.* scraps, trifles, minu-

mant, (*-au*), *n.m.f.* mouth, lip

mantach, *a.* toothless

mantais, (*-eision*), *n.f.* advantage

manteisio, *v.* take advantage, profit

manteisiol, *a.* advantageous

mantell, (*-oedd, mentyll*), *n.f.* mantle

mantellog, *a.* mantled

mantol, (*-ion*), *n.f.* balance

mantoli, *v.* turn scale, balance, weigh

mantolen, (*-ni*), *n.f.* balance-sheet

manwaidd, *a.* delicate, fine

manwl, *a.* exact, precise, strict, particular

manylion, *n.pl.* particulars, details

manylrwydd, *n.m.* exactness, precision

manylu, *v.* go into detail, particularize

manylwch, *n.m.* exactness, precision

marc, (*-iau*), *n.m.* mark

marcio, *v.* mark

march, (*meirch*), *n.m.* horse, stallion

marchnad, (*-oedd*), *n.f.* market

marchnadfa, (*-oedd*), *n.f.* market-place

marchnata, *v.* market, trade

marchnatawr, (*-wyr*), *n.m.* merchant

marchnaty, (*-tai*), *n.m.* market (-house)

marchocáu, *v.* ride a horse

marchog, (*-ion*), *n.m.* horseman, rider; knight

marchogaeth, *v.* ride

marchogwr, (*-wyr*), *n.m.* rider, horseman

marchredyn, *n.pl.* (**-en,** *n.f.*) polypody fern

marchwellt, *n.m.* tall coarse grass

marian, *n.m.* holm, strand, moraine

marlad, *n.m.* drake

marmor, *n.m.* marble

marsiandïaeth, *n.f.* merchandise

marsiandwr, (*-wyr*), *n.m.* merchant

marw, *v.* die

marw, (*meirw, meirwon*), *n. & a.* dead

marwaidd, *a.* lifeless, sluggish

marweidd-dra, *n.m.* deadness, sluggishness

marweiddio, *v.* deaden, mortify

marwhad, *n.m.* mortification

marwhau, *v.* deaden, mortify

marwnad, (*-au*), *n.f.* lament, elegy

marwol, *a.* deadly, mortal, fatal

marwolaeth, (*-au*), *n.f.* death

marwoldeb, *n.m.* mortality

marwolion, *n.pl.* mortals

marwor, *n.pl.* (**-yn,** *n.m.*), embers; charcoal

marwydos, *n.pl.* embers

masgl, (**-au**), *n.f.* shell, pod

masglo, -u, *v.* shell; interlace

masnach, (**-au**), *n.f.* trade, traffic, commerce

masnachdy, (**-dai**), *n.m.* business-house, shop

masnachol, *a.* commercial, business

masnachu, *v.* do business, trade, traffic

masnachwr, (**-wyr**), *n.m.* dealer, merchant

masw, *a.* soft, tender; wanton

maswedd, *n.m.* wantoness, ribaldry

masweddol, *a.* wanton, ribald

mat, (**-iau**), *n.m.* mat

mater, (**-ion**), *n.m.* matter

materol, *a.* material; materialistic

materoliaeth, *n.f.* materialism

matog, (**-au**), *n.f.* mattock

matras, (**-resi**), *n.f.* mattress

math, (**-au**), *n.m.* sort, kind

mathemateg, *n.m.* mathematics

mathru, *v.* trample, tread

mathrwr, (**-wyr**), *n.m.* trampler

mawl, *n.m.* praise

mawn, *c.n.* (**-en,** *n.f.*) peat

mawnog, *a.* peaty: *n.f.* peat-bog

mawr, (**-ion**), *a.* big, great, large

mawredd, *n.m.* greatness, grandeur, majesty

mawreddog, *a.* grand, majestic; grandiose

mawrfrydig, *a.* magnanimous

mawrfrydigrwydd, *n.m.* magnanimity

mawrhau, *v.* magnify, enlarge

mawrhydi, *n.m.* majesty

Mawrth, *n.m.* Mars; March. —**Dydd M.,** Tuesday

mawrygu, *v.* magnify, extol

mebyd, *n.m.* childhood, infancy, youth

mechni, (**-ion**), *n.m.* surety, bail

mechnïaeth, *n.f.* suretyship

mechnïo, *v.* go bail, become surety

mechnïol, *a.* vicarious

mechnïydd, (**-ion**), *n.m.* surety, bail

medel, (**-au**), *n.f.* reaping; reaping party

medelwr, (**-wyr**), *n.m.* reaper

medi, *v.* reap

Medi, *n.m.* September

medr, *n.m.* skill, ability

medru, *v.* know, be able

medrus, *a.* clever, skilful

medrusrwydd, *n.m.* cleverness, skilfulness, skill

medd, *n.m.* mead

medd, *v.* says

meddal, *a.* soft, tender

meddalhau, meddalu, *v.* soften

meddalwch, *n.m.* softness

meddiannol, *a.* possessing, possessive

meddiannu, *v.* possess, occupy

meddiant, (**-iannau**), *n.m.* possession

meddu, *v.* possess, own

meddw, (**-on**), *a.* drunk, intoxicated

meddwdod, *n.m.* drunkenness, intoxication

meddwi, *v.* get drunk, intoxicate, inebriate

meddwl, *v.* think; mean: (**-yliau**), *n.m.* thought; meaning; opinion

meddwol, *a.* intoxicating

meddwyn, (**-won**), *n.m.* drunkard, inebriate

meddyg, (**-on**), *n.m.* physician, doctor

meddyginiaeth, (**-au**), *n.f.* medicine, remedy

meddyginiaethol, *a.* medicinal, remedial

meddyginiaethu, *v.* cure, remedy, heal

meddyglyn, *n.m.* medicine, drug

meddygol, *a.* medicinal; medical

meddylddrych, (**-au**), *n.m.* idea

meddyleg, *n.f.* psychology

meddylfryd, *n.m.* mind, affection, bent

meddylgar, *a.* thoughtful

meddylgarwch, *n.m.* thoughtfulness

meddyliol, *a.* mental, intellectual

meddyliwr, (*-wyr*), *n.m.* thinker

meddylrith, (*-iau*), *n.m.* mental image, idea, conception

mefl, (*-au*), *n.m.* disgrace, blot, blemish

mefus, *n.pl.* (**-en**, *n.f.*), strawberries

megin, (*-au*), *n.f.* bellows

megino, *v.* work bellows, blow

megis, *c. & pr.* as, so as, like a

Mehefin, *n.m.* June

meichiad, (*-iaid*), *n.m.* swineherd

meichiau, (*-iafon*), *n.m.* surety, bail

meidrol *a.* finite

meidroldeb, *n.m.* finiteness

meiddion, *n.pl.* curds and whey

meiddlyd, *a.* wheyey, curdled

meilart, *n.m.* drake

meilwng, (*-yngau*), *n.m.* small of leg, ankle

meillion, *n.pl.* (**-en**, *n.f.*), clover

meinder, *n.m.* fineness, slenderness

meindio, *v.* mind, care

meinedd, *n.m.* slender part, small

meinhau, *v.* grow slender, taper

meingefn, *n.m.* small of the back

meini. See **maen**

meinir, *n.f.* maiden

meinllais, *n.m.* shrill voice, treble

meipen, (*maip*), *n.f.* turnip

meirch. See **march**

meirioli, *v.* thaw

meirw. See **marw**

meistr, (*-iaid*, *-i*, *-adoedd*), *n.m.* master

meistres, (*-i*), *n.f.* mistress

meistrolaeth, *n.f.* mastery

meistrolgar, *a.* masterful, masterly

meistroli, *v.* master

meitin, *n.m.*—**ers m.**, some time since

meitr, (*-au*), *n.m.* mitre

meithder, *n.m.* length

meithrin, *v.* nurture, rear, foster

meithrinfa, (*-oedd*), *n.f.* nursery

mêl *n.m.* honey

mela, *v.* gather honey

melan, *n.f.* melancholy

melen, *a.*, f. of **melyn**

melfaréd, *n.m.* corduroy

melfed, *n.m.* velvet

melin, (*-au*), *n.f.* mill

melinydd, (*-ion*), *n.m.* miller

melodaidd, *a.* melodious

melodi, *n.m.* melody

melyn, *a.* yellow: *f.* **melen:** *n.m.* yellow.—**m. wy**, yolk of egg. **Y clefyd m.**, jaundice

melynaidd, *a.* yellowish, tawny

melynder, **-dra**, *n.m.* yellowness

melynddu, *a.* tawny, swarthy

melyngoch, *a.* yellowish red, orange

melyni, *n.m.* yellowness; jaundice

melynu, *v.* yellow

melynwyn, *a.* yellowish white, cream

melys, *a.* sweet: (*-ion*), *n.pl.* sweets

melyster, **-tra**, *n.m.* sweetness

melysu, *v.* sweeten

mellt, *n.pl.* (**-en**, *n.f.*), lightning

melltennu. *v.* flash lightning

melltigaid, **-edig**, *a.* accursed, cursed

melltith, (*-ion*), *n.f.* curse

melltithio, *v.* curse

memrwn, (*-rynau*), *n.m.* parchment, vellum

men, (*-ni*), *n.f.* wain, waggon, cart

mên, *a.* mean

mendio, *v.* mend, heal, recover

menestr, *n.m.* cup-bearer

menig. See **maneg**

mentr, *n.f.* venture, hazard

mentro, *v.* venture, hazard

mentrus, *a.* venturesome

menu, *v.* mark, impress, affect

menwyd, *n.m.* pleasure, mirth, joy, delight

mêr, (*merion*), *n.m.* marrow

merch, (*-ed*), *n.f.* daughter, woman

merchedaidd, *a.* effeminate

Mercher, *n.m.* Mercury. —**Dydd M.**, Wednesday

merddwr, (*-ddyfroedd*), *n.m.* stagnant water

merf, **-aidd**, *a.* insipid, tasteless, flat

merfdra, **merfeidd-dra**, *n.m.* insipidity

merlyn, (-nod, merlod), n.m. pony: f. **merlen**

merthyr, (-on, -i), n.m. martyr

merthyrdod, n.m. martyrdom

merthyru, v. martyr

merwindod, n.m. numbness, tingling

merwino, v. benumb, tingle, smart

meryw, n.pl. (-en, n.f.), juniper trees

mes, n.pl. (-en, n.f.), acorns

mesa, v. gather acorns

mesur, (-au), n.m. measure; metre; tune; bill

mesur, v. measure, mete

mesureg, n.f. mensuration

mesuriad, (-au), n.m. measurement

mesurwr, (-wyr), n.m. measurer; surveyor

mesurydd, (-ion), n.m. measurer, meter

metel, (-oedd), n.m. metal; mettle

metelaidd, a. metallic

metelydd, (-ion), n.m. metallurgist

metelyddiaeth, n.f. metallurgy

meth, (-ion), n.m. miss, failure

methdaliad, (-au), n.m. bankruptcy

methdalwr, (-wyr), n.m. bankrupt

methedig, (-ion), a. decrepit, infirm, disabled

methiannus, a. failing, decayed

methiant, n.m. failure

methl, n.m. unfair advantage, embarrassment

methu, v. fail, miss

meudwy, (-aid, -od), n.m. hermit, recluse

meudwyaidd, a. hermit-like, retiring

meudwyol, a. eremitic

mewian, v. mew

mewn, pr. in, within

mewnforio, v. import: (-ion), n.pl. imports

mewnol, a. inward, internal; subjective

mi, pn. I, me

mieri, n.pl. (**miaren,** n.f.), brambles

mig, n.f.—**chwarae m.,** play bopeep

mign, -en, n.f. bog, quagmire

migwrn, (-yrnau), n.m. knuckle; ankle

mil, (-od), n.m. animal

mil, (-oedd), n.f. thousand

milain, a. angry, fierce, savage, cruel

mileindra, n.m. savageness, ferocity

mileinig, a. savage, ferocious, malignant

milfed, a. thousandth

milfeddyg, (-on), n.m. veterinary surgeon [number

milfil, n.f. million, an indefinite

milflwyddiant, n.m. millennium

milgi, (-gwn), n.m. greyhound

miliast, (-ieist), n.f. greyhound bitch

miliwn, (-iynau), n.f. million

miliynydd, (-ion), n.m. millionaire

milodfa, (-oedd, -feydd), n.f. menagerie

milofydd, (-ion), n.m. zoologist

milofyddiaeth, n.f. zoology

milofyddol, a. zoological

milwr, (-wyr), n.m. soldier

milwraidd, a. soldierly

milwriad, (-iaid), n.m. colonel

milwriaeth, n.f. warfare

milwriaethus, a. militant

milwrio, v. militate

milwrol, a. military

milyn, (milod), n.m. beast

milltir, (-oedd), n.f. mile

min, (-ion), n.m. edge; brink; lip

mindlws, a. simpering, affected, precious

mingamu, v. grimace

minio, v. edge, sharpen; make impression

miniog, a. sharp, keen, cutting

minnau, pn.c. I (on my part), I also

mintai, (-eioedd), n.f. band, troop

mintys, n.m. mint

mirain, a. fair, beautiful, comely

mireinder, n.m. beauty, comeliness

miri, n.m. merriment, fun, festivity

mis, (-oedd), n.m. month

misio, *v.* miss, fail

misol, (*-ion*), *a.* monthly

miswrn, (*-yrnau*), *n.m.* visor, mask, wimple

miwsig, *n.m.* music

mo, contr. of **dim o.—nid oes mo'i debyg** there is none like him

moch, *n.pl.* (**-yn,** *n.m.*), swine, pigs, hogs

mocha, *v.* pig, litter

mochaidd, *a.* swinish, hoggish

mochynnaidd, *a.* piggish, swinish

modfedd, (*-i*), *n.f.* inch

modrwy, (*-au*), *n.f.* ring

modrwyo, *v.* ring

modrwyog, *a.* ringed

modryb, (*-edd*), *n.f.* aunt

modur, (*-on*), *n.m.* motor

modurdy, (*-dai*), *n.m.* motor-house, garage

modurwr, (*-wyr*), *n.m.* motorist

modd, (*-ion,* *-au*), *n.m.* mode, manner; mood

moddion, *n.pl.* means; medicine

moel, (*-ion*), *a.* bare, bald; hornless, polled

moel, (*-ydd*), *n.f.* hill

moeli, *v.* make or become bald; hang (ears)

moelni, *n.m.* bareness, baldness

moelyn, *n.m.* bald-head

moes, *v. imp.* give, bring hither

moes, (*-au*), *n.f.* morality; (*pl.*) manners, morals

moeseg, *n.f.* ethics

Moesenaidd, *a.* Mosaic

moesgar, *a.* mannerly, polite

moesgarwch, *n.m.* politeness

moesol, *a.* moral, ethical

moesoldeb, *n.m.* morality

moesoli, *v.* moralize

moesolwr, (*-wyr*), *n.m.* moralist

moeswers, (*-i*), *n.f.* moral

moeth, (*-au*), *n.m.* luxury, indulgence

moethi, *v.* pamper, indulge

moethlyd, *a.* pampered, spoilt

moethus, *a.* luxurious, pampered

moethusrwydd, *n.m.* luxuriousness, luxury

molawd, *n.m.f.* eulogy, panegyric

moled, (*-au*), *n.f.* kerchief; muffler

moli, moliannu, *v.* praise, laud

moliannus, *a.* praised, to be praised

moliant, (*-iannau*), *n.m.* praise

mollt, (*myllt*), *n.m.* wether

molltgig, *n.m.* mutton

moment, (*-au*), *n.f.* moment

monni, *v.* sulk, pout

mopren. See **ymotbren**

môr, (*moroedd*), *n.m.* sea, ocean

mor, *adv.* how, so, as

mordaith, (*-deithiau*), *n.f.* voyage

mordeithiwr, (*-wyr*), *n.m.* voyager

mordwyaeth, *n.f.* navigation

mordwyo, *v.* go by sea, voyage, sail

mordwywr, (*-wyr*), *n.m.* mariner, sailor

morddwyd, (*-ydd*), *n.f.m.* thigh

morfa, (*-feydd*), *n.m.* moor, fen, marsh

morfil, (*-od*), *n.m.* whale

môr-forwyn, (*-forynion*), *n.f.* mermaid

morfran, (*-frain*), *n.f.* cormorant

morgainc, (*-geinciau*), *n.f.* gulf

môr-gerwyn, *n.f.* whirlpool, vortex, abyss

morglawdd, (*-gloddiau*), *n.m.* embankment, mole

morgrug, *n.pl.* (**-yn,** *n.m.*), ants

morio, *v.* voyage, sail

môr-ladrad, (*-au*), *n.m.* piracy

môr-leidr, (*-ladron*), *n.m.* pirate

morlo, (*-loi*), *n.m.* sea-calf, seal

morllyn, (*-noedd*), *n.f.m.* lagoon

moron, *n.pl.* (**-en,** *n.f.*), carrots

mortais, (*-eisiau*), *n.f.* mortise

morteisio, *v.* mortise

morter, (*-au*), *n.m.* mortar

morthwyl, (*-ion*), *n.m.* hammer

morthwylio, *v.* hammer

morthwyliwr, (*-wyr*), *n.m.* hammerer

morwr, (*-wyr*), *n.m.* seaman, sailor, mariner

morwriaeth, *n.f.* seamanship, navigation

morwydd, *n.pl.* **(-en,** *n.f.*), mulberry-trees

morwyn, (*-ynion*), *n.f.* maid, virgin

morwyndod, *n.m.* virginity

morwynig, *n.f.* maiden

morwynol, *a.* virgin, maiden

moryd, (*-iau*), *n.f.* estuary

moryn, (*-nau*), *n.m.* billow, breaker, a 'sea'

muchudd, *n.m.* jet

mud, *a.* dumb, mute; dull

mudan, (*-od*), *n.m.* mute

mudandod, *n.m.* muteness

mudanes, (*-au*), *n.f.* dumb woman

mudiad, (*-au*), *n.m.* removal; movement

mudo, *v.* move, remove

mudwr, (*-wyr*), *n.m.* remover

mul, (*-od*), *a.* mule; donkey

mulaidd, *a.* mulish, asinine

mules, (*-au*), *n.f.* she-mule, she-ass

mulfran, (*-frain*), *n.f.* cormorant

mun. See **bun**

muner, *n.m.* lord

munud, (*-au*), *n.m.f.* minute, moment

munud, (*-iau*), *n.m.* sign, gesture; nod

munudio, *v.* make gestures, gesticulate

mur, (*-iau*), *n.m.* wall

murddun, (*-od*), *n.m.* ruin, ruins

murio, *v.* wall

murlen, (*-ni*), *n.f.* poster, placard

murmur, *v.* murmur: (*-on*), *n.m.* murmur

murn, *n.m.* injury; murder

mursen, (*-nod*), *n.f.* coquette; prude

mursendod, *n.m.* prudery, affectation

mursennaidd, *a.* prudish, affected

mursennu, *v.* coquette, mince

musgrell *a.* feeble, decrepit

musgrellni, *n.m.* feebleness, debility

mwd, *n.m.* mud

mwdwl, (*mydylau*), *n.m.* cock (of hay)

mwg, *n.m.* smoke

mwgwd, (*mygydau*), *n.m.* blind mask

mwng, (*myngau*), *n.m.* mane

mwlwg, *n.m.* refuse, sweepings, chaff

mwll, *a.* close, warm, sultry

mwmian, *v.* hum, mumble

mŵn. See **mwyn**

mwnci, (*-ïod*), *n.m.* monkey

mwnciaidd, *a.* monkeyish, apish

mwnglawdd. See **mwyn-**

mwnwgl, (*mynyglau*) *n.m.* neck

mwnws, *c.n.* small particles, dust, debris

mwrllwch, *n.m.* fog, mist, vapour

mwrn, *a.* sultry, close, warm

mwrndra, *n.m.* sultriness

mwrthwl, (*myrthylau*), *n.m.* hammer

mws, *a.* stale, rank, stinking

mwsg, *n.m.* musk

mwsged, (*-i*), *n.m.f.* musket

mwsogl, -wgl, *n.m.* moss

mwstard, -tart, *n.m.* mustard

mwstro, *v.* fidget, hurry

mwstwr, *n.m.* muster; bustle, commotion

mwth, *a.* swift, ready

mwy, *a.* more, bigger: *adv.* more, again

mwyach, *adv.* any more, henceforth

mwyafrif, (*-au*), *n.m.* majority

mwyalch, -en, (*-od*), *n.f.* blackbird

mwyar, *n.pl.* **(-en,** *n.f.*), blackberries

mwyara, *v.* gather blackberries

mwydion, *n.pl.* crumb; pith, pulp

mwydo, *v.* moisten, soak, steep

mwydro, *v.* moider, bewilder

mwyfwy, *adv.* more and more

mwygl, *a.* tepid; warm, sultry

mwyhau, *v.* increase, enlarge, magnify

mwyn, *n.m.* sake

mwyn, mŵn, (*-au*), *n.m.* ore, mineral

mwyn, *a.* kind, gentle, mild; dear

mwynder, (*-au*), *n.m.* gentleness; (*pl.*) delights

mwyneidd-dra, *n.m.* kindness, gentleness

mwynglawdd, (*-gloddiau*), *n.m.* mine

mwyngloddio, *v.* mine

mwynhad, *n.m.* enjoyment, pleasure

mwynhau, *v.* enjoy

mwyniant, (*-iannau*), *n.m.* pleasure

mwynofydd, (*-ion*), *n.m.* mineralogist

mwynwr, (*-wyr*), *n.m.* miner

mwys, *a.* ambiguous, equivocal

mwythau, *n.pl.* indulgence, caresses

mwytho, *v.* pet, fondle, pamper

mwythus, *a.* pampered

mydr, (*-au*), *n.m.* metre, verse

mydryddiaeth, *n.f.* versification

mydryddol, *a.* metrical

mydryddu, mydru, *v.* versify

mydylu, *v.* cock

myfi, *pn.* I, me, myself

myfïaeth, *n.f.* egotism

myfïol, *a.* egotistic

myfyrdod, (*-au*), *n.m.* meditation

myfyrfa, (*-feydd*), *n.f.* study

myfyrgar, *a.* studious, contemplative

myfyrgell, (*-oedd*), *n.f.* study

myfyrio, *v.* meditate, study

myfyriol, *a.* meditative

myfyriwr, (*-wyr*), *n.m.* student

mygedol, *a.* honorary

mygfa, (*-feydd*), *n.f.* suffocation

myglyd, *a.* smoky; close; asthmatic

myglys, *n.m.* tobacco

mygu, *v.* smoke; suffocate, stifle, smother

mygydu, *v.* blindfold

mygyn, *n.m.* a smoke

myngial, *v.* mumble, mutter

myngog, *a.* maned

myngus, *a.* indistinct, mumbling

myllni, *n.m.* sultriness

mympwy, (*-on*), *n.m.* whim, caprice, fad   [cious

mympwyol, *a.* arbitrary, capri-

mymryn, (*-nau*), *n.m.* particle, bit, mite

myn, *pr.* by (in swearing)

myn, (*-nod*), *n.m.* kid

mynach, (*-aich, -od*), *n.m.* monk

mynachaeth, *n.f.* monasticism

mynachdy, (*-dai*), *n.m.* monastery, convent

mynachlog, (*-ydd*), *n.f.* monastery, abbey

mynawyd, (*-au*), *n.m.* awl

mynci, (*-iau*), *n.m.* hame(s)

myned, mynd, *v.* go, proceed

mynedfa, (*-oedd, -feydd*), *n.f.* entrance, passage

mynediad, *n.m.* going; access, admission

mynegai, (*-eion*), *n.m.* index, exponent

mynegair, (*-eiriau*), *n.m.* concordance

mynegfys, (*-edd*), *n.m.* forefinger, index

mynegi, *v.* tell, express, relate, declare

mynegiad, (*-au*), *n.m.* statement, declaration

mynegiant, *n.m.* expression

mynnu, *v.* will, wish; insist; get, obtain

mynor, (*-ion*), *n.m.* marble

mynwent, (*-au, -ydd*), *n.f.* churchyard, graveyard

mynwes, (*-au*), *n.f.* breast, bosom

mynwesol, *a.* bosom

mynwesu, *v.* cherish

mynych, *a.* frequent, often

mynychiad, *n.m.* frequenting; repetition

mynychu, *v.* frequent, attend; repeat

mynydd, (*-oedd*), *n.m.* mountain

mynydd-dir, *n.m.* hill-country

mynyddig, -og, *a.* mountainous, hilly

mynyddwr, (*-wyr*), *n.m.* mountaineer

myrdd, -iwn, (*-iynau*), *n.m.* myriad

myrllyd, *a.* myrrhy

myrndra, *n.m.* sultriness

myrr, *n.m.* myrrh

myrtwydd, *n.pl.* (**-en,** *n.f.*) myrtles

mysg, *n.m.* middle, midst.—**ymysg,** among

mysgu, *v.* loose, undo

myswynog, (-*ydd*), *n.f.* barren cow

mysyglog, *a.* mossy

N

na, *c.* nor, neither; than: *adv.* no, not

nabl, (-*au*), *n.m.* psaltery

nac, *adv.* no, not: *c.* nor, neither

nacâd, *n.m.* refusal, denial

nacaol, *a.* negative

nacáu, *v.* refuse, deny

nad, *adv.* not

nâd, (*nadau*), *n.f.* cry, howl; clamour

Nadolig, *n.m.* Christmas

nadu, *v.* cry (out), howl

nadu, *v.* stop, hinder

nadd, *a.* hewn, wrought

naddion, *n.pl.* chips; shreds; lint

naddo, *adv.* no (to questions in preterite tense)

naddu, *v.* hew, chip, whittle

Naf, *n.m.* Lord

nag, *c.* than

nage, *adv.* not so, no

nai, (*neiaint*), *n.m.* nephew

naid, (*neidiau*), *n.f.* jump, leap, bound

naill, *dem.pn.* the one: *c.* either

nain, (*neiniau*), *n.f.* grandmother

nam, (-*au*), *n.m.* mark, blemish, flaw

namyn, *pr.* except, but, save

nant, (*nentydd*), *n.f.* brook; gorge, ravine

napcyn, (-*au*), *n.m.* napkin

nard, -us, *n.m.* nard, spikenard

natur, *n.f.* nature; temper

naturiaeth, (-*au*), *n.f.* nature

naturiaethwr, (-*wyr*), *n.m.* naturalist

naturiol, *a.* natural

naturioldeb, *n.m.* naturalness

naturus, *a.* angry, quick-tempered

naw, *a. & n.m.* nine

nawdd, *n.m.* protection; patronage

nawddogaeth, *n.f.* patronage, protection

nawfed, *a.* ninth

nawn, *n.m.* noon

naws, *n.f.* nature, disposition; essence, tincture

nawseiddio, *v.* temper, soften

neb, *n.m.* any one; (with negative understood) no one

nedd, *n.pl.* (-*en, n.f.*), nits

neddau, neddyf, (*neddyfau*), *n.f.* adze

nef, (-*oedd*), *n.f.* heaven

nefol, -aidd, *a.* heavenly, celestial

nefoli, *v.* make or become heavenly

neges, (-*au, -euau*), *n.f.* errand, message

negesa, -eua, *v.* run errands; trade

negeseuwr, (-*wyr*), *n.m.* messenger

negyddol, *a.* negative

neidio, *v.* leap, jump; throb

neidiwr, (-*wyr*), *n.m.* leaper, jumper

neidr, (*nadroedd, nadredd*), *n.f.* snake

neilltu, *n.m.* one side.—**or n.,** aside, apart

neilltuad, *n.m.* separation

neilltuaeth, *n.f.* separation, privacy, seclusion

neilltuedig, *a.* separated, secluded

neilltuo, *v.* set apart, separate

neilltuol, *a.* particular, peculiar, special

neilltuolion, *n.pl.* peculiarities

neilltuolrwydd, *n.m.* peculiarity, distinction

neina, *n.f.* grandmamma

neis, *a.* nice

neisied, (-*i*), *n.f.* kerchief

neithdar, *n.m.* nectar

neithior, (-*au*), *n.f.* marriage feast

neithiwr, *adv.* last night

nemor, *a.* few. —**nid n.,** hardly any

nen, (-*nau, -noedd*), *n.f.* ceiling; heaven.—**n. tŷ,** house-top

nenbren, *n.m.* roof-tree

nenfwd, (-*fydau*), *n.m.* ceiling

nenlen, (-*ni*), *n.f.* canopy

nepell, *adv.* far.—**nid n.,** not far

Nêr, *n.m.* Lord

nerf, (*-au*), *n.f.* nerve

nerfwst, *n.m.* neurasthenia

nerth, (*-oedd*), *n.m.* might, power, strength

nerthol, *a.* strong, powerful, mighty

nerthu, *v.* strengthen

nes, *a.* nearer.— **yn n. ymlaen,** further on

nes, *adv.* till, until

nesáu, *v.* draw near, approach

nesaf, *a.* nearest, next

nesnes, *adv.* nearer and nearer

nesu, *v.* draw near.—**n. draw,** move away

neu, *c.* or

neuadd, (*-au*), *n.f.* hall

newid, *v.* change, alter: *n.m.* change

newydd, *a.* new, novel; fresh: (*-ion*), *n.m.* news

newyddbeth, (*-au*), *n.m.* novelty

newydd-deb, -der, *n.m.* newness, novelty

newyddiadur, (*-on*), *n.m.* newspaper

newyddiaduriaeth, *n.f.* journalism

newyddiadurwr, (*-wyr*), *n.m.* journalist

newyddian, (*-od*), *n.c.* novice, neophyte

newyn, *n.m.* hunger, famine

newynog, *a.* hungry, starving

newynu, *v.* starve, famish

ni, *pn.* we, us

ni, nid, *adv.* not

nidr, *n.m.* hindrance

nidro, *v.* entwine, entangle

nifer, (*-oedd, -i*), *n.m.f.* number

nifwl, *n.m.* mist, fog; nebula

ninnau, *pn.c.* we (on our part), we also

nis, *adv.* not ... it.—**n. cafodd,** he did not find it

nith, (*oedd*), *n.f.* niece

nithio, *v.* sift, winnow

nithiwr, (*-wyr*), *n.m.* sifter, winnower

nithlen, (*-ni*), *n.f.* winnowing-sheet

niwed, (*-eidiau*), *n.m.* harm, injury

niweidio. *v.* harm, hurt, injure, damage

niweidiol, *a.* harmful, injurious

niwl, (*-oedd*), *n.m.*, **-en,** *n.f.* mist, fog, haze

niwliog, niwlog, *a.* misty, foggy, hazy

nod, (*-au*), *n.m.f.* note; mark, token

nodachfa, (*-feydd*), *n.f.* bazaar

nodedig, *a.* appointed, set; remarkable

nodi, *v.* mark, note, appoint, state

nodiad, (*-au*), *n.m.* note

nodiant, *n.m.* notation

nodwedd, (*-ion*), *n.f.* character, characteristic, feature

nodweddiadol, *a.* characteristic

nodweddu, *v.* characterize

nodwydd, (*-au*), *n.f.* needle

nodyn, (*-nau, nodau, nodion*), *n.m.* note

nodd, (*-ion*), *n.m.* moisture; juice, sap

nodded, *n.m.* refuge, protection

noddfa, (*-fâu, -feydd*), *n.f.* refuge

noddi, *v.* protect

noddlyd, *a.* juicy, sappy

noddwr, (*-wyr*), *n.m.* protector; patron

noe, (*-au*), *n.f.* dish; kneading-trough

noeth, *a.* naked, bare, exposed, raw

noethder, *n.m.* bareness, nakedness

noethi, *v.* bare, denude

noeth lymun, *a.* stark-naked, nude

noethni, *n.m.* nakedness, nudity

nofel, (*-au*), *n.f.* novel

nofelwr, -ydd, (*-wyr*), *n.m.* novelist

nofiadwy, *a.* swimmable

nofiedydd, (*-ion*), *n.m.* swimmer

nofio, *v.* swim; float

nofiwr, (*-wyr*), *n.m.* swimmer

nogio, *v.* jib

noglyd, *a.* jibbing

nôl, *v.* fetch, bring

nos, (*-au, nosweithiau*), *n.f.* night

nosi, *v.* become night

noson, noswaith, (*nosweithiau*), *n.f.* a night, an evening

noswyl, (*-iau*), *n.f.* eve of festival, vigil

noswylio, *v.* cease work at eve

nudden, *n.f.* fog, mist, haze

nwy, (*-on*), *n.m.* gas

nwyd, (*-au*), *n.m.* passion; emotion

nwydd, (*-au*), *n.m.* substance, article; (*pl.*) goods

nwyf, *n.m.* vivacity, energy, vigour

nwyfiant, *n.m.* vivacity, vigour

nwyfre, *n.m.* sky, firmament

nwyfus, *a.* sprightly, spirited, lively

nwyol, *a.* gaseous

nychdod, *n.m.* feebleness, infirmity

nychlyd, *a.* sickly, feeble

nychu, *v.* sicken, pine, languish

nydd-dro, (*-droeau, -droeon*), *n.m.* twist

nydd-droi, *v.* twist, screw

nyddu, *v.* spin, twist

nyddwr, (*-wyr*), *n.m.* spinner

nyf, *c.n.* snow

nyni, *pn.* we, us

nyth, (*-od*), *n.m.f.* nest

nythu, *v.* nest, nestle

O

o, *pr.* from; of, out of; by

o, *i.* oh, O!

oblegid, *c. & pr.* because, for

obry, *adv.* beneath, below

ocraeth, *n.f.* usury

ocrwr, (*-wyr*), *n.m.* usurer

och, *i.* oh, alas, woe

ochain, *v.* groan

ochenaid, (*-eidiau*), *n.f.* sigh

ocheneidio, ochneidio, *v.* sigh

ochr, (*-au*), *n.f.* side

ochri, *v.* side

ôd, *n.m.* snow

od, *a.* odd, remarkable

odfa. See **oedfa**

odi, *v.* snow

odiaeth, *a.* excellent, exquisite: *adv.* very, most, extremely

odid, *adv.* perchance, peradventure

odl, (*-au*), *n.f.* rhyme; ode, song

odlaw, *n.m.* sleet

odli, *v.* rhyme

Odydd, (*-ion*), *n.m.* Oddfellow

Odyddiaeth, *n.f.* Oddfellowship

odyn, (*-au*), *n.f.* kiln

oddeutu, *pr.* **o ddeutu,** *adv.* about

oddi, *pr.* out of, from

oddieithr, oddigerth, *pr.* except, unless

oed, (*-au*), *n.m.* age; time

oedfa, (*-on, -feuon*), *n.f.* meeting, service

oedi, *v.* delay; postpone, defer

oediad, (*-au*), *n.m.* delay

oedran, *n.m.* age, full age

oedrannus, *a.* aged

oedd, *v.* was, were

oen, (*ŵyn*), *n.m.* lamb

oena, *v.* lamb, yean

oenig, *n.f.* ewe-lamb

oer, *a.* cold, chill, frigid; sad

oeraidd, *a.* coldish, cool, chilly

oerder, *n.m.* coldness

oerfel, *n.m.* cold

oerfelgarwch, *n.m.* coolness, coldness

oerfelog, *a.* cold, chilly

oeri, *v.* cool, chill

oerllyd, *a.* chilly, frigid; cool

oernad, (*-au*), *n.f.* howl, wail, lamentation

oernadu, *v.* howl, wail, lament

oerni, *n.m.* cold, coldness, chillness

oes, (*-oedd, -au*), *n.f.* age, lifetime. **-yn o. oesoedd,** for ever and ever

oes, *v.* there is, there are; is there?

oesi, *v.* live

oesol, *a.* age-long, perpetual

ofer, *a.* vain, idle; prodigal, dissipated; waste

ofera, *v.* waste, squander, idle

oferedd, *n.m.* vanity, dissipation

ofergoel, (*-ion*), *n.f.* superstition

ofergoeledd, -iaeth, *n.m.* superstition

ofergoelus, *a.* superstitious

oferwr, (*-wyr*), *n.m.* idler, waster

ofn, (*-au*), *n.m.* fear, dread

ofnadwy, *a.* awful, terrible, dreadful

ofnadwyaeth, *n.f.* awe, terror, dread

ofni, *v.* fear, dread

ofnog, *a.* fearful, timorous

ofnus, *a.* timid, nervous

ofnusrwydd, *n.m.* timidity, nervousness

ofydd, (*-ion*), *n.m.* ovate

offeiriad, (*-iaid*), *n.m.* priest, clergyman

offeiriadaeth, *n.f.* priesthood

offeiriades, (*-au*), *n.f.* priestess

offeiriadol, *a.* priestly, sacerdotal

offeiriadu, *v.* officiate, minister

offer, *n.pl.* implements, tools, gear

offeren, (*-nau*), *n.f.* mass

offeryn, (*-nau, offer*), *n.m.* instrument, tool

offerynnol, *a.* instrumental

offerynoliaeth, *n.f.* instrumentality

offrwm, (*-ymau*), *n.m.* offering, oblation

offrymu, *v.* offer, sacrifice

offrymwr, (*-wyr*), *n.m.* offerer, sacrificer

og, (*-au*), **oged**, (*-au, -i*), *n.f.* harrow

ogof, (*-au, -fâu, -feydd*), *n.f.* cave, cavern; den

ogylch, *pr.* about

ongl, (*-au*), *n.f.* angle, corner

onglog, *a.* angled, angular

oherwydd, *c. & pr.* because, for

ôl, *a.* back, hind, hindmost: **olion**, *n.m.* mark, print, trace, track. **Yn ôl**, according to; ago

olddodiad, (*-iaid*), *n.m.* suffix, affix

ôl-ddyddio, *v.* post-date

olew, (*-au*), *n.m.* oil

olewydd, *n.pl.* (**-en**, *n.f.*), olive-trees

olifaid, *n.pl.* olive-berries

olrhain, *v.* trace

olwyn, (*-ion*), *n.f.* wheel

olwyno, *v.* wheel, cycle

olwynog, *a.* wheeled

olyniaeth, *n.f.* succession, sequence

olynol, *a.* successive, consecutive

olynu, *v.* succeed (to)

olynwr, (*-wyr*), **-ydd**, (*-ion*), *n.m.* successor

ôl-ysgrif, (*-au*), *n.f.* postscript

oll, *adv.* all, wholly; ever, at all

ond, *c.* but, only: *pr.* except, save, but

onest, *a.* honest

onestrwydd, *n.m.* honesty

oni, onid, *adv.* not? is it not? *c.* if not, unless: *pr.* except, save, but

onid e, *adv.* otherwise, else; is it not?

onis, *c.* if it is not. —**o. caiff,** if he does not get it

onnen, (*onn, ynn*), *n.f.* ash

opiniwn, (*-ynau*), *n.m.* opinion

opiniynllyd, -iynus, *a.* opinionated

oracl, (*-au*), *n.m.* oracle

oraclaidd, *a.* oracular

oraens, *n.m.* orange

ordeiniad, (*-au*), *n.m.* ordination, ordinance

ordeinio, *v.* ordain

ordinhad, (*-au*), *n.f.* ordinance, sacrament

organ, (*-au*), *n.f.m.* organ

organaidd, *a.* organic

organydd, (*-ion*), *n.m.* organist

orgraff, (*-au*), *n.f.* orthography

orgraffyddol, *a.* orthographical

oriadur, (*-on*), *n.f.* watch

oriadurwr, (*-wyr*), *n.m.* watchmaker

oriawr, (*oriorau*), *n.f.* watch

oriel, (*-au*), *n.f.* gallery

orig, *n.f.* little while

oriog, *a.* fickle, changeable, inconstant

orlais, (*-leisiau*), *n.m.* clock

ornest, (*-au*), *n.f.* duel, combat, contest

orohïan, *n.m.* doting lover

os, *c.* if

osai, *n.m.* wine (of Osey)

osgo, *n.m.* slant, slope, inclination

osgoi, *v.* swerve, avoid, evade, shirk

osio, *v.* offer to do, essay; dare

oslef, *n.f.* tone, voice

ow, *i.* oh! alas!

owmal, *n.m.* enamel

P

pa, *a.* what, which

pab, (*-au*), *n.m.* pope

pabaeth, *n.f.* papacy

pabaidd, *a.* papal, popish

pabell, (*pebyll*), *n.f.* tent, tabernacle

pabellu, *v.* tent, tabernacle, encamp

pabi, *n.m.* poppy

pabwyr, *n.pl.* (**-en,** *n.f.,* **-yn,** *n.m.*), rushes

pabwyr, *n.m.* wick, candle-wick

pabydd, (*-ion*), *n.m.* papist, Roman Catholic

pabyddiaeth, *n.f.* popery, papistry

pabyddol, *a.* papistic, Roman Catholic

pac, (*-iau*), *n.m.* pack, bundle

pacio, *v.* pack

padell, (*-au, -i, pedyll*), *n.f.* pan, panmug

padellaid, (*-eidiau*), *n.f.* panful

pader, (*-au*), *n.m.* paternoster, Lord's Prayer

padera, *v.* repeat prayers, patter

pae, *n.m.* pay, wage

paent, *n.m.* paint

paentiad, (*-au*), *n.m.* painting

paffio, *v.* box, fight

paffiwr, (*-wyr*), *n.m.* boxer

pagan, (*-iaid*), *n.m.* pagan, heathen

paganaidd, *a.* pagan, heathen

paganiaeth, *n.f.* paganism, heathenism

pang, (*-au*), *n.m.* **pangfa,** (*-feydd*), *n.f.* pang, fit

paham, *adv.* why, wherefore

paill, *n.m.* flour; pollen

pair, (*peiriau*), *n.m.* cauldron, furnace

pais, (*peisiau*), *n.f.* coat, petticoat

paith, (*peithiau*), *n.m.* prairie

pâl, (*palau*), *n.f.* spade

paladr, (*pelydr*), *n.m.* ray, beam; staff; stem

palas, (*-au*), *n.m.* palace

palf, (*-au*), *n.f.* palm, hand; paw

palfais, (*-eisiau*), *n.f.* shoulder

palfalu, *v.* feel, grope

palfod, (*-au*), *n.f.* smack, slap, buffet

palff, *n.m.* fine, well-built man

pali, *n.m.* silk brocade

palis, (*-au*), *n.m.* pale, partition, wainscot

palmant, (*-mentydd*), *n.m.* pavement

palmantu, *v.* pave

palmwydd, *n.pl.* (**-en,** *n.f.*), palm-trees

palu, *v.* dig, delve

palwr, (*-wyr*), *n.m.* digger

pall, (*-au*), *n.m.* mantle; tent

pall, *n.m.* fail, failing; lack; lapse

pallu, *v.* fail, cease; neglect; refuse

pam, *adv.* why, wherefore (**paham**)

pamffled, (*-i, -au*), **-yn,** *n.m.* pamphlet

pan, *c.* when

pân, *n.m.* bog down; fur

pandy, (*-dai*), *n.m.* fulling-mill

pannas, *n.pl.* (**panasen,** *n.f.*), parsnips

pannu, *v.* full cloth

pannwl, (*panylau*), *n.m.* dimple, hollow

pannwr, (*panwyr*), *n.m.* fuller

pant, (*-iau*), *n.m.* hollow, valley

pantio, *v.* depress, dent, sink

pantiog, *a.* hollow, sunken; dimpled

papur, (*-au*), *n.m.* paper

papuro, *v.* paper

papurwr, (*-wyr*), *n.m.* paperer, paperhanger

papuryn, *n.m.* scrap of paper

pâr, (*parau*), *n.m.* pair; suit

pâr, (*peri*), *n.m.* spear, lance

para, *v.* last, endure, continue

parabl, (*-au*), *n.m.* speech, discourse

parablu, *v.* speak

paradwys, *n.f.* paradise

paradwysaidd, *a.* paradisean

paragraff, (*-au*), *n.m.* paragraph

paratoad, (*-au*), *n.m.* preparation

paratoi, *v.* prepare, get ready

parc, (*-iau*), *n.m.* park, field

parch, *n.m.* respect, reverence

parchedig, (*-ion*), *a.* reverend; reverent

parchedigaeth, *n.f.* reverence

parchu, *v.* respect, revere, reverence

parchus, *a.* respectful; respectable

parchusrwydd, *n.m.* respectability

pardwn, (*-ynau*), *n.m.* pardon

pardynu, *v.* pardon

parddu, *n.m.* fire-black, smut; soot

pardduo, *v.* blacken, vilify, defame

pared, (*parwydydd*), *n.m.* partition wall, wall

parhad, *n.m.* continuance, continuation

parhaol, *a.* lasting, perpetual

parhau, *v.* last, continue; persevere

parhaus, *a.* lasting; continual, perpetual

parlwr, (*-yrau*), *n.m.* parlour

parlys, *n.m.* paralysis, palsy

parlysu, *v.* paralyse

parod, *a.* ready, prepared; prompt

parodrwydd, *n.m.* readiness, willingness

parsel, (*-i, -ydd*), *n.m.* parcel

parti, (*-ïon*), *n.m.* party

partïaeth, *n.f.* partisanship

partïol, *a.* partial, biassed, partisan

parth, (*-au*), *n.m.* part, region; floor

parthed, *pr.* about, concerning

parthu, *v.* part, divide

parwyden, (*-nau*), *n.f.* wall, side; breast

pas, *n.m.* whooping-cough

Pasg, *n.m.* Passover, Easter

pasgedig, (*-ion*), *a.* fatted, fattened, fat

pasiant, (*-iannau*), *n.m.* pageant

pasio, *v.* pass

past, *n.m.* paste

pastai, (*-eiod*), *n.f.* pasty, pie

pastio, *v.* paste   [cudgel

pastwn, (*-ynau*), *n.m.* baton, club,

pastynu, *v.* club, cudgel, bludgeon

patriarch, (*-iaid, patrieirch*), *n.m.* patriarch

patriarchaeth, (*-au*), *n.f.* patriarchate

patriarchaidd, *a.* patriarchal

patrwm, (*-ymau*), *n.m.* pattern

pathew, (*-od*), *n.m.* dormouse

pau, *n.f.* country

paun, (*peunod*), *n.m.* peacock

pawb, *pn.* everybody, all

pawen, (*-nau*), *n.f.* paw

pawl, (*polion*), *n.m.* pole, stake

pe, *c.* if

pebyll. See **pabell**

pecyn, (*-nau*), *n.m.* packet, package

pech-aberth, (*-au*), *n.m.* sin-offering   [offender

pechadur, (*-iaid*), *n.m.* sinner,

pechadures, (*-au*), woman sinner

pechadurus, *a.* sinful, wicked

pechadurusrwydd, *n.m.* sinfulness

pechod, (*-au*), *n.m.* sin, offence

pechu, *v.* sin, offend

ped, *c.* if

pedair, *a.,* f. of **pedwar**

pedeirongl, *a.* foursquare

pedi, *v.* worry, grieve

pedol, (*-au*), *n.f.* horseshoe

pedoli, *v.* shoe

pedrain, *n.f.* haunches, crupper

pedrongl, *a.* square: (*-au*), *n.f.* square

pedronglog, *a.* quadrangular

pedryfan, *a.* four-cornered: **-noedd,** *n.m.* four quarters

pedryfwrdd, (*-fyrddau*), *n.m.* quarter-deck

pedwar, *a.* four: f. **pedair**

pedwarawd, *n.m.* quartette

pedwarcarnol, (*-ion*), *a.* four-footed, quadruped

pedwaredd, *a.* f. of **pedwerydd**

pedwarplyg, *a.* fourfold, quarto

pedwerydd, *a.* fourth: f. **pedwaredd**

peddestr, *n.m.* pedestrian

peddestrig, *n.m.* walking; pedestrian

pefr, *a.* radiant, bright, beautiful

pefrio, *v.* radiate, sparkle

peg, (*-iau*), *n.m.* peg

pegio, *v.* peg

pegor, (*-au*), *n.m.* manikin; dwarf; imp

pegwn, (*-ynau*), *n.m.* pivot, pole, axis

pegynol, *a.* axial, polar

peidio, *v.* cease, stop, desist

peilliaid, *n.m.* fine flour, wheat flour

peillio, *v.* bolt, sift

peint, (*-iau*), *n.m.* pint

peintio, *v.* paint

peintiwr, (*-wyr*), *n.m.* painter

peipen, (*peipiau*), *n.f.* pipe

peirianneg, *n.m.* engineering

peiriannol, *a.* mechanical

peiriannydd, (*-ianyddion*), *n.m.* engineer

peiriant, (*-iannau*), *n.m.* machine, engine

peirianwaith, *n.m.* mechanism

peiswyn, *n.m.* chaff

peithyn, (*-au*), *n.m.* roofing-tile

pêl, (*pelau, peli*), *n.f.* ball

pelen, (*-nau, -ni*), *n.f.* pill

pelten, (*pelts*), *n.f.* blow

pelydr, (*-au*), *n.m.* ray, beam

pelydru, *v.* beam, gleam, radiate

pelydryn, *n.m.* ray, beam

pell, *a.* far, distant, remote, long

pellebru, *v.* telegraph

pellebyr, *n.m.* telegraph, telegram

pellen, (*-nau, -ni*), *n.f.* ball (of yarn)

pellennig, *a.* far, distant, remote

pellhau, *v.* put or remove far off

pellseinydd, (*-ion*), *n.m.* telephone

pellter, (*-au, -oedd*), *n.m.* distance

pen, (*-nau*), *n.m.* head; chief; end; top

pen, *a.* head, chief, supreme

penadur, (*-iaid*), *n.m.* sovereign

penaduriaeth, *n.f.* sovereignty

penagored, *a.* open, indefinite, undecided

penaig, *n.m.* chief, leader

penarglwyddiaeth, *n.f.* sovereignty

penbaladr, *a.* general, universal

penben, *adv.* at loggerheads

penbleth, *n.f.* perplexity, quandary

penboeth, *a.* hot-headed, fanatical

penboethni, *n.m.* fanaticism

penboethyn, (*-boethiaid*) *n.m.* fanatic

penbwl, (*-byliaid*), *n.m.* blockhead; tadpole

pencadlys, *n.m.* head-quarters

pen-campwr, (*-wyr*), *n.m.* champion

pencawna, *v.* trifle, dally

pencerdd, (*-ceirddiaid*), *n.m.* chief musician

penchwiban, *a.* giddy, flighty

pendant, *a.* positive, emphatic

pendantrwydd, *n.m.* positiveness

pendefig, (*-ion*), *n.m.* prince, peer, noble

pendefigaeth, *n.f.* aristocracy, peerage

pendefigaidd, *a.* noble, aristocratic

pendefiges, (*-au*), *n.f.* peeress

penderfyniad, (*-au*), *n.m.* determination, resolution

penderfynol, *a.* determined, resolute

penderfynu, *v.* determine, resolve

pendew, *a.* thick-headed, stupid

pendifaddau, *a.—yn b.*, especially

pendil, (*-iau*), *n.m.* pendulum

pendramwnwgl, *a.* topsyturvy; headlong

pendraphen, *a.* helter-skelter, confused

pendro, *n.f.* giddiness, vertigo; staggers

pendroni, *v.* perplex oneself, worry over

pendrwm, *a.* top-heavy; drowsy

pendrymu, *v.* drowse, droop

pendwmpian, *v.* nod, doze, slumber

penddaredd, *n.m.* giddiness

penddaru, *v.* make or become giddy

pendduyn, (*-nod*), *n.m.* botch, boil

penelin, (*-oedd*), *n.m.f.* elbow

penelino, *v.* elbow

penffol, *a.* silly, idiotic

penffrwyn, (*-au*), *n.m.f.* head-stall, halter

pengaled, *a.* headstrong: *n.f.* knapweed

pengaledwch, *n.m.* stubbornness

pengam, *a.* wrong-headed, perverse

pengemi, *n.m.* wrong-headedness, perverseness

penglog, (*-au*), *n.f.* skull

pengryf, *a.* headstrong, stubborn

pengryniad, (*-iaid*), *n.m.* round-head

penigamp, *a.* excellent, splendid

penisel, *a.* downcast, crestfallen

penlin, (*-liniau*), *n.m.f.* knee

penlinio, *v.* kneel

penllad, *n.m.* supreme good

penllwyd, *a.* grey-headed

penllwydni, *n.m.* grey hair, white hair

pen-llywydd, (*-ion*), *n.m.* sovereign

penllywyddiaeth, *n.f.* sovereignty

pennaeth, (*penaethiaid*), *n.m.* chief

pennaf, *a.* chief, principal

pennawd, (*penawdau*), *n.m.* heading

pennill, (*penillion*), *n.m.* verse, stanza

pennod, (*penodau*), *n.f.* chapter

pennoeth, *a.* bare-headed

pennog, (*penwaig*), *n.m.* herring

pennu, *v.* specify, appoint, determine

penodi, *v.* appoint

penodiad, (*-au*), *n.m.* appointment

penodol, *a.* particular, specific

penrhydd, *a.* unbridled, loose

penrhyddid, *n.m.* licence, licentiousness

penrhyn, (*-noedd, -nau*), *n.m.* cape

pensaer, (*-seiri*), *n.m.* architect

pensiwn, (*-iynau*), *n.m.* pension

pen-swyddog, (*-ion*), *n.m.* chief officer

pensyfrdan, *a.* stunned, dazed

pensyfrdandod, *n.m.* giddiness, dizziness

pensyfrdanu, *v.* stun, daze

pentan, (*-au*), *n.m.* hob; abutment

penteulu, (*pennau teuluoedd*), *n.m.* head of family

pentewyn, (*-ion*), *n.m.* firebrand

pentir, (*-oedd*), *n.m.* headland

pentis, *n.m.* pentice, penthouse

pentref, (*-i, -ydd*), *n.m.* village, homestead

pentrefol, *a.* village

pentrefwr, (*-wyr*), *n.m.* villager

pentwr, (*-tyrrau*), *n.m.* heap, pile

penty, (*-tai*), *n.m.* cottage, shed

pentyrru, *v.* heap, pile, accumulate

penuchel, *a.* proud, haughty

penwan, *a.* weak-minded

penwyn, *a.* white-headed

penwynni, *n.m.* white hair, grey hair   [ment

penyd, (*-iau*), *n.m.* penance, punish-

penyd-wasanaeth, *n.m.* penal servitude

penysgafn, *a.* light-headed, giddy, dizzy

penysgafnder, *n.m.* giddiness, dizziness

pêr, *a.* sweet, delicious, luscious

peraidd, *a.* sweet, mellow

perarogl, (*-au*), *n.m.* perfume, fragrance

perarogli, *v.* perfume; embalm

perchen, -nog, (*perchenogion*), *n.m.* owner

perchenogaeth, *n.f.* ownership

perchenogi, *v.* possess, own

perchi, *v.* respect, revere

pereidd-dra, *n.m.* sweetness

pereiddio, *v.* sweeten

pererin, (*-ion*), *n.m.* pilgrim

pererindod, (*-au*), *n.m.f.* pilgrimage

pererinol, *a.* pilgrim

perfedd, (*-ion*), *n.m.* guts, bowels

perffaith, *a.* perfect

perffeithio, *v.* perfect

perffeithrwydd, *n.m.* perfection

perffeithydd, (*-ion*), *n.m.* perfecter

perhôn, *c.* granted (that)

peri, *v.* cause, bid

periglor, (*-ion, -iaid*), *n.m.* priest, incumbent

perl, (*-au*), *n.m.* pearl

perlewyg, (*-on*), *n.* ecstasy, trance

perlysiau, *n.pl.* aromatic herbs; spices

perllan, (*-nau*), *n.f.* orchard

perori, *v.* make melody

peroriaeth, *n.f.* melody, music

persain, *a.* euphonious, melodious; (*-seinian*), *n.f.* euphony

persawr, (*-au*), *n.m.* fragrance

perseiniol, *a.* melodious

persli, *n.m.* parsley

person, (*-au*), *n.m.* person

person, (*-iaid*), *n.m.* parson, clergy-man

persondy, (*-dai*), *n.m.* parsonage

personol, *a.* personal

personoli, *v.* personify

personoliaeth, (*-au*), *n.f.* personality; parsonage, benefice

perswâd, *n.m.* persuasion

perswadio, *v.* persuade

pert, *a.* quaint, pretty; pert

perth, (*-i*), *n.f.* bush, hedge

perthyn, *v.* belong, pertain, be related

perthynas, (*-au*), *n.f.* relation; relationship

perthynasol, *a.* relevant

perthynol, *a.* relative

perwig, (*-au*), *n.f.* periwig, wig

perwyddiad, (*-iaid*), *n.m.* verb

perwyl, *n.m.* purpose, effect

perygl, (*-on*), *n.m.* danger, peril, risk

peryglu, *v.* endanger, imperil

peryglus, *a.* dangerous, perilous

pes, *c.* if . . . it.—**p. adwaenasent**, had they known him

pesgi, *v.* feed, fatten

pestl, (*-au*), *n.m.* pestle

peswch, *n.m.* cough

pesychiad, (*-au*), *n.m.* cough

pesychu, *v.* cough

petris, *n.pl.* (*-en*, *n.f.*), partridges

petrual, *n.m.* & *a.* square

petrus, *a.* hesitating; doubtful

petruso, *v.* hesitate, doubt

petruster, *n.m.* hesitation, doubt

peth, (*-au*), *n.m.* thing; part, some

petheuach, *n.pl.* odds and ends, trifles

peues, *n.f.* country

peunes, (*-od*), *n.f.* peahen

peuo, *v.* puff; bellow

pi, pia, (*pîod*), *n.f.* magpie

piau, *v.* own, possess

pib, (*-au*), *n.f.* pipe, tube; diarrhœa

pibell, (*-au*, *-i*), *n.f.* pipe, tube

pibo, *v.* pipe; squirt

pibonwy, *c.n.* icicles

pibydd, (*-ion*), *n.m.* piper

picell, (*-au*), *n.f.* dart, javelin, spear

picellu, *v.* spear, stab

picfforch, (*-ffyrch*), *n.f.* pitchfork

picio, *v.* dart, hie

piff, (*-iau*), *n.m.* puff, sudden blast

piffian, *v.* snigger, giggle

pig, (*-au*), *n.f.* point, spike; beak; spout

pigdwr, (*-dyrau*), *n.m.* spire, steeple

pigiad, (*-au*), *n.m.* prick, sting

pigion, *n.pl.* pickings, selections

piglas, *a.* pale-faced, blue

pigo, *v.* pick; peck; prick; sting

pigog, *a.* prickly

pigyn, *n.m.* thorn, prickle; stitch

pilcod, *n.pl.* (*-yn*, *n.m.*) minnows

pilen, (*-nau*), *n.f.* membrane, film; cataract

piler, (*-au*, *-i*), *n.m.* pillar

pilio, *v.* peel, pare

pili-pala, *n.m.* butterfly

pilyn, *n.m.* garment, rag, clout

pill, *n.m.* bit of poetry, snatch of song

pill, *n.m.* branch, post; defence

pîn, *n.m.* pine, fir

pin, (*-nau*), *n.m.f.* pin: *n.m.* pen

pinacl, (*-au*), *n.m.* pinnacle

pinaclog, *a.* pinnacled

pinc, (*-od*), *n.m.* finch, chaffinch

pincio, *v.* pink.—**parlwr p.**, beauty parlour

pincyn, *n.m.* sprig

pinsiad, (*-au*), *n.m.* pinch

pinsio, *v.* pinch

pioden, piogen, (*pîod*), *n.f.* magpie

piser, (*-au*, *-i*), *n.m.* pitcher, jug, can

pistyll, (*-oedd*), *n.m.* spout; cataract

pistyllio, *v.* spout, gush

pisyn, (*-nau*, *pisiau*), *n.m.* piece

piti, *n.m.* pity

pitw, *a.* petty, puny, paltry

piw, (*-od*), *n.m.* dug, udder

Piwritan, (*-iaid*), *n.m.* Puritan

piwritanaidd, *a.* puritan, puritanical

piwritaniaeth, *n.f.* puritanism

pla, (*plâu*), *n.m.f.* plague, pestilence; nuisance

pladur, (*-iau*), *n.f.* scythe

pladurwr, (*-wyr*), *n.m.* mower

plaen, *a.* plain, clear

plaen, (*-au*), *n.m.* plane

plaenio, *v.* plane

plag, *n.* plague, nuisance

plagio, *v.* plague, tease, torment

plagus, *a.* annoying, troublesome

plaid, (*pleidiau*), *n.f.* side, party

planced, (*-i*), *n.f.* blanket

planed, (*-au*), *n.f.* planet

planedydd, (*-ion*), *n.m.* astrologer

planfa, planhigfa, (*-feydd*), *n.f.* plantation

planhigyn, (*-higion*), *n.m.* plant

plannu, *v.* plant; dive

plannwr, (*planwyr*), *n.m.* planter

plant, *n.pl.* (**plentyn,** *n.m.*), children

planta, *v.* beget or bear children

plantos, *n.pl.* (little) children

plas, (*-au*), *n.m.* hall, mansion, palace

plasaidd, *a.* palatial

plastr, (*-au*), *n.m.* plaster

plastro, *v.* plaster

plastrwr, (*-wyr*), *n.m.* plasterer

plât, plat, (*-iau*), *n.m.* plate

ple, *n.m.* plea

pledio, *v.* plead, argue

pledren, (*-nau, -ni*), *n.f.* bladder

pleidgarwch, *n.m.* partisanship

pleidio, *v.* side with, support

pleidiol, *a.* favourable, partial

pleidiwr, (*-wyr*), *n.m.* partisan, supporter

pleidlais, (*-leisiau*), *n.f.* vote, suffrage

pleidleisio, *v.* vote

pleidleisiwr, (*-wyr*), *n.m.* voter

plentyn, (*plant*), *n.m.* child, infant

plentyndod, *n.m.* childhood, infancy

plentyneiddiwch, *n.m.* childishness

plentynnaidd, *a.* childish, puerile

plentynrwydd, *n.m.* childishness

pleser, (*-au*), *n.m.* pleasure

pleserdaith, (*-deithiau*), *n.f.* trip, excursion

pleserus, *a.* pleasurable, pleasant

plesio, *v.* please

plet, pleten, (*pletiau*), *n.f.* pleat

pletio, *v.* pleat

pletiog, *a.* pleated

pleth, (*-au*), *n.f.* plait

plethdorch, (*-au*), *n.f.* wreath

plethu, *v.* plait, weave, fold

plicio, *v.* pluck, peel, strip

plisg, *c.n.* (**-yn,** *n.m.*), shells, husks, pods

plisgo, *v.* shell, husk

plisman, -mon, (*-myn*), *n.m.* policeman

plith, *n.m.* midst

plod, *a. & n.m.* plaid, tartan

ploryn, (*-nod*), *n.m.* pimple

plu, *n.pl.* (**-en,** *n.f.*), **pluf,** *n.pl.* (**-yn,** *n.m.*), feathers.—**p. eira,** snow-flakes

pluo, plufio, *v.* pluck, deplume; plume

pluog, *a.* feathered, fledged

plwc, (*plyciau*), *n.m.* pluck; space, while

plwm, *n.m.* lead

plwyf, (*-i, -ydd*), *n.m.* parish

plwyfol, *a.* parochial

plwyfolion, *n.pl.* parishioners

plycio, *v.* pluck

plyg, (*-ion*), *n.m.* fold, double; hollow

plygain, *n.m.* cock-crow, dawn; matins

plygeiniol, *a.* dawning; very early

plygiad, (*-au*), *n.m.* folding, fold

plygu, *v.* fold; bend, stoop; bow

plymen, *n.f.* plummet

plymio, *v.* plumb, sound

plymydd, (*-ion*), *n.m.* plumber

po, particle used before superlative. —**gorau po gyntaf,** the sooner the better

pob, *a.* each, every; all

pobi, *v.* bake; roast; toast

pobiad, (*-au*), *n.m.* baking, batch

pobl, (*-oedd*), *n.f.* people

poblog, *a.* populous

poblogaeth, (-au), n.f. population

poblogaidd, a. popular

poblogeiddio, v. popularize

poblogi, v. people, populate

poblogrwydd, n.m. popularity

pobwr, (-wyr), **-ydd,** (-ion), n.m. baker

poced, (-i), n.f. pocket

pocedu, v. pocket

poen, (-au), n.m.f. pain, torment

poenedigaeth, n.f. torment

poeni, v. pain, torment; worry, grieve

poenus, a. painful

poenwr, (-wyr), n.m. tormentor, torturer

poenydio, v. torment, torture; fret, vex

poenydiwr, (-wyr), n.m. tormentor

poer, (-ion), n.m. spittle, saliva

poeri, v. spit, expectorate

poeryn, n.m. spittle

poeth, a. hot; burning.—**dŵr p.,** heart-burn

poethder, -ni, n.m. hotness, heat

poethi v. heat

polyn, (polion), n.m. pole

pomgranad, (-au), n.m. pomegranate

pompiwn, (-iynau), n.m. pumpkin, gourd

pompren, n.f. plank bridge, footbridge

ponc, (-iau), **-en,** n.f. **-yn,** n.m. hillock, tump; bank

pont, (-ydd), n.f. bridge, arch

pontio, v. bridge

poplys, n.pl. (**-en,** n.f.) poplartrees

popty, (-tai), n.m. bakehouse; oven

porchell, (perchyll), n.m. little pig

porfa, (-feydd), n.f. pasture, grass

porffor, a. & n.m. purple

pori, v. graze, browse; eat

portread, (-au), n.m. portrayal, pattern

portreadu, v. portray

porth, n.m. aid, help, succour

porth, (pyrth), n.m. gate, gateway; porch

porth, (pyrth), n.f. ferry; port

porthfa, (-feydd), n.f. port, harbour; ferry

porthi v. feed

porthiannus, a. well-fed, high-spirited

porthiant, n.m. food, sustenance, support

porthladd, (-oedd), n.m. port, harbour, haven

porthmon, (-myn), n.m. cattle-dealer

porthor, (-ion), n.m. porter, doorkeeper

porthwr, (-wyr), n.m. feeder

pos, (-au), n.m. riddle, conundrum, puzzle

posel, n.m. posset

posibilrwydd, n.m. possibility

posibl, a. possible

post, (pyst), n.m. post; pillar

postio, v. post

pot, (-iau), n.m. pot

potel, (-i) n.f. bottle

potelaid, (-eidiau), n.f. bottleful

potelu, v. bottle

poten, (-ni), n.f. paunch; pudding

potes, n.m. pottage, broth, soup

potio, v. pot; tipple

pothell, (-au, -i), n.f. blister

powdr, (-au), n.m. powder

powl, -en, (powliau), n.f. bowl, basin

powlio, v. roll; wheel, trundle

praff, a. thick, stout

praffter, n.m. thickness, stoutness, girth

praidd, (preiddiau), n.m. flock

pranc, (-iau), n.m. frolic, prank

prancio, v. caper, prance

pratio, v. pat, stroke, caress

praw, prawf, (profion), n.m. trial, proof, probation

preblan, v. chatter, babble

pregeth, (-au), n.f. sermon, discourse

pregethu, v. preach

pregethwr, (-wyr), n.m. preacher

pregethwrol, a. preacher-like

pregowtha, v. jabber, rant

preiddin, *n.m.* booty

preifat, *a.* private

preimin, *n.m.* ploughing match

prelad, (*-iaid*), *n.m.* prelate

preladiaeth, *n.f.* prelacy

pren, (*-nau*), *n.m.* tree, timber; wood

prentis, (*-iaid*), *n.m.* apprentice

prentisiaeth, *n.f.* apprenticeship

prentisio, *v.* apprentice

prepian, *v.* babble, blab

pres, *n.m.* brass; bronze; copper: money

present, (*-au*), *n.m.* present, gift

preseb, (*-au*), *n.m.* crib, stall

presennol, *a. & n.m.* present

presenoldeb, *n.m.* presence; attendance

presenoli, *v.* be present (reflexive)

preswyl, *n.m.,* **-fa,** (*-feydd*), *n.f.,* **-fod,** *n.m.* abode, dwelling

preswylio, *v.* dwell, reside, inhabit

preswylydd, (*-ion, -wyr*), *n.m.* dweller, inhabitant

pric, (*-iau*), *n.m.* stick, chip

pricsiwn, *n.m.* laughing-stock, butt

prid, *a.* dear, costly: *n.m.* price, value

pridwerth, *n.m.* ransom

pridd, *n.m.* mould, earth, soil, ground

priddell, (*-au, -i*), *n.f.* clod

priddfaen, (*-feini*), *n.m.* brick

priddlech, (*-au, -i*), *n.f.* tile

priddlestr, (*-i*), *n.m.* earthenware vessel

priddlyd, *a.* earthy

priddo, *v.* earth

priddyn, *n.m.* earth, soil, mould

prif, *a.* prime, principal, chief

prifardd, (*-feirdd*), *n.m.* chief bard

prifathro, (*-athrawon*), *n.m.* headmaster, principal

prifddinas,(*-oedd*), *n.f.* metropolis, capital

prifiant, *n.m.* growth

prifio, *v.* grow

prifodl, (*-au*), *n.f.* chief rhyme

prifysgol, (*-ion*), *n.f.* university

priffordd, (*-ffyrdd*), *n.f.* highway

primas, *n.m.* primate, chief

prin, *a.* scarce, rare: *adv.* scarcely

prinder, -dra, *n.m.* scarceness, scarcity

prinhau, *v.* make or grow scarce, diminish

print, (*-iau*), *n.m.* print

printio, *v.* print

printiwr, (*-wyr*), *n.m.* printer

priod, *a.* own; proper; married: *n.c.* husband or wife

priodas, (*-au*), *n.f.* marriage, wedding

priodasfab, (*-feibion*), *n.m.* bridegroom

priodasferch, (*-ed*), *f.* bride n.

priodasol. *a.* matrimonial, married

priod-ddull, (*-iau*), *n.m.* idiom

priodfab, (*-feibion*), *n.m.* bridegroom

priodferch, (*-ed*), *n.f.* bride

priodi, *v.* marry

priodol *a.* proper, appropriate

priodoldeb, (*-au*), *n.m.* propriety

priodoledd, (*-au*), *n.f.* attribute

priodoli, *v.* attribute

priodoliaeth, (*-au*), *n.f.* attribute

prior, (*-iaid*), *n.m.* prior

priordy, (*-dai*), *n.m.* priory

pris, (*-iau*), *n.* price, value

prisiad, -iant, *n.m.* valuation

prisio, *v.* price, value; prize

prisiwr, (*-wyr*), *n.m.* valuer

problem, (*-au*), *n.f.* problem

proc, (*-iau*) *n.m.* poke

procer, (*-au, -i*), *n.m.* poker

procio, *v.* poke; throb

profedigaeth, (*-au*), *n.f.* trial, temptation

profedigaethus, *a.* beset with trials

profi, *v.* prove; taste; try; experience

profiad, (*-au*), *n.m.* experience

profiadol, *a.* experienced

proflen (*-ni*), *n.f.* proof-sheet

profocio, *v.* provoke, tease

profwr, (*-wyr*), *n.m.* taster, tester

proffes, (*-au*), *n.f.* profession

proffesu, *v.* profess

proffeswr, (*-wyr*), *n.m.* professor
proffid, *n.f.* profit
proffidio, *v.* profit, benefit
proffidiol, *a.* profitable
proffwyd, (*-i*), *n.m.* prophet
proffwydes, (*-au*), *n.f.* prophetess
proffwydo, *v.* prophesy
proffwydol, *a.* prophetic
proffwydoliaeth, (*-au*), *n.f.* prophecy
Protestannaidd, *a.* Protestant
Protestant, (*-aniaid*), *n.m.* Protestant
prudd, *a.* grave, serious, sad; wise
pruddaidd, *a.* sad, gloomy, mournful
prudd-der, *n.m.* sadness, gloom
pruddglwyf, *n.m.* depression, melancholy
pruddglwyfus, *a.* depressed, melancholy
pruddhau, *v.* sadden, depress
pryd, (*-iau*), *n.m.* time, season: (*-au*), *n.m.* meal
pryd, *adv.* while, when, since
pryd, *n.m.* form, aspect; complexion
Prydeinig *a.* British
Prydeiniwr, (*-wyr*), *n.m.* Briton, Britisher
pryder, (*-on*), *n.m.* anxiety, solicitude
pryderu, *v.* be anxious
pryderus, *a.* anxious, solicitous
prydferth, *a.* beautiful, handsome
prydferthu, *v.* beautify
prydferthwch, *n.m.* beauty
prydles, (*-au, -i, -ydd*), *n.f.* lease
prydlon, *a.* timely, punctual
prydlondeb, *n.m.* punctuality
prydnawn. See **prynhawn**
prydweddol, *a.* comely, handsome
prydydd, (*-ion*), *n.m.* poet
prydyddes, (*-au*), *n.f.* poetess
prydyddiaeth, *n.f.* poetry
prydyddol, *a.* poetical, metrical
prydyddu, *v.* compose poetry, poetize

pryddest, (*-au*), *n.f.* poem in free metre
pryf, (*-ed*), *n.m.* insect; worm; vermin
pryfedog, *a.* verminous
pryfyn, *n.m.* worm
prŷn, *a.* bought, purchased
prynedigaeth, *n.f.m.* redemption
prynhawn, (*-au*), *n.m.* afternoon
prynhawnol, *a.* afternoon, evening
pryniad, *n.m.* purchase
prynu, *v.* buy, purchase; redeem
prynwr, (*-wyr*), *n.m.* buyer; redeemer
prys, *n.m.* bush, wood
prysgwydd, *n.pl.* brushwood
prysur, *a.* busy, hasty; diligent; serious
prysurdeb, *n.m.* haste, hurry; busyness
prysuro, *v.* hurry, hasten
publican, (*-od*), *n.m.* publican (New Test.)
pulpud, (*-au*), *n.m.* pulpit
pum, pump, *a.* five
pumed, *a.* fifth
punt, (*punnoedd, punnau*), *n.f.* pound, £
pupur, *n.m.* pepper
pur, *a.* pure, sincere: *adv.* very, fairly
purdan, *n.m.* purgatory
purdeb, *n.m.* purity, sincerity
puredigaeth, *n.f.* purification
puredd, *n.m.* purity, innocence
purion, *a.* very well; right enough
puro, *v.* purify, cleanse
puror, *n.m.* harpist
purwr, (*-wyr*), *n.m.* purifier, refiner
putain, (*-einiaid*), *n.f.* harlot, prostitute
puteindra, *n.m.* harlotry, prostitution
puteinio, *v.* commit fornication
puteinwr, (*-wyr*), *n.m.* fornicator
pw, *i.* pooh
pwdin, *n.m.* pudding
pwdr, *a.* rotten, corrupt, putrid
pwdu, *v.* pout, sulk
pŵer, (*-au*), *n.m.* power

pwerus, *a.* powerful

pwff, (*pyffiau*), *n.m.* puff, blast

pŵl, *a.* blunt, obtuse; dull, dim

pwl, (*pyliau*), *n.m.* fit, attack, paroxysm

pwll, (*pyllau*), *n.m.* pit, pool, pond

pwn, (*pynnau*), *n.m.* pack, burden

pwnc, (*pynciau*), *n.m.* point, subject, question

pwniad, (*-au*), *n.m.* nudge, dig

pwnio, *v.* nudge; beat, thump, wallop

pwrcas, (*-au*), *n.m.* purchase

pwrcasu, *v.* purchase

pwrffil, *n.m.* purfle, train

pwrpas, (*-au*), *n.m.* purpose

pwrpasol, *a.* suitable

pwrpasu, *v.* purpose, intend

pwrs, (*pyrsau*), *n.m.* purse, bag; udder

pwt, (*pytiau*), *n.m.* anything short; stump

pwt, *n.m.* **-ian,** *v.* prod, poke

pwy, *pn.* who

pwyll, *n.m.* sense, discretion

pwyllgor, (*-au*), *n.m.* committee

pwyllgorwr, (*-wyr*), *n.m.* committee-man

pwyllo, *v.* pause, consider, reflect

pwyllog, *a.* discreet, prudent, deliberate

pwynt, (*-iau*), *n.m.* point

pwyntil, *n.m.* tab, tag; pencil

pwyntio, *v.* point; fatten

pwyo, *v.* beat, batter, pound

pwys, (*-au*, *-i*), *n.m.* weight, burden, pressure; pound (lb.); importance

pwysau, *n.m.* weight

pwysedd, *n.m.* pressure

pwysi, (*-ïau*), *n.m.* posy

pwysig, *a.* important

pwysigrwydd, *n.m.* importance

pwyslais, (*-leisiau*), *n.m.* emphasis

pwysleisio, *v.* emphasize

pwyso, *v.* weigh, press: lean, rest; rely

pwyswr, (*-wyr*), *n.m.* weigher

pwyth, (*-au*), *n.m.* stitch.— **talu'r p.,** requite

pwytho, *v.* stitch

pwythwr, (*-wyr*), *n.m.* stitcher

pybyr, *a.* strong, stout, staunch, valiant

pybyrwch, *n.m.* stoutness, vigour, valour

pyd, *n.m.* danger

pydew, (*-au*), *n.m.* well, pit

pydredig, *a.* rotten, putrid

pydredd, *n.m.* rottenness, putridity, rot

pydrni, *n.m.* rottenness, putrefaction

pydru, *v.* rot, putrefy

pyg, *n.m.* pitch, bitumen

pygddu, *a.* pitch-black

pygu, *v.* pitch

pyngad, pyngu, *v.* cluster

pylni, *n.m.* bluntness, dullness

pylor, *n.m.* dust, powder

pylu, *v.* blunt, dull

pyllog, *a.* full of pits

pyllu, *v.* pit

pymtheg, *a. & n.m.* fifteen

pymthegfed, *a.* fifteenth

pyncio, *v.* sing, play, make melody

pynfarch, (*-feirch*), *n.m.* pack-horse; mill-race

pynio, *v.* burden, load

pys, *n.pl.* (*-en,* *n.f.*), peas

pysgod, *n.pl.* (*-yn,* *n.m.*), fishes, fish

pysgodfa, (*-feydd*), *n.f.* fishery

pysgota, *v.* fish

pysgotwr, (*-wyr*), *n.m.* fisherman

pystylad, *v.* stamp with the feet

pytaten, (*-tws*), *n.f.* potato

pythefnos, (*-au*), *n.m.f.* fortnight

PH

Pharisead, (*-aid*), *n.m.* Pharisee

Phariseaeth, *n.f.* Pharisaism

Phariseaidd, *a.* Pharisaic(al)

Philistiad, (*-iaid*), *n.m.* Philistine

Philistiaeth, *n.f.* Philistinism

philosophi, *n.m.* philosophy

phiol. See **ffiol**

physygwr, -iaeth. See **ffis-**

R

rabbi, (*-niaid*), *n.m.* rabbi
rabbinaidd, *a.* rabbinical
ras, (*-ys*), *n.f.* race
record, (*-iau*), *n.f.m.* record
reiat, *n.f.* row, riot
reis, *n.m.* rice
reit, *adv.* right, very, quite
ridens, *n.f.* fringe
riwl, *n.f.* ruler
robin y gyrrwr, *n.* gadfly
ruban, (*-au*), *n.m.* ribbon
rwbel, *n.m.* rubble, rubbish
rwber, *n.m.* rubber
rwdins, *n.pl.* (**rwden,** *n.f.*), swedes

RH

rhaca, (*-nau*), *n.f.* rake: **-nu,** *v.* rake
rhactal, (*-au*), *n.m.* frontlet
rhad, *a.* free; cheap
rhad, (*-au*), *n.m.* grace, favour, blessing
rhadlon, *a.* gracious, kind; genial
rhadlondeb, -rwydd, *n.m.* graciousness, cheapness
rhaeadr, (*-au*), *n.f.* cataract, waterfall
rhaeadru, *v.* pour, gush
rhaff, (*-au*), *n.f.* rope, cord
rhaffo, -u *v.* rope
rhag, *pr.* before, against; from; lest: *px.* pre-, fore-, ante-
rhagarfaethiad, *n.m.* predestination
rhagarfaethu, *v.* predestine
rhagarweiniad, *n.m.* introduction
rhagarweiniol, *a.* introductory, preliminary [tend
rhagarwyddo, *v.* foretoken, por-
rhagbaratoawl, *a.* preparatory
rhagbrawf, (*-brofion*), *n.m.* foretaste
rhagderfynu, *v.* predetermine
rhagdraeth, (*-au*), *n.m.* preface, introduction

rhagdybied, -io, *v.* presuppose
rhagddodiad, (*-iaid*), *n.m.* prefix
rhagddor, (*-au*), *n.f.* outer door, hatch
rhagddywedyd, *v.* foretell
rhagenw, (*-au*), *n.m.* pronoun
rhagfarn, (*-au*), *n.f.* prejudice
rhagfarnllyd, *a.* prejudiced
rhagferf (*-au*), *n.f.* adverb
rhagflaenor, (*-iaid*), *n.m.* forerunner
rhagflaenu, *v.* precede, anticipate, forestall
rhagflaenydd, (*-ion, -wyr*), *n.m.* predecessor, precursor
rhagflas, *n.m.* foretaste
rhagfur, (*-iau*), *n.m.* bulwark
rhagfyfyrio, *v.* premeditate
rhagfynegi, *v.* foretell
Rhagfyr, *n.m.* December
rhaglaw, (*-iaid, -lofiaid*), *n.m.* prefect, viceroy
rhaglawiaeth, *n.f.* prefecture
rhaglen, (*-ni*), *n.f.* programme
rhaglith, (*-iau, -oedd*), *n.f.* preface
rhagluniaeth, (*-au*), *n.f.* providence
rhagluniaethol, *a.* providential
rhaglunio, *v.* predestine, predestinate
rhagod, *v.* hinder, meet, waylay
rhagofnau, *n.pl.* forebodings
rhagolwg, (*-ygon*), *n.m.* prospect
rhagor, (*-au, -ion*), *n.m.* difference; more
rhagorfraint, (*-freintiau*), *n.f.* privilege
rhagori, *v.* exceed, excel, surpass
rhagoriaeth, (*-au*), *n.f.* superiority; excellence
rhagorol, *a.* excellent, splendid
rhagoroldeb, *n.m.* excellence
rhagorsaf, (*-oedd*), *n.f.* out-station; outpost
rhagredegydd, (*-ion*), *n.m.* forerunner
rhagrith, (*-ion*), *n.m.* hypocrisy
rhagrithio, *v.* practise hypocrisy
rhagrithiol, *a.* hypocritical
rhagrithiwr, (*-wyr*), *n.m.* hypocrite

rhagrybuddio, v. forewarn
rhagweled, v. forsee
rhagwelediad, n.m. foresight, prescience
rhagwybod, v. foreknow
rhagwybodaeth, n.f. foreknowledge
rhagymadrodd, (-ion), n.m. preface, introduction
rhai, pn. ones: a. some
rhaib, n.m. rapacity, greed; spell
rhaid, (rheidiau), n.m. need, necessity
rhaidd, (rheiddiau), n.f. spear; antler
rhain, pn. these
rhamant, (-au), n.f. romance
rhamantus, a. romantic
rhampio, v. romp
rhan, (-nau), n.f. part, portion; fate
rhanbarth, (-au), n.m. division, district
rhandir, (-oedd), n.m.f. division, district
rhangymeriad, (-iaid), n.m. participle
rhaniad, (-au), n.m. division
rhannu, v. divide, share, distribute
rhannwr, (rhanwyr), n.m. divider, sharer
rhathell, (-au), n.f. rasp
rhathiad, n.m. friction
rhathu, v. rub, rasp, file
rhaw, (-iau, rhofiau), n.f. spade, shovel
rhawd, n.f. course, career
rhawg, adv. for a long time (to come)
rhawio, rhofio, v. shovel
rhawn, c.n. coarse long hair, horse-hair
rhedeg, v. run; flow
rhedegfa, (-feydd), n.f. racecourse, race
rhedegog, a. running, flowing
rhedegydd, (-ion, -wyr), n.m. runner
rhedfa, n.f. running, course, race
rhediad, n.m. running, trend; slope
rhedweli, (-ïau), n.f. artery
rhedyn, n.pl. (-en, n.f.), fern

rhefder, rhefedd, n.m. thickness
rhefr, n.m. rectum
rheffyn, (-nau), n.m. cord; string, rigmarole
rheg, (-au, -feydd), n.f. curse
rhegen yr ŷd, rh. ryg, n.f. corncrake
rhegi, v. curse   [fane
rheglyd, a. given to cursing, pro-
rheng, (-au, -oedd), n.f. row, rank
rheibio, v. raven, ravage, ravish
rheibus, a. rapacious, of prey
rheidiol, a. necessary, needful
rheidrwydd, n.m. necessity, need
rheidus, a. necessitous, needy
rheilffordd, (-ffyrdd), n.f. railway
rheini, pn. those
rheitheg, n.f. rhetoric
rheithegydd, (-ion, -wyr), n.m. rhetorician
rheithfarn, (-au), n.f. verdict
rheithiwr, (-wyr), n.m. juryman, juror
rheithor, (-ion, -iad), n.m. rector
rhelyw, n.m. residue, rest, remainder
rhemp, n.f. excess; defect
rhent, (-i), n.m. rent
rhentu, v. rent
rheol, (-au), n.f. rule, regulation
rheolaeth, n.f. rule, management, control
rheolaidd, a. regular
rheoleiddio, v. regulate
rheoli, v. rule, govern, control
rheolwr, (-wyr), n.m. ruler, controller
rhes, (-i), n.f. line, stripe; row, rank
rhesen, (rhesi), n.f. line, streak, stripe
rhesin, (-au, -ingau), n.m. raisin
rhesog, a. striped; ribbed
rhestl, (-au), n.f. rack
rhestr, (-au, -i), n.f. list; row
rhestru, v. list
rheswm, (-ymau), n.m. reason
rhesymeg, n.f. logic
rhesymegol, a. logical
rhesymegydd, (-ion, -wyr), n.m. logician

rhesymol, *a.* reasonable, rational

rhesymoldeb, *n.m.* reasonableness

rhesymoliaeth, *n.f.* rationalism

rhesymolwr, (*-wyr*), *n.m.* rationalist

rhesymu, *v.* reason

rhetoreg, rhethreg, *n.f.* rhetoric

rhew, (*-oedd, -ogydd*), *n.m.* frost, ice

rhewfryn, (*-iau*), *n.m.* iceberg

rhewi, *v.* freeze

rhewllyd, *a.* icy, frosty, frigid

rhewydd, *a.* wanton, lustful

rhi, *n.m.* king, lord

rhiain, (*rhianedd*), *n.f.* maiden

rhialtwch, *n.m.* pomp; festivity, jollity

rhibidirês, *n.f.* rigmarole

rhibin, *n.m.* streak

rhic, (*-iau*), *n.m.* notch, nick; groove

rhiciog, *a.* notched; grooved; ribbed

rhidyll, (*-iau*), *n.m.* riddle, sieve

rhidyllio, -u, *v.* riddle, sift

rhieingerdd, (*-i*), *n.f.* love-poem

rhieni, *n.pl.* parents

rhif, (*-au*), *n.m.* **rhifedi,** *n.m.* number, numeral

rhifo, *v.* number, count, reckon

rhifol, (*-ion*), *n.m.* numeral

rhifyddeg, -yddiaeth, *n.f.* arithmetic

rhifyddwr, (*-wyr*), *n.m.* arithmetician

rhifyn, (*-nau*), *n.m.* number

rhigol, (*-au, -ydd*), *n.f.* rut, groove

rhigwm, (*-ymau*), *n.m.* rigmarole: rhyme

rhigymu, *v.* rhyme, versify

rhigymwr, (*-wyr*), *n.m.* rhymester

rhingyll, (*-iaid*), *n.m.* sergeant, bailiff

rhimyn, (*-nau*), *n.m.* strip, string

rhin, (*-iau*), *n.f.* virtue, essence

rhincian, *v.* creak; gnash

rhiniog, (*-au*), *n.m.* threshold

rhinwedd, (*-au*), *n.m.f.* virtue

rhinweddol, *a.* virtuous

rhip, *n.m.* strickle

rhisgl, *n.m.* bark

rhith, (*-iau*), *n.m.* form, guise, appearance, image

rhithio, *v.* appear

rhithyn, *n.m.* atom, particle, scintilla

rhiw, (*-iau*), *n.f.* hill, acclivity

rhoch, *n.f.* grunt, groan; death-rattle

rhochain, -ian, *v.* grunt

rhod, (*-au*), *n.f.* wheel, orb; ecliptic

rhodfa, (*-feydd*), *n.f.* walk, promenade, avenue

rhodiad, *n.m.* walk

rhodianna, *v.* stroll

rhodio, *v.* walk, stroll

rhodres, *n.m.* ostentation, affectation

rhodresa, *v.* behave ostentatiously

rhodresgar, *a.* ostentatious, affected

rhodreswr, (*-wyr*), *n.m.* swaggerer

rhodd, (*-ion*), *n.f.* gift, present

rhoddi, *v.* give, bestow, yield; put

rhoddwr, (*-wyr*), *n.m.* giver, donor

rhoi, *v.* give, bestow, yield; put

rhôl, (*-iau*), *n.f.* **rholyn,** *n.m.* roll

rhôl, *n.f.* rule

rholbren, (*-ni*), *n.m.* rolling-pin

rholio, *v.* roll

rhonc, *a.* rank, stark, out-and-out

rhos, (*-ydd*), *n.f.* moor, heath; plain

rhos, *n.pl.* (*-yn, n.m.*), roses

rhost, *a.* roast, roasted

rhostio, *v.* roast

rhuad, (*-au*), *n.m.* roaring, roar

rhuadwy, *a.* roaring

rhuchen, (*rhuchion*), *n.f.* husk; film, pellicle

rhudd, *a.* red, crimson

rhuddell, *n.f.* rubric

rhuddin, *n.m.* heart of timber

rhuddion, *n.pl.* bran

rhuddygl, *n.m.* radish

Rhufeinaidd, *a.* Roman

Rhufeiniad, (*-iaid*), **-iwr,** (*-wyr*), *n.m.* Roman

Rhufeinig, *a.* Roman

rhugl, *a.* free, fluent, glib

rhuglen, (*-ni*), *n.f.* rattle

rhuglo, *v.* rattle
rhumen, *n.f.* belly, paunch
rhuo, *v.* roar, bellow, bluster
rhusio, *v.* start, scare, take fright
rhuthr, (*-au*), *n.m.* rush; attack; sally
rhuthro, *v.* rush; attack, assault
rhwbio, *v.* rub, chafe
rhwd, *n.m.* rust
rhwng, *pr.* between, among
rhwnc, *n.m.* snort, snore; death-rattle
rhwth, *a.* gaping, distended
rhwyd, (*-au*, *-i*), *n.f.* net, snare
rhwydo, *v.* net, ensnare
rhwydog, *a.* reticulated, netted
rhwydd, *a.* easy, expeditious, prosperous
rhwyddhau, *v.* facilitate
rhwyddineb, *n.m.* ease, facility
rhwyf, (*-au*), *n.f.* oar
rhwyflong, (*-au*), *n.f.* galley
rhwyfo, *v.* row; sway, toss about
rhwyfus, *v.* restless
rhwyfwr, (*-wyr*), *n.m.* rower, oarsman
rhwyg, (*-iadau*), *n.f.* rent, rupture; schism
rhwygo, *v.* rend, tear
rhwyll, (*-au*), *n.f.* **-yn,** *n.m.* buttonhole, aperture
rhwym, *a.* bound: (*-au*), *n.m.* bond, tie; obligation
rhwymedig, *a.* bound, obliged
rhwymedigaeth, (*-au*), *n.f.* bond, obligation
rhwymedd, *n.m.* constipation
rhwymiad, (*-au*), *n.m.* binding
rhwymo, *v.* bind, tie; constipate
rhwymwr, (*-wyr*), *n.m.* binder
rhwymyn, (*-nau*), *n.m.* band, bond, bandage
rhwysg, (*-au*), *n.m.* sway; pomp
rhwysgfawr, *a.* pompous, ostentatious
rhwystr, (*-au*), *n.m.* hindrance, obstacle
rhwystro, *v.* hinder, prevent, obstruct   [fused
rhwystrus, *a.* embarrassed, con-

rhy, *adv.* too
rhybedio, *v.* rivet; reverberate
rhybudd, (*-ion*), *n.m.* notice, warning
rhybuddio, *v.* warn, admonish, caution
rhybuddiwr, (*-wyr*), *n.m.* warner
rhych, (*-au*), *n.m.f.* furrow, rut, groove
rhychog, *a.* furrowed, seamed
rhychwant, (*-au*), *n.m.* span
rhychwantu, *v.* span
rhyd, (*-au*, *-iau*), *n.f.* ford
rhydio, *v.* ford
rhydlyd, *a.* rusty
rhydu, *v.* rust
rhydd, *a.* free; loose; liberal
Rhyddfrydiaeth, *n.f.* Liberalism
rhyddfrydig, *a.* liberal, generous
rhyddfrydol, *a.* liberal (in politics)
Rhyddfrydwr, (*-wyr*), *n.m.* Liberal, Radical
rhyddhad, *n.m.* liberation, emancipation
rhyddhau, *v.* free, release, liberate
rhyddhawr, (*-wyr*), *n.m.* liberator
rhyddiaith, *n.f.* prose
rhyddid, *n.m.* freedom, liberty
rhyddieithol, *a.* prose, prosaic
rhyddni, *n.m.* looseness, diarrhœa
rhyfedd, *a.* strange, queer, wonderful
rhyfeddnod, (*-au*), *n.m.* note of exclamation
rhyfeddod, (*-au*), *n.m.f.* wonder, marvel   [lous
rhyfeddol, *a.* wonderful, marvel-
rhyfeddu, *v.* wonder, marvel
rhyfel, (*-oedd*), *n.m.f.* war, warfare
rhyfela, *v.* wage war, war
rhyfelgar, *a.* warlike, bellicose
rhyfelgri, *n.m.* war-cry, battle-cry
rhyfelgyrch, (*-oedd*), *n.m.* campaign
rhyfelwr, (*-wyr*), *n.m.* warrior
rhyferthwy, *n.m.* torrent, inundation
rhyfon, *n.pl.* currants
rhyfyg, *n.m.* presumption, foolhardiness

rhyfygu, *v.* presume, dare

rhyfygus, *a.* presumptuous; foolhardy

rhyg, *n.m.* rye

rhyglyddu, *v.* deserve, merit

rhygnu, *v.* rub, grate, jar; harp

rhygyngu, *v.* amble; caper, mince

rhyngu, *v.*—**rh. bodd,** please

rhyngwladwriaethol, *a.* international

rhyndod, *n.m.* shivering, chill

rhynion, *n.pl.* grits, groats

rhynllyd, *a.* shivering, chilly

rhynnu, *v.* starve with cold

rhysedd, *n.m.* abundance, excess

rhyswr, (*-wyr*), *n.m.* hero, champion

rhython, *n.pl.* cockles

rhythu, *v.* gape; stare

rhyw, *a.* some, certain: (*-iau*), *n.f.m.* sort; sex

rhywiog, *a.* kindly, genial: fine: tender

rhywogaeth, (*-au*), *n.f.* species, sort, kind

rhywyr, *a.* high time

S

Sabath, -oth, (*-au*), *n.m.* Sabbath

Sabothol, *a.* Sabbath, sabbatic(al)

sacrament, (*-au*), *n.m.f.* sacrament

sacramentaidd, *a.* sacramental

sach, (*-au*), *n.f.m.* sack

sachaid, (*-eidiau*), *n.f.* sackful

sachlen, *n.f.* **sachliain,** *n.m.* sackcloth

sachu, *v.* sack, bag

sad, *a.* firm, steady, solid; sober

sadio, *v.* firm, steady

sadrwydd, *n.m.* firmness, steadiness

Sadwrn, (*-yrnau*), *n.m.* Saturn; Saturday

saer, (*seiri*), *n.m.* wright, mason, carpenter

saernïaeth, *n.f.* workmanship, construction

saernïo, *v.* fashion, construct

Saesneg, *n.f. & a.* English

Saesnes, (*-au*), *n.f.* Englishwoman

saets, *n.m.* sage

saeth, (*-au*), *n.f.* arrow, dart

saethu, *v.* shoot, dart; blast

saethwr, (*-wyr*), *n.m.* shooter, shot

saethydd, (*-ion*), *n.m.* shooter, archer

saethyddiaeth, *n.f.* archery

safadwy, *a.* stable

safbwynt, (*-iau*), *n.m.* standpoint

safiad, *n.m.* standing; stature; stand

safio, *v.* save

safle, (*-oedd*), *n.m.* position, station, situation

safn, (*-au*), *n.f.* mouth, jaws

safnrhwth, *a.* open-mouthed, gaping

safnrhythu, *v.* gape, stare

safon, (*-au*), *n.f.* standard, criterion

saffir, *n.m.* sapphire

saffwy, *n.f.* javelin, spear

sagrafen, (*-nau*), *n.f.* sacrament

sang, (*-au*), *n.f.* pressure, tread

sangu, *v.* tread, trample

saib, (*seibiau*), *n.m.* leisure; pause, rest

saig, (*seigiau*), *n.f.* mess, meal, dish

sail, (*seiliau*), *n.f.* base, foundation

saim, (*seimiau*), *n.m.* grease

sain, (*seiniau*), *n.f.* sound, tone

Sais, (*Saeson*), *n.m.* Saxon, Englishman

saith, *a. & n.m.* seven

sâl, *a.* poor; poorly, ill

saldra, *n.m.* poorness; illness

salm, (*-au*), *n.f.* psalm

salmydd, (*-ion*), *n.m.* psalmist

saltring, *n.m.* psaltery

salw, *a.* poor, mean, vile; ugly

salwch, *n.m.* illness

Sallwyr, *n.m.* Psalter

Sanct, *n.m.* the Holy One

sanctaidd, *a.* holy

sancteiddhad, -eiddiad, *n.m.* sanctification

sancteiddio, *v.* sanctify, hallow

sancteiddrwydd, *n.m.* holiness, sanctity

sandal, (-au), *n.m.* sandal

sant, (*saint, seintiau*), *n.m.* saint

santes, (-au), *n.f.* female saint

sarff, (*seirff*), *n.f.* serpent

sarhad, (-au), *n.m.* insult, disgrace, injury

sarhau, *v.* insult, affront, injure

sarhaus, *a.* insulting, offensive, insolent

sarn, (-au), *n.f.* causeway: *n.m.* litter

sarnu, *v.* trample; litter

sarrug, *a.* gruff, surly, morose

sarugrwydd, *n.m.* gruffness, surliness

sasiwn, (-*iynau*), *n.m.* C.M. Association

sathredig, *a.* common, vulgar

sathru, *v.* tread, trample

sawdl, (*sodlau*), *n.m.f.* heel

sawdring, sawdur, *n.m.* solder

sawl, *pn.* whoso, he that. **—Pa s.**, how many

sawr, sawyr, *n.m.* savour

sawrio, -u, *v.* savour

sawrus, *a.* savoury

saws, *n.m.* sauce

sbâr, (*sbarion*), *n.m.* spare; (*pl.*) leavings

sbario, *v.* spare, save

sbectol, *n.f.* spectacle(s)

sbeit, *n.f.* spite

sbeitio, *v.* spite

sbeitlyd, *a.* spiteful

sbel, (-*iau*), *n.f.* spell

sbon, *adv.***—newydd s.**, span-new, brand-new

sbort, *n.f.* sport, fun, game

sbwylio, *v.* spoil

sebon, (-au), *n.m.* soap

seboni, *v.* soap, lather; soft-soap

sebonwr, (-*wyr*), *n.m.* soapman; flatterer

sect, (-au), *n.f.* sect

sectyddiaeth, *n.f.* sectarianism

sectyddol, *a.* sectarian

sech, *a.*, f. of **sych**

sedd, (-au), *n.f.* seat, pew

seddu, *v.* seat, instal

sef, *c.* that is to say, namely, to wit

sefnig, *n.m.* pharynx

sefydledig, *a.* established

sefydliad, (-au), *n.m.* establishment, institution

sefydlog, *a.* fixed, settled, stationary, stable

sefydlo(w)grwydd, *n.m.* stability

sefydlu, *v.* establish, found, settle

sefyll, *v.* stand; stop

sefyllfa, (-*oedd*), *n.f.* situation, position

sefyllian, *v.* stand about, loiter

segur, *a.* idle

segura, *v.* idle

segurdod, *n.m.* idleness

segurwr, (-*wyr*), *n.m.* idler

seguryd, *n.m.* idleness

sengi, *v.* tread, trample

sengl, *a.* single

seiat, (-*adau*), *n.f.* fellowship meeting, 'society'

seibiant, *n.m.* leisure, respite

seiliad, *n.f.* foundation

seilio, *v.* ground, found

seimlyd, *a.* greasy

seinber, *a.* melodious, euphonious

seindorf, (-*dyrf*), *n.f.* band

seineg, *n.f.* phonetics

seinfforch, (-*ffyrch*), *n.f.* tuning-fork

seinio, *v.* sound, resound

seintio, *v.* saint, canonize

seintwar, *n.f.* sanctuary

seinyddiaeth, *n.f.* phonology

seinyddol, *a.* phonetic

Seisnig, *a.* English

Seisnigaidd, *a.* Englishy, Anglicized

Seisnigeiddio, -igo, *v.* Anglicize

seithblyg, *a.* sevenfold

seithfed, *a.* seventh

seithongl, (-au), *n.f.* septangle, heptagon

seithug, *a.* futile, fruitless, bootless

seithugo, *v.* frustrate, balk, thwart

sêl, *n.f.* zeal

sêl, (*seliau*), *n.f.* seal

seld, (-au), *n.f.* dresser, sideboard, bookcase

seler, (-au, -*ydd*), *n.f.* cellar

selio, *v.* seal
selni, *n.m.* illness
selog, *a.* zealous, ardent
selsig, (*-od*), *n.f.* black-pudding, sausage
seml, *a.,* f. of **syml**
sen, (*-nau*) *n.f.* reproof, rebuke, censure
senedd, (*-au*), *n.f.* senate; parliament [tary
seneddol, *a.* senatorial, parliamen-
seneddwr, (*-wyr*), *n.m.* senator
sennu, *v.* rebuke, censure
sêr. See **seren**
seraff, (*-iaid*), *n.m.* seraph
serch, *c. & pr.* although, notwithstanding
serch, (*-iadau*), *n.m.* affection, love
serchog, *a.* affectionate, loving
serchowgrwydd, *n.m.* affectionateness, love
serchu, *v.* love
serchus, *a.* loving, affectionate, pleasant
sêr-ddewin, (*-iaid*), *n.m.* astrologer
sêr-ddewiniaeth, *n.f.* astrology
seremoni, (*-ïau*), *n.f.* ceremony
seremonïol, *a.* ceremonial
seren, (*sêr*), *n.f.* star; asterisk
serennog, *a.* starry
serennu, *v.* sparkle, scintillate
serfyll *a.* unsteady
seri, *n.* causeway, pavement
serio, *v.* sear
serth, *a.* steep, precipitous; obscene
serthedd, *n.m.* ribaldry, obscenity
seryddiaeth, *n.f.* astronomy
seryddol, *a.* astronomical
seryddwr, (*-wyr*), *n.m.* astronomer
sesbin, *n.m.* shoehorn
set, (*-iau*), *n.f.* set
sêt, (*seti*), *n.f.* seat, pew.—**s. fawr,** deacons' pew
setl, (*-au*), *n.f.* settle
setlo, *v.* settle
seth, *a.,* f. of **syth**
sethrydd, (*-ion*), *n.m.* treader, trampler
sew, (*-ion*), *n.m.* juice; pottage; delicacy

sg-. See also **ysg-**
sgâm, (*sgamiau*), *n.f.* scheme, dodge
sgamio, *v.* scheme, dodge
sgaprwth, *a.* uncouth, rough
sgîl, *n.m.* pillion
sgrech y coed, *n.f.* jay
sgwd, (*sgydiau*), *n.f.* cataract, waterfall
sgwrs, (*sgyrsiau*), *n.f.* talk, chat, conversation
sgwrsio, *v.* talk, chat
si, *n.m.* whiz, buzz; rumour, murmur
siaced, (*-i*), *n.f.* jacket, coat
siâd, (*sidau*), *n.f.* pate
sialc, *n.m.* chalk
sialens, *n.f.* challenge
sialensio, *v.* challenge
siambr, *n.f.* chamber
sianel, (*-i, -ydd*), *n.f.* channel
siâr, *n.f.* share
siarad, *v.* talk, speak: *n.m.* talk
siaradus, *a.* talkative, garrulous
siaradwr, (*-wyr*), *n.m.* talker, speaker
siario, *v.* share
siars, *n.f.* charge, command
siarsio, *v.* charge, enjoin, warn
siartr, (*-au*), *n.f.* charter
siasbi, *n.m.* shoehorn
siawns, *n.f.* chance
siawnsio, *v.* chance
sibrwd, *v.* whisper, murmur: (*-ydion*), *n.m.* whisper, murmur
sicl, (*-au*), *n.m.* shekel
sicr, *a.* sure, certain; secure
sicrhau, *v.* assure, affirm, confirm; secure [ance
sicrwydd, *n.m.* certainty, assur-
sidan, (*-au*), *n.m.* silk
sidanaidd *a.* silky
sidanbryf, (*-ed*), *n.m.* silkworm
siêd, *n.m.* escheat, forfeit
siesbin, *n.m.* shoehorn
siew, *n.f.* show
siffrwd, *v.* rustle, shuffle
sigledig, *a.* shaky, rickety, unstable
siglen, (*-nydd*), *n.f.* swing; bog, swamp

siglo, *v.* shake, quake, rock, swing, wag

sil, (*-od*), *n.m.* spawn, fry

silff, (*-oedd*), *n.f.* shelf

silwair, *n.m.* silage

sill, (*-iau*), **-af**, (*-au*), *n.f.* syllable

sillafiaeth, *n.f.* spelling

sillafu, *v.* spell

sillgoll, (*-au*), *n.f.* apostrophe

simnai, (*-neiau*), *n.f.* chimney

simsan, *a.* unsteady, tottering, rickety

sinach, (*-od*), *n.f.* balk, waste ground; skinflint

sinsir, *n.m.* ginger

sïo, *v.* hiss, whiz; murmur, purl

sioe, (*-au*), *n.f.* show

siol, (*-au*), *n.f.* skull, pate

siôl, (*siolau*), *n.f.* shawl

siom, (*-au*), *n.m.* disappointment

siomedig, *a.* disappointed, disappointing

siomedigaeth, (*-au*), *n.f.* disappointment

siomi, *v.* disappoint; balk, thwart; deceive

siomiant, *n.m.* disappointment

sionc, *a.* brisk, nimble, agile, active

sioncio, *v.* brisk

sioncrwydd, *n.m.* briskness, agility

sioncyn y gwair, *n.m.* grasshopper

siop, (*-au*), *n.f.* shop

siopwr, (*-wyr*), *n.m.* shopman, shopkeeper

sipian, *v.* sip, sup, suck

siprys, *n.m.* mixed corn (oats and barley)

sipsiwn, *n.pl.* gipsies

sir, (*-oedd*), *n.f.* shire, county

sirig, *n.m.* silk

siriol, *a.* cheerful, bright, pleasant

sirioldeb, *n.m.* cheerfulness

sirioli, *v.* cheer, brighten

sirydd, **-yf**, (*-ion*), *n.m.* sheriff

siryddiaeth, *n.f.* shrievalty

sisial, *v.* whisper

siswrn, (*-yrnau*), *n.m.* scissors

siwglaeth, *n.f.* jugglery

siwgr, *n.m.* sugar

siwr, *a.* sure, certain

siwrnai, (*-eiau*), *n.f.* journey: *adv.* once

slaf, (*slafiaid*), *n.m.* slave, drudge

slotian, *v.* paddle, dabble; tipple

slumyn. See **ystlum**

smocio, *v.* smoke (tobacco)

smociwr, (*-wyr*), *n.m.* smoker

snisin, *n.m.* snuff

snwffian, *v.* snuff, sniff; snuffle; whimper

sobr, *a.* sober, serious

sobreiddio, sobri, *v.* sober

sobrwydd, *n.m.* sobriety, soberness

socas, (*-au*), *n.f.* gaiter, legging

sodr, *n.m.* solder

soddi, *v.* sink, submerge

soeg, *n.m.* brewers' grains, draff

sofl, *n.pl.* (*-yn*, *n.m.*), stubble

sofliar, (*-ieir*), *n.f.* quail

sofren, (*sofrod*), *n.f.* sovereign (coin)

solas, *n.m.* solace, joy

sol-ffa, *n.m.*; **solffaeo**, *v.* sol-fa

sôn, *v. & n.m.* talk, mention, rumour

soned, (*-au*), *n.f.* sonnet

soniarus, *a.* melodious, tuneful; loud

soriant, *n.m.* indignation, displeasure

sorod, *n.pl.* dross, dregs, refuse

sorri, *v.* chafe, sulk, be displeased

sosban, (*-nau*, *-benni*), *n.f.* saucepan

soser, (*-i*), *n.f.* saucer

sosialaeth, *n.f.* socialism

sothach, *c.n.* refuse, rubbish, trash

st-. See also **yst-**

staen, (*-au*), *n.m.*: **-io**, *v.* stain

stâl, (*-au*), *n.f.* stall

stamp, (*-iau*), *n.m.f.* stamp

stampio, *v.* stamp

starts, *n.m.* starch

stên, (*stenau*), *n.f.* pitcher

stesion, (*-au*), *n.f.* station

sticil, **-ill**, *n.f.* stile

stomp, *n.f.* bungle, mess, muddle

stompio, *v.* beat, pound; bungle, mess

stompiwr, (*-wyr*), *n.m.* bungler

stori, (*-ïau, -ïâu, straeon*), *n.f.* story, tale

stor(o)m, (*stormydd*), *n.f.* storm

straegar, *a.* gossiping, gossipy

stwc, (*stycau*), *n.m.* pail, bucket

stwff, (*styffiau*), *n.m.* stuff

stwffio, *v.* stuff, thrust

stwffwl, (*styffylau*), *n.m.* post; staple

su, *n.m.* buzz, murmur, hum

suad, *n.m.* buzzing, lulling; hum

sucan, *n.m.* gruel

sudd, (*-ion*), *n.m.* juice, sap

suddgloch, (*-glychau*), *n.f.* diving-bell

suddlong, (*-au*), *n.f.* submarine

suddo, *v.* sink, dive; invest (money)

sug, (*-ion*), *n.m.* juice, sap

sugn, *n.m.* suck; suction; sap

sugno, *v.* suck, imbibe, absorb

Sul, (*-iau*), *n.m.* Sunday

Sulgwyn, *n.m.* Whitsunday

suo, *v.* buzz, hum; lull, hush

sur, (*-ion*), *a.* sour, acid: *n.m.* acid

surdoes, *n.m.* leaven

surni, *n.m.* sourness, staleness, tartness

suro, *v.* sour

sut, *n.m.* manner; plight.—**pa sut? sut?** how?

swalpio, *v.* flounder, jump, bounce

swci, *a.* tame, pet

swcro, *v.* succour

swcwr, *n.m.* succour

swch, (*sychau*), *n.f.* ploughshare; tip, grimble

swil, *a.* shy, bashful

swilder, *n.m.* shyness, bashfulness

swllt, (*sylltau*), *n.m.* shilling

swm, (*symiau*), *n.m.* sum, bulk

swmbwl, (*symbylau*), *n.m.* goad

swmer, (*-au*), *n.m.* beam; pack

swn, *n.m.* noise, sound

swnian, *v.* murmur, grumble, nag

swnio, *v.* sound, pronounce

swnllyd, *a.* peevish, querulous

swnt, *n.m.* sound, strait

swp, (*sypiau*), *n.m.* mass, heap; cluster

swper, (*-au*), *n.m.f.* supper

swpera, -u, *v.* give or take supper

swrn, (*syrnau*), *n.f.* fetlock, ankle; *n.m.* good number

swrth, *a.* heavy, sluggish; sullen

swta, *a.* abrupt, curt

swydd, (*-au, -i*), *n.f.* office; county

swyddfa, (*-feydd*), *n.f.* office

swyddog, (*-ion*), *n.m.* officer, official

swyddogaeth, *n.f.* office

swyddogol, *a.* official

swyn, (*-ion*), *n.m.* charm, fascination, spell, magic

swyngyfaredd, (*-ion*), *n.f.* sorcery, witchcraft

swyngyfareddwr, (*-wyr*), *n.m.* sorcerer

swyno, *v.* charm, enchant, bewitch

swynol, *a.* charming, fascinating

swynwr, (*-wyr*), *n.m.* magician, wizard

swynwraig, (*-wragedd*), *n.f.* sorceress

syber, *a.* sober, decent; clean, tidy

syberw, *a.* proud, courteous

sych, *a.* dry: *f.* **sech**

sychder, *n.m.* dryness, drought

syched, *n.m.* thirst

sychedig, *a.* thirsty, parched, dry

sychedu, *v.* thirst

sychlyd, *a.* dry

sychu, *v.* dry, dry up; wipe dry, wipe

sydyn, *a.* sudden, abrupt

sydynrwydd, *n.m.* suddenness

sydd, *v.* is, are

syfi, *n.pl.* (**syfïen,** *n.f.*), strawberries

syflyd, *v.* stir, move, budge

syfrdan, *a.* giddy, dazed, stunned

syfrdandod, *n.m.* giddiness, stupor

syfrdanu, *v.* daze, stupefy, stun

sylfaen, (*-feini*), *n.f.* foundation

sylfaenu, *v.* found

sylfaenwr, (*-wyr*), **-ydd,** (*-ion*), *n.m.* founder

sylw, (*-adau*), *n.m.* notice, attention, remark

sylwadaeth, *n.f.* observation

sylwedydd, (*-ion*), *n.m.* observer

sylwedd, (*-au*), *n.m.* substance, reality

sylweddol, *a.* substantial, real
sylweddoli, *v.* realize
sylweddoliad, *n.m.* realization
sylwi, *v.* observe, regard, notice
syllu, *v.* gaze
symbal, (*-au*), *n.m.* cymbal
symbyliad, *n.m.* stimulus, encouragement
symbylu, *v.* goad, spur, stimulate
symbylydd, (*-ion*), *n.m.* stimulant
symio, *v.* sum
syml, *a.* simple: *f.* **seml**
symledd, *n.m.* simplicity
symleiddio, *v.* simplify
symlrwydd, *n.m.* simplicity
symol, *a.* middling, fair
symud, *v.* move, remove
symudiad, (*-au*), *n.m.* movement, removal
symudol, *a.* moving, movable, mobile
syn, *a.* amazed; astonishing, surprising
synagog, (*-au*), *n.m.* synagogue
synamon, *n.m.* cinnamon
syndod, *n.m.* marvel, amazement, surprise
synfyfyrdod, *n.m.* reverie
synfyfyrio, *v.* muse
synhwyrol, *a.* sensible
syniad, (*-au*), *n.m.* notion, idea, view
synied, -io, *v.* think, believe, feel
synnu, *v.* marvel, be amazed, surprise, be surprised
synnwyr, (*synhwyrau*), *n.m.* sense
synwyroldeb, *n.m.* sensibleness
sypio, *v.* pack, heap, bundle
sypyn, (*-nau*), *n.m.* package, packet
syr, *n.m.* sir
syrffed, *n.m.* surfeit
syrffedu, *v.* surfeit
syrthiedig, *a.* fallen
syrthio, *v.* fall, tumble
syrthni, *n.m.* listlessness, sloth; inertia
syth, *a.* stiff; straight: *f.* **seth**
sythu, *v.* stiffen, straighten; starve with cold

T

tabernacl, (*-au*), *n.m.* tabernacle
tabl, (*-au*), *n.m.* table
tablen, *n.f.* ale, beer
tabwrdd, (*-yrddau*), *n.m.* drum
tabyrddu, *v.* drum, thrum
taclau, *n.pl.* (**teclyn,** *n.m.*), tackle, gear
taclo, *v.* tackle
taclu, *v.* put in order, trim
taclus, *a.* neat, trim, tidy
tacluso, *v.* trim, tidy
taclusrwydd, *n.m.* tidiness
Tachwedd, *n.m.* November
tad, (*-au*), *n.m.* father. — **tad-cu,** grandfather
tadmaeth, (*-au*, *-od*), *n.m.* foster-father [tion
tadogaeth, *n.f.* paternity; deriva-
tadogi, *v.* father
tadol, *a.* fatherly, paternal
taenelliad, *n.m.* sprinkling, affusion
taenellu, *v.* sprinkle
taenellwr, (*-wyr*), *n.m.* sprinkler
taenu, *v.* spread, expand, stretch
taenwr, (*-wyr*), *n.m.* spreader, disseminator
taeog, *a.* churlish, blunt: (*-au*, *-ion*), *n.m.* churl
taeogaidd, *a.* churlish, rude
taer, *a.* earnest, importunate, urgent
taerineb, taerni, *n.m.* earnestness, importunity
taeru, *v.* insist, maintain; contend, wrangle
tafarn, (*-au*), *n.f.m.* tavern, inn, public-house
tafarndy, (*-dai*), *n.m.* public-house
tafarnwr, (*-wyr*), *n.m.* inn-keeper, publican
tafell, (*-au*, *-i*, *tefyll*), *n.f.* slice
tafl, (*-au*), *n.f.* cast; scale.—**ffon d.** sling
tafleisiaeth, *n.f.* ventriloquism
tafleisydd, (*-ion*, *-wyr*), *n.m.* ventriloquist

taflen, (*-nau, -ni*), *n.f.* table, list, leaflet

taflennu, *v.* tabulate

tafliad, (*-au*), *n.m.* throw; set-back

taflod, (*-ydd*), *n.f.* loft.—**t. y genau,** palate

taflu, *v.* throw, fling, cast, hurl

tafod, (*-au*), *n.m.* tongue

tafodi, *v.* rate, scold

tafodiaith, (*-ieithoedd*), *n.f.* speech, language, dialect

tafod-leferydd, *n.m.* speech, utterance,—**ar d.,** by rote

tafol, *n.f.* scales

tafol, *c.n.* dock

tafotrwg, *a.* foul-mouthed, abusive

tafotrydd, *a.* garrulous, flippant

tagell, (*-au, tegyll*), *n.f.* gill; wattle; dewlap; double chin

tagellog, *a.* wattled; double-chinned

tagfa, (*-feydd*), *n.f.* choking, strangling

tagu, *v.* choke, stifle; strangle

tangnefedd, *n.m.f.* peace

tangnefeddu, *v.* make peace; appease

tangnefeddus, *a.* peaceable, peaceful

tangnefeddwr, (*-wyr*), *n.m.* peacemaker

tai. See **tŷ**

taid, (*teidiau*), *n.m.* grandfather

tail, *n.m.* dung, manure

tair, *a.* f. of **tri**

taith, (*teithiau*), *n.f.* journey, voyage, progress

tal, *a.* tall, high, lofty

tâl, (*talau, taloedd*), *n.m.* end, forehead

tâl, (*taliadau*), *n.m.* pay, payment. **Taloedd,** rates

talaith, (*-eithiau*), *n.f.* diadem; province, state

talar, (*-au*), *n.f.* headland in field

talcen, (*-nau, -ni*), *n.m.* forehead; gable

taldra, *n.m.* tallness, loftiness, stature

taleb, (*-au, -ion*), *n.f.* receipt, voucher

taledigaeth, *n.f.* payment, recompense

taleithiol, *a.* provincial

talent, (*-au*), *n.f.* talent

talentog, *a.* talented

talfyriad, (*-au*), *n.m.* abbreviation, abridgement

talfyrru, *v.* abbreviate, abridge

talgryf, *a.* sturdy, robust; impudent

taliad, (*-au*), *n.m.* payment

talm, *n.m.* space, while; quantity, number.—**er ys t.,** long ago

talog, *a.* jaunty

talp, (*-au, -iau*), *n.m.* mass, lump

talpiog, *a.* lumpy

talu, *v.* pay, render; answer, suit; be worth

talwr, (*-wyr*), *n.m.* payer

tamaid, (*-eidiau*), *n.m.* morsel, bit, bite

tan, *pr.* to, till, until, as far; under

tân, (*tanau*), *n.m.* fire

tanbaid, *a.* fiery, hot, fervent; brilliant

tanbeidrwydd, *n.m.* fierce heat, ardour

tanchwa, (*-oedd*), *n.f.* fire-damp; explosion

tanddaearol, *a.* underground, subterranean

tanforol, *a.* submarine

tanio, *v.* fire, stoke

taniwr, (*-wyr*), *n.m.* firer, fireman, stoker

tanlli, *a.*—**newydd sbon danlli;** brand new

tanllwyth, (*-i*), *n.m.* blazing fire

tanllyd, *a.* fiery

tanodd, *adv.* below, beneath

tant, (*tannau*), *n.m.* chord, string

tanwydd, *c.n.* firewood, fuel

tanysgrifiad, (*-au*), *n.m.* subscription

tanysgrifio, *v.* subscribe

tanysgrifiwr, (*-wyr*), *n.m.* subscriber

taradr, (*terydr*), *n.m.* auger.—**t. y coed,** woodpecker

taran, tran, *adv.* rather, somewhat

taran, (*-au*), *n.f.* (peal of) thunder

taranfollt, (-au), n.f. thunderbolt

taranu, v. thunder

tarawiad. See **trawiad**

tarddiad, (-au), n.m. source, derivation

tarddle, (-oedd), n.m. source

tarddu, v. sprout, spring; derive, be derived

tarfu, v. scare, scatter

tarian, (-au), n.f. shield

tario, v. tarry

taro, v. strike, smite, hit, knock; tap; stick; hot; suit

tarren, (tarenni, -ydd), n.f. knoll, rock

tarth, (-oedd), n.m. mist, vapour

tarw, (teirw), n.m. bull

tas, (teisi), n.f. rick, stack

tasg, (-au), n.f. tax, task

tasgu, v. tax, task; start; splash, spirt

tato, tatws, n.pl. (**taten, tatysen,** n.f.), potatoes

taw, n.m. silence.—**rhoi t. ar** silence

taw c. that

tawch, n.m. vapour, haze, mist, fog

tawdd, a. melted, molten, dissolved

tawedog, a. silent, taciturn

tawel, a. calm, quiet, still, tranquil

tawelu, v. calm; grow calm

tawelwch, n.m. calm, quiet, tranquillity

tawlbwrdd, n.m. chessboard, draughtboard

te, n.m. tea

tebot, (-au), n.m. teapot

tebyg, a. similar, like, likely

tebygol, a. likely, probable

tebygolrwydd, n.m. likelihood, probability

tebygrwydd, n.m. likeness, resemblance

tebygu, v. liken, resemble; suppose

tecáu, v. beautify, adorn, embellish

techneg, n.f. technique: **-ol,** a. technical

teg, a. fair, beautiful, fine

tegan, (-au), n.m. plaything, toy, bauble

tegell, (-au, -i), n.m. kettle, tea-kettle

tegwch, n.m. fairness, beauty

teigr, (-od), n.m. tiger

teilchion, n.pl. fragments, atoms, shivers

teiliwr, (-eilwriaid), n.m. tailor

teilo, v. dung, manure

teilwng, a. worthy; deserved

teilwra, v. tailor

teilwres, (-au), n.f. tailoress

teilwriaeth, n.f. tailoring

teilyngdod, n.m. worthiness, merit

teilyngu, v. deserve, merit; deign

teimlad, (-au), n.m. feel, feeling, sensation, emotion: **-ol,** a. emotional

teimladrwydd, n.m. feelingness, sensibility

teimladwy, a. feeling; sensitive

teimlo, v. feel, touch, handle, manipulate

teip, (-iau), n.m. type

teipiedydd, (-ion), n.m. typewriter

teipydd, (-ion), n.m. typist

teisen, (-nau), n.f. cake

teitl, (-au), n.m. title

teithi c.n. traits, characteristics, qualities

teithio, v. travel, journey

teithiol, a. travelling, itinerant

teithiwr, (-wyr), n.m. traveller, passenger

telaid, a. beautiful, comely

telediw, a. handsome

teledu, n.m. television: v. televise

teler, (-au), n.m. term, condition

telm, (-au), n.f. snare

telori, v. warble, quaver

telyn, (-au), n.f. harp

telyneg, (-ion), n.f. lyric

telynor, (-ion), n.m. harpist

teml, (-au), n.f. temple

Temlydd, (-ion), n.m. Templar

Temlyddiaeth, n.f. Templarism

temtasiwn, (-iynau), n.m.f. temptation

temtio, v. tempt

temtiwr, (-wyr), n.m. tempter

tenant, (-iaid), n.m. tenant

tenantiaeth, *n.f.* tenancy

tenau, *a.* thin, lean; slender; rarified; sensitive

tendio, *v.* tend, mind

teneuo, *v.* thin

teneuwch, *n.m.* thinness, leanness; tenuity

tenewyn, (*-nau*), *n.m.* flank

tenlli(**f**), *n.m.* lining

tennyn, (*tenynnau*), *n.m.* cord, rope, halter

têr, *a.* clear, refined, pure, fine

terfyn, (*-au*), *n.m.* end, extremity, bound

terfyniad, (*-au*), *n.m.* ending, termination

terfynol, *a.* final; conclusive

terfynu, *v.* end, terminate, determine

terfysg, (*-oedd*), *n.m.* tumult, riot

terfysgaidd, -lyd, *a.* riotous, turbulent

terfysgu, *v.* riot, rage, surge

terfysgwr, (*-wyr*), *n.m.* rioter, insurgent

term, (*-au*), *n.m.* term

teru, *v.* clear, refine, clarify

terrwyn, *a.* brave, fierce, mighty

terwyn, *a.* fiery, ardent

tes, *n.m.* sunshine, warmth, heat; haze

tesog, *a.* sunny, hot, close, sultry

testament, (*-au*), *n.m.* testament

testamentwr, (*-wyr*), *n.m.* testator

testun, (*-au*), *n.m.* text, theme, subject

testunio, *v.* taunt, deride

teth, (*-au*), *n.f.* teat

teulu, (*-oedd*), *n.m.* family

teuluaidd, *a.* family, domestic

tew, *a.* thick, fat, plump

tewdra, -dwr, *n.m.* thickness, fatness

tewhau, *v.* thicken, fatten

tewi, *v.* keep silence, be silent

tewychu, *v.* thicken, fatten; condense

tewyn, (*-ion*), *n.m.* ember, brand

teyrn, (*-edd, -oedd*), *n.m.* monarch, sovereign

teyrnas, (*-oedd*), *n.f.* kingdom, realm

teyrnasiad, (*-au*), *n.m.* reign

teyrnasu, *v.* reign

teyrnfradwr, (*-wyr*), *n.m.* traitor

teyrnfradwriaeth, *n.f.* (high) treason

teyrngadair, *n.f.* throne

teyrngarol, *a.* loyal

teyrngarwch, *n.m.* loyalty

teyrnged, (*-au*), *n.f.* tribute

teyrnwialen, (*-wiail*), *n.f.* sceptre

ti, *pn.* thou, thee

ticed, (*-i*), *n.m.f.* ticket

tician, *v.* tick

tid, (*-au*), *n.f.* chain

tila, *a.* feeble, puny, insignificant

tîm, (*timau*), *n.m.* team

tin, (*-au*), *n.f.* bottom; rump; tail

tinc, (*-iadau*), *n.m.* clang, tinkle

tincian, *v.* tinkle, chink, clink, clank

tipian, *v.* tick

tipyn, (*-nau, tipiau*), *n.m.* bit

tir, (*-oedd*), *n.m.* land, ground, territory

tirf, *a.* fresh, luxuriant, fat

tirio, *v.* land, ground

tiriog, *a.* landed

tiriogaeth, (*-au*), *n.f.* territory

tiriogaethol, *a.* territorial

tirion, *a.* kind, tender, gentle, gracious   [ness

tiriondeb, *n.m.* kindness, tender-

tirol, *a.* relating to land

tisian, *v.* sneeze

titw, *n.f.* puss, pussy

tithau, *pn.c.* thou (on thy part), thou also

tiwn, (*-iau*), *n.f.* tune

tiwnio, *v.* tune

tlawd, (*tlodion*), *a.* poor

tlodaidd, *a.* poorish, mean, dowdy

tlodi, *v.* impoverish: *n.m.* poverty

tlos, *a.,* f. of **tlws**

tloty, (*-ai*), *n.m.* poorhouse, workhouse

tlotyn, (*tlodion*), *n.m.* pauper

tlws, *a.* pretty: f. **tlos**

tlws, (*tlysau*), *n.m.* jewel, gem; medal

tlysni, *n.m.* prettiness

to, (*toeau*), *n.m.* roof; generation

toc, *adv.* shortly, presently, soon

tocio, *v.* clip, dock, prune

tocyn, (*tociau*), *n.m.* pack, heap, hillock

tocyn, (*-nau*), *n.m.* ticket

toddedig, *a.* molten; melting

toddi, *v.* melt, dissolve, thaw

toddion, *n.pl.* dripping

toddwr, (*-wyr*), **-ydd,** (*-ion*), *n.m.* melter

toes, *n.m.* dough

toi, *v.* cover; roof; thatch

tolach, *v.* fondle

tolc, (*-iau*), *n.m.* dent, dinge

tolcio, *v.* dent, dinge

tolciog, *a.* dented, dinged

toll, (*-au*), *n.f.* toll, custom

tolli, *v.* take toll

tom, *n.f.* dirt, mire, dung

tomen, (*-nydd*), *n.f.* heap; dunghill

tomlyd, *a.* dirty, miry

ton, (*-nau*), *n.f.* wave, billow, breaker

ton, (*-nau*), *n.m.* lay-land

tôn, (*tonau*), *n.f.* tone; tune

tonc, (*-iau*), *n.f.* tinkle, ring, clash

toncio, -ian, *v.* tinkle, ring

tonfedd, (*-i*), *n.f.* wavelength

tonnen, (*tonennydd, -au*), *n.f.* skin; sward; bog

tonni, *v.* wave, undulate

tonnog, *a.* wavy, billowy

tonyddiaeth, *n.f.* tone, intonation

topio, *v.* plug, stop up

topyn, *n.m.* plug, stopper

tor, (*-ion*), *n.m.* break, interruption

tor, (*-rau*), *n.f.* belly; palm (of hand)

toraeth. See **toreth**

torcalonnus, *a.* heart-breaking

torch, (*-au*), *n.f.* wreath; coil

torchi, *v.* wreathe; coil; roll, tuck

torchog, *a.* wreathed; coiled

tordyn, *a.* tight-bellied; hectoring

toreithiog, *a.* abundant, teeming

toreth, *n.f.* abundance

torf, (*-eydd*), *n.f.* crowd, multitude

torfynyglu, *v.* break neck of; behead

torheulo, *v.* bask

tori, (*-ïaid*), *n.m.* tory

toriad, (*-au*), *n.m.* cut, break; fraction

torïaeth, *n.f.* torysim

torïaidd, *a.* tory, conservative

torlan, (*-nau, -lennydd*), *n.f.* river bank

torllwyth, (*-i*), **torraid,** *n.f.* litter

torogen, (*-ogod*), *n.f.* tick (in cattle)

torri, *v.* break, cut; dig; write, trace

torrwr, (*torwyr*), *n.m.* breaker, cutter

torsyth, *a.* swaggering

torsythu, *v.* strut, swagger

torth, (*-au*), *n.f.* loaf

tost, *a.* severe, sharp, sore; ill

toster, *n.m.* severity

tosturi, (*-aethau*), *n.m.* compassion, pity

tosturio, *v.* compassionate, pity

tosturiol, *a.* compassionate

tosyn, (*tosau*), *n.m.* pimple

tra, *adv.* over; very: *c.* while, whilst

tra-arglwyddiaeth, (*-au*), *n.f.* tyranny

tra-arglwyddiaethu, *v.* tyrannize

tra-awdurdodi, *v.* lord it over, domineer

trabludd, *n.m.* trouble, tumult, turmoil

trachefn, *adv.* again

trachwant, (*-au*), *n.m.* lust; covetousness

trachwanta, -tu, *v.* lust, covet

trachwantus, *a.* covetous

tradwy, *adv.* three days hence

traddodi, *v.* deliver; commit

traddodiad, (*-au*), *n.m.* tradition; delivery

traddodiadol, *a.* traditional

traddodwr, (*-wyr*), *n.m.* deliverer

traean, *n.m.* one third, the third part

traed. See **troed**

traeth, (*-au*), *n.m.* strand, shore, beach

traethawd, (*-odau*), *n.m.* treatise, essay; tract   [bank

traethell, (*-au*), *n.f.* strand, sand-

traethodydd, (*-ion*), *n.m.* essayist

traethu, *v.* utter, declare; treat

trafael, (*-ion*), *n.f.* travail, trouble

trafaelio, *v.* travel

trafaeliwr, (*-wyr*), *n.m.* traveller

trafaelu, *v.* travel; travail

traflyncu, *v.* guzzle, gulp, devour

trafnidiaeth, *n.f.* traffic

trafod, *v.* handle; discuss; transact

trafodaeth, (*-au*), *n.f.* discussion, transaction

trafferth, (*-ion*), *n.f.m.* trouble

trafferthu, *v.* trouble

trafferthus, *a.* troublesome; troubled

tragwyddol, *a.* everlasting, eternal

tragwyddoldeb, *n.m.* eternity

tragywydd, *a.* everlasting, eternal

traha, *n.m.* arrogance, presumption

trahaus, *a.* arrogant, haughty

trahauster, *n.m.* arrogance, presumption

trai, *n.m.* ebb

trais, *n.m.* oppression, force, violence

trallod, (*-ion*, *-au*), *n.m.* trouble, tribulation

t1allodi, *v.* afflict, vex, trouble

trallodus, *a.* troubled; troublous

trallodwr, (*-wyr*), *n.m.* troubler, afflicter

tramgwydd, (*-iadau*), *n.m.* stumbling; offence

tramgwyddo, *v.* stumble; offend; take offence

tramgwyddus, *a.* scandalous; offensive

tramor, *a.* transmarine; foreign

tramorwr, (*-wyr*), *n.m.* foreigner

tramwy, -o, *v.* pass, traverse

tramwyfa, (*-feydd*), *n.f.* passage, thoroughfare

tranc, *n.m.* end, dissolution, death

trancedig, *a.* deceased

trancedigaeth, *n.f.* death, decease

trannoeth, *adv.* next day: *n.m.* the morrow

traphlith, *adv.*—**blith d.,** higgledy-piggledy

tras, *n.f.* kindred, affinity

traul, (*treuliau*), *n.f.* wear; cost, expense

trawiad, (*-au*), *n.m.* stroke, beat

trawiadol, *a.* striking

traws, *a.* cross; froward, perverse

trawsblannu, *v.* transplant

trawsenwad, *n.m.* metonymy

trawsfeddiannu, *v.* usurp

trawsfudo, *v.* transmigrate

trawsffurfio, *v.* transform

trawsgludo, *v.* transport

trawsgyweirio, *v.* transpose, change key

trawslif, *n.m.* cross-saw

trawslythrennu, *v.* transliterate

traws-sylweddiad, *n.m.* transubstantiation

trawst, (*-iau*), *n.m.* beam

trawster, *n.m.* violence, oppression

trebl, *n.m. & a.* treble

treblu, *v.* treble

trech, *a.* superior, stronger, mightier

trechu, *v.* overpower, overcome, conquer

tref, (*-i*, *-ydd*), *n.f.* home; town

trefedigaeth, (*-au*), *n.f.* settlement, colony

trefgordd, (*-au*), *n.f.* township

treflan (*-nau*), *n.f.* small town, townlet

trefn (*-au*), *n.f.* order, method, system

trefniad, (*-au*), *n.m.* arrangement, ordering

trefniant, *n.m.* arrangement, organization

trefnu, *v.* order, arrange, dispose

trefnus, *a.* orderly, methodical

trefnusrwydd, *n.m.* orderliness

trefnydd, (*-ion*), *n.m.* arranger; Methodist

Trefnyddiaeth, *n.f.* Methodism

trefol, *a.* town, urban

treftadaeth, *n.f.* patrimony, inheritance

trengholiad, (*-au*), *n.m.* coroner's inquest

trengholydd, (*-ion*), *n.m.* coroner

trengi, *v.* die, perish, expire

treial, (*-on*), *n.m.* trial

treiddgar, *a.* penetrating, keen

treiddgarwch, *n.m.* penetration, acumen

treiddio, *v.* pass, penetrate

treiddiol, *a.* penetrating

treigl, (*-au*), *n.m.* turn, revolution, course

treigl(i)ad, (*-au*), *n.m.* mutation; inflection

treiglo, *v.* roll; mutate; inflect; decline

treio, *v.* ebb

treio, *v.* try

treisiad, (*-iedi*), *n.f.* heifer

treisio, *v.* force, ravish, violate, oppress

treisiwr, (*-wyr*), *n.m.* violator, oppressor

trem, (*-iau*), *n.f.* sight, look, aspect

tremio, *v.* look, gaze

tremygu, *v.* insult, contemn, despise [tuous

tremygus, *a.* insulting, contemp-

tremynt, *n.m.* sight, view

tremynu, *v.* walk, travel

trên, (*trenau*), *n.m.* train

trennydd, *adv.* day after to-morrow

tres, (*-i*), *n.f.* trace, chain; tress

tresbasu, tresmasu, *v.* trespass

tresglen, *n.f.* thrush

treth, (*-i*), *n.f.* rate, tax, tribute

trethdalwr, (*-wyr*), *n.m.* ratepayer

trethu, *v.* tax, rate, assess

trethwr, (*-wyr*), *n.m.* taxer

treuliad, *n.m.* digestion

treulio, *v.* wear, consume; spend; digest

trew, *n.m.* sneeze

trewlwch, *n.m.* snuff

tri, *a.* & *n.m.* three: *f.* **tair**

triagl, *n.m.* treacle, balsam, balm

triawd, (*-au*), *n.m.* trio

triban, (*-nau*), *n.m.* triplet (metre)

tribiwnlys, (*-oedd*), *n.m.* tribunal

tric, (*-iau*), *n.m.* trick

tridiau, *n.pl.* three days

trigain, *a.* & *n.m.* sixty

trigfa (*-feydd*), **-fan,** (*-nau*), *n.f.* dwelling-place, abode

trigiannol, *a.* residentiary

trigiannu, *v.* reside, dwell

trigiannydd, (*-ianwyr*), *n.m.* resident

trigo, *v.* stay, abide; dwell; die

trigolion, *n.pl.* inhabitants, dwellers

trin, (*-oedd*), *n.f.* battle

trin, *v.* handle; treat; dress; till; transact

trindod, (*-au*), *n.f.* trinity

triniaeth, (*-au*), *n.f.* treatment

trioedd, *n.pl.* triads

triongl, (*-au*), *n.m.f.* triangle

trist, *a.* sad, sorrowful

tristáu, *v.* sadden, grieve

tristwch, *n.m.* sadness, sorrow

tro, (*troeau, troeon*), *n.m.* turn, twist; conversion

troad, (*-au*), *n.m.* bend, turning

trobwll, (*-byllau*), *n.m.* whirlpool

trobwynt, (*-iau*), *n.m.* turning-point

trochfa, (*-feydd*), *n.f.* plunge, immersion

trochi, *v.* dip, plunge, immerse; soil

trochion, *n.pl.* lather, suds, foam

trochioni, *v.* lather, foam

trochwr, (*-wyr*), *n.m.* immerser, immersionist

troed, (*traed*), *n.m.f.* foot; leg; handle

troedfainc, (*-feiniau*), *n.f.* footstool

troedfedd, (*-i*), *n.f.* foot (= 12 inches)

troëdig, *a.* turned, converted

tröedigaeth, (*-au*), *n.f.* turning, conversion

troedio, *v.* foot, tread, trudge

troednoeth, *a.* barefoot, barefooted

troedwst, *n.f.* gout

troell, (*-au*), *n.f.* wheel, spinning-wheel

troelli, *v.* spin; twist, wind

troellog, *a.* winding, tortuous

troetffordd, (*-ffyrdd*), *n.f.* footway, footpath

trofa, (*-feydd*), *n.f.* turn; bend, turning

trofan, (*-nau*), *n.f.* tropic

trofannol *a.* tropical

trofaus, *a.* perverse

trogen. See **torogen**

trogylch, (*-au*), *n.m.* orbit

troi, *v.* turn, revolve; convert; plough

trol, (*-iau*), *n.f.* cart

trolian, -io, *v.* roll

troliwr, (*-wyr*), *n.m.* carter

trom *a.,* f. of **trwm**

tros, *pr.* over, for, instead of, on behalf of

trosedd, (*-au*), *n.m.* transgression, offence, crime

troseddu, *v.* transgress, trespass, offend

troseddwr, (*-wyr*), *n.m.* transgressor, trespasser, offender; criminal

trosglwyddiad, *n.m.* transference, transfer

trosglwyddo, *v.* hand over, transfer

trosi, *v.* turn; translate; convert (a goal)

trosiad, (*-au*), *n.m.* translation; metaphor

trosodd, *adv.* over, beyond

trosol, (*-ion*), *n.m.* lever, crow-bar, bar; staff

trostan, (*-au*), *n.f.* pole

trothwy, (*-au*), *n.m.* threshold

trowr, (*-wyr*), *n.m.* ploughman

trowynt, (*-oedd*), *n.m.* whirlwind, tornado

tru, truan, (*truain*), *a.* poor, wretched, miserable: (*trueiniaid*), *n.m.* wretch: *f.* **truanes**

trueni, *n.m.* wretchedness; misery; pity

truenus, *a.* wretched, miserable

trugaredd, (*-au*), *n.f.m.* mercy, compassion

trugareddfa, *n.f.* mercy-seat

trugarhau, *v.* have mercy, take pity

trugarog, *a.* merciful, compassionate

trugarowgrwydd, *n.m.* mercifulness

trulliad, (*-iaid*), *n.m.* butler, cupbearer

trum, (*-au, -iau*), *n.m.* ridge

truth, *n.m.* flattery; rigmarole

trwbl, *n.m.* **-o,** *v.* trouble

trwch, *n.m.* thickness. —**t. y blewyn,** hair's breadth

trwch, *a.* broken; unfortunate; wicked

trwchus, *a.* thick

trwm, (*trymion*), *a.* heavy: *f.* **trom**

trwnc, *n.m.* urine, lye

trwnc, (*trynciau*) *n.m.* trunk

trwodd, *adv.* through

trwsgl, *a.* awkward, clumsy, bungling

trwsiad, *n.m.* dress, attire

trwsiadus, *a.* well-dressed, smart

trwsio, *v.* dress, trim; mend, repair

trwsiwr, (*-wyr*), *n.m.* mender, repairer

trwst, *n.m.* noise, din, tumult

trwstan, *a.* awkward, clumsy, untoward [ness

trwstaneiddiwch, *n.m.* awkward-

trwy, *pr.* through, by, by means of

trwyadl, *a.* thorough

trwydded, (*-au*), *n.f.* leave, licence

trwyddedu, *v.* license

trwyddew, *n.m.* auger, borer

trwyn, (*-au*), *n.m.* nose, snout; point, cape

trwyndwn, *a.* broken-nosed

trwyno, *v.* nose, nuzzle, sniff

trwynol, *a.* nasal

trwynsur, *a.* sour, morose

trwyth, (*-i*), *n.m.* decoction

trwytho, *v.* steep, saturate, imbue

trybedd, trybed, *n.f.* tripod, trivet

trybelid, *a.* bright, brilliant

trybestod, *n.m.* commotion, bustle, fuss

trybini, *n.m.* trouble, misfortune, misery

tryblith, *n.m.* muddle, chaos

trychfil, (*-od*), *n.m.* insect, animalcule

trychiad, (*-au*), *n.m.* cutting

trychineb, (*-au*), *n.m.f.* disaster, calamity

trychinebus, *a.* disastrous, calamitous

trychu, v. cut, hew, pierce, lop

trydan, n.m. electric fluid, electricity

trydaniaeth, n.f. electricity; thrill

trydanol, a. electric, electrical

trydanu, v. electrify

trydar, n.m. & v. chirp, chatter

trydydd, a. third: f. **trydedd**

tryfer, (-i), n.f. harpoon, trident

tryferu, v. spear, harpoon

tryfesur, n.m. diameter

tryfrith, a. speckled; swarming, teeming

tryloyw, a. pellucid, transparent

tryloywder, n.m. transparency

trylwyr, a. thorough

trylwyredd, n.m. thoroughness

trymaidd, a. heavy, close, oppressive

trymder, n.m. heaviness, drowsiness

trymfryd, n.m. sadness, sorrow

trymhau, v. make or grow heavy

trymllyd, a. heavy, close, oppressive

trysor, (-au), n.m. treasure

trysordy, (-dai), n.m. treasure-house

trysorfa, (-feydd), n.f. treasury, fund

trysori, v. treasure

trysorlys, n.m. treasury, exchequer

trysorydd, (-ion), n.m. treasurer

trystio, v. make a noise

trystiog, a. noisy, rowdy

trythyll, a. wanton, lascivious

trythyllwch, n.m. lasciviousness

trywanu, v. transfix, stab, pierce

trywel, n.m. trowel

trywydd, n.m. scent, trail

tu, n.m. side, part, direction

tua, tuag, pr. towards; about

tuchan, v. grumble, groan, murmur

tudalen, (-nau), n.m.f. page

tudded, (-i), n.f. covering; pillow-case

tuedd, (-iadau), n.f. tendency, inclination

tueddfryd, n.m. inclination, bent

tueddol, a. inclined, apt

tueddu, v. incline, tend, trend

tufewnol, a. inward, internal

tugel, n.m. ballot

tulath, (-au), n.f. beam, rafter

tunnell, (tunelli), n.f. ton; tun

turio, v. root up, burrow, delve

turn, n.m. lathe

turniwr, (-wyr), n.m. turner

turs, (-iau), n.m. snout, bill; frown

turtur, (-od), n.f. turtle-dove

tusw, (-ŵau), n.m. wisp, bunch

tuth, (-iau), n.m. trot

tuthio, v. trot

twb, (tybiau), n.m. tub

twca, n.m. tuck-knife

twlc, (tylciau), n.m. sty

twlcio, v. horn, butt, gore

twlciog, a. given to horning

twll, (tyllau), n.m. hole

twmpath, (-au), n.m. tump, hillock; bush

twn, a. broken, f. **ton**

twnffed, (-i), n.m. funnel

twnnel, (twnelau), n.m. tunnel

twp, a. stupid, dull, obtuse

twr, (tyrau), n.m. tower

twr, (tyrrau), n.m. heap; group, crowd

Twrc, (Tyrciaid), n.m. Turk

twrci, (-îod), n.m. turkey

twrch, (tyrchod), n.m. hog. — **t. daear,** mole

twrf, (tyrfau), n.m. noise; (pl.) thunder

twrnai, (-eiod), n.m. attorney, lawyer

twrw, n.m. noise (**twrf**)

twt, i. tut!

twt, a. tidy, neat, smart

twtio, v. tidy

twyll, n.m. deceit, deception, fraud

twyllo, v. deceive, cheat, swindle

twyllodrus, a. deceitful, false

twyllresymeg, n.f. sophism

twyllresymiad, (-au), n.m. sophistry

twyllwr, (-wyr), n.m. deceiver

twym, a. warm, hot, sultry

twymdra, n.m. warmness, warmth

twymgalon, a. warm-hearted

twymo, twymno, v. warm, heat

twymyn, (-au), n.f. fever

twyn, (-i), n.m. hill, hillock, knoll; bush

twysged, n.f. lot, quantity

tŷ, (tai, teiau), n.m. house

tyaid, (-eidiau), n.m. houseful

tyb, (-iau), n.m.f. opinion, notion, surmise

tybaco, n.m. tobacco

tybed, adv. I wonder; is that so?

tybiaeth, (-au), n.f. supposition

tybied, tybio, v. suppose, think, imagine

tybiedig, a. supposed, putative

tycio, v. prosper, succeed, avail

tydi, pn. thou, thyself

tyddyn, (-nod), n.m. (small) farm, holding

tyddynnwr, (-ynwyr), n.m. small-holder

tyfadwy, a. growing

tyfiant, n.m. growth

tyfu, v. grow

tynged, n.f. destiny, fate

tynghedu, v. destine, fate; adjure

tyngu, v. swear, vow

tyngwr, (-wyr), n.m. swearer

tylath. See **tulath**

tyle, n.m. slope, hill; n.f. couch

tylino, v. knead

tylinwr, (-wyr), n.m. kneader

tylwyth, (-au), n.m. household, family.—**t. teg,** fairies

tyllog a. holey

tyllu, v. hole, bore, perforate, pierce

tylluan, (-od), n.f. owl

tyllwr, (-wyr), n.m. borer

tymer, (-herau), n.f. temper

tymestl, (-hestloedd), n.f. tempest, storm

tymheredd, n.m. temperature

tymherus, a. temperate

tymhestlog, a. tempestuous, stormy

tymhoraidd, a. seasonable

tymhorol, a. temporal

tymor, (-horau), n.m. season

tymp, n.m. (appointed) time, season

tympan, (-au), n.f. drum; timbrel

tymyr, n.m. land, territory, region

tyn, a. tight: f. **ten**

tynder, -dra, n.m. tightness, tension

tyner, a. tender, gentle

tyneru, v. make tender, soften

tynerwch, n.m. tenderness, gentleness

tynfa, (-feydd), n.f. draw, attraction

tynfaen, (-feini), n.m. loadstone, magnet

tynhau, v. tighten, strain

tynnu, v. draw, pull; take off, remove

tyno, n.m. hollow; tenon

tyrchu, v. root up, burrow

tyrchwr, (-wyr), n.m. mole-catcher

tyrfa, (-oedd), n.f. multitude, host, crowd

tyrfo, tyrfu, v. make a noise or commotion

tyrpant, n.m. turpentine

tyrpeg, n.m. turnpike

tyrru, v. heap, amass; crowd together

tyst, (-ion), n.m. witness

tysteb, (-au), n.f. testimonial

tystio, v. testify, witness

tystiolaeth, (-au), n.f. testimony, evidence

tystiolaethu, v. bear witness, testify

tystlythyr, (-au), n.m. testimonial

tystysgrif, (-au), n.f. certificate

tywallt, v. pour, shed, spill

tywalltiad, (-au), n.m. outpouring

tywarchen, (tywyrch), n.f. sod, turf

tywod, n.m. sand

tywodfaen, n.m. sandstone

tywodlyd, -odog, a. sandy

tywodyn, n.m. grain of sand

tywydd, n.m. weather

tywyll, a. dark, obscure; blind

tywyllu, v. darken, obscure

tywyllwch, n.m. darkness

tywyn, (-au), n.m. sea-shore, strand

tywynnu, v. shine

tywys, v. lead, guide

tywysen, (-nau, tywys), n.f. ear of corn

tywysog, (*-ion*), *n.m.* prince
tywysogaeth, (*-au*), *n.f.* principality
tywysogaidd, *a.* princely
tywysoges, (*-au*), *n.f.* princess
tywysydd, (*-ion*), *n.m.* leader, guide

TH

thema, (*themâu*), *n.f.* theme
thermomedr, *n.m.* thermometer
thus, *n.m.* frankincense
thuser, (*-au*), *n.f.* censer

U

ubain, *v.* howl, wail, moan; sob
uchaf, *a.* uppermost, highest
uchafbwynt, (*-iau*), *n.m.* climax; zenith
uchafiaeth, *n.f.* supremacy; ascendancy
uchafiaid, *n.pl.* superiors
uchafion, *n.pl.* heights
uchafrif, (*-au*), *n.m.* maximum
uchanianaeth, *n.f.* metaphysics
uchder, *n.m.* height; top
uchel, *a.* high, lofty; uppish; loud
uchelder, (*-au*), *n.m.* highness, height
ucheldir, (*-oedd*), *n.m.* highland
uchelfa, (*-feydd*), *n.f.* high place
uchelfar, *n.m.* mistletoe
uchelfryd, *a.* high-minded
uchelgais, *n.m.f.* ambition
uchelgeisiol, *a.* ambitious
uchelion, *n.pl.* heights
uchelradd, *a.* of high degree, superior
uchelryw, *a.* superior
uchelwr, (*-wyr*), *n.m.* gentleman, nobleman
uchelwydd, *c.n.* mistletoe
uchenaid, (*-eidiau*), *n.f.* sigh
ucheneidio, *v.* sigh
uchgapten, (*-teiniaid*), *n.m.* major
uchod, *adv.* above
udfil, (*-od*), *n.m.* hyena

udganu, &c. See **utganu**
udo, *v.* howl
udd, *n.m.* lord
ufel, *n.m.* fire
ufudd, *a.* obedient, humble
ufudd-dod, *n.m.* obedience, humility
ufuddgar, *a.* dutiful
ufuddhau, *v.* obey
ufyll, *a.* humble, meek
uffern, *n.f.* hell
uffernol, *a.* infernal, hellish
ugain, (*ugeiniau*), *a. & n.m.* twenty, score
ulw, *c.n.* ashes, powder: *adv.* utterly
un, *a.* one, only; same: (*-au*), *n.c.* one, unit
unawd, (*-au*), *n.m.f.* solo
unawdwr, (*-wyr*), *n.m.* soloist
unbeiniaeth, *n.f.* supremacy, despotism
unben, (*-iaid*, *unbyn*), *n.m.* sovereign lord, despot unit
unbenaethol, *a.* despotic
unbennaeth, *n.f.* sovereignty, despotism
undeb, (*-au*), *n.m.* unity, union
undebaeth, *n.f.* unionism
undebol, *a.* united, union
undebwr, (*-wyr*), *n.m.* unionist
undod, (*-au*), *n.m.* unity; unit
Undodaidd, *a.* Unitarian
Undodiaeth, *n.f.* Unitarianism
Undodwr, (*-wyr*, *-iaid*), *n.m.* Unitarian
undonedd, *n.m.* monotony
undonog, *a.* monotonous
uned, (*-au*), *n.f.* unit
unfarn, *a.* unanimous
unfryd, -ol, *a.* unanimous
unfrydedd, *n.m.* unanimity
unffurf, *a.* uniform
unffurfiaeth, *n.f.* uniformity
uniaith, *a.* monoglot
uniawn, *a.* straight; right, upright; just
unig, *a.* sole, only; alone, lonely
unigedd, *n.m.* loneliness, solitude
unigol, *a.* singular; individual: (*-ion*), *n.m.* individual

unigoliaeth, *n.f.* **-rwydd,** *n.m.*
individuality

unigrwydd, *n.m.* loneliness, solitude

union, *a.* straight, direct; just,
exact

uniondeb, *n.m.* straightness; rectitude

uniongred, *a.* orthodox

uniongrededd, *n.m.f.* orthodoxy

uniongyrch, -ol, *a.* immediate,
direct

unioni, *v.* straighten; rectify; make
for

unionsyth, *a.* straight, direct; erect

uno, *v.* join, unite, amalgamate

unol, *a.* united

unoli, *v.* unify

unoliaeth, *n.f.* unity, oneness,
identity

unplyg, *a.* of one fold; folio;
simple, ingenuous

unplygrwydd, *n.m.* sincerity

unrhyw, *a.* same; any

unrhywiaeth, *n.m.f.* sameness,
monotony

unsain, *a.* unison.—**yn u.,** in unison

unsill, *a.* monosyllabic

unswydd, *a.* of one purpose

unwaith, *adv.* once

unwedd, *a.* like; *adv.* likewise

urael, *n.m.* asbestos; asbestos cloth

urdd, *(-au), n.f.* order; rank

urddas, *(-au), n.m.* dignity, honour

urddasol, *a.* dignified, noble

urddiad, *(-au), n.m.* ordination

urddo, *v.* ordain, confer degree or
rank

us, *c.n.* chaff

ust, *i. & n.m.* hush

ustus, *(-iaid), n.m.* justice, magistrate

usuriaeth, *n.f.* usury

usuriwr, *(-wyr), n.m.* usurer

utganu, *v.* sound a trumpet

utganwr, *(-wyr), n.m.* trumpeter

utgorn, *(-gyrn), n.m.* trumpet

uthr, *a.* wonderful, terrible

uwch, *a.* higher: *pr.* above, over

uwchradd, *n.m. & a.* superior

uwchraddol, *a.* superior

uwd, *n.m.* porridge

W

waldio, *v.* wallop, beat

wdwart, *n.m.* woodward, forester

wedi, *pr.* after: *adv.* afterwards

wedyn, *adv.* afterwards, then

weithian, -ion, *adv.* now, now at
length

weithiau, *adv.* sometimes

wel, *i,* well

wele, *i.* behold, lo

wermod, *n.f.* wormwood

wfft, *i.* fie, for shame

wfftio, *v.* cry fie, flout, scout

wmbredd, *n.m.* abundance

wns, *(-iau), n.f.* ounce

wrth, *pr.* by; with; to; because,
since

wtres, *n.f.* luxury, prodigality;
carousal

wy, *(-au), n.m.* egg

wybr, *(-au),* **wybren,** *(-nau, -nydd)*
n.f. sky; cloud

wybrennol, *a.* firmamental, celestial

wyf, *v.* I am

wylo, *v.* weep, cry

wylofain, *v.* wail, weep: *n.m.* wailing

wylofus, *a.* wailing, doleful, tearful

ŵyll, *n.f.* owl

ŵyn. See **oen**

wyneb, *(-au), n.m.* face, surface;
front

wyneb-ddalen, *n.f.* title-page

wynebgaled, *a.* barefaced, impudent

wynebgaledwch, *n.m.* impudence

wyneblun, *(-iau), n.m.* frontispiece

wynebu, *v.* face, front

wynepryd, *n.m.* countenance

wynwyn, *n.pl.* onions

ŵyr, *(wyrion), n.c.* grandchild,
grandson

wysg, *n.m.* track.—**yn w. ei gefn,**
backwards

wystn, *n.m.* stump

wystrys, *n.pl. & c.n.* oysters

wyth, (*-au*) *a. & n.m.* eight

wythawd, (*-au*, *-odau*), *n.f.* octave

wythblyg, *a.* octavo

wythfed, *a.* eighth

wythnos, (*-au*) *n.f.* week

wythnosol, (*-ion*), *a.* weekly

wythnosolyn, (*-olion*), *n.m.* weekly paper

wythongl, (*-au*), *n.f.* octagon

Y

y, yr, 'r, *a.* the

y, yr, preverbal and relative particle

ych, (*-en*), *n.m.* ox

ychwaith, *adv.* (nor) either, neither

ychwaneg, *n.m.* more

ychwanegiad, (*-au*), *n.m.* addition

ychwanegol, *a.* additional

ychwanegu, *v.* add, augment, increase

ychydig, *a., adv., & n.m.* little, few

ychydigyn, *n.m.* a very little

ŷd, (*ydau*), *n.m.* corn

ydlan, (*-nau*), *n.f.* stack-yard, rick-yard

ydwyf, *v.* I am

ydys, *v.—yr ydys yn disgwyl,* it is expected

yfed, *v.* drink; absorb

yfory, *adv.* to-morrow

yfwr, (*-wyr*), *n.m.* drinker

yfflon, *n.pl.* (**yfflyn**, *n.m.*), shivers, pieces, bits

yng, *pr.* in (mutation of **yn**)

yngan, -u, utter, speak

ynghyd, *adv.* together

ynghylch, *pr.* about, concerning

ynglŷn â, *pr.* in connexion with

yngo(d), *adv.* close by

ym, *pr.* in (mutation of **yn**)

ym-, *px.*, usu. reflexive or reciprocal

yma, *adv.* here, in this place; this

ymadael, ymadaw, *v.* depart

ymadawedig, *a.* departed, deceased

ymadawiad, *n.m.* departure; decease

ymadawol, *a.* farewell, valedictory

ymadferth, (*-oedd*), *n.f.* effort, exertion

ymadnewyddu, *v.* renew oneself

ymado, *v.* depart

ymadrodd, (*-ion*), *n.m.* speech, saying, expression

ymadroddi, *v.* speak, discourse

ymadroddus, *a.* eloquent

ymadroddwr, (*-wyr*), *n.m.* speaker

ymaelodi, *v.* become a member, join

ymaelyd, ymafael, ymaflyd, *v.* take hold

ymagor, *v.* open, unfold, expand

ymaith, *adv.* away, hence

ymannerch, *v.* greet

ymarfer, *v.* practise, exercise: (*-ion*), *n.f.* practice, exercise

ymarferiad, (*-au*), *n.m.* exercise

ymarhous, *v.* dilatory; long-suffering, patient

ymaros, *v.* bear with, endure: *n.m.* long-suffering, patience

ymarwar, *n.m.* conversation, discussion: *v.* discuss

ymarweddiad, *n.m.* conduct, behaviour

ymarweddu, *v.* conduct oneself, behave

ymatal, *v.* forbear, refrain, abstain

ymateb, *v.* answer, respond, correspond

ymbalfalu, *v.* grope

ymbaratoi, *v.* get oneself ready

ymbil, (*-iau*), *n.m.* supplication, entreaty

ymbil, -io, *v.* implore, beseech, entreat

ymboeni, *v.* take pains

ymborth, *n.m.* food, sustenance

ymborthi, *v.* feed

ymbriodi, *v.* marry; intermarry

ymbwyllo, *v.* pause, reflect

ymchweliad, *n.m.* return, reversion

ymchwelyd, *v.* turn, return; overturn

ymchwil *n.f.* search, research, quest

ymchwiliad, (*-au*), *n.m.* investigation

ymchwydd, (*-iadau*), *n.m.* swelling, surge

ymchwyddo, *v.* swell; surge

ymdaith, *v.* journey, march : (*-deithiau*), *n.f.* journey, march

ymdaro, *v.* shift for oneself

ymdebygu, *v.* grow like; resemble

ymdeimlad, *n.m.* feeling, sense

ymdeimlo, *v.* feel; be conscious of

ymdeithio, *v.* travel, journey; sojourn

ymdeithydd, (*-ion*), *n.m.* sojourner

ymdoddi, *v.* melt, become dissolved

ymdopi, *v.* manage

ymdrafodaeth, *n.f.* discussion

ymdrech, (*-ion*), *n.m.f.* effort, endeavour, struggle

ymdrechgar, *a.* striving, energetic

ymdrechu, *v.* wrestle; strive, endeavour

ymdreiglo, *v.* roll; wallow

ymdrin, *v.* treat, deal with

ymdriniaeth, *n.f.* treatment; discussion

ymdrochi, *v.* bathe

ymdrochwr, (*-wyr*), *n.m.* bather

ymdroi, *v.* linger, loiter, dawdle

ymdrybaeddu, *v.* wallow

ymdynghedu, *v.* vow

ymdyrru, *v.* crowd together

ymddadlau, *v.* dispute, contend

ymddangos, *v.* appear, seem

ymddangosiad, (*-au*), *n.m.* appearance

ymddangosiadol, *a.* seeming, apparent

ymddarostwng, *v.* humble oneself, submit

ymddarostyngiad, *n.m.* humiliation, submission

ymddatod, *v.* dissolve

ymddatodiad, *n.m.* dissolution

ymddeol, *v.* resign, retire

ymddeoliad, (*-au*), *n.m.* resignation

ymddibyniad, *n.m.* dependence

ymddibynnu, *v.* depend

ymddiddan, *v.* talk, converse: (*-ion*), *n.m.* talk, conversation

ymddigrifo, *v.* delight

ymddihatru, *v.* divest, undress

ymddiheuriad, (*-au*), *n.m.* apology

ymddiheuro, *v.* apologize

ymddiosg, *v.* strip, undress

ymddiried, *v.* trust: *n.m.* trust, confidence

ymddiriedaeth, *n.f.* trust, confidence

ymddiriedolwr, (*-wyr*), *n.m.* trustee

ymddisgleirio, *v.* shine forth

ymddiswyddo, *v.* resign

ymddwyn, *v.* behave, act

ymddŵyn, *v.* bear; conceive

ymddygiad, (*-au*), *n.m.* behaviour, conduct; (*pl.*) actions

ymddyrchafu, *v.* exalt oneself; rise, ascend

ymegnïo, *v.* exert oneself

ymehangu, *v.* become enlarged

ymennydd, (*ymenyddiau*), *n.m.* brain

ymenyn, *n.m.* butter

ymerawdwr, (*-wvr*), *n.m.* emperor

ymerodraeth, (*-au*), *n.f.* empire

ymerodres, (*-au*), *n.f.* empress

ymerodrol, *a.* imperial

ymesgusodi, *v.* excuse oneself, apologize

ymestyn, *v.* stretch, extend, reach

ymfalchïo, *v.* pride oneself

ymfudo, *v.* emigrate

ymfudwr, (*-wyr*), *n.m.* emigrant

ymffrost, *n.m.* boast

ymffrostio, *v.* boast, vaunt

ymffrostiwr, (*-wyr*), *n.m.* boaster

ymgadw, *v.* keep oneself (from), forbear

ymgais, *n.m.f.* effort, attempt

ymgasglu, *v.* gather together

ymgecru, *v.* quarrel, wrangle

ymgeinio, *v.* scold, revile

ymgeisio, *v.* try, apply; aim at

ymgeisydd, (*-wyr*), *n.m.* applicant, candidate

ymgeledd, *n.m.* succour, care; helpmeet

ymgeleddu, *v.* cherish, succour

ymgeleddwr, (*-wyr*), *n.m.* succourer; tutor, guardian

ymgilio, *v.* retreat, recede

ymgiprys, *v. & n.m.* scramble

ymglywed, *v.* feel (oneself), be inclined

ymgnawdoli, *v.* become flesh, become incarnate

ymgnawdoliad, *n.m.* incarnation

ymgodi, *v.* rise

ymgodymu, *v.* wrestle, fight

ymgofleidio, *v.* embrace mutually

ymgom, (*-ion*), *n.f.* chat, conversation

ymgomio, *v.* chat, converse

ymgorfforiad, *n.m.* embodiment

ymgosbol, *a.* ascetic

ymgreinio, *v.* prostrate oneself; grovel

ymgroesi, *v.* cross oneself; beware

ymgryfhau, *v.* strengthen oneself, be strong

ymgrymu, *v.* bow down, stoop

ymgrynhoi, *v.* gather together

ymguddfa, *n.f.* shelter, hiding-place

ymguddio, *v.* hide (oneself)

ymgyfathrachu, *v.* have commerce with

ymgyfeillachu, *v.* associate

ymgyfoethogi, *v.* get rich

ymgynghori, *v.* consult, confer

ymgynghoriad, *n.m.* consultation

ymgymeriad, (*-au*), *n.m.* undertaking

ymgymryd, *v.* undertake

ymgynddeiriogi, *v.* rage, rave

ymgynnal, *v.* bear up; support oneself; control oneself

ymgynnull, *v.* assemble, congregate

ymgyrch, (*-oedd*), *n.m.f.* campaign, expedition

ymgyrraedd, *v.* stretch, strive after

ymgystlwn, *v.* associate with

ymhel, *v.* meddle

ymhelaethu, *v.* abound; enlarge

ymhell, *adv.* far, afar

ymhellach, *adv.* further, furthermore

ymherodr, &c. See **ymerawdwr**

ymhlith, *pr.* among

ymhoffi, *v.* take delight; boast

ymholi, *v.* inquire

ymholiad, (*-au*), *n.m.* inquiry

ymhonni, *v.* lay claim to, pretend

ymhonnwr, (*-honwyr*), *n.m.* pretender

ymhŵedd, *v.* beseech, implore, crave

ymhyfhau, *v.* grow bold

ymhyfrydu, *v.* delight (oneself)

ymiacháu, *v.* become healed, get well

ymladd, *v.* fight: (*-au*), *n.m.* fighting

ymlâdd, *v.* kill oneself (with exertion), tire oneself out.—**wedi y.**, dead beat

ymladdfa, (*-feydd*), *n.f.* fight

ymladdgar, *a.* pugnacious, warlike

ymladdwr, (*-wyr*), *n.m.* fighter, combatant

ymlaen, *adv.* on, onward

ymlafnio, *v.* toil, strive, struggle

ymlawenhau, *v.* rejoice

ymledu, *v.* spread, expand

ymlenwi, *v.* fill oneself

ymlid, *v.* pursue, chase

ymlidiwr, (*-wyr*), *n.m.* pursuer

ymliw, -io, *v.* reproach, expostulate

ymlonyddu, *v.* grow calm or still

ymluosogi, *v.* multiply

ymlusgiad, (*-iaid*), *n.m.* reptile

ymlusgo, *v.* creep, crawl

ymlwybro, *v.* make one's way

ymlyniad, *n.m.* attachment

ymlynu, *v.* attach, adhere, cleave (to)

ymlynwr, (*-wyr*), *n.m.* adherent

ymneilltuad, *n.m.* retirement

Ymneilltuaeth, *n.f.* Nonconformity

ymneilltuo, *v.* retire

Ymneilltuol, *a.* Nonconformist

Ymneilltuwr, (*-wyr*), *n.m.* Nonconformist

ymnesáu, *v.* approach, draw near

ymochel, -yd, *v.* shelter; beware

ymod, -i, *v.* move, stir

ymofidio, v. grieve

ymofyn, v. ask, inquire, seek: (-ion), n.m. inquiry [quirer

ymofynnydd, (-ofynwyr), n.m. inquirer

ymogelyd, v. beware, avoid

ymohebu, v. correspond

ymolchfa, (-feydd), n.f. wash; lavatory

ymolchi, v. wash oneself: bathe

ymollwng, v. sink, drop, give way, collapse

ymollyngdod, n.m. relaxation; collapse

ymorchestu, v. strive, labour

ymorffwys, v. rest, repose

ymorol, v. seek; take care, attend to, see to it

ymosod, v. attack, assail, assault

ymosodiad, (-au), n.m. attack, assault

ymosodol, a. aggressive, offensive

ymosodwr, (-wyr), n.m. attacker, assailant

ymostwng, v. stoop; humble oneself; submit

ymostyngar, a. submissive

ymostyngiad, n.m. submission

ymotbren, n.m. stirrer, ladle

ympryd, (-ion), n.m. fast

ymprydio, v. fast

ymprydiwr, (-wyr), n.m. faster

ymrafael, (-ion), n.m. quarrel, contention

ymrafaelgar, a. quarrelsome, contentious

ymrafaeliwr, (-wyr), n.m. quarreller

ymraniad, (-au), n.m. division, schism

ymrannu, v. part, divide, separate

ymrannwr, (-ranwyr), n.m. separatist

ymreolaeth, n.f. self-government, Home Rule

Ymreolwr, (-wyr), n.m. Home Ruler

ymrestriad, n.m. enlistment

ymrestru, v. enlist

ymresymiad, (-au), n.m. reasoning, argument

ymresymu, v. reason, argue

ymresymwr, (-wyr), n.m. reasoner

ymrithio, v. appear

ymroad, n.m. application, devotion

ymrodio, v. walk about, perambulate

ymroddedig, a. devoted

ymroddgar, a. of great application

ymroddi, ymroi, v. apply or devote oneself; yield or resign oneself, surrender

ymroddiad, n.m. application, devotion

ymron, adv. nearly, almost

ymrwyfo, v. struggle, toss about

ymrwygo, v. tear, burst

ymrwymiad, (-au), n.m. engagement

ymrwymo, v. bind or engage oneself

ymryson, v. contend, strive: (-au), n.m. contention, strife, rivalry

ymrysonfa, (-feydd), n.f. contest, match

ymrysongar, a. contentious

ymsefydlu, v. establish oneself, settle

ymsefydlwr, (-wyr), n.m. settler

ymserchu, v. cherish, dote

ymson, v. soliloquize: (-au), n.m. soliloquy

ymswyno, v. cross oneself; beware

ymsymud, v. move

ymunioni, v. straighten oneself, become straight

ymuno, v. join, unite

ymwacâd, n.m. kenosis

ymwacáu, v. empty oneself

ymwadiad, n.m. denial, abnegation

ymwadu, v. deny (oneself); renounce

ymwahanu, v. part, divide, separate [tist

ymwahanwr, (-wyr), n.m. separa-

ymwared, n.m. deliverance

ymwasgaru, v. spread, scatter

ymwasgu, v. embrace, hug

ymweled, v. visit

ymweliad, (-au), n.m. visit, visitation

ymwelwr, -ydd, (-*wyr*), *n.m.* visitor, visitant

ymwng, ymwnc, *a.* frequent, many, ample

ymwingo, *v.* writhe, wriggle

ymwneuthur, *v.* make oneself, become; deal

ymwrando, *v.* hearken

ymwroli, *v.* take heart, be of good courage

ymwrthod, *v.* abstain; renounce

ymwrthodiad, *n.m.* abstinence

ymwthgar, *a.* pushing, obtrusive

ymwthio, *v.* push oneself, obtrude

ymwthiol, *a.* obtrusive, intrusive

ymwthiwr, (-*wyr*), *n.m.* intruder, interloper

ymwybodol, *a.* conscious

ymwybyddiaeth, *n.f.* consciousness

ymwylltio, *v.* fly into a passion

ymyfed, *v.* tipple: *n.m.* tippling

ymyl, (-*au*, -*on*), *n.m.f.* edge, border, margin

ymylu, *v.* border

ymylwe, *n.f.* selvedge

ymyrgar, *a.* meddlesome, officious

ymyrraeth, ymyrru, -yd, *v.* meddle, interfere: *n.f.* interference

ymyrrwr, (-*yrwyr*), *n.m.* meddler

ymysg, *pr.* among, amid

ymysgaroedd, *n.pl.* bowels

ymysgwyd, *v.* bestir oneself

yn, *pr.* in, at, into; for: also introduces verb-nouns

yn, *a.* particle

yna, *adv.* there; then; thereupon; that

ynad, (-*on*), *n.m.* judge, justice, magistrate [tracy

ynadaeth, *n.f.* judicature, magis-

ynadol, *a.* judicial, magisterial

yn awr, *adv. phrase,* now, at present

ynfyd, (-*ion*), *a.* foolish, rash

ynfydrwydd, *n.m.* foolishness, folly

ynfydu, *v.* rave, be mad

ynfytyn, (-*fydion*), *n.m.* fool, madman

ynni, *n.m.* energy, vigour

ynnill. See **ennill**

yno, *adv.* there

yntau, *pn.c.* he (on his part), he also

ynteu, ynte, *c.* or, or else, otherwise; then

Ynyd, *n.m.* Shrovetide

ynys, (-*oedd*), *n.f.* island, river meadow

ynysfor, (-*oedd*), *n.m.* archipelago

ynysol, *a.* island, insular

ynyswr, (-*wyr*), *n.m.* islander

yr. See **y**

yrhawg, *adv.* for a long time (to come)

yrŵan, *adv.* now (N.W.)

ys, *v.* it is: *c.* as

ysbaid, (-*beidiau*), *n.m.f.* space (of time)

ysbail, (-*beiliau*), *n.f.* spoil, plunder

ysbardun, (-*au*), *n.m.f.* spur

ysbarduno, *v.* spur

ysbeilio, *v.* spoil, plunder

ysbeiliwr, (-*wyr*), *n.m.* spoiler, robber

ysbienddrych, (-*au*), *n.m.* spying-glass

ysbïo, *v.* spy, look

ysbïwr, (-*wyr*), *n.m.* spy

ysblander, *n.m.* splendour

ysbleddach, *n.m.f.* merriment, festivity

ysblennydd, *a.* splendid

ysbonc, (-*iau*), *n.f.* jump, bound; spurt

ysboncio, *v.* jump, bounce; spurt, splash

ysbrigyn, *n.m.* sprig, twig

ysbryd, (-*ion*, -*oedd*), *n.m.* spirit, ghost

ysbrydegaeth, *n.f.* spiritualism

ysbrydegol, *a.* spiritualistic

ysbrydegydd, (-*ion*), *n.m.* spiritualist

ysbrydiaeth, *n.f.* encouragement, inspiration

ysbrydol, *a.* spiritual; high-spirited

ysbrydoli, *v.* spiritualize; inspire; inspirit

ysbrydoliaeth, *n.f.* inspiration

ysbrydolrwydd, *n.m.* spirituality

ysbwng, *n.m.* sponge

ysbwrial, -iel, *n.m.* rubbish, refuse

ysbwylio, *v.* spoil

ysbyty, *(-tai), n.m.* hospital; hospice

ysfa, *(-feydd), n.f.* itching; hankering

ysg-. See also **sg-**

ysgadan, *n.pl.* (**-enyn,** *n.m.*) herrings

ysgafala, *a.* secure, careless, free

ysgafell, *(-au), n.f.* ledge, shelf; brow

ysgafn, *a.* light: *n.m.* stack

ysgafnder, *n.m.* lightness, levity

ysgafnhau, ysgafnu, *v.* lighten

ysgafnu, *v.* heap, pile

ysgall, *n.pl.* (**-en,** *n.f.*), thistles

ysgar, *(-ant, -geraint), n.m.* enemy

ysgar, *v.* part, separate, divorce

ysgariad, *n.m.,* **-iaeth,** *n.f.* separation, divorce

ysgarlad, *n.m.* scarlet

ysgarlys, *n.m.* divorce court

ysgarmes, *(-oedd, -au), n.f.* skirmish

ysgaru, *v.* separate, divorce

ysgatfydd, *adv.* perhaps, peradventure

ysgaw, *c.n.* (**-en,** *n.f.*), elder

ysgegio, -ian, *v.* shake, jerk, jolt

ysgeler, *a.* wicked, villainous, infamous

ysgelerder, *(-au), n.m.* wickedness, infamy

ysgerbwd, *(-bydau), n.m.* skeleton, carcase

ysgîn, *n.m.f.* long, loose mantle

ysgithr, *(-edd), n.m.* tusk, fang

ysgithrog, *a.* fanged, tusked ; craggy, rugged

ysglefrio, *v.* slide (on ice); skate

ysglent, *(-iau), n.f.* slide

ysglisen, *(ysglisiau), n.f.* slice

ysglisio, *v.* slice

ysglyfaeth, *(-au), n.f.* prey, spoil; carrion, filth

ysglyfaethu, *v.* plunder, spoil

ysglyfaethus, *a.* of prey; rapacious

ysglyfio, *v.* prey on, snatch

ysgogi, *v.* move, stir

ysgogiad, *(-au), n.m.* movement, motion

ysgol, *(-ion), n.f.* school; schooling

ysgol, *(-ion), n.f.* ladder

ysgoldy, *(-dai), n.m.* schoolhouse, schoolroom

ysgolfeistr, *(-i, -iaid), n.m.* schoolmaster

ysgolfeistres, *(-i), n.f.* schoolmistress

ysgolhaig, *(-heigion), n.m.* scholar

ysgolheictod, *n.m.* scholarship

ysgolheigaidd, *a.* scholarly

ysgolor, *(-ion), n.m.* scholar

ysgoloriaeth, *(-au), n.f.* scholarship

ysgolwr, *(-wyr), n.m.* schoolman

ysgorpion, *(-au), n.m.* scorpion

Ysgotyn, *(-gotiaid), n.m.* Scot, Scotchman

ysgothi, *v.* squirt, spirt; purge

ysgrafell, *(-od, -i), n.f.* scraper; curry-comb

ysgrafellu, *v.* scrape, curry

ysgraff, *(-au), n.f.* boat, barge, ferry-boat

ysgraffinio, *v.* scarify, graze, abrade

ysgrech, *(-feydd), n.f.* scream, shriek

ysgrechain, -in, *v.* scream, shriek

ysgrepan, *(-au), n.f.* wallet, scrip

ysgrif, *(-au), n.f.* writing, article, essay

ysgrifbin, *(-nau), n.m.,* **-grifell,** *(-au), n.f.* pen

ysgrifen, -eniad, *(-iadau), n.f.* writing

ysgrifennu, *v.* write

ysgrifennwr, *(-enwyr), n.m.* writer

ysgrifennydd, *(-enyddion), n.m.* scribe, secretary

ysgrifenyddiaeth, *n.f.* secretaryship

ysgriflyfr, *(-au), n.m.* codex, manuscript

ysgrifrwym, *(-au), n.m.* bond

ysgrîn, *(ysgriniau), n.f.* settle; coffin

ysgriw, *(-iau), n.f.* screw

ysgriwio, *v.* screw

ysgrubl, *(-iaid), n.m.* beast

ysgrublaidd, *a.* animal, brute, brutish

ysgrublyn, *n.m.* small piece

ysgrwbio, *v.* scrub

ysgryd, *n.m.* shiver

ysgrytian, *v.* shiver, shudder

ysgrythu, *v.* shiver, shudder, quake

ysgrythur, (*-au*), *n.f.* scripture

ysgrythurol, *a.* scriptural

ysgrythurwr, (*-wyr*), *n.m.* scripturist

ysgub, (*-au*), *n.f.* sheaf; broom

ysgubion, *n.pl.* sweepings

ysgubo, *v.* sweep

ysgubol, *a.* sweeping

ysgubor, (*-iau*), *n.f.* barn, granary

ysgubwr, (*-wyr*), *n.m.* sweeper, sweep

ysgum, *n.m.* scum

ysgutor, (*-ion*), *n.m.* executor

ysguthan, (*-od*), *n.f.* wood-pigeon; jade

ysgwâr, *a. & n.f.* square

ysgwario, *v.* square

ysgŵd, *n.m.* jerk, toss, fling, shove

ysgwïer, (*-iaid*), *n.m.* squire

ysgwrfa, *n.f.* scouring, lathering

ysgwrio, *v.* scour, scrub; lather

ysgwyd, *v.* shake; flutter; wag

ysgwydd, (*-au*), *n.f.* shoulder

ysgwyddo, *v.* shoulder, jostle

ysgydwad, *n.m.* shaking, shake

ysgyfaint, *n.pl.* lungs, lights

ysgyfarnog, (*-od*), *n.f.* hare

ysgymun, *a.* excommunicate, accursed

ysgymundod, *n.m.* excommunication, ban

ysgymuno, *v.* excommunicate

ysgyrion, *n.pl.* staves, splinters, shivers

ysgyrnygu, *v.* grind the teeth, snarl

ysgytiad, (*-au*), *n.m.* shock

ysgytio, *v.* shake violently, shock

ysgythru, *v.* cut, carve; prune

ysictod, *n.m.* contusion; sprain

ysig, *a.* bruised, sore, sprained

ysigo, *v.* bruise, crush; sprain

yslotian, *v.* dabble, tipple

ysmala, *a.* droll, funny, amusing

ysmaldod, *n.m.* fun, drollery

ysmalio, *v.* joke, jest

ysmaliwr, (*-wyr*), *n.m.* joker, wit

ysmotyn, (*ysmotiau*), *n.m.* spot

ysmwddio, *v.* iron

ysmygu, *v.* smoke (tobacco)

ysmygwr, (*-wyr*), *n.m.* smoker

ysnoden, (*-ni*), *n.f.* fillet, band, ribbon

ysol, *a.* consuming, devouring; corrosive

yst-. See also **st-**

ystabl, (*-au*), *n.f.* stable

ystad, (*-au*), *n.f.* state; estate; furlong

ystadegau, *n.pl.* statistics

ystradegol, *a.* statistical

ystadegydd, (*-ion*), *n.m.* statistician

ystaen, *n.m.* tin

ystafell, (*-oedd*), *n.f.* chamber, room

ystafellog, *a.* chambered [lain

ystafellydd, (*-ion*), *n.m.* chamber-

ystalwyn, (*-i*), *n.m.* stallion

ystarn, (*-au*), *n.f.* stern

ystelcian, *v.* skulk, loaf, loiter

ystelciwr, (*-wyr*), *n.m.* loafer, loiterer

ystig, *a.* willing, obliging, diligent

ystinos, *n.m.* asbestos

ystiwart, (*-wardiaid*), *n.m.* steward

ystlen, (*-i*), *n.f.* sex

ystlum, (*-od*), *n.m.* bat

ystlys, (*-au*), *n.f.* side, flank

ystod, (*-ion*), *n.f.* course; swath. **Yn y.,** during

ystof, *n.m.f.* warp

ystofi, *v.* warp; weave, plan

ystôl, (*-olion*), *n.f.* stool, chair

ystor, *n.m.* resin

ystôr, (*-orau*), *n.m.* store, abundance

ystordy, (*-dai*), *n.m.* storehouse, warehouse

ystorfa, (*-feydd*), *n.f.* store, storehouse

ystorio, *v.* store

ystoriwr, (*-iwyr*), *n.m.* historian; storyteller

ystorm, (*-ydd*), *n.f.* storm

ystormus, *a.* stormy

ystrad, (*-au*), *n.m.f.* vale, flat

ystranc, (*-iau*), *n.f.* trick

ystrancio, *v.* play tricks; jib

ystremp, (*-iau*), *n.f.* dash, streak, mess

ystrodur, (*-iau*), *n.f.* cart-saddle

ystryd, (*ystrydoedd*), *n.f.* street

ystrydebol, *a.* stereotyped

ystrydebu, *v.* stereotype

ystryw, (*-iau*), *n.f.* wile, craft, ruse

ystrywgar, *a.* wily, crafty

ystudfach, (*-au*), *n.m.* stilt

ystum, (*-iau*), *n.m.f.* bend; form; posture; (*pl.*) grimaces

ystumio, *v.* bend, distort; pose

ystumog, (*-au*), *n.f.* stomach

ystŵr, *n.m.* stir, noise, bustle, fuss

Ystwyll, *n.m.* Epiphany

ystwyrian, *v.* stretch and yawn, stir

ystwyth, *a.* flexible, pliant, supple

ystwythder, *n.m.* flexibility, pliancy

ystwytho, *v.* make flexible; bend, soften

ystyfnig, *a.* obstinate, stubborn

ystyfnigo, *v.* behave obstinately

ystyfnigrwydd, *n.m.* obstinacy

ystyffylu, *v.* balk

ystyr, (*-on*), *n.f.m.* sense, meaning

ystyrgar, *a.* thoughtful, meditative

ystyriaeth, (*-au*), *n.f.* consideration, heed

ystyried, *v.* consider, regard, heed

ystyriol, *a.* mindful, heedful

ysu, *v.* eat, consume; hanker; itch

yswain, (*-weiniaid*), *n.m.* esquire

yswil, *a.* shy, bashful, timid

yswildod, *n.m.* shyness, bashfulness

yswilio, *v.* be abashed

yswiriant, *n.m.* insurance

yswirio, *v.* insure

yswitian, *v.* chirp, twitter

ysywaeth, *adv.* more's the pity

yw, *v.* is, are

yw, *n.pl. & c.n.* (**-en,** *n.f.*) yew

ENWAU PERSONAU   PERSONAL NAMES

Adda, Adam
Anghrist, Antichrist
Ahasferus, Ahasuerus
Andreas, Andrew
Awstin, Augustine
Bartholomeus, Bartholomew
Beda, Bede
Buddug, Boadicea; Victoria
Cadi, Catherine, Kate
Caradog, Caratacos, Caractacus
Caswallon, Cassivellaunus
Catrin, Catherine
Cesar, Caesar
Crist, Christ
Cystennin, Constantine
Dafydd, Dewi, David
Efa, Eve
Elen, Helen, Ellen
Eleias, Elijah, Elias
Eliseus, Elisha, Eliseus
Emrys, Ambrose
Ercwlff, Hercules
Eseia, Esay, Isaiah
Esyllt, Iseult
Fychan, Vaughan
Fyrsil, Fferyll, Virgil
Ffowc, Foulkes
Ffraid, Bride, Bridget
Geraint, Gerontius
Gruffudd, Gruffydd, Griffith
Gwallter, Walter
Gwener, Venus
Gwilym, William
Gwrtheyrn, Vortigern
Harri, Harry, Henry
Hu, Huw, Hugh
Iago, James
Iau, Jove, Jupiter
Iesu Grist, Jesus Christ
Ieuan, Evan
Ioan, John
Iorwerth, Edward
Iwan, John
Lowri, Laura

Luc, Lug, Luke
Llwyd, Lloyd
Mabli, Mabel
Mair, Mary
Mali, Molly
Marc, Mark
Marged, Margred, Margaret
Mari, Mary
Mawrth, Mars
Mercher, Mercury
Mererid, Margaret
Meurig, Morris
Mihangel, Michael
Modlen, Magdalene
Moesen, Moses
Myrddin, Merlin
Neifion, Neptune
Ofydd, Ovid
Oswallt, Oswald
Owain, Owen
Padrig, Patrick
Pedr, Peter
Prys, Price, Preece
Puw, Pugh
Pyrs, Pierce
Rhisiart, Richard
Rhobert, Robert
Rhonwen, Rowena
Rhys, Rees, Rice
Sadwrn, Saturn
Sebedeus, Zebedee
Selyf, Solomon
Siân, Jane
Siarl, Charles
Siencyn, Jenkin
Siôn, John
Sioned, Janet
Siôr, George
Steffan, Stephen
Timotheus, Timothy
Tomos, Thomas
Tudur, Tudor
Twm, Tom
Wmffre, Humphrey

ENWAU LLEOEDD PLACE-NAMES

Aberdaugleddyf, Milford Haven
Abergwaun, Fishguard
Aberhonddu, Brecon
Abermo, Barmouth
Abertawe, Swansea
Aberteifi, Cardigan
Amwythig, Shrewsbury
Athen, Athens
Awstralia, Australia
Awstria, Austria
Babilon, Babylon
Brycheiniog, Brecknock
Brynbuga, Usk
Bryste, Bristol
Caerdroea, Troy
Caerdydd, Cardiff
Caeredin, Edinburgh
Caerefrog, York
Caerfyrddin, Carmarthen
Caergaint, Canterbury
Caergrawnt, Cambridge
Caergybi, Holyhead
Caergystennin, Constantinople
Caerliwelydd, Carlisle
Caerloyw, Gloucester
Caerludd, London
Caerlleon, Chester
Caerllion, Caerleon
Caernarfon, Caernarvon
Caerodor, Bristol
Caersalem, Jerusalem
Caerwrangon, Worcester
Caint, Kent
Calfaria, Calvary
Casllwchwr, Loughor
Casnewydd, Newport, Mon.
Castell-nedd, Neath
Castellnewydd, Newcastle
Ceredigion, Cardiganshire
Cernyw, Cornwall
Conwy, Conway
Croesoswallt, Oswestry
Crucywel, Crickhowell
Cydweli, Kidwelly

Cymru, Wales
Dinbych, Denby
Dinbych-y-pysgod, Tenby
Dolgellau, Dolgelley
Dulyn, Dublin
Dyfed, Demetia
Dyfnaint, Devon
Dyfrdwy, Dee
Efrog, York
Eryri, Snowdonia
Ewrob, Europe
Fflandrys, Flanders
Fflint, Flint
Ffrainc, France
Gâl, Gaul
Groeg, Greece
Gwent, part of Monmouthshire
Gwlad-yr-haf, Somerset
Gwy, Wye
Gwynedd, North West Wales
Gŵyr, Gower
Hafren, Severn
Henffordd, Hereford
Hisbaen, Spain
Hwlffordd, Haverfordwest
Iorddonen, Jordan
Isalmaen, Holland
Iwerddon, Ireland
Iwerydd, The Atlantic
Lerpwl, Liverpool
Libanus, Lebanon
Llanbedr (Pont Steffan), Lampeter
Llandaf, Landaff
Llanelwy, St. Asaph
Llanfair-ym-Muallt, Builth
Llangrallo, Coychurch
Llanilltud Fawr, Llantwit Major
Llanllieni, Leominster
Llanymddyfri, Llandovery
Lloegr, England
Llundain, London
Llwydlo, Ludlow
Llydaw, Brittany

Llyn Tegid, Bala Lake
Maesyfed, Radnor
Manaw, Isle of Man
Manceinion, Manchester
Meirionnydd, Merioneth
Môn, Anglesey
Môr y Canoldir, Mediterranean Sea
Morgannwg, Glamorgan
Mynwy, Monmouth
Mynyw, St. David's
Penarlâg, Hawarden
Penfro, Pembroke
Penrhyn Gobaith Da, Cape of Good Hope
Pen-y-bont ar Ogwr, Bridgend
Pontarfynach, Devil's Bridge
Porthaethwy, Menai Bridge
Porthmadog, Portmadoc
Prwsia, Prussia
Prydain, Britain
Pwyl, Poland
Rhufain, Rome
Rhuthun, Ruthin
Rhydychen, Oxford
Rwsia, Russia
Tafwys, Thames
Trefaldwyn, Montgomery
Trefdraeth, Newport, Pem.
Treforys, Morriston
Trefyclo(dd), Knighton

Treffynnon, Holywell
Twrci, Turkey
Tyddewi, St. David's
Tywi, Towy
Wrecsam, Wrexham
Wysg, the Usk
Y Bermo, Barmouth
Y Bont-faen, Cowbridge
Y Cei Newydd, New Quay
Y Fenni, Abergavenny
Y Gelli (Gandryll), Hay
Y Môr Canoldir, Mediterranean Sea
Y Môr Coch, Red Sea
Y Môr Marw, Dead Sea
Y Môr Tawel, Pacific Ocean
Y Waun, Chirk
Ynys Enlli, Bardsey Island
Ynys Wyth, Isle of Wight
Yr Aifft, Egypt
Yr Alban, Scotland
Yr Almaen, Germany
Yr Alpau, Alps
Yr Amerig, America
Yr Eidal, Italy
Yr Unol Daleithiau, United States
Yr Wyddfa, Snowdon
Yr Wyddgrug, Mold
Ystrad-fflur, Strata Florida
Ystrad Marchell, Strata Marcella
Y Trallwng, Welshpool

ENGLISH—WELSH DICTIONARY

ENGLISH—WELSH DICTIONARY

a, an, *a.* **a man**, dyn.—**an ass,** asyn

aback, *adv.* yn ôl.—**taken a.**, wedi synnu

abaft, *adv.* yn ôl; ym mhen ôl llong

abandon, *v.t.* rhoi'r gorau i, gadael

abandoned, *a.* ofer, afradlon

abase, *v.t.* darostwng, iselu, gostwng

abash, *v.t.* cywilyddio

abate, *v.* gostwng, lleihau; gostegu

abbess, *n.* abades

abbey, *n.* abaty, mynachlog

abbot, *n.* abad

abbreviate, *v.t.* byrhau, talfyrru

abdicate, *v.* ymddeol

abdomen, *n.* bol

abdominal, *a.* perthynol i'r bol

abduct, *v.t.* dwyn ymaith drwy drais

aberration, *n.* cyfeiliorn, gwyriad

abet, *v.t.* cefnogi, cynorthwyo, ategu

abeyance, *n.* dirymedd dros dro

abhor, *v.t.* ffieiddio, casáu

abhorrence, *n.* ffieidd-dod, atgasrwydd

abide, *v.* aros, trigo; goddef

abiding *a.* arhosol, gwastadol

ability *n.* gallu, medr

abject, *a.* distadl, dirmygedig

abjure, *v.t.* gwadu ar lw; ymwrthod â

ablative, *n.* abladol

ablaze, *adv.* ar dân, yn wenfflam

able, *a.* abl, galluog

ablution, *n.* golchiad; puredigaeth

abnegation, *n.* (hunan)ymwadiad

abnormal, *a.* anghyffredin, annormal

aboard, *adv.* ar fwrdd (llong)

abode, *n.* annedd, trigfa, cartrefle

abolish, *v.t.* diddymu, dileu

abominable, *a.* ffiaidd

abomination, *n.* ffieidd-dra

aborigines, *n.pl.* cyn-drigolion

abortion, *n.* erthyliad; erthyl

abound, *v.i.* amlhau, heigio; ymhelaethu

about, *pr.* am, oddeutu, tua; *adv.* o ddeutu

above, *pr.* uwch, uwchlaw; *adv.* fry

abridge, *v.t.* talfyrru, cwtogi

abroad, *adv.* allan, ar led, ar daen

abrogate, *v.t.* diddymu, dileu

abrupt, *a.* disymwth, sydyn, swta; serth

abscess, *n.* cornwyd, casgliad, crynhofa

abscond, *v.i.* rhedeg i ffwrdd, dianc

absence, *n.* absenoldeb

absent, *a.* absennol: *v.t.* absenoli

absolute, *a.* cwbl, hollol; diamodol; *n.* y diamod, absolwt

absolution, *n.* gollyngdod; maddeuant

absolve, *v.t.* rhyddhau, gollwng; maddau

absorb, *v.t.* yfed, llyncu, sugno, sychu

abstain, *v.* ymatal, ymgadw

abstemious, *a.* cymedrol, sobr

abstention, *n.* ymataliad

abstinence, *n.* dirwest, ymataliad

abstinent, *a.* cymedrol, sobr

abstract, *v.t.* tynnu: *a.* haniaethol : *n.* crynodeb

abstraction, *n.* haniaeth; synfyfyrdod

abstruse, *a.* tywyll, dyrys, astrus

absurd, *a.* gwrthun, afresymol

abundance, *n.* digonedd, helaethrwydd

abundant, *a.* aml, helaeth, digonol

abuse, *v.t.* camddefnyddio; difrïo

abuse, *n.* camddefnydd; difrïaeth
abut, *v.i.* cydio, ffinio, ymylu ar
abutment, *n.* ateg; pentan (pont)
abyss, *n.* y dyfnder, agendor
academic, -al, *a.* athrofaol, academig
academy, *n.* ysgol, athrofa, academi
accede, *v.i.* cytuno, cydsynio
accelerate, *v.t.* cyflymu, chwimio
accelerator, *n.* ysbardun, chwimiadur
accent, *n.* acen; llediaith: *v.t.* acennu
accentuate, *v.t.* acennu; pwysleisio
accept, *v.t.* derbyn (yn gymeradwy)
acceptable, *a.* derbyniol, cymeradwy
access, *n.* dyfodfa, dyfodiad
accessary, *n.* cynorthwywr, cefnogydd
accessible, *a.* hygyrch; hawdd nesu ato
accession, *n.* esgyniad (i'r orsedd)
accessory, *a.* cynorthwyol, cyfranogol; atodol
accidence, *n.* ffurfiant
accident, *n.* damwain
acclaim, *v.t.* bloeddio cymeradwyaeth
acclamation, *n.* bloddest, cymeradwyaeth
accommodate, *v.t.* cymhwyso; lletya
accommodation, *n.* lle, llety
accompaniment, *n.* cyfeiliant
accompanist, *n.* cyfeilydd
accompany, *v.* hebrwng; cyfeilio
accomplice, *n.* cynorthwywr mewn trosedd
accomplish, *v.t.* cyflawni, cwblhau
accord, *v.* cytuno; cyflwyno: *n.* cydfod
accordance, *n.*—**in a. with,** yn unol â
according, *adv.* **a. to,** yn ôl
accordingly, *adv.* felly, gan hynny
accost, *v.t.* cyfarch
account, *v.* cyfrif: *n.* cyfrif; hanes
accountable, *a.* cyfrifol, atebol

accountant, *n.* cyfrifydd
accoutre, *v.t.* taclu, arfogi
accredit, *v.t.* coelio, credu; awdurdodi
accrue, *v.t.* deillio, codi, digwydd
accumulate, *v.* casglu, pentyrru, cronni
accumulator, *n.* cronadur
accuracy, *n.* cywirdeb
accurate, *a.* cywir
accursed, *a.* melltigedig, melltigaid
accusative, *a.* gwrthrychol (*gram.*); cyhuddol
accuse, *v.t.* cyhuddo
accustom, *v.t.* arfer, ymarfer, cynefino
ache, *v.i.* poeni, gwynio: *n.* poen, cur
achieve, *v.t.* cyflawni, gorffen, cwpláu, cwblhau
achievement, *n.* cyflawniad, camp
acid, *a.* siarp, sur: *n.* suryn, asid
acidic, *a.* asidig
acknowledge, *v.t.* cydnabod, cyfaddef
acknowledgment, *n.* cydnabyddiaeth
acorn, *n.* mesen
acquaint, *v.t.* hysbysu
acquaintance, *n.* cydnabod, cydnabyddiaeth
acquiesce, *v.i.* dygymod, cydsynio
acquire, *v.t.* cael, ennill
acquisition, *n.* caffaeliad
acquit, *v.t.* rhyddhau
acre, *n.* erw, cyfair, acer
acrid, *a.* chwerw, llymsur
acrimonious, *a.* chwerw, sarrug, cecrus
across, *adv. & pr.* yn groes, ar draws; trosodd
act, *v.* gweithredu, actio: *n.* act, gweithred, deddf
action, *n.* gweithred, gweithrediad
active, *a.* bywiog; gweithredol
activity, *n.* gweithgarwch, gweithgaredd
actor, *n.* actor, actiwr
actress, *n.* actores

actual, *a.* gwir, gwironeddol
actuary, *n.* ystadegydd, cyfrifydd
actuate, *v.t.* ysgogi, cymell, cyffroi
acumen, *n.* treiddgarwch, craffter
acute, *a.* llym, tost; craff
adage, *n.* dihareb, dywediad
adamant, *n.* adamant, diemwnt
adapt, *v.t.* cyfaddasu
add, *v.* chwanegu, atodi; adio
adder, *n.* neidr, gwiber
addict, *v.t.* ymroddi
addition, *n.* ychwanegiad
additional, *a.* ychwanegol
addle, *a.* gwag, clwc, gorllyd
address, *v.* annerch; cyfeirio: *n.* anerchiad; cyfeiriad
adduce, *v.t.* dwyn ymlaen; nodi
adept, *n.* un cyfarwydd; campwr
adequate, *a.* digonol
adhere, *v.i.* ymlynu, glynu wrth
adhesion, *n.* glyniad, ymlyniad
adhesive, *a.* glynol, ymlynol
adieu, *i.* bydd wych! ffarwel!
adjacent, *a.* cyfagos, gerllaw
adjective *n.* ansoddair
adjoin, *v.t.* cydio, cyffwrdd â
adjourn, *v.t.* gohirio, oedi
adjudge, *v.t.* dyfarnu, barnu
adjudicate, *v.t.* beirniadu, barnu
adjudicator, *n.* beirniad
adjunct, *n.* atodiad, ychwanegiad
adjure, *v.t.* tynghedu, tyngu
adjust, *v.t.* cymhwyso, addasu, unioni
administer, *v.t.* gweinyddu
administration, *n.* gweinyddiaeth
admirable, *a.* rhagorol, campus
admiral, *n.* llyngesydd
admiralty, *n.* morlys
admiration, *n.* edmygedd
admire, *v.t.* edmygu
admission, *n.* derbyniad; addefiad
admit, *v.t.* derbyn; addef, cyfaddef
admittance, *n.* derbyniad; trwydded
admixture, *n.* cymysgiad, cymysgedd
admonish, *v.t.* rhybuddio, ceryddu
admonition, *n.* rhybudd, cerydd
ado, *n.* helynt, heldrin, ffwdan

adolescence, *n.* llencyndod, adolesens
adolescent, *n.* adolesent, llencyn, llances
adopt, *v.* mabwysiadu
adoption, *n.* mabwysiad
adore, *v.t.* addoli
adorn, *v.t.* addurno
adroit, *a.* medrus, deheuig, hyfedr
adulation, *n.* gweniaith, truth
adult, *n.* (un) mewn oed, oedolyn
adulterate, *v.t.* llygru
adulterer, *n.* godinebwr
adulteress, *n.* godinebwraig
adultery, *n.* godineb
advance, *v.* symud ymlaen; dyrchafu; rhoi benthyg: *n.* benthyg, echwyn [budd
advancement, *n.* dyrchafiad; lles,
advantage, *n.* mantais
advantageous, *a.* manteisiol
advent, *n.* dyfodiad; yr Adfent
adventitious, *a.* damweiniol
adventure, *n.* antur, anturiaeth
adverb, *n.* adferf
adversary, *n.* gwrthwynebydd
adverse, *a.* adfydus, gwrthwynebus, croes
adversity, *n.* adfyd, drygfyd
advertise, *v.t.* hysbysu, hysbysebu
advertisement, *n.* hysbysiad, hysbyseb
advice, *n.* cyngor, cyfarwyddyd
advisable, *n.* doeth, buddiol
advise, *v.t.* cynghori, annog; hysbysu
advocate, *n.* eiriolwr, bargyfreithiwr: *v.t.* eiriol, dadlau, cefnogi, pleidio
adze, *n.* neddau, neddyf
aerate, *v.t.* awyru
aerial, *a.* awyrol, wybrol
aeroplane, *n.* awyren
aesthetic, *a.* esthetig
aesthetics, *n.* estheteg
afar, *adv.* pell, hirbell
affable, *a.* hynaws, caruaidd, clên
affair, *n.* achos; mater; helynt
affect, *v.t.* effeithio; cymryd arno, ffugio**

affectation, *n.* mursendod, rhodres, ffug

affection, *n.* serch, cariad; clefyd, haint; affeithiad (*gram.*)

affectionate, *a.* serchog, caruaidd

affiliate, *v.t.* mabwysiadu, tadogi; uno

affinity, *n.* cyfathrach; tebygrwydd

affirm, *v.* haeru, taeru; sicrhau, gwirio

affirmative, *a.* cadarnhaol

affix, *v.t.* sicrhau, gosod

afflict, *v.t.* cystuddio

affliction, *n.* cystudd, adfyd

affluent, *a.* goludog, cyfoethog, cefnog

afford, *v.t.* rhoddi; fforddio

afforestation, *n.* coedwigaeth

affray, *n.* ymryson, ffrwgwd, ysgarmes

affright, *v.t.* dychrynu, brawychu

affront, *v.t.* sarhau, tramgwyddo: *n.* sarhad

afield, *adv.* **far a.,** ymhell

aflame, *adv.* ar dân

afloat, *adv.* yn nofio; ar daen, ar led

afoot, *adv.* ar droed

afraid, *a.* ag ofn arno, ofnus

afresh, *adv.* o'r newydd, eilwaith

after, *pr. & c.* wedi, ar ôl, yn ôl; *adv.* wedyn

aftermath, *n.* adladd, adlodd

afternoon, *n.* prynhawn,

afterwards, *adv.* wedi hynny, wedyn

again, *adv.* eilwaith, drachefn, eto

against, *pr.* erbyn, yn erbyn

age, *n.* oed, oedran; oes; henaint: *v.* heneiddio

aged, *a.* hen, oedrannus

agency, *n.* goruchwyliaeth, cyfrwng

agent, *n.* goruchwyliwr; gweithredydd

aggrandise, *v.t.* mawrhau, mwyhau

aggravate, *v.t.* gwneuthur yn waeth

aggregate, *n.* cyfanswm, crynswth

aggression, *n.* ymosodiad, gormes

aggressive, *a.* ymwthiol, gormesol

aggrieve, *v.t.* blino, tramgwyddo

aghast, *a.* syn, brawychedig

agile, *a.* heini, sionc, gwisgi

agitate, *v.t.* cynhyrfu, aflonyddu, cyffroi

agnostic, *n.* agnostig, anffyddiwr

ago, *adv.* yn ôl. —**long a.,** ers talm

agony, *n.* ing, poen

agrarian *a.* tirol, gwledig

agree, *v.i.* cytuno; dygymod; cyfateb

agreeable, *a.* clên, dymunol, hyfryd

agreement, *n.* cytundeb

agriculture, *n.* amaethyddiaeth

aground, *adv.* ar lawr, ar dir, i dir

ague, *n.* y cryd

ahead, *adv.* ymlaen, o flaen

aid, *v.t.* cynorthwyo, helpu: *n.* cymorth, cynhorthwy

ail, *v.* clafychu; blino, poeni

ailment, *n.* dolur, afiechyd, anhwyldeb

aim, *v.* anelu, amcanu: *n.* amcan, nod

air, *n.* awyr; osgo; cainc, alaw: *v.t.* awyru

aisle, *n.* ystlys eglwys; llwybr; eil

ajar, *adv.* cilagored

akin, *adv. & a.* perthynol, perthynasol

alack, *i.* och fi

alacrity, *n.* bywiogrwydd, parodrwydd

alarm, *v.t.* dychrynu: *n.* braw, dychryn; rhybudd; larwm

alas, *i.* och!

albeit, *c.* er, er hynny, eto

album, *n.* albwm

albumen, *n.* gwyn wy

alcohol, *n.* alcohol

alcove, *n.* cilfach wely; hafdy, deildy, alcof

alder, *n.* gwernen

alderman, *n.* henadur

ale, *n.* cwrw

alert, *a.* esgud, effro, gwyliadwrus

algebra, *n.* algebra

alien, *a.* estronol: *n.* estron

alight, *v.i.* disgyn
align, *v.* cyfunioni
alike, *a.* yr un fath : *adv.* yn gyffelyb
aliment, *n.* maeth, ymborth
alive, *adv. & a.* yn fyw, byw
alkali, *n.* alcali
alkaline, *a.* alcalïaidd
all, *a.* holl; oll, i gyd : *adv.* yn hollol
   n. y cwbl, y cyfan; pawb
allay, *v.t.* lleddfu, lliniaru; tawelu
allege, *v.t.* honni, haeru
allegiance, *n.* teyrngarwch, gwrogaeth
allegory, *n.* alegori
alleviate, *v.t.* ysgafnhau, esmwytho
alley, *n.* llwybr, ale
alliance, *n.* cyfathrach, cynghrair
alliteration, *n.* cyflythreniad,
   cyseinedd
allocate, *v.t.* cyfleu, rhannu, dosbarthu
allot, *v.* gosod, penodi
allotment, *n.* cyfran; rhandir
allow, *v.t.* caniatáu, goddef
allowance, *n.* goddefiad; dogn;
   lwfans
alloy, *n.* aloi
allude, *v.i.* cyfeirio, sôn
allure, *v.* hudo, denu, llithio
allusion, *n.* crybwylliad, cyfeiriad
   (at)
alluvium, *n.* llif bridd, dolbridd
ally, *v.t.* cynghreirio : *n.* cynghreiriad
almighty, *a.* hollalluog, hollgyfoethog
almoner, *n.* elusennwr
almost, *adv.* bron, agos, braidd
alms, *n.* elusen, cardod
aloft, *adv.* yn uchel, fry, i fyny
alone, *adv. & a.* unig, ar ei ben ei
   hun
along, *adv.* ymlaen ; ar hyd.—**all a.**,
   o'r cychwyn
aloof, *adv. & a.* yn cadw draw; pell
aloud, *adv.* yn uchel, yn groch
alphabet, *n.* egwyddor, abiéc
already, *adv.* eisoes, yn barod
also, *adv.* hefyd
altar, *n.* allor
alter, *v.* newid, altro

alteration, *n.* newid, cyfnewidiad
altercation, *n.* ymryson, ffrae
alternate, *a.* bob yn ail : *v.* digwydd
   bob yn ail; eilio
although, *c.* er
altitude, *n.* uchder
altogether, *adv.* oll, i gyd, yn gyfan
   gwbl
altruism, *n.* allgarwch, allgaredd
always, *adv.* yn wastad(ol), bob
   amser
amalgamate, *v.* cymysgu, cyfuno,
   uno
amanuensis, *n.* ysgrifennydd dros
   arall
amass, *v.t.* casglu, cronni, pentyrru
amateur, *n.* amatur
amatory, *a.* carwriaethol
amaze, *v.t.* synnu, rhyfeddu,
   aruthro
ambassador, *n.* llysgennad
ambidextrous, *a.* deheuig â'i
   ddwy law
ambiguity, *n.* amwysedd
ambiguous, *a.* amwys
ambition, *n.* uchelgais
ambitious, *a.* uchelgeisiol
amble, *v.i.* rhygyngu ; *n.* rhygyng
ambulance, *n.* ambiwlans
ambush, *n. & v.* cynllwyn, rhagod
ameliorate, *v.t.* gwella, diwygio
amenable, *a.* hydrin ; atebol;
   cyfrifol
amend, *v.* gwella, diwygio, cywiro
amendment, *n.* gwelliant
amends, *n.* iawn
amenity, *n.* hyfrydwch ; hynawsedd
amerce, *v.t.* dirwyo
amiable, *a.* hawddgar, serchus
amicable, *a.* cyfeillgar
amid, -st, *pr.* ynghanol, ymhlith,
   ymysg
amiss, *adv.* ar fai, o'i le
amity, *n.* cyfeillgarwch
ammunition, *n.* arlwy rhyfel;
   pylor, &c.
amnesty, *n.* maddeuant
among, -st, *pr.* ymhlith, ymysg,
   rhwng
amorous, *a.* hoff o garu

amorphous, *a.* di-ffurf, amorffus
amount, *v.i.* cyrraedd; codi: *n.* swm
amour, *n.* carwriaeth
ample, *a.* helaeth, eang; cyflawn, digon
amplify, *v.t.* helaethu, ehangu
amputate, *v.t.* torri aelod, trychu
amulet, *n.* swyngyfaredd
amuse, *v.t.* difyrru, diddanu
amusement, *n.* difyrrwch, digrifwch
an, Gwêl **a**
anachronism, *n.* camamseriad
anaemia, *n.* diffyg gwaed
anaemic, *a.* di-waed, diwryg
anaesthesia, *n.* dideimladrwydd
anaesthetic, *a. & n.* anesthetig
analogy, *n.* cyfatebiaeth, cydweddiad   [fennu
analyse, *v.t.* dadansoddi, dadel-
analysis, (-*yses*) *n.* dadansoddiad
analyst, *n.* dadansoddwr
analytical, *a.* dadansoddol
anarchic, -al, *a.* anarchol
anarchist, *n.* anarchydd, terfysgwr
anarchy, *n.* anhrefn, aflywodraeth, anarchaeth
anatomy, *n.* anatomeg
ancestor, *n.* cyndad, (*pl.*) hynafiaid
ancestry, *n.* ach, achau; hynafiaid
anchor, *n.* angor: *v.* angori
anchoret, -ite, *n.* meudwy, ancr
ancient, *a.* hen, hynafol; oesol
and, *c.* a, ac
anecdote, *n.* hanesyn, chwedl
anent, *pr.* ynghylch
anew, *adv.* o'r newydd
angel, *n.* angel
anger, *n.* dicter, llid: *v.t.* digio, llidio
angle, *n.* ongl: *v.i.* genweirio, pysgota
Anglican, *a.* perthynol i Eglwys Loegr, Anglicanaidd
angry, *a.* dig, llidiog
anguish, *n.* ing
angular, *a.* onglog
animadvert, *v.i.* beirniadu, ceryddu, sennu

animal, *n.* anifail, mil: *a.* anifeilaidd
animate, *a.* byw: *v.t.* bywhau; ysgogi
animation, *n.* bywiogrwydd
animosity, *n.* gelyniaeth, digasedd
animus, *n.* drwgdeimlad, gelyniaeth
ankle, *n.* migwrn, ffêr, swrn
annals, *n.pl.* cofnodion blynyddol
anneal, *v.* anelio
annex, *v.t.* cysylltu, cydio; meddiannu
annihilate, *v.t.* diddymu, difodi
annihilation, *n.* diddymiant, difodiant
anniversary, *n.* pen blwydd; cylchwyl flynyddol
annotate, *v.* gwneud nodiadau
announce, *v.t.* datgan, cyhoeddi
announcement, *n.* cyhoeddiad, hysbysiad
announcer, *n.* cyhoeddwr
annoy, *v.t.* poeni, blino, cythruddo
annual *a.* blynyddol
annuity, *n.* blwydd-dâl
annul *v.t.* diddymu, dileu, dirymu
annular *a.* crwn fel modrwy, modrwyol
anoint *v.t.* eneinio, iro
anomaly *n.* peth croes i reol, afreoleidd-dra
anon *adv.* yn union, toc, yn y man
anonymity *n.* cyflwr dienw
anonymous *a.* dienw, anhysbys
another *pn. & n.* arall
answer *v.* ateb: *n.* ateb, atebiad
answerable, *a.* atebol, cyfrifol
ant, *n.* morgrugyn
antagonism, *n.* gwrthwynebiaeth
antagonist, *n.* gwrthwynebydd
antarctic, *a.* o gylch y pegwn deheuol
ante-, *px.* cyn, o flaen, rhag-
antecedent, *a.* blaenorol
antediluvian, *a.* cynddilywaidd
antelope, *n.* gafrewig, antelop
anterior, *a.* blaen, blaenorol, cynanthology,** *n.* blodeugerdd
anthracite, *n.* glo caled, glo carreg

anthropology, *n.* anthropoleg

anti-, ant-, *px.* gwrth-, yn erbyn

antibiotic, *n. & a.* gwrthfiotig

antics, *n.pl.* castiau digrif, campau

antichrist, *n.* anghrist

anticipate, *v.t.* achub y blaen, disgwyl

antidote, *n.* gwrthwenwyn

antipathy, *n.* gwrthnaws; casineb, gwrthnaws

antipodes, *n.pl.* pellafoedd byd, eithafoedd

antiquarian, *a.* hynafiaethol: *n.* hynafiaethydd

antiquated, *a.* hen a di-les

antique, *a.* hen, hynafol, hen-ffasiwn

antiquity, *n.* hynafiaeth; y cynoesoedd

antiseptic, *a. & n.* antiseptig

antithesis, (-*es*), *n.* gwrthgyferbyniad

antler, *n.* cainc o gorn carw, rhaidd

anvil, *n.* eingion, einion

anxiety, *n.* pryder

anxious, *a.* pryderus, awyddus

any, *a.* un, unrhyw, rhyw, peth, dim

apace, *adv.* ar garlam, ar ffrwst, ar frys

apart, *adv.* o'r neilltu, ar wahân

apartment, *n.* rhandy, llety

apathetic, *a.* difraw, difater, didaro

apathy, *n.* difrawder, difaterwch

ape, *n.* epa: *v.t.* dynwared

aperture, *n.* bwlch, twll, agorfa

apex, *n.* blaen, brig, pen, copa

aphis, (*aphides*) *n.* pryf gwyrdd

aphorism *n.* gwireb, dihareb

apiary, *n.* gwenynfa

apiece, *adv.* un bob un

apocalypse, *n.* datguddiad

apocryphal, *a.* anghanonaidd, apocryffaidd

apologize, *v.i.* ymddiheuro, ymesgusodi

apology, *n.* ymddiheuriad, esgusawd

apoplexy, *n.* parlys mud, strôc

apostasy, *n.* gwrthgiliad

apostate, *n.* gwrthgiliwr

apostle, *n.* apostol

apostolic, -al, *a.* apostolaidd

apostrophe, *n.* sillgoll, collnod (')

apothecary, *n.* apothecari, fferyll-ydd

apotheosis, *n.* dwyfoliad

appal, *v.t.* brawychu, digalonni

apparatus, *n.* offer, aparatws

apparel, *n.* dillad, gwisg

apparent, *a.* amlwg, eglur

apparition, *n.* drychiolaeth, ysbryd

appeal, *v.i.* apelio, erfyn: *n.* apêl

appear, *v.i.* ymddangos, ymrithio

appearance, *n.* ymddangosiad

appease, *v.t.* llonyddu, tawelu, dofi

appellation, *n.* enw, teitl

append, *v.t.* atodi, ychwanegu

appendicitis, *n.* enyniad y coluddyn crog

appendix, *n.* atodiad, ychwanegiad

appertain, *v.i.* perthyn

appetite, *n.* archwaeth, chwant, awydd

applaud, *v.t.* cymeradwyo, curo dwylo

applause, *n.* cymeradwyaeth

apple, *n.* afal.—**a. of the eye,** cannwyll llygad

appliance, *n.* offeryn, dyfais

applicant, *n.* ymgeisydd

application, *n.* cymhwysiad; cais; ymroddiad

applied, *a.* cymwysedig

apply, *v.* cymhwyso; ymroi; cynnig (am), ymgeisio

appoint, *v.* gosod, penodi, pennu

appointment, *n.* cyhoeddiad; penodiad

apportion, *v.t.* rhannu, dosbarthu

apposite, *a.* addas, priodol

appraise, *v.t.* prisio

appreciate, *v.t.* prisio, gwerthfawrogi

apprehend, *v.t.* ymaflyd mewn; dirnad; ofni

apprehension, *n.* dirnadaeth; ofn

apprehensive, *a.* ofnus, pryderus

apprentice, *n.* prentis, dysgwr: *v.t.* prentisio

apprise, *v.* hysbysu

approach, v. nesáu, dynesu: n. dyfodfa

approbation, n. cymeradwyaeth

appropriate, v.t. meddiannu: a. priodol

approval, n. cymeradwyaeth

approve, v.t. cymeradwyo; profi

approximate, v.i. agosáu: a. agos

appurtenance, n. peth perthynol

apricot, n. bricyllen

April, n. Ebrill

apron, n. (ar)ffedog, barclod

apt, a. tueddol; cymwys, parod

aquarium, n. pysgodlyn, pysgoty

aquatic, a. dyfrol, dyfriog

aqueduct, n. dyfrffos

aquiline, a. eryraidd; crwbi, bachog

arable, a. **a. land,** tir âr

arbiter, n. dyddiwr, brawdwr, beirniad

arbitrament, n. rhaith, dedfryd

arbitrary, a. gormesol, mympwyol

arbitrate, v. cyflafareddu, athrywyn

arbour, n. deildy

arc, n. bwa, arc

arch, n. bwa, pont; nen: v.t. pontio

arch-, px. arch-, carn-, prif-

arch, a. direidus, cellweirus, ysmala

archaeology, n. hynafiaeth, archaeoleg

archaic, a. hynafol, henaidd

archangel, n. archangel

archbishop, n. archesgob

archdeacon, n. archddiacon, archddiagon

archdruid, n. archdderwydd

archer, n. saethydd, saethwr

archery, n. saethyddiaeth

archipelago, n. twr ynysoedd, ynysfor

architect, n. pensaer

architecture, n. pensaernïaeth

architrave, n. amhiniog

arctic, a. gogleddol

ardent, a. gwresog, poeth, angerddol

ardour, n. angerdd, aidd

arduous, a. llafurus, blin, caled

area, n. arwynebedd, wyneb

argue, v. dadlau, ymresymu

argument, n. dadl, ymresymiad

arid, a. sych, crin, cras, gwyw

aright, adv. yn iawn, yn briodol

arise, v.i. cyfodi, codi

aristocracy, n. pendefigaeth

aristocrat, n. pendefig, gŵr mawr

aristocratic, a. pendefigaidd, bonheddig

arithmetic, n. rhifyddeg

arithmetician, n. rhifyddwr

ark, n. arch

arm, n. braich; cainc

arm, n. arf: v. arfogi

armament, n. offer rhyfel; arfogaeth

armful, a. coflaid, ceseiliaid

armistice, n. cadoediad

armour, n. arfogaeth, arfwisg

armoury, n. arfdy

army, n. byddin

aroma, n. perarogl(au)

aromatic, a. peraroglaidd, pêr, persawrus

around, adv. & pr. am, o amgylch

arouse, v.t. deffro(i), dihuno; cyffroi

arraign, v.t. cyhuddo o flaen brawdle

arrange, v. trefnu

arrangement, n. trefn, trefniad, trefniant

arrant, a. dybryd, cywilyddus

array, v.t. trefnu, cyfleu; gwisgo: n. trefn; gwisg

arrears, n.pl. ôl-ddyled

arrest, v.t. atal; dal, dala, restio

arrive, v.i. cyrraedd, dyfod

arrogance, n. balchder, traha

arrogant, a. balch, trahaus

arrogate, v.t. hawlio, trawshawlio

arrow, n. saeth

arsenal, n. arfdy, ystordy neu ffatri arfau

arson, n. llosgiad, llosg

art, n. celfyddyd; ystryw

artery, n. rhedweli

artful, a. ystrywgar, dichellgar, cyfrwys

article, *n.* erthygl; nwydd; bannod
articulate, *v.* cymalu; cynanu
artifice, *n.* dyfais; ystryw, dichell
artificer, *n.* saer, crefftwr, celfydd-ydwr
artificial, *a.* celfyddydol; gosod, dodi
artillery, *n.* offer rhyfel, magnelau
artisan, *n.* crefftwr
artist, *n.* celfyddydwr, arlunydd, artist
artistic, *a.* celfydd, celfyddgar, artistig
as, *c. & adv.* megis, fel; cyn, mor; â, ag
asbestos, *n.* ystinos, asbestos
ascend, *v.* esgyn, dringo, dyrchafu
ascendancy, *n.* goruchafiaeth, uchafiaeth,
ascension, *n.* esgyniad, dyrchafael
ascent, *n.* esgynfa, rhiw, gorifyny
ascertain, *v.t.* cael gwybod, mynnu gwybod
ascetic, *n.* meudwy: *a.* meu-dwyaidd, ymgosbol, asgetig
ascribe, *v.t.* cyfrif i, priodoli, rhoddi
ash, *n.* onnen, onn
ash, *(-es) n.* lludw, ulw. —*a.* **tray,** plat lludw
ashamed, *a.* ag arno gywilydd
ashore, *adv.* i'r lan, ar y lan
aside, *adv.* o'r neilltu
ask, *v.* gofyn, holi; ceisio
askew, *adv.* ar osgo, ar letraws
askance, *adv.* yn llygatraws, yn gam
aslant, *adv.* ar ei ogwydd
asleep, *adv.* yng nghwsg, yn cysgu
aspect, *n.* golwg, golygwedd, wyneb, agwedd
aspen, *n.* aethnen
asperity, *n.* gerwindeb, llymder
asperse, *v.t.* taenellu; gwarad-wyddo
aspersion, *n.* difrïad, enllib
asphyxiate, *v.t.* mygu, tagu
aspirate, *v.t.* seinio ag anadl: *n.* yr *(h)*
aspiration, *n.* dyhead

aspire, *v.i.* dyheu
ass, *n.* asyn; asen
assail, *v.t.* ymosod ar, rhuthro ar
assailant, *n.* ymosodwr
assassin, *n.* bradlofrudd, llofrudd
assassinate, *v.t.* bradlofruddio
assault, *n.* ymosodiad: *v.t.* ymosod
assay, *n.* praw(f): *v.* profi; cynnig, ceisio
assemble, *v.* cynnull, ymgynnull
assembly, *n.* cynulliad, cymanfa
assent, *v.i.* cydsynio: *n.* cydsyniad
assert, *v.t.* haeru, honni, mynnu
assess, *v.t.* trethu, prisio
assets, *n.pl.* eiddo, meddiannau
asseverate, *v.t.* haeru ar ei wir, tyngu
assiduous, *a,* dyfal, diwyd
assign, *v.t.* gosod, penodi; tros-glwyddo
assimilate, *v.* cymathu; tebygu
assist, *v.* cynorthwyo, cymorth, helpu
assize, *n.* brawdlys
associate, *v.* cymdeithasu, cyfeill-achu: *n.* cydymaith
association, *n.* cymdeithas, cym-deithasfa
assort, *v.* trefnu, dosbarthu
assuage, *v.t.* llonyddu, lliniaru, lleddfu
assume, *v.t.* cymryd ar; tybied; honni
assumption, *n.* tyb(iaeth), bwr-iant, honiad
assurance, *n.* sicrwydd; hyder, hyfder
assure, *v.t.* sicrhau; yswirio
asterisk, *n.* serennig, seren (*)
asthma, *n.* caethder, diffyg anadl
asthmatic, *a.* byr ei wynt, caeth ei frest
astir, *adv.* yn symud, wedi codi, mewn cyffro
astonish, *v.t.* synnu
astound, *v.t.* synnu, syfrdanu
astral, *a.* serol
astray, *adv.* ar gyfeiliorn, ar grwydr
astride, *adv.* â'r traed ar led
astrologer, *n.* sêr-ddewin

astrology, n. sêr-ddewiniaeth

astronomer, n. serydd, seryddwr

astronomy, n. seryddiaeth

astute, a. craff, cyfrwys, call

asunder, adv. ar wahân, yn ddryll-iau

asylum, n. noddfa.—**lunatic a.,** gwallgofdy

at, pr. yn, wrth, ger, ar

atheist, n. anffyddiwr

athlete, n. mabolgampwr

athletics, n.pl. mabolgampau

atlas, n. llyfr mapiau, atlas

atmosphere, n. awyrgylch

atom, n. mymryn, gronyn, atom

atone, v.i. gwneuthur iawn

atonement, n. iawn, cymod

atrocious, a. erchyll, anfad, ysgeler

atrophy, n. annhyfiant

attach, v. gosod, glynu; atafaelu

attachment, n. ymlyniad, serch

attack, v.t. ymosod ar: n. ymosod-iad

attain, v.t. ennill; cyrraedd; cael gafael

attainment, n. cyrhaeddiad

attempt, v.t. ceisio, cynnig: n. cynnig, ymgais

attend, v. gweini; ystyried; dilyn

attendance, n. gwasanaeth; presen-oldeb

attention, n. sylw, ystyriaeth

attentive, a. astud, ystyriol

attenuate, v.t. teneuo, lleihau

attest, v. tystio, gwirio; ardystio

attic, n. nenlofft, nennawr

attire, v.t. gwisgo: n. gwisg, dillad

attitude, n. ystum, agwedd, osgo

attorney, n. twrnai

attract, v.t. tynnu, atynnu, denu, hudo

attraction, n. atyniad

attribute, n. priodoledd

attribute, v.t. priodoli, cyfrif i

attrition, n. rhathiad, treuliad, traul

attune, v.t. hwylio, cyweirio

auburn, a. gwinau, browngoch

auction, n. arwerthiant, ocsiwn

auctioneer, n. arwerthwr

audacious, a. hy, digywilydd, haerllug

audacity, n. hyfdra, ehofndra, beiddgarwch

audible, a. hyglyw, clywadwy

audience, n. gwrandawyr, cynu-lleidfa

audit, v.t. archwilio cyfrifon: n. ar-chwiliad

auditor, n. gwrandawr; archwilydd

auger, n. taradr, ebill

aught, n. dim

augment, v.t. ychwanegu, atodi

augur, n. dewin: v. darogan; argoeli

August, n. Awst

august, a. urddasol, mawreddog

aunt, n. modryb

auricular, a. **a. confession,** clust-gyffes

auspices, n.pl. nawdd

auspicious, a. yn argoeli'n dda, ffafriol

austere, a. gerwin, llym, tost, caled

authentic, a. dilys, gwir

author, n. awdur, awdwr

authority, n. awdurdod

authorize, v.t. awdurdodi

auto-, px. hunan-, ym-

autobiography, n. hunangofiant

autocracy, n. unbennaeth

autocrat, n. unben; dyn aw-durdodol

autograph, n. llofnod

automatic, a. hunanysgogol, awto-matig

automaton, (-ta) n. ymsymudydd, peiriant dienaid

autonomy, n. ymreolaeth

autumn, n. hydref

auxilliary, a. cynorthwyol, ategol: n. cynorthwywr

avail, v. llesáu, tycio: n. lles, budd

avalanche, n. syrthfa, cwymp (eira, &c.)

avarice, n. cybydd-dod, trachwant

avaricious, a. cybyddlyd, ariangar

avenge, v.t. dial cam

avenue, n. mynedfa, rhodfa

aver, v.t. gwirio, haeru

average, n. canolbris; cyfartaledd
averse, a. gwrthwynebol, gelynol
aversion, n. gwrthwynebiad; casbeth
avert, v.t. troi heibio, gochel
aviary, n. adardy
avidity, n. awydd, awch, gwanc
avocation, n. gorchwyl, galwedigaeth
avoid, v.t. gochel, osgoi, arbed
avouch, v.t. gwirio, haeru; arddelwi
avow, v.t. addef; cydnabod
await, v.t. disgwyl, aros
awake, v. deffro, dihuno: a. effro
award, v.t. dyfarnu: n. dyfarniad
aware, a. hysbys, ymwybodol
awareness, n. arwybod
away, adv. ymaith, i ffwrdd
awe, n. (parchedig) ofn: v.t. rhoi arswyd
awful, a. ofnadwy, arswydus
awhile, adv. am ennyd, am dro
awkward, a. trwsgl, lletchwith, anghyfleus
awl, n. mynawyd
awning, n. cysgodlen
awry, adv. ar letraws, o chwith
axe, n. bwyall, bwyell
axiom, n. gwireb
axis, (axes) n. echel, pegwn
axle, n. echel
ay, adv. ie
aye, adv. yn wastad(ol), byth
azure, n. glas y ffurfafen, asur: a. asur

B

babble, v. baldordd, clebran: n. baldordd
babe, n. baban, plentyn bach
baby, n. baban, maban, babi
bachelor, n. dyn dibriod, hen lanc; baglor
back, n. cefn: v. cefnogi; bacio: adv. yn ôl
backslide, v.i. gwrthgilio
backward, adv. yn ôl: a. hwyrfrydig; digynnydd; araf

bacon, n. cig moch, bacwn
bad, a. drwg, drygionus; gwael, sâl
badge, n. bathodyn
badger, n. mochyn daear, broch: v.t. profocio, poeni
badinage, n. cellwair, ysmaldod
baffle, v.t. drysu, siomi, trechu
bag, n. cwd, cod, bag
baggage, n. clud, celfi, pac.
bah, i. pw !
bail, n. meichiau, gwystl: v.t. mechnïo
bail, bale, v.t. hysbyddu cwch
bailiff, n. beili; hwsmon, goruchwyliwr
bait, v.t. abwydo; baeddu, eirthio: n. abwyd
bake, v. pobi, crasu
baker, n. pobydd
balance, n. clorian, mantol; gweddill: v.t. mantoli; cydbwyso
balcony, n. oriel, balcon
bald, a. moel, penfoel
balderdash, n. lol, ffregod, ffiloreg
bale, n. pwn, sypyn
baleful, a. alaethus, gresynol, galarus
balk, baulk, n. balc; siom: v.t. balcio; siomi
ball, n. pêl, pellen
ball, n. dawns, dawnsfa
ballad, n. baled
ballast, n. balast
balloon, n. balŵn
ballot, n. balot, tugel
balm, n. balm, triagl
bamboozle, v. twyllo, llygaddynnu
ban, v.t. gwahardd, ysgymuno
banal, a. cyffredin, sathredig
band, n. band, rhwymyn; mintai; seindorf
bandage, n. rhwymyn: v.t. rhwymo, rhwymynnu
bandbox, n. bocs hetiau
bandit, n. herwr, ysbeiliwr
bandy, v.t. taflu (pêl, &c) yn ôl a blaen
bandy-legged, a. coesgam
bane, n. dinistr, melltith

baneful, *a.* dinistriol, andwyol

bang, *v.* curo, dulio, clepian: *n.* ergyd, twrf

bangle, *n.* breichled

banish, *v.t.* alltudio, deol

bank, *n.* mainc; rhes

bank, *n.* glan, torlan; traethell

bank, *n.* banc, ariandy: *v.* bancio

banker, *n.* bancwr

bankrupt, *n.* methdalwr

bankruptcy, *n.* methdaliad

banner, *n.* baner, lluman

banns, *n.pl.* gostegion

banquet, *n.* gwledd: *v.* gwledda

bantam, *n.* coriar, dandi

banter, *n.* ysmaldod, cellwair: *v.* cellwair, profocio

baptism, *n.* bedydd

Baptist, *n.* Bedyddiwr

baptize, *v.t.* bedyddio

bar, *n.* bar, bollt; rhwystr; traethell: *v.t.* bario; eithrio

barb, *n.* barf; adfach

barbarian, *n.* barbariad, anwariad

barber, *n.* barbwr

bard, *n.* bardd, prydydd

bare, *a.* noeth, llwm, moel, prin: *v.t.* dinoethi

barely, *adv.* prin, o'r braidd

bargain, *n.* bargen: *v.* bargeinio

barge, *n.* bad mawr

bark, *n.* barc, llong, llestr

bark, *v.i.* cyfarth, coethi: *n.* cyfarthiad

bark, *n.* rhisgl: *v.t.* dirisglo, digroeni

barley, *n.* haidd, barlys

barm, *n.* burum, berem, berman

barn, *n.* ysgubor

barometer, *n.* hinfynegydd, baromedr

baron, *n.* barwn, arglwydd

baronet, *n.* barwnig

barrack, *n.* lluest, lluesty, gwersyllty

barrage, *n.* argae, clawdd

barrel, *n.* baril, casgen

barren, *a.* diffrwyth; amhlantadwy

barricade, *n.* atalglawdd: *v.t.* cau

barrier, *n.* atalfa, rhwystr, terfyn, ffin

barrister, *n.* bargyfreithiwr

barrow, *n.* berfa, whilber; crug

barter, *v.* cyfnewid, ffeirio: *n.* cyfnewid

base, *a.* isel, gwael, distadl, gau

base, *n.* sylfaen; bôn: *v.t.* sylfaenu, seilio

bashful, *a.* swil, gwylaidd

basin, *n.* basn, cawg, dysgl

basis, *(bases)* *n.* sail, sylfaen

bask, *v.i.* ymheulo, torheulo

basket, *n.* basged, cawell

basketful, *n.* basgedaid

bass, *n.* bas, isalaw

bastard, *n.* bastart, plentyn gordderch

baste, *v.t.* iro, brasteru; ffusto, ffonodio

bastinado, *n. & v.t.* ffonodio gwadnau'r traed

bat, *n.* ystlum

bat, *n.* bat: *v.i.* batio

batch, *n.* pobiad, ffyrnaid; swp, sypyn

bath, *n.* ymolchfa, badd, baddon; bath

bathe, *v.* ymdrochi, ymolchi, golchi

baton, *n.* llawffon, byrllysg, arweinffon　　　　[iwn

battalion, *n.* byddin, mintai, batal-

batten, *v.i.* ymfrasáu, ymbesgi

batter, *v.t.* curo, pwyo: *n.* defnydd crempog

battery, *n.* magnelfa; batri

battle, *n.* brwydr, cad: *v.i.* brwydro

battlement, *n.* canllaw, murganllaw

bauble, *n.* ffril, tegan

baulk. Gwêl **balk**

bawl, *v.i.* gweiddi, crochlefain, bloeddio

bay, *n.* bae

bay, *v. & n.* cyfarth

bay, *n.* llawryf

bay, *a.* gwinau, gwineugoch

bayonet, *n.* bidog: *v.t.* bidogi

bazaar, *n.* basâr

be, *v.i.* bod

beach, *n.* traeth, traethell: *v.t.* gyrru ar y traeth

beacon, n. gwylfa, goleudy; coel-
certh
bead, n. glain. —**beads,** paderau
beadle, n. rhingyll
beak, n. pig, gylfin, duryn
beam, n. trawst, paladr; pelydryn:
v.i. pelydru
bean, n. ffäen, ffeuen
bear, n. arth; arthes
bear, v.t. dwyn, cludo; geni;
dioddef, goddef
beard, n. barf; col ŷd
beast, n. bwystfil, anifail
beat, v.t. curo: n. cur, curiad
beatific, a. gwynfydus, gwynfydedig
beatitude, n. gwynfyd
beau, n. coegyn
beautiful, a. prydferth, hardd, teg
beauty, n. prydferthwch, harddwch,
tegwch. —**b. parlour,** parlwr
pincio
beaver, n. afanc, llostlydan
becalm, v.t. tawelu, llonyddu
because, adv. & c. oherwydd,
oblegid, o achos; gan, am
beck, n. amnaid, awgrym
beckon, v. amneidio
become, v. dyfod; gweddu
becoming, a. gweddus
bed, n. gwely; cefn, pâm
bedeck, v.t. addurno, trwsio
bedew, v.t. gwlitho, gwlychu
bedizen, v.t. addurno, gwychu
bedrid(den), a. gorweiddiog
bedroom, n. ystafell wely, llofft
bedstead, n. pren neu haearn gwely
bee, n. gwenynen
beech, n. ffawydden   [biff
beef, (beeves) n. eidion; cig eidion,
beehive, n. cwch, gwenyn
beer, n. cwrw
beestings, n.pl. llaeth newydd,
llaeth tor
beet, n. betys
beetle, n. chwilen
befall, v. digwydd
befit, v. gweddu
before, pr. o flaen, gerbron, cyn:
adv. o'r blaen

beforehand, adv. ymlaen llaw
befriend, v.t. ymgeleddu, bod yn
gefn
beg, v. erfyn, deisyf, ymbil; cardota
beget, v. cenhedlu, creu, peri
beggar, n. cardotyn: v.t. tlodi,
llymhau
begin, v. dechrau
beginning, n. dechreuad
beguile, v.t. hudo, twyllo; swyno,
difyrru
behalf, n. plaid, rhan, achos, tu
behave, v. ymddwyn
behaviour, n. ymddygiad
behead, v.t. torri pen
behest, n. arch, archiad
behind, adv. & pr. ar ôl, yn ôl, tu
ôl, tu cefn
behold, v.t. edrych, gweled: v. imp.
wele
behoof, n. mantais, elw, budd, lles
behove, v.t. bod yn rhwymedig ar
being, n. bod
belabour, v. curo, baeddu
belated, a. diweddar; wedi ei ddal
gan y nos
belch, v. bytheirio
beleaguer, v.t. gwarchae ar
belfry, n clochdy
belie, v.t. anwireddu, siomi
belief, n. cred, crediniaeth, coel
believe, v. credu. coelio
believer, n. credwr, credadun
belittle, v.t. bychanu
bell, n. cloch
belle, n. merch brydweddol,
meinwen
bellicose, a. rhyfelgar, ymladdgar
belligerent, a. rhyfelog: n. rhyfel-
blaid
bellow, v. rhuo, bugunad
bellows, n.pl. megin
belly, n. bol, bola; cest, tor: v. bolio
belong, v.i. perthyn
belongings, n. meddiannau, eiddo
beloved, a. annwyl, cu: n. anwylyd
below, adv. & pr. is, islaw, isod,
obry, oddi tanodd
belt, n. gwregys
bemoan, v.t. galaru am, arwylo

bench, n. mainc

bend, v. plygu, camu: n. tro, camedd

beneath, adv. & pr. is, tan, oddi tanodd

benediction, n. bendith

benefactor, n. cymwynaswr, noddwr

benefice, n. bywoliaeth eglwysig

beneficent, a. daionus, llesfawr

beneficial, a. buddiol, llesol

benefit, n. budd, lles, elw: v. llesáu, elwa

benevolent, a. daionus, haelionus

benighted, a. a ddaliwyd gan y nos; tywyll

benign, a. tirion, mwyn

bent, n. tuedd, gogwydd

benumb, v.t. merwino, fferru, diffrwytho

bequeath, v.t. cymynnu, cymynroddi

bequest, n. cymynrodd

bereave, v.t. difuddio, amddifadu

berry, n. aeronen, mwyaren

berth, n. lle llong; gwely llongwr; swydd

beseech, v.t. atolygu, deisyf, erfyn

beseem, v.t. gweddu

beset, v.t. cynllwyn; amgylchynu

beside, pr. gerllaw, wrth, yn ymyl

besides, adv. & pr. heblaw, gyda

besiege, v.t. gwarchae ar

besmirch, v.t. llychwino, pardduo

besom, n. ysgubell

bespeak, v.t. ymofyn ymlaen llaw

best, a. & adv. gorau

bestial, a. bwystfilaidd

bestir, v.t. cyffroi, ymysgwyd

bestow, v.t. rhoddi, cyflwyno, anrhegu

bestride, v.t. eistedd neu gamu yn groes i

bet, n. bet, cyngwystl: v. betio, dal am

betide, v. damweinio, digwydd

betimes, adv. yn brydlon, yn fore

betoken, v.t. arwyddo, argoeli

betray, v.t. bradychu

betrayal, n. brad

betroth, v.t. dyweddïo

better, a. gwell, rhagorach: adv. yn well: v.t. gwella

between, -twixt, pr. rhwng, cydrhwng

beverage, n. diod

bevy, n. haid o adar; twr o enethod

bewail, v.t. cwyno, cwynfan, galaru am

beware, v.i. gochel, ymogelyd

bewilder, v.t. drysu, mwydro, pensyfrdanu

bewitch, v.t. rheibio

beyond, adv. & pr. tu hwnt

bi-, px. dau-, deu-

bias, n. tuedd, gogwydd, rhagfarn: v.t. tueddu

bib, v.i. llymeitian, diota

Bible, n. Beibl

bibliography, n. llyfryddiaeth

bibulous, a. yfgar, llymeitgar

bicker, v.i. ffraeo, ymrafaelio, ymgecru [beic

bicycle, n. ceffyl haearn, deurod,

bid, v. erchi; gwahodd; cynnig

bide, v. aros, disgwyl

biennial, a. dwyflynyddol

bier, n. elor

big, a. mawr; braisg

bigamy, n. dwywreigiaeth

bigot, n. penboethyn

bilberries, n.pl. llus

bile, n. bustl, geri

bilingual, a. dwyieithog

bilingualism, n. dwyieithedd; dwyieitheg

bill, n. bil; mesur; rhaglen; hysbyslen

bill, n. pig, gylfin, duryn

billet, n. llety (milwr): v.t. lletya

billow, n. ton, gwaneg, moryn: v.i. tonni

billy-goat, n. bwch gafr

bin, n. cist

bind, v.t. rhwymo, caethiwo

biography, n. bywgraffiad, cofiant

biology, n. bywydeg, bioleg

biped, a. & n. (creadur) deudroed

birch, n. bedw, bedwen; gwialen fedw: v.t. chwipio

bird, *n.* aderyn
birth, *n.* genedigaeth
biscuit, *n.* bisgeden
bisect, *v.t.* dwyrannu, rhannu
bisector, *n.* dwyrannydd
bishop, *n.* esgob
bishopric, *n.* esgobaeth
bison, *n.* ych gwyllt, bual
bit, *n.* tamaid; tipyn, dernyn; genfa, bit
bitch, *n.* gast
bite, *v.* cnoi, brathu: *n.* cnoad, brath; tamaid
bitter, *a.* chwerw, bustlaidd, tost
bittern, *n.* aderyn y bwn, bwmp y gors
bitterness, *n.* chwerwedd
bitumen, *n.* pyg
bituminous, *a.* pyglyd
bizarre, *a.* rhyfedd, od, chwithig
blab, *v.* prepian, clepian: *n.* clepgi
black, *a.* du: *n.* du, dyn du: *v.t.* duo
blackamoor, *n.* dyn du
blackberries, *n.pl.* mwyar duon
blackbird, *n.* aderyn du, mwyalchen
blacken, *v.t.* duo, pardduo; tywyllu
blackguard, *n.* dihiryn: *v.t.* difrïo
blackmail, *n.* arian bygwth
blacksmith, *n.* gof, gof du
bladder, *n.* pledren, chwysigen
blade, *n.* llafn; eginyn, blewyn
blame, *v.t.* beio: *n.* bai
blanch, *v.t.* gwynnu, cannu
bland, *a.* mwyn, tyner, tirion
blandish, *v.t.* gwenieithio, truthio
blank, *a.* gwag, syn —**b. verse,** mesur di-odl
blanket, *n.* blanced, gwrthban
blare, *v.* canu utgorn: *n.* sain utgorn
blarney, *n.* gweniaith, truth
blaspheme, *v.* cablu, difenwi
blasphemy, *n.* cabledd, cabl
blast, *n.* chwa, chwythiad, deifiad: *v.t.* deifio; saethu.—**b. furnace,** ffwrnais chwythu
blatant, *a.* stwrllyd, digywilydd, haerllug   [ffaglu
blaze, *n.* fflam, ffagl: *v.i.* fflamio,

bleach, *v.* cannu, gwynnu
bleak, *a.* oer, digysgod, noeth, noethlwm
blear, *a.* pŵl, dolurus, dyfriog
bleat, *v.* brefu: *n.* bref
bleed, *v.* gwaedu
blemish, *v.t.* anafu, anurddo: *n.* anaf, bai, mefl
blend, *v.* cymysgu: *n.* cymysgedd
bless, *v.t.* bendithio
blessed, *a.* bendigedig, gwyn ei fyd
blessing, *n.* bendith
blight, *n.* malltod: *v.t.* mallu, deifio
blind, *a.* dall, tywyll: *v.t.* dallu: *n.* llen, bleind
blindness, *n.* dallineb
blink, *v.* cau'r llygaid, ysmicio, amrantu
bliss, *n.* gwynfyd, dedwyddyd
blister, *n.* chwysigen, pothell: *v.* pothellu
blithe, *a.* llawen, llon, hoenus
blizzard, *n.* ystorm erwin o wynt ac eira
bloat, *v.* chwyddo, chwythu
blob, *n.* ysmotyn, bwrlwm
block, *n.* plocyn, cyff: *v.t.* cau, rhwystro
blockade, *n.* gwarchae: *v.* gwarchae ar
blockhead, *n.* penbwl, hurtyn
blood, *n.* gwaed; gwaedoliaeth
bloom, *n.* blodeuyn; gwawr, gwrid: *v.i.* blodeuo
blossom, *n.* blodeuyn: *v.i.* blodeuo
blot, *n.* ysmotyn du, blot, mefl: *v.* blotio
blotch, *n.* ysmotyn, blotyn, ystremp
blow, *n.* dyrnod, ergyd
blow, *v.* chwythu
blubber, *n.* braster morfil
blubber, *v.i.* nadu, wylo, gweflo
bludgeon, *n.* pastwn
blue, *n. & n.* glas: *v.t.* glasu
bluff, *a.* garw, brochus
blunder, *n.* amryfusedd: *v.* amryfuso
blunt, *a.* pŵl, di-fin; plaen: *v.t.* pylu

blur, *n.* ysmotyn, ystaen

blurt, *v.t.* rhuthro dywedyd

blush, *v.i.* cochi, gwrido: *n.* gwrid

bluster, *v.i.* trystio, brochi: *n.* brawl, broch

boar, *n.* baedd

board, *n.* bwrdd, bord; ymborth: *v.* byrddio

boast, *n.* ymffrost: *v.* ymffrostio

boat, *n.* bad, cwch

bob, *v.i.* hercian, siglo

bobbin, *n.* gwerthyd

bode, *v.t.* darogan, argoeli

body, *n.* corff

bog, *n.* cors, mignen, siglen

boggle, *v.i.* petruso; rhusio, ffwndro

bogus, *a.* ffug, gau, ffuantus

bogy, -ey, *n.* bwbach, bwci, bwgan

boil, *n.* cornwyd, casgliad

boil, *v.* berwi

boiler, *n.* pair, crochan

boisterous, *a.* terfysglyd, trystiog, brochus

bold, *a.* hy, eofn; hyderus; eglur

bolster, *n.* gobennydd: *v.t.* ategu

bolt, *n.* bollt: *v.* bolltio; dianc; traflyncu

bomb, *n.* bom

bombast, *n.* chwyddiaith

bombastic, *n.* chwyddedig

bond, *n.* rhwymyn; ysgrifrwym: *a.* caeth

bondage, *n.* caethiwed

bone, *n.* asgwrn

bonfire, *n.* coelcerth, banffagl

bonnet, *n.* penguwch, bonet

bonny, *a.* braf, nobl

booby, *n.* hurtyn, penbwl

book, *n.* llyfr

boom, *n.* bŵm

boom, *v.* trystio, utganu: *n.* trwst, swae

boon, *n.* ffafr, bendith, caffaeliad

boor, *n.* taeog

boot, *n.* botasen, esgid

boot, *n.* lles, elw: *v.t.* llesáu

booth, *n.* bwth, lluest, lluesty, caban

booty, *n.* ysglyfaeth, anrhaith, ysbail

booze, *v.i.* diota, meddwi: *n.* diod feddwol

border, *n.* ffin, goror, ymyl: *v.* ymylu

bore, *v.* tyllu, ebillio: *n.* twll

bore, *n.* pla, dyn diflas: *v.t.* blino, diflasu

borough, *n.* bwrdeistref

borrow, *v.t.* benthyca

bosh, *n.* lol, dyli, ffwlbri, gwiriondeb

bosom, *n.* mynwes, côl

boss, *n.* meistr

botany, *n.* llysieueg

botch, *n.* ystomp: *v.* ystompio, bwnglera

both, *a., pn. & adv.* y ddau, ill dau

bother, *v.* blino, trafferthu: *n.* helynt, trafferth

bottle, *n.* potel, costrel: *v.t.* potelu, costrelu

bottom, *n.* gwaelod, godre, tin

bough, *n.* cainc, cangen

boulder, *n.* carreg fawr, clogfaen

bounce, *v.* neidio, adlamu; bostio, ymffrostio

bound, *n.* terfyn, ffin, cyffin: *v.t.* ffinio

bound, *v.i.* llamu, neidio

boundary, *n.* ffin, terfyn

bounty, *n.* daioni, haelioni, ced

bouquet, *n.* blodeuglwm, pwysi

bout, *n.* sbel, term; ornest, ffrwgwd

bow, *n.* bwa; dolen

bow, *v.* plygu, crymu, ymgrymu: *n.* moesymgrymiad

bow, *n.* pen blaen llong, bow

bowels, *n.pl.* ymysgaroedd, perfedd

bower, *n.* deildy

bowl *n.* cawg, basn

box, *n.* bocs, pren bocs

box, *n.* bocs, blwch, cist; sedd, côr; bwth

box, *n.* bonclust: *v.* taro bonclust; paffio

boy, *n.* bachgen, hogyn, mab, gwas

boyhood, *n.* bachgendod, mebyd

brace, *n.* rhwymyn; pâr: *v.t.* tynhau, cryfhau

bracelet, *n.* breichled

bracket, n. braced, cromfach

bracken, n. rhedyn ungoes

brackish, a. hallt

brag, n. brol, ymffrost, bocsach: v. brolio, ymffrostio

braid, n. pleth, brwyd: v.t. plethu, brwydo

brain, n. ymennydd

brake, n. dryslwyn, prysglwyn

brake, n. brêc: v.t. rhoi'r brêc

bramble, n. miaren

bran, n. eisin, bran, rhuddion

branch, n. cangen, cainc: v.i. canghennu

brand, n. pentewyn; nod: v.t. gwarthnodi

brandish, v. ysgwyd, chwifio

brass, n. pres, efydd

brat, n. crwt, crwtyn; croten

bravado, n. gwagymffrost, bocsach, gorchest

brave, a. dewr, gwrol, glew: v.t. herio

bravo, i. da iawn! campus!

brawl, v.i. ffraeo, terfysgu: n. ffrae, ffrwgwd

brawn, n. cnawd

bray, v.t. pwyo, briwio, malurio

bray, v.i. brefu (megis asyn), nadu

brazen, a. haerllug, hy

breach, n. adwy, rhwyg, tor; trosedd

bread, n. bara

breadth, n. lled

break, v. torri: n. toriad, tor

breakfast, n. brecwast: v. brecwesta

breakwater, n. morglawdd

breast, n. bron, dwyfron, mynwes: v.t. wynebu, ymladd â

breath, n. anadl, gwynt

breathe, v. anadlu, chwythu

breech, n. tin, bôn

breeches, n.pl. llodrau, clos

breed, v. magu; epilio; bridio: n. rhywogaeth, brid

breeze, n. awel, awelan, chwa

brethren, n.pl. brodyr (ffigurol yn bennaf)

brevity, n. byrder, byrdra

brew, v.t. darllaw, bragu

brewer, n. darllawydd, bragwr

bribe, n. llwgrwobrwy : v.t. llwgrwobrwyo

brick, n. bricsen, priddfaen: v.t. bricio

bride, n. priodferch, priodasferch

bridegroom, n. priodfab

bridesmaid, n. morwyn briodas

bridge, n. pont: v.t. pontio

bridle, n. ffrwyn: v.t. ffrwyno

brief, a. byr

brier, briar, n. miaren, drysïen

brigade, n. brigâd, mintai, torf

brigand, n. ysbeiliwr, carnleidr, herwr

bright, a. disglair, claer, gloyw, hoyw

brilliant, a. disglair, llachar: n. gem

brim, n. ymyl, min, cyfor; cantel

brimstone, n. brwmstan

brindled, a. brith, brych

brine, n. heli

bring, v.t. dwyn, cyrchu, dyfod â

brink, n. min, ymyl, glan

brisk, a. bywiog, heini, sionc

bristle, n. gwrychyn, gwrych: v.i. codi gwrychyn

British, a. Prydeinig, Brytanaidd

Briton, n. Brython, Prydeiniwr

brittle, a. brau, bregus

broach, v.t. agor baril, gollwng; agor ymddiddan

broad, a. llydan; eang; bras

broaden, v. lledu, ehangu

brogue, n. llediaith (Gwyddelod)

broil, n. terfysg, ymrafael, ymryson

broil, v.t. briwlio

bronze, n. pres, efydd

brooch, n. tlws

brood, n. nythaid; hil, epil: v.i. deor; synfyfyrio

brook, n. nant, cornant, afonig

brock, v.t. goddef, cyd-ddwyn â

broom, n. banadl; ysgub, ysgubell

broth, n. potes, cawl

brother, (-s, brethren) n. brawd

brotherly, a. brawdol.—**b. love** brawdgarwch

brow, n. ael, talcen; crib

brown, *a.* brown, llwyd, gwinau

browse, *v.i.* brigbori, pori, blewynna

bruise, *v.* cleisio, ysigo: *n.* clais

brush, *n.* brws: *v.t.* brwsio, ysgubo

brushwood, *n.* manwydd, prysgwydd

brusque, *a.* cwta, anfoesgar, taeog

brutal, *a.* creulon, bwystfilaidd

brute, *n.* anifail, creadur (direswm)

bubble, *n.* bwrlwm: *v.* byrlymu

buccaneer, *n.* môr-leidr, môrherwr

buck, *n.* bwch: coegyn: *v.* llamsachu

bucket, *n.* bwced, ystwc

buckle, *n.* bwcl, gwäeg: *v.* byclu, gwäegu

bucolic, *a.* bugeiliol, gwladaidd

bud, *n.* blaguryn, eginyn: *v.* blaguro, egino

budge, *v.* syflyd, chwimio

budget, *n.* cwd, coden; cyllideb

buff, *a.* llwydfelyn

buffalo, *n.* bual

buffer, *n.* byffer; llob, cono

buffet, *n.* cernod: *v.t.* cernodio, baeddu

buffoon, *n.* digrifwas, croesan, ysgentyn

bug, *n.* drewbryf, bwg

bugbear, *n.* bwgan, bwbach, bwci

bugle, *n.* corn, utgorn

build, *v.t.* adeiladu: *n.* corffolaeth

building, *n.* adail, adeilad, adeiladaeth

bulge, *n.* chwydd: *v.t.* chwyddo

bulk, *n.* swm, crynswth

bull, *n.* tarw

bullet, *n.* bwled, bwleden

bulletin, *n.* bwletin

bullfinch, *n.* coch y berllan

bullion, *n.* aur neu arian clamp, bwliwn

bullock, *n.* bustach, eidion, ych

bully, *n.* gormeswr, bwli: *v.t.* gormesu, erlid

bulrushes, *n.pl.* llafrwyn, hesg

bulwark, *n.* gwrthglawdd; canllaw

bumbailiff, *n.* bwmbeili

bumble-bee, *n.* cacynen

bump, *v.* bwmpio, hergydio: *n.* bwmp, hergwd

bumpkin, *n.* lleban, llabwst, llelo

bumptious, *a.* hunanol, rhodresgar

bun, *n.* bynsen, bynnen, teisen

bunch, *n.* swp; cwlwm, pwysi: *v.* sypio

bundle, *n.* bwndel, coflaid: *v.t.* bwndelu

bung, *n.* bwng, topyn casgen

bungalow, *n.* tŷ unllawr, byngalo

bungle, *v.* bwnglera, ystompio: *n.* bwnglerwaith

bunkum, *n.* lol, ffiloreg, truth

bunting, *n.* (defnydd) banerau

buoy, *n.* bwi: *v.t.* cynnal, cadw rhag suddo

buoyant, *a.* hynawf; calonnog

burden, *n.* baich: *v.t.* beichio, llwytho

bureau, *n.* ysgrifgist; swyddfa

burgess, burgher, *n.* dinesydd, bwrdais

burglar, *n.* torrwr tŷ, bwrgler

burgomaster, *n.* maer

burial, *n.* claddedigaeth, angladd

burke, *v.t.* osgoi, mygu; tagu

burlesque, *n.* digrifwawd, gwatwargerdd

burly, *a.* corffol, praff, mawr

burn, *v.* llosgi, ysu: *n.* llosg, llosgiad

burnish, *v.t.* caboli, llathru, gloywi

burrow, *n.* twll cwningen: *v.* tyllu, tyrchu

bursary, *n.* amneriaeth, ysgoloriaeth

burst, *v.* byrstio, ymrwygo, ymddryllio, torri: *n.* rhwyg

bury, *v.t.* claddu

bush, *n.* perth, llwyn; prysgwydd, drysi

bushel, *n.* bwysel, mesur wyth galwyn

business, *n.* busnes, masnach, gwaith

bust, *n.* penddelw; mynwes

bustle, *v.i.* trafferthu, ffwdanu: *n.* ffwdan

busy, *a.* prysur

busybody, *n.* ymyrrwr, dyn busneslyd

but, *c. & pr.* ond, eithr

butcher, *n.* cigydd: *v.t.* cigyddio, lladd

butler, *n.* trulliad, bwtler

butt, *n.* nod, targed; cyff clêr

butt, *v.t.* cornio, hyrddu, twlcio, hwylio

butt, *n.* casgen, baril

butter, *n.* ymenyn: *v.t.* rhoi ymenyn ar

buttercup, *n.* blodeuyn yr ymenyn

butterfly, *n.* glöyn byw, iâr fach yr haf, pili-pala

buttermilk, *n.* llaeth enwyn

buttery, *n.* bwtri

buttock, *n.* ffolen

button, *n.* botwm: *v.t.* botymu

buttress, *n.* ateg, gwanas: *v.t.* ategu

buxom, *a.* glandeg, gweddgar, nwyfus

buy, *v.t.* prynu

buzz, *v.* suo, sisial, mwmian: *n.* su, sŵn gwenyn

by, *pr.* gan, wrth, trwy, ger, gerllaw; *adv.* heibio, yn agos: *px.* rhag-, is-

byre, *n.* beudy

C

cab, *n.* cab

cabal, *n.* clymblaid: *v.i.* clymbleidio

cabbage, *n.* bresychen, bresych

cabin, *n.* caban: *v.t.* cabanu, caethiwo

cabinet, *n.* cell, cist; cabinet

cable, *n.* rhaff fferf; cebl tanforol

cackle, *v.i.* clegar

cad, *n.* taeog, bryntyn, cenau

cadaverous, *a.* fel corff, corffaidd

caddie, *n.* gwas chwaraeydd golff

cadence, *n.* oslef, diweddeb

cadet, *n.* mab ieuengaf; cadlanc

café, *n.* tŷ bwyta, caffe

cage, *n.* cawell, caets: *v.t.* cau, carcharu

cairn, *n.* carn, carnedd, crug

cajole, *v.t.* twyllo drwy weniaith

cake, *n.* teisen, cacen: *v.* torthi; caglu

calamity, *n.* adfyd, trallod, trychineb

calcareous, *a.* calchaidd, calchog

calcine, *v.* llosgi'n galch

calculate, *v.* cyfrif, bwrw cyfrif, clandro

calendar, *n.* calendr, almanac

calf, *(calves)* *n.* llo

calf, *(of the leg),* *n.* croth (coes)

calibre, *n.* calibr

call, *v.* galw: *n.* galwad, galw; ymweliad

calling, *n.* galwedigaeth

callous, *a.* croendew, dideimlad, caled

callow, *a,* di-blu, croenllwm, noeth

calm, *a.* tawel: *n.* tawelwch: *v.* tawelu

calumny, *n.* anair, enllib, athrod, cabl

calve, *v.i.* bwrw llo

Calvinism, *n.* Calfiniaeth

Cambrian, *a.* Cymreig

cambric, *n.* lliain main, camrig

camera, *n.* ystafell; teclyn tynnu lluniau, camera

camp, *n.* gwersyll: *v.i.* gwersyllu

campaign, *n.* ymgyrch, rhyfelgyrch

can, *n.* tyn, piser, stên

canal, *n.* camlas; pibell

cancel, *v.t.* dileu, dirymu, diddymu

cancer, *n.* dafad wyllt, cancr, cranc

candid, *a.* teg, onest, plaen

candidate, *n.* ymgeisydd

candle, *n.* cannwyll

candlestick, *n.* canhwyllbren

candour, *n.* onestrwydd, didwylledd

cane, *n.* corsen, cansen: *v.t.* curo â chansen

canine, *a.* perthynol i'r ci

canister, *n.* tyn cadw te

canker, *n.* cancr: *v.* cancro

cannibal, *n.* canibal

cannon, *n.* magnel

canny, *a.* call, cyfrwys, ffel

canoe, *n.* ceufad, canŵ

canon, *n.* canon, rheol

canopy, *n.* gortho, nenlen

cant, *n.* ffugsancteiddrwydd: *v.i.* rhagrithio

cantankerous, *a.* cwerylgar, cynhennus

cantata, *n.* cantata, cantawd

canteen, *n.* cantîn

canter, *v.i.* rhygyngu: *n.* rhygyng

canticle, *n.* cantigl, canig, cân, emyn

canto, *n.* cân, adran o gân

canton, *n.* rhandir, talaith

canvas, *n.* cynfas, lliain bras

canvass, *v.* trafod; ymofyn pleidleisiau, canfasio

canyon, *n.* ceunant

cap, *n.* cap, capan: *v.t.* capio

capable, *a.* galluog, cymwys, cyfaddas

capacious, *a.* helaeth, eang

capacity, *n.* gallu, cymhwyster; cynnwys

caparison, *n.* addurnwisg march

cape, *n.* penrhyn, pentir, trwyn

cape, *n.* mantell, cêp

caper, *n.* pranc: *v.i.* prancio

capital, *a.* prif, pen: *n.* pen; priflythyren; prifddinas; cyfalaf

capitulate, *v.i.* ymostwng ar amodau

capon, *n.* ceiliog disbaidd, capwllt

caprice, *n.* mympwy, chwilen

capsize, *v.* dymchwelyd, troi

captain, *n.* capten

captious, *a.* hoff o weld bai, cecrus

captivate, *v.t.* swyno, hudo, denu

captive, *a.* caeth: *n.* carcharor

captivity, *a.* caethiwed; caethglud

captor, *n.* daliwr, deiliad

capture, *n.* daliad: *v.t.* dal

car, *n.* car, cerbyd

caravan, *n.* carafán; men

carbine, *n.* dryll byr, byrddryll

carbon, *n.* carbon

carbuncle, *n.* carbwncl

carcass, -ase, *n.* celain, ysgerbwd

card, *n.* cerdyn, carden

card, *v.t.* cribo gwlân

cardiac, *a.* perthynol i'r galon

cardinal, *a.* prif, arbennig: *n.* cardinal [malio

care, *n.* gofal, pryder: *v.i.* gofalu,

career, *n.* gyrfa, hynt: *v.i.* carlamu

careful, *a.* gofalus, gwyliadwrus

careless, *a.* diofal, esgeulus

caress, *n.* anwes, mwythau: *v.t.* anwesu

caret, *n.* gwallnod, diffygnod (^)

cargo, *n.* llwyth (llong), cargo

caricature, *n.* gwawdlun, digriflun

carnage, *n.* galanastra, lladdfa

carnal, *a.* cnawdol

carnival, *n.* carnifal

carnivorous, *a.* cigysol, rheibus

carol, *n.* carol: *v.i.* caroli, canu

carouse, *v.i.* gloddesta, cyfeddach

carp, *v.i.* pigo beiau, cecru, cadw swn

carpenter, *n.* saer coed

carpet, *n.* carped: *v.t.* carpedu

carriage, *n.* cerbyd; cludiad; ymarweddiad

carrier, *n.* cariwr, cludydd

carrion, *n.* burgyn, celain, ysgerbwd

carrot, *n.* moronen

carry, *v.* cario, cludo, cywain

cart, *v.* men, trol, cert, cart, car

cartilage, *n.* madruddyn

cartoon, *n.* digriflun, cartŵn

cartridge, *n.* cetrisen

carve, *v.t.* cerfio, naddu; torri cig

cascade, *n.* rhaeadr

case, *n.* achos, cyflwr; dadl

case, *n.* cas, gwain; cist wydr

casement, *n.* ffenestr adeiniog, casment

cash, *n.* arian parod

cashier, *n.* ariannwr, trysorydd

cashier, *v.t.* diswyddo

cask, *n.* casgen, baril

casket, *n.* cistan, prenfol, blwch

cassock, *n.* llaeswisg ddu offeiriad, casog

cast, *v.* bwrw, taflu: *n.* tafliad.
—**c. iron,** haearn bwrw

caste, *n.* llwyth; gradd, braint; cast

castigate, *v.t.* cystwyo
castle, *n.* castell: *v.i.* castellu
castrate, *v.t.* disbaddu
casual, *a.* damweiniol, achlysurol
casuistry, *n.* achosionaeth
cat, *n.* cath
cataclysm, *n.* dilyw, dylif, rhyferthwy
catacomb, *n.* claddgell, claddogof
catalepsy, *n.* llesmeirglwyf
catafalque, *n.* llwyfan arch; elor
catalogue, *n.* catalog
catapult, *n.* blif
cataract, *n.* rhaeadr, sgwd; pilen
catarrh, *n.* llif annwyd, gormwyth
catastrophe, *n.* trychineb
catch, *v.t.* dal: *n.* bach, cliced; dalfa
catching, *a.* heintus
catechism, *n.* holwyddoreg, catecism
category, *n.* trefn, dosbarth
cater, *v.i.* arlwyo, darmerth
caterpillar, *n.* lindys
caterwaul, *v.i.* catherica
cathartic, *n.* carthlyn
cathedral, *n.* eglwys gadeiriol
catholic, *a.* catholig; pabyddol: *n.* catholigydd; pabydd
catkins, *n.pl.* cenawon cyll, cywion gwyddau
cattle, *n.pl.* gwartheg, da
caucus, *n.* clymblaid
caudle, *n.* sucan
cauldron, *n.* crochan, pair, callor
cauliflower, *n.* blodfresychen
caulk, *v.t.* cyweirio agennau, calcio
causality, *n.* achosiaeth
cause, *n.* achos: *v.t.* achosi, peri
causeway, *n.* sarn, cawsai
caustic, *a.* ysol, llosg, deifiol
cauterize, *v.t.* serio
caution, *n.* pwyll, gwyliadwriaeth; rhybudd: *v.t.* rhybuddio
cautious, *a.* gwyliadwrus
cavalcade, *n.* mintai o farchogion
cavalier, *n.* marchog, marchfilwr
cavalry, *n.* gwŷr meirch, marchfilwr
cave, *n.* ogof

cavern, *n.* ceudwll, ogof
cavil, *v.i.* cecru
cavity, *n.* ceudod, gwagle
caw, *v.i.* crawcian
cease, *v.* peidio, darfod
cedar, *n.* cedrwydden
cede, *v.t.* rhoi i fyny, gildio, trosglwyddo
ceiling, *n.* nen, nenfwd
celebrate, *v.t.* clodfori; dathlu; gweinyddu
celebrated, *a.* clodfawr, enwog, hyglod
celebrity, *n.* bri, enwogrwydd; gŵr o fri
celestial *a.* nefol, nefolaidd
celibate, *a.* dibriod
cell, *n.* cell
cellar, *n.* seler
cement, *n.* sment: *v.t.* smentio; cadarnhau
cemetery, *n.* mynwent, claddfa
censer, *n.* thuser
censor, *n.* beirniad; sensor
censure, *n.* cerydd, sen: *v.t.* ceryddu
census, *n.* cyfrifiad
centenarian, *n.* canmlwyddiad
centenary, *n.* canmlwyddiant
centipede, *n.* neidr gantroed
central, *a.* canol, canolog
centre, *n.* canol, canolfan, canolbwynt: *v.* canolbwyntio
centre-forward, *n.* canolwr blaen
centre-threequarter, *n.* canolwr
centrifugal, *a.* allgyrchol
centripetal, *a.* mewngyrchol
centurion, *n.* canwriad
century, *n.* canrif
cereal, *n.* grawn, ŷd
cerebral, *a.* ymenyddiol
ceremony, *n.* seremoni, defod
certain, *a.* sicr; neilltuol; rhyw, rhai
certainty, *n.* sicrwydd
certificate, *n.* tystysgrif
certify, *v.t.* hysbysu, tystio
cesspool, *n.* carthbwll
chafe, *v.* rhwbio; llidio: *n.* llid, cythrudd

chaff, *n.* us, manus, mân us
chaffer, *v.i.* edwica, bargeinio, bargenna
chaffinch, *n.* gwinc, asgell fraith
chagrin, *n.* cythrudd, siom
chain, *n.* cadwyn: *v.t.* cadwyno
chair, *n.* cadair: *v.t.* cadeirio
chairman, *n.* cadeirydd
chaise, *n.* cerbydan
chalice, *n.* cwpan cymun, caregl
chalk, *n.* sialc: *v.t.* sialcio
challenge, *n.* her, sialens: *v.t.* herio, sialensio
chamber, *n.* ystafell, siambr
chamberlain, *n.* gwas ystafell, siambrlen
champ, *v.t.* cnoi, dygnoi
champion, *n.* pencampwr; pleidiwr: *v.t.* cymryd plaid
chance, *n.* damwain, siawns: *v.t.* digwydd
chancel, *n.* cangell
chancellor, *n.* canghellor
chandelier, *n.* canhwyllyr
chandler, *n.* canhwyllydd, masnachydd
change, *v.* newid, cyfnewid: *n.* newid
channel, *n.* sianel, gwely; rhigol
chant, *v.t.* corganu: *n.* corgan, salmdon
chaos, *n.* tryblith, anhrefn
chap, *v.t.* agennu, torri (am ddwylo)
chapel, *n.* capel
chaplain, *n.* caplan
chapter, *n.* pennod; cabidwl
char, *v.* golosgi, deifio
character, *n.* cymeriad; nod, arwydd
characteristic, *a.* nodweddiadol: *n.* nodwedd
charcoal, *n.* marwor, golosg, sercol
charge, *v.* siarsio; cyhuddo; rhuthro; codi; llwytho: *n.* siars; gofal; cyhuddiad; rhuthr; pris; ergyd
charger, *n.* march rhyfel, cadfarch
chariot, *n.* cerbyd
charity, *n.* cariad; cardod, elusen

charlatan, *n.* crachfeddyg; cwac
charm, *n.* swyn, cyfaredd: *v.t.* swyno
charnel-house, *n.* esgyrndy
chart, *n.* siart
charter, *n.* siarter, breinlen: *v.t.* breinio; llogi
chary, *a.* gwagelog, gochelgar, gofalus
chase, *v.t.* ymlid, erlid, hel: *n.* helwriaeth
chasm, *n.* hafn, ceunant, agendor
chaste, *a.* diwair, pur, dillyn
chasten, *v.t.* puro, coethi: ceryddu
chastise, *v.* ceryddu, cosbi, cystwyo
chastity, *n.* diweirdeb, purdeb
chat, *v.i.* sgwrsio, ymgomio: *n.* sgwrs, ymgom
chattel, *n.* catel
chatter, *v.i.* trydar, cogor; clebran; rhincian
chatterbox, *n.* clebryn, clebren
cheap, *a.* rhad, salw
cheat, *n.* twyll; twyllwr: *v.t.* twyllo
check, *n.* rhwystr, atalfa: *v.t.* atal, ffrwyno
cheek, *n.* grudd, boch; digywilydd-dra
cheeky, *a.* digywilydd, haerllug, eg(e)r
cheer, *n.* calondid, cysur; arlwy: *v.* llonni, sirioli, sirio
cheerful, *a.* llon, siriol
cheese, *n.* caws
chemical, *a.* cemegol: *n.* cyffur
chemise, *n.* crys merch
chemist, *n.* fferyllydd; cemegwr
chemistry, *n.* cemeg
cheque, *n.* archeb (ar fanc), siec
chequer, *v.t.* amryliwio, britho
cherish, *v.t.* meithrin, coleddu, mynwesu
cherry, *n.* ceiriosen
cherub, *n.* ceriwb
chest, *n.* cist, coffr; brest
chestnut, *n.* castan
chevalier, *n.* marchog
chew, *v.* cnoi. —**c. the cud,** cnoi cil
chick, chicken, *n.* cyw (iâr)
chide, *v.t.* ceryddu, dwrdio

chief, *a.* pen, pennaf, prif: *n.* pennaeth

chieftain, *n.* blaenor, pennaeth

chilblain, *n.* llosg eira, cibwst, malaith

child, (*-ren*) *n.* plentyn

childhood, *n.* plentyndod, mebyd

chill, *n.* oerni, annwyd: *a.* oer, anwydog: *v.* oeri, fferru, rhynnu

chime, *n.* sain clychau: *v.* canu (clychau)

chimera, *n.* anghenfil; bwgan, bwbach

chimney, *n.* corn mwg, simnai

chin, *n.* gên

china, *n.* llestri te (tsieni)

chink, *n.* agen, hollt

chip, *v.* hacio, naddu: *n.* asglodyn, pric

chirp, *v.i.* yswitian, grillian, trydar

chisel, *n.* cŷn, gaing

chivalry, *n.* urddas marchog; sifalri

choice, *n.* dewis, dewisiad: *a.* dewisol, dethol

choir, *n.* côr; cafell

choke, *v.* tagu; mygu; topio, cau

choler, *n.* geri, bustl; dicter, llid

cholera, *n.* y geri marwol

choose, *v.* dewis, dethol, ethol

chop, *v.t.* torri: *n.* golwyth

choral, *a.* corawl

chord, *n.* tant; cord

chortle, *v.* crechwenu, chwerthinial

chorus, *n.* côr, cytgan, byrdwn, corws

christen, *v.t.* bedyddio, enwi

Christendom, *n.* (gwledydd) Cred

Christian, *a.* Cristionogol: *n.* Cristion

Christianity, *n.* Cristionogaeth

Christmas, *n.* Nadolig

chronic, *a.* parhaol (am anhwyldeb)

chronicle, *n.* cronicl: *v.t.* croniclo

chronology, *n.* amseryddiaeth

chrysalis, *n.* chwiler

chubby, *a.* wynepgrwn, tew

chuck, *v.t.* taro dan yr ên; taflu, lluchio

chuckle, *v.i.* chwerthin yn nwrn dyn

chum, *n.* cyfaill mebyd: *v.i.* cyfrinachu

chunk, *n.* tafell dew, toc

church, *n.* eglwys, llan: *v.t.* eglwysa

churchyard, *n.* mynwent

churl, *n.* taeog, costog, cerlyn

churlish, *a.* afrywiog, taeogaidd

churn, *n.* buddai: *v.* corddi

chute, *n.* llithrigfa, llithren

cicatrice: *n.* craith

cider, *n.* seidr

cincture, *n.* gwregys, rhwymyn

cinder, *n.* marworyn, colsyn

cinema, *n.* sinema

cipher, *n.* gwagnod (O); ysgrifen ddirgel: *v.i.* cyfrif

circle, *n.* cylch: *v.* cylchu

circuit, *n.* cylch, amgylchedd; cylchdaith

circular, *a.* crwn: *n.* cylchlythyr

circulate, *v.* cylchredeg, lledaenu

circum-, *px.* cylch-, am-

circumcise, *v.t.* enwaedu

circumference, *n.* amgylchedd

circumflex, *n.* cylchedd; cylchyn to, acen grom to (^)

circumlocution, *n.* cylchymadrodd

circumscribe, *v.t.* cyfyngu

circumspect, *a.* gwyliadwrus, gofalus

circumstance, *n.* amgylchiad

circumstantial, *a.* amgylchus

circumvent, *v.* twyllo

circus, *n.* syrcas

cistern, *n.* dyfrgist, pydew

citadel, *n.* castell, amddiffynfa, caer

cite, *v.t.* gwysio; dyfynnu

citizen, *n.* dinesydd, bwrdais

city, *n.* dinas

civic, *a.* dinesig

civil, *a.* gwladol; moesgar

civilian, *n.* dinesydd (anfilwrol)

civilization, *n.* gwareiddiad

civilize, *v.t.* gwareiddio

clack, *v.i.* clecian, clepian, clegar

claim, *v.t.* hawlio: *n.* hawl

clamber, *v.i.* dringo, cribo

clammy, *a.* gludiog, cleiog, toeslyd

clamour, *n.* gwaedd, dadwrdd: *v.i.* crochlefain

clamp, *n.* ystyffwl, craff

clan, *n.* tylwyth, llwyth

clandestine, *a.* lladradaidd

clang, clank, *v.* cloncio: *n.* clonc

clap, *n.* twrf, trwst: *v.* curo; taro; clepian

clarify, *v.t.* gloywi, puro; egluro

clarion, *n.* utgorn

clash, *v.* taro, gwrthdaro: *n.* tyrfu

clasp, *n.* gwäeg, bach, clesbyn: *v.t.* gwaëgu; cofleidio

class, *n.* dosbarth: *v.t.* dosbarthu

classical, *a.* clasurol

classics, *n.pl.* clasuron

classify, *v.* dosbarthu

clatter, *v.* clewtian, clepian, trystio: *n.* trwst

clause, *n.* adran, cymal

claw, *n.* crafanc, ewin: *v.t.* crafangu, cripio

clay, *n.* clai

clean, *a.* glân, glanwaith: *v.t.* glanhau

cleanly, *a.* glanwaith

cleanse, *v.t.* glanhau

clear, *a.* clir, eglur, gloyw; croyw: *v.t.* clirio

cleave, *v.i.* glynu (wrth)

cleave, *v.t.* hollti; fforchogi

cleff, *n.* allwedd, cleff

cleft, *n.* hollt, agen

clement, *a.* tyner, tirion, trugarog

clench, *v.t.* cau yn dynn, clensio

clergy, *n.* offeiriaid

clergyman, *n.* clerigwr, offeiriad

clerical, *a.* clerigol; perthynol ı glerc

clerk, *n.* clerc

clever, *n.* medrus, deheuig, clyfar

cleverness, *n.* medr, deheurwydd, clyfrwch

click, *v.i.* clician, clepian: *n.* clic

client, *n.* cyflogydd cyfreithiwr, cwsmer

cliff, *n.* clogwyn, allt

climate, *n.* hinsawdd

climax, *n.* uchaf bwynt

clinch, *v.t.* clensio; cau, cloi

cling, *v.i.* glynu, cydio

clinic, *n.* meddygfa, clinig

clinical, *a.* clinigol

clink, *v.i.* tincian

clip, *v.t.* cneifio, tocio, clipio

clique, *n.* clic, clymblaid

cloak, *n.* mantell, clogyn, clog: *v.t.* cuddio, celu

clock, *n.* cloc

clod, *n.* tywarchen

clog, *n.* clocsen: *v.t.* llesteirio; tagu

cloister, *n.* clwysty

close, *v.* cau; terfynu: *n.* diwedd, diweddglo

close, *a.* agos, clòs; caeth, tyn

close, *n.* clas, clos, buarth, clwt, cae

closet, *n.* cell, ystafell; geudy

clot, *n.* tolchen: *v.* tolchi, ceulo

cloth, *n.* brethyn, lliain

clothe, *v.t.* dilladu, gwisgo

clothes, *n.pl.* dillad, gwisgoedd

clothier, *n.* brethynnwr, dilledydd

cloud, *n.* cwmwl: *v.t.* cymylu

clout, *n.* cernod, clewt; clwt: *v.t.* clewtian; clytio

clover, *n.* meillion, clofer

clown, *n.* lleban; croesan, clown

cloy, *v.t.* digoni, syrffedu

club, *n.* pastwn; clwb: *v.* pastynu; clybio

cluck, *v.i.* clwcian, clochdar

clue, *n.* pen llinyn, arwydd

clump, *n.* clwmp, clamp, cyff

clumsy, *a.* trwsgl, anfedrus, llet-chwith　　　　　　　　　　[tyrru

cluster, *n.* clwstwr, swp. *v.* casglu, clymu

clutch, *n.* crafanc; gafael, (*pl*). hafflau: *v.* crafangu

clutter, *n.* dadwrdd, helynt

co-, *px.* cyd-

coach, *n.* cerbyd; hyfforddwr: *v.* hyfforddi

coadjutor, *n.* cynorthwyydd

coagulate, *v.* ceulo

coal, *n.* glöyn, glo

coalesce, *v.i.* cyfuno, cyd-doddi

coalition, *n.* cyfuniad; cynghrair, clymblaid

coarse, *a.* garw, aflednais; bras
coast, *n.* arfordir, glan: *v.i.* hwylio gyda'r tir
coat, *n.* cot, cob
coating, *n.* caen, golchiad
coax, *v.t.* hudo, denu, perswadio
cobble, *v.t.* coblo, coblan
cobble, -stone, *n.* carreg balmant
cobbler, *n.* coblwr, cobler, crydd
cobweb, *n.* gwe pryf cop, gwe'r cor
cock, *n.* ceiliog: *v.* codi, picio, cocio
cock, *n.* mwdwl: *v.t.* mydylu
cockerel, *n.* cyw ceiliog, ceiliogyn
cockles, *n.pl.* cocos, cocs, rhython
cockroach, *n.* chwilen ddu
cock-sure, *a.* gorbendant, gor-hyderus
cocoa, *n.* coco
cod, *n.* y penfras
coddle, *v.t.* codlo, panso, llochi
code, *n.* rheithlyfr: cyfundrefn, dosbarth   [ewyllys
codicil, *n.* atodiad at ewyllys, ôl-
codify, *v.t.* cyfundrefnu, dosbarthu
coefficient, *n.* cyfernod
coerce, *v.t.* gorfodi, gorthrechu
coffee, *n.* coffi
coffer, *n.* cist, coffr
coffin, *n.* arch, ysgrîn
cog, *n.* dant olwyn gocos, còg
cogent, *a.* cryf, grymus, argyhoedd-iadol
cogitate, *v.* meddwl, myfyrio
cognate, *a.* perthynol, cytras
cognizant, *a.* hysbys
cohabit, *v.i.* cyd-fyw, cyd-drigo, cytal
cohere, *v.i.* cydlynu, cyflynu
cohesion, *n.* cydlyniad, cyflyniad
cohort, *n.* mintai o filwyr
coil, *v.* torchi: *n.* torch
coin, *n.* bath, arian bath: *v.t.* bathu
coincide, *v.i.* cytuno, cyd-ddigwydd
coiner, *n.* bathwr
coke, *n.* golosg, côc
cold, *a.* oer: *n.* oerfel, oerni, annwyd
colic, *n.* bolwst
collaborate, *v.i.* cydlafurio, cyd-gyfansoddi

collapse, *v.i.* cydymollwng: *n.* cwymp
collar, *n.* coler: *v.t.* coleru
collate, *v.t.* cymharu, cyfleu
collateral, *a.* cyfochrol, cyfystlys
colleague, *n.* cyd-swyddog, cyd-weithiwr
collect, *v.* casglu, cynnull, crynhoi
collect, *n.* colect
collection, *n.* casgliad
college, *n.* coleg
collide, *v.i.* gwrthdaro
collie, *n.* ci defaid
collier, *n.* glowr; llong lo
colliery, *n.* gwaith glo, pwll glo, glofa
collision, *n.* gwrthdrawiad
colloquial, *a.* ymddiddanol; llafar
colon, *n.* gorwahannod, colon (:)
colonel, *n.* milwriad, cyrnol
colony, *n.* trefedigaeth, gwladfa
colossal, *a.* cawraidd, anferth
colour, *n.* lliw; baner: *v.* lliwio; cochi
colporteur, *n.* Beibl-gludydd
colt, *n.* ebol
column, *n.* colofn
comb, *n.* crib: *v.t.* cribo
combat, *n.* brwydr: *v.t.* brwydro; gwrthladd
combine, *v.* cyfuno
combustion, *n.* llosgiad
come, *v.i.* dyfod
comedy, *n.* comedi
comely, *a.* glân, prydweddol, teg
comet, *n.* seren gynffon, comed
comfort, *n.* cysur, diddanwch: *v.t.* cysuro, diddanu
comic, *a.* digrif, ysmala
comma, *n.* rhagwahannod (,)
command, *v.* gorchymyn: *n.* gor-chymyn; llywodraeth
commandeer, *v.t.* atafaelu, medd-iannu
commandment, *n.* gorchymyn
commemorate, *v.t.* coffáu, dathlu
commence, *v.* dechrau
commend, *v.t.* cymeradwyo, can-mol
commensurate, *a.* cymesur

comment, *v.i.* sylwi, esbonio: *n.* sylw

commentary, *n.* esboniad

commentator, *n.* esboniwr

commerce, *n.* masnach

commination, *n.* bygythiad, cominasiwn

commingle, *v.* cymysgu, cydgymysgu

commiserate, *v.t.* cydofidio â, cyd-dosturio â

commission, *n.* comisiwn, dirprwyaeth

commit, *v.t.* cyflawni; traddodi; cyflwyno; cymynnu

committal, *n.* cymyndod

committee, *n.* pwyllgor

commodious, *a.* cyfleus, eang, helaeth

commodity, *n.* nwydd (masnachol)

common, *a.* cyffredin: *n.* tir cyffredin, cytir, comin

commons, *n.pl.* y cyffredin

commonwealth, *n.* cymanwlad

commotion, *n.* cyffro, terfysg

commune, *v.i.* ymddiddan; cymuno

communicate, *v.* cymuno; cyfrannu

communion, *n.* cymun, cymundeb, cymdeithas

communism, *n.* comiwnyddiaeth

community, *n.* cymdeithas, cymuned

commute, *v.t.* cyfnewid, newid

compact, *n.* cytundeb, cyfamod

compact, *a.* cryno: *v.t.* crynhoi

companion, *n.* cydymaith

company, *n.* cymdeithas, cwmni

comparative, *a.* cymharol

compare, *v.t.* cymharu, cyffelybu

comparison, *n.* cymhariaeth

compartment, *n.* adran, rhan

compass, *n.* cwmpawd; cwmpas: *v.t.* amgylchu

compassion, *n.* tosturi

compassionate, *a.* tosturiol: *v.t.* tosturio

compatible, *a.* cydweddol, cyson

compatriot, *n.* cyd-wladwr

compeer, *n.* cyfurdd, cydradd

compel, *v.t.* cymell, gorfodi

compendium, *n.* crynodeb, talfyriad edu

compensate, *v.t.* talu iawn, digolli

compete, *v.i.* cydymgeisio, cystadlu

competent, *a.* cymwys, digonol

competition, *n.* cystadleuaeth

compile, *v.t.* casglu, cynnull, cyfansoddi

complacent, *a.* hunan-foddhaus, digonol

complain, *v.i.* cwyno, achwyn, grwgnach

complaint, *n.* cwyn, achwyniad; anhwyldeb

complaisant, *a.* moesgar, hynaws

complement, *n.* cyflawnder, cyflenwad

complete, *a.* cyflawn: *v.t.* cyflawni

complex, *a.* cymhleth, dyrys

complexion, *n.* gwedd, pryd, gwawr

complicate, *v.t.* cymhlethu; drysu

complicity *n.* cyfranogaeth (mewn drwg)

compliment, *n.* cyfarchiad; canmoliaeth

comply, *v.i.* cydsynio, ufuddhau

comport, *v.* ymddwyn, ymarweddu

compose, *v.t.* cyfansoddi; cysodi; tawelu

composite, *a.* cyfansawdd

composition, *n.* cyfansoddiad; cymysg

compositor, *n.* cysodydd

compost, *n.* gwrtaith, compost

composure, *n.* tawelwch, hunanfeddiant

compound, *a.* cyfansawdd: *n.* cymysg: *v.* cymysgu

comprehend, *v.t.* cynnwys; amgyffred

comprehension, *n.* amgyffred, dirnadaeth

compress, *v.t.* gwasgu, crynhoi

comprise, *v.t.* amgyffred, cynnwys

compromise, *n.* cymrodedd, cytundeb: *v.* cymrodeddu; peryglu

compulsion, *n.* gorfodaeth

compulsory, *a.* gorfodol

compunction, *n.* dwysbigiad cydwybod, gofid

compute, *v.t.* cyfrif

comrade, *n.* cydymaith

concave, *a.* cau, cafnog

conceal, *v.* cuddio, celu, dirgelu

concede, *v.t.* caniatáu, addef

conceit, *n.* tyb, mympwy; hunan-dyb, hunanoldeb, cysêt

conceive, *v.* dirnad; tybied, synied; beichiogi

concentrate, *v.t.* crynhoi, canol-bwyntio

conception, *n.* syniad; beichiogiad

concern, *v.t.* perthyn, bod a wnelo â: *n.* busnes, diddordeb; gofal, pryder

concert, *n.* cyngerdd: *v.t.* cyd-drefnu

concession, *n.* caniatâd, goddefiad

conciliate, *v.t.* cymodi, heddychu

concise, *a.* byr, cryno, cynhwys-fawr

conclave, *n.* cyfarfod dirgel

conclude, *v.* diweddu; casglu, barnu

conclusion, *n.* diwedd; casgliad

concoct, *v.t.* llunio, dyfeisio

concoction *n.* cymysgedd

concomitant, *a.* cyfredol

concord, *n.* cytgord, cydfod

concordance, *n.* mynegair

concourse, *n.* tyrfa, torf

concrete, *a.* diriaethol, concrit

concubine, *n.* gordderch

concupiscence, *n.* chwant, trach-want

concur, *v.i.* cydredeg; cydfyned, cytuno

concussion, *n.* cyd-drawiad, ysgytiad

condemn, *v.* condemnio, collfarnu

condense, *v.* tewychu; crynhoi

condescend, *v.i.* ymostwng

condescension, *n.* iselfrydedd

condign, *a.* dyledus, haeddiannol; llym

condiment, *n.* cyffaith

condition, *n.* cyflwr, ansawdd; amod

condole, *v.i.* cydofidio, cydym-deimlo

condone, *v.t.* maddau (bai), pasio heibio (i)

conduce, *v.i.* arwain, tueddu

conduct, *n.* ymddygiad, ymar-weddiad

conduct, *v.t.* arwain; dwyn ymlaen

conductor, *n.* arweinydd

conduit, *n.* pibell ddwfr, cwndid

cone, *n.* pigwrn, côn

confabulate, *v.i.* ymgomio, ym-ddiddan

confection, *n.* cyffaith

confederate, *n.* cynghreirio, cyd-fwriadu: *n.* cynghreiriad

confer, *v.* ymgynghori; rhoddi

conference, *n.* cynhadledd

confess, *v.* cyffesu, cyfaddef

confession, *n.* cyffesiad, cyffes

confide, *v.* ymddiried

confidence, *n.* ymddiried, hyder

confine, *v.t.* cyfyngu, carcharu, caethiwo

confirm, *v.t.* cadarnhau; conffirmio

confiscate, *v.t.* atafaelu

conflagration, *n.* goddaith, tan-llwyth

conflict, *n.* ymladdfa; gwrth-drawiad

conflict, *v.i.* anghytuno, gwrthdaro

confluence, *n.* cymer, aber

conform, *v.* cydymffurfio; cydffurf-io

confound, *v.t.* cymysgu; drysu; gwaradwyddo

confront, *v.t.* wynebu

confuse, *v.t.* cymysgu, drysu

confute, *v.t.* gwrthbrofi, dym-chwelyd

congeal, *v.* rhewi, fferru; tewychu, ceulo

congenial *a.* cydnaws, hynaws

congenital, *a.* genedigol, cynhwyn-ol

congeries, *n.* crug, crugyn, crug-lwyth

congest, *v.* cronni; gorlanw

conglomerate v. pentyrru, dirwyn
congratulate, v.t. llongyfarch
congregate, v. ymgynnull
congregation, n. cynulleidfa
congress, n. cyngres, cymanfa
conjecture, n. tyb, dychymyg: v. dyfalu
conjugal, a. cydweddog, priodasol
conjugate, v.t. cydieuo; treiglo berf
conjunction, n. cysylltiad
conjure, v.t. tynghedu
conjure, v. consurio
connect, v. cysylltu, cydio
connexion, n. cysylltiad; cyfundeb
connive, v.i. goddef, cau llygaid rhag
connotation, n. cynodiad
connote, v.t. dynodi, arwyddo
connubial, a. cydweddog, priodasol
conquer, v.t. gorchfygu, trechu
conqueror, n. gorchfygwr, concwerwr
conquest, n. buddugoliaeth, concwest
conscience, n. cydwybod
conscientious, a. cydwybodol
conscious, a. ymwybodol
consciousness, n. ymwybyddiaeth
conscription, n. gorfodaeth filwrol
consecrate, v.t. cysegru
consecutive, a. olynol
consent, v.i. cydsynio: n. cydsyniad, caniatâd
consequence, n. canlyniad; pwys
conservative, a. ceidwadol: n. ceidwadwr
conservatory, n. tŷ gwydr
conserve, v.t. cadw, diogelu, amddiffyn
consider, v. ystyried
considerable, a. cryn
considerate, a. ystyriol, tosturiol
consideration, n. ystyriaeth
consign, v.t. traddodi, trosglwyddo
consist, v.t. cynnwys, bod
consistent, n. cyson
consistory, n. llys eglwysig
console, v.t. cysuro, diddanu
consolidate, v. caledu, cyfnerthu, cyfuno

consonant, a. cysain; cyson: n. cytsain
consort, n. cydwedd, cymar
consort, v.i. cymdeithasu, cyfeillachu
conspicuous, a. amlwg
conspiracy, n. bradwriaeth, brad, cynllwyn
conspire, v. bradfwriadu, cynllwyn
constable, n. cwnstabl, heddgeidwad
constant, a. cyson; dianwadal
constellation, n. cytser
consternation, n. braw, dychryn
constipate, v.t. rhwymo
constituency, n. cynrychiolaeth, etholaeth
constituent, a. cyfansoddol: n. defnydd; etholwr
constitute, v.t. cyfansoddi
constitution, n. cyfansoddiad
constrain, v.t. cymell, gorfodi
constrict, v.t. gwasgu, tynhau
construct, v.t. ffurfio, llunio, adeiladu, saernïo
construe, v.t. cyfieithu; dehongli
consul, n. ynad, rhaglaw; consul
consult, v. ymgynghori
consume, v. treulio, difa, ysu; nychu
consummate, a. perffaith, cyflawn
consummate, v.t. perffeithio, cyflawni
consumption, n. traul; darfodedigaeth
contact, n. cyffyrddiad
contagion, n. haint
contagious, a. heintus
contain, v.t. cynnwys, dal; amgyffred
contaminate, v.t. halogi, llygru, heintio
contemplate, v. ystyried, myfyrio; bwriadu
contemporary, a. cyfoes(ol): n. cyfoeswr
contempt, n. dirmyg, diystyrwch
contend, v. ymryson, cynhennu
content, a. bodlon: v.t. bodloni

contention, *n.* cynnen, ymryson
contentment, *n.* bodlonrwydd
contents, *n.pl.* cynnwys, cynhwysiad
contest, *n.* cystadleuaeth, ymryson
contest, *v.* amau, ymryson, ymladd
context, *n.* cyd-destun
contiguous, *a.* cyffiniol, cyfagos
continent, *a.* cymedrol; diwair
continent, *n.* cyfandir
contingency, *n.* damwain, digwyddiad
contingent, *a.* damweiniol: *n.* mintai
continual, *a.* parhaus, gwastadol
continue, *v.* parhau, para, aros
continuous, *a.* parhaol, di-fwlch, di-dor
contort, *v.t.* nydd-droi; dirdynnu
contour, *n.* amlinell, tro
contra-, *px.* gwrth-, croes-
contraband, *a. & n.* (nwyddau), gwaharddedig
contract, *n.* cytundeb, cyfamod
contract, *v.* byrhau; cytuno, cyfamodi
contraction, *n.* talfyriad, cywasgiad
contradict, *v.t.* gwrthddywedyd
contrary, *a.* gwrthwyneb, croes
contrast, *n.* gwrthgyferbyniad: *v.* gwrthgyferbynnu
contravene *v.t.* torri, troseddu
contribute, *v.* cyfrannu
contrite, *a.* drylliedig, edifeiriol
contrive, *v.* dyfeisio, llwyddo, trefnu
control, *v.t.* llywodraethu: *n.* llywodraeth
controversy, *n.* dadl
controvert, *v.t.* gwrthbrofi, dymchwelyd
contumacious, *a.* gwrthnysig
contumely, *n.* sarhad, anfri, gwarth
contuse, *v.t.* cleisio
conundrum, *n.* dychymyg, pôs
convalesce, *v.i.* ymadfer, gwella, hybu
convene, *v.t.* galw, gwysio, cynnull
convenience, *n.* cyfleustra, hwylustod

convenient, *a.* cyfleus, gweddus, hwylus
convent, *n.* cwfaint, lleiandy
conventicle, *n.* tŷ cwrdd
convention, *n.* cytundeb; cymanfa; defod, confensiwn
converge, *v.i.* cydgyfeirio
conversant, *a.* cyfarwydd, cynefin
conversation, *n.* ymddiddan
conversazione, *n.* ymgomwest
converse, *v.i.* ymddiddan
converse, *a. & n.* gwrthwyneb, cyferbyniol
conversion, *n.* tröedigaeth, tro
convert, *v.t.* troi, dychwelyd; newid
convex, *a.* crwm
convey, *v.t.* cludo; trosi, trosglwyddo; cyfleu
convict, *v.t.* barnu'n euog; argyhoeddi
convict, *n.* troseddwr, penydgarcharor
convince, *v.t.* argyhoeddi
convivial *a.* llawen
convocation, *n.* confocasiwn
convoke, *v.t.* gwysio
convolution, *n.* troelliad, dirwyniad
convolvulus, *n.* cwlwm coed
convoy, *v.t.* hebrwng: *n.* gosgordd
convulse, *v.t.* dirgrynu, dirdynnu
coo, *v.i.* lleisio fel colomen
cook, *n.* cogydd, cogyddes: *v.* coginio, gwneud bwyd
cookery, *n.* coginiaeth
cool, *a.* oer, oeraidd; hunanfeddiannol: *v.* oer, ymoeri
coop, *n.* cawell, cut ieir: *v.t.* cutio
cooper, *n.* cylchwr, cowper
co-operate, *v.i.* cydweithio, cydweithredu
co-opt, *v.t.* cyfethol
co-ordinate, *a.* cyfurdd: *v.t.* cyfurddo
cope, *n.* cochl
cope, *v.i.* ymdaro â
copious, *a* helaeth, dibrin
copper, *n.* copr: efyddyn, pair
copse, *n.* prysgwydd, prysglwyn
copula, *n.* cyplad

copy, n. copi: v.t. copïo
copyright, n. hawlfraint
coquette, n. hoeden, mursen
coracle, n. cwrwgl
coral, n. cwrel
cord, n. cortyn, rheffyn, tennyn:
v.t. rheffynnu
cordial, a. o galon, calonnog: n.
cordial, gwirod
cordon, n. rhes, cadwyn
corduroy, n. melfaréd, rib
core, n. calon, perfedd
cork, n. corc, corcyn: v.t. corcio,
topio
cormorant, n. mulfran, bilidowcar; gloddestwr
corn, n. ŷd, llafur
corn, n. corn (ar droed)
corncrake, n. rhegen ryg, rhegen
yr ŷd
corner, n. congl, cornel, cil: v.t.
cornelu
cornice, n. cornis
coronation, n. coroniad
coroner, n. trengholydd, crwner
coronet, n. coronig, talaith
corporal, a. corfforol
corporate, a. yn un corff, corffor-
edig
corporation, n. corfforaeth; cest
corporeal, a. corfforol; materol
corps, n. corfflu
corpse, n. corff (marw), celain
corpulent, a. corffol, cestog, boliog,
tew
corpuscle, n. corffilyn
correct, a. cywir: v.t. cywiro,
ceryddu
correlate, v.t. cydberthnasu
correspond, v.i. cyfateb; gohebu
corridor, n. llwybr, rhodfa
corroborate, v.t. cyfnerthu, cadarnhau
corrode, v. ysu, rhydu, treulio
corrugate, v.t. crychu, rhychu,
crebachu
corrupt, a. llygredig, pwdr: v.
llygru
corset, n. staes
coruscate, v.i. fflachio, gwreichioni

cost, v.i. costio: n. cost, traul
costive, a. bolrwym, rhwym
costly, a. drudfawr, drud, prid
costume, n. gwisg
cosy, a. cysurus, clyd
cot, n. gwely bychan
coterie, n. cyfrinfa, clymblaid
cottage, n. bwth, bwthyn, tŷ
cotton, n. cotwm; edau
cotyledon n. had-ddeilen
couch, n. gorweddfa, glwth: v. gorwedd
cough, n. peswch: v. pesychu
coulter, n. cwlltwr
council, n. cyngor
counsel, n. cyngor; dadleuydd:
v.t. cynghori
count, n. cyfrif: v. rhifo, cyfrif
count, n. iarll
countenance, n. wynepryd; cefnogaeth v.t. cefnogi
counter, n. cownter
counter-, px. gwrth-
counteract, v.t. gwrthweithio
counterfeit, a. gau, ffug: v.t. ffugio
counterfoil, n. gwrthddalen
countermand, v.t. gwrthorchymyn
counterpane, n. cwrlid, cwilt
gwely
counterpart, n. rhan gyfatebol,
cymar
countervail, v. gwrthbwyso; tycio
yn erbyn
countess, n. iarlles
country, n. gwlad, bro
county, n. sir, swydd
coup, n. ergyd, trawiad, strôc
couple, n. cwpl: v.t. cyplu, cyplysu
couplet, n. cwpled
coupon, n. cwpon
courage, n. gwroldeb, dewrder
courier, n. cennad
course, n. cwrs, treigl; ystod; gyrfa
court, n. llys; cwrt; cyntedd: v.t.
caru; gwahodd
courteous, a. cwrtais
courtesy, n. cwrteisrwydd, cwrteisi
courtier, n. gŵr llys, llyswr
courtly, a. llysaidd
courtship, n. carwriaeth

courtyard, n. buarth, cwrt, clos, iard

cousin, n. cefnder; cyfnither

cove, n. cil, cilfach

covenant, n. cyfamod: v. cyfamodi

cover, v.t. gorchuddio, toi: n. gorchudd

coverlet, -lid, n. cwrlid, cwilt

covert, a. cêl, cudd, dirgel

covert, n. lloches; prysglwyn

covet, v.t. chwennych, chwenychu

covey, n. nythaid o betris, haid

cow, n. buwch

cow, v.t. bygylu, torri ysbryd

coward, n. llwfrddyn, llwfryn, llwfrgi

cowardice, n. llwfrdra

cowardly, a. llwfr

cower, v.i. yswatio, cyrcydu

cowl, n. cwcwll, cwfl

cowpox, n. brech y fuwch

cowslip, n. briallu Mair

coxcomb, n. coegyn, ysgogyn, pefryn

coxswain, n. llywydd cwch

coy, a. yswil, gwylaidd

cozen, v.t. twyllo, hudo, hocedu

crab, n. cranc   [crabas

crab (apple), n. afal sur, afal

crack, v. cracio; brolio: n. crac

crackle, v.i. clindarddach

cradle, n. crud, cawell; cadair fedi

craft, n. crefft; cyfrwystra, dichell; llong, llestr

crafty, a. cyfrwys, dichellgar

crag, n. craig, clegr, clogwyn

cram, v. gorlenwi, stwffio, saco

cramp, n. cwlwm gwythi, cramp; creffyn: v.t. caethiwo, gwasgu

crane, n. garan, creyr, crychydd, craen: v.t. estyn (gwddf)

cranium, (-ia) n. penglog

cranny, n. agen, hollt, agennig

crape, n. crêp

crash, v. chwilfriwio: n. twrf, gwrthdrawiad

crass, a. tew, praff; dybryd

crate, n. cawell llestri

crater, n. safn llosgfynydd; ceudod, cawg

cravat, n. cadach gwddf, crafat

crave, v. crefu, deisyf, chwennych

craven, a. & n. llwfr

craving, n. blys, chwant

crawl, v.i. ymlusgo, cropian

craze, n. ysfa, chwilen

creak, v.i. grillian, gwichian, crecian

cream, n. hufen

creamery, n. hufenfa

crease, n. ôl plygu, plyg: v.t. crychu

create, v.t. creu

creation, n. cread, creadigaeth

creator, n. crëwr, creawdwr

creature, n. creadur

credence, n. cred, coel, ffydd

credentials, n.pl. credlythyrau

credible, a. credadwy, hygoel, hygred

credit, n. coel, cred; clod, credyd: v.t. coelio

creditor, n. gofynnwr, echwynnwr

credulous, a. hygoelus

creed, n. credo

creek, n. cilfach

creep, v.i. ymlusgo, cropian, ymgripio

cremate, v.t. amlosgi

crematorium, n. amlosgfa

crescent, n. hanner lleuad: a. cynyddol

cress, n. berwr

crest, n. crib; mwng; arfau bonedd

crevice, n. agen, hollt, rhigol

crew, n. criw, gwerin llong; haid

crewel, n. edau fain o wlân

crib, n. preseb; caban; gwely plentyn: v.t. caethiwo

cricket, n. criced; cricsyn

crime, n. trosedd

criminal, a. troseddol: n. troseddwr

crimp, v.t. crychu, crebachu, crimpio

crimson, a. & n. rhuddgoch

cringe, v.i. cynffonna, ymgreinio

cripple, n. cloff, efrydd: v.t. cloffi; llyffetheirio, llesteirio

crisis, (crises) n. argyfwng

crisp, a. cras, crych

criterion, (*-ia*) *n.* maen prawf, safon

critic, *n.* beirniad

critical, *a.* beirniadol; pryderus; peryglus

criticism, *n.* beirniadaeth

criticize, *v.t.* beirniadu

croak, *v.i.* crawcian: *n.* crawc

crochet, *v.* crosio

crock, *n.* llestr pridd, priddell

crock, *n.* ewach

crocodile, *n.* crocodil [tyddyn

croft, *n.* llain, crofft; cadlas

crony, *n.* cyfaill agos, cydymaith

crook, *n.* crwca, bagl, ffon fugail

crooked, *a.* crwca, cam

croon, *v.* mwmian canu, grwnan

crop, *n.* cnwd, cynnyrch; crombil: *v.t.* tocio, torri

crosier, *n.* bagl esgob

cross, *n. & a.* croes: *v.* croesi

crotchet, *n.* cromfach; crosiet; mympwy

crouch, *v.i.* gŵyro i lawr, cyrcydu

croup, *n.* crŵp

crow, *n.* brân; trosol haearn

crow, *v.i.* canu fel ceiliog; ymffrostio

crowd, *n.* torf, tyrfa: *v.* tyrru, heidio

crown, *n.* coron; corun: *v.t.* coroni

crucial, *a.* hanfodol; terfynol

crucifix, *n.* delw Crist ar y groes, crog

crucifixion, *n.* croeshoeliad

crucify, *v.t.* croeshoelio

crude, *a.* cri, crai; llymrig, amrwd

cruel, *a.* creulon

cruise, *v.i.* morio: *n.* mordaith

cruiser, *n.* gwiblong

crumb, *n.* briwsionyn; mwydion (torth)

crumble, *v.* briwsioni, malurio

crumple, *v.* crychu, gwasgu

crunch, *v.* cnoi neu sathru yn drystiog

crupper, *n.* pedrain, crwper, pen ôl

crusade, *n.* rhyfel y groes, croesgad

crush, *v.* gwasgu, ysigo, llethu: *n.* ymwasg, torf

crust, *n.* crawen, crofen, crystyn

crutch, *n.* bagl, ffon fagl

cry, *v.* llefain, wylo: *n.* llef, dolef, cri

cryptic, *a.* dirgel, cyfrin

crystal, *n.* grisial: *a.* grisialaidd

crystallisation, *n.* crisialiad

cub, *n.* cenau

cube, *n.* ciwb

cubicle, *n.* cuddygl

cubit, *n.* cufydd

cuckoo, *n.* cog, cwcw; gwirionyn

cud, *n.* cil

cuddle, *v.* anwylo, anwesu, tolach

cudgel, *n.* ffon, pastwn: *v.t.* ffonodio

cue, *n.* awgrym; ciw

cuff, *n.* torch llawes

cuff, *v.t.* cernodio: *n.* cernod, dyrnod

cuirass, *n.* dwyfronneg, llurig

culinary, *a.* coginiol

cull, *v.t.* dewis, pigo

culminate, *v.i.* cyrraedd ei anterth

culpable, *a.* beius, camweddus

culprit, *n.* troseddwr, drwgweithredwr

cult, *n.* addoliad, cwlt

cultivate, *v.t.* diwyllio, trin, meithrin

culture, *n.* diwylliant, gwrtaith

cultured, *a.* diwylliedig, coeth

cumber, *v.t.* beichio, llesteirio

cumbersome, *a.* afrosgo, beichus

cunning, *a.* cywrain; cyfrwys: *n.* medr; cyfrwystra

cup, *n.* cwpan, cwpanaid

cupboard, *n.* cwpwrdd

cupidity, *n.* gwanc am elw, trachwant

cur, *n.* corgi, costog; taeog

curate, *n.* curad

curb, *n.* genfa, atalfa: *v.t.* ffrwyno

curd, *n.* caul, ceuled; caws

curdle, *v.* ceulo, cawsio, cawsu

cure, *n.* iachâd; meddyginiaeth; gofal: *v.* iacháu, gwella; halltu

curfew, *n.* dyhuddgloch, hwyrgloch

curiosity, *n.* cywreinrwydd, chwilfrydedd

curious, *a.* cywrain; chwilfrydig; hynod

curl, *v.* crychu, modrwyo: *n.* cudyn, cwrlyn

curlew, *n.* gylfinir

curmudgeon, *n.* cerlyn, taeog, cybydd

currants, *n.pl.* grawn Corinth, cyrains

currency, *a.* arian breiniol

current, *a.* rhedegol: *n.* ffrwd, llif

current money, *n.* arian treigl

curriculum, *n.* cwrs addysg

curry, *v.t.* trin lledr; ysgrafellu, cribo

curse, *n.* melltith, rheg: *v.* melltithio, rhegi

cursory, *a.* brysiog, diofal

curt, *a.* cwta, byr, cryno

curtail, *v.t.* cwtogi, talfyrru; prinhau

curtain, *n.* llen

curtsy, *n.* cyrtsi

curve, *v.* camu, gŵyro, troi: *n.* tro; cromlin

cushion, *n.* clustog

custard, *n.* cwstart

custodian, *n.* ceidwad

custody, *n.* dalfa, cadwraeth

custom, *n.* defod; cwsmeriaeth; toll

customer, *n.* cwsmer

cut, *v.* torri: *n.* toriad, archoll, briw

cutaneous, *a.* croenol

cuticle, *n.* croen, pilen

cutler, *n.* cyllellwr

cutlet, *n.* golwyth

cycle, *n.* cylch, olwyn: *v.i.* olwyno

cyclone, *n.* trowynt

cygnet, *n.* cyw alarch, alarchen

cylinder, *n.* rhol; silindr

cymbal, *n.* symbal

cynic, *n.* gwawdiwr, sinig

D

dab, *v.t.* dabio, dwbio: *n.* dab

dabble, *v.* yslotian, diblo, dablo

dad, dada, daddy, *n.* tad, tada, tyta, dada

daffodil, *n.* cenhinen Bedr

daft, *a.* hurt, gwirion

dagger, *n.* dagr, bidog

daily *a.* dyddiol, beunyddiol

dainty, *n.* danteithfwyd, amheuthun: *a.* danteithiol, dillyn, del

dairy, *n.* llaethdy

daisy, *n.* llygad y dydd [bro

dale, *n.* dyffryn, glyn, dôl, cwm,

dally, *v.i.* cellwair; ymdroi, swmera

dam, *n.* argae, cronfa: *v.t.* argáu, cronni

dam, *n.* mamog, mam (anifail)

damage, *n.* niwed, difrod: *v.t.* niweidio

dame, *n.* arglwyddes, meistres, gwraig

damn, *v.* damnio

damnation, *n.* damnedigaeth

damp, *a.* llaith: *n.* lleithder: *v.* lleitho

damsel, *n.* llances, morwyn, herlodes

dance, *v.* dawnsio: *n.* dawns

dandelion, *n.* dant y llew

dandruff, -iff, *n.* mardon, cen

dandy, *n.* dandi, coegyn

danger, *n.* perygl, enbydrwydd

dangerous, *a.* peryglus, enbyd

dangle, *v.* hongian; siglo

dapper, *a.* del, twt, sionc, heini

dapple, *v.* ysmotio, britho

dare, *v.* beiddio, anturio

daring, *a.* beiddgar, mentrus: *n.* beiddgarwch

dark, *a.* tywyll: *n.* tywyllwch, nos

darkness, *n.* tywyllwch

darling, *n.* anwylyd, cariad: *a.* annwyl

darn, *v.t.* cyweirio, trwsio

dart, *n.* picell, saeth: *v.* gwanu, picio

dash, *v.* rhuthro, chwalu, chwilfriwio: *n.* rhuthr; llinell (—)

dastard, *n.* llwfryn

date, *n.* dyddiad, amseriad: *v.* dyddio

daub, *v.* dwbio, iro

daughter, *n.* merch

daunt, *v.t.* dantio, digalonni, llwfrhau

dawdle, *v.i.* ymdroi, swmera

dawn, *v.i.* gwawrio, dyddio: *n.* gwawr

day, *n.* diwrnod, dydd

daze, *v.t.* synnu, syfrdanu; dallu

dazzle, *v.* disgleirio, pelydru; dallu

dazzling, *a.* disglair, llachar

deacon, *n.* diacon, blaenor

dead, *a.* marw; difywyd: *adv.* hollol

deadly, *a.* marwol, angheuol

deaf, *a.* byddar

deal, *v.* delio; trin: *n.* trafodaeth; llawer

dealer, *n.* masnachwr

dean, *n.* deon

dear, *a.* annwyl, cu, hoff; drud: *n.* anwylyd, cariad

dearth, *n.* prinder, drudaniaeth

death, *n.* angau, marwolaeth, tranc

debar, *v.t.* atal, lluddias, cau allan

debase, *v.t.* iselu, darostwng, llygru

debate, *v.* dadlau, ymryson: *n.* dadl

debauch, *v.t.* llygru; treisio: *n.* cyfeddach

debility, *n.* gwendid

debit, *n.* dyled: *v.t.* dyledu, codi ar

debris, *n.* malurion, ysbwrial

debt, *n.* dyled

debtor, *n.* dyledwr

decadence, *n.* dirywiad, adfeiliad

decalogue, *n.* y deg gorchymyn

decamp, *v.i.* ffoi, dianc, cilio

decapitate, *v.t.* torri pen

decay, *v.i.* dadfeilio: *n.* dadfeiliad

decease, *n.* tranc, marwolaeth: *v.i.* marw, trengi

deceit, *n.* twyll, dichell, hoced

deceive, *v.t.* twyllo, hocedu, siomi

December, *n.* Rhagfyr

decency, *n.* gwedduster, gwedd-eidd-dra

decent, *a.* gweddus, gweddaidd

deception, *n.* twyll, ffug, dichell

decide, *v.* penderfynu

decimal, *a.* degol

decimate, *v.t.* degymu

decipher, *v.t.* dadrys, dehongli, darllen

decision, *n.* penderfyniad

decisive, *a.* penderfynol, pendant

deck, *n.* bwrdd llong, dec

deck, *v.t.* trwsio, addurno, pincio

declare, *v.* mynegi, datgan, cyhoeddi

decline, *v.* dadfeilio; gwrthod: *n.* dadfeiliad; darfodedigaeth

declivity, *n.* goriwaered, llethr

decoct, *v.t.* berweddu, trwytho

decompose, *v.* pydru, braenu; dadelfennu

decorate, *v.t.* addurno, arwisgo

decorous, *a.* gweddus, gweddaidd

decorum, *n.* gwedduster, gwedd-eidd-dra

decoy, *n.* hud, magl: *v.t.* hudo, llithio

decrease, *v.* lleihau, gostwng: *n.* lleihad

decree, *n. & v.* gorchymyn

decrepit, *a.* musgrell, llegach, llesg

decry, *v.t.* gogan, difrïo

dedicate, *v.t.* cysegru, cyflwyno

deduce, *v.t.* tynnu, casglu, diddwytho

deduct, *v.t.* tynnu ymaith, tolli, toli

deed, *n.* gweithred

deem, *v.t.* meddwl, ystyried, barnu

deep, *a.* dwfn; dwys: *n.* dwfn, dyfnder

deepen, *v.* dyfnhau, trymhau, dwysáu

deer, *(deer),* *n.* carw

deface, *v.t.* difwyno, anurddo, hagru

defalcate, *v.i.* celcio, darnguddio, lladrata

defame, *v.t.* difenwi, difrïo, athrodi

default, *n.* diffyg, gwall, pall, meth

defeat, *v.t.* gorchfygu: *n.* gorchfygiad

defect, *n.* diffyg, nam

defence, *n.* amddiffyn, amddiffyniad

defend, *v.t.* amddiffyn

defendant, *n.* diffynnydd

defer, *v.* oedi, gohirio

defer, *v.i.* ymostwng, gwrogi, parchu

defiance, *n.* her, herfeiddiad

defiant, *a.* herfeiddiol
deficient, *a.* diffygiol, prin, yn eisiau
deficit, *n.* diffyg
defile, *v.i.* symud yn rhes: *n.* culffordd, bwlch, ceunant
defile, *v.t.* halogi, difwyno
define, *v.t.* penderfynu; diffinio, darnodi
definite, *a.* penodol, pendant
definition, *n.* diffiniad, darnodiad
deflect, *v.* gwyro, osgoi
deform, *v.t.* anffurfio, hagru, aflunieiddio
deformity, *n.* anffurfiad
defraud, *v.t.* twyllo, hocedu; ysbeilio
defray, *v.t.* talu (treuliau)
deft, *a.* medrus, hylaw, deheuig
defunct, *a.* marw, trancedig
defy, *v.t.* beiddio, herfeiddio, herio
degenerate, *v.i.* dirywio: *a.* dirywiedig
degrade, *v.t.* diraddio, difreinio
degree, *n.* gradd
deify, *v.t.* dwyfoli
deign, *v.* ymostwng, teilyngu
deity, *n.* duwdod; duw
deject, *v.t.* digalonni, llwfrhau
delay, *v.* oedi, gohirio: *n.* oediad
delectable, *a.* hyfryd, hyfrydlon
delegate, *v.t.* dirprwyo: *n.* dirprwy
delete, *v.t.* dileu
deleterious, *a.* niweidiol
deliberate, *v.* ystyried yn bwyllog: *a.* pwyllog, bwriadol
delicate, *a.* tyner; cain; gwanllyd
delicious, *a.* danteithiol, blasus
delight, *v.* difyrru; ymhyfrydu: *n.* hyfrydwch
delightful, *a.* hyfryd, braf
delimit, *v.t.* gosod terfynau
delineate, *v.t.* darlunio, portreadu
delinquency, *n.* bai, trosedd
delirium, *n.* syfrdandod, gwallgofrwydd
deliver, *v.t.* traddodi; gwaredu; danfon
deliverance, *n.* gwaredigaeth
delivery, *n.* traddodiad; danfoniad

dell, *n.* glyn, pant, ceunant, cwm
delude, *v.t.* twyllo, hudo, llithio, hocedu
deluge, *n.* dilyw, dylif: *v.t.* gorlifo
delusion, *n.* twyll, cyfeiliornad; lledrith
delve, *v.* cloddio, palu, chwilio
demand, *v.t.* gofyn, hawlio, mynnu: *n.* gofyn, hawl
demarcation, *n.* gosodiad terfynau; ffin
demean, *v.t.* ymddwyn
demeanour, *n.* ymddygiad
demented, *a.* gwallgof, gorffwyll
demerit, *n.* anhaeddiant
demesne, *n.* treftadaeth, tiriogaeth; bro
demi-, *px.* hanner
demise, *n.* trosglwyddiad; marwolaeth
democracy, *n.* gweriniaeth; gwerin
democrat, *n.* gwerinydd, gweriniaethwr
demolish, *v.t.* dymchwelyd, distrywio
demon, *n.* cythraul, ysbryd drwg
demonstrate, *v.* arddangos, profi
demoralize, *v.t.* anfoesoli, llygru; anwroli
demur, *v.i.* codi gwrthwynebiad, petruso
demure, *a.* swil; mursennaidd
den, *n.* ffau, gwâl, lloches
denial, *n.* gwad; nacâd, gwrthodiad
denizen, *n.* dinesydd, preswylydd
denominate, *v.t.* enwi, cyfenwi, galw
denomination, *n.* enw, enwad
denote, *v.t.* arwyddo, dynodi, hynodi
denounce, *v.t.* lladd ar, cyhuddo, condemnio
dense, *a.* tew, dwys; pendew, hurt
density, *n.* dwysedd
dent, *n.* tolc: *v.t.* tolcio
dental, *a.* deintiol
dentist, *n.* deintydd
denude, *v.t.* noethi, dinoethi
deny, *v.t.* gwadu, gomedd, gwrthod
depart, *v.i.* ymadael; cychwyn

department, *n.* adran, dosbarth

departure, *n.* ymadawiad; cychwyniad

depend, *v.i.* dibynnu

depict, *v.t.* darlunio

deplete, *v.t.* gwacáu, gwagu, hysbyddu

deplore, *v.t.* gresynu, gofidio

deponent, *n.* tyst ar lw; deponent

depopulate, *v.t.* diboblogi

deport, *v.t.* ymarweddu; alltudio

deportation, *n.* alltudiaeth

deportment, *n.* ymddygiad, ymarweddiad

depose, *v.t.* tystio, tyngu; deol, diswyddo

deposit, *v.t.* dodi i lawr, adneuo, gwaddod

deposit, *n.* adnau, gwaddod

depot, *n.* ystorfa; gorsaf

deprave, *v.t.* llygru, halogi

deprecate, *v.t.* anghymeradwyo

depreciate, *v.* dibrisio; bychanu

depredation, *n.* lladrad, ysbeiliad

depress, *v.t.* gostwng, iselu; digalonni

deprive, *v.t.* amddifadu, difuddio, difreinio

depth, *n.* dyfnder

deputation, *n.* dirprwyaeth

depute, *v.t.* dirprwyo

deputy, *n.* dirprwy

derange, *v.t.* drysu, anhrefnu

deride, *v.t.* gwatwar, gwawdio

derision, *n.* gwatwar, gwawd, dirmyg

derive, *v.* derbyn, cael; tarddu, deillio

derogate, *v.i.* tynnu oddi wrth, bychanu

descant, *v.i.* desgant, cyfalaw

descend, *v.i.* disgyn

descent, *n.* disgyniad, disgynfa; hil, ach

describe, *v.t.* disgrifio, darlunio

description, *n.* disgrifiad, darluniad

descry, *v.t.* canfod

desecrate, *v.t.* digysegru, halogi

desert, *n.* haeddiant

desert, *a.* diffaith, anial: *n.* diffeithwch

desert, *v.* gadael, cefnu ar; encilio

deserve, *v.* haeddu, teilyngu, rhyglyddu

desiccate, *v.* disychu

desiderate, *v.t.* chwenychu

design, *n.* arfaeth; cynllun: *v.* arfaethu; cynllunio

designate, *v.t.* dynodi, penodi

desirable, *a.* dymunol, dewisol

desire, *v.* dymuno: *n.* dymuniad, chwant

desist, *v.i.* ymatal, peidio

desk, *n.* desg

desolate, *a.* anghyfannedd: *v.t.* anghyfanheddu

despair, *n.* anobaith: *v.i.* anobeithio

desperado, *n.* rhyfygwr

desperate, *a.* diobaith, anobeithiol; gorffwyll

despicable, *a.* dirmygedig, ffiaidd

despise, *v.t.* dirmygu, diystyru, tremygu

despite, *pr.* er, er gwaethaf

despoil, *v.t.* anrheithio, ysbeilio

despond, *v.i.* anobeithio, digalonni

despondent, *a.* digalon, isel-ysbryd

despot, *n.* unben, gormeswr

destination, *n.* pen taith, cyrchfan, nod

destine, *v.t.* bwriadu, arfaethu

destiny, *n.* tynged, tynghedfen

destitute, *a.* anghenus, amddifad

destroy, *v.t.* distrywio, difetha, dinistrio

destruction, *n.* distryw, dinistr

desultory, *a.* anghysylltiol, didrefn

detach, *v.t.* datod, gwahanu

detachment, *n.* adran; didoliad; annibyniaeth

detail, *n.* manylyn, *(pl.)* manylion

detain, *v.t.* cadw, atal, caethiwo

detect, *v.t.* canfod, darganfod, dal

detective, *n.* cuddswyddog, ditectif

detention, *n.* carchariad, ataliad

deter, *v.t.* cadw rhag, atal, rhwystro

deteriorate, *v.* dirywio, gwaethygu

determination, *n.* penderfyniad

determine, v. terfynu, penderfynu

determinism, n. rheidoliaeth, penderfyniaeth

detest, v.t. ffieiddio, casáu, atgasu

dethrone, v.t. diorseddu

detour, n. cylch, cwmpas

detract, v.t. tynnu oddi wrth, bychanu

detriment, n. colled, niwed, anfantais

devastate, v.t. diffeithio, difrodi

develop, v. datblygu

deviate, v.i. gwyro, troi o'r neilltu

device, n. dyfais

devil, n. diafol, diawl, cythraul

devilish, a. dieflig

devious, a. diarffordd, troellog; cyfeiliornus

devise, v.t. dyfeisio; cymynroddi

devoid, a. amddifad

devolution, n. trosglwyddiad, treiglad

devolve, v. treiglo; disgyn, syrthio

devote, v.t. cysegru, cyflwyno; diofrydu

devoted, a. ffyddlon, ymroddgar

devotion, n. defosiwn

devour, v.t. ysu, difa, traflyncu

devout, a. duwiol, crefyddol, defosiynol

dew, n. gwlith: v. gwlitho

dewlap, n. tagell

dexterous, a. deheuig, medrus, celfydd

diabolical a. dieflig

diaconate, n. diaconiaeth

diadem, n. coron, talaith, coronbleth

diagonal, n. croeslin: a. croeslinol

diagram, n. darlun eglurhaol, diagram

dial, n. deial

dialect, n. tafodiaith

dialectic, n. dilechdid

dialogue, n. ymddiddan; dadl

diameter, n. tryfesur, diamedr

diamond, n. diemwnt, adamant

diaphragm, n. llengig, llieingig

diarrhoea, n. rhyddni, dolor rhydd

diary, n. dyddiadur, dyddlyfr

dichotomous, a. deubarthol, fforchog

dichotomy, n. deubarthiad

dictate, v. adrodd; gormesu

dictate, n. arch, galwad, gorchymyn

dictation, n. arddywediad

diction, n. ieithwedd, geirwedd, iaith

dictionary, n. geiriadur, geirlyfr

didactic, a. hyfforddiadol, athrawiaethol

diddle, v.t. twyllo, hocedu

die, n. (dice) dis; (dies) bath

die, v.i. marw, trengi, trigo, darfod

diet, n. ymborth, lluniaeth, deiet; dogn: v. dogni

dietetics, n. deieteg

differ, v.i. gwahaniaethu

difference, n. gwahaniaeth

different, a. gwahanol

differentiate, v. gwahaniaethu

difficult, a. anodd, caled

difficulty, n. anhawster

diffidence, n. anymddiried, anhyder

diffident, a. petrusgar, anhyderus

diffuse, v. gwasgaru, lledaenu

diffuse, a. anghryno, gwasgarog

dig, v. palu, cloddio, ceibio; plannu

digest, v. treulio, toddi; cymathu

digest, n. crynhoad

digestion, n. treuliad, traul

dignify, v.t. anrhydeddu, urddasu

dignity, n. urddas, teilyngdod

digress, v.i. gwyro, crwydro

dike, dyke, n. clawdd, ffos; argae

dilapidate, v. adfeilio, malurio

dilate, v. ymhelaethu, lledu

dilatory, a. hwyrfrydig, anniben

dilemma n. dilema

diligence, n. diwydrwydd, dyfalwch

diligent, a. diwyd, dyfal

dilute, v.t. cymysgu â dwfr, teneuo, gwanhau

dim, a. pŵl, aneglur: v. tywyllu, cymylu

dimension, n. mesur, maintioli, dimensiwn

diminish, *v.* lleihau, prinhau

diminution, *n.* lleihad, prinhad

diminutive, *a.* bychan; bachigol; *n.* bachigyn

dimple, *n.* pannwl, pant: *v.* panylu

din, *n.* twrf, dadwrdd, mwstwr

dine, *v.i.* ciniawa

dingle, *n.* cwm, glyn, pant

dingy, *a.* tywyll, dilewyrch; tlodaidd

dinner, *n.* cinio

dint, *n.* tolc; grym: *v.t.* tolcio

diocesan, *a.* esgobaethol: *n.* esgob

diocese, *n.* esgobaeth

dioxide, *n.* deuocsid

dip, *v.* trochi, gwlychu; gostwng: *n.* trochfa

diphthong, *n.* deusain, dipton

diploma, *n.* breinlen, tystysgrif, diploma

diplomatist, *n.* llysgennad, diplomydd

dire, *a.* dygn, arswydus, echryslon

direct, *a.* union, uniongyrchol: *v.t.* cyfarwyddo, cyfeirio [iad

direction, *n.* cyfarwyddyd; cyfeir-

director, *n.* cyfarwyddwr

dirge, *n.* galargan, galarnad, marwnad

dirt, *n.* baw

dirty, *a.* budr, brwnt: *v.t.* budro, diwyno, maeddu

dis-, *px.* dad-, di-, an-, &c.

disable, *v.t.* analluogi; efryddu

disabuse, *v.t.* didwyllo

disadvantage, *n.* anfantais

disagree, *v.i.* anghytuno

disagreeable, *a.* annymunol, cas

disappear, *v.i.* diflannu

disappoint, *v.t.* siomi

disapprove, *v.* anghymeradwyo

disaster, *n.* trychineb, aflwydd

disavow, *v.t.* gwadu, diarddel

disband, *v.* dadfyddino; gwasgaru

disbelieve, *v.* anghredu, anghoelio

disburse, *v.t.* gwario, talu arian

discard, *v.t.* rhoi heibio, gwrthod

discern, *v.t.* canfod, dirnad

discharge, *v.* gollwng: *n.* gollyng-dod; ergyd

disciple, *n.* disgybl

discipline, *n.* disgyblaeth: *v.t.* disgyblu

disclaim, *v.t.* diarddel, gwadu

disclose, *v.t.* dadlennu, datguddio

discomfit, *v.t.* gorchfygu, dymchwelyd

discomfort, *v.t.* anghysuro: *n.* anghysur

discompose, *v.t.* aflonyddu, cyffroi

disconcert, *v.t.* aflonyddu, cyffroi, tarfu

disconsolate, *a.* digysur, anniddan, galarus

discord, *n.* anghytgord

discount, *n.* disgownt: *v.t.* anghyfrif

discountenance, *v.t.* anghefnogi

discourage, *v.t.* digalonni, anghefnogi

discourse, *n.* ymddiddan; araith: *v.* traethu

discourteous, *a.* anghwrtais

discover, *v.t.* darganfod, canfod

discredit, *n.* anfri, anghlod, amarch: *v.t.* anghoelio; amau, difrio

discreet, *a.* call, synhwyrol, pwyllog

discrepant, *a.* gwahanol, anghyson

discretion, *n.* barn, pwyll, synnwyr

discriminate, *v.* gwahaniaethu

discursive, *a.* crwydrol, anghysylltiol

discuss, *v.t.* trin, trafod

disdain, *v.* diystyru, dirmygu, ysgornio: *n.* dirmyg

disease, *n.* afiechyd, clefyd, clwyf

disembark, *v.* glanio

disentangle, *v.* datod, datrys

disestablish, *v.t.* datgysylltu

disfigure, *v.t.* anffurfio, anharddu, hagru

disfranchise, *v.t.* difreinio

disgorge, *v.* chwydu, arllwys

disgrace, *v.t.* gwaradwyddo: *n.* gwaradwydd, gwarth

disguise, *v.t.* dieithrio, ffugio, lledrithio: *n.* rhith

disgust, n. diflastod, ffieidd-dod: v.t. diflasu

disgusting, a. ffiaidd, brwnt

dish, n. dysgl; dysglaid

dishearten, v.t. digalonni

dishevelled, a. anhrefnus, aflêr, anniben

disintegrate, v. datod, chwalu

disk, disc, n. coeten

dislike, v.t. casáu: n. casineb

dislocate, v.t. rhoi o'i le, dadgymalu

dislodge, v.t. symud, syflyd, gwared

dismal, a. tywyll, dilewyrch, digalon

dismay, v.t. brawychu, siomi, digalonni: n. braw, siom, chwithdod

dismiss, v.t. gollwng; diswyddo

dismount, v. disgyn, dymchwelyd

disobedient, a. anufudd

disobey, v. anufuddhau

disorder, n. anhrefn: anhwyldeb: v.t. anhrefnu

disown, v.t. gwadu, diarddel

disparage, v.t. amharchu, bychanu, difrio

disparity, n. anghyfartaledd, rhagor

dispatch, v. anfon; diweddu: n. neges

dispel, v.t. chwalu, gwasgaru

dispense, v. rhannu; gweinyddu; hepgor

disperse, v. gwasgaru, chwalu, taenu

dispirit, v.t. digalonni, llwfrhau

display, v.t. arddangos: n. arddangosiad

displease, v.t. anfodloni, anfoddio, digio

displeasure, n. anfodlonrwydd, dicter

disport, v. difyrru, chwarae

dispose, v.t. tueddu; trefnu, dosbarthu

disprove, v.t. gwrthbrofi

dispute, v. dadlau, ymryson: n. dadl

disregard, v.t. diystyru, esgeuluso

disrespect, n. amarch

dissatisfy, v.t. anfoddio, anfodloni

dissect, v. difynio, trychu; dadansoddi

dissemble, v. ffugio, rhagrithio, celu

disseminate, v.t. hau, taenu, lledaenu

dissent, v.i. anghytuno, anghydolygu: n. anghytundeb; ymneilltuaeth

dissimulation, n. rhagrith; dadfathiad

dissipate, v.t. chwalu, gwasgaru, afradloni

dissociate, v.t. anghysylltu, gwahanu, diaelodi

dissolute, a. penrhydd, afradlon, ofer

dissolution, n. ymddatodiad, datodiad

dissolve, v. toddi, datod; datgorffori

distance, n. pellter

distant, a. pell, pellennig

distemper, n. anhwyldeb; lliw

distend, v.t. estyn, lledu, chwyddo

distension, n. ymlediad, chwydd, tyndra

distil, v. distyllu, defnynnu, dihidlo

distinct, a. gwahanol; eglur, croyw

distinguish, v. gwahaniaethu; hynodi

distort, v.t. ystumio, anffurfio, gwyrdroi

distract, v. tynnu ymaith, drysu, mwydro

distrain, v.i. atafaelu

distress, n. cyfyngder, ing, trallod

distribute, v.t. rhannu, dosbarthu

district, n. dosbarth, ardal, rhandir

disturb, v.t. aflonyddu, cyffroi

disturbance, n. aflonyddwch, cyffro, terfysg

ditch, n. ffos

ditto, adv. eto, yr un, yr un peth

ditty, n. cân, canig

dive, v.i. ymsuddo, soddi

diverge, v.i. ymwahanu, ymrannu

diverse, *a.* gwahanol; annhebyg

diversion, *n.* difyrrwch, adloniant

divert, *v.t.* troi o'r neilltu; difyrru

divest, *v.t.* diosg, dihatru

divide, *v.* rhannu, dosbarthu, gwahanu

dividend, *n.* buddran; difidend

divination, *n.* dewiniaeth

divine, *a.* dwyfol: *n.* diwinydd: *v.* dewinio, dyfalu

divinity, *n.* duwdod; diwinyddiaeth

division, *n.* rhan, rhaniad; cyfraniaeth

divorce, *v.t.* ysgar: *n.* ysgariaeth

divulge, *v.t.* datguddio, dadlennu

dizzy, *a.* penysgafn, pensyfrdan

do, *v.* gwneuthur

docile, *a.* dof, hywedd, hydrin

dock, *n.* (dail) tafol

dock, *v.t.* tocio, cwtogi

dock, *n.* doc, porthladd: *v.t.* docio; cwtogi

dock, *n.* brawdle

doctor, *n.* doctor, meddyg: *v.* doctora

doctrine, *n.* athrawiaeth

document, *n.* ysgrif, gweithred, dogfen

dodge, *v.* osgoi, twyllo: *n.* cast, ystryw

doe, *n.* ewig

doff, *v.t.* tynnu, diosg

dog, *n.* ci

dogged, *a.* cyndyn, ystyfnig

doggerel, *a.* salw, crach; *n.* rhigwm

dogma, *n.* pwnc (athrawiaeth)

dogmatic, *a.* athrawiaethol: awdurdodol, pendant

dole, *n.* cyfran, dogn, cardod: *v.t.* dogni

doleful, *a.* trist, prudd, galarus

doll, *n.* dol, doli

dollar, *n.* doler

dolt, *n.* delff, penbwl, hurtyn

domain, *n.* tiriogaeth, maes

dome, *n.* cromen, cryndo

domestic, *a.* teuluaidd, cartrefol; gwâr, dof

domicile, *n.* anheddle, trigfa, cartref

dominate, *v.* arglwyddiaethu

domineer, *v.i.* tra-arglwyddiaethu, gormesu

dominion, *n.* rheolaeth; dominiwn, tiriogaeth

don, *v.t.* gwisgo (dilledyn)

donation, *n.* rhodd

donkey, *n.* asyn, mul

donor, *n.* rhoddwr

doom, *n.* dedfryd, barn, tynged: *v.t.* dedfrydu, tynghedu, collfarnu

door, *n.* drws, dôr, porth

dormant, *a.* ynghwsg; di-rym

dormitory, *n.* ystafell gysgu, hundy

dose, *n.* dogn: *v.t.* dogni

dot, *n.* dot: *v.* dotio

dotage, *n.* penwendid, plentynrwydd henaint

dote, *v.i.* dotio, gwirioni, ffoli, dylu

double, *a. & n.* dwbl: *v.* dyblu, plygu

doubt, *v.* amau, petruso: *n.* amheuaeth, (*pl.*) amheuon

dough, *n.* toes

doughty, *a.* pybyr, glew, dewr

dove, *n.* colomen

dowager, *n.* gweddw waddolog

dowdy, *a.* tlodaidd, salw, aflêr

down, *n.* manblu

down, *n.* gwaun, rhos, mynydd-dir

down, *adv.* i lawr, i waered, obry

dowry, *n.* gwaddol

doxology, *n.* mawlgan

doyen, *n.* aelod hynaf, hynafddyn

doze, *v.i.* hepian: *n.* cyntun

dozen, *n.* deuddeg, dwsin

drab, *a.* llwydwyn, llwydaidd, salw

draft, *n.* cynllun, drafft; archeb; mintai: *v.t.* tynnu

drag, *v.* llusgo: *n.* car llusg

dragon, *n.* draig

dragon-fly, *n.* gwas y neidr

dragoon, *n.* marchfilwr: *v.t.* erlid

drain, *n.* traen, carthffos

drain, *v.* treinio, sychu, disbyddu

drake, *n.* ceiliog hwyad, meilart

drama, *n.* drama

dramatic, *a.* dramatig

dramatist, *n.* dramodydd

drape, *v.t.* gwisgo

draper, n. dilledydd
drastic, a. cryf, llym, trwyadl
draught, n. llymaid, llwnc; gwynt, drafft
draw, v. tynnu, llusgo; denu
drawer, n. drâr, drôr
drawl, v. llusgo (geiriau)
dray, n. men bragwdas
dread, v. ofni, arswydo: n. ofn, arswyd
dream, v. breuddwydio: n. breu-ddwyd
dreary, a. llwm, diflas, digysur
dredge, v. glanhau
dregs, n.pl. gwaddod, gwaelodion, gwehilion
drench, v.t. gwlychu, trochi
dress, v. gwisgo, trwsio, cyweirio: n. gwisg
dribble, v. defnynnu, diferu, diferynnu
drift, n. rhediad; lluchfa: v. myned gyda'r llif
drill, v. drilio: n. dril
drink, v. yfed: n. diod, llymaid
drip, v. diferu, defnynnu: n. diferiad
dripping, a. diferol: n. toddion, saim
drive, v. gyrru; gwthio, ymlid
drivel, v.i. glafoerio, driflan, dreflu
drizzle, v.i. defnynnu, gwlitho: n. glaw mân
droll, a. digrif, ysmala
dromedary, n. dromedari
drone, n. gwenynen ormes; diogyn
droop, v.i. llaesu, ymollwng; nychu
drop, v. disgyn; diferu: n. diferyn, dafn
dropsy, n. dyfrglwyf, dropsi
dross, n. sorod, sothach
drought, n. tywydd sych, sychder, sychdwr
drove, n. gyr, diadell, cenfaint, mintai
drover, n. porthmon, gyrrwr
drown, v. boddi   [swrth
drowsy, a. cysglyd, marwaidd,
drub, v.t. baeddu, ffusto, cystwyo
drudge, n. slaf: v.i. slafio
drug, n. cyffur

druid, n. derwydd
drum, n. tabwrdd, drwm: v. tabyrddu
drunk, a. meddw, brwysg
drunkard, n. meddwyn
dry, a. sych, hysb, cras: v. sychu
dual, a. deuol
dub, v.t. urddo, galw, llysenwi; dwbio
dubious, a. amheus, petrus
duchess, n. duges
duchy, n. dugiaeth
duck, n. hwyad, hwyaden
duck, v. trochi; gostwng pen, gwyro
duckling, n. cyw hwyaden
ductile, a. hydyn, ystwyth, hyblyg
dude, n. coegyn
dudgeon, n. natur ddrwg, llid, dig
due, a. dyledus, dyladwy: n. dyled, haeddiant
duel, n. ornest
duet, duett, n. deuawd
duffer, n. hurtyn, penbwl, brebwl
duke, n. dug
dulcet, a. melys, hyfryd, pêr
dull, a. dwl, hurt; marwaidd; diflas; cymylog; pŵl: v. pylu, lleddfu
dumb, a. mud
dumbfound, v.t. syfrdanu, drysu
dummy, n. mudan; delw; ffug
dumpling, n. tymplen, poten
dumps, n.pl. iselder ysbryd
dun, v.t. gwasgu am dalu dyled
dunce, n. hurtyn, delff, penbwl
dunderhead, n. hurtyn, penbwl
dune, n. tywodfryn, tywyn
dung, n. tom, tail: v. teilo, tomi
dungeon, n. daeardy, daeargell
dunghill, n. tomen dail
duoglot n. dwyieithog
dupe, n. ehud: v.t. twyllo
duplicate, a. dyblyg: n. copi: v.t. dyblygu
duplicity, n. dichell, rhagrith
durable, a. parhaol, parhaus, cryf
duration, n. parhad
during, pr. yn ystod
dusk, n. cyfnos, gwyll
dusky, a. tywyll, croenddu, pygddu

dust, *n.* llwch: *v.t.* taenu neu sychu llwch
dutiful, *a.* ufudd, ufuddgar
duty, *n.* dyled, dyletswydd; toll
dwarf, *n.* cor, corrach: *a.* corachaidd
dwell, *v.i.* trigo, preswylio
dwelling, *n.* annedd, preswyl
dwindle, *v.i.* darfod, lleihau, dirywio
dye, *v.* lliwio, llifo: *n.* lliw, lliwur
dyer, *n.* lliwydd
dynamic, *a.* dynamig
dynamics, *n.* dynameg
dynasty, *n.* brenhinlin, teyrnach
dysentery, *n.* gwaedlif
dyspepsia, *n.* diffyg traul, camdreuliad

E

each, *a. & pn.* pob, pob un
eager, *a.* awyddus, awchus
eagle, *n.* eryr
ear, *n.* clust, dolen
ear, *n.* tywysen
earl, *n.* iarll
early, *a.* cynnar, bore, boreol: *adv.* yn fore
earn, *v.t.* ennill, elwa
earnest, *a.* difrif, difrifol, taer
earnest, *n.* ern, ernes: *v.* gwystl
earth, *n.* daear, pridd: *v.t.* priddo
earthly, *a.* daearol, ar wyneb daear
earthquake, *n.* daeargryn
ease, *n.* esmwythdra, esmwythyd; rhwyddineb: *v.* esmwytho
east, *n.* dwyrain
Easter, *n.pl.* y Pasg
eastern *a.* dwyreiniol
easy, *a.* hawdd, rhwydd, esmwyth
eat, *v.t.* bwyta, ysu
eaves, *n.pl.* bargod, bondo
ebb, *n.* trai: *v.i.* treio
ebullition, *n.* berw
eccentric, *a.* od, hynod; echreiddig
ecclesiastic, *a.* eglwysig: *n.* clerigwr
echo, *n.* atsain, carreg ateb: *v.* atseinio

eclipse, *n.* diffyg: *v.t.* cymylu, tywyllu
economic, *a.* economaidd
economical, *a.* cynnil, darbodus
economics, *n.* economeg
economize, *v.* cynilo
economy, *n.* cynildeb, darbodaeth
ecstacy, *n.* gorfoledd, gorawen, hwyl
eddy, *n.* trobwll: *v.* troi, chwyrlïo
edge, *n.* min, ymyl: *v.* minio, hogi
edible, *a.* bwytadwy
edict, *n.* cyhoeddiad, gorchymyn
edification, *n.* adeiladaeth
edifice, *n.* adail, adeilad
edify, *v.t.* adeiladu
edit, *v.t.* golygu, paratoi i'r wasg
edition, *n.* argraffiad
editor, *n.* golygydd
educate, *v.t.* addysgu
education, *n.* addysg
eduction, *n.* edwythiad
eel, *n.* llysywen
efface, *v.t.* dileu
effect, *n.* effaith; canlyniad: *v.t.* effeithio
effectiveness, *n.* effeithiolrwydd
effectual, *a.* effeithiol
effeminate, *a.* merchedaidd
effervesce, *v.i.* eferwi
effervescence, *n.* eferwad
effete, *a.* darfodedig, diffrwyth, dirym
efficacious, *a.* effeithiol
efficiency, *n.* effeithlonrwydd
efficient, *a.* effeithiol, cymwys
effigy, *n.* llun, delw
effort, *n.* ymdrech, ymgais
effrontery, *n.* digywilydd-dra
effulgence, *n.* disgleirdeb, llewyrch
effuse, *v.t.* tywallt; alledu
egg, *n.* wy
egg, *v.t.* annog, annos
egoism, *n.* myfïaeth, egoistiaeth
egregious, *a.* hynod, amlwg, dybryd
egress, *n.* mynediad allan; allanfa
eight, *a. & n.* wyth
eighteen, *a. & n.* deunaw, un deg wyth

eighty, *a. & n.* pedwar ugain, wyth deg

either, *a.* un o'r ddau: *c.* naill ai

ejaculate, *v.* saethu; gweiddi, ebychu

eject, *v.t.* bwrw allan; diarddel

eke, *v.t.* estyn allan; hel neu grafu

elaborate, *a.* llafurfawr, manwl

elaborate, *v.* manylu

elapse, *v.i.* myned heibio, treiglo

elastic, *a.* hydwyth, ystwyth

elation, *n.* gorawen

elbow, *n.* elin, penelin

elder, *n.* ysgaw

elder, *n.* henuriad, hynafgwr

elect, *v.t.* ethol, dewis: *a.* etholedig

election, *n.* etholiad; etholedigaeth

elector, *n.* etholwr

electorate, *n.* etholaeth

electricity, *n.* trydan

electrify, *v.t.* gwefreiddio, trydanu

elegant, *a.* cain, dillyn, lluniaidd

elegy, *n.* marwnad, galarnad

element, *n.* elfen; egwyddor

elephant, *n.* cawrfil, eliffant

elevate, *v.t.* dyrchafu

elevation, *n.* uchder, codiad; drychiad

eleven, *a. & n.* un ar ddeg

elf, (*elves*), *n.* ellyll, coblyn

elide, *v.t.* seingolli

eligible, *a.* cymwys, etholadwy, dewisol

eliminate, *v.t.* dileu, deol

elision, *n.* seingoll

ellipse, *n.* hirgylch, elips

elliptical, *a.* hirgrwn, eliptig

elm, *n.* llwyf, llwyfen

elocution, *n.* areithyddiaeth

elocutionist, *n.* adroddwr

elongate, *v.t.* hwyhau, estyn

eloquent, *a.* huawdl

else, *adv.* arall, amgen, pe amgen

elsewhere, *adv.* mewn lle arall

elucidate, *v.t.* goleuo, egluro

elude, *v.t.* osgoi

elusive, *a.* di-ddal, gwibiog, ansafadwy

elysium, *n.* gwynfa, gwynfyd, paradwys

emaciate, *v.t.* teneuo, culhau, curio

emanate, *v.i.* deillio, tarddu, llifo

emancipate, *v.t.* rhyddfreinio, rhyddhau

emasculate, *v.t.* disbaddu

embalm, *v.t.* pararogli corff

embankment, *n.* clawdd, cob

embargo, *n.* gwaharddiad i hwylio

embark, *v.* myned neu osod ar long; hwylio

embarrass, *v.t.* rhwystro, drysu

embassy, *n.* llysgenhadaeth

embellish, *v.t.* addurno, trwsio, prydferthu

embers, *n.pl.* marwor, marwydos

embezzle, *v.t.* celcio, darnguddio, lladrata

embitter, *v.t.* chwerwi

emblazon, *v.t.* addurno, gwychu

emblem, *n.* arwyddlun

embody, *v.t.* corffori

emboss, *v.t.* boglynnu

embrace, *v.t.* cofleidio

embrocate, *v.t.* iro, eneinio

embroider, *v.t.* brodio

embroil, *v.t.* tynnu i ymrafael

embryo, *n.* cynelwad, embryo

emend, *v.t.* cywiro, diwygio

emerald, *n.* emrallt

emerge, *v.i.* dyfod allan, dyfod i'r golwg

emergency, *n.* cyfyngder, taro

emetic, *a.* yn codi cyfog: *n.* cyfoglyn

emigrate, *v.i.* ymfudo, mudo

eminent, *a.* uchel, enwog, clodfawr

emissary, *n.* cennad

emit, *v.t.* rhoddi neu fwrw allan

emollient, *a.* meddalhaol: *n.* meddalydd

emolument, *n.* tâl, cyflog, elw, ennill

emotion, *n.* cyffro, teimlad, emosiwn

emperor, *n.* ymerawdwr, ymherodr

emphasis, *n.* pwys, pwyslais

emphasize, *v.t.* pwysleisio

emphatic, *a.* pwysleisiol, pendant

empire, *n.* ymerodraeth

empirical, *a.* empeiraidd

empiricism, *n.* empeiraeth

employ, *v.t.* cyflogi; arfer, defnydd-io: *n.* gwasanaeth

employment, *n.* gwaith, gorchwyl

empower, *v.t.* awdurdodi, galluogi

empress, *n.* ymerodres

empty, *a.* gwag, coeg: *v.* gwagu, arllwys

emulate, *v.t.* ymgystadlu â; efel-ychu

enable, *v.t.* galluogi

enact, *v.t.* deddfu, ordeinio; cyf-lawni

enamour, *v.t.* ennyn serch, ymserchu

encamp, *v.* gwersyllu

enchant, *v.t.* swyno, cyfareddu, hudo, rheibio

enclose, *v.t.* cau i mewn, amgau

enclosure, *n.* lle caeëdig

encompass, *v.t.* amgylchu, cylchynu

encounter, *v.t.* cyfarfod, taro ar: *n.* ymgyfarfod, brwydr

encourage, *v.t.* cefnogi, calonogi, annog

encouragement, *n.* cefnogaeth, calondid

encroach, *v.i.* cyfyngu, gormesu

encumber, *v.t.* llesteirio, beichio

encyclopaedia, *n.* gwyddoniadur

end, *n.* diwedd, diben: *v.* diweddu, dibennu

endanger, *v.t.* peryglu, enbydu

endear, *v.t.* anwylo

endeavour, *v.i.* ymdrechu: *n.* ymdrech

endorse, *v.t.* cefnogi, ategu

endow, *v.t.* gwaddoli, cynys-gaeddu, donio

endowment, *n.* gwaddol, cynhys-gaeth

endue, *v.t.* gwisgo, donio, cynys-gaeddu

endurance, *n.* dioddefgarwch

endure, *v.* parhau; dioddef, goddef, ymaros

enemy, *n.* gelyn

energetic, *a.* grymus, egnïol

energy, *n.* ynni, egni

enervate, *v.t.* gwanhau, gwanychu

enfeeble, *v.t.* eiddilo, gwanychu

enforce, *v.t.* rhoi mewn grym; gorfodi

enfranchise, *v.t.* breinio; rhyddhau

engage, *v.* ymrwymo, dyweddïo; cyflogi

engender, *v.t.* cenhedlu; magu; peri

engine, *n.* peiriant

engineer, *n.* peiriannydd

English, *a.* Saesneg; Seisnig: *n.* Saesneg

Englishman, (*-men*), *n.* Sais (*pl.* Saeson)

engrain, *v.t.* dwfnliwio; greddfu

engrave, *v.t.* ysgythru

engraving, *n.* ysgythrad

engulf, *v.t.* llyncu

enhance, *v.* chwanegu, mwyhau, chwyddo

enjoin, *v.t.* siarsio, gorchymyn; erchi

enjoy, *v.t.* mwynhau; meddu

enjoyment, *n.* mwynhad

enkindle, *v.t.* ennyn

enlarge, *v.t.* ehangu, helaethu

enlighten, *v.t.* goleuo; hysbysu

enlist, *v.* ymrestru, listio; ennill

enliven, *v.t.* bywiogi; sirioli

enmity, *n.* gelyniaeth, digasedd

ennoble, *v.t.* urddasu, urddasoli, urddo

ennui, *n.* diflastod   [erder

enormity, *n.* anfadrwydd, ysgel-

enormous, *a.* dirfawr, anferth

enough, *a.*, *n.* & *adv.* digon

enquire, *v.* ymofyn, ymholi, gofyn, holi

enrage, *v.t.* ffyrnigo, cynddeiriogi

enrich, *v.t.* cyfoethogi

enrol, -ll, *v.t.* rhestru, cofrestru

ensign, *n.* lluman, baner; llumanwr

enslave, *v.t.* caethiwo, dwyn yn gaeth

ensue, *v.i.* dilyn, canlyn

ensure, *v.t.* diogelu, cadarnhau

entail, *v.t.* gorfodi, gofyn

entangle, *v.t.* drysu, maglu, rhwydo

enter, *v.* myned i mewn, treiddio; cofnodi

enterprise, *n.* anturiaeth
entertain, *v.t.* lletya; difyrru; coleddu
entertainment, *n.* difyrrwch, adloniant
enthrone, *v.t.* gorseddu
enthusiasm, *n.* brwdfrydedd, aidd
enthusiastic, *a.* brwdfrydig, eiddgar
entice, *v.* hudo, denu, llithio
entire, *a.* cyfa, cyfan, cyflawn
entity, *n.* hanfod, endid
entomb, *v.t.* claddu
entrails, *n.pl.* coluddion, perfedd
entrance, *n.* mynediad, mynedfa
entrance, *v.t.* taflu i berlewyg
entreat, *v.t.* erfyn, ymbil, deisyf
entrust, *v.t.* ymddiried
entry, *n.* mynediad, mynedfa; cofnodiad
entwine, *v.t.* cyfrodeddu, cordeddu
enumerate, *v.t.* cyfrif, rhifo, nodi
enunciate, *v.t.* datgan, mynegi; seinio
envelop, *v.t.* amgáu
envelope, *n.* amlen
envious, *a.* cofigennus
environment, *n.* amgylchoedd
envoy, *n.* cennad, negesydd
envy, *n.* cenfigen: *v.t.* cenfigennu
ephemeral, *a.* undydd, byrhoedlog
epic, *a.* arwraidd: *n.* arwrgerdd
epidemic, *a.* heintus: *n.* haint
epilepsy, *n.* yr haint digwydd
episcopal, *a.* esgobol, esgobaidd
episcopalian, *a.* esgobyddol: *n.* esgobydd
episcopate, *n.* esgobaeth
episode, *n.* digwyddiad
epistle, *n.* epistol, llythyr
epitaph, *n.* beddargraff
epithet, *n.* ansoddair
epitome, *n.* crynodeb
epoch, *n.* cyfnod
equable, *a.* gwastad, cyfartal
equal, *a.* cyfartal: *n.* cydradd: *v.t.* bod yn gyfartal
equanimity *n.* tawelwch
equate, *v.t.* cyfartalu, cymharu
equation, *n.* hafaliad

equator, *n.* y cyhydedd
equestrian, *a.* marchogol: *n.* marchog
equilibrium, *n.* cydbwysedd, cymantoledd
equine, *n.* marchol
equinox, *n.* cyhydedd dydd a nos, cyhydnos
equip, *v.t.* taclu, paratoi, cymhwyso
equipoise *n.* cydbwysedd
equitable, *a.* teg, uniawn, cyfiawn
equity, *n.* cyfiawnder, uniondeb, tegwch
equivalent, *a.* cyfwerth, cywerth
equivocal, *a.* amwys
equivocate, *v.i.* celwyddo
era, *n.* cyfnod
eradicate, *v.t.* diwreiddio, dadwreiddio
erase, *v.t.* dileu, rhwbio allan
ere, *pr.* cyn
erect, *a.* syth, unionsyth: *v.t.* codi, adeiladu
ermine, *n.* carlwm; ermyn
erode, *v.* ysu, treulio
erotic, *a.* serchol, nwydol
err, *v.i.* cyfeiliorni
errand, *n.* neges, cenadwri
erratic, *a.* gwibiog, ansefydlog, od
erroneous, *a.* cyfeiliornus
error, *n.* cyfeiliornad, camgymeriad, bai, gwall
erudite, *a.* dysgedig   [iant
eruption, *n.* toriad allan; tardd-
erysipelas, *n.* tân iddwf, fflamwydden
escapade, *n.* pranc, direidi
escape, *v.* dianc, osgoi: *n.* dihangfa
eschew, *v.t.* gochel, osgoi, ymochel rhag
escort, *v.t.* hebrwng: *n.* gosgordd
escutcheon, *n.* pais arfau, arfbais
especial, *a.* arbennig, neilltuol
espionage, *n.* ysbïaeth
esplanade, *n.* rhodfa
espouse, *v.t.* dyweddïo, priodi; noddi, pleidio, cefnogi
espy, *v.* canfod, ysbïo, gwylio
esquire, *n.* yswain
essay, *n.* ymgais; traethawd, ysgrif

essay, *v.t.* profi, ymgeisio

essence, *n.* hanfod; nodd; naws

essential, *a.* hanfodol

establish, *v.t.* sefydlu, cadarnhau

estate, *n.* etifeddiaeth, ystad

esteem, *v.t.* parchu; cyfrif: *n.* parch, bri

estimate, *v.t.* amcangyfrif, mesuroni: *n.* amcangyfrif, mesuroniad

estrange, *v.t.* dieithrio

estuary, *n.* aber

eternal, *a.* tragwyddol, bythol

eternity, *n.* tragwyddoldeb

ether, *n.* ether

ethics, *n.* moeseg

etiquette, *n.* defod, moesgarwch

etymology, *n.* geirdarddiad

eucharist, *n.* cymun, cymundeb

eulogy, *n.* canmoliaeth, molawd

euphony, *n.* perseinedd

evacuate, *v.t.* ymgilio, ymadael (â)

evade, *v.t.* gochelyd, osgoi

evanescent, *a.* diflanedig, darfodedig

evangelical, *a.* efengylaidd

evangelist, *n.* efengylydd

evangelize, *v.t.* efengylu

evaporate, *v.* ymageru, anweddu

evasion, *n.* osgoad, gocheliad

eve, *n.* min nos, noswyl

even, *a.* gwastad, cydwastad, cyfartal: *adv.* hyd yn oed

evening, *n.* hwyr, noswaith

evensong, *n.* prynhawnol weddi, gosber

event, *n.* digwyddiad; canlyniad

ever, *adv.* bob amser, erioed, byth

everlasting, *a.* tragwyddol, bythol

evermore, *adv.* byth, byth bythoedd

every, *a.* pob

evict, *v.t.* troi allan, didyo

evidence, *n.* tystiolaeth, prawf

evident, *a.* amlwg, golau, eglur

evil, *a.* drwg, drygionus: *n.* drwg, drygioni

evince, *v.t.* dangos, amlygu

eviscerate, *v.t.* diberfeddu

evoke, *v.t.* galw neu dynnu allan; gwysio

evolution, *n.* datblygiad, esblygiad; tro

evolve, *v.* datblygu; ymagor

ewe, *n.* dafad, mamog

ex-, *px.* allan o, wedi bod, gynt, cyn-

exact, *a.* manwl, cywir, union

exact, *v.t.* hawlio, mynnu, codi

exaggerate, *v.t.* chwyddo, gorliwio

exalt, *v.t.* dyrchafu, codi; mawrygu

examine, *v.t.* holi, arholi, profi, archwilio

example, *n.* esiampl, enghraifft

exasperate, *v.t.* cyffroi, llidio, cythruddo

excavate, *v.t.* cloddio

exceed, *v.t.* bod yn fwy na, myned dros

excel, *v.* rhagori

excellent, *a.* rhagorol, ardderchog, godidog, campus

except, *v.t.* eithrio: *pr.* ond, oddieithr: *c.* oddieithr

exception, *n.* eithriad

excerpt, *n.* dyfyniad, detholiad

excess, *n.* gormod, gormodedd

exchange, *v.t.* cyfnewid, ffeirio: *n.* cyfnewid, cyfnewidfa

exchequer, *n.* trysorlys; cyllid

excise, *n.* toll: *v.t.* gosod toll

excite, *v.t.* cynhyrfu, cyffroi, cymell

exclaim, *v.t.* llefain, gweiddi, bloeddio

exclamation, *n.* llef, gwaedd

exclude, *v.t.* cau allan, bwrw allan

exclusion, *n.* gwaharddiad, gwrthodiad

excommunicate, *v.t.* ysgymuno

excrement, *n.* carth, tom, baw

excrete, *v.t.* ysgarthu

excruciate, *v.t.* arteithio, dirdynnu

exculpate, *v.t.* difeio, dieuogi, esgusodi

excursion, *n.* gwibdaith, pleserdaith

excuse, *v.t.* esgusodi: *n.* esgus, esgusawd

execrate, *v.t.* melltithio, rhegi, cablu, ffieiddio

execute, *v.t.* cyflawni; dienyddio

executive, *a.* gweithiol, gweinyddol

executor, *n.* ysgutor

exegesis, *n.* esboniad, esboniadaeth

exemplar, *n.* esiampl, cynllun, patrwm

exemplify, *v.t.* egluro, dangos

exempt, *a.* rhydd, esgusodol: *v.t.* e sgusodi

exercise, *n.* ymarfer, ymarferiad: *v.* ymarfer

exert, *v.t.* ymegnïo; gweithredu

exhale, *v.* anadlu allan

exhaust, *v.t.* gwacáu, hysbyddu; lluddedu

exhaustion, *n.* gwacâd; lludded

exhibit, *v.t.* dangos, arddangos

exhibition, *n.* arddangosfa; ysgoloriaeth

exhilarate, *v.t.* llonni, sirioli, bywiogi

exhort, *v.t.* cynghori, annog, cymell

exhume, *v.t.* dadgladdu

exigence, -cy, *n.* angen, gofyn, galwad

exiguous, *a.* bychan, eiddil, main, prin   [alltudio

exile, *n.* alltud; alltudiaeth: *v.t.*

exist, *v.i.* bod, bodoli

exit, *n.* mynediad allan; allanfa

exodus, *n.* mynediad allan, ymadawiad

exonerate, *v.t.* esgusodi, difeio

exorbitant, *a.* afresymol, gormodol

exorcise, *v.t.* bwrw allan gythreuliaid

exotic, *a.* estron, tramor

expand, *v.* lledu, ymagor, datblygu

expanse, *n.* ehangder; ymlediad

expansion, *n.* ymlediad

expatiate, *v.i.* ymhelaethu

expatriate, *v.t.* alltudio

expect, *v.* disgwyl

expectation, *n.* disgwyliad

expectorate, *v.t.* poeri

expedient, *a.* manteisiol, buddiol: *n.* dyfais

expedite, *v.t.* hyrwyddo, hwyluso

expedition, *n.* cyflymdra; ymgyrch

expeditious, *a.* hyrwydd, hwylus

expel, *v.t.* bwrw allan, deol, diarddel

expend, *v.t.* talu, gwario, treulio

expense, *n.* traul, cost

experience, *n.* profiad: *v.t.* profi

experiment, *n.* arbrawf: *v.i.* arbrofi

expert, *a.* cyfarwydd, hyfedr

expiate, *v.t.* gwneuthur iawn; dioddef cosb

expire, *v.* anadlu allan; darfod, marw

explain, *v.t.* egluro, esbonio

explanation, *n.* eglurhad, esboniad

expletive, *n.* gair llanw, gair segur

explicit *a.* eglur, manwl, pendant

explode, *v.* ffrwydro, chwalu

exploit, *n.* camp, gorchest: *v.t.* gweithio, gwneud elw o, ymelwa ar

explore, *v.t.* chwilio, archwilio

explosion, *n.* ffrwydriad; tanchwa

exponent, *n.* esboniwr, dehonglwr

export, *v.t.* allforio: *n.* allfor

expose, *v.t.* arddangos, dinoethi; peryglu

exposition, *n.* esboniad; arddangosiad

expositor, *n.* esboniwr

expostulate, *v.i.* ymliw, cyfymliw

expound, *v.t.* esbonio

express, *v.t.* mynegi, datgan: *a.* penodol, pendant; cyflym

expression, *n.* ymadrodd; mynegiant

expulsion, *n.* troad allan, diarddeliad

expunge, *v.t.* dileu, croesi allan

expurgate, *v.t.* coethi, puro, glanhau

exquisite, *a.* odiaeth, rhagorol; coeth

extant, *a.* yn bod

extempore, *adv. & a.* byrfyfyr, o'r frest

extend, *v.* estyn, ymestyn; ehangu

extent, *n.* ehangder, maint, hyd, mesur

extenuate, *v.t.* lleihau, lleddfu; esgusodi

exterior, *a.* allanol: *n.* tu allan

exterminate, *v.t.* difodi, dileu

external, *a.* allanol

extinct, *a.* wedi diffodd, wedi darfod, diflanedig

extinguish, *v.t.* diffodd; diddymu, dileu

extirpate, *v.t.* distrywio, difodi

extol, *v.t.* moli, moliannu, clodfori

extort, *v.t.* cribddeilio, gwasgu

extra, *a.* ychwanegol: *adv.* tu hwnt, dros ben: *n.* peth dros ben, ychwanegiad

extract, *v.t.* tynnu, gwasgu: *n.* dyfyniad; trwyth

extraneous, *a.* allanol, amherthynol

extraordinary, *a.* hynod, anghyffredin

extravagant, *a.* gwastraffus; gwyllt

extreme, *a.* i'r eithaf, eithafol: *n.* eithaf

extremity, *n.* pen, eithaf; cyfyngder

extricate, *v.t.* rhyddhau, dadfaglu

exuberant, *a.* toreithiog, afieithus

exude, *v.* chwysu

exult, *v.i.* gorfoleddu, ymffrostio

eye, *n.* llygad; crau; dolen: *v.t.* llygadu

F

fable, *n.* chwedl, dameg; anwiredd

fabric, *n.* adail, adeilad, defnydd

fabricate, *v.t.* llunio, dyfeisio, ffugio

fabulous, *a.* chwedlonol; anhygoel

façade, *n.* wyneb adeilad

face, *n.* wyneb, wynepryd: *v.* wynebu

facetious, *a.* cellweirus, ffraeth

facile, *a.* hawdd, hwylus, rhwydd

facilitate, *v.t.* hwyluso, hyrwyddo

facility, *n.* hwylustod, rhwyddineb

fact, *n.* gweithred, ffaith

faction, *n.* plaid, clymblaid

factious, *a.* cynhennus

factor, *n.* goruchwyliwr; gweithredydd

factory, *n.* gweithfa, ffatri

faculty, *n.* cynneddf; cyfadran; trwydded

fad, *n.* mympwy, chwilen

fade, *v.* diflannu, gwywo; colli ei liw

fag, *v.* slafio, ymlâdd, baeddu: *n.* caledwaith

faggot, *n.* ffagod, ffasgell

fail, *v.i.* ffaelu, methu, pallu, diffygio   [iant

failure, *n.* methiant, pall, aflwydd-

faint, *a.* gwan, diffygiol: *v.i.* diffygio, llewygu: *n.* llewyg

fair, *n.* ffair

fair, *a.* teg, glân; gweddol, symol

fairy, *n.* un o'r tylwyth teg

faith, *n.* ffydd, cred, coel

faithful, *a.* ffyddlon, cywir

falcon, *n.* hebog, curyll

fall, *v.i.* cwympo, syrthio: *n.* cwymp

fallacy, *n.* cyfeiliornad, geudyb, hoced

fallible, *a.* ffaeledig

fallow, *n.* braenar: *v.t.* braenaru

false, *a.* gau, ffug, ffals, twyllodrus

falsehood, *n.* anwiredd, celwydd

falsify, *v.t.* anwireddu, siomi

falter, *v.* petruso, methu, pallu

fame, *n.* enwogrwydd, clod, bri

familiar, *a.* cynefin, cyfarwydd; eofn

family, *n.* teulu, tylwyth

famine, *n.* newyn

famish, *v.* newynu

famous, *a.* enwog, hyglod

fan, *n.* gwyntyll: *v.t.* gwyntyllio, chwythu

fanatic, *n.* penboethyn

fanaticism, *n.* penboethni, ffanatigiaeth

fancy, *n.* dychymyg, ffansi: *v.t.* dychmygu, ffansïo

fane, *n.* teml, eglwys (bardd.)

fang, *n.* ysgithr, dant, pig, blaen

fantastic, *a.* penchwiban, mympwyol

far, *a. & adv.* pell

farce, *n.* ffars, rhith

fare, *n.* cost, pris; ymborth: *v.i.* bod, byw

farewell, *i.* yn iach, ffarwel: *n.* ffarwel

farm, *n.* fferm, amaethdy: *v.t.* amaethu, ffarmio

farmer, *n.* amaethwr, ffarmwr

farrier, *n.* ffarier, meddyg ani-feiliaid

farthing, *n.* ffyrling

fascinate, *v.t.* rheibio, hudo, swyno

fashion, *n.* llun, ffasiwn: *v.t.* llunio

fast, *v.i.* ymprydio: *n.* ympryd

fast, *a.* tyn, sownd; buan, cyflym, clau

fasten, *v.* sicrhau, cau, clymu, ffasno

fastidious, *a.* cysetlyd, dicra, misi

fastness, *n.* amddiffynfa, lloches, caer

fat, *a.* tew, bras: *n.* braster, gwêr, bloneg

fatal, *a.* angheuol, marwol; an-dwyol

fatality, *n.* trychineb, marwolaeth

fate, *n.* tynged, tynghedfen, rhan: *v.t.* tynghedu

father, *n.* tad: *v.t.* tadogi

fathom, *n.* gwryd: *v.t.* plymio

fatigue, *n.* lludded: *v.t.* lluddedu

fatuous, *a.* ynfyd, disynnwyr

fault, *n.* bai, diffyg, nam, anaf

favour, *n.* ffafr, cymwynas: plaid: *v.t.* ffafrio

favourite, *a.* cu, hoff: *n.* ffafryn

fawn, *n.* elain: *v.i.* llydnu: *a.* llwyd

fawn, *v.i.* cynffonna, ffalsio, gwen-ieithio

fear, *n.* ofn: *v.* ofni

fearful, *a.* ofnus; ofnadwy

feasible, *a.* dichonadwy

feast, *n.* gwledd, ffest; gŵyl: *v.* gwledda

feat, *n.* camp, gorchest

feather, *n.* pluen, plufyn: *v.t.* pluo, plufio; dibluo

feature, *n.* arwedd, golygwedd, nodwedd

February, *n.* Chwefror

fecund, *a.* epilgar, toreithiog, hiliog

federal, *a.* cynghreiriol, ffederal

federate, *v.* uno, cynghreirio

fee, *n.* gwobr, tâl, cyflog: *v.t.* talu

feeble, *a.* gwan, eiddil

feed, *v.* porthi, ymborthi, bwydo

feel, *v.* teimlo, clywed, profi

feign, *v.* cymryd arno, ffugio

felicity, *n.* dedwyddwch, ded-wyddyd

feline, *n.* fel cath, cathaidd

fell, *a.* creulon, ysgeler, erch

fellow, *n.* cymar; cymrawd; dyn, creadur: *px.* cyd-

felon, *n.* drwgweithredwr

female, *a. & n.* benyw

feminine, *a.* benywaidd, benywol

fen, *n.* cors, morfa

fence, *n.* clawdd, ffens: *v.* cau, amgáu

fend, *v.* cadw draw; ymdaro

ferment, *n.* eples, gwaith, berw: *v.* gweithio, eplesu

fern, *n.* rhedynen, rhedyn

ferocious, *a.* ffyrnig, gwyllt, milain

ferret, *n.* ffured: *v.t.* ffuredu, chwilota

ferry, *n.* porth, fferi: *v.* cludo dros

fertile, *a.* ffrwythlon, toreithiog

fertilize, *v.* ffrwythloni, gwrteithio

fervent, *a.* brwd, gwresog, tanbaid, taer

fervid, *a.* brwd, gwresog, hwyliog

fester, *v.i.* crawni, gori, crynhoi

festival, *n.* gŵyl, dydd gŵyl

festive, *a.* gwleddol, llawen

fetch, *v.t.* cyrchu, dwyn, nôl

fete, *n.* gŵyl, miri: *v.i.* gwledda

fetid, *a.* drewllyd

fetter, *n.* llyffethair, hual: *v.t.* llyffetheirio

fettle, *n.* graen, cyflwr

feud, *n.* cynnen

feudal, *a.* ffiwdal

fever, *n.* twymyn, clefyd, gwres

few, *a.* ychydig, prin, anaml

fib, *n.* anwiredd, celwydd

fibre, *n.* edefyn, ffibr

fickle, *a.* anwadal, oriog, gwamal

fiction, *n.* ffug, ffugchwedlau

fictitious, *a.* ffug, ffugiol

fiddle, *n.* ffidil, crwth: *v.i.* ffidlo

fidelity, *n.* ffyddlondeb, cywirdeb

fidget, *v.t.* ffwdanu, gwingo

fiduciary, *a.* ymddiriedol

field, *n.* cae, maes

fiend, *n.* cythraul, ellyll, ysbryd drwg

fierce, *a.* ffyrnig, milain; tanbaid

fiery, *a.* tanllyd, tanbaid

fife, *n.* chwibanogl

fifteen, *a.* & *n.* pymtheg

fifty, *a.* & *n.* hanner cant, deg a deugain

fig. *n.* ffigysen

fight, *v.* ymladd, cwffio, rhyfela: *n.* ymladdfa, brwydr

figment, *n.* ffug, dyfais, dychymyg

figurative, *a.* ffigurol, cyffelybiaethol

figure, *n.* ffigur, llun, ffurf: *v.* cyfrif; llunio; ymddangos

filch, *v.i.* lladrata, dwyn

file, *n.* ffeil: *v.t.* ffeilio

file, *n.* rhes, rhenc; ffeil: *v.i.* ffeilio

filial, *a.* mabol, mabaidd

fill, *v.* llenwi: *n.* llonaid, gwala

fillet, *n.* ffunen; tafell, golwyth

fillip, *n.* symbyliad: *v.* symbylu

filly, *n.* eboles

film, *n.* pilen, caenen, rhuchen, ffilm

filter, *n.* hidl, hidlydd: *v.* hidlo, ffiltro

filth, *n.* brynti, budreddi, baw, tom

fin, *n.* adain, asgell

final, *a.* diwethaf, terfynol, olaf

finance, *n.* cyllid

find, *v.t.* canfod, cael: *n.* darganfyddiad, caffaeliad

fine, *a.* main; mân; gwych; braf: *v.t.* coethi

fine, *n.* dirwy: *v.t.* dirwyo

finesse, *n.* ystryw, dichell

finger, *n.* bys: *v.t.* bysio, bodio

finical, -icking, *a.* cymhenllyd, cysetlyd

finish, *v.* diweddu, gorffen: *n.* diwedd; gorffeniad

finite, *a.* meidrol

fir, *n.* ffynidwydden

fire, *n.* tân: *v.* tanio

firm, *n.* masnachdy, cwmni, ffyrm

firm, *a.* cadarn, sad: *v.* caledu, sadio

firmament, *n.* ffurfafen

first, *a.* cyntaf, blaenaf: *adv.* yn gyntaf

fiscal, *a.* cyllidol

fish, *n.* pysgodyn, pysgod: *v.* pysgota

fisherman, *n.* pysgodwr, pysgotwr

fishing-rod *n.* genwair, gwialen bysgota

fissure, *n.* hollt, agen: *v.* hollti, agennu

fist, *n.* dwrn

fit, *n.* ffit, gwasgfa, haint

fit, *a.* ffit, addas, cymwys, gweddus; *v.* ffitio: *n.* ffit

five, *a.* pum: *n.* pump

fix, *v.* sicrhau, sefydlu, gosod: *n.* cyfyngder

fizz, *v.i.* sïo, ffrïo

flabbergast, *v.t.* synnu, syfrdanu

flabby, *a.* llipa, meddal, masw

flaccid, *a.* llipa, gwyw, llaes

flag, *n.* llechfaen, fflag: *v.t.* fflagio

flag, *v.i.* llesgáu, llaesu, diffygio

flag, *n.* lluman, baner

flagellate, *v.t.* fflangellu, ffrewyllu

flagon, *n.* fflagen, ffiol, costrel

flagrant, *a.* amlwg, dybryd, gwarthus

flail, *n.* ffust

flake, *n.* tafell, caenen; pluen (eira)

flame, *n.* fflam: *v.i.* fflamio, ffaglu

flank, *n.* tenewyn, ystlys, ochr: *v.* ymylu, ystlysu

flannel, *n.* gwlanen

flap, *n.* llabed, fflap: *v.* fflapio

flare, *v.* fflachio, ffaglu: *n.* fflach, ffagl

flash, *v.* fflachio, melltennu: *n.* fflach

flask, *n.* costrel, fflasg; corn pylor

flat, *a.* & *n.* fflat, gwastad: *v.* fflatio

flatter, *v.t.* gwenieithio, truthio

flattery, *n.* gweniaith, truth

flatulence, *n.* gwynt (yn y cylla)

flaunt, *v.* chwifio, fflawntio, rhodresa

flavour, *n.* blas, sawr: *v.t.* blasu

flaw, *n.* crac, bai, diffyg, nam

flax, *n.* llin

flay, *v.t.* blingo

flea, *n.* chwannen

fledge, *v.t.* magu plu

flee, *v.* ffoi, cilio, dianc, diflannu

fleece, *n.* cnu: *v.t.* cneifio; ysbeilio

fleet, *n.* llynges, fflyd

fleet, *a.* cyflym, buan

flesh, *n.* cig, cnawd; croen noeth

flexible, *a.* hyblyg, ystwyth

flick, *v.t.* cyffwrdd â blaen chwip, cnithio

flight, *n.* hedfa; ffo, ffoedigaeth

flighty, *a.* gwamal, penchwiban

flimsy, *a.* masw, gwan, gwael, bregus

flinch, *v.i.* cilio yn ôl, gwingo, llwfrhau

fling, *v.t.* taflu, bwrw, lluchio: *n.* rhwysg

flint, *n.* callestr, carreg dân

flip, *v.* cnithio: *n.* cnith

flippant, *a.* tafodrydd, ysgafn, gwamal

flirt, *v.* cellwair caru

flit, *v.i.* symud, mudo; gwibio

flitch, *n.* hanerob, ystlys mochyn

float, *v.* nofio; *n.* cart, trol

flock, *n.* diadell, praidd: *v.i.* heidio

flog, *v.t.* fflangellu, ffrewyllu, chwipio

flood, *n.* llif, dilyw, cenllif: *v.* llifo, gorlifo

floor, *n.* llawr: *v.t.* llorio

floral, *a.* blodeuol

florid, *a.* blodeuog, gorwych; gwritgoch

florin, *n.* deuswllt

floss, *n.* manblu, sidanblu

flounce, *v.i.* swalpio, ysboncio: *n.* llam, ysbonc

flounder, *n.* llythïen

flounder, *v.i.* ymdrybaeddu, swalpio, ffwndro

flour, *n.* blawd, can

flourish, *v.* blodeuo; ffynnu; ysgwyd

flout, *v.* gwawdio, wfftio, diystyru

flow, *v.i.* llifo, llifeirio: *n.* llif, llanw

flower, *n.* blodeuyn, blodyn: *v.i.* blodeuo

fluctuate, *v.i.* codi a gostwng, amrywio, anwadalu

flue, *n.* pibell simnai, ffliw

fluent, *a.* rhwydd, llithrig, rhugl

fluff, *n.* blewiach, fflwcs

fluid, *a.* hylif, gwlyb: *n.* hylif, gwlybwr

fluke, *n.* llythïen; ffliwc, lwc

flummery, *n.* llymru; truth

flunkey, *n.* gwas gŵr bonheddig; cynffonnwr

flurry, *n.* cyffro, ffwdan

flush, *a.* llawn, cydwastad, cyfwyneb

flush, *v.* golchi, carthu; gwrido: *n.* gwrid

fluster, *v.* ffwdanu, rhusio: *n.* ffwdan

flute, *n.* chwibanogl, ffliwt

flutter, *v.* curo, dychlamu, siffrwd

fly, *n.* gwybedyn, cleren, pryf

fly, *v.* ehedeg, ehedfan; ffoi. —**fly into a passion,** ymwylltio, gwylltu

foal, *n.* ebol, eboles: *v.* bwrw ebol

foam, *n.* ewyn: *v.i.* malu ewyn, ewynnu

focus, *n.* canolbwynt, ffôc: *v.* canoli

fodder, *n.* ebran, gogor: *v.t.* ebrannu

foe, *n.* gelyn

fog, *n.* niwl

fogy, -gey, *n.* cono

foible, *n.* gwendid, y man gwan

foil, *v.t.* rhwystro, siomi, trechu

foist, *v.t.* gwthio ar (drwy ddichell)

fold, *n.* corlan, ffald: *v.t.* corlannu

fold, *v.* plygu: *n.* plyg

foliage, *n.* dail

folio, *n.* dalen, dalen unplyg

folk, folks, *n.pl.* pobl, dynion

folklore, *n.* llên gwerin

follow, *v.* canlyn, dilyn

folly, *n.* ffolineb, ynfydrwydd

foment, *v.t.* cyffroi, ennyn

fomentation, *n.* powltis

fond, *a.* hoff, annwyl

fondle, *v.t.* anwylo, anwesu

font, *n.* bedyddfaen

food, *n.* bwyd, ymborth, lluniaeth

fool, *n.* ffŵl, ynfytyn: *v.* castio; ofera

foolhardy, *a.* rhyfygus

foolish, *a.* ffôl, ynfyd, annoeth, angall

foot, (*feet*) *n.* troed; troedfedd: *v.* troedio

fop, *n.* coegyn, ysgogyn

for, *pr.* i, at, am, dros, yn lle, rhag: *c.* canys, oblegid

forage, *n.* gogor, ebran, porthiant: *v.* herwa

forasmuch, *c.* yn gymaint

forbear, *v.* ymatal, peidio; ymaros

forbid, *v.t.* gwahardd, gwarafun, gomedd

force, *n.* grym; trais, gorfod: llu: *v.t.* gorfodi

forceps, *n.* gefel fain

forcible, *a.* grymus; gorfodol

ford, *n.* rhyd: *v.t.* rhydio

fore, *a.* blaen, blaenaf: *adv.* ymlaen

forebode, *v.t.* rhagargoeli, rhag-arwyddo

forecast, *v.t.* rhagfynegi: *n.* rhag-fynegiad

forecastle, *n.* caban blaen, fforcas

forefather, *n.* cyndad

forehead, *n.* talcen

foreign, *a.* estronol, tramor

forenoon, *n.* bore

forensic, *a.* cyfreithiol

forerunner, *n.* rhagredegydd

foresee, *v.t.* rhagweled, rhagwybod

forest, *n.* coedwig, fforest: *v.t.* fforestu

forestall, *v.t.* achub y blaen

foretaste, *n.* blaenbrawf, rhag-brawf

foretell, *v.t.* rhagfynegi

forethought, *n.* darbodaeth, rhag-fwriad

forfeit, *n.* fforffed: *v.t.* fforffedu, colli

forge, *n.* gefail, morthwylfa: *v.* morthwylio, gyrru; ffugio

forget, *v.t.* anghofio

forgive, *v.t.* maddau

forgiveness, *n.* maddeuant

forgo, *v.t.* gadael, gildio, hepgor

fork, *n.* fforch, fforc: *v.* fforchio; fforchogi

forlorn, *a.* amddifad, truan, ano-beithiol

form, *n.* ffurf; mainc; ffurflen: *v.* ffurfio

former, *a.* blaenaf, blaenorol

formidable, *a.* arswydus, ofnadwy

formula, *n.* rheol, fformwla

fornicate, *v.i.* puteinio

forsake, *v.t.* gadael, ymadael â, gwrthod

forsooth, *adv.* wir! bondigrybwyll

forswear, *v.t.* tyngu anudon

fort, *n.* caer, castell, amddiffynfa

forte, *n.* man cryf dyn

forth, *adv.* allan, ymlaen

forthwith, *adv.* rhag blaen, yn ddioed

fortification, *n.* amddiffynfa

fortify, *v.t.* cadarnhau, cryfhau

fortitude, *n.* gwroldeb, dewrder

fortnight, *n.* pythefnos

fortress, *n.* amddiffynfa, caer, castell

fortuitous, *a.* damweiniol

fortunate, *a.* ffodus, ffortunus

fortune, *n.* ffawd; ffortun

forty, *a. & n.* deugain

forward, *a.* blaen, blaenllaw: *adv.* ymlaen: *v.t.* anfon

fossil, *n.* ffosil

foster, *v.t.* magu, meithrin, coleddu

foul, *a.* aflan; annheg; afiach: *v.t.* difwyno

found, *v.t.* seilio, sylfaenu, sefydlu

foundation, *n.* sail, sylfaen, sawd

founder, *v.* suddo; ffwndro; cloffi

fountain, *n.* ffynnon, ffynhonnell

four, *a. & n.* pedwar (*f.* pedair)

fourteen, *a & n.* pedwar (pedair) ar ddeg

fowl, *n.* aderyn, edn, ehediad: *v.i.* adara

fox, *n.* cadno, llwynog

foxglove, *n.* bysedd cochion, bysedd y cŵn

fraction, *n.* toriad; ffracsiwn

fractious, *a.* cecrus, croes, afrywiog

fracture, *n.* toriad, drylliad: *v.t.* torri

fragile, *a.* brau

fragment, *n.* dryll, darn, briwsionyn

fragrance, *n.* perarogl, persawr

frail, *a.* brau, bregus, gwan, eiddil

frame, *n.* ffrâm; agwedd: *v.t.* fframio, llunio

franchise, *n.* rhyddfraint, etholfraint   [didwyll

frank, *a.* rhydd, calon-agored,

frankincense, *n.* thus

frantic, *a.* cyffrous, gorffwyll, gwallgof

fraternal, *a.* brawdol

fraternity, *n.* brawdoliaeth

fratricide, *n.* brawdladdiad; brawdleiddiad

fraud, *n.* twyll, hoced, ystryw

fraudulent, *a.* twyllodrus

fraught, *a.* llwythog, llawn

fray, *n.* ymryson, ymgiprys, ffrae

fray, *v.* treulio, rhwbio

freak, *n.* pranc, mympwy; anghenfil

freckle, *n.* brych, brychni

free, *a.* rhydd: *v.t.* rhyddhau

freebooter, *n.* herwr, ysbeiliwr

freedom, *n.* rhyddid; dinasfraint

freestone, *n.* tywodfaen, carreg nadd

freeze, *v.* rhewi, fferru

freight, *n.* llwyth llong: *v.t.* llwytho llong

French, *a.* Ffrengig: *n.* Ffrangeg

frenzy, *n.* gorffwylltra, cynddaredd

frequent, *a.* mynych, aml: *v.t.* mynychu

fresh, *a.* ffres, crai, cri, croyw, newydd

fret, *v.* rhwbio, ysu; poeni, poenydio

fretwork, *n.* rhwyllwaith

friable, *a.* hyfriw, bregus, brau

friar, *n.* brawd, mynach

fricative, *a.* affrithiol

friction, *n.* rhathiad, rhwbiad, ffrithiant

Friday, *n.* dydd Gwener

friend, *n.* cyfaill

friendship, *n.* cyfeillgarwch

fright, *n.* dychryn, ofn, braw

frigid, *a.* oer, rhewllyd; oeraidd, oerllyd

fringe, *n.* ymyl, ymylwe

frippery, *n.* coegwychder

frisk, *v.t.* crychneidio, campio

fritter, *v.t.* briwsioni, afradu, ofera

frivolous, *a.* gwamal; diystyr, disylwedd

fro, *adv.* **to and f.,** yn ôl ac ymlaen

frock, *n.* ffrog

frog, *n.* llyffant (melyn), broga

frolic, *v.i.* prancio, campio: *n.* pranc

from, *pr.* o, oddi, oddi wrth, gan

frond, *n.* deilen (rhedyn, &c.)

front, *n.* wyneb, blaen, ffrynt: *v.* wynebu

frontier, *n.* ffin, terfyn, goror

frontispiece, *n.* wyneb-ddarlun, wyneblun

frost, *n.* rhew

froth, *n.* ewyn: *v.i.* ewynnu

froward, *a.* cyndyn, gwrthnysig

frown, *v.i.* cuchio, gwgu: *n.* cuwch, gwg

fructify, *v.* cnydio; ffrwythloni

frugal, *a.* cynnil, darbodus

fruit, *n.* ffrwyth, ffrwythau

fruitful, *a.* ffrwythlon

fruition, *n.* mwyniant, mwynhad

frustrate, *v.t.* rhwystro, llesteirio

frustration, *n.* llesteiriant

fry, *n.* sil, silod

fry, *v.* ffrio

fudge, *n.* lol, sothach, ffiloreg

fuel, *n.* tanwydd, cynnud

fugitive, *a.* ar ffo, diflanedig; *n.* ffoadur

fugue, *n.* ffiwg

fulcrum, *n.* ffwlcrwm, pwysbwynt

fulfil *v.t.* cyflawni

full, *a.* llawn, cyflawn: *n.* llonaid

fuller, *n.* pannwr

fulminate, *v.* melltennu, taranu; bygwth

fulsome, *a.* ffiaidd, diflas (am weniaith, &c.)

fumble, *v.* palfalu, bwnglera

fume, *n.* tarth, mwg; llid: *v.* mygu; llidio, sorri

fumigate, *v.t.* myctarthu, mygu

fun, *n.* difyrrwch, digrifwch, cellwair

function, *n.* swydd, swyddogaeth; ffwythiant (mathemateg)

fund, *n.* cronfa, trysorfa

fundamental *a.* sylfaenol

funeral, *n.* angladd, cynhebrwng, claddedigaeth

funereal, *a.* angladdol, prudd, tywyll

fungus, *n.* ffwng

funnel, *n.* ffynnel, twnffed, twndis, corn [hynod

funny, *a.* digrif, ysmala; rhyfedd,

fur, *n.* blew, ffwr

furbish, *v.t.* gloywi, caboli, trwsio

furious, *a.* cynddeiriog, ffyrnig, gwyllt

furl, *v.t.* plygu, rholio, cau

furlong, *n.* ystad, wythfed ran milltir

furnace, *n.* ffwrn, ffwrnais

furnish, *v.t.* dodrefnu; cyflenwi

furniture, *n.* dodrefn, celfi

furrow, *n.* cwys, rhych: *v.t.* cwyso, rhychu

further, *a.* pellach: *adv.* ymhellach: *v.t.* hyrwyddo

furtive, *a.* lladradaidd

fury, *n.* cynddaredd, ffyrnigrwydd

furze, *n.* eithin

fuse, *v.* toddi, ymdoddi; chwythu

fuse, *n.* ffiws

fuss, *n.* ffwdan, helynt, stŵr: *v.* ffwdanu

fustian, *n.* ffustian, chwyddiaith

futile, *a.* ofer, di-les

future, *a. & n.* dyfodol

G

gabble, *v.* bregliach, clebran: *n.* cleber

gable, *n.* piniwn, talcen tŷ

gad, *v.i.* crwydro, gwibio, rhodianna

gadfly, *n.* cleren lwyd, robin y gyrrwr

gaff, *n.* tryfer, bach pysgota

gag, *n.* cau ceg

gage, *n.* gwystl: *v.t.* gwystlo, arwystlo

gaiety, *n.* llonder, difyrrwch, miri

gain, *v.* ennill, elwa: *n.* ennill, elw

gainsay, *v.t.* gwrthddywedyd, gwadu

gait, *n.* cerddediad, osgo

gale, *n.* awel, gwynt cryf; tymestl

gall, *n.* bustl, geri

gall, *n.* dolur, cig noeth: *v.* blino, cythruddo

gallant, *a.* gwrol, dewr: *n.* carwr

gallery, *n.* oriel, llofft

galley, *n.* rhwyflong, gali

gallon, *n.* galwyn, galwynaid

gallop, *n.* carlam: *v.* carlamu

gallows, *n.* crocbren, dienyddfa

galore, *n. & adv.* digonedd

galvanize, *v.t.* galfaneiddio, trydaneiddio

gamble, *v.* hapchwarae, gamblo

gambol, *n.* crychnaid, pranc: *v.* prancio

game, *n.* chwarae, camp; helwriaeth: *v.* gamblo

gammon, *n.* lol, sothach, ffiloreg

gammon, *n.* halfais (mockyn)

gamut, *n.* seinradd, gamwt

gander, *n.* ceiliagwydd, clacwydd

gang, *n.* mintai, torf, haid

gangway, *n.* mynedfa, tramwyfa

gaol, *n.* carchar: *v.t.* carcharu

gap, *n.* bwlch, adwy

gape, *v.i.* rhythu, dylyfu gên

garage, *n.* modurdy, garais

garb, *n.* gwisg, trwsiad, diwyg

garbage, *n.* ysgarthion, ysbwrial, sothach

garble, *v.t.* darnio, llurgunio

garden, *n.* gardd: *v.i.* garddu

garish, *a.* coegwych

garland, *n.* coronbleth, garlant

garlic, *n.* garlleg

garment, *n.* dilledyn, gwisg

garner, *n.* ysgubor: *v.t.* ysguborio, cywain

garnish, *v.t.* addurno, harddu, trwsio

garret, *n.* nenlofft

garrison, *n.* gwarchodlu

garrotte, *v.t.* llindagu

garrulous, *a.* tafodrydd, siaradus

garter, *n.* gardas, gardys

gas, *n.* nwy; bocsach

gash, *n.* archoll, hollt, hac: *v.t.* archolli, hacio

gasp, *v.* ebychu, dyheu: *n.* ebwch

gastronomy, *n.* ymbortheg

gate, *n.* porth, llidiart, clwyd, gât, iet

gather, *v.* casglu, cynnull, crynhoi, hel

gaudy, *a.* coegwych, gorwych

gauge, *n.* mesur; lled; meidrydd: *v.t.* mesur, meidryddu

gaunt, *a.* cul, llwm

gauntlet, *n.* dyrnfol, maneg ddur

gawky, *a.* llebanaidd, trwsgl, llibin

gay, *a.* gwych, hoenus; ofer, afradlon

gaze, *v.i.* edrych, syllu, tremio: *n.* golwg, trem

gazelle, *n.* gafrewig

gazette, *n.* newyddiadur (swyddogol)

gazetteer, *n.* geiriadur daearyddol

gear, *n.* gêr, offer, celfi, taclau

gearbox, *n.* gergist

geld, *v.t.* disbaddu, cyweirio

gelding, *n.* adfarch, ceffyl

gem, *n.* glain, gem, tlws

gender, *n.* cenedl

genealogy, *n.* achau; achyddiaeth

general, *a.* cyffredin, cyffredinol: *n.* cadfridog

generate, *v.t.* cenhedlu, cynhyrchu

generation, *n.* cenhedliad; cenhedlaeth

generator, *n.* cynhyrchydd; generadur

generic, *a.* tylwythol, rhywiogaethol

generous, *a.* hael, haelionus, haelfrydig

genesis, *n.* dechreuad, tarddiad

genetics, *n.* geneteg

genial, *a.* hynaws, rhadlon, tyner, tirion

genitive, *a.* genidol

genius, *n.* athrylith, anian, awen; dyn o athrylith

genteel, *a.* bonheddig, crachfonheddig

gentile, *a.* cenhedlig: *n.* cenedlddyn

gentle, *a.* bonheddig; mwyn, tyner

gentleman, *n.* gŵr bonheddig

genuflect, *v.i.* plygu glin, penlinio

genuine, *a.* dilys, diffuant, diledryw

genus, (*genera*) *n.* rhywogaeth, tylwyth

geography, *n.* daearyddiaeth

geology, *n.* daeareg

geometry, *n.* meintoniaeth, geometreg

germ, *n.* hedyn, eginyn

German, *a.* Almaenaidd: *n.* Almaenwr; Almaeneg

germane, *a.* perthynasol

germinate, *v.i.* egino

gesticulate, *v.i.* gwneuthur ystumiau, munudio

gesture, *n.* ystum, arwydd, mosiwn

got, *v.* cael; ceisio; ennill

ghastly, *a.* erchyll, annaearol; gwelw

ghost, *n.* ysbryd, drychiolaeth, bwgan

giant, *n.* cawr: *a.* cawraidd

gibberish, *n.* ffregod, clebar, baldordd

gibbet, *n.* crocbren, sibed: *v.t.* crogi, sibedu

gibe, *v.* gwawdio: *n.* gwawd

giddiness, *n.* pendro, madrondod, dot

giddy, *a.* penfeddw, penchwiban

gift, *n.* rhodd, dawn, anrheg, gwobr

gigantic, *a.* cawraidd, dirfawr, anferth

gild, *v.t.* euro, goreuro

gill, *n.* tagell

gimlet, *n.* ebill, gimbill, whimbil

ginger, *n.* sinsir

gingerly, *a. & adv.* gochelgar, gwyliadwrus

gipsy, gy-, *n.* sipsiwn

gird, *v.t.* gwregysu
girder, *n.* trawst
girdle, *n.* gwregys, rhwymyn: *v.t.* gwregysu
girl, *n.* geneth, hogen, merch
girth, *n.* cengl; cylchfesur, cwmpas
gist, *n.* cnewyllyn pwnc, ergyd, sylwedd
give, *v.* rhoddi, rhoi.—**g.up,** rhoi'r gorau i
glacier, *n.* afon rew, rhewlif, iäen
glad, *a.* llawen, llon, balch
glade, *n.* llannerch
gladiator, *n.* cleddyfwr, ymladdwr
glamour, *n.* swyn, cyfaredd, hud
glance, *v.* llithro, osgoi; taflu cipolwg: *n.* cipolwg, trem
gland, *n.* chwarren, cilchwyrnen, gland
glare, *v.* disgleirio; rhythu: *n.* disgleirdeb, tanbeidrwydd
glass, *n.* gwydr; gwydraid
glaze, *v.t.* gwydro; sgleinio: *n.* sglein
gleam, *n.* pelydryn, llewyrch: *v.i.* pelydru
glean, *v.* lloffa
glebe, *n.* clastir, tir eglwys; gweryd
glee, *n.* hoen, afiaith; cytgan, canig
glen, *n.* glyn, cwm, dyffryn
glib, *a.* llyfn, llithrig, hylithr, rhugl
glide, *v.i.* llithro, llifo
glimmer, *v.i.* godywynnu: *n.* gwawr, llewyrch, eiliw, godywyn
glimpse, *n.* trem, cipolwg, cipdrem
glint, *v.* fflachio: *n.* fflach, llewyrch
glisten, *v.i.* disgleirio, caneitio
glitter, *v.i.* disgleirio, serennu, pelydru
gloaming, *n.* cyfnos
globe, *n.* pêl, pelen
globule, *n.* pelen; defnyn, seren, llygad
gloom, *n.* caddug, gwyll; prudd-der
gloomy, *a.* prudd, pruddaidd, digalon
glorify, *v.t.* gogoneddu
glorious, *a.* gogoneddus
glory, *n.* gogoniant: *v.i.* ymogoneddu

gloss, *n.* disgleirdeb arwynebol, sglein; glos, esboniad
glossary, *n.* geirfa
glove, *n.* maneg
glow, *v.i.* twymo, gwrido: *n.* gwres, gwrid
glower, *v.i.* cuchio, gwgu
glue, *n.* glud: *v.t.* gludio, asio
glum, *a.* prudd, digalon, swrth, sarrug
glut, *v.t.* gorlenwi, glythu: *n.* gormodedd
gluten, *n.* glud
glutinous, *a.* gludiog
glutton, *n.* glwth
gluttony, *n.* glythineb
gnarled, *a.* clymog, cygnog, garw
gnash, *v.* rhincian; ysgyrnygu
gnat, *n.* gwybedyn, cylionen
gnaw, *v.* cnoi, cnofain, deintio
gnome, *n.* gwireb; ysbryd, coblyn
go, *v.i.* myned, cerdded, rhodio: *n.* tro
goad, *n.* swmbwl: *v.t.* symbylu, gyrru
goal, *n.* gôl, cyrchnod, nod
goat, *n.* gafr
gobble, *v.* bochio bwyd, traflyncu
goblet, *n.* ffiol, cwpan
goblin, *n.* ellyll, drychiolaeth, coblyn
god, *n.* duw.—**G.,** Duw
godfather, *n.* tad bedydd
godhead, *n.* duwdod
godly, *a.* duwiol
godmother, *n.* mam fedydd
godspeed, *n.* llwyddiant, ffyniant
gold, *n.* aur: *a.* aur, euraid
good, *a.* da, daionus; cryn: *n.* da, daioni, lles
good-bye, *i. & n.* yn iach! ffarwel
goodly, *a.* hardd, teg
goodness, *n.* daioni
goods, *n.pl.* nwyddau, eiddo
goodwill, *n.* ewyllys da: braint (fasnachol)
goose, (*geese*), *n.* gŵydd
gooseberry, *n.* eirinen Fair, gwsberen
gore, *n.* gwaed

gore, *v.t.* cornio, twlcio

gorge, *n.* safn; hafn, nant, ceunant: *v.* safnio, gwancio, gorlenwi

gorgeous, *a.* gorwych

gormandize, *v.i.* bolera, glythu

gorse, *n.* eithin

gosling, *n.* cyw gŵydd

gospel, *n.* efengyl

gossamer, *n.* gwawn

gossip, *n.* clebryn, clebren; clap, clec, clonc; *v.i.* clepian, clecian, hel straeon

gouge, *n.* gaing gau, cŷn llwy: *v.t.* cafnio, cafnu

gourd, *n.* cicaion, pompiwn

gourmand, *n.* glwth, bolerwr

gout, *n.* gowt

govern, *v.* llywodraethu, rheoli, llywio

government, *n.* llywodraeth

governor, *n.* llywodraethwr

gown, *n.* gŵn

grab, *v.* crafangu, gwancio, rheibio: *n.* gwanc, rhaib

grace, *n.* gras, rhad, graslonrwydd; teleidrwydd: *v.t.* harddu, prydferthu, addurno

gracious, *a.* graslon, grasol, rhadlon

grade, *n.* gradd

gradual, *a.* graddol

graduate, *v.* graddio, graddoli: *n.* gŵr gradd

graft, *n.* impyn: *v.t.* impio

grail, *n.* greal

grain, *n.* grawn, gronyn; mymryn; graen: *v.* graenu, graenio

grammar, *n.* gramadeg

grammarian, *n.* gramadegwr, gramadegydd

grammatical, *a.* gramadegol

granary, *n.* ysgubor

grand, *a.* mawreddog, ardderchog, crand

grandchild, *n.* ŵyr

grandee, *n.* pendefig, uchelwr

grandeur, *n.* mawredd, crandrwydd

grandfather, *n.* taid, tad-cu

grandiloquence, *n.* chwyddiaith

grandiose, *a.* mawreddog, rhodresgar

grandmother, *n.* nain, mam-gu

grange, *n.* maerdy; ydlan

granite, *n.* gwenithfaen, ithfaen

grant, *v.t.* rhoddi, caniatáu: *n.* rhodd

granule, *n.* gronyn, greyenyn

grapes, *n.* grawnwin

graphic, *a.* darluniadol; byw

grapple, *v.* bachu, ymgodymu

grasp, *v.* gafael; amgyffred: *n.* gafael

grass, *n.* glaswellt, gwelltglas, gwellt

grasshopper, *n.* ceiliog y rhedyn, sioncyn y gwair

grate, *n.* grat

grate, *v.* rhygnu, rhincian, gratio

grateful, *a.* diolchgar; dymunol, hyfryd

gratify, *v.t.* boddio, boddhau

gratis, *adv.* am ddim, yn rhad, yn rhodd

gratitude, *n.* diolchgarwch

gratuitous, *a.* rhad; di-alwamdano

gratuity, *n.* rhodd, gwobr

grave, *a.* difrifol, dwys

grave, *n.* bedd, beddrod

gravel, *n.* graean, gro, grafel

graven, *a.* cerfiedig

graveyard, *n.* mynwent

gravitate, *v.i.* disgyrchu, treiglo

gravity, *n.* disgyrchiant; pwys, pwysau; difrifwch

graze, *v.* pori; porfelu

graze, *v.* rhwbio, crafu, ysgythru

grease, *n.* saim, iraid: *v.t.* iro

great, *a.* mawr.—**a g. many,** llawer iawn

greed, *n.* bâr, trachwant, gwanc, rhaib

greedy, *a.* barus, gwancus, blysig

Greek, *n.* Groeg; Groegwr: *a.* Groeg

green, *a.* gwyrdd, glas, ir: *v.* glasu

greet, *v.t.* annerch, cyfarch

gregarious, *a.* heidiol, heidiog

grey, *a.* llwyd, llwydwyn, glas

greyhound, *n.* milgi

grid, *n.* rhwyll, grid, sinc

griddle, gridiron, *n.* gradell

grief, *n.* gofid, galar, hiraeth

grievance, *n.* cwyn

grieve, *v.* gofidio, galaru, hiraethu

grievous, *a.* trwm, gofidus, poenus, blin

grill, *v.t.* briwlio: *n.* gradell

grim, *a.* sarrug, milain; penderfynol

grimace, *n.* gwep: *v.i.* gwneud gwep

grime, *n.* parddu

grin, *v.* gwenu o glust bwygilydd: *n.* gwên

grind, *v.* malu (ŷd, &c.); llifo (arf), llifanu

grip, *v.* gafael, gwasgu: *n.* gafael, craff

gripe, *v.* gwasgu, cnoi: *n.* cnoi

grisly, *a.* erch, erchyll, hyll, milain

grist, *n.* ŷd i'w falu; mâl; elw

gristle, *n.* madruddyn

grit, *n.* grud, grut, graean; pybyrwch

grizzled, grizzly, *a.* llwyd, llwydwyn

groan, *v.i.* & *n.* griddfan

grocer, *n.* groser

groin, *n.* cesail morddwyd

groove, *n.* rhigol, rhych: *v.t.* rhychu

grope, *v.i.* palfalu, ymbalfalu

gross, *a.* tew, bras: braisg; dybryd

gross, *n.* deuddeg dwsin, gros: *a.* crynswth

grotesque, *a.* gwrthun

grotto, *n.* ogof, ogofdy

ground, *n.* llawr, daear, tir; sail; gwaelod: *v.t.* seilio, sylfaenu

group, *n.* twr, bagad: *v.t.* cydosod, sypio

grouse, *n.* iâr y rhos, grugiar

grouse, *v.i.* grwgnach

grove, *n.* llwyn, celli

grovel, *v.i.* ymgreinio

grow, *v.* tyfu, prifio, cynyddu; myned

growl, *v.i.* chwyrnu

growth, *n.* twf, tyfiant, cynnydd

grub, *n.* pryf, cynrhonyn

grub, *v.* cloddio, chwilota, chwynnu

grudge, *v.t.* gwarafun, grwgnach: *n.* dig

gruel, *n.* grual, griwel

gruesome, *a.* erchyll, hyll, ffiaidd

gruff, *a.* sarrug, garw, gwrthgroch

grumble, *v.i.* grwgnach, tuchan

grumpy, *a.* sarrug, taeog, anynad

grunt, *v.i.* rhochian, rhochain: *n.* rhoch

guarantee, *n.* gwarant, mach: *v.t.* gwarantu

guard, *n.* gwyliadwriaeth, gard: *v.* cadw, gwarchod, gwylied

guardian, *n.* gwarcheidwad

guerdon, *n.* gwobr, gwobrwy

guess, *v.* dyfalu, dyfeisio: *n.* amcan

guest, *n.* gwestai

guffaw, *n.* & *v.* crechwen

guide, *n.* arweinydd: *v.t.* arwain, cyfarwyddo

guild, *n.* cymdeithas, cofforaeth, urdd

guile, *n.* twyll, dichell, hoced, ystryw

guilt, *n.* euogrwydd, bai

guilty, *a.* euog

guinea, *n.* gini

guise, *n.* dull, modd, rhith, diwyg

gulf, *n.* morgainc; llynclyn; agendor

gull, *n.* gwylan; gwirionyn: *v.t.* hocedu

gullet, *n.* corn gwddf, sefnig, corn pori

gullible, *a.* hygoelus, ehud, hydwyll

gully, *n.* rhigol, ffos

gulp, *v.t.* llawcian, traflyncu: *n.* llawc

gum, *n.* gwm, glud: *v.t.* gymio, gludio

gums, *n.pl.* cig y dannedd, gorcharfanau

gun, *n.* gwn, dryll, magnel

gurgle, *v.i.* byrlymu

gush, *v.* ffrydio, pistyllio: *n.* ffrwd: truth

gust, *n.* awel, chwa, hyrddwynt

gusto, *n.* awch, blas

gut, *n.* perfeddyn, coluddyn: *v.t.* diberfeddu; difrodi, ysbeilio

gutter, *n.* ffos, cwter, rhigol, rhewyn

guttural, *a.* gyddfol

guzzle, *v.* llawcio, traflyncu

gymnasium *n.* gymnasium

gyrate, *v.i.* troi, amdroi, chwyldroi

H

habiliment, *n.* gwisg

habit, *n.* arferiad; anian; gwisg: *v.t.* gwisgo, dilladu

habitable, *a.* cyfannedd, cyfanheddol

habitat, *n.* cartref, cynefin

habitation, *n.* trigfa, preswylfa

habitual, *a.* arferol, cyson

habituate, *v.t.* arfer, cynefino

hack, *v.* hacio, torri: *n.* hac

hack, *n.* hurfarch; cystog, slaf

hackney, *n.* hacnai: *v.t.* mynychu, rhygnu

hades, *n.* hades, annwn

haemorrhage, *n.* gwaedlin, diferlif gwaed

haemorrhoids, *n.pl.* clwyf y marchogion

haft, *n.* carn

hag, *n.* gwrach, gwiddon

haggard, *a.* gwyllt, curiedig

haggle, *v.i.* taeru, bargenna, bargeinio

hail, *n.* cenllysg, cesair: *v.* bwrw cesair

hail, *i.* henffych well: *v.* cyfarch, galw

hair, *n.* gwallt, blew, rhawn

hale, *a.* iach, cryf, hoenus

half, (*halves*), *n.* hanner

half-back, *n.* hanerwr

halfpenny, *n.* dimai

hall, *n.* llys, neuadd, plas

hallow, *v.t.* cysegru, sancteiddio

hallucination, *n.* geuddrych, lledrith

halo, *n.* corongylch, gogoniant

halt, *v.* sefyll: *n.* safiad: gorsaf

halter, *n.* cebystr, tennyn

halve, *v.t.* haneru

ham, *n.* morddwyd, ham

hames, *n.pl.* mynci

hamlet, *n.* pentref

hammer, *n.* morthwyl, mwrthwl, gordd: *v.* morthwylio

hamper, *n.* cawell, hamper

hamper, *v.t.* rhwystro, llesteirio

hand, *n.* llaw: *v.t.* estyn, trosglwyddo

handcuff, *n.* gefyn

handicap, *n.* rhwystr, llestair, anfantais; blaen. —**handicapped children,** plant dan anfantais

handicraft, *n.* llawgelfyddyd, crefft

handiwork, *n.* gwaith llaw

handkerchief, *n.* cadach poced, hances

handle, *n.* carn, coes, troed, dolen, clust, dwrn: *v.t.* trin, trafod; teimlo

handmaid, -en *n.* llawforwyn

handrail, *n.* canllaw

handsome, *a.* hardd, prydferth; hael

handwriting, *n.* llawysgrifen

handy, *a.* hylaw, deheuig, cyfleus

hang, *v.* crogi, hongian, dibynnu

hank, *n.* cengl

hanker, *v.i.* blysio, dyheu, hiraethu

hap, *n.* hap, damwain

haphazard, *n.* damwain (noeth): *a. & adv.* damweiniol

haply, *adv.* efallai, hwyrach

happen, *v.i.* digwydd, damweinio

happiness, *n.* dedwyddwch, hapusrwydd

happy, *a.* dedwydd, hapus

harangue, *n.* araith, arawd: *v.* areithio

harass, *v.t.* poeni, blino, gofidio

harbinger, *n.* rhagredegydd

harbour, *n.* porthladd, harbwr: *v.* llochesu

hard, *a.* caled, anodd

hardihood, *n.* hyfdra, digywilydd-dra

hardly, *adv.* prin, braidd

hardship, *n.* caledi; cam

hardy, *a.* caled, cryf, gwydn; hy, eofn

hare, *n.* ysgyfarnog, ceinach
hark, *i.* gwrando! clyw!—**h. back,** dychwelyd
harlot, *n.* putain
harm, *n.* niwed, drwg, cam: *v.t.* niweidio, drygu
harmony, *n.* harmoni, cynghanedd
harness, *n.* harnais, gêr: *v.t.* harneisio
harp, *n.* telyn: *v.i.* canu'r delyn
harpoon, *n.* tryfer: *v.t.* tryferu
harpy, *n.* hudoles reibus
harrow, *n.* og: *v.t.* llyfnu; rhwygo, dryllio
harry, *v.t.* anrheithio, difrodi, blino
harsh, *a.* garw, gerwin, aflafar
hart, *n.* hydd
harvest, *n.* cynhaeaf: *v.t.* cynaeafu
hash, *n.* briwgig; cymysgfa, cybolfa
hasp, *n.* hesben
haste, *n.* brys, hast: *v.i.* brysio, prysuro
hasten, *v.* brysio, prysuro, hastu
hasty, *a.* brysiog, byrbwyll
hat, *n.* het
hatch, *v.* deor, gori: *n.* dehoriad
hatch, *n.* gorddrws, rhagddor, dôr
hatchet, *n.* bwyellan, bwyell (fach)
hate, *v.t.* casáu: *n.* cas, casineb
hatred, *n.* cas, casineb, digasedd
haughty, *a.* balch, ffroenuchel, trahaus
haul, *v.* tynnu, llusgo, halio: *n.* dalfa
haulm *n.* callod, gwrysg, gwlydd
haunch, *n.* morddwyd, pedrain
haunt, *v.t.* cyniwair, mynychu; trwblu, aflonyddu: *n.* cyniweirfa, cynefin
have, *v.t.* cael, meddu
haven, *n.* hafan, porthladd
havoc, *n.* hafog, difrod
hawk, *n.* hebog, cudyll, curyll: *v.* heboca
hawk, *v.t.* gwerthu o dy i dŷ, pedlera
haws, *n.pl.* crawel y moch, criafol y moch
hawthorn, *n.* ysbyddaden, draenen wen
hay, *n.* gwair

hazard, *n.* enbydrwydd; antur; damwain: *v.t.* anturio, peryglu
haze, *n.* niwl, tarth, tawch
hazel, *n.* collen: *a.* gwinau golau
he, *pn.* ef, efe; efo, fo, o
head, *n.* pen: *v.* blaenori
headache, *n.* dolur (cur) yn y pen, pen tost
heading, *n.* pennawd
headland, *n.* pentir, penrhyn; talar
headlong, *adv.* pendramwnwgl
headstrong, *a.* cyndyn
heal, *v.* iacháu, meddyginiaethu
health, *n.* iechyd
healthy, *a.* iach, iachus
heap, *n.* crug, pentwr: *v.t.* crugio, pentyrru
hear, *v.* clywed
hearken, *v.i.* gwrando, clustymwrando
hearse, *n.* elor-gerbyd, hers
heart, *n.* calon
hearten, *v.* calonogi, sirioli
hearth, *n.* aelwyd
hearty, *a.* calonnog, cynnes
heat, *n.* gwres, poethder: *v.* twymo, poethi
heath, *n.* rhos, rhostir
heathen, *a.* cenhedlig, paganaidd: *n.* pagan
heather, *n.* grug
heave, *v.* codi, dyrchafu; chwyddo; taflu
heaven, *n.* nef, nefoedd
heavenly, *a.* nefol, nefolaidd
heavy, *a.* trwm, trymaidd, trymllyd
Hebrew, *n.* Hebrëwr; Hebraeg: *a.* Hebraeg; Hebreig
hedge, *n.* clawdd, gwrych, perth
hedgehog, *n.* draenog
heed, *v.t.* ystyried, talu sylw: *n.* ystyriaeth
heel, *n.* sawdl: *v.* sodli
heifer, *n.* anner, heffer, treisiad
height, *n.* uchder, uchelder
heinous, *a.* dybryd, anfad, ysgeler
heir, *n.* etifedd
hell, *n.* uffern
helm, *n.* llyw; llywyddiaeth
helmet, *n.* helm

help, *v.t.* helpu, cymorth, cynorthwyo: *n.* help, cymorth, cynhorthwy

helpless, *a.* diymadferth

helter-skelter, *adv.* blith-draphlith

hem, *n.* hem, ymyl: *v.t.* hemio

hemi-, *px.* hanner

hemlock, *n.* cegid

hemp, *n.* cywarch

hen, *n.* iâr

henchman, *n.* gwas, canlynwr, cefnogydd

hence, *adv.* oddi yma: *i.* ymaith!

henceforth, -forward, *adv.* rhag llaw

hepta-, *px.* saith

herald, *n.* herald: *v.t.* cyhoeddi; rhagflaenu

herb, *n.* llysieuyn

herd, *n.* gyr, cenfaint, gre: *v.* heidio

here, *adv.* yma

hereditary, *a.* etifeddol

heredity, *n.* etifeddeg

heresy, *n.* heresi, camgred

heretic, *n.* heretic, camgredwr

heritage, *n.* etifeddiaeth, treftadaeth

hermit, *n.* meudwy

hernia, *n.* y fors

hero, *n.* arwr, gwron

heroic, *a.* arwrol

heroine, *n.* arwres

heron, *n.* creyr, crychydd

herring, *n.* pennog, ysgadenyn

hesitate, *v.i.* petruso

hesitation, *n.* petruster

heterodox, *a.* anuniongred

heterogeneous, *a.* anghydryw, afryw, heterogenus

hew, *v.t.* naddu, torri, cymynu

hexa-, *px.* chwech

heyday, *n.* anterth

hibernate, *v.i.* gaeafu

hiccup, *n.* yr ig: *v.i.* igian

hide, *v.* cuddio, celu, ymguddio

hide, *n.* croen

hideous, *a.* hyll, erchyll

hierarchy, *n.* gradd, offeiriadaeth

higgle, *v.i.* taeru, bargenna

high, *a.* uchel; mawr; cryf; llawn

highness, *n.* uchder, uchelder

high-priest, *n.* archoffeiriad

hilarious, *a.* llawen, llon, siriol, hoenus

hill, *n.* bryn, allt, gorifyny

hillock, *n.* bryncyn, ponc, twmpath

hilt, *n.* carn cleddyf

hind, *a.* ôl

hind, *n.* ewig

hinder, *v.t.* rhwystro, atal, lluddias, llesteirio

hindrance, *n.* rhwystr, llestair, lludd

hinge, *n.* colyn drws: *v.* troi, dibynnu

hint, *n.* awgrym: *v.t.* awgrymu

hip, *n.* clun, pen uchaf y glun

hippopotamus, (-*muses*, -*mi*), *n.* afonfarch

hips, *n.pl.* egroes

hire, *v.t.* cyflogi, hurio, llogi: *n.* cyflog, hur

hirsute, *a.* blewog, cedenog, garw

hiss, *v.* chwythu, sïo, hysio, hisian

history, *n.* hanes, hanesiaeth, hanesyddiaeth

hit, *v.* taro: *n.* ergyd, trawiad

hitch, *v.* bachu: *n.* cwlwm; atalfa, rhwystr

hither, *adv.* yma, hyd yma, tuag yma

hitherto, *adv.* hyd yma, hyd yn hyn

hive, *n.* cwch gwenyn

hoar, *a.* llwyd, penllwyd: *n.* llwydrew, barrug

hoard, *n.* cronfa, cuddfa: *v.t.* cronni

hoarse, *a.* cryg, cryglyd

hoax, *v.t.* twyllo: *n.* cast, tric, twyll

hob, *n.* pentan

hobble, *v.* hercian; hualu

hobby, *n.* difyrwaith, hyfrydwch, hobi

hobgoblin, *n.* bwbach, bwci, bwgan

hoe, *n.* chwynnogl, hof: *v.* hofio

hog, *n.* mochyn

hoist, *v.t.* codi, dyrchafu

hold, *v.* dal; atal; cadw: *n.* gafael, dalfa

hold, *n.* ceudod llong, howld
holding, *n.* deiliadaeth; tyddyn
hole, *n.* twll, ffau
holiday, *n.* dydd gŵyl
holiness, *n.* sancteiddrwydd
hollow, *a.* cau, gwag: *n.* ceudod: *v.t.* tyllu, cafnio
holly, *n.* celyn, celynnen
holocaust, *n.* poethoffrwm; lladdfa
holy, *a.* sanctaidd, glân, cysegr-lân
homage, *n.* gwrogaeth
home, *n.* cartref: *adv.* adref. —at h.,** gartref
homely, *a.* cartrefol
home-sick, *a.* hiraethus
homestead, *n.* cartref, tŷ, tyddyn
homicide, *n.* dynleiddiad, llofrudd; dynladdiad
homily, *n.* pregeth, homili
homogeneous, *a.* cydryw, homogenus
homosexual, *a. & n.* cyfunrhywiol
homosexuality, *n.* cyfunrhywoliaeth [honio
hone, *n.* calen hogi; hôn: *v.t.* hogi,
honest, *a.* onest, didwyll
honey, *n.* mêl
honeycomb, *n.* dil mêl, crwybr: *v.t.* tyllu, britho
honeysuckle, *n.* gwyddfid
honorary, *a.* mygedol
honour, *n.* anrhydedd: *v.t.* anrhydeddu
honourable, *a.* anrhydeddus
hood, *n.* cwfl, cwcwll, penguwch
hoodwink, *v.t.* mygydu, dallu, twyllo
hoof, *n.* carn
hook, *n.* bach; cryman: *v.* bachu
hooker, *n.* bachwr
hoop, *n.* cylch, cant: *v.t.* cylchu, cantio
hoot, *v.* hwtian, hwtio: *n.* hwt
hop, *v.* hercian: *n.* llam, herc
hope, *n.* gobaith: *v.* gobeithio
horde, *n.* torf, haid, mintai
horizon, *n.* gorwel
horizontal, *a.* gwastad, llorwedd
horn, *n.* corn: *v.t.* cornio, twlcio
hornet, *n.* gwenynen feirch

horrible, *a.* erchyll, ofnadwy
horrid, *a.* erchyll, echrydus, anferth
horrify, *v.t.* brawychu
horror, *n.* arswyd, erchylltod
horse, *n.* march, ceffyl
horse-hair, *n.* rhawn
horseshoe, *n.* pedol
horticulture, *n.* garddwriaeth
hose, (*hose*), *n.* hosan: (*hoses*) *n.* pibell ddŵr
hospitable, *a.* lletygar, croesawus
hospital, *n.* ysbyty, clafdy
hospitality, *n.* lletygarwch, croeso
host, *n.* llu, byddin
host, *n.* lletywr, gwesteiwr
hostage, *n.* mach, gwystl
hostel, *n.* llety efrydwyr, neuadd breswyl
hostile, *a.* gelyniaethus, gelynol
hot, *a.* poeth, twym, brwd, gwresog
hotch-potch, *n.* cymysgfa, cybolfa
hotel, *n.* gwesty
hound, *n.* bytheiad, helgi: *v.t.* hela, erlid, annos
hour, *n.* awr
house, *n.* tŷ, annedd: *v.* lletya
household, *n.* teulu, tylwyth
hovel, *n.* penty, hofel
hover, *v.i.* hofran, ehedfan, gwibio
how, *adv.* pa mor, pa fodd, pa sut, sut
howbeit, *adv.* er hynny
however, *adv.* pa fodd bynnag, sut bynnag
howl, *v.i.* udo, oernadu: *n.* udiad, oernad
hoyden, *n.* rhampen, hoeden
hub, *n.* both olwyn; canolbwynt
hubbub, *n.* dwndwr, dadwrdd, wbwb
huddle, *v.* tyrru, gwthio
hue, *n.* lliw, eiliw, gwawr, gwedd
huff, *v.* sorri, tramgwyddo: *n.* soriant
hug, *v.t.* cofleidio, gwasgu
huge, *a.* anferth, enfawr, dirfawr
hulk, *n.* corff llong, llong foel, hwlc
hull, *n.* corff llong; cibyn, plisgyn
hullabaloo, *n.* dadwrdd, helynt, heldrin

hum, *v.* mwmian: *n.* si, sibrwd

human. *a.* dynol   [garog

humane, *a.* tirion, tosturiol, tru-

humanism, *n.* hiwmaniaeth

humanity, *n.* dynoliaeth

humble, *a.* gostyngedig, ufudd: *v.t.* darostwng

humble-bee, *n.* cacynen

humbug, *n.* twyll, ffug, hoced; twyllwr: *v.t.* twyllo

humdrum, *a.* difwynd, diflas

humid, *a.* gwlyb, llaith, gwlybyrog

humiliate, *v.t.* darostwng, iselu

humiliation, *n.* darostyngiad

humility, *n.* gostyngeiddrwydd

humour, *n.* hwyl, donioldeb: *v.t.* boddio

hump, *n.* crwmach, crwmp, crwbi

hundred, *a.* cant, can: *n.* cant; cantref

hunger, *n.* newyn, chwant bwyd: *v.i.* newynu

hungry, *a.* newynog

hunt, *v.* hela: *n.* helwriaeth

hurdle, *n.* clwyd, pleiden

hurl, *v.t.* hyrddio

hurly-burly, *n.* hwrli-bwrli, dwndwr

hurricane, *n.* hyrddwynt, corwynt

hurry, *v.* brysio: *n.* brys

hurt, *v.* niweidio, dolurio, brifo: *n.* niwed, dolur

hurtle, *v.* gwrthdaro, chwyrlïo

husband, *n.* gŵr, priod: *v.t.* cynilo

husbandry, *n.* amaethyddiaeth, hwsmonaeth

hush, *i.* ust: *v.* distewi: *n.* distawrwydd

husk, *n.* plisgyn, cibyn: *v.t.* plisgo

husky, *a.* sych, cryglyd

hussy, *n.* maeden

hustle, *v.* cilgwthio, prysuro

hut, *n.* bwth, caban, cwt

hutch, *n.* cwt cwningen, cwb

hybrid, *a.* cymysgryw, croesryw

hydro-, *px.* dwfr

hydrophobia, *n.* y gynddaredd

hygiene, *n.* iechydaeth, gwyddor glendid

hymeneal, *a.* priodasol

hymn, *n.* emyn, hymn: *v.* emynu

hyper-, *px.* gormod, gor-, tra-

hyperbole, *n.* gormodiaith

hyphen, *n.* cyplysnod (-)

hypnotism, *n.* swyngwsg, hypnotiaeth

hypnotize, *v.t.* swyno, rheibio

hypochondria, *n.* pruddglwyf

hypocrisy, *n.* rhagrith

hypocrite, *n.* rhagrithiwr

hypothesis, (-*theses*), *n.* damcaniaeth

hyssop, *n.* isop

hysteria, *n.* y famwst, hysteria

I

I, *pn.* mi, myfi; fi, i; minnau, innau

ice, *n.* ia, rhew: *v.t.* taenu (megis) a rhew

iceberg, *n.* mynydd rhew, rhewfryn

ice-cream, *n.* hufen iâ

ichthyology, *n.* pysgyddiaeth

icicle, *n.* clöyn iâ, cloch iâ, pibonwy

iconoclast, *n.* delwdorrwr

icy, *a.* rhewllyd

idea, *n.* drychfeddwl, syniad, idea

ideal, *a.* delfrydol, ideal: *n.* delfryd

idealism, *n.* idealaeth, delfrydiaeth

idealize, *v.* delfrydu

identical, *a.* yr un (yn union)

identify, *v.t.* adnabod (fel yr un un); uniaethu

identity, *n.* unfathiant

idiocy, *n.* gwiriondeb, penwendid

idiom, *n.* priod-ddull, idiom

idiosyncrasy, *n.* tymer, anianawd

idiot, *n.* gwirionyn, hurtyn

idle, *a.* segur, ofer: *v.* segura, ofera

idol, *n.* eilun

idolater, *n.* eilunaddolwr

idolatry, *n.* eilunaddoliaeth

idyll, *n.* bugeilgerdd; canig

if, *c.* os, pe

ignite, *v.* ennyn, tanio, cynnau

ignoble, *a.* anenwog, isel, gwael, salw

ignominious, *a.* gwarthus, gwaradwyddus

ignorance, *n.* anwybodaeth

ignorant, *a.* anwybodus

ignore, *v.t.* anwybyddu, diystyru

il-, *px.* di-, an-,

ill, *a.* drwg; gwael, claf: *adv.* yn ddrwg: *n.* drwg, niwed

illegal, *a.* anghyfreithlon

illegible, *a.* annarllenadwy, aneglur

illegitimate, illicit, *a.* anghyfreithlon

illiterate, *a.* anllythrennog

illness, *n.* afiechyd, anhwyldeb

illuminate, *v.t.* goleuo, addurno

illusion, *n.* rhith, lledrith, camganfod, rhithganfyddiad

illustrate, *v.t.* egluro; darlunio

illustration, *n.* eglureb; darlun

illustrious, *a.* ardderchog, enwog, hyglod

im-, *px.* di, an-

image, *n.* delw, llun; delwedd

imagination, *n.* dychymyg, darfelydd

imagine, *v.t.* dychmygu, tybio

imbecile, *a. & n.* (un) penwan

imbibe, *v.t.* yfed, sugno, llyncu

imbue, *v.t.* trwytho

imitate, *v.t.* dynwared, efelychu

immaculate, *a.* difrycheulyd, pur, glân

immanent, *a.* mewnfodol

immature, *a.* anaeddfed

immediate, *a.* digyfrwng; uniongyrchol

immemorial, *a.* er cyn cof

immense, *a.* eang, dirfawr

immerse, *v.t.* trochi, suddo

immigrate, *v.i.* ymfudo, ymsefydlu

imminent, *a.* gerllaw, agos, wrth y drws

immobile, *a.* diymod

immolate, *v.t.* aberthu, offrymu

immoral, *a.* anfoesol

immortal, *a.* anfarwol

immune, *a.* rhydd rhag

immure, *v.t.* caethiwo, carcharu

immutable, *a.* anghyfnewidiol, digyfnewid

imp, *n.* dieflyn, cenau

impact, *n.* gwrthdrawiad, ymwrdd

impair, *v.t.* amharu

impale, *v.t.* trywanu

impart, *v.t.* cyfrannu, rhoddi

impartial, *a.* diduedd, amhleitgar, teg

impassioned, *a.* brwd, hwyliog, cyffrous

impassive, *a.* dideimlad, digyffro, didaro

impatient, *a.* diamynedd

impeach, *v.t.* cyhuddo

impecunious, *a.* heb arian, tlawd

impede, *v.t.* atal, rhwystro, llesteirio

impediment, *n.* atalfa, rhwystr

impel, *v.t.* gyrru, hyrddio, cymell

impenitent, *a.* anedifeiriol

imperative, *a.* gorchmynnol, gorfodol

imperfect, *a.* amherffaith

imperial, *a.* ymerodrol

imperil, *v.t.* peryglu

imperious, *a.* awdurdodol, trahaus

impersonal, *a.* amhersonol

impersonate, *v.t.* personoli

impertinent, *a.* amherthynasol; digywilydd

imperturbable, *a.* tawel, digyffro

impetuous, *a.* byrbwyll, nwydwyllt

impetus, *n.* cymhelliad, symbyliad

impinge, *v.i.* taro yn erbyn, gwrthdaro

impious, *a.* annuwiol, diras

implacable, *a.* anghymodlon

implant, *v.t.* plannu, gwreiddio

implement, *n.* offeryn, arf

implicate, *v.t.* gwneuthur yn gyfrannog [iad

implication *n.* ymhlygiad, goblyg-

implicit, *a.* dealledig; ymhlyg, goblygedig

implore, *v.t.* atolygu, ymbil, erfyn, crefu

imply, *v.t.* arwyddo, awgrymu

import, *v.t.* dwyn i mewn, mewnforio; arwyddo: *n.* (*pl.*) mewnforion; arwyddocâd; pwys

importance, *n.* pwys, pwysigrwydd

important, *a.* pwysig

importunate, *a.* taer

importune, *v.t.* dyfal geisio, taer erfyn

impose, *v.* gosod ar; twyllo

impossible, *a.* amhosibl, annichonadwy

impost, *n.* toll, treth

imposture, *n.* twyll, hoced

impotent, *a.* di-rym, analluog

impound, *v.i.* ffaldio; atafaelu

impoverish, *v.t.* tlodi, llymhau

impracticable, *a.* annichonadwy

imprecate, *v.t.* rhegi, melltithio

impregnable, *a.* cadarn, di-syfl

impregnate, *v.t.* ffrwythloni; trwytho

impress, *v.t.* argraffu: *n.* argraffiad

impression, *n.* argraff

imprint, *v.t.* argraffu: *n.* argraff, delw

imprison, *v.t.* carcharu

impromptu, *a. & adv.* difyfyr, byrfyfyr

improper, *a.* amhriodol, anweddus

improve, *v.* gwella, diwygio

impudent, *a.* digywilydd, haerllug

impugn, *v.t.* gwrthwynebu, amau

impulse, *n.* cymhelliad, ysgogiad

impulsive, *a.* cymhellol; byrbwyll

impunity, *n.* angherydd, angosb.— **with i.,** yn ddi-gosb

impure, *a.* amhûr, aflan

impute, *v.t.* cyfrif i; priodoli; bwrw ar

in, *pr.* yn, mewn, i mewn, o fewn

in-, *px.* di-, an-

inadvertent, *a.* anfwriadol, amryfus

inane, *a.* gwag, gwageddus, ofer

inanimate, *a.* difywyd, dienaid

inasmuch, *adv.* yn gymaint (â)

inaugurate, *v.t.* urddo, cysegru, agor, dechrau

incandescent, *a.* gwynias

incantation, *n.* swyn, swyngyfaredd

incapacitate, *v.t.* anghymhwyso, analluogi

incarcerate, *v.t.* carcharu

incarnation, *n.* ymgnawdoliad

incendiary, *a.* enynnol, llosg

incense, *n.* arogl-darth

incense, *v.t.* llidio, cythruddo

incentive, *a.* cymelliadol: *n.* cymhelliad

inception, *n.* dechreuad

incessant, *a.* di-baid, di-dor

incest, *n.* llosgach

inch, *n.* modfedd

incident, *n.* digwyddiad, tro

incipient, *a.* dechreuol

incise, *v.t.* torri, trychu

incisive, *a.* llym, miniog

incite, *v.t.* annog, cyffroi, annos

inclement, *a.* gerwin, garw, drycinog

incline, *v.* tueddu, gogwyddo: *n.* llethr

include, *v.t.* cynnwys

incoherent, *a.* digyswllt, anghysylltus

income, *n.* incwm

incongruous, *a.* anghydweddol, anaddas

incontestable, *a.* diymwad, diamheuol

inconvenience, *n.* anghyfleustra, anhwylustod

inconvenient, *a.* anghyfleus, anhwylus

incorporate, *v.* corffori, cyfuno, uno

incorrigible, *a.* heb ddim diwygio arno, anwelladwy

incorruptible, *a.* anllygradwy

increase, *v.* cynyddu: *n.* cynnydd

incredible, *a.* anhygoel, anghredadwy

increment, *n.* cynnydd, ychwanegiad

incriminate, *v.t.* cyhuddo, euogi

incubate, *v.* deor

incubus, *n.* hunllef, baich, bwrn

inculcate, *v.t.* cymell, gwasgu, pwyso

incumbent, *a.* rhwymedig ar: *n.* periglor

incur, *v.t.* rhedeg i, gosod yn agored i

incursion, *n.* ymgyrch
indebted, *a.* dyledus; rhwymedig
indecent, *a.* anweddus
indeed, *adv.* yn wir; iawn, dros ben
indefatigable, *a.* diflin, dyfal
indelible, *a.* annileadwy
indelicate, *a.* aflednais
indemnify, *v.* digolledu
indemnity, *n.* iawn
indenture, *n.* cytundeb, cyfamod
independent, *a.* annibynnol: *n.* annibynnwr
indescribable, *a.* annisgrifiadwy
indeterminate, *a.* amhenodol, penagored
index, *n.* mynegai; mynegfys
indicate, *v.t.* dangos, arwyddo
indict, *v.t.* cyhuddo
indifference, *n.* difaterwch, difrawder
indifferent, *a.* difater; dibwys; canolig
indigenous, *a.* genedigol, cynhenid
indigent, *a.* anghenus, tlawd, rheidus
indigestion, *n.* diffyg traul, camdreuliad
indignant, *a.* dig, digofus, dicllon
indignation, *n.* dig, digofaint, llid
indignity, *n.* amarch, sarhad, anfri
indirect, *a.* anuniongyrchol
indiscreet, *a.* annoeth, di-farn
indiscriminate, *a.* diwahaniaeth
indispensable, *a.* anhepgorol
indisposed, *a.* anhwylus
indissoluble, *a.* annatodol
indistinct, *a.* aneglur, anhyglyw, bloesg
indite, *v.t.* cyfansoddi, ysgrifennu
individual, *a.* unigol: *n.* un, unigolyn
indolence, *n.* seguryd, syrthni
indolent, *a.* segur, swrth, dioglyd
indomitable, *a.* anorchfygol, di-ildio
indubitable, *a.* diamheuol
induce, *v.t.* darbwyllo, denu, cymell
induct, *v.t.* sefydlu; anwytho
induction, *n.* anwythiad
indulge, *v.* boddio; maldodi

indulgence, *n.* ymfoddhad; maldod
industrial, *a.* diwydiannol, gweithfaol
industrious, *a.* diwyd, dyfal, gweithgar
industry, *n.* diwydrwydd; diwydiant   [wyn
inebriate, *v.t.* meddwi: *n.* medd-
ineffable, *a.* anhraethol, anhraethadwy
inept, *a.* heb fod yn taro, gwrthun, gwirion
inert, *a.* swrth, diynni, diegni
inestimable, *a.* amhrisiadwy
inevitable, *a.* anocheladwy, anesgorol
inexorable, *a.* di-ildio, anhyblyg
inexperience, *n.* diffyg profiad
inexperienced, *a.* amhrofiadol, dibrofiad
infallible, *a.* anffaeledig
infamous, *a.* gwaradwyddus, gwarthus
infancy, *n.* mabandod, mebyd, maboed
infant, *n.* maban, baban; un dan oed
infantry, *n.* gwŷr traed, milwyr traed
infatuate, *v.t.* gwirioni, ffoli, dylu
infect, *v.t.* heintio, llygru
infer, *v.t.* casglu
inferior, *a.* is, israddol, gwaelach: *n.* isradd
infernal, *a.* uffernol, dieflig
infest, *v.t.* bod yn bla, heigio
infidel, *n.* anffyddiwr
infidelity, *n.* anffyddiaeth; anffyddlondeb
infinite, *a.* anfeidrol
infinitesimal, *a.* anfeidrol fach
infinitive, *a.* annherfynol
infirm, *a.* egwan, gwan, gwanllyd
infirmary, *n.* ysbyty, clafdy
infirmity, *n.* gwendid, llesgedd
inflame, *v.* ennyn, cyffroi, llidio
inflamed, *a.* llidus
inflammable, *a.* hylosg
inflammation, *n.* enyniad, enynfa, llid

inflate, *v.t.* chwythu, chwyddo
inflect, *v.t.* plygu; treiglo
inflexible, *a.* anhyblyg
inflict, *v.t.* peri, gweinyddu (cosb, poen, &c.) [wadu
influence, *n.* dylanwad: *v.t.* dylan-
influenza, *n.* anwydwst, ffliw
influx, *n.* dylifiad
inform, *v.* hysbysu
infra-, *px.* is-
infringe, *v.t.* torri, troseddu
infuriate, *v.t.* ffyrnigo, cynddeiriogi
infuse, *v.t.* tywallt, arllwys; trwytho
ingenious, *a.* medrus, cywrain, celfydd
ingenuous, *a.* didwyll, diddichell
ingrained, *a.* wedi greddfu; cynhenid
ingratiate, *v.t.* ennill ffafr
ingratitude, *n.* anniolchgarwch
ingredient, *n.* cyffur, defnydd, elfen
inhabit, *v.t.* cyfanheddu, trigo, preswylio
inhale, *v.t.* tynnu anadl, anadlu
inhere, *v.i.* glynu, ymlynu, bod
inherent, *a.* cynhenid, greddfol
inherit, *v.t.* etifeddu
inheritance, *n.* etifeddiaeth
inheritor, *n.* etifedd, etifeddwr
inhibit, *v.t.* gwahardd, atal
inhuman, *a.* annynol, creulon, brwnt
inimical, *a.* gelynol, gelyniaethus
inimitable, *a.* digyffelyb
iniquity, *n.* anwiredd, camwedd
initial, *a.* dechreuol: *n.* llythyren gyntaf
initiate, *v.t.* egwyddori; derbyn; dechrau
inject, *v.t.* chwistrellu
injunction, *n.* gorchymyn, gwaharddiad
injure, *v.t.* niweidio, drygu, anafu
injury, *n.* niwed, cam, anaf
injustice, *n.* anghyfiawnder, cam
ink, *n.* inc: *v.t.* incio
inkling, *n.* awgrym, amnaid, arwydd

inland, *a.* canoldirol: *n.* canoldir
inlet, *n.* cilfach, bae
inmate, *n.* lletywr, trigiannydd, preswylydd
inmost, *a.* nesaf i mewn, dyfnaf
inn, *n.* tafarn, tafarndy, gwesty
innate, *a.* cynhenid, cynhwynol, greddfol
inner, *a.* mewnol
innings, *n.pl.* cyfle, tro
innocence, *n.* diniweidrwydd
innocent, *a.* diniwed, gwirion, dieuog
innocuous, *a.* diniwed, diberygl
innovate, *v.i.* newyddu, newid
innovation, *n.* cyfnewidiad; newyddbeth
innuendo, *n.* ensyniad
innumerable, *a.* aneirif, afrifed, dirifedi
inoculate, *v.t.* rhoi'r frech; brechu
inordinate, *a.* anghymedrol, di-rôl
inquest, *n.* cwest; trengholiad
inquietude, *n.* anesmwythder
inquire, *v.* ymofyn, ymholi, gofyn, holi
inquisition, *n.* ymchwiliad; chwillys
inquisitive, *a.* ymofyngar, holgar,
insane, *a.* gwallgof, gorffwyll, ynfyd
insatiable, *a.* anniwall
inscribe, *v.t.* arysgrifennu; cyflwyno
inscription, *n.* arysgrif
inscrutable, *a.* anolrheiniadwy, anchwiliadwy
insect, *n.* pryf, trychfil
insenate, *a.* dideimlad, disynnwyr
insensible, *a.* annheimladwy, dideimlad
insert, *v.t.* dodi i mewn
inside, *n.* tu mewn: *a.* mewnol
inside-half, *n.* mewnwr
insidious, *a.* lladradaidd, llechwraidd
insight, *n.* dirnadaeth, dealltwriaeth, mewnweliad
insignificant, *a.* di-nod, distadl, dibwys

insincere, *a.* ffuantus, rhagrithiol

insinuate, *v.* ymwthio; ensynio

insipid, *a.* diflas, merfaidd

insist, *v.i.* mynnu, haeru

insolent, *a.* haerllug, digywilydd

insolvent, *a.* yn methu talu, wedi torri

insomnia, *n.* diffyg cwsg, anhunedd

inspect, *v.t.* edrych, chwilio, archwilio

inspiration, *n.* ysbrydoliaeth

inspire, *v.* tynnu anadl; ysbrydoli

install, *v.t.* sefydlu, gorseddu

instalment, *n.* cyfran, rhandal

instance, *n.* enghraifft: *v.t.* enwi, nodi

instant, *a.* taer, dyfal; ebrwydd: *n.* eiliad, moment

instantaneous, *a.* yn y fan; disymwth

instead, *adv.* yn lle

instep, *n.* mwnwgl troed, cefn troed

instigate, *v.t.* annog, cymell, annos

instil, *v.t.* defnynnu; argymell

instinct, *n.* greddf

institute, *v.t.* sefydlu: *n.* sefydliad

instruct, *v.t.* addysgu, hyfforddi

instrument, *n.* offeryn; gweithred

insubordinate, *a.* anufudd, gwrthryfelgar

insular, *a.* ynysol, cul

insulate, *v.t.* ynysu, didoli

insult, *v.t.* sarhau: *n.* sarhad

insuperable, *a.* anorfod

insurance, *n.* yswiriant

insure, *v.* yswirio

insurgent, *a.* gwrthrygelfar: *n.* gwrthryfelwr

insurrection, *n.* terfysg, gwrthryfel

intact, *a.* cyfan, dianaf

integral, *a.* cyfan, cyflawn

integrate, *v.* cyfannu

integrity, *n.* cywirdeb, onestrwydd

integument, *n.* croen, croenyn, pilen

intellect, *n.* deall

intelligence, *n.* deallgarwch, deallusrwydd; hysbysrwydd

intelligent, *a.* deallus, deallgar

intelligible, *a.* dealladwy

intend, *v.t.* bwriadu, amcanu, golygu

intense, *a.* angerddol, dwys

intent, *a.* dyfal, diwyd, astud

intent, *n.* bwriad, amcan; ystyr; diben

intention, *n.* bwriad

inter, *v.t.* claddu, daearu

inter-, *px.* rhwng, cyd

intercede, *v.i.* cyfryngu, eiriol

intercept, *v.t.* rhwystro, rhagod

intercession, *n.* cyfryngdod, eiriolaeth

interchange, *v.t.* cyfnewid, cydgyfnewid   [ach

intercourse, *n.* cyfeillach, cyfathr-

interdict, *v.t.* gwahardd: *n.* gwaharddiad

interest, *n.* budd, buddiant; diddordeb; llog: *v.t.* diddori

interesting, *a.* diddorol

interfere, *v.t.* cyfryngu, ymyrraeth, ymhel

interim, *n.* cyfamser, cyfwng

interior, *a.* mewnol: *n.* tu mewn, canol

interject, *v.t.* bwrw i mewn; ebychu

interlock, *v.* cydgloi, cydymgloi

interloper, *n.* ymwthiwr, ymyrrwr

interlude, *n.* egwyl; anterliwt

intermediary, *n.* canolwr, cyfryngwr

intermediate, *a.* canol, canolradd

intern, *v.t.* carcharu

internal, *a.* mewnol

international, *a.* cydwladol

interpolate, *v.t.* dodi i mewn, rhyngosod

interpose, *v.* gosod rhwng, cyfryngu

interpret, *v.t.* dehongli; cyfieithu

interrogate, *v.t.* holi

interrupt, *v.t.* torri ar, torri ar draws

intersect, *v.* croesi ei gilydd; croestorri

interstice, *n.* cyfrwng, cyfwng; agen

interval, *n.* cyfwng; seibiant

intervene, *v.i.* cyfryngu

interview, *n.* cyfweliad

intestate, *a.* diewyllys

intestines, *n.pl.* perfedd, coluddion

intimacy, *n.* agosatrwydd

intimate, *a.* cyfarwydd, agos: *n.* cydnabod

intimate, *v.t.* arwyddo, hysbysu

intimidate, *v.t.* dychrynu, brawychu

into, *pr.* i, i mewn i

intolerable, *a.* annioddefol

intonation, *n.* tôn, tonyddiaeth, oslef

intone, *v.t.* llafarganu

intoxicate, *v.t.* meddwi

intractable, *a.* anhydyn, anhywaith   [dewr

intrepid, *a.* di-ofn, diarswyd, gwrol

intricate, *a.* dyrys, cymhleth, astrus

intrigue, *v.i. & n.* cynllwyn

intrinsic, *a.* priodol, hanfodol

introduce, *v.t.* rhagarwain; cyflwyno

introspection, *n.* mewnsylliad

intrude, *v.* ymyrraeth, ymyrryd

intrusion, *n.* ymwthiad

intuition, *n.* sythweliad, sythweledidad

inundate, *v.t.* gorlifo, boddi

inure, *v.t.* cynefino, arfer, caledu

invade, *v.t.* goresgyn

invalid, *a.* di-rym

invalid, *n.* un afiach, un methedig

invaluable, *a.* amhrisiadwy

invariable, *a.* gwastad, dieithriad

invasion, *n.* goresgyniad

invective, *n.* difriaeth, cabl, cabledd

inveigh, *v.i.* difrio, cablu, sennu

inveigle, *v.t.* twyllo, llithio, hudo

invent, *v.t.* dyfeisio, dychmygu

inventory, *n.* rhestr

inverse, *a.* (yn y) gwrthwyneb

inversion, *n.* gwrthdro

invert, *v.t.* troi wyneb i waered, gwrthdroi

invest, *v.t.* gwisgo; gwarchae; buddsoddi

investigate, *v.t.* chwilio

inveterate, *a.* cyndyn, dygn

invidious, *a.* eiddiglyd

invigorate, *v.t.* cryfhau, grymuso

invincible, *a.* anorchfygol

inviolable, *a.* dihalog, cysegredig

invisible, *a.* anweledig, anweladwy

invitation, *n.* gwahoddiad

invite, *v.t.* gwahodd, denu

invoice, *n.* infois

invoke, *v.t.* galw ar, galw am

involuntary, *a.* o anfodd, anfwriadol, annirfoddol

involve, *v.t.* drysu; cynnwys

inward, *a.* mewnol

iodine, *n.* ïodin

ion, *n.* ïon

ir-, *px.* di-, an-

irate, *a.* dig, llidiog

ire, *n.* dig, dicter, llid, soriant

iris, *n.* enfys; elestr

Irish, *a.* Gwyddelig: *n.* Gwyddeleg

irksome, *a.* blin, trafferthus, diflas

iron, *n. & a.* haearn: *v.t.* smwddio

irony, *n.* coegni, gwatwareg

irradiate, *v.t.* pelydru, goleuo, disgleirio

irrefragable, *a.* diwrthbrawf, diymwad

irrefutable, *a.* anwrthbrofadwy

irreparable, *a.* anadferadwy

irreproachable, *a.* diargyhoedd

irresistible, *a.* anorchfygol

irretrievable, *a.* anadferadwy

irrevocable, *a.* di-alw-yn-ôl

irrigate, *v.t.* dyfrhau, mwydo

irritable, *n.* croendenau, anniddig, llidiog

irritate, *v.t.* cythruddo, llidio, ffyrnigo

irruption, *n.* rhuthr

is, *v.i.* mae, sydd, yw, ydyw, oes

island, isle, *n.* ynys

islet, *n.* ynysig

isolate, *v.t.* neilltuo, gwahanu, unigo

Israelite, *n.* Israeliad

issue, *n.* mynediad allan; llif; agorfa, arllwysfa; had, hilogaeth; canlyniad, diwedd; pwnc mewn dadl: v. tarddu, deillio; rhoi allan, cyhoeddi

isthmus, n. culdir

it, pn. efe, fe, ef, efo, fo, o; hi

italics, n.pl. llythrennau italaidd

itch, v.i. ysu, cosi: n. y crafu, ysfa

item, n. peth, pwnc, ban, darn, tamaid

iterate, v.t. ailadrodd

itinerant, a. teithiol

itinerary, n. teithlyfr: a. teithiol

itinerate, v.i. teithio, cylchdeithio

itself, pn. ei hun, ei hunan

ivory, n. ifori

ivy, n. eiddew, eiddiorwg, iorwg

J

jabber, v.i. bragawthan, clebran: n. clebar

jackass, n. asyn gwryw; penbwl, hurtyn [do

jackdaw, n. cogfran, corfran, jac-y-

jacket, n. siaced

jade, v.t. blino, lluddedu

jagged, a. danheddog, ysgithrog

jail, n. carchar

jam, n. cyffaith, jam

jam, v.t. gwasgu, saco

jamb, n. ystlysbost, gorsin

jangle, v.i. clochdar

janitor, n. porthor, drysor

January, n. Ionawr

jar, n. anghytsain; anghydfod: v. rhygnu

jar, n. jar

jargon, n. bregiaith, jargon

jasper, n. maen iasbis

jaundice, n. y clwyf melyn, y clefyd melyn

jaunt, v.i. gwibio, rhodio: n. gwib-daith

jaunty, a. hoenus, talog

javelin, n. picell, gwaywffon

jaw, n. gên, car yr ên; tafod; (pl.) safn

jay, n. piogen y coed, sgrech y coed

jealous, a. eiddigus, cenfigennus, gwenwynllyd

jeer, v. gwawdio, gwatwar

jejune, a. sych, diffrwyth, diflas

jeopardy, n. perygl, enbydrwydd

jerk, n. ysbonc, ysgytiad: v. ysbonc-io; ysgytio

jest, n. cellwair, ysmaldod: v.i. cellwair, ysmalio

jet, n. muchudd

jet, n. ffrwd: v. ffrydio, pistyllio

jettison, v.t. taflu (llwyth) dros y bwrdd

jetty, n. morglawdd, glanfa

Jew, n. Iddew

jewel, n. gem, glain, tlws

jib, n. hwyl flaen llong, jib

jib, v.i. nogio, strancio

jig, n. dawns fywiog, jig

jilt, v.t. siomi mewn cariad

jingle, v. tincian: n. sŵn tincian, tinc

jinks, n. miri

job, n. tasg, gorchwyl

jobbery, n. dichellwaith

jockey, n. joci

jocose, a. cellweirus, direidus, ysmala

jocular, a. digrif, ffraeth, ysmala

jocund, a. llon, hoyw, difyr

join, v. cydio, cysylltu, uno, ymuno, asio

joiner, n. asiedydd, saer coed

joint, n. cyswllt, cymal: a. cyd-ysmalio

joist, n. dist

joke, n. cellwair, maldod: v. cell-wair,

jolly, a. braf, difyr, llawen

jolt, v. ysgytio, ysgegio, honcian

jostle, v.t. ysgwyddo, cilgwthio

jot, n. iod, tipyn: v.t. nodi

journal, n. dyddlyfr; newyddiadur

journalist, n. newyddiadurwr

journey, n. taith, siwrnai: v.i. teithio

journeyman, n. gweithiwr, huriwr

joust, v.i. & n. ymwan

jovial, a. llon, llawen

joy, n. llawenydd, gorfoledd

jubilant, a. gorfoleddus

jubilee, n. jiwbili, jiwbil

Judaism, n. Iddewaeth
judge, n. barnwr, beirniad: v. barnu, beirniadu
judgment, n. barn, dyfarniad: dedfryd
judicature, n. ynadaeth, barnwriaeth
judicial, a. barnol, barnyddol, ynadol
judicious, a. call, synhwyrol, doeth
jug, n. jwg
juggle, v. consurio, castio, twyllo
juggler, n. siwglwr
juice, n. sug, sugn, sudd, nodd
July, n. Gorffennaf
jumble, v. cymysgu, cyboli: n. cymysgfa, cybolfa
jump, v. neidio, llamu: n. naid, llam
junction, n. cydiad; uniad; cyffordd
juncture, n. cyfwng
June, n. Mehefin
jungle, n. coedwig; drysi
junior, a. iau, ieuengach; ieuaf
jurisdiction, n. awdurdod, llywodraeth
jurisprudence, n. deddfeg
juror, juryman, n. rheithiwr
jury, n. rheithwyr
just, a. cyfiawn, uniawn, teg: adv. yn union; prin, braidd; newydd
justice, n. cyfiawnder; ynad, ustus
justify, v.t. cyfiawnhau
jut, v.i. taflu allan
juvenile, a. ieuanc
juxtapose, v.t. cyfosod, gosod ochr yn ochr

K

keel, n. gwaelod llong
keen, a. craff, llym, awchus
keep, v. cadw, cynnal: n. cadw; amddiffynfa
keepsake, n. cofrodd, crair
ken, v.t. canfod, dirnad: n. golwg; dirnadaeth

kennel, n. cenel, cwb ci, cwt ci
kerb, n. ymyl, cwrbyn
kerchief, n. cadach, neisied, hances
kernel, n. cnewyllyn
kettle, n. tegell
key, n. agoriad, allwedd; cywair
kick, v. cicio, gwingo: n. cic
kid, n. myn; hogyn, plentyn, crwt
kidnap, v.t. lladrata
kidney, n. aren, elwlen
kill, v.t. lladd
kiln, n. odyn
kin, n. perthynas, tras, carennydd
kind, n. rhyw, rhywogaeth, math
kind, a. caredig, caruaidd
kindergarten, n. ysgol i blant bach
kindle, v. ennyn, cynnau
kindly, a. caredig, hynaws, tirion
kindness, n. caredigrwydd
kindred, n. perthynas; perthynasau: a. perthynol
kine, n.pl. buchod, gwartheg
king, n. brenin
kingdom, n. teyrnas, brenhiniaeth
kink, n. tro, dolen; mympwy, chwilen
kirk, n. eglwys
kiss, v.t. cusanu: n. cusan
kit, n. pac,
kitchen, n. cegin
kite, n. barcut, barcutan
kitten, n. cath fach: v. bwrw cathod
kleptomania, n. ysfa ladrata
knack, n. cast, arferiad, cnac, medr
knacker, n. prynwr hen geffylau
knapsack, n. ysgrepan milwr, cnapsach
knapweed, n. pengaled
knave, n. cnaf, dihiryn
knead, v.t. tylino
knee, n. glin, pen-lin, pen-glin
kneel, v.i. penlinio
knell, n. cnul, clul
knickerbockers, n.pl. clos pen-glin
knick-knack, n. tegan
knife, (knives): n. cyllell
knight, n. marchog: v.t. urddo yn farchog
knit, v. gwau, gweu; clymu, cysylltu

knob, n. cnap, cnwc; dwrn

knock, v. cnocio, taro, curo: n. cnoc

knoll, n. bryn, bryncyn, twyn

knot, n. cwlwm; cymal, cwgn, cainc; v.t. clymu

knout, n. fflangell Rwsiaidd

know, v. gwybod, adnabod

knowledge, n. gwybodaeth

knuckle, n. cymal, migwrn, cwgn

L

label, n. llabed, label: v.t. llabedu, enwi

labial, a. gwefusol

laboratory, n. gweithfa, labordy

laborious, a. llafurus

labour, n. llafur; gwewyr esgor: v. llafurio

labyrinth, n. drysfa

lace, n. las, les; carrai: v. cau (esgidiau)

lacerate, v.t. rhwygo, llarpio, dryllio

lachrymal, a. dagreuol

lack, n. eisiau, diffyg, gwall: v. bod mewn eisiau

laconic, a. byreiriog, byr, cwta

lacteal, a. llaethog, llaethol

lacuna, (-ae), n. bwlch

lad, n. bachgen, hogyn, llanc, gwas

ladder, n. ysgol

lade, v.t. llwytho

ladle, n. lletwad, llwy

lady, n. arglwyddes; boneddiges

lag, v.i. llusgo ar ôl, ymdroi, llercian

laggard, n. ymdrowr, llusgwr, diogyn

lagoon, n. morllyn

lair, n. gwâl, lloches, ffau

laird, n. meistr tir yn yr Alban

laity, n. lleygwyr

lake, n. llyn

lamb, n. oen: v. bwrw ŵyn

lambent, a. lleibiol, llyfol

lame, n. cloff: v.t. cloffi

lament, v. galaru, cwynfan, cwyno

lamentation, n. galar, galarnad

lamp, n. lamp, llusern

lampoon, n. dychangerdd, gogangerdd

lance, n. gwaywffon, picell: v.t. lansio, agor dolur

lancet, n. fflaim, lansed

land, n. tir, gwlad: v. tirio, glanio

landlord, n. meistr tir; lletywr, tafarnwr

landscape, n. tir-olygfa, tirlun

lane, n. heolan, lôn, wtre, beidr

language, n. iaith

languid, a. egwan, llesg, llegach

languish, v.i. nychu, dihoeni, llesgáu

languor, n. gwendid, llesgedd, nychdod

lank, a. cul, tenau, main, llipa

lantern, n. llusern

lap, n. arffed, glin

lap, v. plygu, lapio: n. plyg, tro, cylch

lap, v. llepian, lleibio

lapel, n. llabed

lapidary, n. gemydd

lappet, n. llabed

lapse, n. cwymp, gwall: v.i. llithro, cwympo

larceny, n. lladrad

lard, n. bloneg: v.t. blonegu

larder, n. bwtri, pantri

large, a. mawr, helaeth, eang, maith

lark, n. ehedydd

lark, n. sbort, difyrrwch, miri: v.i. cellwair, prancio

larva, (-ae), n. cynrhonyn

larynx, n. afalfreuant, bocs llais

lascivious, a. anllad, trythyll, anniwair

lash, n. llach, fflangell: v. llachio, fflangellu; rhwymo

lass, n. llances

lassitude, n. blinder, lludded, llesgedd

lasso, n. dolenraff: v.t. dolenraffu

last, a. olaf, diwethaf: adv. yn olaf, yn ddiwethaf

last, v.i. parhau, para

latch, n. cliced: v.t. clicedu

late, *a.* hwyr, diweddar.—**l. developers,** plant hwyrgynnydd

latent, *a.* dirgel, cudd

lateral, *a.* ystlysol, ochrol

lath, *n.* aseth, eisen, dellten

lathe, *n.* turn

lather, *n.* trochion: *v.* seboni, trochioni; golchi

Latin, *a. & n.* Lladin

latitude, *n.* lledred; ehangder; penrhyddid

latter, *a.* diwethaf

lattice, *n.* dellt, rhwyllwaith

laud, *v.t.* canmol, clodfori, moli

laugh, *v.* chwerthin: *n.* chwerthiniad

laughter, *n.* chwerthin

launch, *v.* lansio, bwrw, ymfwrw

laundry, *n.* golchdy

laureate, *a.* llawryfog

laurel, *n.* llawryf

lavatory, *n.* ymolchfa, ystafell ymolchi

lavender, *n.* lafant [traffus

lavish, *a.* hael, afradlon, gwas-

law, *n.* cyfraith, deddf

lawful, *a.* cyfreithlon

lawn, *n.* lawnt, llannerch

lawn, *n.* lliain main, bliant

lawyer, *n.* cyfreithiwr, twrnai

lax, *a.* llac, esgeulus, diofal

laxative, *n.* carthlyn

lay, *n.* cân, cerdd, cathl

lay, *v.t.* gosod, dodi; gostwng, gostegu; dodwy

lay, *a.* lleyg, llyg

layer, *n.* haen, trwch

laziness, *n.* diogi

lazy, *a.* diog, dioglyd

lea, *n.* tir glas, doldir, dôl

lead, *n.* plwm; plymen

lead, *v.* arwain, tywys; blaenori: *n.* blaenoriaeth

leader, *n.* arweinydd, blaenor

leaf, (*leaves*), *n.* deilen, dalen

league, *n.* cynghrair: *v.i.* cynghreirio

league, *n.* tair milltir

leak, *n.* twll: *v.i.* gollwng, diferu, colli

lean, *a.* tenau, cul: *n.* cig coch

lean, *v.* pwyso, gogwyddo

leap, *v.* neidio, llamu: *n.* naid, llam

learn, *v.* dysgu

learned, *a.* dysgedig, hyddysg

learning, *n.* dysg, dysgeidiaeth

lease, *n.* prydles: *v.t.* prydlesu

leash, *n.* cynllyfan, tennyn: *v.t.* cynllyfanu

leather, *n.* lledr

leave, *n.* cennad, caniatâd

leave, *v.* gadael, ymadael

leaven, *n.* lefain: *v.t.* lefeinio

lectern, *n.* darllenfa eglwys

lecture, *n.* llith, darlith: *v.* darlithio

ledge, *n.* silff, ysgafell; crib, trum

ledger, *n.* llyfr cyfrifon

lee, *n.* ochr gysgodol, cysgod gwynt

leech, *n.* gêl, gelau, gelen

leek, *n.* cenhinen

leer, *v.i.* cilwenu

lees, *n.pl.* gwaddod, gwaelodion

left, *a.* aswy, chwith

leg, *n.* coes

legacy, *n.* cymynrodd

legal, *a.* deddfol, cyfreithiol, cyfreithlon

legate, *n.* llysgennad pab

legatee, *n.* derbynnydd cymynrodd

legation, *n.* llysgenhadaeth

legend, *n.* chwedl, traddodiad

legerdemain, *n.* siwglyddiaeth

legible, *a.* darllenadwy, eglur

legion, *n.* lleng, llu

legislate, *v.i.* deddfu

legislation, *n.* deddfwriaeth

legitimate, *a.* cyfreithlon

leisure, *n.* seibiant, hamdden

lend, *v.t.* benthyca, rhoi benthyg

length, *n.* hyd, meithder

lengthen, *v.* estyn, hwyhau

lengthy, *a.* hir, maith

lenient, *a.* tyner, tirion, trugarog

Lent, *n.* y Grawys

leonine, *a.* llewaidd

leopard, *n.* llewpart

leper, *n.* dyn gwahanglwyfus

leprosy, *n.* gwahanglwyf

less, *a. & adv.* llai

lessen, *v.* lleihau

lesson, *n.* gwers, llith
lest, *c.* rhag, rhag ofn, fel na
let, *v.t.* gadael, goddef; gollwng; gosod
lethal, *a.* marwol, angheuol
lethargy, *n.* cysgadrwydd, difrawder
letter, *n.* llythyren; llythyr
lettuce, *n.* letys
level, *n. & a.* lefel, gwastad: *v.t.* lefelu
lever, *n.* trosol
leveret, *n.* ysgyfarnog ieuanc
Levite, *n.* Lefiad
levity, *n.* ysgafnder, gwamalrwydd
levy, *v.t.* codi, trethu: *n.* treth
lewd, *a.* anllad, anniwair, anweddus
lexicon, *n.* geiriadur, geirlyfr
liable, *a.* rhwym, atebol, agored
liar, *n.* celwyddwr
libation, *n.* diod-offrwm
libel, *n.* athrod, enllib: *v.t.* athrodi, enllibio
liberal, *a.* hael, rhyddfrydig, rhyddfrydol: *n.* rhyddfrydwr
liberate, *v.t.* rhyddhau
libertine, *n.* oferwr, anlladwr
liberty, *n.* rhyddid; hyfdra
librarian, *n.* llyfrgellydd
library, *n.* llyfrgell
licence, *n.* trwydded; penrhyddid
license, *v.t.* trwyddedu
licentiate, *n.* trwyddedog
licentious, *a.* penrhydd, ofer, anllad
lick, *v.t.* llyfu, llyo; lleibio, llepian; curo
lid, *n.* caead, clawr
lie, *n.* celwydd, anwiredd: *v.i.* dywedyd celwydd
lie, *v.i.* gorwedd
liege, *a.* ffyddlon, ufudd
lieu, *n.* lle
lieutenant, *n.* is-gapten; rhaglaw
life, *(lives), n.* bywyd, einioes, oes, buchedd, hoedl
lifetime, *n.* oes, einioes, hoedl
lift, *v.t.* codi, dyrchafu: *n.* codiad
ligament, *n.* rhwymyn, giewyn, gewyn

light, *n.* golau, goleuni: *a.* golau: *v.* goleuo, cynnau
light, *a.* ysgafn
light, *v.i.* disgyn, taro ar
lighthouse, *n.* goleudy
lightning, *n.* mellt, lluched
lights, *n.pl.* ysgyfaint
like, *a.* tebyg, cyffelyb
like, *v.* caru, hoffi
likelihood, *n.* tebygolrwydd
likely, *a. & adv.* tebygol, tebyg
liken, *v.t.* cyffelybu
likeness, *n.* tebygrwydd; llun
likewise, *adv.* yn gyffelyb: *c.* hefyd
lily, *n.* lili, alaw
limb, *n.* aelod, cainc
lime, *n.* calch
limit, *n.* terfyn, ffin: *v.t.* cyfyngu
limp, *a.* llipa, masw, ystwyth, hyblyg
limp, *v.i.* hercian, cloffi
limpet, *n.* brenigen
limpid, *a.* gloyw, tryloyw, grisialaidd
line, *n.* llinyn, tennyn; llin, llinell; rhes; llinach: *v.t.* llinellu, rhesu
lineage, *n.* ach, llinach, llin, hil
lineament, *n.* llinell; prydwedd
linear, *a.* llinellog, llinellaidd
linen, *n.* lliain
linger, *v.* oedi, aros, sefyllian, ymdroi
linguist, *n.* ieithydd
liniment, *n.* ennaint, eli
lining, *n.* leinin
link, *n.* dolen, modrwy: *v.* cydio, cysylltu
linnet, *n.* llinos
linseed, *n.* had llin, llinad
lintel, *n.* capan drws
lion, *n.* llew
lip, *n.* gwefus, min, gwefl
liquid, *n.* gwlyb, gwlybwr, llyn, hylif: *a.* gwlyb, hylif
liquidate, *v.* talu, clirio (dyled), dirwyn i ben
liquor, *n.* llyn, gwlybwr, diod, gwirod
lisp, *n.* bloesgni: *v.* bloesgi, siarad yn floesg

list, *n.* rhestr, llechres: *v.t.* rhestru

list, *n.* gogwydd, goledd: *v.i.* pwyso, gwyro, gogwyddo

listen, *v.i.* gwrando

listless, *a.* llesg, diynni, diofal

litany, *n.* litani

literal, *a.* llythrennol

literary, *a.* llenyddol

literature, *n.* llenyddiaeth

lithe, lithesome, *a.* ystwyth, hyblyg

lithograph, *n.* maenargraff

litigate, *v.* cyfreithio

litter, *n.* elorwely; llaesod, gwasarn; torllwyth

little, *a.* bach, bychan; mân, ychydig; *n.* ychydig, tipyn

liturgy, *n.* ffurfwasanaeth

live, *a.* byw, bywiol, bywiog

live, *v.i.* byw, bucheddu, oesi

livelihood, *n.* bywoliaeth, cynhaliaeth

livelong, *a.* maith, hirfaith

lively, *a.* bywiog, hoyw, heini, sionc

liven, *v.* bywiogi, sirioli

liver, *n.* yr au, yr iau, yr afu

livery, *n.* lifrai

livid, *a.* dulas, cleisiog

living, *n.* bywoliaeth; personiaeth

lizard, *n.* madfall, genau-goeg, modrchwilen

lo, *i.* wele

load, *n.* llwyth: *v.* llwytho

loadstone, lode-, *n.* ehedfaen, tynfaen

loaf, *(loaves), n.* torth

loaf, *v.* ystelcian, sefyllian, diogi

loam, *n.* tywotglai, marl, priddglai

loan, *n.* benthyg, echwyn

loath, loth, *a.* anewyllysgar, anfodlon

loathe, *v.t.* ffieiddio, casáu

lobby, *n.* cyntedd, porth, lobi

lobster, *n.* cimwch

local, *a.* lleol

locality, *n.* lle, safle, ardal, cymdogaeth

locate, *v.t.* lleoli, sefydlu, gosod

loch, *n.* llyn, llwch

lock, *n.* clo; loc, llifddor: *v.* cloi, cau

lock, *n.* cudyn; *(pl.)* gwallt

locomotion, *n.* ymsymudiad

locomotive, *a.* ymsymudol: *n.* peiriant rheilffordd

locust, *n.* locust

lodge, *n.* lluest, llety, cyfrinfa: *v.* lletya

lodger, *n.* lletywr

lodging, *n.* **lodgings,** *n.pl.* llety

loft, *n.* taflod, llofft

lofty, *a.* uchel, aruchel, dyrchafedig

log, *n.* cyff, boncyff, pren

logic, *n.* rhesymeg

loin, *n.* llwyn, lwyn

loiter, *v.i.* ymdroi, ystelcian, sefyllian

loll, *v.i.* sefyllian, gorweddian, diogi

lonely, *a.* unig

long, *a. & adv.* hir, maith, llaes

long, *v.i.* hiraethu, dyheu

longevity, *n.* hirhoedledd

longing, *n.* hiraeth, dyhead

longitude, *n.* hyd; hydred

long-suffering, *a.* hirymarhous: *n.* hirymaros

look, *v.* edrych, syllu: *n.* edrychiad, golwg

looking-glass, *n.* drych

loom, *n.* gwŷdd

loom, *v.i.* ymrithio, ymddangos

loon, *n.* gwirionyn, dihiryn

loop, *n.* dolen: *v.* dolennu

loose, *a.* rhydd, llac: *v.t.* gollwng, rhyddhau, datod

loot, *n.* anrhaith, ysbail: *v.* ysbeilio, anrheithio

lop, *v.t.* ysgythru, brigladd, tocio

loquacious, *a.* siaradus, tafodrydd

lord, *n.* arglwydd: *v.* arglwyddiaethu

lordship, *n.* arglwyddiaeth

lore, *n.* dysg, llên

lorry, *n.* lori

lose, *v.* colli

loss, *n.* colled

lot, *n.* coelbren, rhan, tynged. **—a l.,** llawer

loud, *a.* uchel, croch

lounge, *v.i.* segura, gorweddian
louse, (*lice*), *n.* lleuen
lout, *n.* lleban, llabwst, delff
love, *n.* cariad, serch: *v.t.* caru
lovely, *a.* hawddgar, teg, hyfryd
loving, *a.* cariadus, serchog
loving-kindness, *n.* trugaredd
low, *a.* isel
low, *v.i.* brefu: *n.* bref (buwch)
lower, *v.* gostwng, darostwng, iselu
lower, *v.i.* gwgu, duo, hel cymylau
lowly, *a.* isel, iselfrydig, gostyngedig
loyal, *a.* teyrngarol
lozenge, *n.* losin
lubricate, *v.t.* iro, llithrigo, seimio
lucid, *a.* eglur, clir
luck, *n.* lwc, damwain, hap, ffawd
lucrative, *a.* enillgar, enillfawr
lucre, *n.* elw, ennill
ludicrous, *a.* chwerthinllyd, gwrthun
lug, *v.* llusgo, tynnu
luggage, *n.* clud, teithglud, celfi
lugubrious, *a.* galarus, alaethus, dolefus
lukewarm, *a.* claear, llugoer
lull, *v.t.* suo, gostegu: *n.* gosteg
lullaby, *n.* hwiangerdd
lumbago, *n.* llwynwst
lumber, *n.* llanastr, anialwch
lumber, *v.i.* llusgo
luminary, *n.* goleuad
luminous, *a.* golau, disglair, llachar
lump, *n.* lwmp, clamp, clap, talp
lunacy, *n.* lloerigrwydd, gwallgofrwydd
lunar, *a.* lloerol, lleuadol
lunatic, *n.* lloerig, gwallgofddyn
lunch, *v.* ciniawa (ganol dydd)
lunch, luncheon, *n.* byrbryd, cinio canol dydd
lung, *n.* ysgyfaint
lunge, *n.* hergwd, gwth, rhuthr
lurch, *n.* cyfyngder, dryswch, trybini
lure, *n.* hud: *v.t.* hudo, denu
lurid, *a.* erch, erchyll, erchliw, fflamgoch
lurk, *v.i.* cynllwyn, llercian, llechu

luscious, *a.* melys
lust, *n.* chwant, trachwant: *v.i.* trachwantu
lustre, *n.* gloywder, disgleirdeb, llewyrch
lusty, *a.* heini, cryf, pybyr, grymus
luxuriant, *a.* toreithiog, bras, ffrwythlon
luxurious, *a.* moethus
luxury, *n.* moeth, moethusrwydd, amheuthun
lyre, *n.* telyn
lyric, *a.* telynegol: *n.* telyneg

M

ma'am, *n.* madam, mam
mace, *n.* brysgyll, byrllysg
macerate, *v.* meddalu, mwydo; nychu, curio
machinate, *v.i.* cynllwyno
machine, *n.* peiriant
mackerel, *n.* macrell
mad, *a.* cynddeiriog, gwallgof, gwyllt, ynfyd
madam, *n.* madam, meistres
madrigal, *n.* madrigal
magazine, *n.* ystorfa, arfdy; cylchgrawn
maggot, *n.* cynrhonyn
magic, *a.* cyfareddol: *n.* hud, dewiniaeth, swyngyfaredd
magician, *n.* swynwr, dewin
magistrate, *n.* ynad
magnanimous, *a.* mawrfrydig
magnet, *n.* magned
magnificent, *a.* gwych, ysblennydd
magnify, *v.t.* mawrhau, mwyhau, chwyddo
magnitude, *n.* maint, maintioli
magpie, *n.* pi, pia, pioden, piogen
mahout, *n.* gyrrwr eliffant
maid, *n.* merch, morwyn, morwynig
maiden, *n.* morwynig: *a.* morwynol, gwyryfol
mail, *n.* y post
mail, *n.* arfogaeth [gunio
maim, *v.t.* anafu, efryddu, llur-

main, *n.* prif bibell; prif gebl; cefnfor. **—in the m.,** yn bennaf
main, *a.* pennaf, prif, mwyaf
mainland, *n.* y tir mawr
maintain, *v.t.* dal, cynnal, maentumio
maintenance, *n.* cynhaliaeth, gofalaeth
majesty, *n.* mawrhydi, mawredd
major, *a.* mwy, mwyaf, pennaf: *n.* uchgapten
majority, *n.* mwyafrif; oedran llawn
make, *v.t.* gwneuthur, peri: *n.* gwneuthuriad
maker, *n.* gwneuthurwr, creawdwr
mal-adjustment, *n.* diffyg ymaddasiad
mal-, *px.* drwg, cam
malady, *n.* drwg, anhwyldeb, dolur
malcontent, *a.* anfoddog: *n.* anfoddogwr
male, *n. & a.* gwryw
malediction, *n.* melltith
malefactor, *n.* drwgweithredwr
malevolent, *a.* drygnaws, maleisus
malformation, *n.* camffurfiad
malice, *n.* malais
malign, *a.* niweidiol; llidiog: *v.t.* enllibio
malignant, *a.* drygnaws, digasog, llidiog
mallet, *n.* gordd
malt, *n.* brag: *v.* bragu
mammal, *n.* mamal
mammoth, *a.* anferth
man, *(men), n.* dyn, gŵr
manacle, *n.* gefyn: *v.t.* gefynnu
manage, *v.* trin, llywodraethu, rheoli; ymdaro, ymdopi, llwyddo
mandate, *n.* gorchymyn, arch
mane, *n.* mwng
mange, *n.* clafr, clefri, brech y cŵn
manger, *n.* mansier, preseb
mangle, *v.t.* llurgunio
mangle, *n.* mangl
manhood, *n.* dyndod, dynoliaeth
mania, *n.* gwallgofrwydd, cynddaredd
maniac, *n.* gwallgofddyn

manifest, *a.* amlwg: *v.t.* amlygu, dangos
manifold, *a.* amryw, amrywiol
manikin, *n.* dynyn, corryn
manipulate, *v.t.* trin, trafod
mankind, *n.* dynolryw
manly, *a.* dynol, gwrol
manner, *n.* modd; moes
mannerism, *n.* munudedd, dullwedd
manœuvre, *n.* symudiad, tro, ystryw
man-of-war, *n.* llong ryfel
manor, *n.* maenor, maenol
manse, *n.* tŷ gweinidog, mans
mansion, *n.* plas; *(pl.)* trigfannau
manslaughter, *n.* dynladdiad
mantel, *n.* mantell simnai
mantelpiece, *n.* silff ben tân
mantle, *n.* mantell: *v.t.* mantellu
manual, *a.* perthynol i'r llaw: *n.* llawlyfr
manufactory, *n.* gwaith, gweithfa
manufacture, *n.* gwaith, nwydd: *v.t.* gwneuthur
manure, *n.* tail, gwrtaith: *v.t.* teilo, gwrteithio
manuscript, *n.* llawysgrif
many, *a.* llawer. **—how m.,** pa sawl
map, *n.* map
maple, *n.* masarnen
mar, *v.t.* difetha, andwyo, hagru
maraud, *v.* ysbeilio, anrheithio
marble, *n.* marmor, mynor; marblen
March, *n.* (mis) Mawrth
march, *v.* ymdeithio: *n.* ymdaith
march, *n.* mers, goror, cyffin
marchioness, *n.* ardalyddes
mare, *n.* caseg
margarine, *n.* margarîn
margin, *n.* ymyl, cwr, goror
marigold, *n.* gold Mair, gold
marine, *a.* morol: *n.* môr-filwr; llynges [dwywr]
mariner, *n.* morwr, llongwr, mormarital,** *a.* priodasol
maritime, *a.* morol, arforol
mark, *n.* nod, marc: *v.t.* nodi, marcio, craffu, sylwi

market, *n.* marchnad: *v.* marchnata

maroon, *v.* rhoi a gadael ar ynys anial

marquee, *n.* pabell fawr

marquis, *n.* ardalydd

marriage, *n.* priodas

marrow, *n.* mêr

marry, *v.* priodi

marsh, *n.* morfa, cors, mignen

marshal, *n.* cadlywydd: *v.t.* byddino, trefnu

mart, *n.* marchnadfa, arwerthfa

martial, *a.* milwraidd, milwrol

martinet, *n.* disgyblwr llym

martyr, *n.* merthyr: *v.t.* merthyru

martyrdom, *n.* merthyrdod

marvel, *n.* rhyfeddod: *v.i.* rhyfeddu, synnu

masculine, *a.* gwryw, gwrywaidd

mash, *n.* cymysg, stwns: *v.t.* stwnsio

mask, *n.* mwgwd: *v.t.* mygydu, cuddio

mason, *n.* saer maen, masiwn, meiswn

mass, *n.* pentwr, talp, crynswth, mas; (*pl.*) y werin

mass, *n.* offeren

massacre, *n.* cyflafan: *v.t.* cyflafanu

massive, *a.* trwm, cadarn, ffyrf, praff

mass-production, *n.* masgynhyrchu

mast, *n.* hwylbren

master, *n.* meistr, athro: *v.t.* meistroli

masticate, *v.t.* cnoi, malu

mastiff, *n.* gafaelgi, cystowci, catgi

mat, *n.* mat: *v.t.* matio, plethu

match, *n.* matsen

match, *n.* cymar; priodas; ymrysonfa, gêm: *v.* cystadlu; cyfateb

matchless, *n.* digymar, digyffelyb

mate, *n.* cymar, cydymaith; mêt: *v.t.* cymharu

material, *a.* materol; o bwys: *n.* defnydd

materialism, *n.* materoliaeth

maternal, *a.* mamol; o du'r fam

mathematics, *n.pl.* mathemateg

matins, *n.pl.* boreol weddi, plygain

matriculate, *v.* ymaelodi mewn prifysgol

matrimony, *n.* priodas

matron, *n.* gwraig briod, meistres

matter, *n.* mater; crawn: *v.i.* bod o bwys

mattock, *n.* caib, matog

mattress, *n.* matras

mature, *a.* aeddfed; mewn oed: *v.* aeddfedu

maudlin, *a.* lledfeddw; masw, merfaidd

maul, *v.t.* baeddu, pwyo

maunder, *v.i.* llusgo, ymlusgo; grymial

mausoleum, *n.* beddadail

mauve, *n.* lliw porffor

maw, *n.* crombil, cylla

mawkish, *a.* diflas, merfaidd

maxim, *n.* dihareb, gwireb, rheol

maximum, *n.* uchafswm, uchafrif

May, *n.* Mai

may, *n.* blodau drain gwynion

mayor, *n.* maer

maze, *n.* drysfa

mazy, *a.* dyrys, troellog

me, *pn.* myfi, mi, fi, i; minnau

mead, *n.* medd

meadow, *n.* dôl, gwaun, gweirglodd

meagre, *a.* cul, tenau, prin, tlodaidd, llwm

meal, *n.* blawd

meal, *n.* pryd o fwyd

mean, *n.* cyfrwng, modd; canol; cymedr

mean, *v.t.* meddwl, golygu, bwriadu

mean, *a.* gwael, isel, crintach, iselwael

meander, *v.i.* dolennu, troelli, ymdroelli

meaning, *n.* ystyr, meddwl

meantime, -while, *adv.* yn y cyfamser

measles, *n.pl.* y frech goch

measure, *v.t.* & *n.* mesur

meat, *n.* ymborth, bwyd; cig

mechanic, *n.* peiriannydd
mechanical, *a.* peiriannol, peirianyddol
mechanics, *n.pl.* mecaneg
mechanism, *n.* peirianwaith
medal, *n.* bathodyn, medal
meddle, *v.i.* ymyrraeth, ymhel
mediaeval *a.* canoloesol
medial, *a.* canol, canolog
mediate, *v.i.* canoli, cyfryngu
medical, *a.* meddygol
medicine, *n.* meddyginiaeth; ffisig, moddion
mediocre, *a.* canolig, cyffredin
meditate, *v.* myfyrio
meditation, *n.* myfyrdod
medium, *n.* canol; cyfrwng: *a.* canol, canolig
medley, *n.* cymysgfa, cybolfa; cymysgedd
meek, *a.* llariaidd, addfwyn
meet, *v.* cyfarfod, cwrdd: *a.* addas
meeting, *n.* cyfarfod, cyfarfyddiad
melancholy, *a.* prudd, pruddglwyfus: *n.* pruddglwyf, y felan
mêlée, *n.* ymgiprys, ysgarmes
mellifluous, *a.* melyslais, melysber
mellow, *a.* aeddfed, meddal: *v.* aeddfedu
melody, *n.* peroriaeth, melodi
melt, *v.* toddi, ymdoddi
member, *n.* aelod
membrane, *n.* pilen, croenyn
memento, *n.* cofeb, cofarwydd
memoir, *n.* cofiant
memorable, *a.* cofiadwy, bythgofiadwy
memorandum, *n.* cofnod, cofnodiad
memorial, *a.* coffadwriaethol: *n.* coffadwriaeth; cofeb; deiseb
memory, *n.* cof; coffadwriaeth
menace, *n.* bygythiad: *v.t.* bygwth
menagerie, *n.* milodfa, sioe (siew) anifeiliaid
mend, *v.* gwella, cyweirio, trwsio, helpu
mendacity, *n.* anwiredd, celwydd
mendicant, *a.* cardotlyd: *n.* cardotyn

menial, *a.* gwasaidd, isel: *n.* gwas
mensuration, *n.* mesureg
mental, *a.* meddyliol
mention, *v.t.* crybwyll, sôn: *n.* crybwylliad
mentor, *n.* cynghorwr
menu, *n.* rhestr bwydydd, bwydrestr   [nachol
mercantile, *a.* marchnadol, masmercenary,** *a.* ariangar, chwannog i elw: *n.* huriwr, milwr cyflog
merchandise, *n.* marsiandiaeth
merchant, *n.* masnachwr, marsiandwr
merciful, *a.* trugarog, tosturiol
mercuric, *a.* mercurig
mercury, *n.* arian byw, mercwri
mercy, *n.* trugaredd. — **m-seat,** trugareddfa
mere, *a.* unig, pur, moel, noeth, hollol
mere, *n.* llyn, llwch
merge, *v.* soddi, suddo, colli, ymgolli
meridian, *n.* nawn; cyhydedd; anterth
merit, *n.* haeddiant, teilyngdod: *v.t.* haeddu, teilyngu
mermaid, *n.* môr-forwyn
merriment, *n.* digrifwch, difyrrwch
merry, *a.* llawen, llon
mesh, *n.* masgl, magl
mess, *n.* saig; llanastr, annibendod: *v.* bwyta; ymhel; maeddu
message, *n.* cenadwri, neges
messenger, *n.* cennad, negesydd
messieurs (Messrs.), *n.pl.* meistri
metabolism, *n.* metaboleg, metabolaeth
metal, *n.* metel
metamorphosis, (-ses), *n.* trawsffurfiad, metamorffosis
metaphor, *n.* trosiad
metaphysics, *n.pl.* metaffiseg
meteor, *n.* seren wib
meter, *n.* mesurydd
method, *n.* trefn, method, dull
meticulous, *a.* gorfanwl
metonymy, *n.* trawsenwad

metre, *n.* mesur, mydr
metrical *a.* mydryddol
metric system, *n.* system fedrig
metropolis, *n.* prifddinas
mettle, *n.* metel, anian, arial
mew, *v.i.* mewian
miasma, *n.* tawch heintus
Michaelmas, *n.* gŵyl Fihangel
microbe, *n.* trychfilyn, meicrob
microphone, *n.* meicroffon, meic
microscope, *n.* chwyddwydr, meicrosgob
mid, *a.* canol
midden, *n.* tomen
middle, *n. & a.* canol
middling, *a.* canolig, gweddol, symol
midge, *n.* gwybedyn
midget, *n.* corrach
midnight, *n.* canol nos, hanner nos
midriff, *n.* llengig
midst, *n.* canol, plith
midwife, (*-wives*), *n.* bydwraig
mien, *n.* golwg, pryd, gwedd, agwedd
might, *n.* nerth, cadernid, gallu
mighty, *a.* cadarn, galluog, nerthol
migrate, *v.i.* symud, mudo
milch, *a.* blith, llaethog
mild, *a.* tyner, tirion, mwyn; gwan, ysgafn
mildew, *n.* llwydi, llwydni
mile, *n.* milltir
militant, *a.* milwriaethus
military, *a.* milwrol
militate, *v.i.* milwrio
militia, *n.* milisia
milk, *n.* llaeth, llefrith: *v.t.* godro
mill, *n.* melin: *v.t.* melino, malu
millennium, *n.* mil blynyddoedd
miller, *n.* melinydd
milliner, *n.* hetwraig
million, *n.* miliwn
millionaire, *n.* miliynydd
mime, *n.* meim
mimic, *v.t.* dynwared, gwatwar
mince, *v.t.* malu: *n.* briwgig, briwfwyd
mind, *n.* meddwl, bryd, cof: *v.* gofalu, cofio

mine, *n.* mwynglawdd, pwll
mineral, *a.* mwynol: *n.* mwyn
mingle, *v.* cymysgu, britho
miniature, *n.* mân ddarlun: *a.* bychan
minimize, *v.t.* lleihau, bychanu
minimum, *n.* lleiafrwm, isafrif
minion, *n.* anwylyn, ffafryn; gwas
minister, *n.* gweinidog: *v.* gwasanaethu, gweinidogaethu
ministry, *n.* gweinidogaeth, gweinyddiaeth, gwasanaeth
minnow, *n.* pilcodyn, pilcyn
minor, *a.* llai, lleiaf: un dan oed
minority, *n.* maboed, mebyd; lleiafrif
minster, *n.* mynachlog; eglwys gadeiriol
minstrel, *n.* clerwr, cerddor
mint, *n.* bathdy: *v.t.* bathu
mint, *n.* mintys
minus, *a. & pr.* llai, heb, yn fyr o; minws
minute, *a.* bach, bychan, mân, manwl
minute, *n.* munud; cofnod
minx, *n.* coegen, mursen, maeden
miracle, *n.* gwyrth
miraculous, *a.* gwyrthiol
mire, *n.* llaid, llaca, tom, baw
mirror, *n.* drych: *v.t.* adlewyrchu
mirth, *n.* llawenydd, digrifwch, afiaith
mis-, *px.* cam-
misadventure, *n.* amryfusedd
misanthropist, *n.* dyngaswr
miscarry, *v.i.* erthylu; aflwyddo; colli
miscellaneous, *a.* amrywiol, amryfath
mischance, *n.* anffawd, damwain
mischief, *n.* drwg, drygioni, direidi
mischievous, *a.* drygionus, direidus
miscreant, *n.* dihiryn, adyn
misdeed, *n.* drwgweithred, camwedd
misdemeanour, *n.* camwedd, trosedd
miser, *n.* cybydd

miserable, *a.* truenus, gresynus, anhapus

misery, *n.* trueni, gresyni, adfyd

misfortune, *n.* anffawd, aflwydd

misgivings, *n.pl.* amheuon, ofnau

mishap, *n.* anap, anffawd, aflwydd

misinterpret, *v.* camesbonio

misnomer, *n.* camenw

misrepresent, *v.t.* camddarlunio, camliwio

miss, *v.t.* methu, ffaelu, colli: *n.* meth

missal, *n.* llyfr offeren

missing, *a.* yn eisiau, yngholl, ar goll

mission, *n.* cenhadaeth

missionary, *n.* cenhadwr: *a* cenhadol

missive, *n.* llythyr

mist, *n.* niwl, nudden; tarth; caddug

mistake, *v.t.* camgymryd, methu: *n.* camgymeriad, gwall

mistletoe, *n.* uchelwydd

mistress, *n.* meistres

mite, *n.* hatling; mymryn, tamaid

mitigate, *v.t.* lleddfu, lliniaru, lleihau

mitre, *n.* meitr

mitten, *n.* dyrnfol, maneg heb fysedd

mix, *v.* cymysgu

mixture, *n.* cymysgedd, cymysgfa

moan, *n. & v.* ochain, griddfan, udo

moat, *n.* ffos (castell)

mob, *n.* torf, tyrfa, haid: *v.t.* ymosod ar, baeddu

mobile, *a.* symudol, symudadwy; mudol (cemeg)

mobilize, *v.t.* dygyfor, byddino

mock, *v.* gwatwar: *a.* gau, ffug

mockery, *n.* gwatwar; ffug

mode, *n.* modd, dull

model, *n.* cynllun, patrwm: *v.t.* llunio

moderate, *a.* cymedrol: *v.t.* cymedroli

modern, *a.* modern, diweddar

modest, *a.* gwylaidd; diymhongar

modesty, *n.* gwylder, gwyleidd-dra

modify, *v.t.* newid, lleddfu

modulate, *v.* cyweirio neu reoli llais

moiety, *n.* hanner, hanereg

moil, *v.i.* ymlâdd, ymfaeddu

moist, *a.* llaith, gwlyb

moisture, *n.* lleithder, gwlybaniaeth, gwlybwr

molar, *n.* cilddant

mole, *n.* man geni

mole, *n.* gwadd, twrch daear

mole, *n.* morglawdd

molecule, *n.* molecwl: *a.* molecylig

molest, *v.t.* molestu, aflonyddu, blino

mollify, *v.t.* meddalu, tyneru, dyhuddo

molten, *a.* tawdd

moment, *n.* moment; pwys, pwysigrwydd

momentum, *n.* momentwm

monarch, *n.* brenin, teyrn, penadur

monastery, *n.* mynachlog, mynachdy

monastic, *a.* mynachaidd

Monday, *n.* dydd Llun

monetary, *a.* ariannol

money, *n.* arian, pres

mongrel, *a.* cymysgryw: *n.* mwngrel

monitor, *n.* monitor

monk, *n.* mynach

monkey, *n.* mwnci

mono-, *px.* un-

monogamy, *n.* unwreigiaeth

monoglot, *a.* uniaith

monolith, *n.* maen hir

monologue, *n.* ymson

monopoly, *n.* monopoli

monosyllable, *n.* gair unsill

monotheism, *n.* undduwiaeth

monotone, *a. & n.* unsain

monotonous, *a.* undonog

monotony, *n.* undonedd, unrhywiaeth

monsoon, *n.* monsŵn

monster, *n.* anghenfil; clamp: *a.* anferth

monstrous, *a.* angenfilaidd, anferth, gwrthun

month, *n.* mis

monthly, *a.* misol: *n.* misolyn

monument, *n.* cofadail, cofgolofn

mood, *n.* hwyl, tymer; modd

moody, *a.* oriog, cyfnewidiol

moon, *n.* lleuad, lloer

moonlight, *n.* golau leuad

moonshine, *n.* ffiloreg, gwegi, lol

moor, *n.* morfa, rhos, gwaun

moor, *v.t.* angori, bachu, sicrhau

mop, *n.* mop: *v.t.* mopio, sychu

mope, *v.i.* pendrymu, delwi

moraine, *n.* marian

moral, *a.* moesol: *n.* moeswers, addysg

morality, *n.* moesoldeb

morass, *n.* cors, mignen

morbid, *a.* afiach

mordant, *a.* brathog, llym

more, *a.* mwy, ychwaneg, rhagor: *adv.* mwy, mwyach

moreover, *adv.* heblaw hynny, hefyd

moribund, *a.* ar farw, ar dranc

morning, *n.* bore: *a.* bore, boreol

morose, *a.* sur, sarrug, afrywiog, blwng

morphology, *n.* ffurfianneg

morrow, *n.* trannoeth

morsel, *n.* tamaid, tameidyn

mortal, *a.* marwol, angheuol: *n.* dyn marwol

mortar, *n.* cymrwd, morter; breuan, morter

mortgage, *n.* arwystl, morgais: *v.t.* arwystlo, morgeisio

mortify, *v.* marwhau; blino, siomi

mortise, *n.* mortais: *v.t.* morteisio

mortuary, *n.* marwdy

Mosaic, *a.* Moesenaidd

mosaic, *a.* brith, amryliw: *n.* brithwaith

mosque, *n.* mosg, teml Fahometan-aidd

moss, *n.* mwswgl, mwsogl

most, *a.* mwyaf, amlaf

mostly, *adv.* gan mwyaf, fynychaf

mote, *n.* brycheuyn, llychyn, fflewyn

moth, *n.* gwyfyn

mother, *n.* mam

motion, *n.* symudiad, ysgogiad; cynigiad

motive, *a.* symudol, ysgogol: *n.* cymhelliad, amcan, motif

motley, *a.* brith, cymysg

motor, *n.* modur

mottle, *v.t.* britho, brychu

motto, *n.* arwyddair

mould, *n.* pridd, daear, gweryd: *v.t.* priddo

mould, *n.* mold; delw: *v.t.* moldio, llunio, delweddu

mould, *n.* llwydni, llwydi

moulder, *v.i.* malurio, adfeilio

moult, *v.* bwrw plu, mudo

mound, *n.* twmpath, clawdd, crug

mount, *n.* mynydd, bryn

mount, *v.* esgyn, dringo, codi, myned ar gefn; gosod

mountain, *n.* mynydd

mountebank, *n.* ymhonnwr, ffŵl ffair

mourn, *v.* galaru

mournful, *a.* galarus, dolefus, alaethus

mourning, *n.* galar; galarwisg

mouse, *(mice), n.* llygoden: *v.* llygota

moustache, *n.* trawswch, mwstas

mouth, *n.* genau, safn, ceg: *v.* cegu, safnu

move, *v.* symud, syflyd; cymell; cynnig; cyffroi

movement, *n.* symudiad; ysgogiad

mow, *v.t.* lladd (gwair): *n.* mwdwl, medel

much, *a.* llawer: *adv.* yn fawr

mucilage, *n.* glud, llys, llysnafedd

muck, *n.* tail, tom, baw: *v.t.* tomi, baeddu

mucus, *n.* llys, llysnafedd

mud, *n.* mwd, llaid, llaca, baw

muddle, *v.i.* drysu: *n.* dryswch

muff, *n.* mwff

muff, *n.* hurtyn, penbwl, llelo

muffin, *n.* math o deisen, chwiogen

mug, *n.* cwpan, godart

mulberry, *n.* morwydden

mulct, *n.* dirwy: *v.t.* dirwyo

mule, *n.* mul, bastart mul
mullion, *n.* post ffenestr
multi-, *px.* aml, lluosog
multifarious, *n,* amryfath, lluosog
multiple, *a.* amryfal: *n.* cynhwysrif
multiplicand, *n.* lluosrif
multiplication, *n.* amlhad, lluosogiad, lluosiad
multiplicity, *n.* lluosowgrwydd
multiply, *v.* amlhau, lluosogi, lluosi
multitude, *n.* lliaws, tyrfa
mumble, *v.* grymial, myngial
mummy, *n.* mwmi
mumps, *n.* clwy'r pennau, y dwymyn doben
munch, *v.t.* cnoi
mundane, *a.* bydol, daearol
municipal, *a.* dinesig, bwrdeisiol
munificent, *a.* hael, haelionus
munitions, *n.pl.* arfau neu offer rhyfel
mural, *a.* murol
murder, *v.t.* llofruddio: *n.* llofruddiaeth
murderer, *n.* llofrudd
murky, *a.* tywyll, cymylog, dudew
murmur, *v. & n.* murmur, grwgnach
muscle, *n.* cyhyr, cyhyryn
muscular, *a.* cyhyrog
muse, *n.* awen, awenydd
muse, *v.i.* myfyrio, synfyfyrio
museum, *n.* amgueddfa
mushroom, *n.* caws llyffant, madarch
music, *n.* miwsig, cerdd, cerddoriaeth, peroriaeth
musician, *n.* cerddor
musk, *n.* mwsg
musket, *n.* mwsged
musketry, *n.* saethyddiaeth
must, *v.def.* rhaid
mustang, *n.* ceffyl gwyllt
mustard, *n.* mwstart
muster, *v.* casglu, cynnull, byddino: *n.* cynulliad, mwstwr
musty, *a.* wedi llwydo, hendrwm, mws
mutable, *a.* anwadal, cyfnewidiol

mutate, *v.* treiglo (llythrennau)
mutation, *n.* cyfnewidiad, treiglad
mute, *a.* mud: *n.* mudan
mutilate, *v.t.* anafu, hagru, llurgunio
mutiny, *n.* terfysg, gwrthryfel
mutter, *v.* myngial, grymial, mwmian
mutton, *n.* cig dafad, cig mollt, cig gwedder
mutual, *a.* cyd, o boptu, y naill a'r llall
muzzle, *n.* genau, ffroen; pennor: *v.t.* cau safn, rhoi taw ar
my, *pn.* fy
myriad, *n.* myrdd
myrmidon, *n.* anfadwas, dihiryn
myrrh, *n.* myrr
myrtle, *n.* myrtwydd
myself, *pn.* myfi fy hun
mystery, *n.* dirgelwch
mystic, *n.* cyfriniwr, cyfrinydd
mystify, *v.t.* synnu, syfrdanu
myth, *n.* dameg, chwedl, myth
mythology, *n.* chwedloniaeth

N

nadir, *n.* isafbwynt, ory
nag, *v.* cecru, ffraeo, cadw sŵn
nail, *n.* hoel, hoelen; ewin: *v.t.* hoelio
naïve, *a.* diniwed, diddichell, gwirion
naked, *a.* noeth
namby-pamby, *a.* merf, merfaidd, llipa
name, *n.* enw; *v.t.* enwi, galw
namely, *adv.* sef, nid amgen
namesake, *n.* cyfenw
nap, *v.i.* cysgu, pendwmpian; *n.* cyntun
nape, *n.* gwar, gwegil
napkin, *n.* napcyn, cadach, cewyn
narcotic, *a. & n.* cysgbair
narrate, *v.t.* adrodd (hanes)
narrative, *n.* hanes, chwedl, stori
narrow, *a.* cul, cyfyng: *v.* culhau, cyfyngu

nasal, *a.* trwynol

nasty, *a.* cas, brwnt, budr, ffiaidd

natal, *a.* genedigol

nation, *n.* cenedl

national, *a.* cenedlaethol

native, *n.* brodor: *a.* brodorol; cyn-henid

nativity, *n.* genedigaeth

natty, *a.* del, destlus, deheuig

natural *a.* anianol, naturiol

naturalist, *n.* naturiaethwr

naturalize, *v.* naturioli, breinio, cywladu

nature, *n.* anian, natur; naturiaeth

naught, *n.* dim

naughty, *a.* drwg, drygionus

nausea, *n.* clefyd y môr; cyfog; ffieidd-dod

nauseous, *a.* cyfoglyd, ffiaidd, atgas

nautical, *a.* morwrol, mordwyol

naval, *a.* llyngesol, morol

nave, *n.* corff eglwys

nave, *n.* both, bŵl

navel, *n.* bogail

navigate, *v.t.* morio, mordwyo

navvy, *n.* cloddiwr, ceibiwr

navy, *n.* llynges

nay, *adv.* na, nage; nid hynny yn unig

Nazarite, *n.* Nasaread

naze, *n.* trwyn, penrhyn, pentir

neap, *a. & n.* **n. tide,** nêp, llanw isel

near, *a., adv. & pr.* agos: *v.* agosáu, nesu

neat, *a.* del, destlus, twt, trefnus; pur

neat, *n.* ych, eidion

nebula, (*-ae*), *n.* niwlen; niwl sêr

nebulous, *a.* niwlog

necessary, *a.* angenrheidiol

necessitate, *v.t.* gorfodi

necessitous, *a.* anghenus, rheidus

necessitude, *n.* angenoctid

necessity, *n.* angen, anghenraid, rhaid

neck, *n.* gwddf, mwnwgl, gwar

necromancy, *n.* dewiniaeth

nectar, *n.* neithdar

need, *n. & v.* (bod mewn) angen, eisiau

needful *a.* rheidiol, angenrheidiol

needle, *n.* nodwydd; gwaell

needless, *a.* afreidiol, dianghenraid

nefarious, *a.* anfad, drygionus, ysgeler

negation, *n.* nacâd, gwadiad, negyddiad

negative, *a.* nacaol, negyddol

neglect, *v.t.* esgeuluso: *n.* esgeulustra

negligent, *a.* esgeulus

negotiate, *v.* negeseua, trafod, trefnu

negro, *n.* dyn du, negro

neigh, *v.i.* gweryru: *n.* gweryriad

neighbour, *n.* cymydog

neighbourhood, *n.* cymdogaeth

neither, *c.* na, nac, ychwaith: *a. & pn.* na'r naill na'r llall, nid yr un o'r ddau

Nemesis, *n.* dialedd

neo-, *px.* newydd, diweddar

neophyte, *n.* newyddian

nephew, *n.* nai

nepotism, *n.* neigaredd

nerve, *n.* giewyn, gewyn, nerf: *v.t.* gwroli

nervous, *a.* gieuol; nerfus, ofnus

nest, *n.* nyth: v. nythu

nestle, *v.* nythu

net, *n.* rhwyd, rhwyden

net, *a.* union, cywir, net

nether, *a.* isaf

nettle, *n.* danadl: *v.t.* pigo; llidio

neuralgia, *n.* gieuwst

neurasthenia, *n.* nerfwst

neuritis, *n.* newritis

neurosis, *n.* newrosis

neuter, *a.* diryw

neutral, *a.* amhleidiol: *n.* amhleidydd

neutralize, *v.t.* dieffeithio, dirymu

never, *adv.* ni . . . erioed, ni . . .byth

nevertheless, *adv. & c.* eto, er hynny

new, *a.* newydd

news, *n.* newydd, newyddion, hanes

newspaper, *n.* papur newydd, newyddiadur

newt, *n.* madfall, genau-goeg, modrchwilen

next, *a.* nesaf: *adv.* yn nesaf

nib, *n.* blaen, nib

nibble, *v.* deintio, cnoi

nice, *a.* neis, hardd, tlws; manwl, cynnil

niche, *n.* cloer

nickname, *n.* llysenw: *v.t.* llysenwi

niece, *n.* nith

niggard, *n.* cybydd: *a.* cybyddlyd, crintach

nigger, *n.* dyn du (mewn dirmyg)

nigh, *a. & adv.* agos

night, *n.* nos; noson, noswaith

nightfall, *n.* y cyfnos, yr hwyr

nightingale, *n.* eos

nightmare, *n.* hunllef

nil, *n.* dim

nimble, *a.* gwisgi, heini, sionc

nincompoop, *n.* penbwl, gwirionyn

nine, *a. & n.* naw

nineteen, *a. & n.* pedwar (pedair) ar bymtheg, un deg naw

ninety, *a. & n.* deg a phedwar ugain, naw deg

nip, *v.* brathu, cnoi; deifio

nipple, *n.* diden, teth, tethan

nit, *n.* nedden

nitrate, *n.* nitrad

nitre, *n.* neitr

nitrogen, *n.* nitrogen

nitrous, *n.* nitrus

no, *a.* ni . . . neb, dim: *adv.* ni, &c., dim; nac oes, nage, naddo

nobility, *n.* bonedd, urddas, mawredd

noble, *a.* ardderchog, urddasol, pendefigaidd: *n.* pendefig

nobleman, *n.* pendefig

nobody, *n.* neb

nocturnal, *a.* nosol

nod, *v.* amneidio; pendrymu: *n.* amnaid

noddle, *n.* penglog, clopa, clol, siol

noise, *n.* swn, twrf, trwst

noisome, *a.* niweidiol, atgas, ffiaidd

nomad, *n.* crwydrwr: *a.* crwydrol

nom de plume, *n.* ffugenw

nomenclature, *n.* cyfundrefn enwau

nominal *a.* enwol, mewn enw

nominate, *v.t.* enwi, enwebu

nominative, *a.* enwol

non-, *px.* an-, di-

nonagenarian, *n.* un deng mlwydd a phedwar ugain

nonce, *n.* y tro

nonchalance, *n.* difrawder, difaterwch

nonchalant, *a.* didaro, difater

nonconformist, *n.* anghydffurfiwr, ymneilltuwr

nonconformity, *n.* anghydffurfiaeth, ymneilltuaeth

nondescript, *a.* anodd ei ddarlunio, od

none, *pn.* neb, dim, dim un

nonentity, *n.* dyn dibwys, neb

nonplus, *v.t.* drysu, dymchwelyd

nonsense, *n.* lol, dyli, gwiriondeb

noodle, *n.* gwirionyn, ffwlcyn

nook, *n.* congl, cornel, cilfach

noon, *n.* nawn, hanner dydd, canol dydd

noose, *n.* cwlwm rhedeg, byddag(l), magl

nor, *c.* na, nac

normal, *a.* rheolaidd, cyffredin, safonol

north, *n.* gogledd: *a.* gogleddol

nose, *n.* trwyn: *v.* trwyno, ffroeni, gwyntio

nosegay, *n.* blodeuglwm, pwysi

nostalgia, *n.* hiraeth

nostril, *n.* ffroen

not, *adv.* na, nac, nad, ni, nid

notable, *a.* nodedig, hynod, enwog

notary, *n.* nodiadur, nodiedydd

notation, *n.* nodiant

notch, *n.* rhic, bwlch, hecyn, rhwgn, rhint

note, *n.* nod, nodyn: *v.t.* nodi, sylwi

noted, *a.* nodedig, hynod, enwog

nothing, *n.* dim

notice, *n.* sylw, rhybudd: *v.t.* sylwi

notify, *v.t.* hysbysu, rhoi rhybudd

notion, *n.* tyb, amcan, syniad
notorious, *a.* hynod, carn, rhemp
notwithstanding, *c.* er: *pr.* er, er gwaethaf
nought, *n.* dim; gwagnod (0)
noun, *n.* enw
nourish, *v.t.* maethu, meithrin
nourishing, *a.* maethlon
nourishment, *n.* maeth
novel, *a.* newydd: *n.* nofel
November, *n.* Tachwedd
novice, *n.* newyddian
now, *adv.*, *c.* & *n.* yn awr, yr awron, yrŵan, weithian, bellach
nowadays, *adv.* yn y dyddiau hyn
nowhere, *adv.* dim yn unlle
noxious, *a.* niweidiol, afiach
nozzle, *n.* trwyn, ffroen, genau
nucleus, *n.* cnewyllyn, bywyn
nude, *a.* noeth, noeth lymun
nudge, *v.t.* pwnio, penelino
nugatory, *a.* ofer, disylwedd, di-rym
nugget, *n.* clap aur
nuisance, *n.* pla, poenod, budreddi
null, *a.* diddim, dirym, ofer
numb, *a.* diffrwyth, cwsg: *v.t.* fferru, merwino
number, *n.* nifer, rhif, rhifedi; rhifyn; *v.t.* rhifo, cyfrif
numeral, *n.* rhifol, rhifnod
numeration, *n.* cyfrifiad
numerator, *n.* rhifiadur
numerous, *a.* niferog, lluosog, aml
numismatics, *n.pl.* bathofyddiaeth
numskull, *n.* penbwl, clwpa
nun, *n.* lleian, mynaches
nuncio, *n.* llysgennad pab
nuptial, *a.* priodasol, neithiorol
nurse, *n.* mamaeth, gweinyddes, nyrs: *v.t.* magu, meithrin, nyrsio
nursery, *n.* magwrfa, meithrinfa
nurture, *n.* maeth, magwraeth, meithriniad: *v.t.* maethu, meith-rin
nut, *n.* cneuen; gwain, gweinell
nutriment, *n.* maeth
nutrition, *n.* maeth, maethiad
nutritious, *a.* maethlon
nutshell, *n.* plisgyn (masgl) cneuen

nuzzle, *v.* trwyno, turio, ymwasgu
nymph, *n.* duwies, meinwen

O

oaf, *n.* delff, hurtyn, awff, llabwst
oak, *n.* derwen; derw
oakum, *n.* carth, breisgion
oar, *n.* rhwyf
oat, *n.* ceirchen, (*pl.*) ceirch
oath, *n.* llw
oatmeal, *n.* blawd ceirch
obdurate, *a.* caled, cyndyn, ystyfnig, anhyblyg
obedience, *n.* ufudd-dod
obedient, *a.* ufudd
obeisance, *n.* ymostyngiad, moesymgrymiad
obelisk, *n.* colofn
obese, *a.* tew, corfflol
obey, *v.* ufuddhau
obituary, *n.* marwgoffa
object, *n.* gwrthrych; amcan: *v.* gwrthwynebu
objection, *a.* gwrthwynebiad
objectionable, *a.* gwrthwynebus, annymunol
objective, *a.* gwrthrychol; *n.* amcan, nod
objurgate, *v.t.* dwrdio, ceryddu
oblation, *n.* offrwm, aberth
obligation, *n.* dyled, rhwymau
oblige, *v.t.* rhwymo; boddio; gor-fodi
obliging, *a.* caredig, cymwynasgar
oblique, *a.* lleddf, gŵyr, ar osgo
obliterate, *v.t.* dileu
oblivion, *n.* angof, ebargofiant
oblong, *a.* hirgul: *n.* oblong
obloquy, *n.* anair, gwarth, gwar-adwydd
obnoxious, *a.* atgas, ffiaidd
obscene, *a.* serth, anllad, anniwair, brwnt
obscure, *a.* tywyll; anhysbys: *v.t.* tywyllu
obsequies, *n.pl.* angladd
obsequious, *a.* gwasaidd, cyn-ffongar

observance, *n.* cadwraeth; defod
observation, *n.* sylw; sylwadaeth
observatory, *n.* arsyllfa
observe, *v.* sylwi, arsyllu; cadw
obsolete, *a.* anarferedig, ansathredig
obstacle, *n.* rhwystr, atalfa
obstinate, *a.* cyndyn, ystyfnig, gwrthnysig
obstreperous, *a.* trystiog, afreolus
obstruct, *v.t.* cau, tagu; rhwystro, lluddio
obtain, *v.i.* cael, caffael, ennill
obtrude, *v.* gwthio ar, ymwthio
obtrusive, *a.* ymwthgar
obtuse, *a.* pŵl, di-fin, hurt
obviate, *v.t.* symud ymaith, osgoi, arbed
obvious, *a.* eglur, amlwg
occasion, *n.* achlysur: *v.t.* achlysuro
occidental, *a.* gorllewinol
occult, *a.* cudd, dirgel, cêl, cyfrin
occupation, *n.* gwaith, galwedigaeth; meddiant
occupy, *v.i.* meddu, meddiannu; llenwi; dal
occur, *v.i.* digwydd; taro i'r meddwl
occurrence, *n.* digwyddiad
ocean, *n.* môr, cefnfor, cyfanfor, eigion
octagon, *n.* wythongl
octave, *n.* wythawd, octef
octavo, *a.* wythblyg; *n.* llyfr wythblyg
October, *n.* Hydref
octogenarian, *n.* gŵr pedwar ugain mlwydd oed
ocular, *a.* llygadol
oculist, *n.* meddyg llygaid
odd, *a.*₁ od, hynod. —o. **number,** rhif afrwydd
odds, *n.pl.* ots, gwahaniaeth; mantais
ode, *n.* awdl
odious, *a.* atgas, cas, ffiaidd
odium, *n.* atgasrwydd; gwaradwydd; bai
odour, *n.* arogl, aroglau, sawr, sawyr

oecumenical, *a.* cyffredinol, bydeang
of, *pr.* o; gan; am; ynghylch
off, *adv.* ymaith, i ffwrdd: *pr.* oddi, oddi wrth, oddi ar
offal, *n.* syrth, gwehilion, perfedd
offence, *n.* tramgwydd, trosedd, camwedd
offend, *v.* tramgwyddo, troseddu, pechu; digio
offensive, *a.* tramgwyddus, atgas, ffiaidd; ymosodol
offer, *v.* cynnig, cyflwyno; offrymu: *n.* cynnig
offering, *n.* offrwm, aberth
offertory, *n.* offrwm, casgliad
office, *n.* swydd; swyddfa
officer, *n.* swyddog, swyddwr
official, *a.* swyddogol: *n.* swyddog
officiate, *v.i.* gweinyddu
officious, *a.* ymyrgar, busneslyd
offspring, *n.* hiliogaeth, epil, hil, plant
oft, often, *adv.* yn aml, yn fynych
ogle, *v.* cilwenu, ciledrych
ogre, *n.* anghenfil, bwystfil
oh, *i.* O !
oil, *n.* olew, oel: *v.t.* iro, oelio
ointment, *n.* ennaint, eli
old, *a.* hen, oedrannus
olive, *n.* olewydden
omelet, *n.* crempog wyau
omen, *n.* argoel, arwydd, rhagarwydd
ominous, *a.* argoelus, bygythiol
omission, *n.* gwall
omit, *v.t.* gadael allan, esgeuluso
omnibus, *n.* bws
omnipotent, *a.* hollalluog
omnipresent, *a.* hollbresennol
omniscient, *a.* hollwybodol
on, *pr.* ar, ar warthaf: *adv.* ymlaen
once, *adv.* unwaith; gynt
one, *a. & n.* un
onerous, *a.* trwm, beichus, llethol
onion, *n.* wynwynyn, wnionyn
only, *a.* unig: *adv.* yn unig; ond
onset, *n.* ymosodiad, cyrch: cychwyn   [cyrch
onslaught, *n.* ymosodiad, rhuthr,

onus, *n.* baich, dyletswydd, cyfrifoldeb

onward, *a. & adv.,* **onwards,** *adv.* ymlaen

ooze, *n.* llaid, llysnafedd: *v.i.* chwysu

opacity, *n.* afloywder

opaque, *a.* afloyw, tywyll

open, *a.* agored: *v.* agor, ymagor

opening, *n.* agoriad, agorfa

operate, *v.* gweithredu, gweithio

operation, *n.* gweithrediad; gweithred, gweithred lawfeddygol

ophthalmic, *a.* llygadol

opiate, *n.* cysglyn

opine, *v.i.* tybio, tybied, bod o'r farn

opinion, *n.* tyb, meddwl, barn, opiniwn

opponent, *n.* gwrthwynebydd

opportune, *a.* amserol, cyfleus

opportunity, *n.* cyfle, egwyl

oppose, *v.t.* gwrthwynebu, cyferbynnu

opposite, *a., adv. & pr.* gwrthwyneb, cyferbyn

oppress, *v.t.* gorthrymu, llethu

opprobrium, *n.* gwaradwydd, gwarth

optic, -al, *a.* llygadol, golygol

optimism, *n.* optimistiaeth

optimist, *n.* opimist

option, *n.* dewisiad, dewis

opulent, *a.* cyfoethog, goludog, cefnog

or, *c.* neu, ai, ynteu, naill ai

oracle, *n.* oracl

oral, *a.* geneuol, llafar, anysgrifenedig

orange, *n.* oren, oraens: *a.* melyn-

oration, *n.* araith, arawd

orator, *n.* areithiwr, areithydd

oratory, *n.* areithyddiaeth

orb, *n.* pêl, pelen, pellen; y llygad

orbit, *n.* rhod, tro, cylchdro, chwyldro

orchard, *n.* perllan

orchestra, *n.* cerddorfa

ordain, *v.t.* ordeinio, urddo

ordeal, *n.* prawf llym

order, *n.* trefn; gorchymyn, archeb; urdd: *v.* ordeinio, trefnu, gorchymyn; archebu; urddo

orderly, *a.* trefnus: *n.* gwas milwr

ordinal, *a.* trefnol

ordinance, *n.* gosodedigaeth, ordinhad

ordinary, *a.* cyffredin, arferol

ordination, *n.* ordeiniad, urddiad

ordnance, *n.* cyflegrau, magnelau

ordure, *n.* tom, budreddi, aflendid

ore, *n.* mwyn

organ, *n.* organ, offeryn

organist, *n.* organydd

organization, *n.* trefn; cyfundrefn; trefniadaeth

organize, *v.* trefnu

orgy, *n.* gloddest, cyfeddach

oriental, *a.* dwyreiniol: *n.* dwyreiniwr

orientate, *v.* cyfeirio

orifice, *n.* genau, ceg, agorfa

origin, *n.* dechreuad, tarddiad

original *a. & n.* gwreiddiol

ornament, *n.* addurn: *v.t.* addurno

ornate, *a.* addurnedig, mawrwych

ornithology, *n.* adaryddiaeth, adareg

orphan, *a. & n.* amddifad

orthodox, *a.* uniongred

orthography, *n.* orgraff

oscillate, *v.* siglo, dirgrynu, osgiladu

osculate, *v.* cusanu

osier, *n.* mêr-helygen

osseous, *a.* esgyrnog, esgyrnol

ossify, *v.* asgyrnu, esgyrnu

ostensible, *a.* ymddangosiadol, proffesedig

ostentation, *n.* rhodres

ostentatious, *a.* rhodresgar

ostracize, *v.t.* diarddel

ostrich, *n.* estrys

other, *a. & pn.* arall, llall, amgen

otherwise, *adv.* amgen

otiose, *a.* hamddenol, segur; ofer, di-fudd

otter, *n.* dyfrgi

ounce, *n.* wns, owns

our, *pn.* ein, ein . . . ni

oust, *v.t.* cilgwthio, disodli

out, *adv.* allan, i maes

outcome, *n.* canlyniad, ffrwyth

outcry, *n.* gwaedd; dadwrdd; gwrthdystiad

outdo, *v.t.* rhagori ar, trechu

outer, *a.* allanol, nesaf allan

outing, *n.* pleserdaith

outlandish, *a.* dieithr, estronol, anghysbell, diarffordd

outlaw, *n.* herwr

outlay, *n.* traul, cost

outlet, *n.* arllwysfa, allanfa

outline, *n.* amlinelliad, braslun; amlinell

outlook, *n.* rhagolwg, argoel; golygfa

outpost, *n.* rhagorsaf, rhagfintai

outrage, *n.* trais: *v.t.* treisio, ysgelerder

outstanding, *a.* amlwg; dyledus

outward, *a.* allanol

outweigh, *v.t.* gorbwyso

oval, *a.* hirgrwm

ovary, *n.* wygell, wyfa

ovation, *n.* cymeradwyaeth

oven, *n.* ffwrn, popty

over, *pr.* uwch, tros: *adv.* gor, rhy, tra

overbearing, *a.* gormesol

overcast, *a.* cymylog

overflow, *n.* gorlif(iad): *v.* gorlifo

overlook, *v.* edrych dros; esgeuluso

overpower, *v.* trechu

overrun, *v.* goresgyn

overthrow, *n.* dymchweliad: *v.t.* dymchwelyd

overture, *n.* cynnig; agorawd

overturn, *v.t.* troi, dymchwelyd

overweening, *a.* hunanol, trahaus

overwhelm, *v.t.* llethu, gorlethu

owe, *v.t.* bod mewn dyled

owl, *n.* tylluan, gwdihŵ

own, *a.* eiddo dyn ei hun, priod: *v.t.* meddu; arddel, addef

owner, *n.* perchen, perchennog

ox, (-en), *n.* ych, eidion

oxide, *n.* ocsid

oxygen, *n.* ocsigen

oyster, *n.* llymarch, wystrysen

P

pace, *n.* cam, camre; cyflymdra: *v.* camu, cerdded

pacific, *a.* heddychol, tawel

pacify, *v.t.* heddychu, tawelu, dyhuddo

pack, *n.* pac, swp, pwn: *v.* pacio, pynio

packet, *n.* sypyn, paced

pact, *n.* cyfamod, cynghrair

pad, *n.* pad: *v.t.* padio

paddle, *n.* padl, rhodl, rhwyf: *v.* rhodli, padlo

paddock, *n.* marchgae, cae bach

padlock, *n.* clo clap, clo clwt, clo egwyd

pagan, *n.* pagan: *a.* paganaidd

page, *n.* tudalen

pageant, *n.* pasiant

paginate, *v.t.* tudalennu

pail, *n.* ystwc, crwc, bwced

pain, *n.* poen, gwayw, dolur: *v.t.* poeni

painstaking, *a.* gofalus

paint, *n.* paent, lliw: *v.t.* peintio, lliwio

painter, *n.* peintiwr; arlunydd

pair, *n.* pâr, dau, cwpl: *v.* paru

palace, *n.* plas, palas, palasty

palaeo-, paleo-, *px.* hen, hynafol

palatable, *a.* archwaethus, blasus

palate, *n.* taflod y genau: blas, archwaeth,

palatial, *a.* palasaidd, gwych

palatine, *a. & n.* —**count p.,** breiniarll [truth

palaver, *n.* ymddiddan, trafodaeth;

pale, *a.* gwelw, llwyd, glas, gwelwlas: *v.* gwelwi

pale, *n.* pawl, cledr; clawdd, ffin

palfrey, *n.* palffrai

palisade, *n.* palis, gwalc

pall, *n.* pall, mantell, elorlen

pall, *v.* diflasu

pallet, *n.* gwely gwellt, matras

palliate, *v.t.* lleddfu, lliniaru; esgusodi

pallid, *a.* gwelw, llwyd

palm, *n.* palf, cledr llaw: *v.t.* palfu

palm, *n.* palmwydden.—**P. Sunday,** Sul y Blodau

palmistry, *n.* llawddewiniaeth

palpable, *a.* amlwg, dybryd

palpitate, *v.i.* curo, dychlamu

palsy, *n.* parlys: *v.t.* parlysu, diffrwytho

paltry, *a.* distadl, gwael, pitw

pamper, *v.t.* mwytho, maldodi

pamphlet, *n.* pamffled, llyfryn

pan-, *px.* oll-

pan, *n.* padell

pancake, *n.* crempog, cramwythen, ffroisen

pandemonium, *n.* dadwrdd, terfysg

pane, *n.* cwar, cwarel, paen

panegyric, *n.* molawd, arwyrain

panel, *n.* panel

pang, *n.* gloes, gwasgfa, brath, gwayw

panic, *n.* dychryn, cymraw, panig

panoply, *n.* cyflawn arfogaeth

pant, *v.i.* dyheu, hiraethu

pantaloon, *n.* (*pl.*) llodrau

pantheism, *n.* pantheistiaeth

pantry, *n.* bwtri, pantri

papacy, *n.* pabaeth

papal, *a.* pabol, pabaidd

paper, *n.* papur: *v.* papuro

papist, *n.* pabydd

papyrus, (*-i*), *n.* papurfrwyn

par, *n.* cyfartaledd, llawn werth

parable, *n.* dameg

parade, *n.* rhodfa; rhodres, rhwysg

paradise, *n.* paradwys, gwynfa, gwynfyd

paradox, *n.* gwrthddywediad, paradocs

paragraph, *n.* paragraff

parallel, *a.* cyfochrog, cyflin, para-lel

paralyse, *v.t.* parlysu, diffrwytho

paralysis, *n.* parlys

paralytic, *a. & n.* claf o'r parlys

paramount, *a.* pen, pennaf, prif

paramour, *n.* gordderchwr, gor-dderchwraig

parapet, *n.* canllaw, rhagfur

paraphernalia, *n.pl.* meddianna taclau, celfi

paraphrase, *n.* aralleiriad: *v.* aralleirio

parasite, *n.* un yn byw ar gefn u arall, cynffonnwr

parboil, *v.t.* goferwi, lledferwi

parcel, *n.* parsel, swp, sypyn

parch, *v.* crasu, deifio, golosg sychu

parchment, *n.* memrwn

pardon, *n.* maddeuant, pardwr *v.t.* maddau, pardynu

pare, *v.t.* didonni, pilio, digroeni

parent, *n.* tad neu fam, (*pl.*) rhie

parenthesis, (*-ses*) *n.* sangia ymadrodd rhwng cromfachau

pariah, *n.* dyn ysgymun

parings, *n.pl.* pilion, creifion

parish, *n.* plwyf: *a.* plwyf, plwyf

parishioner, *n.* plwyfwr, (*pl* plwyfolion

parity, *n.* cydraddoldeb, cyfa taledd

park, *n.* parc, cae, coetgae

parlance, *n.* ymadrodd

parley, *n.* cyflafaredd, cynhadled

parliament, *n.* senedd

parlour, *n.* parlwr

parochial, *a.* plwyfol

parody, *n.* parodi: *v.* gwatwa dynwared

parole, *n.* gair, addewid

paroxysm, *n.* ffit, gwasgfa, pang

parricide, *n.* tadladdiad; tac leiddiad

parrot, *n.* parot, perot

parry, *v.t.* osgoi, gochelyd, tr heibio

parse, *v.t.* dosbarthu

parsimonious, *a.* crintach, cy byddlyd

parsimony, *n.* crintachrwydd

parsley, *n.* persli

parsnip, *n.* panasen

parson, *n.* person, offeiriad

part, *n.* rhan; parth; plaid: *v* rhannu, parthu; gwahanu ymadael

artake, v. cyfrannu, cyfranogi
artial, a. rhannol; pleidiol, tueddol
articipate, v. cyfranogi
articiple, n. rhangymeriad
article, n. mymryn, gronyn; geiryn
articular, a. neilltuol, penodol; manwl: n. pwnc, (pl.) manylion
art-time, a. rhanamser
artisan, n. pleidiwr
artition, n. canolfur, gwahanfur, palis
artly, adv. mewn rhan
artner, n. partner; cymar
artridge, n. petrisen
arturition, n. esgoriad
arty, n. plaid; parti, mintai
arvenu, n. dyfodiad, newyddian
ass, v. myned heibio, pasio; treulio, bwrw: n. cyflwr, sefyllfa; bwlch; trwydded
assage, n. tramwyfa; mordaith; cyfran
assenger, n. teithiwr
assing, n. ymadawiad
assion, n. dioddefaint; gwŷn, nwyd
assionate, a. angerddol, nwyd-wyllt
assive, a. goddefol
assover, n. pasg
assport, n. trwydded deithio
ast, a. & n. gorffennol: pr. wedi: adv. heibio
aste, n. past: v.t. pastio, gludio
astern, n. egwyd
astime, n. difyrrwch, adloniant
astor, n. bugail (eglwys), gweinidog
astoral, a. bugeiliol: n. bugeil-gerdd [tarten
astry, n. pasteiod, pasteiaeth,
asture, n. porfa: v. porfelu, pori
asty, n. pastai
at, v.t. patio, pratio: a. parod, cymwys, priodol
atch, n. clwt, darn: v.t. clytio
ate, n. siol, pen, copa, iad
aten, n. plat cymundeb

patent, a. agored, cyhoedd, amlwg; breintiedig: n. breintlythyr
paternal, a. tadol
paternoster, n. pader
path, n. llwybr
pathetic, a. gresynus, pathetig
pathos, n. teimlad, dwyster
patience, n. amynedd
patient, a. amyneddgar, dioddefus: n. dioddefydd
patriarch, n. patriarch
patrician, n. uchelwr, gŵr bon-heddig
patrimony, n. treftadaeth; gwadd-ol
patriot, n. gwladgarwr
patrol, n. gwyliadwriaeth, gwylfa
patron, n. noddwr
patronage, n. nawdd, nawddog-aeth
patronize, v.t. noddi, nawddogi
patronymic, n. tadenw
patter, v. curo (fel glaw ar ffenestr)
patter, v. padera: n. clebar, siarad-ach
pattern, n. patrwm, cynllun
patty, n. pasteian
paucity, n. prinder
paunch, n. bol, cest
pauper, n. dyn tlawd, tlotyn
pause, n. saib, seibiant: v.i. aros, sefyll, ymbwyllo
pave, v.t. palmantu
pavilion, n. pabell, pafiliwn
paw, n. palf, pawen: v. palfu, pawennu
pawky, a. direidus
pawn, n. gwystl: v.t. gwystlo
pay, v. talu: n. tâl, cyflog, pae, hur
pea, n. pysen
peace, n. heddwch, tangnefedd: i. gosteg!, ust!
peach, n. eirinen wlanog
peacock, n. paun
peak, n. pig; crib, copa; uchafbwynt
peal, n. sain clychau; twrf (taran): v. canu, darstain
pear, n. gellygen
pearl, n. perl
peasant, n. gwladwr, gwerinwr

peasantry, *n.* gwerin

peat, *n.* mawn

pebble, *n.* gröyn

peccadillo, *n.* beiyn, pechodyn

peck, *n.* pec, pecaid

peck, *v.* pigo, cnocellu: *n.* cnoc, pigiad

pectoral, *a.* dwyfronnol

peculate, *v.t.* celcio, lladrata

peculiar, *a.* priod, priodol; hynod

peculiarity, *n.* hynodrwydd

pecuniary, *a.* ariannol

pedagogue, *n.* athro plant, ysgolfeistr

pedal, *a.* troedol: *n.* troedlath, pedal

pedant, *n.* pedant

peddle, *v.* pedlera

pedestal, *n.* troed, bôn, gwaelod

pedestrian, *a.* ar draed, peddestrig: *n.* gŵr traed, cerddwr

pedigree, *n.* ach, achau, bonedd

pedlar, *n.* pedler

peel, *n.* pil, croen, rhisgl: *v.* pilio

peep, *v.i.* cipedrych, ysbio: *n.* cipolwg, cip

peer, *v.i.* ciledrych, syllu

peer, *n.* gogyfurdd, cydradd; pen-defig

peevish, *a.* anniddig, blin, piwis

peg, *n.* hoel bren, peg: *v.t.* pegio

pelf, *n.* golud

pellet, *n.* peled, pelen, haelsen

pellicle, *n.* croenyn, pilen, rhuchen

pell-mell, *adv.* blith draphlith

pellucid, *a.* gloyw, tryloyw, claer

pelt, *v.t.* lluchio, taflu, peledu, baeddu

pen, *n.* pin, ysgrif bin: *v.t.* ysgrifennu

pen, *n.* lloc, ffald, cwt: *v.t.* ffaldio, llocio

penalty, *n.* cosb, cosbedigaeth

penance, *n.* penyd

pence, *n.pl.* ceiniogau, pres

pencil, *n.* pwyntil, pensel, pensil

pendant, *n.* tlws

pendent, *a.* dibynnol, crog

pendulous, *a.* yn hongian, yn siglo

pendulum, *n.* pendil

penetrate, *v.* treiddio

peninsula, *n.* gorynys

penitent, *a.* edifar, edifarus, edifeir-iol

penitentiary, *n.* penydfa, carchar

penknife, (*-knives*), *n.* pencniff cyllell boced

pennant, pennon, *n.* penwn

penny, (*pence, pennies*), *n.* ceiniog

pension, *n.* blwydd-dâl, pensiwn

pensive, *a.* synfyfyriol, meddylga

pent, *a.* wedi ei gau i mewn, caeth

Pentateuch, *n.* pumllyfr Moses

penult, *n.* goben

penury, *n.* tlodi, angen, eisiau prinder

people, *n.* pobl, gwerin: *v.t.* pobli poblogi

pepper, *n.* pupur

peppermint, *n.* mintys poethion botwm gwyn

per, *pr.* trwy, wrth, yn ôl

peradventure, *adv.* efallai

perambulate, *v.t.* cerdded, rhodi

perceive, *v.t.* canfod, gweled dirnad

percentage, *n.* hyn a hyn y cant canran

perceptible, *a.* canfyddadwy

perception, *n.* canfyddiad

perch, *n.* perc; clwyd: *v.* clwydo

perchance, *adv.* efallai

percolate, *v.* hidlo, diferu

percussion, *n.* trawiad, gwrth drawiad. **—p. band,** seindorf dar

perdition, *n.* colledigaeth, distryw

peregrinate, *v.i.* pererino, teithio

peremptory, *a.* pendant, aw durdodol

perennial, *a.* drwy'r flwyddyn bythol

perfect, *a.* perffaith: *v.t.* perffeithi

perfection, *n.* perffeithrwydd

perfervid, *a.* brwd, tanbaid

perfidy, *n.* brad, dichell, ffalster

perforate, *v.t.* tyllu, rhydyllu

perforce, *adv.* o orfod, drwy drai

perform, *v.* cyflawni; chwarae

perfume, *n.* perarogl: *v.t.* perarog

perfunctory, *a.* o raid, diofa esgeulus

perhaps, *adv.* efallai, hwyrach, ond odid

peril, *n.* perygl, enbydrwydd

perimiter, *n.* amfesur, perimedr

period, *n.* cyfnod; cyfadran (miwsig); diweddnod

peripatetic, *a.* crwydrol, cylchynol, peripatetig [fesur

periphery, *n.* amgylchedd, cylch-

periphrastic, *a.* cwmpasog

perish, *v.i.* colli, trengi, darfod; llygru

periwig, *n.* perwig, gwallt gosod

periwinkle, *n.* gwichiad

perjure, *v.t.* **p. oneself,** tyngu anudon

perjury, *n.* anudon, anudoniaeth

permanent, *a.* parhaol, parhaus, arhosol, sefydlog

permeate, *v.t.* treiddio, trwytho

permission, *n.* caniatâd, cennad

permit, *v.* caniatáu, cenhadu: *n.* trwydded

permutate, *v.* amnewid

pernicious, *a.* niweidiol, aflesol

peroration, *n.* diweddglo araith, perorasiwn

perpendicular, *a.* syth, unionsyth

perpetrate, *v.t.* cyflawni (rhyw ddrwg)

perpetual, *a.* parhaol, parhaus, bythol

perpetuate, *v.t.* parhau, anfarwoli

perplex, *v.t.* drysu, cythryblu, tralldodi

persecute, *v.t.* erlid

persevere, *v.i.* dyfalbarhau, dyfalbara

persist, *v.i.* dal ati; mynnu, taeru

person, *n.* person

perspective, *n.* gwelediad persbectif

perspicacious, *a.* craff

perspicuous, *a.* eglur, clir, golau

perspire, *v.* chwysu

persuade, *v.t.* darbwyllo, perswadio

pert, *a.* eofn, tafodrydd

pertain, *v.i.* perthyn

pertinacious, *a.* dygn, ystyfnig, cyndyn

pertinent, *a.* perthynol, cymwys

perturb, *v.t.* cyffroi, aflonyddu, cythruddo

peruse, *v.t.* darllen, chwilio

pervade, *v.t.* treiddio, trwytho

perverse, *a.* gwrthnysig, trofaus, croes

pervert, *v.t.* gwyrdroi, llygru, camdroi: *n.* gwrthdroëdig

pessimism, *n.* pesimistiaeth

pessimist, *n.* pesimist

pest, *n.* pla, haint

pester, *v.t.* blino, aflonyddu, poeni

pestilence, *n.* haint, pla

pet, *n.* anwylyn, ffafryn: *a.* llywaeth, swci: *v.t.* anwesu

petal, *n.* petal

petition, *n.* deisyfiad; deiseb, petisiwn

petrel, *n.* aderyn drycin

petrify, *v.* caregu

petroleum, *n.* petroliwm

petticoat, *n.* pais

pettifogging, *a.* gwael, isel, brwnt

petty, *a.* bach, bychan, mân, gwael

petulant, *a.* anniddig, anfoddog, anynad

pew, *n.* eisteddle, côr, sedd

pewit, peewit, *n.* cornicyll, cornchwiglen

pewter, *n.* piwter

phalanx, *n.* cadres

phantasm, phantom, *n.* rhith, drychiolaeth

Pharisee, *n.* Pharisead

pharmacy, *n.* fferylliaeth; fferyllfa

pharynx, *n.* sefnig

phase, *n.* golwg, gwedd, agwedd; tro

pheasant, *n.* ceiliog coed, coediar, ffesant

phenomenon, (-*na*). *n.* ffenomen; rhyfeddod

phial, *n.* ffiol

philander, *v.i.* gwamalio caru

philanthropist, *n.* dyngarwr

philanthropy, *n.* dyngarwch

Philistine, *n.* Philistiad

philology, *n.* ieitheg

philosopher, *n.* athronydd

philosophy, *n.* athroniaeth
phlegm, *n.* cornboer, llysnafedd, fflem
phlegmatic, *a.* difraw, digyffro, difywyd
phonetic, *a.* seinegol
phonetician, *n.* seinegwr
phonetics, *n.* seineg
phonograph, *n.* ffonograff
phonography, *n.* llaw-fer Pitman
phonology, *n.* seinyddiaeth
phosphorous, *n.* ffosfforws
photograph, *n.* llun, ffotograff
phrase, *n.* ymadrodd; cymal: *v.t.* geirio   [weddiad
phraseology, *n.* geiriad, geir-
phthisis, *n.* darfodedigaeth
physic, *n.* meddygaeth, meddyginiaeth
physical, *a.* corfforol, materol; ffisegol
physics, *n.* ffiseg
physician, *n.* meddyg, ffisigwr
physiognomy, *n.* wynebofyddiaeth
physiology, *n.* ffisioleg
physique, *n.* corffolaeth, cyfansoddiad
piano, -forte, *n.* piano
pick, *n.* caib: *v.* ceibio
pick, *v.* pigo, dewis, dethol: *n.* dewis
pickaxe, *n.* caib
picket, *n.* polyn, cledren; gwyliwr, gwyliadwriaeth
pickle, *n.* picl, heli: *v.t.* piclo, halltu
picnic, *n.* pleserdaith, picnic
pictorial, *a.* darluniadol
picture, *n.* llun, darlun, pictiwr
picturesque, *a.* darluniaidd, gwych, byw
pie, *n.* pastai
piebald, *a.* brith; brithryw
piece, *n.* darn, dryll, rhan: *v.t.* clytio, asio
piecemeal, *adv.* bob yn damaid
pied, *a.* brith, brithliw
pier, *n.* piler, canbost; pier
pierce, *v.* brathu, gwanu, trywanu
piety, *n.* duwiolfrydedd, duwioldeb
piffle, *n.* lol, oferedd, gwegi

pig, *n.* mochyn: *v.* porchellu, bwrw perchyll
pigeon, *n.* colomen
pigment, *n.* paent, lliw
pike, *n.* gwaywffon; penhwyad
pile, *n.* crug, pentwr: *v.t.* pentyrru
pile, *n.* pawl, cledr
pile, *n.* blew, ceden
piles, *n.pl.* clwyf y marchogion
pilfer, *v.* chwiwladrata
pilgrim, *n.* pererin
pilgrimage, *n.* pererindod
pill, *n.* pelen, pilsen
pillage, *n.* ysbail, anrhaith: *v.t.* ysbeilio, anrheithio
pillar, *n.* colofn, piler
pillion, *n.* sgìl
pillory, *n.* rhigod, pilwri
pillow, *n.* gobennydd, clustog
pillule, *n.* pelen
pilot, *n.* cyfarwyddwr llongau, peilat
pimple, *n.* ploryn, tosyn
pin, *n.* pin: *v.t.* pinio, hoelio
pinafore, *n.* brat
pincers, *n.pl.* gefel
pinch, *v.* pinsio, gwasgu; cynilo: *n.* pins, pinsiad; gwasgfa, cyfyngder
pine, *n.* pinwydden
pine, *v.i.* dihoeni, nychu, curio
pinion, *n.* asgell, adain: *v.t.* torri esgyll
pink, *a. & n.* pinc
pint, *n.* peint
pioneer, *n.* arloeswr, arloesydd
pious, *a.* duwiol, duwiolfrydig
pip, *n.* hedyn afal, &c.
pipe, *n.* pib, pibell: *v.* canu pibell
piping, *a.* **p. hot**, chwilboeth
piquant, *a.* pigog, llym, tost
pique, *v.t.* llidio, cyffroi; ymfalchïo: *n.* soriant
pirate, *n.* môr-leidr
pirouette, *n.* chwyldro: *v.i.* chwyldroi
pistol, *n.* llawddryll, pistol
pit, *n.* pwll, pydew: *v.t.* pyllu
pitch, *n.* pyg: *v.t.* pygu
pitch, *v.* bwrw; gosod; taro (tôn): *n.* gradd, mesur, traw

pitcher, *n.* piser, ystên, cawg

pitchfork, *n.* picfforch, picwarch; seinfforch

piteous, *a.* truenus, gresynus

pitfall, *n.* pyd, magl

pith, *n.* bywyn; mwydion; mêr; grym, sylwedd

pity, *n.* tosturi, trueni, gresyn: *v.t.* tosturio, gresynu

pivot, *n.* colyn, pegwn

placable, *a.* cymodlon, hynaws

placard, *n.* murlen, hysbyslen

placate, *v.t.* cymodi, heddychu, dyhuddo

place, *n.* lle, man, mangre: *v.t.* cyfleu, gosod

placid, *a.* araf, tawel, llonydd

plagiary, *n.* llên-ladrad; llên-leidr

plague, *n.* pla, haint: *v.t.* poeni, blino

plaice, *n.* lleden

plain, *a.* plaen, eglur: *n.* gwastadedd

plaint, *n.* cwyn, achwyniad; cwynfan

plaintiff, *n.* achwynwr, hawlydd

plaintive, *a.* cwynfanus, dolefus, lleddf

plait, *n.* pletl.: *v.t.* plethu

plan, *n.* cynllun, plan: *v.t.* cynllunio, planio

plane, *a. & n.* gwastad, lefel

plane, *n.* plaen: *v.t.* plaenio

planet, *n.* planed

plank, *n.* astell, estyllen, planc

plant, *n.* planhigyn, llysieuyn; offer: *v.t.* plannu

plantation, *n.* planfa

plaster, *n.* plastr: *v.t.* plastro

plat, *n.* darn o dir, clwt, lawnt

plate, *n.* plat; llestri aur, &c.: *v.t.* golchi â metel

plateau, *n.* gwastatir uchel

platform, *n.* llwyfan, esgynlawr

platitude, *n.* sylw hen a diflas, gwireb

platoon, *n.* platŵn

platter, *n.* plat, dysgl, noe

plaudit, *n.* banllef o gymeradwyaeth

plausible, *a.* teg neu resymol yr olwg, ffals

play, *v.* chwarae; canu (offeryn): *n.* chwarae

playful, *a.* chwareus

plea, *n.* ple, dadl, hawl; esgus

plead, *v.* pledio, dadlau, eiriol, ymbil

pleasant, *a.* hyfryd, pleserus, difyr, siriol

please, *v.* boddhau, boddio, rhyngu bodd

pleasure, *n.* pleser, hyfrydwch

pleat, *n.* plet, pleten: *v.t.* pletio

plebeian, *n.* gwerinwr, gwrêng

plebiscite, *n.* pleidlais y bobl

pledge, *n.* gwystl, ernes: *v.t.* gwystlo

plenary, *a.* llawn, cyflawn, diamodol

plenitude, *n.* llawnder, cyflawnder

plenty, *n.* digon, helaethrwydd

plethora, *n.* gorgyflawnder

pleurisy, *n.* eisglwyf, plewrisi

pliable, pliant, *a.* ystwyth, hyblyg

pliers, *n.pl.* gefel fechan

plight, *n.* cyflwr, drych, anghyflwr

plight, *v.t.* addo, gwystlo

plod, *v.* troedio, ymlafnio, llafurio, slafio

plot, *n.* darn o dir; brad, cynllwyn; cynllun, plot, ystofiad: *v.* cynllwyn; cynllunio

plough, *n.* aradr, gwŷdd: *v.* aredig, troi

pluck, *v.t.* tynnu; pluo: *n.* glewder

plug, *n.* topyn, plwg: *v.t.* topio, plygio

plum, *n.* eirinen

plumage, *n.* plu

plumber, *n.* plymwr

plume, *n.* pluen, plufyn: *v.t.* pluo, plufio

plummet, *n.* plymen

plump, *a.* tew, llyfndew, graenus

plunder, *n.* ysbail, anrhaith: *v.t.* ysbeilio

plunge, *v.* trochi, bwrw, ymfwrw

plural, *a.* lluosog

plus, *pr.* plws

plutocrat, *n.* gŵr goludog

ply, *v.* arfer, defnyddio, gyrru; poeni

ply-wood, *n.* pren haenog (tairhaen, pum-haen)

pneumatic, *a.* â'i lond o wynt, awyrog

pneumonia, *n.* llid yr ysgyfaint, niwmonia

poach, *v.* herwhela

poach, *v.t.* berwi (wy) heb ei blisg

pock, *n.* brech, ôl brech

pocket, *n.* poced, llogell: *v.t.* pocedu

pod, *n.* coden, plisgyn, masgl, cibyn

podgy, *a.* byrdew

poem, *n.* cerdd, cân

poet, *n.* bardd, prydydd

poetry, *n.* barddoniaeth, prydyddiaeth

pogrom, *n.* cyflafan

poignant, *a.* llym, tost, llymdost, awchlym

point, *n.* pwynt; man; blaen: *v.* pwyntio; blaenllymu

poise, *v.* mantoli; hofran: *n.* cydbwysedd; ystum

poison, *n.* gwenwyn: *v.t.* gwenwyno

poke, *v.* gwthio, pwnio, procio

pole, *n.* pegwn

pole, *n.* pawl, polyn; pegwn

polemic, *a.* dadleuol: *n.* dadl

police, *n.* heddlu

policeman, *n.* heddwas, heddgeidwad, plisman

policy, *n.* polisi

polish, *v.* caboli, gloywi, llathru

polite, *a.* moesgar, boneddigaidd

politic, *a.* call, cyfrwys, doeth, buddiol

political, *a.* gwleidyddol

politician, *n.* gwleidydd, gwleidyddwr

politics, *n.pl.* gwleidyddiaeth

polity, *n.* ffurflywodraeth, cyfansoddiad

poll, *n.* pen, copa; pôl: *v.* cneifio; pleidleisio, polio

pollen, *n.* paill

pollute, *v.t.* halogi, difwyno, llygru

poltroon, *n.* llwfryn, llwfrgi

polygamy, *n.* amlwreigiaeth

polysyllable, *n.* gair llusosillafog

polytechnic, *n.* ysgol gelfyddydau

polytheism, *n.* amldduwiaeth

pomade, *n.* ennaint pen

pomegranate, *n.* pomgranad

pommel, *n.* dwrn, cnap; pen blaen cyfrwy: *v.t.* dyrnu, pwnio

pomp, *n.* rhwysg

pond, *n.* llyn, pwll

ponder, *v.* ystyried, myfyrio, pwyso

ponderous, *a.* pwysfawr, trwm

poniard, *n.* dagr, bidog

pontiff, *n.* archoffeiriad; y Pab

pontoon, *n.* ysgraff

pony, *n.* merlyn

pooh, *i.* pw!

pool, *n.* pwll, llyn

pool, *n.* cronfa; pwll: *v.t.* cydrannu

poor, *a.* tlawd, truan, gwael, sâl

poorly, *a.* sâl, gwael, claf

pop, *v.* ffrwydro, ysgortio; picio, plannu, taro

pope, *n.* pab

popery, *n.* pabyddiaeth

pop-gun, *n.* gwn clats

popinjay, *n.* parot, perot; coegyn

poplar, *n.* poplysen

poppy, *n.* pabi (coch), llygad y bwgan

populace, *n.* gwerin, gwerinos

popular, *a.* poblogaidd

populace, *v.t.* poblogi

population, *n.* poblogaeth

populous, *a.* poblog

porcelain, *n.* porslen

porch, *n.* porth, cyntedd

porcine, *a.* mochaidd

porcupine, *n.* ballasg

pore, *n.* twll chwys

pore, *v.i.* astudio, myfyrio, synfyfyrio

pork, *n.* cig moch, porc

porker, *n.* mochyn

porous, *a.* tyllog

porpoise, *n.* llamhidydd

porridge, *n.* uwd

porringer, *n.* dysglen

port, *n.* porth, porthfa, porthladd

port, *n.* porth, drws, dôr, agorfa
port, *n.* ymarweddiad, agwedd
port, *n.* ochr aswy llong wrth edrych ymlaen
port, *n.* gwin Oporto, gwin coch
portable, *a.* cludadwy
portal, *n.* porth, cyntedd
portcullis, *n.* porthcwlis
portend, *v.t.* argoeli, rhagarwyddo
portent, *n.* argoel; rhyfeddod, gwyrth
porter, *n.* porthor, drysor
porter, *n.* cludydd, porter
portfolio, *n.* cas papurau; swydd
port-hole, *n.* ffenestr llong; gyndwll
portico, *n.* colofnfa, cyntedd
portion, *n.* rhan, cyfran, gwaddol
portly, *a.* tew, corffol
portmanteau, *n.* bag teithio
portrait, *n.* llun, darlun
portray, *v.t.* portreadu, darlunio
pose, *v.* sefyll, ymddangos: *n.* ystum, rhodres
position, *n.* safle, sefyllfa
positive, *a.* cadarnhaol, pendant, posidiol
posse, *n.* mintai, torf
possess, *v.t.* meddu, meddiannu
possession, *n.* meddiant
possessor, *n.* perchen, perchennog
posset, *n.* posel
possibility, *n.* posibilrwydd
possible, *a.* posibl, dichonadwy
post, *n.* post, cledr: *v.t.* gosod, cyhoeddi
post, *n.* post, llythyrfa; safle, swydd: *v.* postio
post-, *px.* wedi, ar ôl
postage, *n.* cludiad (llythyr, etc.)
poster, *n.* hysbyslen, poster
posterior, *a.* ar ôl, ôl
posterity, *n.* olafiaid; hiliogaeth
postern, *n.* cilborth, cilddor
posthumous, *a.* ôl-anedig; ôl-argraffedig
postilion, *n.* rhagfarchogwr
postpone, *v.t.* gohirio, oedi
postcript, *n.* ôl-ysgrif
postulate, *n.* cynosodiad
posture, *n.* agwedd, ystum

posy, *n.* blodeuglwm, pwysi
pot, *n.* pot, potyn; crochan: *v.* potio
potato, (*-oes*), *n.* cloronen, taten, pytaten
potency, *n.* nerth, grym
potent, *a.* cryf, galluog, grymus, nerthol
potentate, *n.* penadur, pennaeth
potential, *a.* dichonadwy, dichonol: *n.* potensial
pother, *n.* ystŵr, ffwdan, helynt
potion, *n.* dogn, llymaid, llwnc
potsherd, *n.* potyn, cragen
pottage, *n.* cawl, potes
potter, *n.* crochenydd
potter, *v.* diogi, ymdroi, sefyllian, swmera
pottery, *n.* llestri pridd; gwaith llestri pridd; priddweithfa
pouch, *n.* cod, coden, cwd: *v.* cydu
poultice, *n.* powltis
poultry, *n.* dofednod, ffowls
pounce, *v.* disgyn ar, dyfod ar warthaf
pound, *n.* pwys; punt
pound, *n.* ffald: *v.t.* ffaldio
pound, *v.* pwyo, pwnio, malu, malurio
pour, *v.* tywallt, arllwys; bwrw
pout, *v.i.* pwdu, sorri, terru, monni
poverty, *n.* tlodi
powder, *n.* powdr, llwch, pylor: *v.t.* powdro
power, *n.* gallu, nerth; pŵer
pox, *n.* brech
practicable, *a.* dichonadwy
practical, *a.* ymarferol
practice, *n.* arfer, arferiad, ymarferiad
practise, *v.* arfer, ymarfer
practitioner, *n.* meddyg; cyfreithiwr
pragmatical, *a.* ymyrgar; pendant
pragmatism, *n.* pragmatiaeth
prairie, *n.* gwastatir, gweundir, paith
praise, *v.t.* canmol, moli: *n.* canmoliaeth, mawl
prance, *v.i.* prancio, crychneidio

prank, *n.* cast, ystranc, pranc

prate, *v.i.* bragaldian, brygawthan

prattle, *v.* preblan, clebran: *n.* mabiaith [atolwg

pray, *v.* gweddïo. —**I p. thee,**

prayer, *n.* gweddi

pre-, *px.* cyn-, rhag-, blaen-

preach, *v.* pregethu

preacher, *n.* pregethwr

preamble, *n.* rhagymadrodd, rhaglith

precarious, *a.* ansicr, peryglus, enbyd

precaution, *n.* rhagofal, rhagocheliad

precede, *v.* blaenori, blaenu, rhagflaenu

precedent, *n.* cynreol, cynsail

precentor, *n.* arweinydd y gân, codwr canu

precept, *n.* gorchymyn, rheol

preceptor, *n.* athro, hyfforddwr

precinct, *n.* cyffin

preciosity, *n.* mindlysni, gorddetholedd

precious, *a.* gwerthfawr, prid, drud; gorddethol, mindlws

precipice, *n.* dibyn, diffwys, clogwyn

precipitate, *v.t.* bwrw, hyrddio; *v.i.* gwaddodi, gwaelodi: *a.* byrbwyll, anystyriol

precipitation, *n.* hyrddiad, gwaddodiad; byrbwylltra

précis, *n.* crynodeb

precise, *a.* penodol, manwl

preclude, *v.t.* cau allan, atal, rhwystro

precocious, *a.* hen o'i oed, henaidd, henffel

precursor, *n.* rhagredegydd, rhagflaenydd

predatory, *a.* anrheithgar, ysglyfaethus

predecessor, *n.* rhagflaenydd

predestination, *n.* rhagarfaethiad

predicament, *n.* cyflwr, helynt, sefyllfa

predicate, *v.t.* haeru, honni: *n.* traethiad

predict, *v.t.* rhagfynegi, rhagddywedyd

predilection, *n.* hoffter, tuedd, tueddfryd

predominate, *v.i.* bod yn bennaf neu yn fwyaf, arglwyddiaethu, rhagori

pre-eminent, *a.* ar y blaen i bawb

preface, *n.* rhagymadrodd, rhaglith

prefect, *n.* rhaglaw

prefer, *v.t.* dewis yn hytrach, bod yn well gan

preference, *n.* dewis, hoffter, ffafraeth

preferment, *n.* dyrchafiad, codiad

prefix, *v.t.* rhagddodi: *n.* rhagddodiad

pregnant, *a.* beichiog, llawn

prehensile, *a.* yn medru gafael, gafaelog

prejudice, *n.* rhagfarn; niwed: *v.t.* rhagfarnu, niweidio

prelate, *n.* esgob, prelad

preliminary, *a.* arweiniol, rhagarweiniol

prelude, *n.* rhagarweiniad; preliwd (cerdd.)

premature, *a.* anaeddfed, cynamserol

premeditate, *v.t.* rhagfyfyrio, rhagfwriadu

premier, *a.* blaenaf, pennaf, prif: *n.* prifweinidog

premise, *n.* rhagosodiad; (*pl.*) adeiladau, &c.: *v.t.* rhagosod

premium, *n.* gwobr, tâl, taliad

premonish, *v.t.* rhagrybuddio

preoccupy, *v.t.* rhagfeddiannu, llenwi

preparation, *n.* paratoad, darpariaeth

prepare, *v.* paratoi, darparu, darbod, arlwyo

preponderate, *v.i.* gorbwyso

preposition, *n.* arddodiad

prepossess, *v.t.* rhagfeddiannu

preposterous, *a.* afresymol, gwrthun

prerogative, *n.* braint, rhagorfraint

presage, *n.* argoel, rhagargoel: *v.t.* argoeli

presbyter, *n.* henuriad, offeiriad

Presbyterian, *a.* Henadurol, Presbyteraidd: *n.* Presbyteriad

presbytery, *n.* henaduriaeth

prescience, *n.* rhagwybodaeth

prescribe, *v.* gorchymyn, cyfarwyddo

prescription, *n.* cyngor, cyfarwyddyd, presgripsiwn

presence, *n.* gŵydd, presendoldeb

present, *a. & n.* presennol

present, *n.* anrheg: *v.t.* anrhegu; cyflwyno; dangos

presentiment, *n.* rhagargoel

preserve, *v.t.* cadw, diogelu: *n.* jam

preside, *v.i.* llywyddu

president, *n.* llywydd, arlywydd

press, *v.* gwasgu: *n.* gwasg; gwryf; cwpwrdd

pressure, *n.* gwasgiad, gwasgfa, pwys

prestidigitator, *n.* siwgler, consurwr

prestige, *n.* bri, dylanwad, braint

presume, *v.* tybio, tebygu; beiddio, rhyfygu

presumption, *n.* rhyfyg; tyb

presumptuous, *a.* rhyfygus

pretence, *n.* rhith, esgus, ffug

pretend, *v.* ffugio, cymryd ar, cogio; proffesu; honni hawl

pretension, *n.* honiad, hawl

preter-, *px.* tu hwnt i, mwy na

pretext, *n.* esgus, cochl

pretty, *a.* tlws, del, pert: *adv.* cryn, go

prevail, *v.i.* tycio, ffynnu; gorfod, trechu

prevalent, *a.* cyffredin

prevaricate, *v.i.* dywedyd anwiredd, celwyddo

prevent, *v.t.* rhagflaenu; atal, rhwystro

previous, *a.* blaenorol, cynt

prey, *n.* ysglyfaeth, aberth: *v.i.* ysglyfaethu

price, *n.* pris, gwerth: *v.t.* prisio

prick, *n.* pigyn, swmbwl: *v.* pigo; picio, codi

prickle, *n.* draen: *v.* pigo, tymhigo

pride, *n.* balchder: *v.t.* balchio, ymfalchio

priest, *n.* offeiriad

priesthood, *n.* offeiriadaeth

prig, *n.* sychfoesolyn, mursennwr, coethyn

prim, *a.* cymen, cymhenllyd

primal, *a.* bore, cyntefig; prif, sylfaenol

primary, *a.* prif, cyntaf, cysefin: cynradd

primate, *n.* archesgob

prime, *a.* prif, cyntaf; gorau: *n.* anterth

prime, *v.t.* llwytho, llenwi, cyflenwi

primer, *n.* llyfr cyntaf, cynlyfr

primeval, *a.* cynoesol, cyntefig

primitive, *a.* cyntefig; garw, amrwd

primordial, *a.* cyntefig, cysefin

primrose, *n.* briallen, (*pl.*) briallu

prince, *n.* tywysog

principal, *a.* prif: *n.* pen; prifathro; corff

principality *n.* tywysogaeth

principle, *n.* egwyddor, elfen

print, *n.* argraff, print, ôl: *v.* argraffu, printio

prior, *a.* cynt, blaenorol: *n.* prior, priol

priority, *n.* blaenoriaeth

priory, *n.* priordy, mynachdy

prism, *n.* prism

prison, *n.* carchar, carchardy

prisoner, *n.* carcharor

pristine, *a.* hen, cyntefig, cysefin

prithee, *i.* atolwg

private, *a.* preifat, cyfrinachol, personol

privation, *n.* amddifadrwydd, diffyg

privilege, *n.* braint, rhagorfraint

privy, *a.* dirgel, cudd, cyfrin: *n.* geudy

prize, *n.* gwobr: *v.t.* prisio, gwerthfawrogi

prize, *n.* ysbail, caffaeliad

prize, -se, *v.t.* dryllio'n agored â throsol

pro-, *px.* am, yn lle; o blaid

probable, *a.* tebygol, tebyg

probate, *n.* prawf ewyllys

probation, *n.* prawf

probe, *n.* profiedydd: *v.t.* profi, chwilio

probity *n.* uniondeb, cywirdeb

problem, *n.* pwnc, drysbwnc, problem

proboscis, *n.* duryn, trwyn

procedure, *n.* trefn, arfer, defod

proceed, *v.i.* myned, deillio, tarddu; erlyn: *n.* (*pl.*) enillion, elw

process, *n.* gweithrediad, goruchwyliaeth

procession, *n.* gorymdaith; deilliad

proclaim, *v.t.* cyhoeddi, datgan

proclamation, *n.* cyhoeddiad, proclamasiwn

proclivity, *n.* gogwydd, tuedd

proconsul, *n.* rhaglaw

procrastinate, *v.i.* oedi, gohirio

procreate, *v.t.* cenhedlu

procure, *v.* ceisio, caffael, cael

prod, *v.t.* procio, pwnio, symbylu

prodigal, *a.* afradlon, hael

prodigious, *a.* aruthrol, anferth

prodigy, *n.* rhyfeddod, gwyrth

produce, *v.t.* cynhyrchu, epilio; dwyn: *n.* cynnyrch, ffrwyth

product, *n.* cynnyrch, ffrwyth

production, *n.* cynhyrchiad; (*pl.*) cynhyrchion

profane, *a.* anghysegredig, halogedig: *v.t.* anghysegru, halogi

profess, *v.* proffesu, arddel

profession, *n.* proffes, galwedigaeth

professor, *n.* proffeswr; athro

proffer, *v.t. & n.* cynnig

proficient, *a.* hyddysg, cyfarwydd

profile, *n.* ystlyslun, cernlun

profit, *n.* budd, lles, elw, proffid: *v.* llesáu, proffidio

profligate, *a.* afradlon, ofer

profound, *a.* dwfn, dwys, angerddol

profundity, *n.* dyfnder

profuse, *a.* hael, helaeth, toreithiog

progenitor, *n.* cyndad

progeny, *n.* hil, epil, hiliogaeth

prognostic, *n.* argoel, rhagarwydd

programme, *n.* rhaglen

progress, *n.* cynnydd; taith: *v.i.* cynyddu

prohibit, *v.t.* gwahardd

project, *n.* bwriad, cynllun; project

project, *v.* bwrw; bwriadu; ymestyn; taflunio (ffilm)

projectile, *n.* teflyn

projector, *n.* taflunydd

proletariat, *n.* gwerin, gwrêng

prolific, *a.* epiliog, ffrwythlon, toreithiog

prolix, *a.* maith, amleiriog

prologue, *n.* rhagair, prolog

prolong, *v.t.* hwyhau, estyn

promenade, *n.* rhodfa: *v.* rhodianna   [amlwg

prominent, *a.* yn sefyll allan,

promise, *n.* addewid: *v.* addo, argoeli

promissory, *a.* addewidiol

promontory, *n.* pentir, penrhyn

promote, *v.t.* hyrwyddo, meithrin, dyrchafu

promoter, *n.* hyrwyddwr

prompt, *a.* parod, buan: *v.t.* cofweini; cymell

promptitude, *n.* parodrwydd

promulgate, *v.t.* cyhoeddi, lledaenu

prone, *a.* â'i wyneb i waered; tueddol

prong, *n.* fforch, pig fforch

pronominal, *a.* rhagenwol

pronoun, *n.* rhagenw

pronounce, *v.* cynanu, yngan; cyhoeddi, datgan

pronunciation, *n.* cynaniad

proof, *n.* prawf; proflen

prop, *n.* ateg, post, prop: *v.t.* ategu

propaganda, *n.* propaganda

propagate, *v.t.* epilio, cenhedlu; lledaenu

propel, *v.t.* gyrru ymlaen, gwthio

propensity, *n.* tuedd, tueddfryd, gogwydd

proper, *a.* priod, priodol, gweddus

property, *n.* priodoledd; eiddo; priodwedd (cemeg)

prophecy, *n.* proffwydoliaeth

prophesy, *v.* proffwydo

prophet, *n.* proffwyd

propinquity, *n.* agosrwydd, cyfnesafrwydd

propitiate, *v.t.* cymodi, dyhuddo

propitiation, *n.* cymod, iawn

propitious, *a.* tirion, ffafriol

proportion, *n.* cyfartaledd, cyfrannedd

proportional, *a.* cyfrannol

proportionate, *a.* cymesur

propose, *v.* cynnig, bwriadu

proposition, *n.* cynigiad; gosodiad

propound, *v.t.* cynnig, gosod gerbron

proprietor, *n.* perchen, perchennog

propriety, *n.* priodoldeb, gwedduster

propulsion, *n.* gwthiad, gyriad

prorogue, *v.t.* gohirio

prosaic, *a.* rhyddieithol, cyffredin

proscribe, *v.t.* deol, diarddel, gwahardd

prose, *n.* rhyddiaith

prosecute, *v.t.* erlyn, dilyn, dwyn ymlaen

prosecutor, *n.* erlynydd

proselyte, *n.* proselyt

prosody, *n.* mydryddiaeth

prospect, *n.* rhagolwg, golwg, golygfa

prospectus, *n.* rhaglen, hysbyslen

prosper, *v.* llwyddo, tycio, ffynnu

prosperity, *n.* llwyddiant, hawddfyd [wng

prostitute, *n.* putain: *v.t.* darost-

prostrate, *a.* yn gorwedd ar ei wyneb; ar lawr yn lân: *v.t.* bwrw i lawr; ymgrymu

protect, *v.t.* amddiffyn, noddi

protection, *n.* amddiffyn, nawdd, diogelwch

protector, *n.* amddiffynnydd

protest, *v.* gwrthdystio: *n.* gwrthdystiad

prototype, *n.* cynddelw, cynllun

protract, *v.t.* estyn, hwyhau

protrude, *v.* gwthio allan

protuberance, *n.* chwydd

proud, *a.* balch

prove, *v.* profi

provender, *n.* ebran, gogor, porthiant

proverb, *n.* dihareb

provide, *v.t.* darparu, darbod

providence, *n.* rhagluniaeth, darbodaeth

provident, *a.* darbodus

providential, *a.* rhagluniaethol

province, *n.* talaith, tiriogaeth; cylch, maes

provision, *n.* darpariaeth: (*pl.*) darbodion; ymborth

proviso, *n.* amod

provocation, *n.* anogaeth, cyffroad, cythrudd

provoke, *v.t.* annog, cyffroi, cythruddo, profocio

provost, *n.* maer, profost

prow, *n.* pen blaen bad neu long

prowess, *n.* dewrder, glewder, grymuster

prowl, *v.i.* ysglyfaetha, prowlan

proximate, *a.* nesaf, agos at; agos

proximity, *n.* agosrwydd

proxy, *n.* dirprwy

prude, *n.* mursen, coegen

prudence, *n.* pwyll, synnwyr, callineb

prudent, *a.* pwyllog, synhwyrol, call, doeth

prune, *n.* eirinen sech

prurient, *a.* llawn o ysfa; aflan, trythyll

pry, *v.i.* chwilota, chwilenna

psalm, *n.* salm

psalmody, *n.* caniadaeth y cysegr

psalter, *n.* llyfr salmau, sallwyr

pseudo-, *px.* gau, ffug

pseudonym, *n.* ffugenw

pshaw, *i.* wfft, pw, och, ffei

psychology, *n.* seicoleg

puberty, *n.* aeddfedrwydd oed, blaenlencyndod, puberdod

public, *a.* cyhoeddus: *n.* y cyhoedd

publican, *n.* publican; tafarnwr

publicity, *n.* cyhoeddusrwydd

publish, *v.t.* cyhoeddi

pucker, *v.* crychu, crybachu

puddle, *n.* corbwll; pydew, llaca

puerile, *a.* bachgennaidd, plentyn-naidd

puff, *n.* pwff, chwa, chwyth: *v.* pwffio, chwythu

pugilist, *n.* paffiwr, ymladdwr

pugnacious, *a.* ymladdgar, cweryl-gar

puissant, *a.* galluog, grymus, nerthol

pull, *v.t.* tynnu: *n.* tynfa, tyniad

pullet, *n.* cywen

pulley, *n.* chwerfan, troell, pwli

pulmonary, *a.* ysgyfeiniol

pulp, *n.* bywyn, mwydion

pulpit, *n.* pulpud

pulsate, *v.* curo (megis y galon)

pulse, *n.* curiad y galon, curiad y gwaed

pulse, *n.* pys, ffa, &c.

pulverize, *v.t.* malu yn llwch, chwilfriwio

pummel, *v.t.* pwnio, dyrnodio, curo

pump, *n.* sugnedydd, pwmp: *v.* pwmpio

pun, *n.* gair mwys, mwysair

punch, *n.* pwns; dyrnod: *v.* pwnsio, dyrnodio

punctilious, *a.* cysetlyd, gorfanwl

punctual, *a.* prydlon

punctuate, *v.t.* atalnodi

puncture, *n.* twll: *v.t.* tyllu

pundit, *n.* ysgolhaig, doethwr

pungent, *a.* llym, llymdost, siarp

punish, *v.t.* cosbi, ceryddu; poeni

punishment, *n.* cosb, cosbedigaeth

punitive, *a.* cosbol

puny, *a.* eiddil, bychan, tila, pitw

pupil, *n.* ysgolhaig, ysgolor, disgybl; cannwyll llygad

puppet, *n.* delw, dol, pyped; gwas

puppy, *n.* ci bach

purblind, *a.* cibddall, coegddall

purchase, *v.t.* prynu, pwrcasu: *n.* pryniant, pwrcas

pure, *a.* pur, noeth

purgative, *a.* carthol: *n.* carthlyn

purgatory, *n.* purdan

purge, *v.t.* puro, glanhau, carthu, coethi: *n.* carthlyn

purification, *n.* puredigaeth

purify, *v.t.* puro, coethi, glanhau

Puritan, *n.* Piwritan

purity, *n.* purdeb

purl, *v.i.* crychleisio, byrlymu

purlieu, *n.* cyffin, ffin, cymdogaeth

purloin, *v.t.* lladrata, dwyn

purple, *a. & n.* porffor

purport, *n.* ystyr, rhediad, ergyd: *v.t.* arwyddo, proffesu, honni

purpose, *n.* pwrpas, bwriad, ar-faeth: *v.t.* bwriadu, arfaethu

purr, *v.* canu crwth, grwnan

purse, *n.* pwrs, cod: *v.* crychu

pursue, *v.* dilyn, erlyn, erlid, ymlid

pursuit, *n.* ymlidiad; ymchwil, gorchwyl

purulent, *a.* crawnllyd, gorllyd

purvey, *v.* darparu lluniaeth, dar-merth

purview, *n.* amcan, maes, cylch

pus, *n.* crawn, gôr

push, *v.* gwthio: *n.* gwth, ysgŵd; ymdrech [llwfr

pusillanimous, *a.* bychanfrydig,

puss, *n.* titw, pws; ysgyfarnog

pustule, *n.* ploryn, llinoryn

put, *v.* gosod, dodi, rhoddi, rhoi

putative, *a.* tybiedig, cyfrifedig

putrefaction, *n.* pydredd, madredd

putrefy, *v.* pydru, madru

putrid, *a.* pwdr, mall

putty, *n.* pwti: *v.t.* pwtïo

puzzle, *n.* dryswch, penbleth, pos: *v.* drysu, pyslo

pygmy, *n.* corrach

pyramid, *n.* pyramid, bera

pyre, *n.* cynnau angladdol, coel-certh

pyrotechnic, *a. & n.* (o natur) tân gwyllt

Q

quack, n. crachfeddyg, cwac
quack, v.i. lleisio fel hwyad
quadrangle, n. pedrongl
quadrant, n. cwadrant
quadruped, n. pedwarcarnol
quadruple, a. pedwarplyg
quaff, v. drachtio, cofftio, yfed
quagmire, n. siglen, cors, mignen, sybwll
quail, n. sofliar
quail, v.i. llwfrhau, yswatio, cilio
quaint, a. od, hen-ffasiwn
quake, v.i. crynu
Quaker, n. Crynwr
qualification, n. cymhwyster; cymhwysiad
qualified, a. cymwys
qualify, v.t. cymhwyso
quality, n. ansawdd, rhinwedd
qualm, n. petruster, amheuaeth
quandary, n. penbleth, cyfyng-gyngor
quantity, n. swm, maint, mesur
quarantine, n. cwarant
quarrel, n. ymrafael, ffrae, cweryl: v.i. ffraeo
quarry, n. chwarel, cloddfa, cwar: v. cloddio.
quarry, n. ysglyfaeth
quart, n. chwart, cwart
quarter, n. chwarter, cwarter; cwr, man; trugaredd; (pl.) llety
quartet, -te, n. pedwarawd
quarto, a. & n. (llyfr) pedwarplyg
quartz, n. creigrisial, cwarts
quash, v.t. diddymu, dirymu
quaver, v.i. cwafrio, crynu: n. cwafer
quay, n. cei
queen, n. brenhines
queer, a. od, hynod, digrif, ysmala
quell, v.t. llonyddu, gostegu, darostwng
quench, v.t. diffodd, dofi, torri
quern, n. llawfelin, breuan
querulous, a. cwynfanllyd, blin

query, n. holiad, gofyniad: v. holi, amau
quest, n. ymchwil, ymchwiliad, cwest
question, n. gofyniad, cwestiwn: v.t. holi, amau
queue, n. cynffon, cwt, ciw
quibble, n. geirddadl: v.i. geirddadlau, mân-ddadlau
quick, a. byw; buan, cyflym, clau
quiescent, a. distaw, llonydd, digyffro
quiet, a. llonydd, tawel, distaw: n. llonyddwch, tawelwch: v.t. llonyddu, taweli
quill, n. pluen, plufyn, cwilsyn
quilt, n. cwilt, cwrlid: v.t. cwiltio
quintessence, n. naws, rhinwedd, anian
quip, n. gair ffraeth, ateb parod
quit, v.t. gadael, symud: a. rhydd
quite, adv. cwbl, llwyr, hollol
quiver, n. cawell saethau
quiver, v.i. crynu, dirgrynu
quixotic, a. rhamanllyd, mympwyol, gwyllt
quiz, v.t. holi, pyslo, profocio
quoit, n. coeten, coetan
quondam, a. wedi bod, gynt, hen
quorum, n. nifer gofynnol, corwm
quota, n. rhan, cyfran, dogn, cwota
quotation, n. dyfyniad; prisiant
quote, v.t. dyfynnu; nodi (prisiau)
quoth, v.t. meddai, ebe
quotient, n. cyfran (rhifyddeg); cyniferydd (deallusrwydd)

R

rabbit, n. cwningen
rabble, n. ciwed, tyrfa ddireol
rabid, a. cynddeiriog
rabies, n. y gynddaredd
race, n. gyrfa, rhedfa, rhedegfa: v.i. rasio
race, n. hil
racial, a. perthynol i'r hil

rack, *n.* clwyd, rhestl; arteithglwydd: *v.t.* arteithio, dirdynnu

racy, *a.* blasus; arab, ffraeth

raddle, *n.* lliw coch

radiant, *a.* disglair, llachar, tanbaid

radiate, *v.* pelydru, rheiddio

radical, *a.* gwreiddiol, cynhenid; trylwyr: *n.* rhyddfrydwr, radical

radish, *n.* rhuddygl

radius, (-*ii*), *n.* cylch; radius

raft. *n.* cludair

rafter, *n.* tulath, ceibren, trawst

rag, *n.* carp, clwt

rage, *n.* cynddaredd: *v.i.* terfysgu, cynddeiriogi

ragged, *a.* carpiog, bratiog

raid, *n.* rhuthr, cyrch: *v.* anrheithio

rail, *n.* canllaw, cledren, rheilen: *v.* cledru

rail, *v.i.* difrïo, difenwi, cablu

raillery, *n.* difyrrwch, cellwair

railway, *n.* rheilffordd, ffordd haearn

raiment, *n.* dillad, gwisg

rain, *n.* glaw: *v.* glawio, bwrw glaw

rainbow, *n.* enfys

raise, *v.t.* codi, cyfodi, dyrchafu

rake, *n.* cribin, rhaca: *v.* cribinio, crafu

rake, *n.* oferwr, oferddyn

rally, *v.t.* profocio

rally, *v.* atgynnull; gwella: *n.* cynulliad

ram, *n.* hwrdd, maharen: *v.t.* hyrddu, pwnio

ramble, *v.i.* gwibio, crwydro: *n.* gwib

ramify, *v.* canghennu, ymrannu

rampant, *a.* uchel ei ben, rhonc

rampart, *n.* caer, rhagfur, gwrthglawdd

ramshackle, *a.* bregus, candryll

rancid, *a.* â blas cryf arno, mws, drewllyd

rancour, *n.* digasedd, chwerwder

random, *n.* antur, damwain: *a.* damweiniol

range, *n.* ehangder, cylch; *v.* rhestru, cyfleu; crwydro

rank, *n.* rhenc, gradd: *v.* rhestru

rank, *a.* mws; gwyllt, bras; rhonc, noeth

rankle, *v.i.* gori, madru; cnoi, llidio

ransack, *v.t.* chwilio, chwilota, ysbeilio

ransom, *n.* pridwerth: *v.t.* prynu, gwaredu

rant, *v.i.* bragaldian, brygawthan

rap, *n.* cnoc, ergyd: *v.t.* cnocio, curo

rap, *n.* gronyn, mymryn, blewyn

rapacious, *a.* rheibus, ysglyfaethus

rape, *v.t.* treisio, llathruddo: *n.* trais

rapid, *a.* cyflym, buan, chwyrn, gwyllt

rapier, *n.* meingledd

rapine, *n.* trais, anrhaith

rapt, *a.* astud, syn, dwys

rapture, *n.* perlewyg, gorawen

rare, *a.* anaml, prin; godidog; tenau

rascal, *n.* dihiryn, cnaf, gwalch, cenau

rash, *a.* byrbwyll, rhyfygus, anystyriol

rash, *n.* brech, tarddiant

rasher, *n.* ysglisen, sleisen, tafell, golwyth

rasp, *v.* rhasglio, crafu, rhygnu

raspberry, *n.* afanen, mafonen

rat, *n.* llygoden fawr: *v.i.* llygota

rate, *v.t.* ffraeo, dwrdio, dweud y drefn

rate, *n.* cyflymder; cyfartaledd; pris; ardreth

rather, *adv.* braidd, hytrach, go, lled

ratify, *v.t.* cadarnhau

ratio, *n.* cyfartaledd; cymhareb

ration, *n.* dogn, saig: *v.t.* dogni

rational, *a.* rhesymol

rattle, *v.* rhuglo, trystio: *n.* rhugl, rhwnc

raucous, *a.* cryg, garw, aflafar

ravage, *v.t.* anrheithio, diffeithio, difrodi

rave, *v.i.* gwallgofi, ynfydu, gwynfydu

ravel, *v.* drysu; dad-weu, datod

raven, *n.* cigfran
raven, *v.* gwancio, glythu; ysglyfio
ravine, *n.* hafn, ceunant
ravish, *v.t.* treisio, cipio; swyno, hudo
raw, *a.* amrwd; crai, cri; noeth, dolurus, garw: *n.* cig noeth, dolur
ray, *n.* paladr, pelydryn
ray, *n.* cath fôr
raze, *v.t.* llwyr ddymchwelyd, dileu
razor, *n.* ellyn, rasal: *v.t.* eillio
re, *pr.* ym mater, mewn perthynas i
re-, *px.* ad-, ail-
reach, *v.* cyrraedd, estyn: *n.* cyrraedd
react, *v.i.* adweithio
reaction, *n.* adwaith
read, *v.* darllen
ready, *a.* parod, rhwydd
real, *a.* gwir, real, dirweddol
reality, *n.* gwirionedd, sylwedd; dirwedd, realiti
realize, *v.t.* sylweddoli; troi yn arian
realm, *n.* teyrnas, gwlad, bro
reap, *v.* medi
rear, *n.* cefn, pen ôl, ôl
rear, *v.* codi, magu; codi ar ei draed ôl
reason, *n.* rheswm: *v.* rhesymu
reasonable, *a.* rhesymol
reassure, *v.t.* calonogi, cysuro
rebate, *n.* toliant, disgownt
rebel, *v.i.* gwrthryfela: *n.* gwrthryfelwr
rebellion, *n.* gwrthryfel
rebound, *v.i.* adlamu: *n.* adlam
rebuff, *n.* nacâd, sen: *v.t.* nacáu, sennu
rebuke, *v.t.* ceryddu: *n.* cerydd, sen
rebut, *v.t.* gwrthbrofi, gwrthddywedyd
recalcitrant, *a.* cyndyn, anhydyn
recall, *v.t.* galw yn ôl; galw i gof, cofio
recant, *v.* datgyffesu
recapitulate, *v.t.* ailadrodd (yn gryno)
recede, *v.i.* encilio, cilio yn ôl

receipt, *n.* derbyniad; derbynneb
receive, *v.t.* derbyn
recent, *a.* diweddar
receptacle, *n.* llestr; cynheiliad (llysieueg)
reception, *n.* derbyniad, croeso
recess, *n.* cil, encil; cilfach; gwyliau
recessional, *a. & n.* (emyn) ymadawol
Rechabite, *n.* Rechabiad
recipe, *n.* cyfarwyddyd; rysáit
recipient, *n.* derbyniwr, derbynnydd
reciprocal, *a.* cilyddol
reciprocate, *v.* talu'n ôl, cydgyfnewid; cilyddu
recital, *n.* adroddiad, datganiad
recitation, *n.* adroddiad
recitative, *n.* adroddgan
recite, *v.* adrodd
reck, *v.* gofalu, ystyried
reckless, *a.* anystyriol, rhyfygus, dibris
reckon, *v.* cyfrif, barnu, bwrw
reclaim, *v.t.* adennill, diwygio
recline, *v.* lledorwedd, gorwedd, gorffwys
recluse, *n.* meudwy
recognition, *n.* adnabyddiaeth, cydnabyddiaeth
recognizance, *n.* ymrwymiad, gwystl
recognize, *v.t.* adnabod, cydnabod
recoil, *v.i.* adlamu, gwrthneidio, cilio
recollect, *v.t.* galw i gof, atgofio, cofio
recommend, *v.t.* cymeradwyo, argymell
recompense, *v.t.* ad-dalu, gwobrwyo, talu
reconcile, *v.t.* cymodi, cysoni
recondite, *a.* dwfn, cudd, cêl, tywyll
reconnaissance, *n.* archwiliad
reconnoitre, *v.t.* chwilio, archwilio
record, *v.t.* cofnodi, recordio: *n.* cofnod, record

recorder, *n.* cofiadur

recount, *v.t.* adrodd

recoup, *v.* digolledu

recourse, *n.* cyrchfa. **—to have r. to,** myned at, defnyddio

recover, *v.* cael yn ôl, adennill; ymadfer

recreant, *a.* llwfr: *n.* llwfryn, gwrthgiliwr

recreate, *v.* difyrru, adlonni

recreation, *n.* difyrrwch, adloniant

recriminate, *v.i.* gwrthgyhuddo

recrudescence, *n.* ailenyniad

recruit, *n.* ricriwt; newyddian: *v.* codi gwŷr; adennill

rectangle, *n.* petryal

rectangular, *a.* petryalog

rectify, *v.t.* unioni, cywiro; puro, coethi

rectilinear, *a.* unionlin

rectitude, *n.* uniondeb

rector, *n.* rheithor

rectory, *n.* rheithoriaeth; rheithordy

recumbent, *a.* gorweddol, gogwyddol

recuperate, *v.* adfer, ymadfer, cryfhau

recur, *v.i.* ailddigwydd, dychwelyd

recurring, *a.* cylchol

recusant, *n.* anghydffurfiwr

red, *a. & n.* coch, rhudd

redeem, *v.t.* prynu (yn ôl), gwaredu

redemption, *n.* prynedigaeth

redolent, *a.* yn sawru o

redoubtable, *a.* i'w ofni; pybyr

redound, *v.i.* dwyn, peri, adlewyrchu

redress, *v.t.* unioni: *n.* iawn (am gam)

reduce, *v.t.* lleihau, gostwng; rhydwytho

reduction, *n.* lleihad, gostyngiad

redundant, *a.* gormodol

reed, *n.* cawnen, corsen, calaf; pibell

reef, *n.* plyg hwyl, rîff: *v.t.* plygu hwyl

reef, *n.* creigle (yn y môr), creigfa, rîff

reek, *n.* mwg, tarth, drewdod: *v.* mygu, drewi

reel, *n.* ril: *v.* dirwyn

reel, *v.i.* troi, chwyldroi: *n.* dawns

refection, *n.* ymborth, lluniaeth

refer, *v.* cyfeirio, cyfarwyddo

refine, *v.* puro, coethi

reflect, *v.* adlewyrchu: myfyrio

reflex, *n.* adweithred, atgyrch

reflexive, *a.* atblygol

reform, *v.* diwygio, gwella: *n.* diwygiad

reformation, *n.* diwygiad

reformatory, *n.* ysgol ddiwygio

refract, *v.t.* gwrthdorri

refractory, *a.* cyndyn, anhydyn

refrain, *v.* ymatal

refrain, *n.* byrdwn

refresh, *v.t.* adfywio, dadebru, adlonni

refreshment, *n.* adfywiad, adloniant; (*pl.*) ymborth, lluniaeth

refrigerate, *v.t.* rheweiddio

refrigerator, *a.* rhewgell, oergell, oeriedydd

refuge, *n.* noddfa, lloches

refugee, *n.* ffoadur

refuse, *v.* gwrthod

refuse, *n.* ysbwrial, gwehilion, sothach

refute, *v.t.* gwrthbrofi, datbrofi

regal, *a.* brenhinol

regale, *v.* gwledda

regalia, *n.pl.* teyrndlysau

regard, *v.t.* edrych ar, ystyried: *n.* sylw, parch, hoffter

regenerate, *v.t.* aileni

regent, *n.* llywydd, rhaglaw

regicide, *n.* teyrnleiddiad; teyrnladdiad

regime, *n.* trefn, cyfundrefn

regiment, *n.* catrawd

region, *n.* ardal, bro, gwlad

register, *n.* cofrestr: *v.t.* cofrestru

registrar, *n.* cofrestrydd

registry, *n.* cofrestrfa; cofrestriad

regnant, *a.* yn teyrnasu, llywodraethol

regret, *v.t.* gofidio, edifaru: *n.* gofid

regular, *a.* rheolaidd, cyson

regulate, *v.t.* rheoleiddio

regulation, *n.* rheol, trefniant

rehabilitate, *v.t.* adfer i fri neu fraint

rehearsal, *n.* rihyrsal, practis

rehearse, *v.t.* adrodd; ymarfer ymlaen llaw

reign, *v.i.* teyrnasu: *n.* teyrnasiad

reimburse, *v.t.* talu yn ôl, ad-dalu

rein, *n.* afwyn, awen: *v.t.* ffrwyno

reinforce, *v.t.* atgyfnerthu

reinstate, *v.t.* adfer i safle neu fraint

reiterate, *v.t.* ailadrodd, mynychu

reject, *v.t.* gwrthod, bwrw ymaith

rejoice, *v.i.* llawenhau, gorfoleddu

rejoin, *v.* ateb, gwrthateb

rejoinder, *n.* ateb, gwrthateb

relapse, *v.i.* ailglafychu, ailymhoelyd, atglafyrchu

relate, *v.* adrodd, mynegi; perthyn

relation, *n.* adroddiad; perthynas

relative, *a.* perthynasol: *n.* perthynas

relax, *v.* llacio, llaesu, ymollwng

relay, *n.* cyflenwad newydd, cyfnewid: *v.* ailosod

release, *v.t.* rhyddhau, gollwng: *n.* rhyddhad

relegate, *v.t.* alltudio, deol

relent, *v.i.* tyneru, tirioni, llaesu

relevant, *a.* perthnasol

reliable, *a.* y gellir dibynnu arno, dibynadwy

reliance, *n.* ymddiried, hyder, pwys

relic, *n.* crair, (*pl.*) gweddillion

relief, *n.* cynhorthwy; gollyngdod, ymwared

relieve, *v.t.* cynorthwyo; esmwytho, ysgafnhau; rhyddhau, gollwng

religion, *n.* crefydd

religious, *a.* crefyddol

relinquish, *v.t.* gollwng, gildio, gwadu

relish, *n.* blas; enllyn, mwyniant: *v.* blasio, hoffi

reluctant, *a.* anfodlon, anewyllysgar

rely, *v.i.* hyderu, ymddiried, dibynnu

remain, *v.i.* aros, parhau, gorffwys

remainder, *n.* gweddill, rhelyw

remains, *n.pl.* olion, gweddillion

remand, *v.t.* aildraddodi

remark, *v.* sylwi: *n.* sylw

remarkable, *a.* nodedig, hynod, rhyfedd, syn

remedy, *n.* meddyginiaeth: *v.t.* meddyginiaethu, gwella

remember, *v.t.* cofio

remembrance, *n.* cof, coffa, coffadwriaeth

remind, *v.t.* atgofio, atgoffa, cofio

reminiscence, *n.* atgof

remiss, *a.* esgeulus, diofal, llac

remission, *n.* maddeuant

remit, *v.* maddau; arafu, peidio; anfon

remnant, *n.* gweddill

remonstrance, *n.* cwyn, gwrthdystiad

remonstrate, *v.i.* ymliw, gwrthdystio

remorse, *n.* edifeirwch, gofid, atgno

remote, *a.* pell, pellennig, anghysbell

remove, *v.* symud, dileu; mudo

remunerate, *v.t.* talu, gwobrwyo

renaissance, *n.* dadeni

rend, *v.* rhwygo, dryllio, llarpio

render, *v.* talu ; datgan ; gwneuthur; troi, cyfieithu

rendezvous, *n.* cyrchfa, man cyfarfod

renegade, *n.* gwrthgiliwr

renew, *v.t.* adnewyddu

renounce, *v.t.* ymwrthod, ymwadu, gwadu

renovate, *v.t.* adnewyddu

renown, *n.* clod, bri, enwogrwydd

rent, *n.* rhwyg

rent, *n.* ardreth, rhent : *v.t.* ardrethu, rhentu

renunciation, *n.* ymwadiad

repair, *v.i.* cyrchu, myned

repair, *v.i.* atgyweirio, trwsio: *n.* cywair

reparation, *n.* iawn, ad-daliad

repartee, *n.* ateb parod

repast, n. pryd, ymborth, lluniaeth

repatriate, v. adfer i'w wlad ei hun

repeal, v.t. diddymu: n. diddymiad

repeat, v. ailadrodd, ailgyflawni

repel, v.t. bwrw yn ôl

repent, v. edifarhau, edifaru

repentance, n. edifeirwch

repertory, n. ystorfa, trysorfa, cronfa

repetition, n. ailadroddiad

repine, v.i. ymofidio, poenydio

replenish, v.t. ail-lenwi, diwallu

replete, a. llawn, cyflawn, gorlawn

replica, n. copi cywir, cyflun

reply, v.i. ateb: n. ateb, atebiad

report, v.t. adrodd, hysbysu: n. adroddiad; sŵn ergyd

reporter, n. gohebydd

repose, v. gorffwys: n. gorffwys

repository, n. ystorfa, trysorfa

reprehend, v.t. ceryddu, argyhoeddi [ioli

represent, v.t. portreadu; cynrych-

representative, a. yn cynrychioli: n. cynrychiolydd

repress, v.t. atal, gostegu

reprimand, n. cerydd: v.t. ceryddu

reprisal, n. dial

reproach, v.t. ceryddu, gwaradwyddo, edliw: n. gwaradwydd

reprobate, a. ysgymun: n. oferddyn: v.t. condemnio

reproduce, v.t. adgynhyrchu, epilio

reproof, n. cerydd

reprove, v.t. ceryddu, argyhoeddi

reptile, n. ymlusgiad

republic n. gweriniaeth, gwerinlywodraeth

repudiate, v.t. diarddel, diarddelwi, gwadu

repugnance, n. gwrthwynebiad, atgasrwydd

repugnant, a. croes, atgas, gwrthun

repulse, v.t. bwrw'n ôl; nacáu: n. gwrthergyd

repulsion, n. gwrthnysedd

repulsive, a. atgas, ffiaidd

reputable, a. parchus, cyfrifol

reputation, n. gair, cymeriad, enw da

repute, v.t. cyfrif, tybied: n. parch, bri

request, n. cais: v.t. ceisio, gofyn

requiem, n. offeren dros y meirw; galargerdd

require, v.t. gofyn, mynnu

requisite, a. gofynnol, angenrheidiol

requite, v.t. talu, gwobrwyo, talu'r pwyth

rescind, v.t. diddymu, dirymu

rescript, n. adysgrif, ateb, gorchymyn

rescue, v.t. achub: n. achubiad

research, n. ymchwil, ymchwiliad

resemblance, n. tebygrwydd

resemble, v.t. tebygu i

resent, v.t. tramgwyddo, digio, cymryd yn chwith

resentful, a. digofus, llidiog

reserve, v.t. cadw yn ôl: n. yr hyn a gedwir

reservoir, n. cronfa, llyn

reside, v.i. preswylio

residential, a. preswyl

residue, n. gweddill

residuum, n. gweddill, gwaddod

resign, v. rhoddi i fyny, ymddiswyddo, ymddeol

resignation, n. ymddiswyddiad; ymostyngiad

resin, n. ystor, rhwsin

resist, v. gwrthsefyll, gwrthwynebu

resolute, a. penderfynol

resolution, n. penderfyniad

resolve, v. penderfynu: n. penderfyniad

resonant, a. atseiniol

resort, v.i. cyrchu: n. cyrchfa; ymwared

resound, v. atseinio, diasbedain

resource, n. sgil, dyfais; (pl.) adnoddau

respect, v.t. parchu: n. golwg; parch

respective, a. priodol, ar wahân

respire, v. anadlu

respite, n. oediad, saib, seibiant, hamdden [nydd

resplendent, a. disglair, ysblen-

respond, *v.i.* ateb, ymateb; porthi

response, *n.* ateb, atebiad

responsible, *a.* atebol, cyfrifol

responsive, *a.* ymatebol

rest, *n. & v.* gorffwys

rest, *v.i.* aros, parhau: *n.* gweddill

restaurant, *n.* tŷ bwyta, bwyty

restitution, *n.* adferiad; iawn

restive, *a.* ystyfnig, ystranclyd, noglyd

restore, *v.t.* adfer; atgyweirio

restrain, *v.t.* atal, ffrwyno

restraint, *n.* atalfa, ffrwyn, caethiwed

restrict, *v.t.* cyfyngu, caethiwo

result, *v.i.* deillio, canlyn: *n.* canlyniad

resume, *v.t.* ailddechrau

resurrection, *n.* atgyfodiad

resuscitate, *v.* adfywhau, dadebru

retail, *v.t.* mân-werthu, adwerthu: *n.* adwerth

retain, *v.* cadw, dal; llogi

retaliate, *v.* talu'n ôl, talu'r pwyth, dial

retard, *v.* rhwystro, oedi

retch, *v.i.* cyfogi, chwydu

retentive, *a.* yn dal heb ollwng; gafaelgar

reticent, *a.* tawedog, distaw

retina, *n.* rhwyden y llygad

retinue, *n.* gosgordd, gosgorddlu

retire, *v.i.* ymneilltuo, encilio, cilio

retort, *v.* gwrthateb: *n.* ateb parod; ritort (cemeg)

retract, *v.* tynnu'n ôl

retreat, *v.i.* cilio, encilio, ffoi: *n.* encil, ffo

retrench, *v.* cwtogi, cynilo

retribution, *n.* ad-daledigaeth, cosb, dial

retrieve, *v.t.* olrhain; adennill

retro-, *px.* yn l, yôn y gwrthol, gwrth- [dirywio

retrogress, *v.i.* myned yn ôl,

retrospect, *n.* ad-drem, adolwg

return, *v.* dychwelyd: *n.* dychweliad; elw

reveal, *v.t.* datguddio, amlygu, dangos

revel, *v.i.* gloddesta; ymhyfrydu: *n.* gloddest

revenge, *v. & n.* dial

revenue, *n.* cyllid, enillion, incwm

reverberate, *v.* taro'n ôl; atseinio

revere, *v.t.* parchu, anrhydeddu

reverence, *n.* parch, parchedigaeth

reverend, *a.* parchedig

reverent, *a.* parchus, gŵyl, gwylaidd

reverie, *n.* synfyfyrdod

reverse, *a.* gwrthwyneb, chwith: *v.* troi, gwrthdroi: *n.* gwrthdro, aflwydd

revert, *v.* troi yn ôl, dychwelyd

review, *v.t.* adolygu: *n.* adolygiad

revile, *v.t.* difenwi, cablu, gwaradwyddo

revise, *v.t.* cywiro, diwygio

revival, *n.* adfywiad, diwygiad

revive, *v.* adfywio, adnewyddu

revoke, *v.* galw yn ôl, diddymu, dirymu; ffyrnigo (chware cardiau)

revolt, *v.* gwrthryfela: *n.* gwrthryfel

revolting, *a.* gwrthnaws, atgas, ffiaidd

revolution, *n.* chwyldro, chwyldroad

revolve, *v.* troi, amdroi, cylchdroi

revolver, *n.* llawddryll

reward, *n.* gwobr: *v.t.* gwobrwyo

rhapsody, *n.* hwyl, ymfflamychiad

rhetoric, *n.* rhetoreg, rhethreg

rheumatism, *n.* cryd cymalau, gwynegon

rhinoceros, *n.* trwyngornfil

rhombus, *n.* rhombws

rhubarb, *n.* rhiwbob

rhyme, *n.* odl, rhigwm: *v.* odli, rhigymu

rhythm, *n.* rhythm, rhediad

rib, *n.* asen, eisen

ribald, *n.* masweddwr: *a.* maswedd-ol

ribbon, *n.* rhuban, ysnoden

rice, *n.* reis

rich, *a.* cyfoethog, goludog, bras

riches, *n.pl.* cyfoeth, golud

rick, *n.* tas

rickets, *n.pl.* y llech(au)

rickety, *a.* simsan, bregus

rid, *v.t.* gwared

riddle, *n.* dychymyg, pos

riddle, *n.* rhidyll: *v.t.* rhidyllio, gogrwn

ride, *v.* marchogaeth, marchocáu

rider, *n.* marchogwr; atodiad

ridge, *n.* grwn, trum, cefn, crib

ridicule, *n.* gwawd: *v.t.* gwawdio, chwerthin am ben

ridiculous, *a.* chwerthinllyd

rife, *a.* aml, cyffredin

riff-raff, *n.* gwehilion y bobl

rifle, *v.t.* anrheithio, ysbeilio

rifle. *n.* dryll, reiffl

rift, *n.* agen, hollt, rhwyg

rig, *v.* rigio, taclu: *n.* rig

right, *a.* iawn, uniawn; deau; *adv.* yn iawn: *v.t.* unioni, cywiro: *n.* iawnder, hawl

righteous, *a.* cyfiawn

righteousness, *n.* cyfiawnder

rightful, *a.* cyfreithlon, iawn, teg

rigid, *a.* anhyblyg, manwl, caeth

rigmarole, *n.* ffregod, rhibidirês

rigour, *n.* gerwinder, llymder, toster

rile, *v.t.* cythruddo, ffyrnigo, llidio

rill, *n.* cornant, gofer, ffrwd

rim, *n.* ymyl, cylch, cant

rind, *n.* pil, croen, crawen, rhisgl

ring, *n.* modrwy, cylch: *v.* modrwyo

ring, *v.* canu cloch, atseinio: *n.* swn cloch, tinc

rinse, *v.t.* golchi, trochi

riot, *n.* terfysg, gloddest: *v.i.* terfysgu

rip, *v.* rhipio, rhwygo, datod

ripe, *a.* aeddfed

ripple, *n.* crych: *v.* crychu

rise, *v.i.* codi, cyfodi: *n.* codiad

risk, *n.* perygl, enbydrwydd: *v.t.* peryglu, anturio, mentro

rite, *n.* defod

ritual, *a.* defodol: *n.* defod

rival, *n.* cydymgeisydd: *v.* cystadlu

river, *n.* afon

rivet, *n.* rhybed, hem, rifet: *v.* rhybedu, hemio, rifetio

rivulet, *n.* afonig, nant, cornant

road, *n.* ffordd, heol; angorfa

roam, *v.i.* crwydro, gwibio

roan, *a.* brych, gwineulwyd, broc

roar, *v.i.* rhuo: *n.* rhu, rhuad

roast, *v.* rhostio, crasu, pobi, digoni

rob, *v.t.* lladrata, ysbeilio

robber, *n.* lleidr, ysbeiliwr

robe, *n.* gwisg, gŵn

robust, *a.* cadarn, cryf, grymus

rock, *v.* siglo

rock, *n.* craig

rocket, *n.* roced

rod, *n.* gwialen, llath

rodent, *a.* yn cnoi, ysol: *n.* cnowr

roe, *n.* iyrches, ewig

roe, *n.* grawn pysgod, gronell

roebuck, *n.* iwrch

rogue, *n.* gwalch, cnaf

roister, *v.i.* trystio, cadw reiat, wtresa

rôle, *n.* rhan, tasg, cymeriad

roll, *v.* rholio, treiglo: *n.* rhòl

rollick *v.i.* cadw reiat

Roman, *n.* Rhufeiniwr: *a.* Rhufeinaidd, Rhufeinig

romance, *n.* rhamant: *v.i.* rhamanta

romp, *v.i.* rhampio: *n.* rhamp; rhampen

rood, *n.* rhwd; y grog, y groes

roof, *n.* to, nen: *v.t.* toi

rook, *n.* ydfran, brân

room, *n.* lle; ystafell

roost, *n.* clwyd: *v.i.* clwydo

rooster, *n.* ceiliog

root, *n.* gwraidd, gwreiddyn: *v.* gwreiddio; diwreiddio

rope, *n.* rhaff: *v.* rhaffu, rhwymo

rosary, *n.* rhosynfa; rhes baderau

rose, *n.* rhosyn

rosette, *n.* 'rhosyn', ysnoden

rosin, *n.* ystor, rhwsin

rostrum, *n.* llwyfan, areithfa

rosy, *a.* rhosynnaidd, gwritgoch

rot, *v.* pydru, braenu: *n.* pydrni; lol

rotate, *v.i.* troi, cylchdroi, chwyldroi

rote, *n.* tafod-leferydd

rotten, *a.* pwdr, pydredig, sâl

rotund, *a.* crwn, amgrwn, cylch-grwn

rouge, *n.* lliw coch, gruddliw

rough, *a.* garw, gerwin, bras

round, *a.* crwn: *n.* crwn, cylch, tro, rownd: *adv. & pr.* o gylch, o am-gylch: *v.* crynio, rowndio

rouse, *v.* dihuno, deffroi, cyffroi

rout, *n.* rhawt; ffo, dymchweliad: *v.* ymlid, dymchwelyd

route, *n.* ffordd, llwybr, hynt

routine, *n.* defod, arfer

rove, *v.* crwydro, gwibio

row, *n.* rhes, rhestr

row, *v.* rhwyfo

row, *n.* terfysg, cythrwfl, ffrae

rowan, *n.* criafol

rowdy, *a.* trystiog, afreolus

rowel, *n.* troell ysbardun, rhywel

royal, *a.* brenhinol

royalty, *n.* brenhiniaeth; toll, tâl

rub, *v.* rhwbio, rhathu, iro, crafu

rubbish, *n.* ysbwrial, sothach; lol

rubble, *n.* rhwbel

rubicund, *a.* gwridog, gwritgoch

rubric, *n.* rhuddell

ruby, *n.* rhuddem: *a.* coch, rhudd

ruck, *n.* pentwr, crynswth, haid

ruction, *n.* helynt, terfysg

rudder, *n.* llyw

ruddy, *a.* coch, gwridog, gwritgoch

rude, *a.* anfoesgar; anghelfydd, garw

rudiment, *n.* egwyddor, elfen

rue, *v.t.* galaru, gofidio, edifaru

rue, *n.* ryw

ruffian, *n.* adyn, anfadyn, dihiryn

ruffle, *v.* crychu, cyffroi, aflonyddu

rug, *n.* hugan

rugged, *a.* garw, gerwin, clogyrnog

ruin, *n.* distryw, dinistr; adfail: *v.* difetha, andwyo

rule, *n.* rheol, llywodraeth; riwl: *v.* rheoli, llywodraethu; llinellu

rumble, *v.i.* trystio, tyrfu, godyrfu

ruminate, *v.i.* cnoi cil, cilgnoi: myfyrio

rummage, *v.* chwalu a chwilio, chwilota

rumour, *n.* chwedl, gair, sôn

rump, *n.* tin, bôn, cwman, cloren

rumple, *v.t.* crychu, sybachu

rumpus, *n.* helynt, terfysg, brawl

run, *v.* rhedeg, llifo: *n.* rhediad, rhedfa

rung, *n.* ffon ysgol

rupture, *n.* rhwyg; tor llengig: *v.* rhwygo

rural, *a.* gwledig, gwladaidd

ruse, *n.* ystryw, dichell

rush, *n.* brwynen, pabwyryn

rush, *v.* rhuthro: *n.* rhuthr

russet, *a.* llwytgoch

rust, *n.* rhwd: *v.* rhydu

rustic, *a.* gwladaidd, gwledig: *n.* gwladwr

rusticate, *v.t.* anfon adref am dymor

rustle, *v.i.* siffrwd, chwithrwd, rhuglo

rut, *n.* rhych, rhigol

ruthless, *a.* didosturi, diarbed, creulon

rye, *n.* rhyg

S

sable, *n.* sabl, du: *a.* du, dudew, tywyll

sabre, *n.* sabr: *v.t.* sabru, cleddyfu

sac, *n.* coden

sacerdotal, *a.* offeiriadol

sack, *n.* sach, ffetan: *v.t.* sachu; difrodi; diswyddo

sackcloth, *n.* sachlen, sachliain

sacrament, *n.* sacrament, ordin-had

sacred, *a.* cysegredig, glân, sanc-taidd

sacrifice, *n.* aberth, offrwm: *v.* aberthu

sacrilege, *n.* halogiad, cysegr-ysbeiliad

sad, *a.* trist, athrist, prudd, digalon

saddle, *n.* cyfrwy: *v.t.* cyfrwyo; beichio

safe, *a.* diogel, dihangol, saff: *n.* cell, cist

safety, *n.* diogelwch. **—s. pin,** pin dwbl

saffron, *n.* saffrwm: *a.* melyn

sag, *v.* segio, segian, sagio

sagacious, *a.* call, craff, ffel, deallus

sage, *a.* doeth: *n.* gŵr doeth

sage, *n.* saets

sail, *n.* hwyl: *v.* hwylio, morio, mordwyo

sailor, *n.* morwr, llongwr

saint, *n.* sant

sake, *n.* mwyn

salary, *n.* cyflog

sale, *n.* gwerth, gwerthiant, arwerthiant

salient, *a.* yn estyn allan, amlwg

saline, *a.* helïaidd, hallt: *n.* heli

saliva, *n.* haliw, poer

sallow, *a.* melyn afiach

sally, *n.* cyrch, rhuthr: *v.i.* cyrchu, rhuthro

salmon, *n.* eog, gleisiad

saloon, *n.* neuadd, salŵn

salt, *n.* halen, halwyn (cemeg): *a.* hallt: *v.t.* halltu

salubrious, *a.* iach, iachusol

salutory, *a.* iachus, llesol

salute, *v.t.* cyfarch; saliwtio: *n.* cyfarchiad; saliwt

salvation, *n.* iachawdwriaeth

salve, *n.* eli, ennaint: *v.t.* elïo, lleddfu; achub

same, *a.* yr un, yr unrhyw, yr un fath

sample, *n.* sampl, enghraifft: *v.t.* samplu, samplo

sanatorium, (*-ia*) *n.* iechydfa

sanctify, *v.t.* sancteiddio

sanctimonious, *a.* ffug-sanctaidd, sych-dduwiol

sanction, *n.* caniatâd; cosb; sanc-siwn (moeseg): *v.t.* caniatáu; cosbi

sanctity, *n.* sancteiddrwydd

sanctuary, *n.* cysegr; noddfa, nawdd

sanctum, *n.* cafell, myfyrgell

sand, *n.* tywod: *v.t.* tywodi

sane, *a.* iach, call, synhwyrol

sanguinary, *a.* gwaedlyd

sanguine, *a.* gwridog; hyderus, gobeithiol

sanitary, *a.* iechydol

sanitation, *n.* iechydiaeth

sanity, *n.* iechyd meddwl, iawn bwyll

sap, *n.* nodd, sudd, sugn: *v.t.* sugno, hysbyddu

sap, *v.* tangloddio, diseilio

sapient, *a.* doeth, synhwyrol, call

sapling, *n.* pren ieuanc [og

saponaceous, *a.* sebonaidd, sebon-

sarcasm, *n.* gwawdiaith, coegni, gair du

sarcastic, *a.* gwawdlym, coeglyd, brathog

sarcophagus, (*-gi*), *n.* arch garreg

sardonic, *a.* chwerw, gwawdlyd

sartorial, *a.* teilwraidd

sash, *n.* gwregys; ffrâm ffenestr

satchel, *n.* sachell, cod lyfrau

sate, *v.t.* digoni, llenwi, diwallu

satellite, *n.* canlynwr, cynffonnwr; lleuad

satiate, *v.t.* digoni, diwallu, syrffedu

satiety, *n.* syrffed, diflastod

satire, *n.* dychan, gogan

satisfaction, *n.* bodlonrwydd; iawn

satisfactory, *a.* boddhaol; iawnol

satisfy, *v.t.* bodloni, diwallu, digoni

satrap, *n.* llywydd, rhaglaw

saturate, *v.t.* trwytho, mwydo

Saturday, *n.* dydd Sadwrn

saturnine, *a.* Sadyrnaidd, prudd-glwyfus

satyr, *n.* bwystfil o ddyn

sauce, *n.* saws; haerllugrwydd

saucepan, *n.* sosban

saucer, *n.* soser

saucy, *a.* digywilydd, haerllug

saunter, *v.i.* rhodianna, ymdroi, swmera

sausage, *n.* selsig, selsigen

savage, *a.* gwyllt, ffyrnig, milain, anwar: *n.* dyn gwyllt, anwariad, anwarddyn

save, *v.* achub, arbed, gwaredu; cynilo: *pr.* oddieithr, ond

saviour, *n.* achubwr, gwaredwr, iachawdwr
savour, *n.* sawr, blas: *v.* sawru
saw, *n.* llif: *v.* llifio
saw, *n.* dywediad, dihareb
sawdust, *n.* blawd llif
say, *v.* dywedyd, dweud
saying, *n.* dywediad, ymadrodd, gair
scab, *n.* crachen, cramen; clafr
scabbard, *n.* gwain
scabies, *n.* y crafu
scaffold, *n.* ysgaffald; dienyddle
scald, *v.t.* ysgaldio, sgaldan(u): *n.* ysgaldiad
scale, *n.* clorian, tafol, mantol
scale, *n.* graddfa: *v.* dringo
scale, *n.* cen: *v.* cennu; digennu, pilio
scallop, *n.* gylfgragen; gwlf: *v.t.* gylfu, minfylchu
scalp, *n.* copa: *v.t.* penflingo
scamp, *n.* cnaf, gwalch, dihiryn
scamp, *v.t.* brasweithio, taflu drosti
scamper, *v.i.* ffoi, carlamu, brasgamu
scan, *v.* corfannu; edrych, chwilio
scandal, *n.* tramgwydd, gwarth, enllib
scansion, *n.* corfaniad
scant, -y, *a.* prin
scapegoat, *n.* bwch dihangol
scapegrace, *n.* dyn diras, oferwr, dihiryn
scar, *n.* craith: *v.t.* creithio
scarce, *a. & adv.* prin
scarcely, *adv.* prin, braidd, odid, nemor   [dychryn
scare, *v.t.* brawychu, tarfu: *n.*
scarf, *n.* crafat, sgarff
scarify, *v.t.* ysgraffinio
scarlatina, *n.* y dwymyn goch
scarp, *n.* llethr
scathe, *v.t.* deifio, anafu, niweidio
scatter, *v.* gwasgaru, chwalu, taenu
scavenger, *n.* carthwr, carthydd
scene, *n.* lle; golwg, golygfa
scent, *n.* arogl, aroglau; perarogl: *v.t.* arogli

sceptic, *n.* amheuwr
sceptre, *n.* teyrnwialen
schedule, *n.* atodlen, cofrestr, taflen
scheme, *n.* cynllun; cynllwyn: *v.* cynllunio
schism, *n.* rhwyg, ymraniad, sism
scholar, *n.* ysgolhaig, ysgolor
scholarly, *a.* ysgolheigaidd
scholarship, *n.* ysgolheictod; ysgoloriaeth
scholastic, *a.* athrofaol
school, *n.* ysgol, ysgoldy: *v.t.* disgyblu
schooner, *n.* ysgwner
sciatica, *n.* clunwst
science, *n.* gwyddor, gwyddoniaeth
scientific, *a.* gwyddonol
scientist, *n.* gwyddonydd
scimitar *n.* crymgledd
scintilla, *n.* gwreichionen, mymryn
scintillate, *v.i.* gwreichioni, serennu   [fedd
scion, *n.* impyn; disgynnydd, eti-
scissors, *n.pl.* siswrn
scoff, *n.* gwawd: *v.i.* gwawdio, gwatwar
scold, *v.* dwrdio, tafodi, cymhennu: *n.* cecren
scoop, *n.* lletwad: *v.t.* cafnu, cafnio
scope, *n.* ergyd, bwriad; cylch, cwmpas, lle
scorch, *v.* deifio, llosgi, greidio, rhuddo
score, *n.* hac, rhic; cyfrif, dyled; sgôr; ugain
score, *v.* rhicio, cyfrif, sgori(o)
scorn, *n.* dirmyg: *v.* dirmygu, gwatwar
scorpion, *n.* ysgorpion
Scot, *n.* Ysgotyn, Albanwr
scotch, *v.t.* hacio, darnio, trychu
Scotch, *a.* Ysgotaidd, Albanaidd
scot-free, *a.* croeniach, dianaf
scoundrel, *n.* cnaf, dihiryn
scour, *v.t.* carthu, ysgwrio
scour, *v.* rhedeg; chwilio
scourge, *n.* fflangell, pla: *v.t.* fflangellu
scout, *n.* sgowt, ysbïwr: *v.t.* sgowta, ysbïo

scout, *v.t.* gwrthod gyda dirmyg, wfftio

scowl, *v.* cuchio, gwgu: *n.* cilwg, gwg

scragg, *n.* ysgrag, gwddf

scraggy, *a.* esgyrnog, tenau, cul, salw

scramble, *v.i.* & *n.* ciprys, ymgiprys

scrap, *n.* tamaid, tameidyn, dernyn

scrape, *v.* crafu: *n.* helynt, helbul

scratch, *v.* crafu, cripio

scrawl, *v.* ysgriblo, ysgriblan

scream, *v.i.* ysgrechain: *n.* ysgrech, gwawch

screech, *v.i.* ysgrechain: *n.* ysgrech

screed, *n.* rhibidirês

screen, *n.* llen, cysgod: sgrin: *v.t.* cysgodi

screw, *n.* sgriw, hoel dro: *v.* ysgriwio

scribble, *n.* ysgribl: *v.* ysgriblo, ysgriblan

scribe, *n.* ysgrifennydd

scrimmage, *n.* ysgarmes

scrip, *n.* ysgrepan

script, *n.* llawysgrif, ysgrif, sgript

scripture, *n.* ysgrythur

scrofula, *n.* clwy'r brenin

scroll, *n.* rhôl, plyg llyfr

scrub, *n.* prysgwydd; ysgwrfa: *v.t.* ysgwrio

scrubby, *a.* corachaidd, salw

scruff, *n.* gwar, gwegil

scruple, *n.* petruster (moesol): *v.i.* petruso

scrupulous, *a.* gwyliadwrus, manwl

scrutinize, *v.t.* chwilio, archwilio

scud, *v.i.* ysgubo mynd

scuffle, *v.i.* & *n.* ymgiprys, ymryson

scull, *n.* rhwyf unllaw, rhodl: *v.* rhodli

scullery, *n.* cegin fach, cegin gefn

scullion, *n.* ceginwas, golchwr llestri

sculptor, *n.* cerflunydd

sculpture, *n.* cerfluniaeth; cerflun: *v.* cerfio, torri

scum, *n.* sgum; gwehilion, sorod

scurf, *n.* cen, mardon

scurrilous, *a.* bustlaidd, brwnt, difriol

scurry, *v.i.* ffrystio: *n.* ffrwst, ffwdan

scurvy, *a.* crachlyd, crach: *n.* llwg

scutter, *v.i.* ffoi, diengyd

scuttle, *n.* llestr glo

scuttle, *v.t.* tyllu llong i'w suddo

scuttle, *v.i.* heglu ffoi, dianc

scythe, *n.* pladur

sea, *n.* môr, cefnfor; moryn

sea-gull, *n.* gwylan

seal, *n.* morlo

seal, *n.* sêl, insel: *v.t.* selio

seam, *n.* gwnïad, gwrym; haen, gwythïen; craith

seaman, *n.* morwr, llongwr

seamless, *a.* diwnïad

seamstress, *n.* gwniadwraig, gwnïyddes

sear, *a.* sych, crin, gwyw: *v.t.* serio, deifio

search, *v.* chwilio, profi: *n.* ym-chwil

season, *n.* tymor, amser, pryd, adeg: *v.* tymheru; halltu

seat, *n.* sedd, sêt, eisteddle; plas: *v.t.* eistedd

seaweed, *n.* gwymon, gwmon

secede, *v.t.* ymneilltuo, encilio

secession, *n.* ymneilltuad, enciliad

seclude, *v.t.* cau allan, neilltuo

second, *a.* ail: *n.* ail; eiliad: *v.t.* eilio

secret, *a.* dirgel, cyfrinachol: *n.* cyfrinach

secretary, *n.* ysgrifennydd

secrete, *v.t.* cuddio, celu

secretion, *n.* glandlif

sect, *n.* sect, enwad

section, *n.* toriad, trychiad; rhan, adran

sector, *n.* sector

secular, *a.* bydol; lleygol; seciwlar

secure, *a.* sicr, diogel: *v.t.* sicrhau, diogelu

security, *n.* diogelwch, sicrwydd, gwystl

sedate, *a.* tawel, digyffro
sedative, *a.* lleddfol, lliniarol
sedentary, *a.* eisteddol, eisteddog
sedge, *n.* hesg
sediment, *n.* gwaelodion, gwaddod
sedition, *n.* terfysg, brad, gwrthryfel
seduce, *v.t.* llithio, hudo, twyllo
sedulous, *a.* diwyd, dyfal, diesgeulus
see, *n.* esgobaeth
see, *v.* gweled, canfod
seed, *n.* had, hedyn: *v.* hadu, hedeg
seedy, *a.* hadog; salw; sâl, anhwylus
seek, *v.* ceisio, ymofyn, chwilio
seem, *v.i.* ymddangos
seemly, *a.* gweddus, gweddaidd, addas
seer, *n.* gweledydd
seethe, *v.* berwi, byrlymu
segment, *n.* darn, rhan, segment
segregate, *v.t.* didoli, neilltuo, gwahanu
seize, *v.* gafael mewn, atafaelu, dal, achub
seldom, *adv.* anfynych, anaml
select, *v.t.* dewis, dethol
self, (*selves*), *n.* hun, hunan: *px.* hunan-, ym-
selfish, *a.* hunanol
selfsame, *a.* yr un, yr unrhyw
sell, *v.* gwerthu; siomi: *n.* siom
semblance, *n.* tebygrwydd, rhith
semi-, *px.* hanner, lled, go
semicolon, *n.* gwahannod (;)
seminary, *n.* athrofa, ysgol
sempiternal, *a.* bythol, tragwyddol
senate, *n.* senedd
send, *v.t.* anfon, danfon, gyrru
seneschal, *n.* senesgal, distain
senile, *a.* hen a methedig, heneiddiol
senior, *a.* hŷn: *n.* hynaf
sensation, *n.* ymdeimlad, teimlad; cyffro, ias, syndod
sense, *n.* synnwyr, pwyll, ystyr
senseless, *a.* dienaid, disynnwyr, hurt
sensible, *a.* synhwyrol; teimladwy

sensitive, *a.* teimladwy, croendenau
sensual, *a.* cnawdol; trythyll, chwantus
senuous, *a.* teimladol, synhwyrus
sentence, *n.* brawddeg; barn, dedfryd: *v.t.* dedfrydu
sententious, *a.* doetheiriog
sentient, *a.* syniol, canfyddol, dirnadol
sentiment, *n.* syniad, teimlad
sentinel, sentry, *n.* gwyliwr, gwyliedydd
separate, *a.* ar wahân: *v.* gwahanu, neilltuo, ysgar; ymwahanu
sept-, *px.* saith, seith-
September, *n.* Medi
septennial, *a.* seithmlynyddol
septic, *a.* braenol, pydrol, madreddol
septicaemia, *n.* gwenwyniad gwaed
sepulchre, *n.* bedd, beddrod
sepulture, *n.* claddedigaeth, claddiad
sequel, *n.* canlyniad
sequence, *n.* trefn, dilyniad
sequester, *v.t.* neilltuo; atafaelu
seraph, (*-phs, -im*), *n.* seraff
serenade, *n.* hwyrgan, nosgan: *v.t.* hwyrganu
serene, *a.* teg; tawel, digynnwrf
serf, *n.* taeog, bilain, caeth
sergeant, *n.* rhingyll, sersiant
serial, *a.* cyfresol, bob yn rhifyn
series, *n.* rhes, cyfres
serious, *a.* difrifol
sermon, *n.* pregeth
serpent, *n.* sarff
serrated, *a.* danheddog
serried, *a.* tyn yn ei gilydd
serum, *n.* serwm
servant, *n.* gwas; morwyn
serve, *v.* gwasanaethu, gweini
service, *n.* gwasanaeth
serviette, *n.* napcyn
servile, *a.* gwasaidd
servitor, *n.* gweinydd
servitude, *n.* caethiwed, caethwasanaeth

session, *n.* eisteddiad; sesiwn; tymor

set, *v.* gosod, dodi; plannu; sadio; sefydlu; machlud: *n.* set; impyn, planhigyn

settee, settle, *n.* sgiw, setl

settle, *v.* sefydlu; penderfynu; cytuno, setlo; plwyfo; talu

settlement, *n.* cytundeb; gwladfa

seven, *a. & n.* saith

seventeen, *a. & n.* dau (dwy) ar bymtheg, un deg saith

seventh, *a.* seithfed

seventy, *a. & n.* deg a thrigain, saith deg

sever, *v.* gwahanu, datod, torri

several, *a.* amryw; gwahanol

severe, *a.* caled, tost, llym, gerwin

sew, *v.* gwnïo, pwytho

sewage, *n.* carth, budreddi

sewer, *n.* ceuffos, carthffos

sex, *n.* rhyw

sex-, *px.* chwe

sex-education, *n.* addysg ryw

sextet, *n.* chwechawd

sexton, *n.* clochydd; torrwr beddau

sexual, *a.* rhywiol

shabby, *a.* carpiog, gwael, aflêr

shackle, *n.* hual, gefyn, llyffethair

shade, *n.* cysgod; ysbryd: *v.t.* cysgodi

shadow, *n.* cysgod: *v.t.* cysgodi

shaft, *n.* paladr, saeth; llorp, braich; pwll; gwerthyd   [bras

shag, *a.* ceden, hirflew; myglys

shaggy, *a.* cedenog, blewog

shake, *v.* ysgwyd, siglo, crynu

shallow, *a.* bas: *n.* basle, beisle

sham, *v.* ffugio: *a.* ffug, gau, coeg: *n.* ffug, ffugbeth

shamble, *v.i.* llusgo cerdded

shambles, *n.pl.* lladd-dy, cigfa

shame, *n.* cywilydd, gwaradwydd, gwarth: *v.* cywilyddio, gwaradwyddo

shampoo, *v.t.* golchi pen

shank, *n.* coes, gar, esgair; paladr

shanty, *n.* caban, bwthyn, penty

shape, *n.* siâp, llun: *v.t.* siapio, llunio

shapely, *a.* siapus, lluniaidd

share, *n.* rhan, cyfran: *v.* rhannu; cyfranogi

share, *n.* swch aradr

shareholder, *n.* cyfranddaliwr

shark, *n.* siarc, morgi: twyllwr

sharp, *a.* siarp, llym, miniog: *n.* llonnod (cerdd)

sharpen, *v.* hogi, minio, awchlymu

sharper, *n.* siarpwr

shatter, *v.* dryllio, chwilfriwio; ysigo

shave, *v.* eillio, torri barf; rhasglio

shawl, *n.* siôl

she, *pn.* hi: *a. & px.* benyw

sheaf, (*sheaves*), *n.* ysgub

shear, *v.t.* cneifio; siero

shears, *n.pl.* gwellau

sheath, *n.* gwain

sheathe, *v.t.* gweinio

shed, *n.* penty, sied

shed, *v.t.* tywallt; gollwng; colli; dihidlo, bwrw

sheen, *n.* disgleirdeb, llewyrch, gwawr

sheep, (*sheep*), *n.* dafad

sheer, *v.i.* gwyro o'r ffordd, cilio

sheer, *a.* pur, glân, noeth, syth, serth

sheet, *n.* llen; cynfas; hwylraff

shekel, *n.* sicl

shelf, (*shelves*), *n.* silff, astell

shell, *n.* cragen; plisgyn, masgl; tân-belen

shelter, *n.* cysgod, lloches: *v.* cysgodi, llochesu; ymochel; llechu

shelve, *v.i.* llechweddu, llethru

shelve, *v.t.* gosod naill ochr, troi o'r neilltu

shepherd, *n.* bugail: *v.t.* bugeilio

sheriff, *n.* sirydd, siryf

shield, *n.* tarian: *v.t.* cysgodi, amddiffyn

shift, *v.* newid, symud; ymdaro: *n.* newid; dyfais; tro, stem

shilling, *n.* swllt

shilly-shally, *n.* anwadalwch

shimmer, *v.i.* rhithio, caneitio

shin, *n.* crimog, crimp coes

shindy, *n.* helynt, ffrwgwd, terfysg

shine, v. disgleirio, llewyrchu, tywynnu: n. disgleirdeb, llewyrch

shingle, n. graean, gro

shingle, n. peithynen; estyllen

shingles, n.pl. yr eryr, yr eryrod

ship, n. llong: v.t. llongi, trosglwyddo

shipshape, a. & adv. taclus, trefnus, twt

shipwreck, n. llongddrylliad

shire, n. sir

shirk, v.t. gochel, osgoi

shirt, n. crys

shiver, v.i. crynu

shiver, v. dryllio, chwilfriwio

shoal, n. haig: v.i. heigio

shoal, n. basle, beisle

shock, n. ysgafn o ŷd

shock, n. ergyd, ysgytiad: v.t. ysgytio; tramgwyddo

shoddy, n. brethyn eilban: a. ffug, coeg

shoe, n. esgid; pedol: v.t. pedoli

shoemaker, n. crydd

shoot, v. tarddu, egino; saethu: n. ysbrigyn

shop, n. masnachdy, siop: v. siopa

shopkeeper, n. siopwr

shore, n. glan, traeth

short, a. byr, cwta, prin

shortage, n. prinder, diffyg

shortcoming, n. diffyg, bai

shot, n. ergyd: saethwr

shoulder, n. ysgwydd, palfais: v.t. ysgwyddo

shout, v. bloeddio, gweiddi: n. bloedd, gwaedd

shove, v. gwthio, cilgwthio

shovel, n. rhaw: v.t. rhofio

show, v. dangos, arddangos: n. arddangosfa, sioe, siew

shower, n. cawod, cawad: v. cawodi, bwrw

shred, n. llarp, cerpyn: v. rhwygo, torri'n fân

shrew, n. cecren, gwraig anynad; llyg

shrewd, a. ffel, craff, call, cyfrwys

shriek, v. ysgrechain: n. ysgrech

shrievalty, n. siryddiaeth

shrill, a. llym, main, meinllais

shrimp, n. berdysen: v.i. berdysa

shrine, n. ysgrîn; creirfa; cysegr

shrink, v. crebachu, myned i mewn, eilio

shrive, v. gwrando cyffes; cyffesu

shrivel, v. crychu, crebachu

shroud, n. amdo, amwisg; (pl.) rhaffau hwylbren: v.t. amdoi, cuddio, celu

Shrove Tuesday, n. Mawrth Ynyd

shrub, n. prysgwydden

shrug, v. codi'r ysgwyddau

shudder, n. crynfa, echryd, arswyd: v.i. crynu, arswydo

shuffle, v. siffrwd; llusgo; gwingo, gwamalu

shun, v.t. gochelyd

shunt, v. troi o'r neilltu, symud o'r ffordd

shut, v. cau

shutter, n. caead, clawr, gwerchyr

shuttle, n. gwennol (gwëydd)

shy, a. swil: v.i. osgoi, rhusio

shy, v. taflu, lluchio

sibilant, n. sisiad: a. sisiol

sibyl, n. dewines, sibli

sick, a. claf: yn chwydu, â chyfog arno; wedi diflasu

sickening, a. atgas, diflas, cyfoglyd

sickle, n. cryman

sickly, a. afiach, nychlyd

side, n. ochr, ystlys; tu, plaid: v.i. ochri

sidereal, a. serol; yn ôl y sêr

sidle, v.i. cerdded yn wysg ei ochr

siege, n. gwarchae

sieve, n. gogr, gwagr, rhidyll, sife

sift, v.t. gogrwn, nithio, hidlo, rhidyllio

sigh, v. ochneidio: n. ochenaid

sight, n. golwg, golygfa: v.t. gweled

sign, n. arwydd, argoel: v. arwyddo, llawnodi, llofnodi

signal, a. arwyddol, hynod: n. arwydd

signalize, v.t. hynodi, enwogi

signatory, a. arwyddol: n. arwyddwr

signature, n. llofnod

signet, n. sêl, insel
significant, a. arwyddocaol; o bwys
signify, v. arwyddo, arwyddocáu
silence, n. taw, distawrwydd: v.t. rhoi taw ar
silent, a. distaw, tawedog, mud
silhouette, n. llun du, cysgodlun
silk, n. sidan
sill, n. sil
silly, a. gwirion, ffôl, disynnwyr
silt, n. gwaelodion, llaid: v. gwael-odi, tagu
silvan, a. coedog, gwledig
silver, n. arian: v.t. ariannu
similar, a. tebyg, cyffelyb
simile, n. cyffelybiaeth, cymhar-iaeth
similitude, n. cyffelybiaeth, cyffelybrwydd
simmer, v.i. lledferwi, goferwi
simper, v.i. cilwenu, glaswenu
simple, a. syml, unplyg; gwirion, diniwed
simplicity, n. symlrwydd, unplyg-rwydd
simplify, v.t. symleiddio
simulate, v.t. ffugio, dynwared
simultaneous, a. cyfamserol
sin, n. pechod: v. pechu
since, c. gan, yn gymaint: pr. er, er pan
sincere, a. diffuant, didwyll, pur
sinecure, n. segur-swydd
sinew, n. gewyn, giewyn
sing, v. canu
singe, v.t. deifio
single, a. sengl, dibriod, gweddw
singlet, n. gwasgod wlanen, crys isaf
singular, a. unigol; hynod
sinister, a. aswy; ysgeler; chwithig
sink, v. soddi, suddo: n. sinc, ceubwll
sinner, n. pechadur
sinuous, a. dolennog, troellog
sip, v.t. llymeitian: n. llymaid, llym-eidyn
sir, n. syr
sire, n. tad

siren, n. môr-forwyn; hudoles; corn, seiren
sirloin, n. llwyn eidion
sirrah, n. syre
sister, n. chwaer
sit, v. eistedd
site, n. safle, lle
situated, a. yn sefyll
situation, n. lle, safle; sefyllfa
six, a. & n. chwech
sixteen, a. & n. un ar bymtheg, un deg chwech
sixth, a. chweched
sixty, a. & n. trigain, chwe deg
size, n. maint, maintioli
skate, n. cath fôr
skate, n. sgêt: v. ysglefrio
skein, n. cengl, sgain
skeleton, n. ysgerbwd; amlinelliad
sketch, n. llun, braslun: v. tynnu
skewer, n. gwaell, gwachell
skid, v. llithro (naill ochr)
skiff, n. ysgafnfad, ceubal
skill, n. medr, medrusrwydd
skilly, n. potes blawd ceirch
skim, v. tynnu, codi (hufen)
skim-milk, n. llaeth glas
skimp, v. crintachu, cybydda
skin, n. croen: v. blingo
skinny, a. tenau; prin, crintach
skip, v.i. llamu, sgipio
skipper, n. capten llong
skirmish, n. ysgarmes
skirt, n. godre, sgyrt: v.t. dilyn gyda godre
skit, n. gogan
skittish, a. nwyfus, gwantan, anwadal
skittles, n.pl. ceilys
skulk, v.i. llechu, techu
skull, n. penglog
skunk, n. drewgi
sky, n. wybren, wybr, awyr
skylark, n. ehedydd
slab, n. llech
slack, a. llac, diofal, esgeulus: n. glo mân
slag, n. sorod, slag
slake, v.t. torri (syched), slecio
slam, v. cau yn glats, clepian

slander, *n.* enllib: *v.t.* enllibio

slang, *n.* iaith sathredig: *v.t.* difrïo

slant, *v.* gwyro, gogwyddo: *n.* gogwydd

slap, *v.t.* clewtian: *n.* clewt(en), palfod

slash, *n.* slaes, hac: *v.t.* slasio, chwipio

slate, *n.* llech, llechen

slate, *v.t.* sennu, difrïo

slattern, *n.* slwt, slebog, sopen

slaughter, *n.* lladdedigaeth, lladdfa: *v.t.* lladd

slave, *n.* slaf, caethwas: *v.i.* slafio

slavery, *n.* caethiwed, caethwasanaeth

slay, *v.t.* lladd

sled, sledge, sleigh, *n.* car llusg, sled

sledge-hammer, *n.* gordd

sleek, *a.* llyfn, llyfndew, graenus

sleep, *v.* cysgu, huno: *n.* cwsg, hun

sleet, *n.* eirlaw

sleeve, *n.* llawes

sleight, *n.* deheurwydd, cyfrwystra, dichell

slender, *a.* main, eiddil, prin

slice, *n.* tafell, ysglisen: *v.t.* tafellu, ysglisio

slide, *v.* llithro, sglefrio: *n.* llithrigfa, sleid

slight, *a.* ysgafn, eiddil, prin: *v.t.* diystyru: *n.* diystyrwch

slim, *a.* main, eiddil

slime, *n.* llaid, llaca; llys, llysnafedd

sling, *v.t.* taflu, lluchio: *n.* ffon dafl [slip

slip, *v.* llithro, dianc; gollwng·ː *n.*

slipper, *n.* llopan, sliper

slippery, *a.* llithrig, diafael, di-ddal

slit, *v.* hollti, agennu, rhwygo: *n.* hollt

slobber, *v.* glafoerio, slobran

sloe, *n.* eirinen ddu fach, draenen ddu

slogan, *n.* rhyfelgri

sloop, *n.* slŵp

slop, *n.* (*pl.*) golchion: *v.* gwlychu, trochi

slope, *n.* llethr, gogwydd: *v.* gogwyddo

sloppy, *a.* lleidiog, tomlyd; meddal, masw

slot, *n.* agen, twll

sloth, *n.* diogi, seguryd, syrthni

slouch, *v.* llaesu, ymollwng; cerdded yn aflêr

slough, *n.* cors, mignen, siglen

slough, *n.* croen wedi ei fwrw; crawn, gôr

sloven, *n.* dyn aflêr, blerwm

slow, *a.* araf, hwyrfrydig, hwyrdrwm

sludge, *n.* llaid, llaca

slug, *n.* gwlithen, malwoden

sluggard, *n.* diogyn

sluggish, *a.* diog, dioglyd, swrth

sluice, *n.* llifddor

slum, *n.* slym

slumber, *v.* hepian, cysgu: *n.* cwsg

slump, *n.* cwymp, gostyngiad

slur, *v.* slyrio, llithrennu: *n.* llithriad, cyflusg (cerdd.); anfri

slush, *n.* llaid, llaca

slut, *n.* slwt, slebog

sly, *a.* cyfrwys, ffals, dichellgar

smack, *n.* blas: *v.i.* blasio, archwaethu

smack, *n.* smac, palfod: *v.* smacio, chwipio

smack, *n.* llongan, smac

small, *a.* bach, bychan, mân, main

small-pox, *n.* y frech wen

smart, *v.i.* gwynio, dolurio, llosgi: *n.* gwŷn, dolur: *a.* llym, hoyw, bywiog; ffel, ffraeth; crand

smash, *v.* torri, malu, chwilfriwio

smattering, *n.* gwybodaeth fas, crap

smear, *v.t.* iro, dwbio

smell, *n.* arogl, aroglau: *v.* arogli

smelt, *v.t.* toddi

smile, *v.* gwenu: *n.* gwên

smirch, *v.t.* llychwino, difwyno

smirk, *v.i.* cilwenu, glaswenu: *n.* cilwen

smite, *v.* taro

smith, *n.* gof

smithy, n. gefail (gof)

smoke, n. mwg: v. mygu, ysmygu, smocio

smooth, a. llyfn, esmwyth: v.t. llyfnhau

smother, v. mygu, llethu

smoulder, v.i. mudlosgi

smudge, v. llychwino, cluro

smug, a. hunanol, cysetlyd

smuggle, v.t. smyglio

smut, n. parddu, huddygl, smotyn

snack, n. tamaid, byrbryd

snail, n. malwoden, malwen

snake, n. neidr

snap, v. clecian, torri'n glats: n. clec [rhwydo

snare, n. magl, croglath: v.t. maglu,

snarl, v.i. ysgyrnygu, chwyrnu

snatch, v. cipio: n. cip, crap; tamaid

sneak, v.i. llechian: n. llechgi

sneer, v. gwawdio, dirmygu: n. gwawd, ffroenwawd

sneeze, v.i. tisian, taro untrew

sniff, v. ffroeni, gwyntio

snip, v. torri, cynhinio

snipe, n. giach

snippet, n. tamaid, cynhinyn

snob, n. crachfonheddwr, snob

snooze, v. hepian: n. cyntun

snore, v.i. chwyrnu

snort, v.i. ffroeni, ffroenochi

snout, n. trwyn anifail, duryn

snow, n. eira, ôd: v. bwrw eira, odi

snub, v.t. sennu: n. sen

snub, a. pwt, smwt

snuff, v. ffroeni, snwffian: n. trwynlwch, snisyn

snuffle, v.i. siarad drwy'r trwyn

snug, a. cryno, clyd, diddos

snuggle, v. ymwasgu at; llochi, anwesu

so, adv. & c. fel, felly; mor, cyn

soak, v. mwydo, sucio; slotian

soap, n. sebon: v. seboni

soar, v.i. ehedeg, esgyn

sob, v.i. igian, beichio: n. ig, ebwch

sober, a. sobr, sad: v. sobri

sobriety, n. sobrwydd

sobriquet, n. llysenw, ffugenw

sociable, a. cymdeithasgar

social, a. cymdeithasol

socialism, n. sosialaeth

socialist, n. sosialydd

society, n. cymdeithas, cyfeillach

sock, n. socas, socysen, soc

socket, n. twll, crau, soced

sod, n. tywarchen

sodden, a. wedi mwydo, soeglyd

sofa, n. glwth, esmwythfainc, soffa

soft, a. meddal, tyner; distaw; gwirion

soil, n. pridd, daear, gweryd

soil, v.t. difwyno, baeddu: n. baw, tom

soirée, n. hwyrwest

sojourn, v.i. ymdeithio, aros: n. ymdeithiad, arhosiad

solace, n. cysur, diddanwch: v.t. cysuro, diddanu

solar, a. heulog

solder, n. sawdring, sawdur, sodr: v.t. asio, sawdurio, sodro

soldier, n. milwr

sole, a. unig, unigol, un

sole, n. gwadn: v.t. gwadnu

sole, n. lleden chwithig

solecism, n. gwrthuni

solemn, a. difrifol, dwys

solemnize, v.t. dathlu; gweinyddu

sol-fa, n. sol-ffa: v. solffeuo

solicit, v.t. erfyn, ymofyn; llithio

solicitor, n. cyfreithiwr

solicitous, a. gofalus, pryderus

solid, a. caled, sylweddol, solet, cadarn

solid, n. solid

soliloquy, n. ymson

solitary, a. unig; anghyfannedd

solitude, n. unigedd

solo, n. unawd

soluble, a. toddadwy, hydawdd

solution, n. dehongliad, esboniad; toddiant

solve, v.t. dadrys, dehongli

solvent, a. yn gallu talu: n. toddfa

sombre, a. tywyll, prudd

some, a. rhai, rhyw, peth, ychydig: pn. rhywrai, rhywfaint: adv. ynghylch

somnolent, *a.* cysglyd

son, *n.* mab

song, *n.* càn, cathl, cerdd

sonnet, *n.* soned

sonorous, *a.* seinfawr, soniarus

sonship, *n.* mabolaeth

soon, *adv.* buan, ebrwydd, clau

soot, *n.* huddygl, parddu

soothe, *v.t.* lliniaru, lleddfu, dofi, tawelu

soothsayer, *n.* dewin, brudiwr

sop, *n.* tamaid (wedi ei wlychu)

sophism, *n.* soffyddiaeth

sophist, *n.* soffydd

sophistical, *a.* soffyddol

sophisticated, *a.* doethlyd

sorcerer, *n.* swynwr, dewin

sorcery, *n.* swyngyfaredd, dewiniaeth

sordid, *a.* brwnt, cybyddlyd, gwael

sore, *a.* tost, blin, dolurus: *n.* dolur

sorrow, *n.* tristwch, gofid, galar: *v.i.* tristáu, gofidio

sorry, *a.* drwg gan, edifar; salw

sort, *n.* modd; math, bath: *v.t.* trefnu, dosbarthu

sortie, *n.* cyrch

sot, *n.* diotyn, meddwyn: *v.i.* diota

soul, *n.* enaid

sound, *n.* sain, sŵn, trwst: *v.* seinio

sound, *v.* plymio, chwilio

sound, *n.* culfor, swnt

sound, *a.* iach, iachus, dianaf, cyfan, dilys

soup, *n.* potes, cawl

sour, *a.* sur: *v.* suro

source, *n.* ffynhonnell, tarddiad

souse, *v.* rhoi yng ngwlych, trochi

south, *n.* deau, de

southern, *a.* deheuol

souvenir, *n.* cofrodd

sovereign, *a.* pen: *n.* penadur; sofren

sow, *n.* hwch

sow, *v.t.* hau

space, *n.* lle, gwagle, gofod, encyd, ysbaid

spacious, *a.* eang, helaeth

spade, *n.* rhaw, pâl   [wantu

span, *n.* rhychwant: *v.t.* rhych-

spangle, *n.* tlws disglair: *v.t.* serennu

spaniel, *n.* adargi

Spanish, *a.* Ysbaenaidd: *n.* Ysbaeneg

spank, *v.t.* slapio, smacio, palfodi, chwipio tin

spar, *v.i.* cwffio, paffio

spar, *n.* polyn, cledren, ceibren

spare, *a.* prin; tenau; sbâr: *v.t.* arbed; hepgor

spark *n.* gwreichionen

sparkle, *v.i.* gwreichioni, serennu, pefrio

sparrow, *n.* aderyn to

sparse, *a.* tenau, prin, gwasgarog

spasm, *n.* cwlwm gwythi, gwayw, brath

spatter, *v.* ysgeinio, diblo

spawn, *n.* grawn, gronell; grifft; sil: *v.* silio, bwrw grawn

speak, *v.* llefaru, siarad

spear, *n.* gwaywffon, picell: *v.t.* trywanu

special, *a.* neilltuol, arbennig

specialist, *n.* arbenigwr

specie, *n.* arian bathol

species, *(species),* *n.* rhywogaeth

specific, *a.* priodol, penodol, pendant

specify, *v.t.* enwi, penodi

specimen, *n.* enghraifft, cynllun

specious, *a.* teg yr olwg, rhithiol

speck, *n.* brycheuyn, ysmotyn

speckle, *v.t.* britho, brychu

spectacle, *n.* drych, golygfa; *(pl.)* sbectol

spectator, *n.* edrychwr, gwyliwr

spectre, *n.* drychiolaeth

spectrum, *(-ra),* *n.* rhith, spectrwm

speculate, *v.i.* dyfalu; anturio, mentro

speech, *n.* llafar, lleferydd, parabl, ymadrodd, araith

speed, *n.* cyflymder, buander; *v.* prysuro, cyflymu

spell, *n.* cyfaredd, swyn

spell, *n.* sbel

spell, *v.t.* sillafu

spend, *v.* treulio, gwario, bwrw

spendthrift, *n.* afradwr, oferwr, gwastraffwr

sphere, *n.* cronnell, sffêr, pêl; cylch, maes

spice, *n.* perlysiau, peraroglau, sbeis

spider, *n.* cor, corryn, pryf copyn

spike, *n.* pig, hoel, cethren

spikenard, *n.* ysbignard, nard

spill, *v.* colli, tywallt

spin, *v.* nyddu, troi, troelli

spindle, *n.* gwerthyd; echel

spine, *n.* asgwrn cefn; draen, pigyn

spinner, *n.* nyddwr

spinning-wheel, *n.* troell

spinster, *n.* merch ddibriod, hen ferch

spiral, *a.* fel cogwrn tro, troellog

spirant, *a.* llaes: *n.pl.* llaesion

spire, *n.* pigwrn, pigdwr

spirit, *n.* ysbryd; gwirod

spiritual, *a.* ysbrydol

spiritualist, *n.* ysbrydegydd

spirituous, *a.* gwirodol

spit, *n.* bêr

spit, *v.* poeri

spite, *n.* sbeit; gwaethaf: *v.t.* sbeitio

spittle, *n.* poer, poeryn

spittoon, *n.* llestr poeri

splash, *v.* sblasio, tasgu; lleidio

spleen, *n.* y ddueg; pruddglwyf; natur ddrwg, gwenwyn

splendid, *a.* ysblennydd, gwych, campus

splendour, *n.* ysblander, gwychder

splice, *v.t.* cymhlethu, cydgysylltu

splint, *n.* dellten, ysgyren, sblint

splinter, *v.* ysgyrioni: *n.* ysgyren, fflaw

split, *v.* hollti, rhannu

spoil, *n.* ysbail, anrhaith: *v.* ysbeilio, ysbwylio, difetha

spoke, *n.* adain olwyn

spokesman, *n.* llefarwr

spoliation, *n.* ysbeiliad, ysbwyliad

sponge, *n.* ysbwng: *v.* ysbyngu; bolera

sponsor, *n.* mach, hyrwyddwr; tad bedydd, mam fedydd   [mell

spontaneous, *a.* gwirfoddol, digy-

spook, *n.* ysbryd, bwgan, bwci

spool, *n.* gwerthyd

spoon, *n.* llwy

spoor, *n.* brisg

sporadic, *a.* achlysurol, gwasgaro

spore, *n.* had (rhedyn, &c.)

sport, *n.* sbort, chwarae, difyrrwch cellwair

sportive, *a.* chwareus, nwyfus

spot, *n.* man, lle, llecyn; brycheuyn ysmotyn: *v.t.* mannu, brychu, ys motio

spouse, *n.* dyweddi, priod

spout, *v.t.* pistyllio, ffrydio: *n* pistyll

sprain, *v.t.* ysigo

sprawl, *v.i.* ymdaenu, ymdreiglo ymrwyfo

spray, *n.* gwlith, tawch: *v.t.* taenell

spray, *n.* ysbrigyn, cainc

spread, *v.* lledu, taenu, lledaenu gwasgaru

spree, *n.* sbri

sprig, *n.* brigyn, ysbrigyn

sprightly, *a.* bywiog, hoenus nwyfus

spring, *v.* tarddu, codi, deillio llamu, neidio: *n.* ffynnon; llam sbring; gwanwyn

sprinkle, *v.* taenellu, ysgeinio

sprit, *n.* sbryd

sprite, *n.* ysbryd, bwgan, bwci

sprout, *v.* tarddu, egino, glasu

spruce, *a.* twt, taclus, smart, cran

spry, *a.* sionc, heini, hoyw

spume, *n.* ewyn, gorferw

spur, *n.* ysbardun, swmbwl: *t* ysbarduno, symbylu

spurious, *a.* ffug, gau, annilys

spurn, *v.* cicio, dirmygu, tremygu

spurt, *n.* ysbonc

sputter, *v.* poeri siarad, baldordd

spy, *n.* ysbïwr: *v.* ysbïo

squabble, *v.i.* cweryla, ffraeo: *r* ffrwgwd, ffrae

squad, *n.* mintai

squalid, *a.* brwnt, bawlyd, budr

squall, *v.i.* ysgrechain: *n.* gwawch storm o wynt

squalor, *n.* brynti

squander, *v.t.* gwastraffu, afradu

square, *a. & n.* ysgwâr, petryal

squash, *v.t.* gwasgu, llethu: *n.* sitrach, ffradach

squat, *v.i.* yswatio, cyrcydu

squaw, *n.* gwraig (gan yr Indiaid Cochion)

squawk, *v.i.* gwawchio: *n.* gwawch

squeak, *v.i.* gwichian: *n.* gwich

squeal, *v.i.* gwichian

squeamish, *a.* dicra, misi

squeeze, *v.* gwasgu

squelch, *v.t.* llethu, gostegu, rhoi taw ar

squib, *n.* tanen wyllt, fflachen; gogan, dychan

squint, *v.* ciledrych, cibedrych: *n.* llygad croes

squire, *n.* ysgwïer, yswain

squirrel, *n.* gwiwer

squirt, *v.* chwistrellu, tasgu: *n.* chwistrell, gwn dŵr

tab, *v.* brathu, gwanu, trywanu

table, *n.* ystabl

table, *a.* diysgog, sefydlog, safadwy, sad

tack, *n.* tas, bera; corn simnai, stac

taff, *n.* ffon; erwydd; staff

tag, *n.* carw, hydd

tage, *n.* pwynt; gradd, lefel; llwyfan

tage-coach, *n.* y goets fawr

tagger, *v.* honclan, gwegian; syfrdanu

tagnant, *a.* llonydd, marw

tagnate, *v.i.* cronni, sefyll

taid, *a.* sad, sobr

tain, *v.* ystaenio, llychwino: *n.* ystaen

tair, *n.* gris

take, *n.* pawl, ystanc: cyngwystl

tale, *a.* hen, hendrwm; diflas, mws

talk, *v.* torsythu, rhodio'n benuchel

talk, *n.* paladr, gwelltyn, coes

tall, *n.* côr; stondin; talcen glo

tallion, *n.* march, stalwyn

talwart, *a.* cadarn, pybyr, dewr

tamen, *n.* brigeryn

stamina, *n.* saf, ynni

stammer, *v.* bloesgi, siarad ag atal arno

stamp, *n.* stamp, delw, argraff: *v.* stampio; curo traed

stampede, *n.* chwalfa, rhuthr

stanch, *v.t.* atal, sychu (gwaed)

stanchion, *n.* ateg, post, gwanas

stand, *v.* sefyll, bod, aros: *n.* safiad

standard, *n.* lluman, baner; post; safon

stanza, *n.* pennill

staple, *n.* prif nwydd; edefyn (gwlân, &c)

staple, *n.* ystwffwl, stapal

star, *n.* seren: *v.* serennu

starch, *n.* starts

stare, *v.* llygadrythu, synnu

stark, *a.* syth, rhonc: *adv.* hollol

starling, *n.* aderyn drudwy, aderyn yr eira

start, *v.* cychwyn, codi, rhusio, tasgu

startle, *v.t.* brawychu, dychrynu, rhusio

starve, *v.* newynu; fferru, rhynnu

starveling, *n.* edlych

state, *n.* ystad, cyflwr, ansawdd; rhwysg; gwladwriaeth; talaith

state, *v.t.* mynegi, datgan; penodi

stately, *a.* urddasol, mawreddog

statement, *n.* mynegiad, datganiad, haeriad

statesman, *(men) n.* gwladweinydd

station, *n.* gorsaf, stesion; safle, sefyllfa

stationary, *a.* sefydlog, gorsafol

stationer, *n.* gwerthwr papurau

statistics, *n.pl.* ystadegau

statue, *n.* delw, cerfddelw, cerflun

stature, *n.* uchder, taldra, corffolaeth

status, *n.* safle, braint, statws

statute, *n.* deddf, cyfraith, ystatud

staunch, *a.* pybyr, cywir

stave, *n.* estyllen, erwydd: *v.t.* astellu; dryllio.—**s. off,** cadw draw

stay, *v.* aros; ategu; atal: *n.* arhosiad; ateg; *(pl.)* staes

stead, *n.* lle

steadfast, *a.* diysgog, dianwadal

steady, *a.* sad, diysgog; cyson, gwastad

steak, *n.* golwyth

steal, *v.* dwyn, lladrata, cipio

stealth, *n.* lladrad. —**by s.,** yn ddistaw bach

steam, *n.* ager, stêm, tarth: *v.* ageru

steamer, *n.* agerlong, stemar

steed, *n.* march, ceffyl

steel, *n.* dur: *v.t.* caledu

steep, *a.* serth: *n.* dibyn, clogwyn, llethr

steep, *v.t.* rhoi yng ngwlych, mwydo, sucio

steeple, *n.* clochdy

steer, *n.* bustach

steer, *v.* llywio; cyfeirio

stellar, *a.* serol, serennol

stem, *n.* paladr, corsen, coes, bôn; ach; pen blaen

stem, *v.t.* gwrthsefyll, gwrthladd, atal

stench, *n.* drewi, drycsawr

stenography, *n.* llaw-fer

stentorian, *a.* croch

step, *v.i.* camu; cerdded: *n.* cam; gris

step-, *px.* llys-

stereotype, *n.* ystrydeb: *v.t.* ystry-debu

sterile, *a.* diffrwyth

sterilize, *v.* diffrwythloni, di-heintio

sterling, *a.* ysterling; diledryw, diffuant

stern, *a.* llym, penderfynol

stern, *n.* starn, pen ôl llong

stertorous, *a.* chwyrnog

stethescope, *n.* corn meddyg

stevedore, *n.* llwythwr a dadlwyth-wr llongau

stew, *v.* araf ferwi, stiwio: *n.* stiw

steward, *n.* stiward, goruchwyliwr, distain

stick, *n.* pren, ffon, pric, gwialen

stick, *v.* glynu; gwanu, brathu

stiff, *a.* syth, anystwyth, anhyblyg, ystyfnig

stifle, *v.t.* mygu, tagu, diffodd

stigma, *n.* mefl, gwarthnod, stigma

stile, *n.* camfa, sticil, sticill

still, *n.* distyllfa, stil

still, *a.* llonydd; marw: *v.* llonyddu

still, *adv.* eto, er hynny; byth

stilt, *n.* ystudfach

stimulant, *n.* symbylydd; gwirod

stimulate, *v.t.* symbylu

stimulus, (*-li*), *n.* symbyliad, swmbwl

sting, *v.* pigo, brathu, colynnu: *n.* colyn

stingy, *a.* crintach, cybyddlyd

stink *v.i. & v.* drewi

stint, *v.t.* cynilo, cybydda: *n.* prinder

stipend, *n.* cyflog

stipulate, *v.* amodi, mynnu

stir, *v.* cyffroi, cynhyrfu, symud: *n.* ystŵr, cynnwrf

stirrup, *n.* gwarthafl, gwarthol

stitch, *n.* pwyth; gwayw, pigyn: *v.t.* pwytho, gwnïo

stoat, *n.* carlwm

stock, *n.* cyff; stoc, ystôr: *n.pl.* cyffion

stocking, *n.* hosan

stodgy, *a.* toeslyd, trymllyd, diflas

stoke, *v.* edrych ar ôl tân, tanio

stole, *v.* ystola

stolid, *a.* swrth, digyffro

stomach, *n.* cylla, stumog

stone, *n.* carreg, maen: *v.t.* llab-yddio

stool, *n.* ystôl

stoop, *v.* plygu, crymu, gwargrymu, ymostwng

stop, *v.* atal, rhwystro; stopio, cau; aros, sefyll: *n.* atalfa; atalnod

stopper, *n.* topyn

store, *n.* ystôr, ystorfa: *v.t.* ystorio

storey, story, *n.* uchdwr, llofft, llawr

stork, *n.* ciconia, chwibon

storm, *n.* ystorm, tymestl

story, *n.* hanes, chwedl, stori; celwydd

stout, *a.* tew, ffyrf; pybyr, gwrol, glew

stove, n. stof, ffwrn
stow, v.i. cyfleu, pacio, dodi o'r neilltu
straddle, v.i. bongamu, lledu'r traed
straggle, v.i. crwydro, gwasgaru
straight, a. union, syth
straightway, adv. yn ddiatreg, yn y fan
strain, v. straenio, streifio, ysigo; tynhau; hidlo: n. straen
strait, a. cyfyng, cul, caeth: n. cyfyngder; culfor
strand, n. traeth, traethell, tywyn
strand, n. cainc (rhaff), edau
strange, a. dieithr, estronol, rhyfedd
stranger, n. dyn dieithr, estron
strangle, v.t. tagu, llindagu
strap, n. strap, cengl
stratagem, n. ystryw
stratum, (-ta), n. haen
straw, n. gwellt; gwelltyn, blewyn
strawberry, n. mefysen, syfïen
stray, v.i. crwydro, cyfeiliorni
streak, n. llinell, rhes, rhesen; stremp
stream, n. ffrwd: v. ffrydio, llifo
street, n. heol, ystryd
strength, n. cryfder, nerth, grym
strenuous, a. egniol, ymdrechgar
stress, n. pwys, straen, caledi
stretch, v. estyn, tynhau: n. estyniad   [sier
stretcher, n. trestl, elorwely, stret-
strew, v.t. gwasgaru, sarnu, chwalu, taenu
strict, a. cyfyng, caeth, llym
stricture, n. cyfyngiad; cerydd, sen
stride, v. camu, brasgamu: n. cam
strident, a. uchel, croch
strife, n. cynnen, ymryson, ymrafael
strike, v. taro; gostwng: n. taro, streic
string, n. llinyn, tant
stringent, a. caeth, llym, tyn
strip, n. llain, llafn, llefnyn. —**film s.,** striplun, stribed ffilm
strip, v. diosg, ymddiosg, ymddihatru

stripe, n. rhes, rhesen; gwialennod
stripling, n. glaslanc, llanc, llencyn
strive, v.i. ymdrechu; ymryson
stroke, n. dyrnod, ergyd, trawiad; llinell
stroke, v.t. llochi, dylofi, pratio
stroll, v.i. crwydro, rhodianna
strong, a. cryf, grymus, cadarn
stronghold, n. amddiffynfa
strop, n. strap hogi: v.t. hogi, minio
structure, n. adail, adeilad, saernïaeth
struggle, v.i. gwingo: ymdrechu: n. ymdrech
strut, v.i. torsythu
stubble, n. sofl
stubborn, a. cyndyn, ystyfnig
stud, n. boglwm, boglyn
stud, n. gre
student, n. myfyriwr, efrydydd
studio, n. arlunfa, stiwdio
study, n. astudiaeth, efrydiaeth, n.pl. efrydiau; myfyrgell, stydi: v. myfyrio, efrydu, astudio
stuff, n. defnydd, stwff: v. stwffio, gwthio
stuffy, a. myglyd, trymllyd
stumble, v. tramgwyddo, maglu, syrthio
stump, n. bonyn, boncyff
stun, v.t. syfrdanu, byddaru, hurtio
stunt, v.t. crabio
stupefy, v.t. syfrdanu, hurtio, madroni
stupendous, a. aruthrol
stupid, a. hurt, pendew, dwl, twp
stupor, n. syfrdandod, madrondod
sturdy, a. talgryf, pybyr
stutter, v.i. siarad ag atal arno, bloesgi
sty, n. cwt, cut, twlc
style, n. dull, arddull; cyfenw, teitl: v.t. cyfenwi
suasion, n. anogaeth, deniad
suave, a. mwyn, tirion, hynaws, rhadlon
sub-, px. tan-, is-, go-
subaltern, n. is-swyddog
subdue, v.t. darostwng; lleddfu
subject, a. darostyngedig; caeth;

ufudd; agored: n. deiliad; pwnc, testun; goddrych

subject, v.t. darostwng, dwyn dan

subjective, a. goddrychol

subjoin, v.t. cysylltu, atodi

subjugate, v.t. darostwng

subjunctive, a. dibynnol

sublimate, n. sychdarth: v. sychdarthu (cemeg)

sublimation, n. sychdarthiad (cemeg)

sublime, a. aruchel, arddunol

submarine, a. tanforol: n. llong danfor

submerge, v. soddi, suddo

submission n. ymostyngiad; ufudd-dod

submit, v. ymostwng, ymddarostwng; datgan barn; cyflwyno

subordinate, a. israddol : v.t. darostwng

suborn, v.t. llwgrwobrwyo i ddrwg

subscribe, v. tanysgrifio, cyfrannu

subscription, n. tanysgrifiad, cyfraniad

subsequent, a. canlynol, dilynol

subserve, v.t. iswasanaethu

subside, v.i. soddi, ymollwng; darfod

subsidiary, a. israddol; ychwanegol, atodol

subsidy, n. arian cymorth, cymhorthdal

subsist, v. byw, bod, bodoli

subsoil, n. isbridd

substance, n. sylwedd, defnydd; da

substantial, a. sylweddol

substantiate, v.t. sylweddu, profi, gwirio

substitute, n. un yn lle arall: v.t. rhoi yn lle

subterfuge, n. ystryw, cast

subterranean, a. tanddaearol

subtle, a. cyfrin; cyfrwys

subtract, v.t. tynnu ymaith

suburb, n. maestref

subvert, v.t. dymchwelyd, gwyrdroi

subway, n. ceuffordd

succeed, v. dilyn, canlyn, llwyddo, ffynnu

success, n. llwyddiant, llwydd, ffyniant

successful, a. llwyddiannus

succession, n. dilyniad, olyniaeth

successive, a. dilynol, olynol

succinct, a. byr, cryno

succour, v.t. swcro, ymgeleddu: n. swcr, ymgeledd

succulent, a. ir, iraidd, noddlyd

succumb, v.i. ymollwng dan, gildio, marw

such, a. cyfryw, y fath, cyffelyb

suck, v. sugno, dyfnu; llyncu, yfed

suckle, v.t. rhoi bron, sugno

suction, n. sugn, sugniad, sugndyniad

sudden, a. sydyn, disymwth, disyfyd

suds, n.pl. trochion sebon, sucion

sue, v. erlyn; erfyn, deisyf

suet, n. gwêr, swyf, siwed

suffer, v. goddef, dioddef, gadael

suffering, n. dioddef

suffice, v. bod yn ddigon, digoni

sufficient, a. digon, digonol

suffix, n. olddodiad

suffocate, v. mygu, tagu

suffrage, n. pleidlais

suffuse, v.t. taenu, gwasgaru, ymledu

sugar, n. siwgr: v.t. siwgro

suggest, v.t. awgrymu

suggestion, n. awgrym, awgrymiad

suicide, n. hunanladdiad; hunan-leiddiad

suit, n. cwyn, cyngaws, hawl; deisyfiad, cais; siwt, pâr: v. ateb, siwtio, gweddu, taro   [wys

suitable, a. addas, cyfaddas, cymsuite, n. cyfres; gosgordd, nifer

sulk, v.i. sorri, pwdu, mulo

sullen, a. sarrug, cuchiog, blwng

sully, v.t. difwyno, llychwino

sulphur, n. sylffur

sultan, n. swltan

sultry, a. mwrn, mwll, mwygl, clos

sum, n. sum, swm: v.t. crynhoi, symio

summary, a. byr, cryno; di-ymaros: n. crynodeb

summer, n. haf
summit, n. pen, copa, crib
summon, v.t. gwysio, dyfynnu
summons, n. gwŷs, dyfyn
sumptuous, a. treulfawr, moethus
sun, n. haul, huan: v.t. heulo
sunbeam, n. pelydryn
Sunday, n. dydd Sul
sunder, v.t. ysgar, gwahanu
sundry, a. amryw, amrywiol
sunshine, n. heulwen
sup, v. llymeitian ; swpera, swperu: n. llymaid
super-, px. uwch, goruwch, gor-, tra-, ar-
superannuation, n. ymddeoliaeth; pensiwn
superb, a. ysblennydd, godidog
supercilious, a. balch, diystyrllyd
superficial, a. arwynebol, bas
superfine, a. coeth, main, meinwych
superfluous, a. gormodol, afreidiol
superintend, v.t. arolygu
superintendent, n. arolygwr, arolygydd
superior, a. uwch, gwell, rhagorach; uwchraddol: n. uchafiad, uwchradd
superlative, a. uchaf; eithafol
supernatural, a. goruwchnaturiol
supernumerary, a. uwchrifol, amlaw: n. uwchrif
supersede, v.t. diswyddo, disodli
superstition, n. coelgrefydd, ofergoeliaeth
superstitious, a. coelgrefyddol, ofergoelus
supervene, v.i. digwydd
supervise, v.t. arolygu
supervision, n. arolygiaeth
supine, a. diofal, didaro, swrth
supper, n. swper
supplant, v.t. disodli
supple, a. ystwyth, hyblyg
supplement, n. atodiad: v.t. atodi
suppliant, n. ymbiliwr, erfyniwr
supplicate, v. erfyn, ymbil, deisyf
supply, v.t. cyflenwi, cyflawni: n. cyflenwad

support, v.t. cynnal: n. cynhaliaeth
suppose, v.t. tybio, tybied, tebygu, bwrw   [celu
suppress, v.t. llethu, gostegu; atal;
suppurate, v.i. crawni, gori
supreme, a. goruchaf, prif, pennaf
sur-, px. gor-
sure, a. & adv. siwr, sicr; diamau, diau
surely, adv. yn sicr, yn ddiau, yn ddilys
surety, n. mach, meichiau, gwystl
surf, n. traethfor, traethellfor, beiston
surface, n. wyneb, arwyneb, caen
surfeit, n. syrffed: v. alaru, syrffedu
surge, v.i. dygyfor, ymchwyddo: n. ymchwydd
surgeon, n. llawfeddyg
surgery, n. llawfeddygaeth; meddygfa, siop doctor
surgical, a. llawfeddygol
surly, a. sarrug, afrywiog, taeog
surmise, n. tyb: v.t. tybied, amau
surmount, v.t. myned dros, gorchfygu
surname, n. cyfenw: v.t. cyfenwi
surpass, v.t. rhagori ar, trechu
surplice, n. gwenwisg
surplus, n. gweddill, gormod, gwarged
surprise, n. syndod: v.t. synnu
surrender, v. traddodi, ymroddi
surreptitious, a. lladradaidd, llechwraidd
surrogate, n. dirprwy, rhaglaw esgob
surround, v.t. amgylchu
surveillance, n. arolygiaeth, gwyliadwriaeth
survey, v.t. edrych, arolygu; mesur: n. arolwg
survive, v. gor-fyw, goroesi
susceptible, a. parod i, tueddol i
suspect, v.t. drwgdybio, amau
suspend, v.t. crogi; gohirio, atal
suspense, n. pryder, petruster, oediad
suspicion, n. drwgdybiaeth, amheuaeth

suspicious, *a.* drwgdybus, amheus

sustain, *v.t.* cynnal; dioddef, goddef

sustenance, *n.* cynhaliaeth, ymborth

suzerain, *n.* uchdeyrn, penarglwydd

swaddle, *v.t.* rhwymynnu

swagger, *v.* rhodresa, torsythu, swagro

swain, *n.* llanc gwlad; cariadfab

swallow, *n.* gwennol

swallow, *v.t.* llyncu: *n.* llwnc

swamp, *n.* cors: *v.t.* gorlifo, boddi

swan, *n.* alarch

swank, *v.i.* bocsachu, rhodresa: *n.* bocsach

sward, *n.* tywarchen, tonnen, gweryd

swarm, *n.* haid: *v.i.* heidio, heigio

swarm, *v.* dringo

swarthy, *a.* melynddu, croenddu, tywyll

swathe, *v.t.* rhwymo, rhwymynnu

sway, *v.* siglo, gwegian; llywio: *n.* llywodraeth

swear, *v.* tyngu

sweat, *n.* chwys: *v.* chwysu

swede, *n.* rwden, sweden

sweep, *v.* ysgubo: *n.* ysgubiad; ysgubwr

sweet, *a.* melys, pêr, peraidd

sweeten, *v.* melysu, pereiddio

sweetheart, *n.* cariad

sweetmeat, *n.* fferin, melysyn

swell, *v.* chwyddo: *n.* chwydd, ymchwydd; gŵr mawr

swelter, *v.i.* crasu; lluddedu, dyddfu

swerve *v.i.* gwyro, osgoi, cilio, troi

swift, *a.* cyflym, buan, chwyrn, clau

swift, *n.* gwennol ddu

swim, *v.* nofio: *n.* nawf

swimmingly, *adv.* yn braf, yn hwylus

swindle, *v.* twyllo, hocedu: *n.* twyll

swine, (*swine*), *n.* mochyn

swing, *v.* siglo: *n.* sigl, siglen, swing

swinge, *v.t.* llachio, baeddu

swirl, *v.* troi, chwyldroi, chwyrndroi

swish, *v.* chwipio, gwialenodio

switch, *n.* gwialen; troswr: *v.* troi

swivel, *n.* bwylltid

swoon, *v.i.* llewygu, llesmeirio: *n.* llewyg

swoop, *v.* dyfod ar warthaf, disgyn

swop, *v.t.* cyfnewid, ffeirio

sword, *n.* cleddyf, cleddau, cledd

sybarite, *n.* moethyn, masweddwr

sycamore, *n.* sycamorwydden

sycophant, *n.* gwenieithiwr, cynffonnwr

syllable, *n.* sillaf

syllabus, *n.* crynodeb, rhaglen, maes, llafur

syllogism, *n.* cyfresymiad

sylph, *n.* un o'r tylwyth teg, meinwen

symbol, *n.* arwyddlun, symbol, symlen (estheteg)

symbolism, *n.* symboliaeth

symmetrical, *a.* cymesur

symmetry, *n.* cymesuredd

sympathize, *v.i.* cydymdeimlo

sympathy, *n.* cydymdeimlad

symphony, *n.* symffoni

symposium, (*-ia*), *n.* trafodaeth

symptom, *n.* arwydd

synagogue, *n.* synagog

synchronize, *v.* cyfamseru, cydamseru

syncopate, *v.* byrhau gair (yn ei ganol); trawsacennu (cerdd)

syncopation, *n.* trawsacen (cerdd)

syncope, *n.* marwlewyg; byrhad gair

syndicate, *n.* cwmni

synod, *n.* cymanfa, senedd, synod

synonym, *n.* (gair) cyfystyr

synopsis, (*-ses*), *n.* cyfolwg; crynodeb

syntax, *n.* cystrawen

synthesis, (*-ses*), *n.* cyfosodiad, synthesis [trellu

syringe, *n.* chwistrell: *v.t.* chwis-

syrup, *n.* sudd; triagl (melyn)

system, *n.* cyfundrefn; trefn, system

tab 301 **tea**

T

tab, *n.* tafod, clust, llabed, pwyntl

tabby, *n.* cath frech, cath fenyw

tabernacle, *n.* tabernacl, pabell

table, *n.* bwrdd, bord; llech; tabl, taflen

tableau, *n.* golygfa

table-cloth, *n.* lliain bord (bwrdd)

tablet, *n.* llechen, llech; tabled

taboo, *n.* diofryd-beth, ysgymunbeth; gwaharddiad, tabŵ

tabular, *a.* taflennol

tabulate, *v.t.* tablu, taflennu

tacit, *a.* dealledig (ond heb ei grybwyll)

taciturn, *a.* tawedog [tacio

tack, *n.* tac, pwyth, brasbwyth: *v.*

tackle, *n.* taclau, offer: *v.* ymosod ar, taclo

tact, *n.* tact, callineb, doethineb

tactics, *n.pl.* cynlluniau, ystrywiau

tactile, *a.* cyffyrddol

tadpole, *n.* penbwl, penbwla

tag, *n.* pwyntl; clust, dolen

tail, *n.* cynffon, llosgwrn, cwt, godre

tailor, *n.* teiliwr

taint, *v.* llygru, heintio: *n.* llwgr, ystaen, mefl

take, *v.* cymryd, derbyn, cael, ennill

tale, *n.* chwedl, hanes, stori, clec, clep

talent, *n.* talent

talisman, *n.* swyn, cyfaredd

talk, *v. & n.* siarad

talkative, *a.* siaradus

tall, *a.* tal, hir, uchel

tallow, *n.* gwêr

tally, *n.* cyfrif; tocyn: *v.* cyfateb, cytuno

talon, *n.* ewin, crafanc

tame, *a.* dof, gwâr: *v.t.* dofi

tamper, *v.i.* ymhel, ymyrraeth

tan, *v.* trin lledr; llosgi, melynu

tangent, *n.* tangiad

tangible, *a.* cyffyrddadwy, sylweddol

tangle, *v.* drysu: *n.* dryswch

tank, *n.* dyfrgist, tanc

tankard, *n.* diod-lestr, tancr

tannery, *n.* barcerdy, crwyndy, tanerdy

tantalize, *v.t.* poeni, poenydio, pryfocio

tantamount, *a.* cyfwerth, cyfystyr

tantrums, *n.pl.* stranciau, nwydau

tap, *v.* taro yn ysgafn

tap, *n.* tap, feis: *v.t.* tapio, gollwng

tape, *n.* tâp, incil

taper, *n.* cwyren, tapr: *v.* meinhau, tapro

tar, *n.* tar; llongwr, morwr

tardy, *a.* hwyrfrydig, araf, diweddar

target, *n.* tarian; nod, targed

tariff, *n.* toll; pris

tarnish, *v.* pylu, cymylu, llychwino

tarry, *v.* aros, oedi, tario; trigo, preswylio

tart, *n.* pastai, pasteian

tart, *a.* sur, surllyd

tartan, *n.* brithwe, plod

task, *n.* gorchwyl, tasg: *v.t.* tasgu, trethu chwaeth

tassel, *n.* tusw, tasel

taste, *v.* archwaethu, blasu, profi: *n.* blas; chwaeth

tatter, *n.* rhecsyn, cerpyn, carp

tattle, *v.* clebar, cleber

taunt, *v.t.* edliw, dannod, gwatwar: *n.* gwaradwydd, sen

taut, *a.* tyn; taclus

tautologous, *a.* ailadroddol, cyfystyrol

tautology, *n.* tawtologaeth, ailadrodd, cyfystyredd

tavern, *n.* tafarn, tafarndy, tŷ tafarn

tawdry, *a.* coegwych

tawny, *n.* melynddu, melyn

tax, *n.* treth: *v.t.* trethu; cyhuddo

tea, *n.* te

teach, *v.t.* dysgu, addysgu

teacher, *n.* athro

team, *n.* gwedd, pâr, tîm

teapot, *n.* tebot.—**t. cover,** cap tebot

tear, *n.* deigryn, deigr
tear, *v.* rhwygo, llarpio: *n.* rhwyg
tease, *v.t.* pryfocio, plagio, poeni
teat, *n.* teth, diden, bron
technical, *a.* technegol
technique, *n.* techneg
technology, *n.* technoleg
tedious, *a.* blin, anniben, poenus
tedium, *n.* diflastod, blinder
teem, *v.* epilio, hilio, heigio
teethe, *v.i.* torri dannedd
teetotaller, *n.* llwyrymwrthodwr, titotal
telegram, *n.* teligram
telegraph, *n.* teligraff: *v.* teligraffio
teleology, *n.* dibenyddiaeth
telephase, *n.* olgyflwr
telephone, *n.* teliffon, ffôn
telescope, *n.* ysbienddrych, telisgob
television, *n.* teledu
tell, *v.* dywedyd, traethu, adrodd, mynegi; cyfrif, rhifo
temerity, *n.* rhyfyg, hyfdra
temper, *n.* tymer, naws: *v.t.* tymheru [ianawd
temperament, *n.* ardymer, an-
temperance, *n.* dirwest
temperate, *a.* cymedrol; tymherus
temperature, *n.* tymheredd
tempest, *n.* tymestl
tempestuous, *a.* tymhestlog
templar, *n.* temlydd
temple, *n.* teml
temple, *n.* arlais
temporal, *a.* tymhorol
temporary, *a.* dros amser, tymhorol
temporize, *v.i.* oedi, anwadalu
tempt, *v.t.* temtio, profi
temptation, *n.* temtiad, temtasiwn
ten, *a. & n.* deg
tenable, *a.* daliadwy; diffynadwy
tenacious, *a.* tyn ei afael, gwydn, gludiog, cyndyn
tenant, *n.* deiliad, tenant
tend, *v.* tendio, gweini
tend, *v.i.* tueddu, cyfeirio, symud
tendency, *n.* tuedd, gogwydd
tender, *a.* tyner, tirion, mwyn; meddal

tender, *v.* cynnig, cyflwyno: *n.* cynnig
tendon, *n.* gewyn
tendril, *n.* tendril
tenet, *n.* daliad, barn, tyb
tenon, *n.* tyno
tenor, *n.* cyfeiriad, tuedd, rhediad; tenor
tense, *a.* tyn, dirdynnol, dwys, angerddol
tense, *n.* amser (berf)
tension, *n.* tyndra, pwys, tyniant
tent, *n.* pabell
tentative, *a.* arbrofol
tenure, *n.* deiliadaeth
tepid, *a.* claear
term, *n.* terfyn; term; teler, amod; tymor: *v.t.* galw, enwi
terminal, *a.* terfynol, termol
terminate, *v.* terfynu
terminus, *n.* terfyn
terrace, *n.* rhes dai, teras
terrain, *n.* tir, bro, ardal
terrestrial, *a.* daearol
terrible, *a.* dychrynllyd, ofnadwy, arswydus
terrier, *n.* daeargi
terrific, *a.* dychrynllyd, arswydus
terrify, *v.t.* brawychu, dychrynu
territory, *n.* tir, tiriogaeth
terror, *n.* dychryn, braw, arswyd, ofn
terse, *a.* byr a chryno
test, *n.* prawf: *v.t.* profi
testament, *n.* testament, cyfamod, ewyllys
testator, *n.* cymynnwr
testify, *v.* tystiolaethu, tystio
testimonial, *n.* tysteb, tystlythyr
testimony, *n.* tystiolaeth; profiad
testy, *a.* afrywiog, ffrom
tether, *n.* rhaff, tennyn: *v.t.* clymu
text, *n.* testun, adnod
textile, *a.* gweol
texture, *n.* gwe, gwead, cyfansoddiad
than, *c.* na, nag
thank, *v.t. & n.* diolch
thankful, *a.* diolchgar
that, *pn. dem.* hwn (hon) yna (acw),

hwnnw, honno, hynny: *rel.* a,
y(r): *a.* hwn, hon, yma, yna,
acw: *c.* mai, taw

thatch, *n.* to, to gwellt: *v.t.* toi

thaw, *v.* dadlaith, dadmer, meirioli,
toddi

the, *a.* yr, y

theatre, *n.* theatr, chwaraedy;
maes, golygfa

thee, *pn.* ti, tydi, tithau

theft, *n.* lladrad

their, *pn.* eu

theirs, *pn.* yr eiddynt, eiddynt hwy

theism, *n.* duwiaeth, theistiaeth

them, *pn.* hwy, hwynt, hwythau

theme, *n.* testun, pwnc

themselves, *pn.* eu hunain

then, *adv.* y pryd hwnnw, yna: *c.*
yna

thence, *adv.* oddi yno, o hynny

theocracy, *n.* theocratiaeth

theology, *n.* diwinyddiaeth

theorem, *n.* theorem

theoretical, *a.* damcanol, damcaniaethol

theory, *n.* damcaniaeth, tyb

therapeutic, *a.* iachaol, meddygol

there, *adv.* yna, yno, acw; dyna,
dacw

therefore, *c.* gan hynny, am
hynny

thermal, *a.* gwresol, brwd

thermometer, *n.* thermomedr

these, *a.pl.* y rhai hyn, y rhai yma

thesis, (-*ses*), *n.* gosodiad; traethawd, thesis

they, *pn.* hwy, hwynt, hwynt-hwy

thick, *a.* tew, praff, trwchus

thicken, *v.* tewhau, tewychu

thicket, *n.* prysglwyn, llwyn

thief, (*thieves*), *n.* lleidr

thieve, *v.i.* lladrata, dwyn

thigh, *n.* clun, morddwyd

thimble, *n.* gwniadur

thin, *a.* tenau, cul, main; anaml,
prin

thine, *pn.* eiddot ti; dy

thing, *n.* peth, dim

think, *v.* meddwl

third, *a.* trydydd, trydedd

thirst, *n.* syched: *v.i.* sychedu

thirteen, *a. & n.* tri (tair) ar ddeg,
un deg tri (tair)   [deg

thirty, *a. & n.* deg ar hugain, tri

this, *a. & pn.* hwn, hon, hyn

thistle, *n.* ysgallen

thither, *adv.* yno, tuag yno

thong, *n.* carrai

thorax, *n.* y ddwyfron, y frest

thorn, *n.* draen, draenen; pigyn,
swmbwl

thorough, *a.* trwyadl, trylwyr

thoroughfare, *n.* tramwyfa

those, *a.pl.* y rhai hynny, y rhai yna

thou, *pn.* ti, tydi, tithau

though, *c.* er, pe, cyd

thought, *n.* meddwl

thousand, *a. & n.* mil

thrall, *n.* caethwr, caethwas

thrash, *v.t.* dyrnu, ffusto, curo

thread, *n.* edau, edefyn

threadbare, *a.* llwm, caledlwm

threat, *n.* bygwth, bygythiad

threaten, *v.t.* bygwth

three, *a. & n.* tri, tair

thresh, *v.t.* dyrnu, ffusto

thresher, *n.* dyrnwr, ffustwr

threshold *n.* trothwy, rhiniog,
hiniog

thrice, *adv.* teirgwaith

thrift, *n.* darbodaeth, cynildeb

thriftless, *a.* gwastraffus

thrill *v.* gwefreiddio: *n.* ias, gwefr

thrive, *v.i.* llwyddo, ffynnu; prifio

throat, *n.* gwddf

throb, *v.i.* dychlamu, curo

throe, *n.* dolur, poen, gloes, gwewyr

throne, *n.* gorsedd, gorseddfainc

throng, *n.* tyrfa, torf: *v.* tyrru,
heidio

throstle, *n.* bronfraith

throttle, *n.* corn gwynt: *v.t.*
llindagu

through, *pr.* trwy: *adv.* trwodd

throughout, *pr.* trwy: *adv.* trwyddo

throw, *v.* taflu, bwrw, lluchio

thrush, *n.* bronfraith

thrush, *n.* llindag, gân

thrust, *v.* gwthio, gwanu, brathu:
n. gwth

thud, *n.* twrf
thumb, *n.* bawd: *v.t.* bodio
thump, *v.* dyrnodio, pwnio, dulio
thunder, *n.* taran(au), tyrfau, trystau: *v.* taranu
Thursday, *n.* dydd Iau
thus, *adv.* fel hyn, felly
thwart, *v.t.* croesi, gwrthwynebu
thy, *pn.* dy, 'th
thyself, *pn.* dy hun, dy hunan
tiara, *n.* talaith, coron, coronig
tick, *v.i.* tipian, ticio: *n.* tipian, tic
tick, *v.t.* marcio, ticio: *n.* nod, marc, tic
tick, *n.* lliain gwely, tic
ticket, *n.* tocyn, ticed
tickle, *v.* goglais, gogleisio: *n.* goglais
tide, *n.* llanw, teit; amser, pryd
tidings, *n.pl.* newyddion, chwedlau
tidy, *a.* taclus, twt, trefnus, destlus
tie, *v.t.* clymu, rhwymo: *n.* cwlwm, cadach
tier, *n.* rhes, rhenc
tiger, *n.* teigr, dywalgi
tight, *a.* tyn, cryno, twt; cyfyng
tighten, *v.* tynhau
tile, *n.* priddlech, teilsen
till, *pr. & c.* hyd
till, *v.t.* trin, amaethu, llafurio
tiller, *n.* coes llyw; llafurwr, triniwr
tilt, *v.* gogwyddo; gosod (â gwayw)
tilth, *n.* triniaeth tir, âr
timber, *n.* coed, pren
time, *n.* amser: *v.t.* amseru
timely, *a.* amserol, prydlon
timepiece, *n.* cloc, wats
timid, *a.* ofnus, ofnog, llwfr
timorous, *a.* ofnus, ofnog
tin, *n.* alcam, tyn
tinge, *v.t.* lliwio, arlliwio: *n.* arlliw, gwawr
tingle, *v.i.* ysu, llosgi, merwino
tinker, *n.* tincer, eurych: *v.* tincera
tinkle, *v.* tincian
tint, *n.* lliw, arlliw, gwawr: *v.t.* lliwio
tiny, *a.* bychan, bach, pitw
tip, *n.* blaen, pen: *v.t.* blaenu

tip, *v.* troi, dymchwelyd; gwobrwyo: *n.* tip, tomen; cyngor; gwobr, cil-dwrn
tipple, *v.* llymeitian, diota
tipsy, *a.* meddw, penfeddw, brwysg
tiptoe, *n.* **on t.,** ar flaenau ei draed
tire, *v.* blino, lluddedu, diffygio
tire, tyre, *n.* cant, cylch, teiar
tiresome, *a.* blin, diflas, plagus
tiro, tyro, *n.* newyddian, dechreuwr
tissue, *n.* gwe, meinwe
titanic, *a.* cawraidd, anferth, aruthrol
titbit, *n.* tamaid blasus, amheuthun
tithe, *n.* degwm: *v.t.* degymu
titivate, *v.* pincio, ymbincio
title, *n.* teitl, hawl, hawlfraint
title-page, *n.* wyneb-ddalen
titter, *v.i.* cilchwerthin, chwerthinial
tittle, *n.* gronyn, mymryn, tipyn
titular, *a.* yn rhinwedd teitl; mewn enw
to, *pr.* i, at, hyd, er mwyn, wrth, yn
toad, *n.* llyffant du dafadennog
toadstool, *n.* caws llyffant, bwyd y boda, madarch
toady, *n.* cynffonnwr: *v.t.* cynffonna
toast, *n.* tost; llwnc-destun: *v.* tostio, crasu
tobacco, *n.* myglys, tybaco
to-day, *adv.* heddiw
toddle, *v.i.* cropian
toe, *n.* bys troed; blaen carn ceffyl
toffee, *n.* taffi, cyflaith
together, *adv.* ynghyd, gyda'i gilydd
toil, *v.i.* llafurio, poeni: *n.* llafur
toilet, *n.* trwsiad, gwisgiad; ystafell ymolchi
toils, *n.pl.* rhwydi, maglau
token, *n.* arwydd, argoel; tocyn
tolerable, *a.* goddefol; gweddol, symol
tolerate, *v.t.* goddef
toll, *n.* toll, treth
toll, *v.* canu (cloch, cnul)
tomb, *n.* bedd, beddrod
tomboy, *n.* hoeden, rhampen
tome, *n.* cyfrol (fawr)

tomfool *n.* ynfytyn, pen-ffŵl
to-morrow, *adv.* yfory
ton, *n.* tunnell
tonality, *n.* tonyddiaeth
tone, *n.* tôn, oslef: *v.* tyneru, lleddfu
tongs, *n.pl.* gefel
tongue, *n.* tafod; tafodiaith, iaith
tonic, *n.* meddyginiaeth gryfhaol, tonic
tonsil, *n.* tonsil
tonsure, *n.* corun, tonsur
to-night, *adv.* heno
too, *adv.* rhy; hefyd.— **t. much,** gormod
tool, *n.* arf, erfyn
toot, *v.* canu corn
tooth, (*teeth*) *n.* dant
toothache, *n.* dannoedd
toothsome, *a.* danteithiol, blasus
top, *n.* pen, brig, copa: *v.t.* tocio; rhagori ar
top, *n.* cogwrn, top
toper, *n.* diotwr, meddwyn
topic, *n.* pwnc
topography, *n.* daearyddiaeth leol
topple, *v.* syrthio, cwympo, dymchwel
topsyturvy, *adv.* yn bendramwnwgl
torch, *n.* ffagl, tors
torment, *n.* poen, poenedigaeth: *v.t.* poeni, poenydio
tornado, *n.* hyrddwynt, corwynt
torpedo, *n.* torpedo
torpid, *a.* marwaidd, cysglyd, swrth
torrent, *n.* cenllif, llifeiriant, rhyferthwy
torrid, *a.* poeth, crasboeth
tortoise, *n.* crwban
tortuous, *a.* troellog, trofaus
torture, *n.* dirboen, artaith: *v.t.* arteithio
tory, *n.* tori, ceidwadwr: *a.* toriaidd
toss, *v.* taflu, lluchio, bwrw
total, *a.* hollol, cyflawn: *n.* cyfan, cyfanswm
totter, *v.i.* honcian, siglo, gwegian
touch, *v.* teimlo, cyffwrdd: *n.* teimlad

touchy, *a.* croendenau
tough, *a.* gwydn, caled, cyndyn
tour, *n.* tro, taith
tourist, *n.* teithiwr, ymwelydd
tournament, *n.* twrnamaint
tousle, *v.t.* dragio, anhrefnu
tout, *v.i.* poeni pobl am archebion
tow, *n.* carth
tow, *v.t.* llusgo, tynnu
toward, -s, *pr.* tua, tuag at
towel, *n.* lliain sychu, tywel
tower, *n.* tŵr: *v.i.* esgyn, ymgodi
town, *n.* tref
township, *n.* trefgordd
toxic, *a.* gwenwynig
toy, *n.* tegan: *v.i.* chwarae, maldodi
trace, *n.* tres
trace, *v.t.* olrhain, dilyn: *n.* ôl
tracery, *n.* rhwyllwaith (maen, &c.)
trachea, *n.* breuant, corn gwynt
track, *n.* ôl, brisg; llwybr: *v.t.* olrhain
tract, *n.* ardal, rhandir
tract, *n.* traethodyn
tractable, *a.* hydyn, hydrin, hywedd
traction, *n.* tyniad, tyniant, llusgiad
trade, *n.* masnach; crefft: *v.* masnachu
tradition, *n.* traddodiad
traduce, *v.t.* cablu, difenwi, enllibio
traffic, *v.* masnachu, trafnidio: *n.* masnach, trafnidiaeth
tragedy, *n.* trasiedi, trychineb
tragic, *a.* trychinebus, alaethus
trail, *n.* llusg, brisg, ôl: *v.* llusgo
train, *v.* hyfforddi, ymarfer: *n.* gosgordd; godre; trên, cerbydres
training, *n.* hyfforddiant, disgyblaeth
trait, *n.* nodwedd, (*pl.*) teithi
traitor, *n.* bradwr, teyrnfradwr
trajectory, *n.* taflwybr
trammel, *n.* rhwyd; hual: *v.t.* llyffetheirio, hualu
tramp, *v.* crwydro, trampio: *n.* crwydryn
trample, *v.* sathru, sangu, mathru

trance, *n.* llewyg, llesmair, perlewyg

tranquil, *a.* tawel, llonydd, digyffro

trans-, tran-, tra-, *px.* tros-, tra-

transact, *v.t.* trafod, gwneuthur, trin

transcend, *v.t.* rhagori ar, tra-rhagori

transcendent, *a.* trosgynnol

transcribe, *v.t.* copïo

transcript, *n.* copi

transept, *n.* croes (eglwys)

transfer, *v.t.* trosglwyddo: *n.* trosglwyddiad

transfigure, *v.t.* gweddnewid

transfix, *v.t.* trywanu, gwanu

transform, *v.t.* trawsffurfio

transgress, *v.t.* troseddu

transient, *a.* diflanedig, darfodedig

transit, *n.* mynediad dros, trosiad

transition, *n.* trosiad, trawsgyweiriad

transitive, *a.* trosiadol; anghyflawn (berf) [edig

transitory, *a.* diflanedig, darfod-

translate, *v.t.* cyfieithu

transliterate, *v.t.* trawslythrennu

translucent, *a.* tryloyw

transmigrate, *v.i.* trawsfudo

transmit, *v.t.* anfon, trosglwyddo

transmute, *v.t.* trawsnewid

transparent, *a.* tryloyw

transpire, *v.* dyfod yn hysbys

transplant, *v.t.* trawsblannu

transport, *v.t.* trosglwyddo; alltudio: *n.* trosglwyddiad; trosglwyddlong; perlewyg, gorawen

transpose, *v.t.* trawsddodi, trawsgyweirio

transubstantiation, *n.* trawssylweddiad

transverse, *a.* croes, traws

trap, *n.* trap, magl; car bach: *v.t.* dal, maglu

trappings, *n.pl.* harnais, gêr

trash, *n.* sothach, gwehilion, ffwlbri

travail, *v.i.* trafaelu: *n.* trafael, llafur

travel, *v.* teithio, trafaelio: *n.* teithio, (*pl.*) teithiau

traverse, *v.* myned ar draws, croesi

trawl, *v.* llusgrwydo: *n.* llusgrwyd

tray, *n.* hambwrdd

treachery, *n.* brad, bradwriaeth

treacle, *n.* triagl

tread, *v.* sathru, sengi, troedio: *n.* sang

treason, *n.* brad, bradwriaeth

treasure, *n.* trysor: *v.t.* trysori

treasury, *n.* trysorfa, trysordy

treat, *v.* tretio; traethu, trin; cyfamodi: *n.* gwledd, amheuthun

treatise, *n.* traethawd

treatment, *n.* triniaeth, ymdriniaeth

treaty, *n.* cyfamod, cytundeb

treble, *a.* triphlyg: *n.* trebl: *v.* treblu

tree, *n.* pren, coeden

trefoil, *n.* meillionen, meillion

trek, *v.i.* mudo: *n.* mud, mudo

trellis, *n.* delltwaith

tremble, *v.i.* crynu, echrydu, arswydo

tremendous, *a.* dychrynllyd, ofnadwy, anferth

tremor, *n.* crynfa, cryndod, ias

tremulous, *a.* crynedig

trench, *n.* ffos, rhigol, rhych: *v.* ffosi

trenchant, *a.* llym, miniog

trencher, *n.* trensiwr, treinsiwr, plat

trend, *v.i.* tueddu: *n.* tuedd, gogwydd

trepidation, *n.* cryndod, ofn, dychryn

trespass, *v.i.* troseddu: *n.* trosedd

tress, *n.* cudyn gwallt, tres

trestle *n.* trestl

tri-, *px.* tri

triad, *n.* tri, (*pl.*) trioedd

trial, *n.* prawf, profedigaeth, treial

triangle, *n.* triongl

tribe, *n.* llwyth, tylwyth, gwehelyth

tribulation, *n.* trallod, cystudd

tribunal, *n.* brawdle, llys, tribiwnlys

tributary, *a.* dan deyrnged: *n.* rhagafon

tribute, *n.* teyrnged, treth
trice, *n.* munudyn, chwinciad
trick, *n.* tric, cast, ystryw: *v.t.* castio
trickle, *v.i.* diferu, diferynnu
trident, *n.* tryfer
triennial, *a.* tairblynyddol
trifle, *n.* gronyn, mymryn; gwaelbeth: *v.* ofera, cellwair
trifling, *a.* diwerth, dibwys
trigger, *n.* cliced
trigonometry, *n.* trigonomeg
trill, *v.* crychleisio, cwafrio: *n.* crychlais
trillion, *n.* triliwn
trim, *a.* taclus, twt, del: *v.* taclu, trwsio: *n.* diwyg, trefn
trinity, *n.* trindod
trinket, *n.* tegan, tlws
trio, *n.* triawd
trip, *v.* tripio, maglu; disodli: *n.* trip, pleserdaith
tripe, *n.* tripa
triple, *a.* triphlyg
triplet, *n.* tripled, triban
tripod, *n.* trybedd
trite, *a.* cyffredin, sathredig
triumph, *n.* gorfoledd, buddugoliaeth: *v.i.* gorfoleddu; buddugoliaethu
trivet, *n.* trybedd
trivial, *a.* distadl, dibwys, diwerth
trolley, -y, *n.* troli
troop, *n.* byddin, torf, mintai: *v.* tyrru
tropic, *n.* trofan
trot, *v.* tuthio, trotian: *n.* tuth, trot
trouble, *v.t.* blino, trafferthu: *n.* blinder, trallod, helbul, trafferth
trough, *n.* cafn
trounce, *v.t.* ffonodio, cystwyo, baeddu
troupe, *n.* mintai o berfformwyr
trousers, *n.pl.* llodrau, trowsus, trwser
trousseau, *n.* dillad priodasferch
trout, *n.* brithyll
trow, *v.* tybied, meddylied, credu
trowel, *n.* trywel
truant, *n.* truawnt, mitsiwr

truce, *n.* cadoediad
truck, *n.* trwc, gwagen
truck, *v.* cyfnewid, ffeirio
truckle, *v.i.* plygu, ymostwng, ymgreinio
truculent, *a.* ffyrnig, milain
trudge, *v.* cerdded yn ffwdanus, trwmgerdded
true, *a.* gwir, cywir
truism, *n.* gwireb, gwiredd
truly, *adv.* yn wir, yn ddiau, yn gywir
trump, *v.* utganu; twyllo, ffugio
trumpery, *n.* sothach, ffwlbri: *a.* coeg, gwacsaw
trumpet, *n.* utgorn, corn
truncheon, *n.* byrllysg
trundle, *v.* treiglo, rholio
trunk, *n.* cyff, cist; corff; duryn, trwnc
trust, *n.* ymddiried, coel: *v.* hyderu, ymddiried, coelio
trustee, *n.* ymddiriedolwr
truth, *n.* gwir, gwirionedd
try, *v.* profi, cynnig, ceisio, treio
tryst, *n.* oed
tub, *n.* twba, twb, baddon
tube, *n.* pib, pibell, tiwb, corn
tuber, *n.* cloronen, taten
tuberculosis, *n.* darfodedigaeth, dicáu, dicléin
tubular, *a.* tiwbaidd.—**t. bridge,** ceubont
tuck, *v.t.* cwtogi, plygu: *n.* plyg, twc
Tuesday, *n.* dydd Mawrth
tuft, *n.* cobyn, tusw, cudyn
tug, *v.* llusgo, tynnu
tuition, *n.* addysg, hyfforddiant
tulip, *n.* tiwlip
tumble, *v.* cwympo: *n.* codwm, cwymp
tumid, *a.* chwyddedig
tumour, *n.* chwydd, casgliad, cornwyd
tumult, *n.* terfysg, cynnwrf
tune, *n.* tôn, tiwn, cywair: *v.* cyweirio
tunic, *n.* crysbais, siaced
tunnel, *n.* ceuffordd, twnnel
turban, *n.* twrban

turbid, *a.* afloyw, cymysglyd, lleidiog

turbot, *n.* torbwt

turbulent, *a.* terfysglyd, afreolus

turf, *n.* tywyrch

turgid, *a.* chwyddedig

Turk, *n.* Twrc

turkey, *n.* twrci

turmoil, *n.* trafferth, ffwdan, berw

turn, *v.* troi: *n.* tro, trofa

turner, *n.* turniwr

turnip, *n.* erfinen, meipen

turnpike, *n.* tollborth, tyrpeg

turpentine, *n.* twrpant, turpant

turpitude, *n.* gwarthusrwydd, ysgelerder

turret, *n.* twred, tyryn

turtle, *n.* crwban môr

turtle, -dove, *n.* turtur

tusk, *n.* ysgithrddant, ysgithr

tussle, *n.* ymgiprys, ysgarmes

tut, *i.* twt !

tutelage, *n.* gwarchodaeth, nawdd

tutor, *n.* athro, hyfforddwr: *v.t.* hyfforddi

twaddle, *n.* lol, ffiloreg

twang, *v.* clecian, swnio: *n.* sŵn, llediaith   [dau

twelve, *a. & n.* deuddeg, un deg

twenty, *a. & n.* ugain

twice, *adv.* dwywaith

twiddle, *v.t.* chwarae bodiau, cellwair

twig, *n.* brigyn, ysbrigyn, impyn

twilight, *n.* cyfnos, cyfddydd

twill, *n.* brethyn caerog

twin, *n.* gefell

twine, *n.* llinyn: *v.* cyfrodeddu, cordeddu

twinge, *n.* cnofa, brath, gwayw

twinkle, *v.i.* serennu, pefrio

twinkling, *n.* chwinciad

twirl, *v.* chwyrndroi, chwyldroi, nydd-droi

twist, *v.* nyddu, nydd-droi, cyfrodeddu; troi, gwyrdroi: *n.* tro; edau gyfrodedd

twit, *n.* dannod, edliw

twitch, *v.* tymhigo, brathgnoi: *n.* tymig

twitter, *v.i.* trydar

two, *a. & n.* dau, dwy

tympan, *n.* tabwrdd, tympan

type, *n.* math, teip

typescript, *n.* teipysgrif

typewriter, *n.* teipiadur, peiriant teipio

typical, *a.* arwyddol, nodweddiadol

typify, *v.t.* arwyddo, nodweddu

typist, *n.* teipydd

typography, *n.* argraffwaith

tyranny, *n.* tra-arglwyddiaeth, gormes

tyrant, *n.* gormesteyrn, gormeswr

tyro, *n.* newyddian, dechreuwr

U

ubiquitous, *a.* ym mhob man, holl-bresennol

udder, *n.* pwrs, cadair, piw

ugly, *a.* hagr, hyll

ulcer, *n.* casgliad, cornwyd

ulterior, *a.* tu draw i, tu hwnt i, pellach; cudd

ultimate, *a.* diwethaf, olaf, eithaf

ultra, *a.* eithafol: *px.* tu hwnt i, gor-

umbrage, *n.* tramgwydd

umbrella, *n.* ymbrelo, brela, ambarél

umpire, *n.* dyddiwr, canolwr

un-, *px.* an-, am-, ang-, af-, di-, heb

unacceptable, *a.* anghymeradwy, annerbyniol

unaccountable, *a.* anesboniadwy

unaccustomed, *a.* anghyfarwydd, anghynefin

unadulterated, *a.* pur, digymysg

unanimity, *n.* unfrydedd

unanimous, *a.* unfrydol

unawares, *adv.* yn ddiarwybod

unbearable, *a.* annioddefol

unbecoming, *a.* anweddus, anweddaidd

unbeliever, *n.* anghredadun

unbelieving, *a.* anghrediniol

unbounded, *a.* diderfyn

uncanny, *a.* rhyfedd, dieithr, annaearol

uncle, *n.* ewythr
unconscionable, *a.* digydwybod, afresymol
uncouth, *a.* trwsgl, lletchwith, garw, amrwd [hwyl
unction, *n.* eli; eneiniad, arddeliad,
unctuous, *a.* seimlyd; rhagrithiol
under, *pr.* tan, is, islaw: *adv.* tanodd, oddi tanodd: *px.* is-, tan-
underneath, *adv.* oddi tanodd: *pr.* tan
understand, *v.t.* deall, dirnad
undertake, *v.* ymgymryd
undertaker, *n.* ymgymerydd; saer (coffinnau)
undeviating, *a.* diwyro
undignified, *a.* anurddasol, di-urddas
undisturbed, *a.* llonydd, tawel, digyffro
undo, *v.t.* dadwneuthur; datod; an-dwyo, difetha
undoing, *n.* distryw, dinistr
undulate, *v.i.* tonni
uneasy, *a.* anesmwyth, aflonydd, pryderus
uneducated, *a.* annysgedig
unemployed, *a.* di-waith, segur
unemployment, *n.* diweithdra, anghyflogaeth
unequal, *a.* anghyfartal
unequalled, *a.* digymar, dihafal
unexpected, *a.* annisgwyliadwy
unfair, *a.* annheg
unfasten, *v.* datod
unfurnished, *a.* diddodrefn
ungainly, *a.* afrosgo, trwsgl
unguent, *n.* ennaint, eli
uni- *px.* un-
uniform, *a.* unffurf: *n.* gwisg swyddogol
unify, *v.t.* unoli, uno
union, *n.* undeb; uniad
unique, *a.* dihafal, digymar
unison, *n.* unsain, unseinedd
unit, *n.* un, rhif un; uned; undod
Unitarian, *n.* Undodwr: *a.* Undod-aidd
unite, *v.* uno, cyfuno, cyduno, cydio

unity, *n.* undeb, cyfundeb
universal, *a.* cyffredinol
universe, *n.* bydysawd, hollfyd, cyfanfyd
university, *n.* prifysgol, prifathrofa
unkempt, *a.* heb ei gribo, aflêr, anniben
unless, *c.* oni, onid, onis, oddieithr
unmarried, *a.* dibriod
unqualified, *a.* heb gymhwyster, anghymwys, anaddas; digymysg, diamodol
unrestrained, *a.* dilywodraeth, aflywodraethus, penrhydd
until, *pr. & c.* hyd, hyd oni, nes, tan
unto, *pr.* i, at, hyd, hyd at, wrth
unwieldy, *a.* afrosgo
up, *adv., pr & px.* i fyny
upholsterer, *n.* dodrefnwr, clustog-wr
upland, *n.* ucheldir, blaenau
upon, *pr.* ar, ar warthaf, ar uchaf
upper, *a.* uwch, uchaf
uppermost, *a. & adv.* uchaf
upright, *a.* syth, union, unionsyth
uproar, *n.* terfysg, cythrwfl, dad-wrdd
uproot, *v.t.* diwreiddio
upset, *v.* troi, dymchwelyd, cyffroi, gofidio
upshot, *n.* swm, canlyniad, diwedd
upstart, *n.* crach fonheddwr
upward, *a. & adv.,* **upwards,** *adv.* i fyny
urban, *a.* dinasol, dinesig
urbane, *a.* hynaws, mwyn, bonedd-igaidd
urchin, *n.* draenog; crwtyn
urge, *v.t.* cymell, annog
urgent, *a.* taer, pwysig, yn gofyn brys
urine, *n.* troeth, trwnc, piso
urn, *n.* wrn
us, *pn.* ni, nyni, ninnau; 'n
usage, *n.* arfer, defod, triniaeth
use, *n.* iws, arfer, defnydd, gwasan-aeth, diben: *v.* iwsio, arfer, defnyddio
usher, *n.* rhingyll; isathro: *v.t.* arwain i mewn, dwyn ymlaen

usual, a. arferol, cynefin

usurp, v.t. trawsfeddiannu

usury, n. usuriaeth, ocraeth

utensil, n. offeryn, llestr

utilitarianism, n. llesyddiaeth

utility, n. defnyddioldeb, budd, lles

utilize, v.t. defnyddio

utmost, a. eithaf, pellaf

utopian, a. delfrydol, anymarferol

utter, a. eithaf, pellaf; hollol, llwyr

utter, v.t. yngan, traethu, dywedyd

utterance, n. parabl, ymadrodd, lleferydd

uttermost, a. eithaf, pellaf

uvula, n. tafod bach, tafodig

uvular, a. tafodigol

V

vacant, a. gwag; syn, synfyfyriol, hurt

vacate, v.t. ymadael â, gadael yn wag

vacation, n. seibiant, gwyliau

vaccinate, v.t. brechu, bufrechu, torri'r frech

vacillate, v.i. anwadalu, bwhwman

vacuous, a. gwag, syn, hurt

vacuum, n. gwag, gwagle, gwactod

vagabond, n. crwydryn, dihiryn

vagary, n. mympwy

vagrant, a. crwydrol: n. crwydryn

vague, a. amwys, amhenodol

vain, a. balch, coegfalch: ofer

vale, n. dyffryn, glyn, bro, cwm, ystrad

valediction, n. ffarwel

valentine, n. falant, folant

valet, n. gwas

valiant, a. dewr, dewrwych, gwrol, glew

valid, a. digonol, dilys, cyfreithlon, iawn

valley, n. dyffryn, cwm, glyn

valour, n. dewrder, gwroldeb, glewder

valuable, a. gwerthfawr

value, n. gwerth: v.t. gwerthfawrogi, prisio

valve, n. falf

van, n. blaen cad, y rheng flaenaf

van, n. men, fan

vandal, n. fandal

vane, n. ceiliog gwynt

vanguard, n. blaen cad, blaenfyddin

vanish, v.i. diflannu, darfod

vanity, n. gwagedd, gwegi, coegfalchder

vanquish, v.t. gorchfygu, trechu

vantage, n. mantais

vapid, a. diflas, merf, marwaidd, egr

vaporize, v. anweddu

vapour, n. tawch, tarth, ager, anwedd

variable, a. cyfnewidiol, anwadal, oriog

variable, n. newidyn (rhifyddiaeth)

variance, n. anghytundeb, anghydfod, amrywioldeb

varicose, a. chwyddedig (am wythiennau)

variegated, a. brith, brithliw

variety, n. amrywiaeth

various, a. gwahanol, amrywiol

varnish, n. barnais, farnais: v.t. barneisio

vary, v. amrywio; newid

vase, n. cwpan, cawg

vassal, n. caethddeiliad, taeog, aillt

vast, a. dirfawr, anferth

vat, n. cerwyn

vaticinate, v. proffwydo, darogan

vault, n. daeargell, claddgell; cromen: v. neidio, llamu

vaunt, v. ymffrostio, bostio, brolio

veal, n. cig llo

veer, v. troi, cylchdroi; trawshwylio

vegetable, a. llysieuol: n. llysieuyn ymborth

vegetate, v.i. tarddu, tyfu; ofera

vegetation, n. tyfiant llysiau, llystyfiant

vehement, a. angerddol, tanbaid

vehicle, n. cerbyd; cyfrwng, moddion

veil, n. gorchudd, llen: v.t. gorchuddio

vein, *n.* gwythïen

veldt, *n.* anialdir, maestir

vellum, *n.* memrwn

velocity, *n.* buander, cyflymder, buanedd (mathemateg)

velvet, *n.* melfed

vend, *v.t.* gwerthu

veneer, *n.* argaen, wynebiad; rhith, ffug

venerable, *a.* hybarch

venerate, *v.t.* parchu, anrhydeddu

venereal, *a.* gwenerol

vengeance, *n.* dial, dialedd

venial, *a.* maddeuadwy, esgusodol

venison, *n.* cig carw, fenswn

venom, *n.* gwenwyn

venous, *a.* gwythennol

vent, *n.* agorfa, twll, arllwysfa: *v.t.* arllwys, gollwng

ventilate, *v.t.* awyru, gwyntyllu

ventriloquism, *n.* tafleisiaeth

venture, *n.* anturiaeth, mentr: *v.* anturio, mentro

veracious, *a.* cywir, geirwir, gwir

verb, *n.* berf

verbal, *a.* berfol; geiriol

verbatim, *adv.* air am air, air yng ngair

verbiage, *n.* amleiraeth, geiriogrwydd

verbose, *a.* amleiriog

verdant, *a.* gwyrddlas, gwyrdd

verdict, *n.* dyfarniad, dedfryd, rheithfarn

verdure, *n.* gwyrddlesni

verge, *n.* min, ymyl: *v.i.* ymylu

verger, *n.* byrllysgydd, eglwyswas

verify, *v.t.* gwiro, gwireddu

verily, *adv.* yn wir, yn ddiau

veritable, *a.* gwirioneddol

verity, *n.* gwir, gwirionedd

vermin, *n.pl.* pryfed, pryfetach; llygod, &c.

vernacular, *a.* cynhenid, brodorol: *n.* iaith y wlad

vernal, *a.* gwanwynol

versatile, *a.* amryddawn

verse, *n.* gwers, adnod, pennill; prydyddiaeth

versed, *a.* cyfarwydd, hyddysg

versify, *v.* mydru, prydyddu, prydu

version, *n.* cyfieithiad, trosiad; esboniad

versus, *pr.* yn erbyn

vertebra, (*-brae*), *n.* un o gymalau'r asgwrn cefn

vertex, (*-tices*) *n.* pen. crib, copa

vertical, *a.* syth, unionsyth, plwm

vertigo, *n.* y bendro, y ddot

very, *a. & adv.* iawn, pur, tra; diamheuol

vespers, *n.pl.* gosber

vessel, *n.* llestr

vest, *n.* gwasgod, crys isaf: *v.* arwisgo, cynysgaeddu

vestal, *a.* gwyryfol: *n.* lleian, gwyry

vestibule, *n.* porth, cyntedd

vestige, *n.* ôl, ôl troed, brisg

vestment, *n.* gwisg, defodwisg

vestry, *n.* festri

vesture, *n.* gwisg, dilledyn, dillad

veteran, *n.* un hen a chyfarwydd

veterinary, *a.* milfeddygol.—**v. surgeon,** meddyg anifeiliaid, milfeddyg

veto, (*-oes*), *n.* gwaharddiad: *v.t.* gwahardd

vex, *v.t.* blino, poeni, poenydio, cythruddo

vexing, *a.* blin, plagus

viaduct, *n.* pontffordd, fforddbont

vial, *n.* ffiol

viand, *n.* bwyd, ymborth

vibrate, *v.* crynu, dirgrynu

vicar, *n.* ficer

vicarious, *a.* dirprwyol, mechnïol

vice, *n.* drygioni, drygedd, bai, gwŷd

vice, *n.* gwasg, feis

vice-, *px.* rhag-, is-

vicegerent, *n.* rhaglaw, dirprwy

viceroy, *n.* rhaglaw

vicinity, *n.* cymdogaeth

vicious, *a.* drygionus, gwydus

vicissitude, *n.* cyfnewidiad, tro

victim, *n.* aberth, ysglyfaeth

victor, *n.* gorchfygwr

victorious, *a.* buddugol, buddugoliaethus

victory, n. buddugoliaeth
victual, n. (pl.) bwyd, lluniaeth: v.t. bwydo
vie, v.i. cystadlu, cydymgais
view, n. golygfa, golygiad: v.t. edrych
vigil, n. noswyl, gwylnos
vigilant, a. gwyliadwrus
vigour, n. grym, nerth, egni, ynni
vile, a. gwael, brwnt
vilify, v.t. pardduo, difrïo
village, n. pentref
villain, n. cnaf, adyn, dihiryn
vindicate, v.t. amddiffyn, cyfiawnhau
vindictive, a. dialgar
vine, n. gwinwydden
vinegar, n. finegr
vineyard, n. gwinllan
vintage, n. cynhaeaf gwin
vintner, n. gwinwr, gwinydd
violate, v.t. torri, troseddu, treisio
violent, a. gwyllt, tanbaid, angerddol
viola, n. fiola
violet, n. fioled, crinllys
violin, n. ffidil
viper, n. gwiber
virago, n. cecren
virgin, n. gwyry, morwyn
virile, a. gwrol, egnïol
virtue, n. rhinwedd
virulent, a. gwenwynig, ffyrnig
virus, n. gôr, crawn; gwenwyn
visage, n. wyneb, wynepryd
viscid, a. gwydn, gludiog
viscount, n. isiarll
visible, a. gweladwy, gweledig
vision, n. gweledigaeth; golwg, gweled
visionary, n. breuddwydiwr: a. breuddwydiol
visit, v.t. ymweled, gofwyo: n. ymweliad
visitor, n. ymwelwr, ymwelydd
visor, n. miswrn, mwgwd
vista, n. golygfa
visual, a. gweledol, golygol.—v. aids, cyfarpar gweld
vital, a. bywiol, bywydol, hanfodol

vitality, n. bywyd, bywiogrwydd
vitiate, v.t. llygru, difetha, dirymu
vitreous, a. gwydrol, gwydraidd
vituperate, v.t. cablu, difenwi, difrïo
vivacious, a. bywiog, heini, nwyfus
vivid, a. byw, clir, llachar, tanbaid
vivify, v.t. bywhau, bywiocáu
vivisection, n. bywdrychiad, bywddifyniad
vixen, n. cadnawes, llwynoges
viz., adv. sef (talfyriad o videlicet)
vocable, n. gair
vocabulary, n. geirfa
vocal, a. lleisiol, llafarol, llafar
vocalist, n. lleisiwr, cantor
vocalize, v.t. llafarseinio; llafarogi
vocation, n. galwad, galwedigaeth
vocative, a. cyfarchol
vociferate, v. crochlefain
vogue, n. arfer, ffasiwn, bri
voice, n. llais, lleferydd, stad (gram.)
void, a. gwag, ofer, di-rym; amddifad, heb; n. gwagle: v.t. gwagu, gollwng
volatile, a. hedegog; anwadal, gwamal, ysgafn
volcano, n. llosgfynydd, mynydd tân
volition, n. ewyllysiad, ewyllys
volley, n. cawod ergydion
volt, n. undod grym trydanol, folt
voluble, a. rhugl, ymadroddus
volume, n. cyfrol; swm, crynswth, folum (cemeg); cyfaint (mathemateg)
voluntary, a. gwirfoddol
volunteer, n. gwirfoddolwr: v. gwirfoddoli
voluptuary, n. pleserwr, glythwr
voluptuous, a. glwth, trythyll
vomit, v. chwydu, cyfogi
voracious, a. gwancus, rheibus
vortex, n. trobwll, chwyldro
votary, n. addunwr, diofrydwr, pleidiwr
vote, n. pleidlais, llais: v. pleidleisio
votive, a. addunedol, addunol
vouch, v. gwirio, gwarantu
vouchsafe, v.t. caniatáu, rhoddi

vow, n. adduned, diofryd: v. addunedu

vowel, n. llafariad.—**v. affection,** affeithiad. –**v. mutation,** gwyriad

voyage, n. mordaith: v. mordeithio, mordwyo

vulgar, a. cyffredin; isel, di-foes, aflednais

vulnerable, a. archolladwy, hyglwyf

vulture, n. fwltur

W

wad, n. sypyn, wad

waddle, v.i. siglo, honcian

wade, v. beisio, rhydio

wafer, n. afrlladen

waft, v.t. chwifio, cludo, dygludo

wag, v. ysgwyd, siglo, honcian

wag, n. cellweiriwr, wag

wage, v.t. gwneuthur, dwyn ymlaen

wage, n. cyflog, hur

wager, n. cyngwystl: v.t. cyngwystlo

wagon, n. men, gwagen

wail, v. cwynfan, wylofain, udo

wainscot, n. palis

waist, n. gwasg, canol

waistcoat, n. gwasgod

wait, v. aros; gweini: n. arhosfa

wake, v. deffro: n. gwylmabsant, gwylnos

wake, n. ôl, brisg

walk, v. cerdded, rhodio: n. rhodfa; tro

wall, n. mur, gwal, gwal, pared: v.t. murio

wallet, n. ysgrepan, gwaled

wallop, v.t. curo, llachio, baeddu

wallow, v.i. ymdreiglo, ymdrybaeddu

walnut, n. cneuen Ffrengig

walrus, n. morfarch

wan, a. gwelw, gwelwlas, llwyd

wand, n. gwialen, llath, hudlath

wander, v. crwydro, gwibio, cyfeiliorni

wane, v.i. darfod, treio, cilio, lleihau

want, n. angen, eisiau, diffyg: v. bod arno eisiau

wanton, a. anllad, trythyll; diachos

war, n. rhyfel: v. rhyfela

warble, v. telori

ward, n. gwart, gward; gwarchodaeth: v.t. gwarchod, amddiffyn

warden, n. gwarden, gwarcheidwad

warder, n. gwarchodwr, gwyliwr

wardrobe, n. cwpwrdd dillad, gwardrob

ware, n. nwydd; llestri, wâr

warehouse, n. ystordy, ystorfa

warfare, n. milwriaeth, rhyfel

warlike, a. rhyfelgar, milwraidd, milwrol

warm, a. cynnes: v. cynhesu

warmth, n. cynhesrwydd

warn, v.t. rhybuddio

warp, n. ystof, dylif: v. gwyro, lleddfu

warrant, n. gwarant; awdurdod: v.t. gwarantu; cyfreithloni

warrior, n. rhyfelwr

wart, n. dafad, dafaden

wary, a. gwyliadwrus, gochelgar

was, v.i. oedd, bu

wash, v. golchi: n. golchiad, golchfa; golchion

wasp, n. cacynen, gwenynen feirch

waste, v. difrodi, gwastraffu, treulio: n. gwastraff, traul

wastrel, n. oferwr, oferddyn

watch, v. gwylio, gwylied, gwarchod: n. gwyliadwriaeth; oriawr, oriadur, wats

watchful, a. gwyliadwrus

watch-night, n. gwylnos

watchword, n. arwyddair, cyswynair

water, n. dwfr, dŵr: v. dyfrhau

watercress, n. berwr dŵr

waterfall, n. rhaeadr, pistyll, cwymp, sgwd

wattle, n. clwyd, pleiden; tagell ceiliog

wave, v. chwifio; tonni; cyhwfan: n. ton   [gwamalu

waver, v.i. anwadalu, petruso,

wax, *n.* cwyr: *v.t.* cwyro
wax, *v.i.* cynyddu, tyfu
way, *n.* ffordd, modd, arfer
wayfarer, *n.* fforddol, teithiwr, tramwywr
waylay, *v.t.* cynllwyn, rhagod
wayward, *a.* cyndyn, ystyfnig, gwrthnysig
we, *pn.* ni, nyni, ninnau
weak, *a.* gwan, egwan
weaken, *v.* gwanhau, gwanychu
weakling, *n.* un gwan, edlych, ewach
weakly, *a.* gwanllyd
weakness, *n.* gwendid
weal, *n.* llwydd, llwyddiant, lles
wealth, *n.* golud, cyfoeth, da
wean, *v.t.* diddyfnu
weapon, *n.* arf
wear, *v.* gwisgo, treulio: *n.* traul
weary, *a.* blin, blinedig: *v.* blino
weasel, *n.* gwenci, bronwen
weather, *n.* tywydd, hin: *v.t.* dal, dioddef
weave, *v.* gwau, gweu
web, *n.* gwe
wed, *v.* priodi, ymbriodi
wedding, *n.* priodas, neithior
wedge, *n.* cŷn, colpes, gaing, lletem: *v.t.* cynio; gwthio i mewn
wedlock, *n.* ystad priodas, priodas
Wednesday, *n.* dydd Mercher
wee, *a.* bach, bychan, pitw
weed, *n.* chwynnyn, chwyn: *v.* chwynnu
week, *n.* wythnos
weep, *v.* wylo, wylofain, llefain
weft, *n.* anwe
weigh, *v.* pwyso; codi (angor)
weight, *n.* pwys, pwysau
weir, *n.* cored
weird, *a.* annaearol, iasol
welcome, *i. & n.* croeso: *v.t.* croesawu: *a.* derbyniol, dymunol
weld, *v.t.* asio
welfare, *n.* llwydd, lles
well, *adv.* yn dda: *a.* da, iach: *i.* wel
well, *n.* ffynnon, pydew
Welsh, *a.* Cymreig, Cymraeg: *n.* Cymraeg

Welshman, *n.* Cymro
Welshwoman, *n.* Cymraes
welt, *n.* gwald, gwaldas
welter, *v.i.* ymdrybaeddu
wend, *v.i.* myned, cerdded
west, *n.* gorllewin: *a.* gorllewinol
wet, *a.* gwlyb: *v.t.* gwlychu: *n.* gwlybaniaeth, gwlybwr
wether, *n.* mollt, gwedder
whack, *v.* llachio, baeddu, ffonodio
whale, *n.* morfil
wharf, *n.* porthfa, llwythfa
what, *a. & pn.* yr hyn; pa beth, pa faint
whatever, *pn.* beth bynnag
whatsoever, *pn.* pa beth bynnag
wheat, *n.* gwenith
wheedle, *v.t.* denu, hudo, llithio, truthio
wheel, *n.* olwyn, rhod, troell: *v.* olwyno, powlio
wheelbarrow, *n.* berfa (drol), whilber
wheelwright, *n.* saer troliau
wheeze, *v.i.* gwichian: *n.* gwich
whelk, *n.* chwalc, gwalc
whelp, *n.* cenau
when, *adv.* pan, pa bryd
whence, *adv.* o ba le, o ba un
whenever, *adv.* bryd bynnag
where, *adv.* ym mha le; yn y lle, lle
whereas, *c.* gan, yn gymaint
wherefore, *adv.* paham, am hynny
wheresoever, wherever, *adv.* pa le bynnag
whereupon, *adv.* ar hynny
wherewithal, *n.* modd, arian
wherry, *n.* ysgraff, ceubal, porthfad
whet, *v.t.* hogi, minio, awchlymu
whetstone, *n.* carreg hogi, hogfaen, agalen
whether, *c.* pa un
whey, *n.* maidd, gleision
which, *pn.* pa un, pa rai; *a:* *a.* pa
whiff, *n.* chwiff, pwff, chwyth, chwa
Whig, *n.* Chwig, Wig, Rhyddfrydwr
while, *n.* ennyd, talm, amser: *v.t.*

treulio: (hefyd **whilst**), *adv.* cyhyd, tra

whim, *n.* mympwy, chwim

whimper, *v.* swnian crio

whimsical, *a.* ysmala, mympwyol

whine, *v.* swnian crio, cwynfan

whinny, *v.i.* gweryru

whip, *v.* chwipio, ffrewyllu, fflangellu: *n.* chwip, ffrewyll, fflangell

whippet, *n.* corfilgi

whir, *v.i.* chwyrndroi, chwyrnu

whirl, *v.* chwyrlïo, chwyrnellu, chwyrndroi

whirligig, *n.* chwirligwgan, chwyrnell

whirlpool, *n.* pwll tro, trobwll

whirlwind, *n.* trowynt, corwynt

whisk, *n.* tusw: *v.* ysgubo, chwyrlïo

whiskers, *n.pl.* blew, barf

whisky, *n.* chwisgi

whisper, *v. & n.* sibrwd, sisial

whist, *n.* chwist

whistle, *v.* chwibanu: *n.* chwiban, chwibanogl, chwît

whit, *n.* tipyn, gronyn, mymryn

white, *a.* gwyn, can, cannaid

whitewash, *n.* gwyngalch: *v.* gwyngalchu

whither, *adv.* i ba le

whiting, *n.* gwyniad

whitlow, *n.* ffelwm, ffalwm, ewinor, bystwn

Whitsunday, *n.* Sulgwyn

whittle, *v.t.* naddu, lleihau

whiz, *v.i.* sïo, chwyrnellu, chwyrlïo

who, *pn.* a, pwy

whoever, *pn.* pwy bynnag

whole, *a.* cyfan; holl; iach, holliach: *n.* cyfan

wholesome, *a.* iach, iachus, iachusol

wholly, *adv.* yn hollol, yn gwbl, yn llwyr

whoop, *v.i.* bloeddio, banllefain: *n.* bloedd

whop, *v.t.* ffusto, baeddu

whore, *n.* putain

whorl, *n.* tro, troell, sidell

whose, *pn.* eiddo pwy? pwy biau?

whosoever, *pn.* pwy bynnag

why, *adv.* paham, pam

wick, *n.* pabwyr, pabwyryn, wic

wicked, *a.* drwg, drygionus, ysgeler

wicker, *n.* gwaith gwiail

wicket, *n.* gwiced, gwiched, clwyd, llidiart

wide, *a.* llydan, eang, helaeth; rhwth

widow, *n. & a.* gweddw: *v.t.* gweddwi

width, *n.* lled, ehangder

wield, *v.t.* llywio, rheoli; ysgwyd, arfer, trin

wife, *(wives),* *n.* gwraig, gwraig briod, priod

wig, *n.* gwallt gosod, perwig, wig

widower, *n.* gŵr gweddw, gwidman, gwidwer

wild, *a.* gwyllt: *n.* diffeithle

wilderness, *n.* anialwch

wile, *n.* dichell, ystryw, cast

wilful, *a.* gwirfoddol, bwriadol; ystyfnig

will, *v.t.* ewyllysio, mynnu: *n.* ewyllys

willing, *a.* ewyllysgar, bodlon

willow, *n.* helygen, pren helyg

wily, *a.* cyfrwys, dichellgar

win, *v.* ennill

wince, *v.i.* gwingo

wind, *n.* gwynt

wind, *v.* dirwyn, troi

window, *n.* ffenestr

wine, *n.* gwin

wing, *n.* adain, asgell

wink, *v.* wincio, cau llygad: *n.* winc; hunell

winnow, *v.t.* nithio, gwyntyllio

winsome, *a.* serchog, deniadol

winter, *n.* gaeaf: *v.* gaeafu

wipe, *v.t.* sychu

wire, *n.* gwifr, gwifren

wisdom, *n.* doethineb

wise, *a.* doeth

wiseacre, *n.* doethyn, ffwlcyn

wish, *v.* dymuno, chwennych: *n.* dymuniad

wishful, *a.* awyddus.–**w. thinking,** breuddwyd gwrach

wisp, *n.* tusw

wistful, *a.* awyddus, hiraethus

wit, *v.* **to w.,** sef, hynny yw, nid amgen

wit, *n.* synnwyr; arabedd; gŵr ffraeth

witch, *n.* dewines, gwrach

witchcraft, *n.* dewiniaeth

with, *pr.* â, ag, gyda, gydag, efo, gan

withdraw, *v.* tynnu yn ôl, encilio; codi arian

withe, *n.* gwden, gwialen helyg

wither, *v.* gwywo, crino

withers, *n.pl.* ysgwydd march

withhold, *v.t.* atal, cadw yn ôl

within, *adv., n. & pr.* i mewn, o fewn

without, *pr.* heb, di-: *adv. & n.* tu allan

withstand, *v.t.* gwrthsefyll

witness, *n.* tyst; tystiolaeth: *v.* tystio

witticism, *n.* ffraethair, ffraetheb

wittiness, *n.* ffraethineb

wittingly, *adv.* trwy wybod, yn fwriadol

witty, *a.* arab, arabus, ffraeth

wizard, *n.* swynwr, dewin

wizened, *a.* gwyw, crin, sybachog

woad, *n.* glaslys

wobble, *v.i.* siglo, honcian, anwadalu

woe, *n.* gwae

wolf, (*wolves*), *n.* blaidd

woman, (*women*), *n.* gwraig, merch

womb, *n.* croth, bru

wonder, *n.* rhyfeddod, syndod: *v.i.* rhyfeddu, synnu

wonderful, wondrous, *a.* rhyfeddol

wont, *v. & n.* arfer: *a.* arferol

woo, *v.t.* caru; deisyf

wood, *n.* coed, coedwig; pren

woodcock, *n.* cyffylog

wood-louse, (*-lice*), *n.* gwrach y lludw, mochyn y coed, tyrchyn llwyd

woodpecker, *n.* taradr y coed

wood-pigeon, *n.* ysguthan

woof, *n.* anwe

wool, *n.* gwlân

word, *n.* gair: *v.t.* geirio

work, *n.* gwaith, gweithred, gorchwyl: *v.* gweithio

workshop, *n.* gweithdy

world, *n.* byd

worm, *n.* pryf, abwydyn; llyngyren: *v.* ymnyddu

wormwood, *n.* wermod

worry, *v.* cnoi, baeddu, blino, poeni, poenydio: *n.* pryder, blinder

worse, *a.* gwaeth

worship, *n.* addoliad: *v.* addoli

worst, *v.t.* gorchfygu, trechu

worsted, *n.* edafedd hirwlan, wstid

worth, *n.* gwerth, teilyngdod

worthy, *a.* teilwng: *n.* gŵr o fri

wound, *n.* archoll, clwyf: *v.t.* archolli, clwyfo

wraith, *n.* cyhiraeth, cyheuraeth

wrangle, *v.* cecru, cweryla, ffraeo: *n.* ffrae

wrap, *v.t.* plygu, amdoi, lapio

wrath, *n.* llid, digofaint, soriant

wreak, *v.t.* tywallt, dial (llid)

wreath, *n.* torch

wreck, *n.* llongddrylliad: *v.* llongddryllio

wren, *n.* dryw, dryw bach

wrench, *v.t.* rhwygo ymaith, tyndroi: *n.* tyndro

wrestle, *v.i.* ymgodymu, ymaflyd codwm

wretch, *n.* adyn, truan; gwalch, dihiryn

wretched, *a.* truan, truenus, gresynus

wriggle, *v.* gwingo, ymnyddu

wright, *n.* saer

wring, *v.t.* troi, gwasgu

wrinkle, *n.* crych, crychni: *v.* crychu

wrinkle, *n.* awgrym, hysbysrwydd

wrist, *n.* arddwrn

writ, *n.* **Holy W.,** yr Ysgrythur Lân

write, *v.* ysgrifennu

writhe, *v.* ymnyddu, gwingo

writing, *n.* ysgrifen

wrong, *a.* cyfeiliornus, cam, anghywir, o'i le: *n.* cam: *v.t.* gwneuthur cam â, niweidio, drygu

wrongful, *a.* anghyfiawn, ar gam

wroth, *a.* dig, dicllon, digofus, llidiog

wrought, *a.* **w. iron,** haearn gyr

wry, *a.* cam, gwyrgam

Y

yacht, *n.* llong bleser, iot

yap, *v.i.* clepian cyfarth

yard, *n.* llath, llathen; hwyl-lath

yard, *n.* iard, buarth, cadlas, clos

yarn, *n.* edau, edafedd; stori, chwedl

yawl, *n.* bad mawr, cwch llong

yawn, *v.i.* dylyfu gên, agor ceg

ye, *pn.* chwi, chwychwi; chwithau

yea, *adv.* ie, yn wir

year, *n.* blwyddyn, blwydd

yearly, *adv.* blynyddol

yearn, *v.i.* hiraethu, dyheu

yeast, *n.* burum, berem, berman

yell, *v.* ysgrechain: *n.* ysgrech, nâd

yellow, *a. & n.* melyn

yelp, *v.i.* cyfarth, gogyfarth, cipial

yeoman, *n.* gwrêng, iwmon; amaethwr

yes, *adv.* ie, do, oes, &c.

yesterday, *n. & adv.* doe

yet, *c. & adv.* er hynny, eto

yew, *n.* yw, ywen

yield, *v.* ildio, gildio, ymroddi, rhoddi: *n.* cynnyrch

yoke, *n.* iau, gwedd: *v.* ieuo

yoke-fellow, *n.* cymar

yokel, *n.* lleban, gwladwr, taeog

yolk, *n.* melyn wy, melynwy

yonder, *a.* acw, draw: *adv.* dacw, acw, draw

yore, *n.* y dyddiau gynt, y cynfyd

you, *pn.* chwi, 'ch; chwychwi; chwithau

young, *a.* ieuanc

youngster, *n.* bachgennyn, plentyn

your, *pn.* eich, 'ch

yours, *pn.* eiddoch, yr eiddoch

youth, *n.* ieuenctid, mebyd; llanc

youthful, *a.* ieuanc, ieuengaidd

Yule, *n.* Nadolig

Yule-tide, *n.* tymor y Nadolig

Z

zeal, *n.* sêl, aidd, eiddgarwch, brwdfrydedd

zealot, *n.* gwynfydwr, penboethyn

zealous, *a.* selog, eiddgar, brwdfrydig

zebra, *n.* sebra

zenana, *n.* gwragedd-dy, gwreicty

zenith, *n.* entrych; anterth

zephyr, *n.* awel dyner (o'r gorllewin)

zero, *n.* dim, diddim, gwagnod (0), sero

zest, *n.* awch, blas, afraith

zigzag, *a. & n.* igam-ogam

zinc, *n.* sinc

zodiac, *n.* sidydd

zone, *n.* gwregys, cylch, rhanbarth

zoo, *n.* sw

zoology, *n.* milofyddiaeth